D1520563

Quantrill of Missouri

CAPT. WILLIAM ANDERSON

CAPT. WILLIAM GREGG

CAPT. DICK YEAGER

COL. WILLIAM QUANTRILL

CAPT. DAVID POOLE

CAPT. JOHN JARRETTE

CAPT. GEORGE TODD

QUANTRILL'S STAFF

Quantrill of Missouri

THE MAKING OF A
GUERRILLA WARRIOR

The Man, the Myth, the Soldier

PAUL R. PETERSEN

CUMBERLAND HOUSE
NASHVILLE, TENNESSEE

Published by
CUMBERLAND HOUSE PUBLISHING, INC.
431 Harding Industrial Drive
Nashville, Tennessee 37211

Cover design by Gore Studio, Nashville, Tennessee.

Library of Congress Cataloging-in-Publication Data

Petersen, Paul R., 1949–
    Quantrill of Missouri : the making of a guerrilla warrior : the man, the myth, the soldier /
Paul R. Petersen.
        p.   cm.
    Includes bibliographical references (p.) and index.
    ISBN 1-58182-359-2 (hardcover : alk. paper)
    1. Quantrill, William Clarke, 1837–1865. 2. Guerrillas—Missouri—Biography. 3. Soldiers—
Missouri—Biography. 4. West (U.S.)—History—Civil War, 1861–1865—Underground
movements. 5. United States—History—Civil War, 1861–1865—Underground movements.
I. Title.
E470.45.P48 2003
973.7'86'092—dc22
                                                                          2003023296

Printed in Canada

1 2 3 4 5 6 7 8 9 10—07 06 05 04 03

To the memory of
Col. William Clarke Quantrill
from a fellow warrior

Through the travail of ages,
Midst the pomp and toils of war;
I fought and strove and perished,
Countless times upon this star.

As if through a glass darkly,
The age-old strife I see;
For I fought in many guises, many names,
But always me.

Contents

Maps

Acknowledgments

I wish to express grateful appreciation to the following people who, from their own personal recollections of their experiences and relationships with William Clarke Quantrill, have contributed greatly to the historical record. Their accounts have been used to bring the truth to light from previously published sources. Their stories have made this book possible.

The following knew Quantrill firsthand, stood beside him, shared his experiences, and preserved his memory in their diaries and postwar memoirs and writings: Sylvester Akers, George Barnett, John Barnhill, James Campbell, Henry Clarke, Jim Cummins, John Newman Edwards, Stephen B. Elkins, Hiram Hicks George, John Hicks George, William H. Gregg, Ike Hall, Sidney Herd, Alexander Franklin James, J. T. Keller, John Koger, N. W. Letton, Andrew J. "Jack" Liddil, Nancy Harris McCorkle Lilly, George T. Maddox, Morgan T. Mattox, John McCorkle, Lee C. Miller, George M. Noland, Otho Offutt, Allen Parmer, J. C. Peters, Caroline Clarke Quantrill, Sarah Catherine "Kate" King Quantrill, George Scholl, W. W. Scott, Frank Smith, William Stockwell, Joseph Talbott, Charles Fletcher Taylor, Harrison Trow, Joseph Vaughn, James Wakefield, Andrew Walker, Morgan Walker, T. J. Walker, Hampton Watts, Warren Welch, Holland Wheeler, Henry Wilson, Rufus Wilson, John A. Workman, and Thomas Coleman Younger.

A special thanks to Wilbur Zink, Claiborne Scholl Nappier, Patrick Marquis, and Emory Cantey of Our Turn Antiques for sharing their Civil War–era images.

Without them, this book would not have been possible.

Introduction

Truth comes to us from the past as gold is washed down to us from the mountains of Sierra Nevada, in minute but precious particles.

—BOVEE

William Clarke Quantrill was a product of his times. He was a man made up by the personalities, passions, and politics that surrounded him. Without the issue of slavery that ignited the nation and the turbulent individuals like John Brown and James Henry Lane that inflamed the border of Kansas and Missouri, history would never have recorded his name. To study the border warfare between Kansas and Missouri is to study the character of the people at the time. Any provocation, however slight, was viewed as a personal insult and easily escalated into a feud, a duel, or a lifetime of hatred between the parties. There was much such personal conflict along the border long before it exploded into hatred and bloodshed. Here personal pride and patriotism controlled individuals, yet hospitality and generosity were also a way of life. Conflict grew, however, between the first to settle in this area—mostly Southerners, and the second wave of settlers—mostly Northerners—who searched for an easy life and a quick fortune. To be a settler was to be an opportunist. Life was hard, and a chance to earn any money that might help to keep a family alive did not come along every day. Many pursued these opportunities through honest endeavors; others sought dollars in lucrative deals or dealings. Some sought fortune in the political future of the new territory, and some sought fortunes in the law. Yet for every individual in pursuit of an honest living there were ten others looking to make a quick dollar by claim jumping or larceny or deceit. Incompatible sectional differences only fueled the growing conflict between Missourians and Kansans.

In my research into the person of William Clarke Quantrill, I was amazed that a man could be reviled as the devil incarnate, lacking any love for either parents or family. His mother was declared to be mother in name only, showing no love for her son. William Elsey Connelley asserted that Quantrill's father was an embezzler and a thief who was despised by his neighbors. Quantrill himself was described as fiendish for skinning the neighbors' cats and for shooting pigs' ears just to hear them squeal. Connelley reported that when Quantrill courted young women, his talk turned sadistic as he commented on how many men he could hang from certain tree limbs. In his life in Kansas before the Civil War, he was described as shiftless and without visible means of support, stealing from his neighbors and local merchants. He was called a bloodthirsty killer, murdering and stealing from those in Missouri as well as Kansas.[1]

Connelley claimed that no one in Quantrill's guerrilla band trusted him, that he made them nervous and edgy. It was said that he had a mistress, and after the war she opened a brothel in St. Louis. When the war was coming to a close, Quantrill was even said to be planning to ride to Washington, D.C., to kill Abraham Lincoln. Historical evidence has never supported these accounts. Many scholars who knew Connelley had read portions of his manuscript prior to publication and warned him against his "extreme statements," but they were ignored.

The contradictions that I discovered in Connelley's work turned my interest into intrigue. How could this alleged fiend have been a respected schoolteacher? How could he have organized and led as many as four hundred men in the most noted band of guerrilla fighters known to history? Why did regular Confederate army officers, who outranked him, yield to him and subordinate themselves to him? How could he be so hated by his own men and still lead them in the van of renowned battles throughout Missouri, winning victories over superior Union forces? Mothers entrusted their sons to him. Citizens served him as spies. Women willingly tended his wounds and those of his men. His followers were intensely loyal to him, even guarding him in battle. Most of his followers were God-fearing farmers trying to live Christian lives. Some may point out that mere association with upright righteous people would not necessarily make Quantrill the same. Yet God-fearing, righteous people would not have followed a depraved, degenerate, psychotic killer.

Only by putting myself in Quantrill's stirrups, so to speak, could I envision the temper of the times. Further research revealed the activities that changed men's minds and stirred the passions of the day in ways that are not known today. Studying the frame of mind of the early settlers and the political and cultural feelings of those who made up the border area is the only way to understand the personality of that era. I did not attempt, as other authors have done, to research everything in print on Quantrill and then put it all in writing. This would only confuse the facts. Researchers present facts. Historians attempt to put the facts together to ascertain how and why something happened so as to explain events. The motives of the authors and the mood of the times are vital questions in assembling an accurate portrayal of William Clarke Quantrill. Too often, writers simply repeat what others have written before them. In this book, I stand back and view Quantrill as a product of his times. What did he actually do compared with what history writers have said he did? What was said of him by those who knew him rather than by those who had only hearsay knowledge of his exploits? If we portray his actions in the light of the times, then stand back to view his motives, does he emerge as a monster or a martyr? How was Quantrill the developer of modern-day guerrilla warfare? Can we judge him fairly, after these many years, in the terms of the terrible troubles of that time between Missouri and Kansas?

After the Civil War, one of Quantrill's men warned: "You who were not there can not realize for a moment the dreadful passions that were roused in the hearts of men during those fearful years." The Missouri border during the war was the scene of the greatest savagery in American history. Never before or since have Americans exhibited such brutality toward fellow Americans. For our purposes, the controversy surrounding William Clarke Quantrill is nothing less than a scandal. In the second half of the nineteenth century the Northern press conspired to blacken his name and those of his followers—a conspiracy that continues even today. In this book I reexamine the facts relating to Quantrill and the conflicts on the Kansas-Missouri border.

Capt. William Gregg, Quantrill's adjutant, reported in a letter after the war: "Quantrill and his men have been unjustly slandered by the people of the North, a people who, even to this day, know nothing of them, except what they have read in irresponsible books and newspapers." Gregg also observed: "It is not enough that their valor is recognized, it is not enough that their honesty be confessed. We ask of our Northern brother, we ask of all mankind and all womankind a recognition of their patriotism, their love of country, and of liberty. . . . We cannot remain silent, so long as any aspersion is cast by the pen of the historian, or the tongue of the orator upon their patriotic motives, or the loftiness of their purposes throughout that mighty struggle. We make no half-hearted apologies for their acts. It is justice for which we plead, not charity."[2] Union Col. R. H. Hunt, who fought against Gregg during the war, said of Gregg after the war: "That in so far as his memory serves him his statements can be depended upon absolutely. He is a man who would not willfully misrepresent."[3]

Quantrill did not act alone, and his followers have suffered a mischaracterization similar to that foisted upon him. According to the Northern press, every guerrilla was a bloodthirsty, brutal, psychotic killer. Their relatives were low-class individuals and criminally natured, and their women had loose morals. Historians refused to acknowledge that Quantrill and his men were soldiers; instead they refer to them as outlaws. From this perspective, Quantrill's partisan rangers could not be credited with military victories in battle, so they were cast as wanton killers who massacred their victims. These accounts were carried down, written by a victorious enemy over a beaten but unbowed foe. John McCorkle, one of Quantrill's men, wrote a book about his wartime experiences, explaining that it was "not published in any spirit of malice or hatred, but in order that the truth may be known, that the world may know that Quantrill and his band were justified in nearly all of their acts and that they were not altogether bad; that they were driven to desperation by brutal outrages committed against them and their friends."[4] Likewise, William Gregg noted: "History after history has been written of Quantrill and his men, none of which can be characterized as true. And that which is not true, is not history."[5]

History is an imperfect record. It is a collective memory of the past with the same faults, distortions, omissions, and exaggerations that mar personal memories. Well-worn history, with many tellings, becomes legend, and legend becomes myth. Necessarily, history is shaped and conditioned by viewpoint and perspective and should not be accepted as absolute truth. There should always be a degree of challenge and skepticism. History will not be knowingly manufactured.[6] That which exists or has existed, events that actually transpired during the war, will claim attention—the true, not the false. It is incumbent on historians to discharge this function in a manner that shall be equally just to all men.

Our understanding of the Civil War is largely viewed through the eyes of the victors, but the majority of the inhabitants along the western border, however, were Southern sympathizers, and their viewpoint has been generally ignored. There is no way to clearly understand the surroundings and character of the men on the western border by today's standards of conduct and values. Ideals such as chivalry and good manners, including kindness toward those younger and weaker, was an ideal that kept the fabric of their society together. Integrity was paramount for a respectful character. Pride, honor, devotion: these intrinsic values that have all but lost their importance, except to a few in today's society, meant everything to the men who had only these values to fight and die for. The very government that was supposed to protect them took everything else they held dear and sacred.

Quantrill's life has been greatly distorted by prejudicial historians and journalists. The hatred of his Kansas enemies and of those he fought against during the war were manifested in writings and grossly exaggerated by those who had never come face to face with him. Only sensational claims previously heard by those who had reason to blacken his name because of their own political views and sectional feelings have been recorded and repeated for the record. Quantrill's critics have painted him in the worst possible light and have collectively and in collusion manufactured or amplified unfounded and unproved stories about him.

Kansans faced an enemy not in the regular Confederate uniform of the Southern army but in the person of William Clarke Quantrill and his guerrilla band. For every brutal act imposed by Federal authorities on the citizens of Missouri to subjugate them, citizens of Kansas knew Quantrill would exact a heavy revenge. When the guerrillas achieved a resounding victory by annihilating their enemy in battle it was called a massacre, but from a military viewpoint, Quantrill's guerrilla tactics were a very efficient use of inferior numbers to exact a higher percentage of enemy casualties. His utilization of fire superiority, cover and concealment, speed of movement, a vast intelligence network, and psychological warfare made his men a force equal in comparison with John S. Mosby's partisan rangers or Nathan Bedford Forrest's regular mounted cavalry. In this century Americans used atomic weapons on Japan, and American troops in Vietnam resorted to Quantrillian tactics but were never viewed as depraved, degenerate killers. In Vietnam, entire villages were burned, old men and young boys bearing arms were killed, entire sections of communities were uprooted and relocated, but our soldiers and marines were never labeled as brutal in their style of fighting. The same is true of Quantrill's raid on Lawrence, Kansas. The answer lies not in accusations toward the raiders but why the raid was planned and executed.

Finding most stories on Quantrill based simply on opinion, I have relied heavily on fact and eyewitness accounts. I have provided quotations and documentation to prove who William Clarke Quantrill was. Jigsaw puzzle manufacturers place a picture on the box that shows how the puzzle should look when completed. Historians have drawn such a picture for us about the life of William Clarke Quantrill. They have given us the pieces to match the picture on the box that they have drawn. After exhaustively researching the complete Quantrill—the son, the youth, the man, the soldier, the husband—I have found a picture quite different from what has been drawn over the years by the writers of history. Time has patiently waited for someone with a knowledgeable background and common experiences to write about Quantrill.

After attending Quantrill's reinterment in the Higginsville, Missouri, Confederate Soldiers Home in 1992, I realized I might be uniquely qualified to write a true history of the guerrilla leader. I was born and raised in the same neighborhood in which Quantrill reunions were held after the war. I attended the same church that was used by Quantrill as a hideout. Church members also rode with him, and the founders of the church all served with Gen. Sterling Price's Missouri State Guards. I discovered I had ancestors living in Chambersburg, Pennsylvania, and Hagerstown, Maryland, at the same time as Quantrill's family.

I spent the summers of my youth with relatives in Howard County, Missouri, where Quantrill spent much of the summer of 1864 with his wife and recovering from wounds. The area had also been the scene of the famous raid on the Fayette courthouse and stockade. I have experienced the same passions and fears from actual combat, fighting the same style of guerrilla warfare that was waged by Quantrill and his men. I have endured the elements, fired shots in anger, led men into combat against a tenacious enemy, and seen comrades fall at my side.

Many writings on Quantrill come from Kansas and Northern writers who lacked military backgrounds or experiences to draw upon. Instead, they merely capitalized on the sensationalism of fictionalized accounts about Quantrill and his men. Many repeat the same worn-out rumors and inaccuracies, but claim they have done exhaustive research. The empathy and insight into guerrilla warfare is from my own personal experiences. A modern military saying is, For those who fight for it, freedom has a flavor the protected never taste. This experience is much more beneficial compared with those authors who have never had military experiences or never walked over the same ground or been familiar with the area known as "Quantrill Country."

By viewing Quantrill through the eyes of an experienced guerrilla fighter, I hope to show Quantrill as he really was: an educated and moral man whose career began by protecting the lives and property of the people who were being daily robbed and killed by enemies who hid their criminal deeds behind the cloak of a flag that they used for their own selfish greed and ambitions. I seek only to dignify Quantrill's life, not to romanticize it.

Loved and respected by his men, hated and feared by his enemies, adored by the young Southern women whom he met, and befriended by those who sought justice and protection: This was William Clarke Quantrill. This is the history of the man and the soldier.

Quantrill of Missouri

1

The Early Years

Honor is what no man can give you,
And no man can take away.
Honor is a man's gift to himself.

—ANONYMOUS

U NNOTICED ON THE STAGE of human events on July 31, 1837, in the small, old-fashioned Ohio village of Canal Dover, pleasantly situated in the broad fertile valley of the Tuscarawas River, a child was born to Caroline Cornelia Clarke and Thomas Henry Quantrill. The Quantrills were of solid English stock. Thomas's father had been a captain in the British army, and in 1812 he had settled in Hagerstown, Maryland. There he raised a company of volunteers for the war in the same year and later married Judith Heiser, the daughter of a wealthy and influential Maryland family. By trade, his son was a tinner, or coppersmith.

Caroline Clarke was born in 1819 in Somerset County, Pennsylvania. Her family then moved to nearby Chambersburg. Thomas Henry Quantrill met Carolina while he was visiting relatives in Chambersburg and fell in love with her. After a brief courtship, they were married on October 11, 1836. Shortly afterward they made a honeymoon trip to Canal Dover and there started a new business venture. Their eldest son, William, was born the following year. Since he undoubtedly was conceived while his parents were still residents of Hagerstown, it isn't hard to understand that young Quantrill often told acquaintances that he had been born in Maryland instead of Ohio.

Shortly after arriving in Canal Dover, Thomas Quantrill, seeking to better himself, obtained a job as a teacher in the Canal Dover school. While a trustee of the school, he wrote a book on tinsmithing—*The Tin-man's Guide* (or *The Tinner's Guide*)—which was a huge success throughout the area. Thomas Quantrill was said to have a brilliant mind, and he was especially noted as a mathematician after writing a book called *The Lightning Calculator*. His neighbors reported that he held the esteem of all who knew him. Abraham Ellis, reporting in the *Topeka Weekly Capital* of February. 3, 1882, noted, "I never heard anything against his character." Thomas later became the school's first principal and continued in that capacity until his death on December 7, 1854.

Thomas and Caroline had eight children, four of whom died in infancy. William was the oldest and exhibited a more mature and brighter personality than his siblings. Factual history records little of his early life in Canal Dover. What is known is that Quantrill was reared in a home presided over by a cultured and genteel mother and a well-educated father, which resulted in his own excellent education.

The *Topeka Mail and Breezem* of April 22, 1898, reported: "William Clarke Quantrill inherited from his father a love for books. He was exceptionally bright in his class and graduated with honor from the school there." Facts about his childhood were presented by his mother, who added:

> He was a handsome boy, slender in build, but muscular. His eyes were blue and his hair soft as silk. As a boy, Quantrill was bright and studious. He attended Union College under his father and graduated when he was sixteen. In the following year he became a teacher in one of the lower departments of the college and later taught for several terms in the district schools about here. . . . He was studious when a boy and was quick and accurate in figures. He was regarded as the best mathematician in Tuscarawas County. He was fond of history and hunting.

Quantrill's mother added: "He was very gentle and kind and affectionate. He was high-minded and I never knew him to manifest a cruel or heartless disposition. He was polite to the ladies, but I don't know of his ever having a love affair." Joseph Talbott of Canal Dover and later a real estate agent in Atchison, Kansas, knew Quantrill well and observed, "As a young man, Quantrill was honorable, well educated and universally esteemed."

William W. Scott was Quantrill's closest childhood friend in Ohio. Scott was a Union soldier during the war and afterward became the editor of the *Iron Valley Reporter* of Dover, Ohio. Scott never offered a disparaging word about young Quantrill, but rather proudly stated, "Quantrill was my earliest playmate, being one year my senior. . . . There was nothing in his conduct or in his letters to indicate his after career." Also in the *Joplin (Mo.) Morning Herald,* Scott reported, "[Quantrill] was strictly temperate and honest . . . and he was remarkably neat in his person."[1] Scott added that Quantrill was "uncommonly precocious intellectually. He was fond of books and quick to learn." Scott described his friend as unassertive and—when it came to women—maybe even lacking self-confidence. Around young girls Quantrill was "ill at ease . . . and generally adverse to their society." Contradicting the general image of the man, Scott noted "Quantrill was a diffident, reserved youth." Most historians asserted that Quantrill had no personal convictions, that he loved theft, destruction, and murder and that he simply lived to kill.[2]

The townspeople who knew Quantrill before the war all described him as a lighthearted, moral boy. He entertained himself like other youths from that section of the country. He was remarkable in that he was well schooled in the social amenities. As a youth, he loved to read and felt at home in the outdoors, hunting in the woods near his home and becoming an outstanding marksman. At fourteen years of age he gained a reputation as the best shot in his section of the country.[3] Like others, Quantrill was greatly influenced by stories of his family's military experiences, especially those of his grandfather who fought in the Revolution.

In December 1854, after a lingering illness, Quantrill's father died, leaving his family in straitened circumstances. As the eldest, William was thrust into the central role of helping to provide for his mother and siblings. Caroline was an expert with needle and thread, so she began to sew for others, but that did not provide sufficient income. Eventually the family was compelled to take in boarders.

Trying to better himself and believing he could contribute more to his family by following in his father's footsteps and furthering his education, seventeen-year-old Quantrill traveled west to Fort Wayne, Indiana. For a year he studied civil engineering, surveying, and Latin. On August 8, 1855, he took a teaching job in Mendota, Illinois, and taught for one winter. After the school term ended he remained in Mendota until the following summer and worked in a lumberyard.

In 1853 the Illinois Central Railroad met the Chicago, Burlington, and Quincy Railroad and the Milwaukee Railroad at Mendota, raising the need for a station when a brisk freight business began. After the job in the lumberyard ended, Quantrill obtained a job from the railroad, unloading railroad cars. In 1856 he returned home and taught school for one term near New

Philadelphia, three miles south of Canal Dover as well as two or three other country schools during the year.

The money that Quantrill and his mother made together barely made ends meet. At the time many who found themselves financially handicapped were encouraged to resettle farther west. Very quickly Quantrill believed that a better life for him lay to the west. He convinced his mother that his chance for success was in resettling and farming in the new Kansas Territory. So in early March 1857, Caroline Quantrill entrusted her nineteen-year-old son to Harmon V. Beeson, a friend and prominent Canal Dover businessmen, who was going to Kansas. Little did she realize she would never see her son again.

When Beeson, his seventeen-year-old son, Richard, and Quantrill came to the Ohio River they took passage on a boat headed downriver then north on the Mississippi for St. Louis, Missouri. There they waited two days for Henry Torrey, another friend from Canal Dover. Torrey had served as a colonel of a New York regiment during the Mexican War[4] and still had business connections in New York. Both Beeson and Torrey planned to establish themselves in Kansas and then have their families join them. While Beeson and the young men waited for Torrey, Quantrill passed the time trying to sell copies of his father's book on tinsmithing. After Torrey joined them, the journey to Kansas continued up the Mississippi by boat. Whenever the vessel stopped along the way, Quantrill went ashore to sell his father's book.

A few short days after leaving home, on March 8, Quantrill wrote to his mother of his experiences. He recounted his book sales experiences, adding that the four men intended to head upriver to Leavenworth. The river, however, was low, too low for the boat to get to Leavenworth. Quantrill and his companions instead landed at Independence, Missouri. There they purchased supplies and outfitted themselves for their new life, adding two ox teams and a few food staples. On March 22 they arrived at the bank of the Marais des Cygnes River in Franklin County, Kansas. Just a year earlier the Marais des Cygnes was the site of a bloody massacre, and feelings were still high when Quantrill and his friends arrived there.

John Brown was an abolitionist who did not hesitate to put his radical philosophy into action. In the winter of 1854–55, after Kansas had been opened for settlement, he brought his family to the area. Earlier his sons—John Jr., Jason, Owen, Frederick—and a half-brother, Salmon, had established themselves in Miami County, near Osawatomie. After they found the life difficult in the new land, they wrote home to ask their father for aid and to urge him to bring weapons and ammunition so they could fight the pro-slavery faction in Kansas. The senior Brown espoused his own brand of religious antislavery fervor,[5] and the aid he sought for his sons was purely military. Brown pleaded eloquently for arms and funds from various Northern antislavery societies, and the abolitionists responded favorably to him. The Massachusetts State Kansas Committee purchased two hundred Sharps carbines and sent them to Brown to sell to "reliable" settlers.

Brown had a curious past. He was born in Connecticut in 1800, but his family moved to northern Ohio when he was five, to an area known for violent antislavery views. As an adult, Brown failed in twenty different business adventures and was sued for so-called sharp practices and dishonesty. After fathering twenty children in two marriages, he filed for bankruptcy while still in his forties. Despite being quite poor he helped finance the publication of a work called *The Call to Rebellion,* which proposed a war against all who supported slavery. He also gave land to fugitive slaves whom he helped through the Underground Railroad. Once he arrived in Kansas, Brown gathered a band of desperate men and led them into Missouri to raid and plunder. Missouri offered a $3,000 reward for his arrest, and the federal government added a personal reward of $250 for his capture. After murdering and plundering along the border, Brown headed back east to lead an ill-conceived assault on the federal arsenal at Harpers Ferry that he hoped might ignite a slave rebellion in Virginia.

Soon after Brown's departure from Kansas, the two Beesons, Torrey, and Quantrill settled on adjoining claims in what is now McCamish Township in Johnson County. On one of the parcels of land they built a cabin, and all of them lived there. On the other claims they erected a pen or put up a few logs to mark their intent to develop the ground in the spring. In memory of their homes in Ohio, they called the settlement Tuscarora Lake.

Territorial laws governing land claims stipulated that claimants had to demonstrate their intent to live on the property through some kind of improvement to the land. Many Missourians had previously entered the territory, cleared some land, cut down some trees to imply that they would be building a residence, then returned across the border to their farms. The earliest confrontations between antislavery and pro-slavery settlers came about when the Missouri farmers returned to find that New England settlers had jumped their claims. Tempers flared, and many seeking to reclaim their land were confronted by armed groups of so-called free-soil settlers. The Free-Soilers then sold these improved farms to newcomers as abandoned claims and turned a handsome profit.

Quantrill described the practice in a January 22, 1858, letter to his mother and added, "The claim north of mine was jumped last Monday by a young fellow from Indiana."[6] In an area lacking reliable government or civil authority to guarantee a level of justice for all, an individual's character and moral code were the only law that existed. Insults and injuries were never forgotten, even in a lifetime. The rugged life endured by the early settlers often caused hostilities and animosities among even the staunchest of friends.

The towns that sprang up in Kansas were not like the quaint and tidy towns of the East. Instead, they became hotbeds of the political abolitionism and greed exhibited by low-class individuals seeking a dollar and not caring how it was made.[7]

James Henry Lane made his home in Lawrence, Kansas, and that settlement soon became the center of abolitionism and jayhawking activity. As a congressional representative from Indiana, Lane's vote in favor of the 1854 Kansas-Nebraska Act wrecked his political career. He went to Kansas to salvage it. Lane's first appearance in Kansas occurred during the organization of a Douglas Democratic Party. Immediately after failing at this, he tried to get the pro-slavery territorial legislature to grant him a divorce from his wife who had followed him from Indiana.[8] Lane was known to be a notorious womanizer as well as being violent, paranoid, and unbalanced. His private life was that of a satyr. Someone observed, "The civilization to which his principles owned origin permitted him the wives of other people if he could win them, and he went about with the quest of a procuress and the encompassment of Solomon."[9] A contemporary of Lane's said that he was morally corrupt and utterly irreligious—except at election time.[10]

In the August 27, 1856, issue of the *Davenport Democrat*, Lane's father-in-law was the source for some interesting information:

> When his precious son-in-law induced his daughter to go to Kansas he sold her property amounting to $10,000 and after reaching Kansas, Lane procured a mistress and treated his wife so badly that she was forced to leave him for home, and he told her that he had paid her passage on the steamboat to Indiana. When in fact, after the boat started she found that such was not the case, and it was with a great difficulty that she raised money enough to pay the passage. Lane had robbed her of her whole fortune, been guilty of adultery with a mistress, and sent her home penniless, and after she left, tried to get a divorce from her through the very Territorial legislature, which he is denouncing as bogus and illegal.

Lane rose quickly in power, which enabled him to become a major general in the free-state militia. His political arm included the newspaper, the

Lawrence Republican, which was operated with funds given to his cohort, John Speer, the paper's owner and editor. Speer's newspaper carried exaggerated accounts of Lane's defense of the free-soil forces in Kansas when in actuality he participated very little and avoided involvement in battle. Lane's oratory was his chief asset. He had a power to sway his audiences by his electrifying manner and tone of voice. His speeches were radical and inflammatory, and he stirred the radical abolitionist element with incendiary words and "talked wildly of [the] wholesale assassination of pro-slavery leaders."[11] In his speeches among the Kansas settlements, Lane said: "Missourians are wolves, snakes, devils, and damn their souls, I want to see them cast into a burning hell! We believe in a war of extermination. . . . There is no such thing as Union men in the border of Missouri. . . . I want to see every foot of ground in Jackson, Cass and Bates Counties [in Missouri] burned over, everything laid waste."[12]

The territorial executive of Kansas, Gov. J. W. Denver, issued a statement against Lane denouncing him as "lawless and restless, never satisfied except when engaged in some broil or exciting trouble" and alleging that Lane had made "insidious attempts to renew the difficulties and troubles . . . with an intention or design of establishing a military dictatorship." Lane was indicted by the territorial grand jury for treason, but he fled to the north whenever an arrest was imminent.

Lane has also been described as a cynical, unscrupulous demagogue who would use any and every kind of chicanery and skullduggery for political or personal gain. His enemies declared that he never paid a debt or told the truth save by accident or under compulsion, that he had no principle he would not sell, that he made no promise he would not break, and that he had no friend he would not betray.[13]

Lane's political rival in Kansas was Charles Robinson, and both men wanted complete control of the territory. Robinson aimed for the governorship and the power involved in granting or bestowing privileges that were left to the prerogatives of the territorial chief executive. Lane wanted to wield power in the territorial legislature as a prelude to returning to Washington and the U.S. Congress. When Kansas entered the Union in 1861, he was elected to the Senate. When war erupted, he wanted to continue to hold his seat in the Senate and at the same time exercise power as the commander in chief of his state's militia, thus allowing him to control both political and military power.

While Lane worked to establish himself in Kansas politics, young Quantrill desperately tried to support his family back in Ohio. Quantrill was very industrious and commonly worked several jobs at the same time to help

out at home. He was accustomed to any kind of labor, whether it was teaching school or manual labor. In a May 16, 1857, letter to his mother, he
recounted his efforts in his new surroundings. He described the hard work in
clearing the land where he intended to put in a crop of potatoes. He mentioned helping plant a ten-acre field of corn, which he and Torrey had
plowed. He noted he planned to plow and plant another twenty-acre field of
corn to help get them through the coming winter. With any spare time that
he had, Quantrill hunted for food in the surrounding woods. His letters
exude his great excitement in seeing his labor bearing fruit. He had big hopes
that he could make a living here and urged his mother to bring the rest of the
family to join him in the new life he had found. He missed his family terribly,
and the last line of his letter states, "All I want is for the rest of you to be
here, and we will live twice as fast."[14]

Henry Torrey acted as a compassionate and sympathetic adviser to
Quantrill. He spent hours talking with him about the family's situation in
Ohio and how it compared to what they could expect in their new life in
Kansas. Torrey concurred that Caroline Quantrill should bring the small clan
to the new land. The businessman from Canal Dover was described as an
honest and good man and was always greatly respected by the people where
he lived. Even though he was from Ohio, Torrey was pro-Southern in his sentiments when he resided in Kansas and remained a friend of Quantrill
throughout the approaching war.[15] Torrey, like Quantrill, apparently changed
his political convictions when he witnessed the lawlessness of the radical
abolitionists as well as the jayhawking raids.

The sympathies of the other men from Canal Dover ran counter to
Quantrill's and Torrey's. During the upcoming war, Beeson's three sons fought
in Kansas jayhawker regiments. After the war Beeson's daughter made every
effort to denounce Quantrill and his actions.

When Quantrill accompanied Beeson and Torrey to Kansas, their business agreement stipulated that each man was to buy a forty-acre section of
land. They also agreed to pay Quantrill's way to the territory, purchase a
claim on his behalf, and hold it for him until his twenty-first birthday.
Beeson's and Torrey's claims involved two forty-acre parcels of prairie land;
Quantrill's claim was half timber and half prairie. Quantrill's working relationship with Beeson and Torrey was based on the understanding that he
would help them to clear and cultivate their claims until his claim was paid
off by his labor.

As thrilled as Quantrill was with life in Kansas, neither Beeson nor Torrey
was as happy. The difficulties and hardships naturally weighed more heavily

upon the older men. To meet the requirements for their claims, they had to immediately clear the land for plowing, plant a crop, and build a residence.

By most standards the Kansas Territory was a harsh environment, but this was especially true between 1857 and 1859, when Kansas experienced one of the worst droughts on record. In the summer of 1860, settlers noted, "The rivers ceased to flow, the ground became like iron, the air was 'the very breath of hell.'" In September 1860 grasshoppers swarmed the fields. The result was an almost universal crop failure and an economic depression, both of which brought much suffering to the already sorely afflicted state.[16]

Many settlers hoping for a rich new life in Kansas pulled up stakes and returned to their former homes in the East. Even so, the tide of immigration continued to flow. In particular, the territory was being overrun with settlers from the New England Emigrant Aid Society, whose characters were not in keeping with the moral standards of the more respected settlers from the Northern states. One early settler observed: "Many of those who came to Kansas under the auspices of this society were undesirable neighbors, looked at from any standpoint. Their ideas on property rights were very hazy, in many cases. Some of them were let out of Eastern prisons to live down a 'past' in a new country. They looked upon a slave owner as legitimate prey, and later when lines became more closely drawn a secessionist was fit game, whether he had owned slaves or not."[17]

Young Quantrill's first taste of treachery was unfortunately from his companions. Even though their families had been friendly in Ohio, there always seemed to be animosity between Beeson and Quantrill. The matter came to a head when Beeson and Torrey tried to cheat Quantrill out of his share of the land that they had farmed together. Trying to take advantage of the boy's youth and lack of legal standing due to his age, both men conspired to keep Quantrill from fully gaining his section of land. Finding himself in strange and hostile surroundings, where now he could not trust the friendship of old family friends, Quantrill looked for redress in the territorial court to win his claim from the injustice done to him. The court found fully in Quantrill's favor, but Beeson and Torrey only attempted a partial settlement with Quantrill, knowing that the territorial judge's decision would be nearly impossible to enforce. Quantrill, with the insight of a youth, took matters into his own hands. He seized property belonging to Beeson and Torrey that equaled what they owed him, and he held it until they satisfied his demands for full payment. This action, however, only antagonized and infuriated the older men. Quantrill was forced to have the matter settled by an arbitrator who ruled in his favor. After the verdict, he returned their property.[18]

Beeson went back to Ohio in early August 1857 to fetch his family. He carried a letter from Quantrill to his mother. In it the young man described the unhappiness expressed by Beeson and Torrey and stated that he was going to go on a claim of his own: "I am going on a claim in a few weeks, and I will probably leave Mr. Torrey this week. . . . I don't think I will see Beeson very often for I am going to do for myself now."[19] Despite the dispute between Torrey and Quantrill, they remained on friendly terms.

In early June 1857 a number of Ohio youths, all former schoolmates of Quantrill's, came to the Kansas Territory and set up adjoining claims. Quantrill joined them, and they all worked together to build a small cabin in which they lived until they could begin working the land in the spring.

Throughout the winter politics was the main topic of conversation. Because of their Northern abolitionist backgrounds, the Ohio men initially favored the free-state tactics of men like James Lane. In a letter to William Scott in Ohio, Quantrill wrote: "Jim Lane, as good a man as we have here, was fighting with U.S. troops at Ft. Scott. . . . The settlers shot two men and wounded 4 or 5, but in self defense, it is a pity they had not shot every Missourian that was there."[20]

Quantrill and the other Ohio youths spent the spring cultivating their claims, but they soon realized that no matter how hard they worked, farming could only provide a meager existence. Despite the promise of a better life in Kansas in the late 1850s, Kansas earned a reputation as the most poverty-stricken region in the country. Thirty thousand settlers returned to their homes back east, and those who remained were unable to return because they could not afford the journey. Much of this was due to the preference of many settlers to make easy money rather than to work at establishing themselves through some honest trade or profession. Some tried to become land speculators, and when this failed many turned a lustful look toward the rich farms across the border in Missouri.

For his part, Quantrill abandoned farming when he heard that jobs could be found in Leavenworth on the wagon trains heading west. In early May 1858 Henry Clay Chiles of Jackson County was hiring bull whackers to handle fifty wagons of freight for the shipping enterprise of Russell, Majors, and Waddell out of Westport, Missouri.[21] The life of most bull whackers was a rough one, and as a result they were very rough men. Alexander Majors was a Presbyterian, and he wanted his employees to become better men so it could not be said that one of his men lost his good name while working for the company. Each bull whacker was given a pair of Colt revolvers for use against Indians and snakes and a Bible for defense against "moral contamination."

These early teamsters were paid a dollar a day, and every day on the trail was considered a workday. Majors's employees, however, received seven days' pay for six days' work. They were then required to attend a meeting on Sunday morning after breakfast, where the Scriptures were read by the wagon master and hymns were sung by all. Then men and animals alike had a full day's rest.

A benefit of this practice of paying for a relatively work-free day gave Majors virtually the pick of the labor market. He probably needed the advantage. He explained: "Being a religious man and opposed to all kinds of profanity and knowing the practice of teamsters to use profane and vulgar language and to travel on the Sabbath Day, another difficulty presented itself which must be overcome. After due reflection . . . I resolved by the help of God to overcome all difficulties that presented themselves . . . whatever the hazards might be. This resolve I carried out, and it was the keynote of my great success in the management of men and animals."

One result of this resolve was the following labor contract: "While I am in the employ of A. Majors, I agree not to use profane language, not to get drunk, not to gamble, not to treat animals cruelly, and not to do anything else that is not compatible with the conduct of a gentleman. I agree, if I violate any of the above conditions, to accept my discharge without any pay for services."

It must have been a "good" contract. Majors noted later, "I do not recall a single instance of a man [being] discharged without pay." Although Majors and his men were armed, he had less Indian trouble than many of his competitors. The company's use of oxen rather than mules was one reason. Another was that the wagons carried no cargoes of whiskey, nor were the men permitted to drink on the trail.[22] Majors's character and employee requirements were in stark contrast to many Kansas entrepreneurs. Early Kansas settler John Ingalls wrote to his father in Massachusetts: "One remarkable feature of the social conditions here is a total disregard of the Sabbath; perhaps because there are no churches. No change of dress or manner indicates the advent of holy time."[23]

After Henry Clay Chiles signed on with Russell, Majors, and Waddell, he hired Quantrill as a bull whacker on a wagon train bound for Utah. The nineteen-year-old Chiles was from the Six Mile Township area of eastern Jackson County, Missouri. Like Majors, he was a religious man, but he was a member of the Six Mile Baptist Church near the historic trading post of Fort Osage in Sibley, where he later helped organize the Buckner Christian Church in Buckner, Missouri. Even though Chiles was but a teenager, he was known for his honesty and executive ability.

During the haul to Utah, Quantrill, for the first time in his life, found himself mostly in the company of Southern men. The wagon train was also escorted by a company of U.S. dragoons, which was led by Maj. Albert Sidney Johnston. At the beginning of the Civil War, Johnston was reputed to be the South's leading general; he died at the April 1862 battle of Shiloh, Tennessee. Two other men who may have been part of the 1858 wagon train were Upton Hays and Adolphus Y. Bennings. Quantrill later stayed with them when they returned to Kansas. Upton Hays was later a Confederate colonel and served with Quantrill. He was the son of Boone Hays, a grandson of Daniel Boone.

Once away from the turbulent and prejudicial surroundings of the Kansas-Missouri border strife, Quantrill for the first time heard the other side of the border issue from Southerners with a stake in the slavery issue.

His job as a bull whacker consisted of walking beside the wagons and snapping his whip overhead to keep the ox teams moving steadily forward. The trip was slow and took several months.

In a letter to his mother, Quantrill described a violent snowstorm in the South Pass of the Rocky Mountains on September 3, 1858. In early October the wagon train made its last stop at Fort Laramie in western Wyoming. When the wagons finally arrived in Salt Lake City, in an October 15 letter to his mother, Quantrill described life in Mormon country:

> I arrived here two weeks ago and I was never so surprised in my life as I was to find a people living here in large cities and towns and farming the lands here which without their untiring labor would be a desert producing neither grass nor timber, nothing but a few stunted weeds, but they have converted it into fine farms and gardens by directing from the mountain streams and watering the whole country. I am going to apply for a school and I think I can obtain one, they pay from $50 to $60 per month and I think that will pay for one winter at least.

In the letter he also noted that in the spring he wanted to go to the Colville gold mines in Canada. Without going into detail, he reported that he had developed some trouble with his throat.

As a loving and devoted son, Quantrill wrote many letters to his mother. In one he assured her: "Bear in mind that I will do what is right, take care of myself, try to make a fortune honestly, which I think I can do in a year or two. I will always let you know where I am and how I am doing and by the next mail I will send you my picture as I appeared in camp coming out here, and also a letter."[24]

A December 1, 1858, letter from Salt Lake City begins with an apology for not writing because he had been ill with "mountain fever." The malady had incapacitated him for three weeks, and his recuperation required two more weeks. The disease apparently struck him in late October, just after he had arrived in Utah. His illness prevented him from taking the teaching job he had mentioned earlier, but he explained that he would be applying for a fifty-dollar-a-month clerking position with the army's quartermaster department. A January 9, 1859, letter reported that he had lost the clerkship but found another job as a cook for twenty-five men. Still, he wanted to find a government job because he had good recommendations from some of the chief men in camp.

Quantrill himself was very optimistic. He was quick with a favorable comment to those whom he met. Although initially naive, only after much experience did he come to evaluate more seriously the true state of things. Upon meeting the Mormons of Utah, he described them as hardworking, clean, without guile, and highly moral. Quantrill was always slow to form a bad opinion of anyone, but after some later life experiences he become disillusioned and realized that he had been deceived, just as he had been about the free-staters back in Kansas. After living with the Mormons for three months, he formed a different opinion and wrote his mother: "They are a very ignorant set of people and generally great rouges and rascals thinking nothing to be too bad to do to a Gentile."[25]

The young man from Canal Dover never made it to the Colfield gold fields. After the winter of 1859, Quantrill decided to try his luck in the Colorado gold fields around Pike's Peak. Much talk circulated about the possibilities of finding gold there, so he left Salt Lake City in the early spring of 1859 with a party of eighteen other men. During that trip they suffered from cold weather, starvation, and hostile Indians. For two months he worked in the gold fields, reporting home he barely made "$1.00 a day in the best diggings. . . . I dug out $54.34 and worked 47 days which money hardly paid my board and expenses."[26] His disillusionment in everything he had anticipated came to a head as he started back to the Tuscarawas Lake region outside Lawrence, Kansas, accompanied by a close friend.[27]

Quantrill had beaten the odds. Of the original group of nineteen men, he was one of seven who survived the experience. Resigning himself to cease rambling in search of his fortune, he decided to settle down in one place and make his living. From Lawrence, Kansas, he wrote to his mother on July 30, 1859, that a friend and he were attacked by a band of jayhawkers on the banks of the Little Cottonwood River and robbed of their horses and all their possessions. Quantrill explained that he was "hunting away from camp about a mile and a half and hearing the firing hurried to camp in time to see my friend lying on the ground apparently dead, but still breathing with difficulty having been shot three times, his leg broke below the knee, shot in the thigh with 7 iron slugs and last shot through the body with an arrow."[28]

Later Quantrill told the story to his followers and elaborated the details enough to suggest that his companion was an older brother—but he had no older brother. William H. Gregg, one of the earliest to join Quantrill's unit, related the story this way:

> Me and my older brother, with a wagon and team and, a negro boy, started for Pike's Peak, arriving at Lawrence, we stopped to make some purchases, leaving some time in the afternoon. Camped near the Kaw River, where we were attacked by [James] Montgomery's Jayhawkers, my brother killed, I wounded and left for dead, the negro, wagon and team appropriated and, after keeping vigil for twenty four hours amidst the hideous howling of hundreds of coyotes, becoming almost famished for water, I managed to crawl to the river and quench my thirst, after which I spied a canoe at the opposite bank, and soon after an Indian approached the canoe to whom I hollered, asking him to come over, which he did, and after hearing my story, buried my dead brother and, took me to his cabin where he and his wife nursed me to health. After which, I [took] myself to Lawrence and joined Montgomery, his officers and men, I next obtained the names of all the men who had taken part in the killing of my brother, etc., I at once went to work in a systematic way to get revenge for the wrongs heaped upon me and my brother, I managed to get one at a time away from the command and never permitted one to get back alive, until, when the war came on, only two were left.[29]

According to many other authors, Quantrill was himself wounded by the jayhawkers in this attack, but he apparently did not relay this information in his letter to his mother, possibly to allay her fears on the subject. He then directed her to send her next letter to him by way of Osawatomie, Lykins County, Kansas Territory.

What prompted this gang of outlaws to make an unprovoked attack upon innocent civilians? Were their actions those of abolitionists or were they motivated as robbers and murderers? As criminals they would be brought to justice, but as abolitionists they were protected from recriminations in Kansas society. In their accounts of the story, John Newman Edwards and William Gregg— both of whom were contemporaries of Quantrill—state that Quantrill and his companion were accompanied by a free black man whose role was general utility person, part hostler and part cook. In their accounts the jayhawkers reacted exactly the same as they had done in previous raids and would do so again in subsequent raids. If it appeared that a man's political persuasion was Southern, then his life and property were forfeit. Edwards states that the jayhawkers left the white men for dead and, after plundering all the goods, took the black man unharmed away with them. Gregg's account expressly claims that Quantrill was attacked by James Montgomery's band of jayhawkers and "the negro, wagon and team [were] appropriated." Gregg added, "Montgomery's band were known to get one hundred dollars for every negro caught and carried back to their headquarters in Osawatomie, Kansas. From there they ran them around to New Orleans and sold them."[30]

Up until this time, Quantrill had only been a spectator in the events transpiring along the border. Swayed by the opinions of those around him before he left for Utah, he had been raised an abolitionist and felt strongly for that cause. While farming in the Kansas Territory, he had only heard stories and rhetoric about the wrongs being done by the pro-slavery side. Now, however, it was he who had been the innocent victim of a cruel jayhawker attack. While suffering the indignation of being robbed and helping his friend to recuperate from his injuries, he now had time to reflect on these injustices heaped on him. He recalled the stories by the Southern men whom he had recently met and accompanied to Utah. He weighed the actions of the pro-slavery men against those of the free-state men and found the preponderance of unjustifiable deeds clearly against the free-state side. Quantrill became a changed man and made a decision that changed his life forever. He decided his future by the old adage, One man with courage makes a majority.[31]

For the next few weeks, Quantrill nursed his friend back to health. A measure of the times was that a man's pride and honor would not allow a personal indignity to be taken lightly or ignored. Feuds were a normal part of life. Duels were commonplace.[32] Caroline Quantrill said that her son was "of a retiring nature, he had a ready smile and a warm heart and was never known to be quarrelsome." William Scott, a boyhood friend, added, "He would fight if drawn into a brawl and obliged to defend himself, but it was not his choice."

After being attacked and robbed of his possessions, Quantrill now felt that he had been drawn into a brawl. He began to formulate a plan. The people who had attacked him and his friend were not Missourians; they were jayhawkers. These people stole from friend and foe alike, and the group that attacked Quantrill's camp supposedly belonged to James Montgomery's band of thieves. Montgomery was a preacher from Linn County, Kansas Territory, and a captain in James Lane's militia. In the late 1850s he was arguably the most feared of the border marauders, and even before the war, he led forays for plunder into Missouri.

In the end, Quantrill decided he would mete out his own kind of justice and revenge. The border situation would never be the same again.

Quantrill knew that he could do nothing alone against so large a party, but he could seek out the individuals involved. First, though, he had to find work, so he found a position in a private school during the fall and winter in the Judge Roberts District in Stanton, Kansas. The school term was six months long, and for the purpose of computing tuition, each term was divided into two three-month sections. Tuition for each section was $2.50 per student. Part of Quantrill's employment agreement was that he would "board around," spending two to three weeks with various patrons and families. He remained with some longer than others, spending two months at the house of Judge Thomas Roberts.

While teaching school, Quantrill continued to plan his revenge. One of his students, Roxey Troxel, said: "Quantrill was a good teacher. . . . [He] talked for the free-state side, but so far as she ever heard he took no part in affairs; dressed neatly, stayed at Bennings Saturday and Sundays; a very quiet man, secretive and peculiar; no one knew how to take him." Evidently the jayhawker attack had affected him visibly, but he was intent on confronting his attackers in a way that would guarantee his success.

Other eyewitness accounts from the students of the 1859–60 winter term indicate that Quantrill was the best teacher they ever had. When he did talk politics, they recalled he talked for the free-state side, but he did not take an active part in political affairs like he was known to do when he first arrived in the territory. When he wrote his mother on January 26, 1860, he told her that, according to his firsthand experience, the newspaper articles she undoubtedly read about the outrages committed by the Southerners in Kansas were false. Quantrill told his mother that the free-state side had caused all the havoc and upheaval in the territory. He added that the trouble-makers sympathized with John Brown and endorsed his actions, and that he found it difficult to have to associate with people who were so corrupt both morally and ethically. Only a few years earlier Daniel Webster had stated, "Justice is the ligament, which holds civilized beings and civilized nations together." For Quantrill, justice did not seem to exist in Kansas.

As an educated man, Quantrill analyzed the border situation and pondered the kind of men who lived in the area as well as their philosophies. The most discussed event at the time was John Brown's unsuccessful attack on the U.S. arsenal at Harpers Ferry. Quantrill thought back to Brown's days in Kansas and looked at the kind of men who gathered around him.

Brown's most notorious act occurred on May 24, 1856, when the abolitionist and his sons and two other men exacted their own brand of revenge for a recent sacking of Lawrence by pro-slavery ruffians. Brown marched his small band by night to some cabins near Pottawatomie Creek. They seized James Doyle and his teenage sons, William and Drury, and dragged them from their cabin and hacked them to death with swords that had been donated by abolitionist backers. Immediately the group moved on to Allen Wilkerson's cabin. Wilkerson was seized from his wife and two children and murdered in the darkness. Lastly Brown's band broke into the home of James Harris, seizing and killing Harris and a guest, William Sherman.

Brown personally knew the men he killed that night. All were advocates of slavery but none owned slaves. In addition to the six murders, Brown's small force stole their victims' weapons, saddles, and horses. Immediately after the murders, Brown allegedly knelt to pray. Many influential abolitionists in the East encouraged Brown's lawlessness by articles and poems. Like Henry David Thoreau, these supporters turned a blind eye to Brown's criminal deeds and praised him for opposing unjust laws and for championing human dignity.

Many of Brown's co-conspirators in the Harpers Ferry attack came from similar backgrounds. Several were foreign revolutionaries, like Austrian John Henry Kagi, who was a leader in one of Brown's gangs and was said to be the best educated but coarse in appearance and an agnostic. He was captured in 1856 by U.S. troops for jayhawking crimes and briefly imprisoned. Kagi immigrated to Kansas with James Lane and enlisted during the Civil War in the Second Kansas Jayhawker Regiment. Kagi had already made a name for himself by associating with John Brown during the winter of 1858, when he and Brown split their forces and launched simultaneous raids into Missouri to free slaves. Kagi's party liberated only one slave, after which he killed the owner.

The Austrian Jewish revolutionary August Bondi accompanied Brown on his jayhawking raids in Kansas. Another member of this group was British revolutionary Richard Realf. Two other Jewish abolitionists also rode with Brown: Theodore Wiener from Poland and Jacob Benjamin from Bohemia. Aaron Dwight Stevens, another associate, had fought in the Mexican War where he was tried for "mutiny, engaging in a drunken riot, and assaulting an officer." He was sentenced to death, but the president commuted it to three years hard labor at Fort Leavenworth. Stevens escaped then joined forces with the free-state settlers in Kansas and became a colonel with the Second

Kansas Jayhawking Regiment during the war. Along with Kagi and Stevens, another conspirator was John E. Cook, who had seen much fighting in prewar Kansas. He was described as reckless, impulsive, and indiscreet. Charles Plummer Tidd was one of Brown's closest associates and was with Brown on many raids into Missouri before the war.

The people living in the Harpers Ferry area before the war were constantly agitated by Northern abolitionists who invaded Virginia to incite a slave rebellion through arson and murder. John Brown had on hand such a large quantity of Sharps carbines from the New England Emigrant Aid Society that he brought 102 with him on his ill-conceived 1859 attack on the arsenal. Brown was reported to be carrying one when he was wounded and captured by Lt. Israel Green, the leader of the assault on the arsenal.

After the Harpers Ferry attack, correspondence was found in Brown's headquarters that revealed the monetary support he received from New Englanders and Ohioans. Two henchmen, Aaron Stevens and John Kagi, were killed when the marines stormed the building in which the raiders had taken shelter. Brown had also brought fifteen hundred pikes with him to Harpers Ferry with which to arm the slaves once they revolted against their masters.

In John Brown's failed raid the South could see its destiny as one of utter subjugation to the North. Southerners witnessed Brown's invasion of a Southern state and saw that many of his associates were murderers and revolutionaries who had already escaped justice by flight, finding protection in the Northern states. They felt they must either submit to degradation and the loss of their property worth many millions or secede from the Union and single-handedly carry on the integrity of the Constitution that their forefathers had made when they separated from England. Brown's raid was an eyeopener for them, and they were disgusted when the North honored Brown as a martyr. The South saw that his purpose was to "apply flames to our dwellings, and the weapons of destruction to our lives."[33] Two of John Brown's party at Harpers Ferry were his own sons. Both escaped. One went back to Ohio, and the other went to Iowa; neither state agreed to surrender them as fugitives from justice charged with murder and inciting insurrection in Virginia.

The August 24, 1859, *Chambersburg (Pa.) Valley Spirit* opined, "What has taken place at Harpers Ferry is but a trifle in comparison with what will some day occur, if conservative men of all political creeds do not unite with the Democracy to put down the sectional party [the Republican Party] that has disturbed the peace of the country." Citizens on both sides of the border between North and South were shocked at the memory of the brutal Pottawatomie murders and the Harpers Ferry insurrectionist, but many Northerners spoke highly of Brown's militant actions. Some eyewitnesses to Brown's deeds chose differently.

While Quantrill was still teaching school in Stanton, Kansas, he wrote his mother on January 26, 1860:

> You have undoubtedly heard of the wrongs committed in this territory by the Southern people, or pro-slavery party, but when one once knows the facts they can easily see that it has been the opposite party that have been the main movers in the troubles and by far the most lawless set of people in the country. They all sympathize for old J. Brown, who should have been hung years ago, indeed hanging was too good for him. May I never see a more contemptible people than those who sympathize for him. A murderer and a robber, made a martyr of, just think of it.[34]

Quantrill's teaching term was over at the end of March 1860. During his term of employment he had healed physically, but his mind was still bent on revenge. As soon as the term was over, he went to live with the Delaware Indians on their reservation on the north side of the Kansas River, which extended upriver to the west of Lawrence. In a letter to his mother he reported that he was employed on a surveying party on the Delaware Indian lands. He stayed with them exclusively for several weeks before venturing into town. In Lawrence he used the name Charles Hart and told people that he was a detective for the Delaware Indians. By this deception he hoped to learn the names of the men who had recently robbed him.

In his last known letter to his mother, dated June 23, 1860, Quantrill revealed that he had sent money to the family in previous letters. In this letter he indicated that he had more money to send and planned to bring it himself, but it would be awhile before he could come home. For the next few months he had committed himself to something. He concluded: "I will say that I will be home any how soon as the 1st of September and probably sooner, by that time I will be done with Kansas."[35]

Quantrill planned to join the jayhawkers. It was the only way he could get justice for the cruel treatment that had been done him. Quantrill knew that only after he had found and punished the last of the jayhawkers that had robbed him would his sense of justice be satisfied, allowing him to return back home to his family.

To initiate his plan, as soon as the school term ended, he began to mingle with the same people he believed were so contemptible in his January 26, 1860, letter. To catch a thief, Quantrill had to become one. The students of his last term, when interviewed after the war, all confirmed that their teacher bore an immaculate appearance and upstanding character in the classroom. Now Quantrill forsook sartorial fastidiousness to carry out his revenge.

William Stockwell knew Quantrill as a schoolteacher in Stanton and recalled, "Quantrill was very quiet . . . dressed neatly, and seemed very particular and careful as to his dress." A description of Quantrill, given by an eyewitness who knew him during the war and later given to the June 10, 1904, *Oak Grove Missouri Banner,* described Quantrill: "In his attire he was scrupulously neat and delighted in kid gloves, until he was forced to take to the part of his hair and to the polishing of his fingernails." In a postwar account Harrison Trow reported that Quantrill "reached Lawrence and went to where Jim Lane was stationed with his company. He wanted to get into the company that murdered his brother and wounded him. After a few days he was taken in and, from outward appearance, he became a full-fledged Redleg, but in his heart he was doing this only to seek revenge on those who had killed his brother and wounded him at Cottonwood, Kansas."

The Redlegs, a paramilitary organization from Lawrence, were known for their brutality and thievery. They were named for the red Moroccan leggings they wore. Sometime during the spring of 1860 Quantrill entered Lawrence wearing a rough woolen shirt and corduroy pants tucked into high leather boots. A slouch hat was pulled low over his face, and he carried a cheap oil-cloth grip.[36]

Using the alias Charley Hart, Quantrill often stayed at the Whitney House Hotel owned by Nathan Stone. It was close to the south ferry ramp on the Kansas River. Holland Wheeler was at the hotel desk when Quantrill entered and registered. As soon as Quantrill left the lobby, Stone showed the guest book to Wheeler, who noted the signature of Charley Hart. Wheeler reported, "Mr. Stone, calling me to the desk, opened the day-book and showed me on the back page the name Wm. C. Quantrill, remarking, 'This is Hart's real name. He is a detective for the Delaware Indians.'" The 1860 census for Lawrence lists a Charley Hart as living in the Whitney Hotel; the census also notes the hotel was the residence of the owner—Stone—and his family, Holland Wheeler, and other guests as of June 6, 1860.

Quantrill's occupation is listed as surveyor, as are two other tenants' besides Wheeler. When questioned about Quantrill, Wheeler recollected that he "had a lady friend who was in town at times. [I] saw him riding with her in a carriage several times. He was always friendly with me."

On June 23, 1860, only two weeks after the census was taken, Quantrill wrote to his mother: "I have been out with a surveying party on the Delaware

Indian lands and was obliged to camp out under rather unfavorable circum-stances." Lydia Stone, a daughter of the hotel proprietor, nursed Quantrill back to health after a severe illness. He was very grateful to her.[37]

There are two explanations for Quantrill's registering at the hotel as a detective for the Delaware Indians. A sale of Indian trust lands was in progress when Quantrill reached Lawrence. One requirement of the sale was that land could only be purchased by actual settlers, but fraud was rampant and rendered this stipulation of little account.[38] Speculation surfaced that James Lane had fraudulently acquired land that legally belonged to the Indi-ans; Quantrill was hired by the Indians to find out how this happened. Lane was accused of stealing the land by abusing political power, and Quantrill—as an educated white man—was in a better position to uncover the facts. For these reasons Quantrill frequently came to town to gain evidence against Lane and about his attackers from the previous summer.

While Quantrill was in Lawrence one day, a white man was attacked by an Indian and severely wounded. Henry Clarke noted: "Quantrill was one of the first to arrive on the scene. [He] assisted for an hour or more in caring for the man."[39] Clarke remembered Quantrill as being "about five feet ten inches tall, rather slight of stature, weighing perhaps, 150 pounds."

Lawrence came to be associated with Quantrill even before the war. It was the home of James Lane, a hotbed of abolitionism, and the center of jay-hawking activities. It was the very place Quantrill needed to be to find out who his attackers had been so they could be brought to justice.

Quantrill learned that the men he was looking for were living in and around Lawrence; they all belonged to James Lane's Kansas militia. Lane's most notorious henchmen, James Montgomery (the so-called preacher from Mound City, Kansas) and Charles Jennison (a small, audacious, brutal physi-cian), were the leaders of the most notorious bands of jayhawkers on the border before the war. Jennison was a vicious jayhawker whose military posi-tion afforded him opportunities for robbery.[40] Even before the war, Jennison had organized the Mound City Sharps Rifle Guards for the purpose of plun-dering neighboring Missouri farms. This military group ultimately became the Seventh Kansas Jayhawker Cavalry. Later on, Jennison also organized the Fifteenth Kansas Jayhawker Cavalry. In each case, Jennison's units were pop-ularly called jayhawkers.

The word *jayhawking* simply meant stealing, but to Missouri slaveholders it had a more precise denotation: It signified planned raids into Missouri with no specific military objective except to plunder farmhouses and steal, kill, and burn anything and anyone as well as to free any slaves who were present.

Lesser-known jayhawkers who were equally cruel and brutal included Eli Snyder of Osawatomie, John E. Stewart of Lawrence, George Hoyt, and Jennison's second-in-command, Daniel Anthony.[41]

John E. Stewart was said to be the chief among the abolitionist extremists. He lived on a farm four miles southeast of Lawrence where runaway slaves were aided on their way to Canada. Men like John H. Kagi made Stewart's farm a frequent rendezvous. Even before the war Stewart had gotten a reputation of being associated with John Brown and James Montgomery in their deprecatory raids across the border. Stewart was said to be second in reputation only to James Montgomery and Charles Jennison. Before coming to Kansas he had been a Methodist minister in New Hampshire, where he had "preached to good acceptance." His frequent forays across the border resulted in the Missouri legislature placing a price on his head, and he was suspected in Kansas of "entertaining loose notions with regard to property in horses as well as negroes." As in the case of all jayhawkers, his professed zeal for abolition caused a large proportion of the settlers to overlook these activities.[42]

Quantrill soon gained the confidence of Eli Snyder and the band of jayhawkers operating out of Osawatomie. Snyder was best known for burning to death four Missourians in their cabin while on a raid with Montgomery. John Dean, a close associate of Snyder, owned a wagon shop in Lawrence. It was here that the jayhawkers obtained the wagons they took into Missouri to haul out plunder and kidnapped slaves. Dean represented an element in Kansas known as the "practical abolitionists": men who believed that only direct and militant action could eradicate slavery. Another jayhawker and former convict, Marshall Cleveland, did not have any quarrel with the Missourians other than his lust for the blooded horses, mules, cattle, and other chattels for which there was a ready market in Kansas. Cleveland's band was described as a "score of dissolute and dirty desperadoes . . . degraded ruffians of the worst type."

Using the guise of a Kansas loafer and ne'er-do-well, Quantrill made quiet inquires into the jayhawkers' secrets and activities. In this way he encountered notable jayhawkers Sidney S. Herd and Walt McGee. Herd operated the north Kansas ferry and knew Quantrill well, often taking him into Lawrence via his ferry. "At first Quantrill appeared to be rather reticent," Herd reported, "but after a time, crossing frequently as he did, he appeared to become more sociable and often stopped and chatted with the boys and after a time became more chummy. . . . [H]e did not strike me as having any braggadocio or desire to make any display in any way."[43]

Many rough characters and criminals hung around the north ferry landing. To gain their confidence Quantrill malingered there also. Practical abolitionist John Dean once asked Quantrill why he associated with such notorious border ruffians and outlaws such as Herd and the McGees, but Quantrill assured him that he did so only to learn their secrets. Dean and Quantrill eventually became so close that Dean assigned Quantrill the task of assassinating Allen Pinks, a Lawrence black who had committed the detestable crime of selling one of his own race back into slavery.[44] If Quantrill had wanted to gain the absolute confidence of the Kansas jayhawkers all he had to do was to kill Pinks, but even while pretending to be a jayhawker, he would not murder a man in cold blood. When Quantrill failed to do the job, Dean decided to kill Pinks himself but only succeeded in wounding him. Ultimately—and fittingly—a mob of Leavenworth blacks lynched Pinks for his treachery to his race.

For several months Quantrill rode as a jayhawker in the Kansas militia. He enlisted as a private, was promoted to orderly sergeant, then rose to the rank of lieutenant. He next associated with the notorious Capt. John Stewart. In Lawrence, Quantrill had finally gained the confidence of the jayhawkers and become a member of their band. While riding with them he discovered the identities of the men who had attacked his camp the previous summer.

The February 24, 1899, *Topeka Capital* related Quantrill's early history after he was attacked by Montgomery's band:

He went to Leavenworth and enlisted in Lane's Jayhawkers. . . . Lane was his friend. He admired the modest, clean-shaven, handsomely dressed young lieutenant who was so prompt to respond to every call. . . . One day Quantrill was sent with a small detail of three men to convoy a train of stolen slaves that was coming out of Missouri via the Underground Railway. . . . When the convoy came back one of the men was missing . . . the man was found dead with a Navy revolver bullet hole in the middle of his forehead.

A little later four companies of Lane's men, including Quantrill's, were ordered down around Fort Scott to check the Missourians who had been doing harm across the Kansas border. When they returned, sixty men were missing, forty-two of whom had fallen in encounters with the enemy. But the other eighteen, every one had fallen mysteriously at night with a bullet hole from a Navy revolver in the center of the forehead . . . still men kept falling at the sentry posts, always with the Navy bullet holes in their foreheads. Every dash after the Indians, every raid across the border counted its one, two or three victims, whom no one saw die and in whose foreheads was always the deadly blue puncture. One night Quantrill and his company commander, Captain Pickens, and two other men were sitting by a campfire.

Pickens went back into their lives and opened pages of their history. The
Captain told with much apparent pleasure of a little foray on which he
had taken his company several years before. They had fallen upon a camping party on the Little Cottonwood River and wiped them out. He mentioned how the plunder was divided, the mules sold, the money put all
together in one pile and gambled for, the kind of a report made to headquarters and the general drunk, which succeeded their return. Three days
later the Captain's body was found with two of his most reliable men along
the banks of Bull Creek, shot like the balance with a bullet hole from a
Navy revolver in their head. Captain Pickens' company along with the
company to which Quantrill belonged had lost thirteen men between
October 1859 and 1860. . . . Even Colonel Jim Lane's orderly had boasted
of the Cottonwood affair in his cups at a banquet one night. The orderly
was found dead soon after.[45]

Quantrill allegedly reported all of this to his followers. One of the men
he tracked down was Jack Winn, a somewhat noted horse thief and abolitionist. An assignment took Quantrill and three men near Wyandotte to
meet a wagonload of freed blacks under the pilotage of Winn. One of
Quantrill's three men failed to return, nor could any account be given of his
absence until his body was found near a creek several days later. In the
center of his forehead was the round, smooth hole of a Navy revolver bullet.
Those who looked for Winn's safe arrival were disappointed, too. Quantrill
reportedly shot an Underground Railroad conductor and two scouts from
Montgomery's command.

Overlooked by historians is the account of a horseman named James
Williams, who rode into Quantrill's camp on October 25, 1862, when
Quantrill was the head of a company of Southern guerrillas headed south for
winter quarters. Harrison Trow, one of Quantrill's most trusted soldiers,
reported Williams's arrival near Dayton, in Cass County:

There came to his camp here a good looking man, clad like a citizen. . . .
Would Quantrill let him become a guerrilla? "Your name?" asked the chief.
The recruit winced under the abrupt question slightly, and Quantrill saw
the start. Quantrill, without looking at the newcomer, appeared yet to be
analyzing him. Suddenly he spoke up. "I have seen you before. Where?"
"Nowhere." "Think again. I have seen you in Lawrence, Kansas." The face
was a murderer's face now. . . . [William] Gregg, standing next to him and
nearest to him, laid his hand on his revolver. "Stop," said Quantrill,

motioning to Gregg, "do not harm him, but disarm him." "You suspect me," he said. . . . "But I have never been in Lawrence in my life."

Quantrill was lost in thought again with the strange man. . . . Quantrill still tried to make out his face, to find a name for that Sphinx in front of him . . . and at last the past returned to him in the light of a swift reveal-ment. "I have it all now," he said, "and you are a Jayhawker. The name is immaterial. I have seen you at Lawrence; I have seen you at Lane's head-quarters; I have been a soldier myself with you; we have done duty together . . . but I have to hang you this hour, by God."

Quantrill's grave voice broke calmly in: "Bring a rope." Blunt brought it. "Make an end fast." The end was made fast to a low-lying limb. In the firelight the noose expanded. "Up with him, men." . . . "So you mean to get rid of me that way? It is like you, Quantrill. I know you, but you do not know me. I have been hunting you for three long years. You killed my brother in Kansas, you killed others there, your comrades. I did not know, till afterwards, what kind of a devil we had around our very messes . . . a devil who prowled about the camp fires and shot soldiers in the night that broke bread with him in the day.

"You do well to disarm me," he said, addressing Gregg, "For I intended to kill your captain. . . . Do your worst," he said, and he folded his arms across his breast and stood stolid as the tree over his head. . . . Even Quantrill's face softened, but only for a moment. Then he spoke harshly to Blunt, "He is one of the worst of a band that I failed to make a finish of before the war came, but what escapes today is dragged up by the next tomorrow. If I had not recognized him he would have killed me. I do not hang him for that, however, I hang him because the whole breed and race to which he belongs should be exterminated. Sergeant, do your duty." Blunt slipped the noose about the prisoner's neck, and the four men who had at first disarmed him, tightened it. No man spoke a word. Something like a huge pendulum swung as though spun by a strong hand, quivered once or twice, and then swinging to and fro and regularly, stopped forever.[46]

In this account, Quantrill admitted he joined the jayhawkers to wipe out the band that attacked him before the war. This account has never before been addressed because to do so would show that Quantrill's story about being attacked and robbed by Kansas jayhawkers was true. Frank Smith, John McCorkle, and Harrison Trow—Quantrill's own soldiers and witnesses to the deed recounted above—all wrote postwar accounts of this incident and described it as witnessed by many of Quantrill's men.[47]

Quantrill brought many of his attackers to justice except the last few. How much longer his vengeance would have continued no one knows, but something soon happened that changed everything. A jayhawker raid was planned on Morgan Walker, a wealthy Missouri slave owner in Jackson County, Missouri.

2

The Pariah Strikes

Injustice anywhere is injustice everywhere.

—ANONYMOUS

QUANTRILL FINALLY HAD THE confidence of the last of the men who had robbed and assaulted him and his friend the summer before. He was now a close friend of John Dean, who was a close friend of John E. Stewart. The latter had little interest in another foray into Missouri due to the bounty placed on his head after his previous jayhawker raids. Dean also associated with a group of young men from Springdale, Iowa, who called themselves the Liberator Club—named after William Lloyd Garrison's abolitionist newspaper. These men—Charles Ball, Chalkey T. Lipsey, Edwin S. Morrison, and Albert Southwick—all came from strict Quaker backgrounds, but they had slid a long way from the peaceful teachings of the pacifist sect and armed themselves with pistols and knives. Presumably, these young zealots had participated only a few short months before with James Montgomery in the attack on Quantrill and his friend on the banks of the Little Cottonwood.

Twenty-three-year-old Ball was a first cousin to the Coppoc brothers who had followed John Brown to Harpers Ferry. Ball had already participated in several Missouri raids to steal slaves and then send them toward Canada via the Underground Railroad.

Twenty-two-year-old Chalkey T. Lipsey, like Quantrill, had worked on farms and taught school. He also had made a trip across the plains with a

29

wagon train and had accompanied his brothers to Pike's Peak in search of gold. Both Ball and Lipsey came to Kansas in 1857.

Twenty-one-year-old Edwin S. Morrison came to Kansas in 1859 with his twenty-three-year-old cousin Albert Southwick. Southwick allegedly rode with the band on the Morgan Walker raid, but at Osawatomie he remained behind with Eli Snyder. Southwick was intellectually limited and somewhat unbalanced, but he managed to serve later in the Tenth Kansas Jayhawker Regiment during the war.[1]

In the winter of 1857–58 John Brown had held abolitionist meetings in Springdale, Ohio, where he had delivered fiery speeches alongside foreign anarchists like Richard Realf and John Kagi. After Ball, Morrison, Lipsey, and Southwick heard these incendiary discourses they feverishly took up the abolitionist cause. They left Ohio for Kansas, settling in Atchison County, where they joined John Dean and participated in the Missouri slave raids.

Settler W. L. Potter claimed that the jayhawkers received sixty dollars for every slave stolen from Missouri and delivered to the Underground Railroad.[2] A. J. Walker recalled that the jayhawkers from Osawatomie, Kansas, received one hundred dollars for every slave they delivered. Rather then send them north to freedom, Walker reported, "They run them around to New Orleans and there sold them."[3] Sen. Stephen A. Douglas noted that more than fifteen thousand slaves had been smuggled into New York and that more than eighty-five vessels had sailed from New York in 1859 to transport more slaves to Southern markets.

During the fall of 1860 three black refugees happened upon the four young men from Springdale and asked for their assistance in rescuing their families from slavery in the Indian Territory (Oklahoma). The four zealots agreed to help and took the fugitive slaves with them to Lawrence to get reinforcements. They first sought out John Dean at his wagon shop. Dean looked up Quantrill and another man, John S. Jones. Dean knew he would naturally need more men, especially for a raid into the Indian Territory, so the seven men rode to Osawatomie and contacted Eli Snyder. They asked the uneducated and rough-spoken Snyder to lead the raid, but he dissuaded them from undertaking the venture because they had little money and the weather might turn against them.

Quantrill silently watched the chance for vengeance slip away. A short time later Charlie Ball took notice of Morgan Walker, a wealthy slave owner from Jackson County, Missouri. Seizing the moment, Quantrill suggested they raid the Walker farm, which employed twenty-five slaves and owned several hundred fine horses and mules. Later Quantrill told his wife he had promised the jayhawkers he would pay with his own life if Walker's slaves were not brought back to Kansas and freed.[4]

Walker was an early Jackson County settler. He was a Virginian by birth and had married in Kentucky. In 1834 he moved to Missouri and built a large farm three miles northeast of Blue Springs. Walker was a product of the Old South, and his outlook on life matched his upbringing.

Walker was one of the wealthiest landowners in the area. In addition to his large acreage, slaves, and thoroughbreds, he was known to keep large sums of money in his home. Walker also had a reputation for kind hospitality. John Newman Edwards noted: "His hands might have been rough and sun-browned, but they were always open. None were ever turned away from his door hungry. Under the old roof of the homestead . . . the last wayfarer got the same comfort as the first, and altogether they got the best." Walker, Newman continued, was, "old fashioned in his courtesies and his hospitalities, he fed the poor, helped the needy, prayed regularly to the good God, did right by his neighbors and his friends, etc."[5]

Like Stewart, Snyder was leery of leading another raid into Missouri because of the price on his head, but the other jayhawkers elected to go. On December 8, 1860, the raiders borrowed a wagon from Dean's wagon shop to carry back the loot. William Gregg commented, "In the name of Abolitionism they took to the highway, and for the sake of freedom in Kansas great freedom was taken with other people's lives and property."[6]

The jayhawkers planned to approach the house first, occupy it, capture the men of the household, commandeer the slaves to hitch up all the wagons and teams, then gallop back to Kansas. Well mounted and armed, the raiders rode by twos but not together, for fear of raising suspicion, until they arrived at a first rendezvous point. Riding mostly after dark and keeping to themselves so as not to attract attention, the raiders took two days to reach the area around the Walker farm. They arrived cold, wet, and hungry from an earlier rain that day. Clouds still filled the sky so that no light came from the stars above. About a mile from the farm they found a place to hide in the dense woods on the Daniel DeWitt farm, and there they made camp for the night.

These young raiders were understandably nervous. They were deep in unfriendly territory. Three miles to the southwest lay the half dozen homes and stores of the village of Blue Springs. Seven miles back to the west was Independence, the county seat of Jackson County. Ten miles farther west was the small town of Kansas City, near the Kansas border. Three miles behind them was the Little Blue River, winding northward to the Missouri River.

The country was covered with thick timber except for the tracts that the farmers had cleared for farming. The mostly open prairie lay farther to the east and south.

For years jayhawkers had raided into Missouri. The mere mention of Kansas was enough to infuriate Missourians. Most of those who lived close to the border had already had a home burned, a loved one shot down in cold blood, or had their smokehouse emptied, their stock driven off, and their slaves kidnapped by the Kansas jayhawkers. Or the same things had happened to their neighbor. Many victims were left destitute and at the mercy of friends or relatives until they could rebuild again. In contrast, the Walker farm was a beautiful homestead with rolling meadows, fertile fields of grain, woodland pastures, and dense timber.

Early on the morning of December 10, Quantrill volunteered to reconnoiter the area. "Boys, you lay low here while I take a look-see at Walker's place," he calmly said. "I'll be back soon." Twice that day Quantrill had left his companions in camp and come back with food, either for the men or the horses. On one of these errands he went directly to Walker's house and laid out the whole plan of attack for the landowner's benefit.

Over the years there have been many explanations of what happened at the Walker farm that day. The following is based on the eyewitness account of Andrew Walker, Morgan's son. He claimed that Quantrill first approached his younger brother, John Riley Walker, who was working in the fields. Quantrill warned him about the upcoming raid and said, "Tonight I betray them; I am coming to the side of your father."[7]

Morgan Walker was not at home at the time. He had gone to Independence that morning on business. John Walker was hesitant to trust Quantrill, so he took him to his older brother, Andrew.

Andrew Walker reported: "I first saw Quantrill in the latter part of November, 1860. . . . I was in the field shucking corn at the time. He told me that he was with a party of three men who had come over from Kansas to rob us."[8] He added: "My visitor wore rather shabby clothes, but had a pleasant dignified appearance. His complexion was light, his hair sandy, and a pair of the brightest, most remarkable eyes you would find in a lifetime looked out at me over his small Roman nose. . . . Quantrill said that his companions were in the woods only a short distance away and they would return after nightfall to do their stealing." When Andrew asked him why he was betraying them, he replied it was for revenge: "He had joined the Kansas militia in order to avenge his brother's murder by the very men who were on this raid with him. There had been thirty-two of them, and these save two, who had quit the jayhawkers and moved to California, were the last of them."[9] Confronted with the peculiar situation, Andrew added, "My natural mistrust of so extraordinary a story was disarmed by the frank manner of the stranger, no less than by the fact that I could think of no reason, in the range of ordinary probabilities, why he should seek to deceive me."

Quantrill pointedly admonished the young men, "Take such action as you see fit, and I warn you they are desperate men, and have taken an oath never to surrender."

When Morgan Walker returned to his home that afternoon he invited Quantrill to stay for supper, but he asked him to remove his pistols, as no one sat to supper armed. During the meal they settled on a plan. The Walkers were especially aroused when Quantrill indicated that Charlie Ball was one of the raiders. They recalled observing Ball, only a few months before, while he huckstered and spied around the area. After supper Quantrill returned to the jayhawkers' camp.

Andrew's son, T. J., recounted later his father's comment on trusting Quantrill: "He didn't recall having any fear of the famous guerrilla, that he appeared to be a kindly and refined man."

The Walker home was a large two-story brick structure that faced east. The front porch ran the length of the house. A small harness room was attached to the south end of the porch, and a small room was attached on the north. On the porch in front of the window of the northern room was a loom. Both rooms had windows overlooking the porch. The house itself had five rooms on the first floor and four on the second. A large passageway separated the two large front rooms, and a stairway led to the sleeping quarters above.

The grand stately home overlooked Andrew's farm, which was a quarter of a mile away. To the north was the business portion of the farm: slave cabins, stable, barn, shop, and smokehouse.

Twenty-four-year-old Andrew sent his wife to her parents' home, then he saddled a horse and raced from neighbor to neighbor to round up men he believed he could trust in the upcoming fight. He returned with four: three farmers and a doctor—Dr. Ashely Neer, D. C. Williams, Lee Koger, and John Tatum. They were all members of the Blue Springs Baptist Church and had farms within two miles of the Walker place.

At 4:30 the sun set. Andrew and Tatum hid behind the loom at the north end of the porch; Koger and Williams positioned themselves in the harness room on the south side of the porch.

The jayhawking raiders—Ball, Lipsey, Morrison, and Quantrill—waited for darkness before riding toward the Walker farm. Clouds made the night darker, again masking the stars. Traces of rain and sleet had fallen during the day, and a cold northern wind chilled the raiders as they advanced on the estate. Fifty yards from the house the men dismounted. Lipsey held the horses while Ball and Morrison drew their pistols and proceeded to the front door. Quantrill left his weapon in his holster.

Around 9 P.M. Quantrill knocked boldly on the front door. It was strange that not a dog barked. The three men were greeted by Morgan Walker and shown into the main room.

Ball bluntly explained: "There is no use to multiply words, Mr. Walker; you have here a people in bondage; I come to take them to Kansas and to free them."

Morgan asked him, "Have you ever consulted [them], to know whether they want to go to Kansas or not?"

Ball replied he had done so. Walker said, "I have told [them] that if any of them wanted to go to Kansas, go and be damned, but if any don't want to go, I want you to leave them here."

Ball added, "We want your money, too, and your horses and mules."

Walker replied, "Then the quicker you get at it the better."

Ball and Morrison turned to leave, but Quantrill said, "I'll stay and take care of the old people, and the things inside."

When Andrew Walker and John Tatum heard the door open, they raised double-barreled shotguns and fired. Morrison was killed immediately. Ball was not hit and leaped off the porch. Lipsey ran, but Williams and Koger fired on him, managing to wound him. He managed to find Ball in the darkness. No one tried to chase down the jayhawkers.

In his memoirs Andrew recorded that the Walkers, their four neighbors, and Quantrill went to bed around midnight but did not get much sleep. Morrison's body was left on the porch until morning.

About Quantrill, Andrew added: "He was not much of a talker, in fact Quantrill was a very quiet man, but he answered our questions good-naturedly, and appeared to be well educated. He carried a sort of self-reliant, commanding look, and appeared to be strong physically. I judged he was two inches under six feet, and would tip the beam at about 150, supple and muscular. He wore a mustache. He was twenty-four years old, he said, just a few weeks older than I."[10]

If it was Walker's money that Quantrill was after, he only had to carry out the raid with the rest of the jayhawkers. Quantrill could have robbed Walker of his money and herded his horses back to Kansas to sell on the streets of Lawrence, like other jayhawkers did, and become a wealthy man.

But he was not after personal gain. What he desired most was justice and the jayhawkers who accompanied him on this raid were the last of the men he had been seeking.

The next morning, December 11, was cold with frost in the air. The men searched all morning for any tracks made by Ball and Lipsey, but no traces could be found. That afternoon a justice of the peace was summoned to hold an inquest over Morrison's body. The coroner's verdict read:

> We, the jury, after holding an inquest over a man found dead at the dwelling of J. M. Walker, and hearing all the evidence that could be produced, found him to come to his death by gun shot. Shot out of a musket or shotgun. He was shot in the right side with twenty buckshot and seven old shot holes in the same side, and in the right arm with three fresh shot and seven old shot holes. We found about his body one silver wach and one bucher knife and one of Allen's pattern Revolver pistols, one small flask of powder, and some pistils balls and some bullet moles, one box of gun caps, one purse with nothing in it, and one pocket knife and one belt.

After the inquest, Morrison's body was transported to Blue Springs. There a doctor dissected it and placed the skeleton in a barrel. Naturally, word of the raid spread like wildfire. When the news reached Independence, Sheriff John T. Burris rode out to the farm and took Quantrill into protective custody. Andrew Walker trailed the two men to Independence.

Passions were duly aroused among the Missourians, and many grabbed their guns and rode for the county seat. Very few did not recollect the previous month's murder of Russell Hinds by jayhawker Charles Jennison, which was allegedly ordered by James Montgomery, who used Scripture to justify the action. Hinds was visiting his mother in Kansas when he was accosted then seized by Jennison. He accused Hinds of capturing and returning a fugitive slave for a twenty-five-dollar reward. Actually Hinds and another man, John O. Turner, persuaded the slave to return to his owner, a close friend of Turner's. When Hinds and Turner accompanied the man to his owner's house, a reward was offered to both men, but both refused. Hinds, however, accepted five dollars as reimbursement for expenses. After Jennison grabbed Hinds, he and nine other men lynched him and left the body dangling beside the highway.[11]

Almost a week later, on November 18, the same ten men and James Lane hanged Sheriff Samuel Scott, a wealthy pro-slavery Missouri resident of Scott Township. About the same time an attempt was made to seize and hang John W. Garrett of Potosi Township.

The two hangings and one near hanging terrorized the countryside. Other Missourians were assaulted and wrestled to the ground by Jennison's men, then Jennison himself cut off their ears. To justify these actions a convention was held on December 8 at Mound City, Kansas. The assembly passed resolutions justifying the hangings of Hinds and Scott and the shooting of another man, L. D. Moore.[12] James Montgomery vowed he "would first exterminate every vestige of pro-slaveryism in Kansas, and then invade Missouri for the purpose of kidnapping and freeing slaves, murdering slave owners and destroying property."

In Independence, Sheriff Burris incarcerated Quantrill. Within a short time an unruly mob formed in the streets to execute vengeance against the jailed jayhawker. Burris feared the mob might storm the jail, so he released Quantrill into Andrew Walker's custody and sent them to a hotel.

Morgan Walker rode into town the next day and found a crowd in the streets and heard that the jayhawkers involved in the assault belonged to Montgomery's band. The Walkers offered to protect Quantrill. While Morgan Walker accompanied Quantrill out of the hotel and into his buggy, Andrew Walker retrieved his horse from the livery stable and noticed a mob gathering on the street corner and planning to lynch Quantrill. He mounted his horse and rode into the unruly crowd, shouting, "I'll kill the first man that puts hands on him." The mob quietly dispersed, but another formed, and again Andrew dispersed them with assurances that Quantrill was with him.

Minutes after the Walkers and Quantrill arrived back at the farm, a neighbor, George Porter, reported that his slave had discovered Ball and Lipsey hiding in the woods about a mile and a half west of the Walker farm. Walker, his two sons, Quantrill, and Porter armed themselves and rode out—with Porter's slave acting as a guide—to find the two jayhawkers. Quantrill warned that Ball was a crack shot.

The men rode to within fifty yards of the fugitives, taking them by surprise. Morgan Walker yelled out to the two men to surrender and he would see that they received a fair trial. Ball raised his gun to fire, but his pistols were no match for the Missourians' rifles. Andrew and his father fired on Ball, striking him in the chest and forehead. Lipsey had been seriously wounded while fleeing the house; Zach Walker and Porter killed him with buckshot. Quantrill did not fire at either man.

Quantrill, Porter, and the Walkers approached the two dead men. They found a horse that had been stolen the day before and a stolen hog that Ball had been cooking on an open fire. The men returned to the Walker house, and Morgan Walker sent some slaves to bury the two jayhawkers where they had fallen.[13] Quantrill's personal vendetta was over, but he now had a price on his head—James Lane offered the reward himself.[14]

Historians and scholars have agonized over Quantrill's motives for betraying his comrades at the Morgan Walker farm. They have condemned him for the false tale of his brother's death by jayhawkers, but Quantrill's embellished story makes sense in light of his account of the jayhawkers' attacked on him and his friend. In a July 20, 1859, letter to his mother, he described his state of mind: "I am now in Lawrence after having spent over $300 and many a day and night when I expected either to be killed or freeze to death and at last when nearly in the settlements to have my horse and all taken from me and a companion of mine shot in three different places and left for dead."[15] The facts that his companion was not his brother and did not die does not negate the sense of retribution that motivated Quantrill to seek out and avenge the wrong done him on the verge of the new life to which he aspired and from which he was waylayed.

For the rest of the winter Quantrill stayed in the area near the Walker farm. He made friends with the surrounding farmers and came to know them quite well. A few weeks after the failed raid on the Walker farm, Morgan Walker showed his appreciation to Quantrill by presenting him with a coal black gelding saddle horse, a bridle and saddle, and a hundred dollars in cash. Andrew Walker gave him a new suit of clothes.

The day after Quantrill received the horse, Walker's fourteen-year-old neighbor, Frank Smith Jr., saw Quantrill ride to his family's store in Blue Springs. Smith's father was one of the founders of Blue Springs and a representative in the Missouri legislature as well as the proprietor of the town's first general store and postmaster.

"He seemed to be a very pleasant sort of fellow," the younger Smith said of Quantrill. "He was laughing and joking with the men in the store and his appearance was any other than that of a killer. We saw him sitting on the porch of a neighbor, sparking a girl."[16] Years later the younger Smith, at the age of seventeen, rode with Quantrill on the Lawrence raid.

Some farmers around the Blue Springs area were not exactly sure how to take Quantrill. For some time they were suspicious of him, knowing he was from Kansas. Now that the jayhawker facade was over, however, Quantrill demonstrated his true character. He visited the home of George M. Noland and relayed the story about the jayhawkers robbing him and killing his companion the year before. Noland remembered, "He was not a savage or bloodthirsty looking boy, but he seemed determined to have revenge." Noland later joined Quantrill's partisan rangers.

John McCorkle wrote, "Quantrill remained in Missouri, assisting the citizens in defending their property and in catching these horse, cattle and negro thieves." William Gregg noted Quantrill's integrity and willingness to protect the Jackson County farmers from the injustices they were experiencing:

> What drew attention to him first was a good piece of work he did in recovering several head of fine breeding stock. The animals had been run off from the owner in this county. Quantrill followed the parties who took them, located them in another Missouri county. The owner offered him a handsome reward, but he refused to accept more than $2 a head. He said that was all the work was worth. After that some trouble was made over the manner in which Quantrill had recovered and returned the property. There were threats that he was to be arrested and taken to the place where he had found the stock. When he heard of them he said that he would try to make things interesting if it was proposed to punish him for returning stolen property.[17]

These generous acts endeared him quickly to the pro-Southern citizens in Jackson County.

Late in March 1861, innocently thinking that his personal vendetta against the injustices of the jayhawkers would go unavenged, Quantrill rode into Kansas to visit his friend John Bennings with whom he had lived while he taught school in Stanton, Lykins County. Word of the failed Walker raid was well-known among the jayhawkers, though, and they were eager to avenge their comrades.

Eli Snyder lived only a few miles from Stanton, and when word reached him on March 26 that Quantrill was staying at Bennings's home, he assembled several gang members and visited Judge Samuel H. Hauser, the justice of the peace. Snyder swore out a warrant for Quantrill's arrest on the charge of horse stealing, because Quantrill was seen riding a horse different from the one on which he had ridden out of Kansas on the previous December. The judge was a jayhawker sympathizer and hated Quantrill as much as Snyder did. His son Peter was the source of Snyder's information on Quantrill's current whereabouts. Hauser wrote out the warrant, but to protect himself from being charged as an accomplice in Quantrill's potential murder "while escaping," Hauser stipulated that the local constable, E. B. Jurd, would serve the warrant.

Jurd deputized Snyder's men, and the posse rode to Bennings's cabin and surrounded it. Jurd called on Quantrill to surrender, but Quantrill saw Snyder and knew he would be killed if he yielded. Quantrill yelled back that he would prefer to die fighting than be killed in cold bold. Jurd promised he would be protected and would be allowed to ride his own horse without constraint. Quantrill gave himself up.

Snyder fully expected Jurd's assistance in killing Quantrill, but Jurd was not as much a friend as Snyder supposed. Jurd escorted his prisoner to the county jail for safekeeping. On the trail back to Stanton, Snyder and his men surrounded Quantrill and tried to provoke him. Knowing that any reaction could be construed as grounds to shoot him, Quantrill remained calm. Frustrated, Snyder attempted to shoot Quantrill in the back, but Jurd knocked the gun aside just as he fired. Another ruffian, John S. Jones, tried to shoot Quantrill in the back; his gun misfired. Only after great difficulty did Jurd get Quantrill safely to the county jail.[18]

As soon as the posse had left Bennings's house, one of Bennings's sons rode for the county seat of Paola to get help. Many citizens there were proslavery and friends of Quantrill's. When the news arrived of his arrest, sixteen men saddled up and rode to Stanton. Lawyers E. W. White, Robert White, Massey, Dr. W. D. Hoover, Tom Kelley, Goodwin Taylor, and merchant Lon Light ran to the livery stable and rode toward Stanton in hacks and buggies and on horseback. They were all willing to risk death to save Quantrill.

The arrival of the Paola men in Stanton almost caused a pitched battle in the streets. A friend of Quantrill's, W. L. Potter, was part of the group that first entered Stanton. He went directly to Tom Wilkerson's store, where Jurd had taken Quantrill. Potter and the men with him were well armed with revolvers, rifles, and shotguns.

Potter went directly to Quantrill and joked, "What are you driving at now? Stealing horses?"

Quantrill replied, "Well, they charge me with it."

Potter sarcastically commented for the benefit of Snyder and his men, "Oh certainly they are all honest men that prefer the charge against you. I suppose they know nothing about stealing horses and [slaves], robbing and burning houses, and murdering citizens, from one end of the land to the other."

To reassure Quantrill, Potter told him that more men were on the way. Quantrill replied that he was not one bit afraid, and Potter remembered that his friend had the same pleasant and cheerful smile on his lips that always accompanied him when in danger.

Quantrill's lawyer friends began a private consultation with the sheriff. Jurd, already uneasy about having Snyder's men as his posse and sensing trouble, showed Potter the warrant and stated that he did not want anything more to do with it. Potter dismissed Snyder and his men and stated that he would be transferring Quantrill to the jail in Paola for safekeeping.[19]

Snyder's men eventually backed off. Once lodged safely in the Paola jail, Quantrill was handed a pistol and a Bowie knife to defend himself should Snyder's men attempt to storm the jail.

Quantrill stayed in the Paola jail for several days. On April 3 he applied for a writ of habeas corpus on the grounds that his arrest was "malicious, false and illegal." His writ stated that the Lykins County judge had no jurisdiction over the charges that were preferred against him and also that the judge failed to attach bail in his case. On the charge of horse stealing, no party was mentioned as the owner of the stolen property.

As a result, the county judge could find no cause to continue holding him and no legal cause for his confinement. He subsequently ordered Quantrill's release. Judge Thomas Roberts was the probate judge and a Republican, but he had also a reputation as an honest and an honorable man.

Quantrill's friends joyously escorted him to the hotel where some ladies packed him a lunch of sandwiches and cake. Meanwhile Snyder swore out another false warrant with a different judge and asked to have the prisoner transferred to a neighboring county jail. While Quantrill's friends advised him to return to Missouri until the current unpleasantness subsided, Snyder and his gang entered town with the new arrest warrant issued by the Douglas County court in Lawrence.

Mounted on Black Bess, the thoroughbred horse given to him by Morgan Walker, Quantrill sped toward the border well ahead of Snyder's riders. From that day on, however, life changed for Quantrill. His enemies from Kansas constantly looked for him, and their vigilance meant he could never return again to visit his old friends in Kansas.

Because of the attempts on his life during his ride into Stanton, Quantrill came to resent the lawlessness of the jayhawkers. From that day his opinion changed toward all Kansans. He chose the only place for a refuge that offered him the justice that he could not find in Kansas and a moral standard like he had been raised on and grown up with. In Jackson County, Missouri, Quantrill finally had found a home. Here the people were glad to have him in their community and made him feel welcomed. At the same time, Jackson County finally found a champion and a leader.

Believing that Snyder was still out to kill him and to retaliate against the peaceful farmers in Jackson County with whom he had been staying, Quantrill decided that it would be best if he left the area for a while. Andrew Walker recorded that Quantrill was well liked and everyone hated to see him go.

Forty-six-year-old Marcus Gill, a farmer and close friend of Morgan Walker's, attended the Bethlehem Baptist Church in Little Santa Fe, where he had a large farm close to the state line in southern Jackson County. Gill and other Missouri farmers sensed that trouble was brewing between the free-staters in Kansas and the slaveholders in Missouri. Many decided to take their families south for protection against Federal military coercion and jayhawker raids. Some months earlier, on December 31, 1860, when Claiborne Jackson took the oath of office as the new governor of Missouri, his inaugural address implied that Missouri would stand behind the Southern states and asserted that the North had already dissolved the Union by nullifying the Fugitive Slave Act. Since Gill owned several slaves, he decided to move them and the rest of his possessions to Texas for safekeeping, just as did several other slave owners in Jackson County. Among them were men like Ben Rice and John Muir from the Brooking Township in Jackson County. They may have traveled with Marcus Gill.

After Gill heard of Quantrill's prowess as a defender of property and his ability with a gun, he hired Quantrill as a guard to accompany him, his wife, and six daughters. During the early spring of 1861 they started south. Just as they arrived at their destination they heard that the seceded states had fired upon Fort Sumter on April 12. Everyone understood that war was eminent. News reached them that Union Capt. Nathaniel Lyon, now a general of militia volunteers in charge of Federal and German immigrant troops, had fired on unarmed civilians as they were taking prisoners away from Camp Jackson in St. Louis. Most Missourians were incensed by this barbaric action.

On June 11, 1861, Lyon arbitrarily issued a statement of war to the state leaders of Missouri. Immediately, state officials headed for Jefferson City. Governor Jackson issued a proclamation on June 12, calling into active service fifty thousand militiamen to repel the invasion. Many young men from the Blue Springs region of Jackson County joined the Missouri State Guard immediately. In the battles that followed, these young men became well acquainted with one another and eventually came to ride together as guerrillas, protecting their homes against Union attacks.

During June, what was to be the first battle in Missouri was forming in Jackson County. Kansas City was overrun by Federal forces from outside the state, and many Secessionists left Kansas City for Independence to join a company of the Missouri State Guard forming there. A Federal company moved toward Independence to break up the militia. Halfway between the two towns, the Federals encountered the State Guards. An accidental shot opened the engagement. Three Missouri officers were killed and one wounded before the Federals withdrew after what was called the battle of Rock Creek.

As these hostilities were taking place, state forces raided a Kansas City warehouse and redirected arms, ammunition, and equipment to Cass County and the Missouri State Guard companies organizing there. A Federal force marched into Cass County to recapture the weapons. They were joined by elements of the First Kansas Jayhawker Regiment. After being attacked by 350 State Guardsmen, the Federals withdrew, low on ammunition, but not before killing fourteen Secessionists with a loss of only one soldier.

Instead of assisting the Federals, jayhawkers Charles Jennison and William Penick attacked Harrisonville—which held not an enemy soldier. They broke into most of the stores and robbed the safe of the county sheriff. The plundered goods were shipped back to Kansas.[20] During this raid, Jennison plundered the farm of Henry Younger with the help of his henchmen Marshall Cleveland and John Stewart.

The jayhawkers were already familiar with the area around southern Jackson and northern Cass Counties. Solomon Young was one of the most prosperous farmers of Jackson County,[21] and he owned a number of large farms that operated with slaves. The previous month James Lane had led a small contingent to one of Young's farms and stole fifteen mules and thirteen horses. Before departing, the jayhawkers shot four hundred Hampshire hogs, cutting off the hams and leaving the rest to rot, then killed the hens and set fire to the hay and stock barns. Lane's raiders threatened to kill an elderly slave to get her to reveal the hiding spot for the family's valuables, then snatched the family silver from its cache in the well. They questioned fifteen-year-old Harrison Young and refused to believe him when he said he did not know where his father was. His father was with a wagon train out west. They hanged Harrison anyway to force him to reveal where his father was hiding. When they tired of the game, they rode off. The boy's mother and a slave cut him down before he died. Subsequent jayhawker raids left the farm bare.[22]

On June 20 James Lane accepted a brigadier general's commission from the Federal government. He hoped to rule Kansas militarily as well as politically, but on June 29 the Senate Judiciary Committee reported his senate seat as vacant. The secretary of war had notified the committee that Lane had accepted the commission, which vacated his senatorial office. Lane could do nothing to change that; he had already taken the military oath and signed the requisite documents. Sensing a loss of his political power, Lane relinquished his military commission and sought a brigadier general's commission of militia volunteers from Indiana Gov. Oliver P. Morton. Lincoln remarked, "I have been reflecting upon [Lane] and have concluded that we need the services of such a man out there at once; that we better appoint him a brigadier general of volunteers today, and send him off with such authority to raise a force . . . as you think will get him into actual work quickest." Lincoln instructed Lane "not [to] be writing or telegraphing back here, but put it through." In this way Lane could wield political power as a senator from Kansas and lead Kansas militia troops along the Missouri border.

Lane traveled via Leavenworth to Fort Scott to take charge of the state troops. His brigade—comprised of the Third, Fourth, and Fifth Kansas Jayhawking Regiments—consisted of twelve hundred men led by Cols. James Montgomery, William Weir, and Hamilton P. Johnson.

While the opposing armies were gathering for the impending storm, Kansas jayhawkers took advantage of the army's departure from the border. Every able-bodied man and boy was in an army on one side or the other—leaving the area vulnerable to attack. Charles Jennison quickly realized the opportunity for another raid. On June 19, 1861, Jennison and one hundred men accompanied a regular army regiment to Kansas City. As the regular soldiers were setting up camp, Jennison led his company into Independence on an independent scouting mission that was nothing more than an expedition for plunder. Shortly thereafter, Montgomery made a quick dash across the border, fought a skirmish with Rebel guerrillas, and marched back with loot and slaves who "happened to walk off on their own accord."[23]

As Southern forces were preparing to meet Lyon's Federals in southern Missouri, Lane, Jennison, and twelve hundred jayhawkers struck across the border at Morristown, which was defended by Col. W. H. Ervin and one hundred recruits. After a brief skirmish, Ervin's men were routed. The jayhawkers killed several citizens. Jennison and Marshall Cleveland plundered the town and stole two thousand dollars, which they divided among themselves the following day. Cleveland shot a Missouri farmer because he wanted his mules and the man protested.

Lane's jayhawkers were causing so many problems along the border that Kansas Gov. Charles Robinson asked Union Gen. John C. Frémont in St. Louis to recall Lane's brigade from the border. To protest the jayhawkers' raids, Union Gen. George Caleb Bingham recounted Jennison's criminal behavior for Missouri congressman James S. Rollins:

> Up to the period of these transactions at Harrisonville, the brigand leader [Jennison] had been murdering and stealing "upon his own hook," having been repelled whenever he attempted to find shelter for his crimes under color of governmental authority. . . . But we next contemplate him as having undergone a complete transition from the condition of an outlaw,

abhorred and avoided by honorable minds, to that of an officer in the
United States Army, empowered to raise a regiment of cavalry, with a view,
as it seemed, to test, upon a more extensive scale, the efficacy of indiscriminate pillage and rapine in crushing out rebellion.[24]

On Thursday, June 13, Nathaniel Lyon (now with the rank of brigadier
general of volunteers) prepared to march on the capital of Missouri at Jefferson City with fifteen hundred men. At 3 P.M. on Saturday, June 15, his men
took possession of the town. Two days earlier Gov. Claiborne Jackson and
Gen. Sterling Price departed on the steamer *White Cloud* upriver to Boonville.
Lyon reembarked his troops on Sunday, June 16, and pursued Price. By the
time Price reached Boonville, his ranks had swelled to around three or four
thousand men, but most were without arms, without officers, and lacking any
kind of training or organization.

Even though the Southerners were vastly outnumbered, an immediate
charge was ordered. Federal cannon tore huge holes in their lines. A brief
engagement between the approximately seventeen hundred troops involved
left the inexperienced Missourians running pell-mell from the battlefield.
Price had no choice but to withdraw his poorly trained army into Arkansas to
seek the aid of regular Confederate troops. They realized that establishing a
line against the Federal onslaught this far north in Missouri would be impossible in the immediate future. Thus defeated but still defiant, the Missouri
State Guardsmen retreated south with their squirrel rifles and shotguns slung
over their tired shoulders.

Lyon made plans to head south and issued orders for all available out-of-
state Federal troops to converge on Price's army. Troops began infiltrating the
state from all sides. Kansas, Iowa, and Illinois troops were summoned. On
June 17 Kansas sent three regiments from the Sixth Kansas Jayhawker Regiment from Fort Scott and the First and Second Kansas Jayhawker Regiments
to join Lyon in Missouri. The Sixth Kansas Jayhawker Regiment plundered
Fort Scott before leaving. Secretary of War Simon Cameron agreed to take
these regiments into Federal service.

In reply to the vast numbers of out-of-state Federal troops in Missouri,
native Francis W. Springer said: "We must remember the majority of Southerners did not own slaves and most certainly did not fight so others could
own them. The real answer is quite simple. The South was fighting because it
was invaded."

Lyon was hoping to be named a general of regular Federal troops, but his
political connections had already expended their efforts on behalf of John C.

Frémont, their protégé, to command the Department of the West. Lyon may not have gotten the recognition he thought he deserved by being named to an important post, but he would try to make up for it by achieving an outstanding victory in the field.

A rump session of the state legislature, overshadowed by Federal bayonets, declared the present state legislature abolished and the offices of governor and other elected officials vacant. The open seats were then filled from the ranks of loyal Union men. Those who did not go along with this travesty of justice were considered disloyal, and almost half of the remaining legislators were arrested for treason when they objected to the illegal operation of the "provisional" government.

While Lyon was pushing south to find Sterling Price's trail, William C. Quantrill was pushing north to enlist with Price. After leaving Marcus Gill's family in Texas, Quantrill enlisted as a volunteer with Col. Joel Mayes, who was recruiting an independent cavalry unit, called the First Cherokee Mounted Regiment. By July Quantrill was riding in another independent cavalry company under a captain named Stewart serving in James S. Rains's division under Price.

As Quantrill's company was moving to join Price, Union Col. Franz Sigel maneuvered to cut off the retreat of Price's army. Sigel met the Missourians in a brief skirmish on July 5 near Carthage, Missouri, at a place the Southerners called Dug Springs. It was here that Pvt. William C. Quantrill received his first lesson in military training. Sigel had assured his men that a few rounds of grapeshot and canister thrown at the somewhat disorganized Confederates would quickly disperse the Southerners. Indeed the bombardment threw the cavalry into confusion and Gov. Claiborne Jackson, as the head of the Southern force, was unable to form battle lines under the artillery attack. Instead, he ordered his infantry, backed by cavalry, to attack the Federal position.

The cavalry, which included Quantrill, dismounted and joined the infantry. Exhibiting an early bravery that was to carry him throughout the war, Quantrill was seen in a bright red shirt on the front lines. His boldly colored shirt was reminiscent of the garb worn by the Italian freedom fighters led by Giuseppe Garibaldi. Later Quantrill's guerrillas adopted the same style sported by Garibaldi's men: a loose-fitting blouse with large breast pockets. Like the Italians, they traveled unencumbered by military gear and accoutrements.

Quantrill flaunted himself at the Union forces, encouraging his comrades to fight bravely and daring the enemy to shoot at him, drawing their fire, causing them to expend their ammunition.[25] The flash of the Union rifles allowed the Southerners to pick out their positions and direct their own fire.

Quantrill's actions also acted as a military feint, luring the enemy toward a strong Confederate defensive line.

The Federals dropped back after the attack and retreated to Carthage with the Confederates close upon their heels. Sigel, fearful and sensing defeat, withdrew another to Rolla, letting the Confederates occupy Carthage. It was here that Quantrill first encountered Cole Younger, then a member of the Missouri State Guard.

New recruits for the South streamed in every day. Many came without arms or uniforms, badly needing supplies of which Price was in short supply. Two thousand of Price's seven thousand soldiers had no weapons. They were instructed to pick up the weapons of fallen comrades on the battlefield. Price rode to Cassville, close to the Arkansas border, to consult with Brig. Gen. Benjamin McCulloch, in charge of the Department of Arkansas.

McCulloch commanded Confederate regulars from Texas and Louisiana and a unit of Arkansas state troops. Initially, McCulloch refused to assist Price in confronting Lyon. He argued that he was under orders not to engage the enemy in Missouri. Even though Lyon had declared war on the sovereign state of Missouri, technically Missouri was still part of the Union and had not yet joined the seceded Southern states.

Price knew he needed the added strength of McCulloch's regulars, but he was prepared to attack Lyon alone if need be. Even though Price was senior in rank, at McCulloch's insistence, he deferred to McCulloch to command their combined forces if he would help Price to launch an immediate attack. "You must either fight beside us," Price told him, "or look on at a safe distance, and see us fight all alone the army, which you dare not attack even with our aid. I must have your answer before dark, for I intend to attack Lyon tomorrow."

After consulting with McCulloch, Price agreed to move their forces north toward Springfield in three separate divisions to reach the invading Northern army. Price and McCulloch rested their forces about ten miles south of their objective at a place called Wilson's Creek. After finally coaxing Franz Sigel out of Rolla, Lyon led six thousand men from Springfield southward to feel out the advance guard of Price's army.

Lyon was pressing for success for the Union and for himself, but events were moving against him. Requested supplies never arrived. Reinforcements from Illinois were compelled to stay where they were to defend against attack from a recent landing of Confederate forces. Lyon overestimated Price's force with the hope that Frémont would respond to his request for reinforcements. He wired Frémont that more than thirty thousand Confederates were converging on Springfield in three separate columns. Frémont replied that Lyon was grossly overestimating the enemy. No reinforcements would be coming from Frémont.

Nonetheless, Lyon intended to attack the Confederate columns before they could unite and defeat them piecemeal. Kansas jayhawkers were attached to Lyon's small force. The Union commander was glad to have the Kansans with him; he was convinced that their intense hatred for the Missourians would prove an asset. Still, he deplored their utter lack of discipline, and both he and Maj. Samuel D. Sturgis employed stringent measures to prevent them from venting their malice on civilians. Because the jayhawkers' raids frequently struck many pro-Union farmers, Lyon issued orders forbidding further "plundering, wanton destruction of property and disregard of personal rights."[26] In explaining his actions to Chester Harding, Lyon wrote, "My misfortunes are greatly due to the rawness of our troops and to the wanton misconduct of many of them. I would not have them in the service if it could be helped."

Lyon also confronted a situation with his German contingent, which had enlisted for a term of three months, and the expiration date was rapidly approaching. With them, Lyon had an effective force of 5,868 supported by three batteries of artillery.[27] On September 14 the First Iowa Infantry was to be mustered out along with a large portion of the Third and Fifth Missouri, which would leave Lyon with around 3,500 effective troops. Pressure was mounting on Lyon to make quick work of any military plans he had. Lyon's aide, Col. John Schofield, recalled that Lyon was overwhelmed by a "morbid sensitiveness" to the thought that Missouri might be lost to the Confederacy if he had to retreat.

Sigel suggested the Federals attack Price's troops from two directions. If attacked from two sides, the enemy would have no choice but to fight. By agreeing with Sigel's strategy, Lyon committed an unforgivable military blunder by dividing his forces in the face of a numerically superior enemy.

Lyon was fully aware that he had no support among the German troops who gave their allegiance to Sigel. "Frémont won't sustain me," he reported. "Sigel has a great reputation, and if I fail against his advice it will give Sigel command and ruin me. Then again, unless he can have his own way, I fear he will not carry out my plans."[28] Lyon acquiesced against his better judgment, knowing that his campaign to punish the Missouri Secessionists would fail unless he could keep the support of Sigel's men.

Sigel moved his forces to the rear of Price's army with the intention of assaulting from the rear while Lyon assaulted Price from the front. As Sigel fired on the Louisiana infantry regiments at 5:30 A.M. on the morning of

August 10, they were driven from their camps in complete surprise. As the Union soldiers swarmed toward the Confederate camp, instead of following up their surprised enemy, they stopped to loot the abandoned site. Because of the Germans' pivotal breakdown in discipline, Confederate cavalry quickly regrouped for a counterattack.

When Price discovered Sigel's forces in his rear, he directed the Louisianans—along with the independent command of Captain Stewart, of which Quantrill was part—to attack Sigel's force. The Germans were shattered by the first volley of Confederate fire. They threw down their weapons, abandoned five cannon, and ran as fast as they could toward Springfield. The Confederate counterattack captured all of Sigel's artillery, his flag, and three hundred men. Confederate cavalry chased the Germans through the open fields until they came to a wooded area; there the Germans attempted to hide from their pursuers. The Southerners continued to run them down. One of Sigel's Germans recorded in his diary: "I do not know who was to blame for this mistake. . . . All who valued their lives sought shelter as quickly as possible."[29]

As a part of the Confederate cavalry, Quantrill gained a great deal of military knowledge that he later put to good use in the upcoming months. He observed how the Southern forces gained fire superiority by unleashing a deadly volley and immediately following it up with a wild Rebel Yell and a fast charge. At Wilson's Creek this tactic routed Sigel's army and enabled the Southern cavalry to ride down the retreating Federals and dispose of them individually, one by one.

By this time Quantrill had been promoted to a sergeant in Company I of the Third Missouri Confederate Cavalry. Brig. Gen. Paul Herbet, the commander of the Louisiana troops under McCulloch, recommended to Price that Quantrill be promoted from sergeant to captain of partisan cavalry for his bravery at Wilson's Creek.[30]

Meanwhile, Price's men, in conjunction with the Third Arkansas Infantry, hammered Lyon's main line. Six times they attacked Lyon's line and almost broke it.

Lyon had earlier been wounded in the leg and was both mentally and physically exhausted. Seated behind his front lines in a despondent mood, he was ready to give up the fight. His aide, Schofield, encouraged him to attack the Southerners "one more time." Lyon personally led his reserves of the Second Kansas Jayhawker Regiment against the determined Confederates.

At the next charge, as the Southerners came within thirty yards of Lyon's troops, Lyon raised his sword and hat and admonished his men, "Come on, my brave boys, I will lead you. Forward!" A few brief seconds later, a murderous volley ripped the Federal line to pieces. Lyon was struck in the chest; the bullet tore through his heart and lungs and exited below his right shoulder blade. As he fell from his horse, his orderly ran to catch him, laid him on the ground, and tried to staunch the wound. A moment later the man who had impetuously waged war on Missouri and launched the state into a bloody conflict was dead.

Trying to hide their commander's death to keep the troops from panicking, Lyon's orderly covered the general's face. It was not enough to keep the news from spreading to the soldiers, and panic set in.

Nathaniel Lyon was the first Union general to die in battle during the Civil War. Many have called him the hero of Missouri for preventing the state from seceding; in fact he declared war on the legally elected government of Missouri and plunged the state into three years of terrible guerrilla warfare. Lyon's decision to make war on Missouri was not a military or political necessity. Without his rash decision, Missouri might have been neutral.

While the Confederates regrouped for another charge, Sturgis pulled his troops out of action and retreated to Springfield under cover of darkness. The exhausted Confederates made no effort to follow. Darkness soon came, and the day's fighting ended. In their efforts to get away as quickly as possible, the Federals left Lyon's body on the field. Price sent the body to Springfield soon afterward, but a rumor of an impending Confederate attack caused them to abandon his body shy of the town.

In the morning the Southern forces found themselves in possession of the field. It was a brilliant victory for the Confederates and might have paved the way for a sweeping Southern victory in Missouri. In lives it was costly for both sides. The Union suffered 223 dead, 721 wounded, and almost 300 missing—dead or deserted. The Confederates lost 265 killed, 800 wounded, and 30 listed as missing. The battle resulted in a 16 percent casualty rate, which at the time stood as one of the highest in the war.

Tactically, the Southerners should have followed up the victory by pressing the demoralized Federal army to abandon the state. Price could have reclaimed Missouri's sovereignty, but McCulloch balked and refused to commit his men. Price was aghast and commented:

The most populous and truest counties of the State lie upon or [are] north of the Missouri River. Had General McCulloch, in response to my earnest entreaties, accompanied me to that river immediately after the battle of Springfield [Wilson's Creek], we could easily have maintained our position there until my army (which was, in fact, augmented from less than 6,000 to more than 16,000 men during the few days we lay there) would have been increased to at least 50,000, and four-fifths of the State would have fallen without a struggle into our possession. As it was, however, I was soon threatened by overwhelming numbers and compelled to fall back again to the southern border of the State, and thousands of those who had flocked to my standard, feeling that they had been betrayed and abandoned by the Confederate government, returned to their homes discontented and disheartened. Again, after the late retreat of the enemy from the southwest, I begged General McCulloch to accompany me to the Missouri, and he again refused to do so. I started thither with my own army and reached the Osage just as the time of service of three-fourths of my own men was expiring. Nearly every one of them had left his home months before without an hour's notice, leaving their families unprotected and unprovided for. A severe winter was at hand; the men were themselves badly clad, and not one of them had ever received a dime in payment of his services. Many of them insisted upon going home for a few weeks to procure clothing for themselves and make some provision for the comfort of their families, who were exposed, not only to the severities of a Missouri winter, but to the fury of an enemy whose barbarity cannot be described.[31]

McCulloch claimed that he was responsible for the defense of Arkansas from the north, but at this early juncture in the war, Arkansas did not need defending. If Arkansas were to face any Northern army, it would naturally have to approach through Missouri, which was the key state of the two that should have been defended at all costs.

To not follow up a victory, but rather withdraw, is a serious blunder for any military commander. McCulloch, however, wanted nothing to do with Price's army. Price claimed that he met McCulloch on five different occasions over three weeks to press him to join him in pushing the Federals out of Missouri. For years afterward, most Missourians blamed McCulloch for the state's not regaining its sovereignty.

McCulloch explained that he interpreted the outstanding victory at Wilson's Creek as sufficient to preclude any further Federal activity in Missouri. Soon after the battle, he abandoned the state to its fate and marched away. On August 20, ten days after the battle of Wilson's Creek, Sterling Price issued a victory proclamation, stating that his army had been organized under the laws of the commonwealth for the maintenance of the rights, dignity, and honor of Missouri and remained in the field for these purposes

alone. He described the battle as a glorious victory over "the well-appointed army, which the usurper at Washington has been more than six months gathering for their subjugation and enslavement . . . and he also warned all evil-disposed persons who might support the usurpation's of anyone claiming to be provisional or temporary governor of Missouri, or who should in any other way give aid or comfort to the enemy, that they would be held as enemies and treated accordingly."[32]

On August 25, with his independent and understrength army—one-third of which had no arms—Price decided to march north without McCulloch. By this time, Quantrill had left Stewart's independent cavalry and joined Price's command. Price knew of the long history of jayhawking raids in Missouri and received regular reports on recent raids.

Holed up at Fort Scott, Kansas, James Lane now headed twelve hundred badly organized, poorly equipped, and undisciplined cavalry and infantry—dubbed the Kansas Brigade. His heaviest weapons were two small cannon. The camp was a pigpen. Lane's line officers were "notoriously incompetent," and the selection of officers in James Montgomery's regiment had been "brought about by corrupt combinations." Some units, notably Capt. John E. Stewart's cavalry, were no better than bandits.[33]

Initially Price intended to march on Kansas directly and attack the jayhawkers. On September 7 his army encountered Lane's troops at Drywood Creek, in Vernon County, Missouri. After a brief skirmish, Price easily swept them aside.

During the fight at Drywood Creek, as Quantrill stood near a cannon, one of Lane's small guns fired on the position, directly hitting the cannon near Quantrill and sending it end over end toward the rear.

Price took his army toward Lexington, Missouri, just north of the Missouri River in Lafayette County. Quantrill, now a cavalry sergeant, advanced as well.

Federals held the Missouri River by a cordon of posts stretching from St. Louis to St. Joseph. Communication was generally maintained between the commands. The object of this line was to prevent five to six thousand Secessionists of northern Missouri from crossing the river and joining Price in southwest Missouri.

Two months earlier, on July 9, troops from the Fifth U.S. Reserve Regiment were taken from Kansas City to Lexington via steamboat. They occupied towns along the way, seizing property and breaking up Secessionist camps. When they arrived in Lexington they set up a defensive position on the high ground at the Lexington Masonic College and sent out patrols to round up hidden caches of guns and powder.

Gen. John Pope led a second force, with volunteer regiments from Kansas, Illinois, and Iowa, into the area to protect the Hannibal and St. Joseph Railroad. Pope levied fines on the citizens to repair the railroad and to ration and quarter his troops.

Pope's Illinois and Kansas troops looted, burned, and generally mistreated the Missourians. The Second Kansas Jayhawker Regiment and the Sixteenth Illinois Infantry especially distinguished themselves in this knavery. Drunken soldiers ran the trains and stole horses and other livestock along the tracks. The animals were shipped to Illinois by rail and sold.

Writing on August 13 about the situation along the Hannibal and St. Joe Railroad, J. T. K. Hayward, a pro-Union general-agent of the line, sent the following remarks to John W. Brooks, who forwarded them to Secretary of War Edwin M. Stanton:

> When there is added to this the irregularities of the soldiery, such as taking poultry, pigs, milk, butter, preserves, potatoes, horses, and in fact everything they want; entering and searching houses, and stealing in many cases; committing rapes on the negroes and such like things, the effect has been to make a great many Union men inveterate enemies, and if these things continue much longer our cause is ruined. These things are not exaggerated by me, and though they do not characterize all the troops, several regiments have conducted in this way, and have also repeatedly fired on peaceable citizens, sometimes from trains as they passed, and no punishment, or none of any account has been meted out to them. . . . If the thing goes on this way much longer, we are ruined. I fear we cannot run the road or live in the country except under military protection. It is enough to drive a people to madness, and it is doing it fast.[34]

The depravity of the Kansas jayhawker troops did not escape Pope's notice. He addressed the following to John C. Frémont, the department commander: "The drunkenness, incapacity, and shameful neglect of duty of many officers of rank in this district have brought matters to a sad state in north Missouri. . . . I have sent Colonel Blair, 2d Kansas, and Major Hays and Captain Ralston, 16th Illinois, to Saint Louis in arrest. Charges will be transmitted as soon as there is a moment's leisure to make them out."[35] Reinforcing the military aspect of the crisis, Missouri's provisional governor, Hamilton Gamble, took the matter to Lincoln and complained about the abuses committed by Federal troops from outside Missouri and by the German Home Guards in the rural areas.

Meanwhile, Sterling Price had several options, but one served his purposes better than the others. Lexington was a prosperous town in the hemp-growing region strategically situated on the south bluffs overlooking the Missouri River. The area was also known to be pro-Southern. According to Price's latest intelligence, Lexington was occupied by a small contingent of Unionist Home Guards. If he could invest the place, Price could blockade the river while the guardsmen from northern Missouri crossed to join him.[36]

On September 2, as Price started north toward Lexington, he sent an advance guard toward Stockton, Missouri, to clear out any marauding bands of jayhawkers. As the Confederates moved north, Lane quickly retreated, believing that Price was moving toward his base at Fort Scott.

Between September 2 and 9, Lane discovered that Price was not marching against him and ordered Charles Jennison into Papinsville, Missouri. Jennison later returned to Kansas laden with plunder and more than two hundred cattle and numerous "freed" slaves.[37]

Reacting to the resurgence of jayhawking raids into Missouri, Price issued a statement threatening to "lay waste the farms and utterly destroy the cities and villages" of Kansas unless the jayhawkers stayed out of Missouri. If forced to do so, Price would pay back the Kansans in kind for what they had been doing in Missouri for years.

As soon as the Federals sensed that Price was marching toward the Missouri River, a train of Federal soldiers from Kansas was run into Missouri to bolster the cordon of river outposts. On September 3 a bridge over the river was burned; the oncoming troop train crashed, causing thirteen deaths and wounding seventy-five.[38]

To counter the jayhawker raids, a Confederate raid was launched into Kansas, as far as Humbolt, which was sacked on September 7. Union Gen. James Blunt managed to overtake the raiders and kill one of the leaders and several of his men.

Lexington was not just a potential river crossing to Price, however. Significant funds were also at stake, specifically funds earmarked to fund the operation of the State Guard. Four months earlier the Missouri legislature had authorized a reappropriation of education funds and had required banks to loan additional funds to the state. Most of this money had never been collected. More than nine hundred thousand dollars sat in Lexington banks. Frémont, as the Federal commander in the state, had impounded the money, but his people had not yet seized the money in Lexington.[39]

Col. James A. Mulligan commanded the Union garrison in Lexington. He was a tall, dark-eyed Irishman and a highly ambitious Chicago lawyer. Mulligan specifically commanded the 800-man Twenty-third Illinois, another aptly named Irish Brigade, since most of the men were immigrants from the Emerald Isle. The Twenty-third Illinois comprised one-third of the garrison; most of the rest were German immigrants. The garrison also included 500 horsemen of the First Illinois Cavalry, commanded by Col. Thomas A. Marshall; 840 men of the Thirteenth Missouri, commanded by Col. Everett Peabody; and 500 men from Federal militia units.

On September 8 Mulligan received orders from Frémont to fortify and hold Lexington and promised reinforcements in two to three days. On September 10 advance elements of Price's army reached Warrensburg, thirty-four miles from Lexington. The few Federals in Warrensburg abandoned it before Price arrived and burned houses and bridges as they fled. On September 12 Price advanced on Lexington. His patrols encountered the Federals five miles out from town, where they tried to make a concerted stand. The Federals lost eight killed and fifteen wounded before being driven back to their entrenchments at Lexington. Price and his army followed the fleeing Federals, arriving at the town on September 13 during a heavy rain. While Price waited for his supply trains to arrive, he ordered a reconnaissance of the area and took the extra time he had to drill his troops. Quantrill was among the latter.

Mulligan realized he faced superior numbers, and he had no immediate hopes of reinforcements. At a council of war, he polled his subordinates, who all recommended abandoning Lexington and withdrawing from the area. Mulligan saw the hopelessness of the situation, but abandoning his position would not bring him glory. He impulsively decided to stand and fight, hoping for reinforcements before defeat. Positioning his meager force on a bluff north of the town, around the area of the Masonic college, Mulligan dug in. Embankments were thrown up around his perimeter, and a deep trench was dug beyond the perimeter to hinder infantry and cavalry attacks. The garrison, however, was in no condition for a lengthy fight. The men had only forty rounds of ammunition each; heavy weapons were limited to six small brass cannon.

While Price continued to wait for his supply wagons to arrive, several of the general's officers recommended an immediate assault against the Federal works. Price, however, decided there should be no useless bloodshed. He knew time was on his side; the Federals could not withstand a lengthy siege. So he waited.

In addition to waiting for his supply wagons, Price was also waiting for the arrival of reinforcements from the north side of the river. Once news spread that a Confederate army had the enemy surrounded, recruits came from every direction to take part in the battle.[40]

Before any shots were fired, Price demanded Mulligan's surrender. The Federal commander was not accommodating. Skirmishers and sharpshooters were deployed against the Federal works; sporadic fire would force the Union troops to keep their heads down and demoralize their fighting spirit. On Wednesday, September 18, Price sent a detachment downriver to capture a steamboat and a ferryboat that were still under Federal control at the base of their fortifications.

In the meantime, Mulligan sent troops into a hospital building (known to locals as the Anderson house) eight hundred yards beyond his lines to fire on the Confederates. Price ordered troops to take the hospital building from the Federal sharpshooters. The Confederates charged, secured the building, and held it for several hours. Mulligan ordered a company of German immigrants to retake it, but they refused. Finally Mulligan sent a company from his Irish Brigade to retake the hospital. They were successful and managed to hold on to the structure for several hours. Southerners mounted a vengeful counter-charge when they learned that Mulligan's men shot down and bayoneted several Confederates after they had surrendered their arms. Overall, the Federals lost more than thirty men out of a total of eighty involved in the action.

By now the Federals were completely surrounded. They also lacked food and water. At 1 A.M. on September 20, in the misty damp darkness that surrounded the town, Price's batteries opened on the Unionists. Mulligan's artillery returned fire, but many shots fell into the town. A cannonball struck one of the Doric columns of the courthouse and embedded itself there.

Even though Mulligan had mined the approach to his entrenchments, sufficient Southern volunteers attempted a storming party. Price, however, refused to needlessly expose his men to such danger given the untenable Federal position. "There is no use in killing the boys now," he said. "Poor fellows! They may, some of them at least, be killed soon enough."

Quantrill distinguished himself during the hottest part of the fight. He raced his horse back and forth in front of the enemy lines, drawing fire and causing the Federals to expend ammunition. The Union fire also revealed their positions. By focusing their fire on the muzzle flashes in the Union lines, Quantrill's comrades could return fire accurately and deadly. Confederate Maj. John Newman Edwards described Quantrill's actions during the battle of Lexington: "Mounted there on a splendid horse, armed with a Sharps carbine and four Navy revolvers, for uniform a red shirt and for oriflamme a sweeping black plume, he advanced with the farthest, fell back with the last, and was always cool, deadly, and omnipresent. It is said that General Price, himself notorious for being superbly indifferent under fire, remarked [on] his bearing and caused mention to be made of it most favorably."[41]

When the Confederates captured the Federal transports on the levee, they found the lower decks of one vessel protected by hemp bales procured from the warehouses on the wharf. On the evening of September 19 some of the Missourians rolled a few hemp bales partway up the bluff and lay down to sleep behind them. After this all the hemp bales in the warehouses were brought to the field and used to powerful effect.[42]

By noon of September 20 the Federal situation was desperate. The Confederates soaked the hemp bales with water, rolled them toward the Federal line, and fired at whatever came into sight. Around 1:30 P.M. one of the German officers raised a white flag above his position, and the Southerners initiated a cease-fire. Mulligan consulted his officers, who voted to surrender. They sent a courier to inform Price. As the word of the surrender spread among the Union troops, some of the Irishmen emptied their rifles toward the Germans.

Mulligan had shown a brave face to the enemy, but to his own officers he looked like a defeated man. Two minor but painful wounds left him perplexed and bewildered. After the battle, rumors circulated that the Union commander's mental condition was so seriously flawed that his wife asked permission to accompany him as a prisoner. She believed he might not be able to make the necessary decisions involved in treating his wounds.[43] The Federals lost 42 men killed and 1,624 men taken captive; the Confederates suffered 25 killed.

Sterling Price was magnanimous in victory. He released all enlisted prisoners who agreed not to take up arms again against Missouri. One of the paroled Federal prisoners was George Caleb Bingham, who would become the state treasurer of the provisional government. After their parole papers were completed, Gov. Claiborne Jackson and Price addressed the Union soldiers. Jackson spoke eloquently, emphasizing that the legal government of Missouri wished to maintain an armed neutrality from the hostilities that were enveloping the Northern and Southern states. He told the Union troops that they "had no business in Missouri; that he would take care of that State, without their assistance, and that they had better go home and mind their own business."

Mulligan's defeat also involved a matter of bad timing. Just prior to the siege at Lexington, Frémont had issued an emancipation proclamation, which politically brought the issue of slavery into the war. At the time, however, neither side was willing to address the issue so bluntly. Kentucky still hung in the balance, and Lincoln hoped to win the state of his birth for the Union. He regarded Frémont's proclamation as a dangerous and premature move, legally indefensible. The president addressed a diplomatic remonstrance to Frémont, but the department commander stubbornly defended his position. Finally, Lincoln issued a direct order. The presidential order so unhinged and embarrassed Frémont personally and politically that Mulligan's pleas for reinforcements were ignored.[44]

After the Lexington victory, Price's army pulled back and marched south toward Arkansas. Quantrill traveled with the army as far as the Osage River in central Missouri.

Winter was not far off, and Price realized that he would not be able to feed and supply his men in winter quarters. The situation was also affected by the short enlistment terms of most of Price's soldiers. Many three-month enlistments had already expired. An alternative, which the general endorsed as a military necessity, was to establish groups of partisan rangers. Partisans protected their own land and provided for themselves. Organized independent ranger companies would keep Union forces in the state occupied and off balance. A fast, well-armed, mobile force existing off the land and supported by friends and family could do more damage to a Federal army of occupation than Price could by trying to maneuver a numerically superior adversary into set-piece battles. Price knew that his army required an intelligence network, and the guerrillas could set themselves up in every county and locale. At the same time, partisans could disrupt the enemy's supply lines and communication.

George T. Maddox fought alongside Quantrill. Guerrilla warfare appealed to him more than the traditional clash of armies in the field. He wrote of his time with Price's command: "That kind of warfare did not suit me. I wanted to get out where I could have it more lively; where I could fight if I wanted to, or run if I so desired: I wanted to be my own general."[45]

Other men wanted a freer hand in the upcoming fighting because "they wanted to avoid the uncertainty of regular battle and know by actual results how many died as a propitiation or a sacrifice. Every other passion became subsidiary to that of revenge. They sought personal encounters that their own handiwork might become unmistakably manifest."[46]

Price determined that Quantrill was the kind of fighter he needed for this kind of irregular warfare. His selection also gained notice for Quantrill in the eyes of the soldiers from the border area who saw his bravery under fire and went on to serve in his independent partisan company in Jackson County. Quantrill sought and received permission to return north to Jackson County.

Partisan fighting promised much risk for the men who responded to the call. On August 30 Frémont had proclaimed death to anyone caught bearing arms in Missouri, but every Missourian knew that few unarmed persons stood any chance of survival in the tumultuous border counties.

With several other Jackson County youths, Quantrill returned to northern Missouri in late 1861. The tides of war were beginning to change.

These men who ventured back home to the already smoking ruins of their once proud and stately homes saw the struggle as a war for hearth and home. They fought a war against the oppression of a government in a way not as glorious as those who stood in long lines of glistening bayonets and advanced toward the enemy in parade-field fashion. Instead these young men followed a less romantic road to glory. Theirs was a personal battle.

In a Border State the inclination to fight in a faraway army was less appealing than an unconventional warfare where the results of their efforts could be seen firsthand. They thought of themselves as waging the same kind of warfare as the early colonists when overpowered and outgunned by the most powerful army in the world, the British army. The early colonists resorted to so-called Indian tactics, avoiding open-field contests for slash-and-dash attacks. Stories of the accomplishments of Francis Marion and the Green Mountain Boys had been shared for generations around hearths and campfires. These tales emboldened young Missourians who found themselves as farmers turned to soldiers in their own back yards.

The area had already suffered frequent jayhawker raids. When the prewar government turned a blind eye and the wartime Federal authorities outright condoned the incursions, a more aggressive strategy was demanded.

In Jackson County, Quantrill gathered eight men from the Blue Springs region as a Home Guard unit. All of them were expert horsemen and marksmen, and they all knew the territory well. They easily inured themselves to the hardships of the elements and the demands that were soon to be placed upon them. In short, they were excellent soldiers. They were also well disciplined. When Quantrill gave an order, it was immediately obeyed or the direst consequences followed.

George T. Maddox recalled, "As a general thing the best soldiers we had were boys; they didn't know what fear was. I would rather take a regiment of boys to go into battle than men, for they never thought of or realized the danger they were in."[47]

To disrupt the enemy's communication the partisans intercepted the mail and destroyed telegraph lines, tore up sections of track and destroyed bridges, and attacked Union patrols and outposts. Price knew that guerrillas would distract the Federals and give him time to rearm, refit, and retrain what remained of his ragged army. Those who remained in the ranks had not been paid since their enlistments, so he gave many furloughs to go home to the fall harvests. Many needed clothing and the barest of equipment.

The only conditions the Confederate government set on organized partisan bands were that they observe the general rules of war. To be commissioned and paid by the government, guerrillas would have to acknowledge their subordination to its authority. Any questions concerning guerrilla warfare were directed to the Confederate secretary of war.

Partisan warfare was an attractive alternative to many Missourians. There was "quite a number of men of undoubted respectability [who were] anxious to serve the government on their own account." They were willing to fight without restraint and without orders, converting any property they captured to their own private use. As long as the government would not interfere with them or look upon them as brigands, they would take care of themselves.[48]

The Union army had already welcomed into its ranks the jayhawkers who had been preying on Missouri prior to the war. Within twelve months of the battle of Lexington, by November 1862, approximately fifty-two thousand men filled the roster of the Enrolled Missouri Militia on the Union side. Confederate guerrillas amounted to only a fraction of that number, but they managed to bedevil and harass these troops and prevented their being sent to the eastern theater against Robert E. Lee's Army of Northern Virginia.

Yet Missouri was not the first scene of guerrilla action. Virginia was the first state to license partisan warfare. Gov. John Letcher was empowered to commission ten companies of partisan rangers, which were to be mustered into state service but allowed to operate as independent units. When irregular warfare came to Missouri, sixty-two guerrilla bands were organized.

After the Confederate victory at Lexington, Kansas jayhawker units raided western Missouri on the pretext of protecting Unionist citizens. In reality all the residents of the area were mistreated without regard for their politics, and marauders confiscated their possessions as they saw fit. Lawlessness "left a red scar on the land." Revenge and reprisal seemed the only recourse for helpless citizens. Survivors determined to set order aside, and each man became a law unto himself.

On October 16 Ella Mercer from Jackson County wrote to a sister in Oregon: "The Jayhawkers of Kansas are robbing the border of everything in the absence of the armies. They robbed Morgan Walker and Henry Chiles of everything they had that could be moved."[49]

Thomas Ewing resigned his position as chief justice of the Kansas Supreme Court to accept an appointment as colonel of the Eleventh Kansas Jayhawker Cavalry. Lane's son-in-law, Charles W. Adams, was made colonel of the Twelfth Kansas Jayhawker Cavalry.

In Missouri the Enrolled Missouri Militia was organized in 1862 to guard the border from bushwhackers and unprincipled soldiers. Suspicion ran high against the soldiers, however, because families with Southern sympathies were too often victimized by the same men who were pledged to protect them. Iowa, Illinois, and Kansas troops made up the larger part of the Union troops stationed in the area; many of them regarded all Missourians as disloyal. The rootless militiamen were obliged to live off the land. Although army regulations required the soldiers to present receipts to householders for grain and other supplies requisitioned, such papers were often "forgotten."[50] In general, when Union forces needed forage for their horses, they confiscated it from Southern farms in the area, which left most of the Southerners' farms denuded of crops and the families destitute.

While Price's army was closing on Lexington, rather than render assistance to Mulligan, Lane and his ragtag army of twelve hundred Kansas jayhawkers marched instead against the small pro-Southern town of Osceola, Missouri, in St. Clair County. The Missouri editor of the *Weston Argus* described the sight of fifty shiftless horsemen riding through his town to join "Lane's Brigade":

> They were nearly naked, and minus shoes and hats in many cases. They were not armed, but a number of them had hams of meat on their backs, which they no doubt had stolen from some man's meat house on the road. There are the kind of men that Lane's Brigade is to be composed of; thieves, cutthroats, and midnight robbers. These hirelings passed through town on a full trot, their eyes looking as big as new moons, as they expected at every corner to be stopped or fired on by the Rebels. On a dark night such soldiers would make a splendid charge on a hen-roost, meat house, negro kitchen or stable, but they can't fight honest Americans in daylight.

Osceola was one of the more prosperous towns in southwest Missouri. At the beginning of the war, the population was greater than 3,000, but by 1865 only 183 called it home.

On September 23, 1861, when Lane entered the area, there wasn't a Confederate soldier within miles of the town. With Lane were Col. William Weir's Fourth Kansas Jayhawker Regiment and Col. James Montgomery's Third Kansas Jayhawker Regiment. A few residents fired on the jayhawkers, so Lane ordered Capt. Thomas Moonlight to shell the town. After the Union guns had reduced the town to rubble, nine male inhabitants were brought to the town square for a drumhead court-martial and shot. Most of the remaining residents were women and children.

Banks were an easy target for the jayhawkers, but the Osceola bank prudently had shipped its funds elsewhere. When Lane found little currency in the bank, he ordered the stores, warehouses, and homes ransacked. His men loaded the loot into government wagons and any other vehicles they could confiscate. Among Lane's personal haul were a number of pianos for his home in Lawrence.

He then set the town afire. Of Osceola's eight hundred buildings all but three were turned to ashes. No consideration was given to political leanings of the homeowners. The plunder included 350 horses, 400 head of cattle, 200 kidnapped slaves, 3,000 sacks of flour, 500 pounds of sugar and molasses, and 50 sacks of coffee. The jayhawkers also took the county records from the courthouse. Lane stole a fine carriage from the home of his colleague, U.S. Sen. Waldo P. Johnson, and sent it to his family in Lawrence along with several silk dresses.

Eyewitnesses noted that the plunder train of 150 wagons was at least a mile long. Property losses were estimated at more than a million dollars.[51] One jayhawker wrote: "As the sun went down Sunday night Osceola was a heap of smoldering ruins. Three thousand people were left homeless when Osceola was burned, and perhaps the fairest city in Missouri had been utterly wiped from the earth."

William Johnson, an Osceola resident whose home was destroyed in the raid, was the son of Senator Johnson. He reported: "The Yankees then loaded all the wagons they could find in Osceola and the vicinity with goods from the stores, and records from the court house, and then burned the court house, and the business houses and most of the residences, and would have burned them all, but for the fact that some of their scouts reported the approach of Confederate troops, a report which was not true. They then made a hasty exit."

The captured slaves were taken into Kansas and assigned to farmers to work in the fields. Their pay was anything they could steal and carry away from their former owners and sell in public-street auctions in the towns where they were taken.

During the autumn of 1861, Kansas farmers prized the slaves brought out of Missouri by the Lane Brigade. The *Lawrence Journal*, however, accused Lane of requiring payment from the farmers for providing them. Almost two years later the *Leavenworth Daily Conservative* affirmed, "The large crop of 1863 was made possible only by negro hands. . . . Almost every farm is supplied with labor in the shape of one or two large, healthy negroes."[52]

Before they left Osceola, Lane's raiders degenerated into a jayhawking rabble. Most were drunk before the raid was ended, and three hundred had to be hauled out of town in the plunder wagons. The brigade's chaplains, including the Rev. Hugh Fisher, helped to loot all the churches in the area before applying the torch. They used the spoils to outfit their Kansas buildings.

The Osceola raid was four times more destructive than the 1863 Lawrence raid. To those who questioned the looting, Lane proudly responded: "When you march through a state you must destroy the property of the men in arms against the Government; destroy, devastate, desolate. This is war. Ours is an army of volunteers who must not be judged by the rules applied to regulars."

Furthermore, Lane encouraged his men to devastate the Missouri towns: "Everything disloyal from a Durham cow to a Shanghai chicken, must be cleaned out." After the Osceola raid, Lane promoted the story that the raid had targeted huge military warehouses in the town. Yet there were no warehouses of war materiel.

At the end of September 1861, Lane received orders from Frémont to march his jayhawkers to Kansas City, Missouri, and confer with Gen. Samuel D. Sturgis. Immediately upon his arrival, Lane argued with Sturgis over who was the senior officer; the jayhawker commander could not countenance being second in command to anyone.

Meanwhile, Lane's army camped on the outskirts of Kansas City and began a wild orgy of plunder and rape. Despite the success of their earlier raids, his regiment lacked uniforms, shoes, blankets, and weapons. They were also as untrained and undisciplined as they had ever been. A camp visitor described the jayhawkers as a "ragged, half-armed, diseased, mutinous rabble, taking votes whether any troublesome or distasteful order should be obeyed or defied."[53]

The men boasted about their plundering. All seemed hard up for cash and eagerly offered to sell Rebel souvenirs at ten cents each. Blacks and Indians mingled with the rowdies. Lt. Seymour D. Thompson of the Third Iowa reported Lane to be "the last man we would have taken for a general. He had on a citizen's pants, a soldier's blouse, and a dilapidated white hat." A woman from Kansas remarked about Lane, "Nobody can study his face without a sensation very much like that which one stands at the edge of a slimy, sedgy, uncertain morass."[54]

On October 28 Charles Jennison established the Seventh Kansas Jayhawker Regiment and soon made it the most notorious of all the jayhawker regiments. John Brown Jr. led one company within the command, and most of his men were radical abolitionists from Ashtabula County, Ohio—home of the elder John Brown. While Cols. William Weir's and Charles W. Adam's men remained in Kansas City, Jennison scouted toward Independence, Missouri. Along the eight miles between the two towns the jayhawkers burned twenty-six homes in Jackson County.

In the meantime, Lane was ordered to move his brigade to Springfield to join Frémont in pursuing Sterling Price, who was making his way toward Arkansas. In Butler, Missouri, on October 28 a detachment of Lane's black soldiers fought the first action of the Civil War with African American troops when they defeated a force of Confederate irregulars who were defending their town from being plundered.

Because of the multiplicity of criminal deeds of wholesale plundering, Capt. Marshall Cleveland was relieved of command in Lane's brigade. Although he relinquished his command, Cleveland continued his lawless behavior from his base in Atchison, Kansas, from where he continued to frequently raid Missouri. Movable wealth was the only motive that lured Cleveland. Allegedly if "a man had an enemy in any part of the country . . . he reported him to Cleveland as a Rebel, and the next night he was robbed of all he possessed and considered himself fortunate if he escaped without personal violence."[55]

With the telegraph wires continually humming about Federal atrocities in Missouri, Lincoln removed Frémont from command of the Department of the West for incompetence and for "gross mismanagement of his office." It helped little that Frémont had been denounced by his old friends, the Blairs. Other charges included irregularities in the disbursement of military funds and the commissioning of officers of questionable military abilities. Frémont had held command for only 122 days when Maj. Gen. David M. Hunter succeeded him on November 2. One week later Maj. Gen. Henry W. Halleck succeeded Hunter, taking command officially on November 19 and setting up his headquarters at St. Louis.

With Price achieving noted military success all across Missouri, the exiled state government, meeting in Neosho, voted on October 28 to leave the Union and join the Confederacy. One month later, on November 28, the Confederate Congress in Richmond sent an official acknowledgment to Gov. Claiborne Jackson accepting Missouri as the twelfth state of the Confederacy.

3

Southern Hopes— A Savior Appears

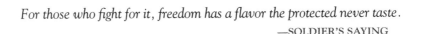

For those who fight for it, freedom has a flavor the protected never taste.
—SOLDIER'S SAYING

QUANTRILL HAD MANY FRIENDS in Jackson County, especially in the Blue Springs neighborhood of the Morgan Walker farm. While he served in Sterling Price's army, he made many new acquaintances from Jackson County. Many of these young men later joined him as part of his partisan rangers.

After leaving Price, Quantrill returned to Blue Springs. The locality was described as one of the most picturesque areas of the state. The Big and Little Blue as well as the Sni Rivers ran through the mountains and hills. Here the dark ravines, impassable gulches, deep defiles, and precipitous canyons rarely saw a human tread. One early settler described the Sni Hills as "an ideal hiding for a band like Quantrills. . . . Here they could make their preparations unobserved and sally forth unheralded."[1]

With most of the local men away in Price's army, Kansans increased their depredatory raids into Missouri. Since the Morgan Walker raid, Lane and his jayhawkers were anxious to pay back Quantrill and the farmers who befriended him. Andrew Walker noted that James Montgomery's band had spread the word that they would burn Walker's property and "kill the whole family."[2] As a result, Morgan Walker hired teenager Jim Little as a lookout to patrol the neighborhood for Montgomery's men and report any news of jayhawker activity.

Because of the Walker property's proximity to the border, jayhawkers continued to attack this area. On Tuesday morning, October 1, 1861, a squad of jayhawkers struck near Walker's farm. They rode from farmhouse to farmhouse and pillaged the farmers of money, silverware, and jewelry. One of the residents rushed word of the raid to Quantrill, and he quickly rode to Walker's farm. There he gathered Andrew Walker, Morgan T. Mattox, John Little, William Haller, John Hampton, and six other youths, and they raced after the jayhawkers.

Quantrill formed his men into an ambush on the Independence and Blue Springs road and waited for the jayhawkers. Somehow the raiders got wind of the trap and detoured to another road with people to rob.

Two miles west of the Walker farm, the jayhawkers attacked the farm of Daniel DeWitt, which had been the last hiding place of Charlie Ball and his raiders prior to the ambush at the Walker farm the previous December. The jayhawkers then moved north toward the Strother Stone farm. Here they insulted Stone's wife, and one of them struck her on the head with his revolver when she protested their actions.[3] After looting the house, they rode to the farm of William Thompson, an elderly gentleman.

As Quantrill and his men came riding up, they saw Stone's wife standing in her yard, her face covered with blood, pointing out which way the jayhawkers had headed. For a brief moment the Southerners were stunned at the sight of the shaken, bleeding woman. James Campbell recalled that Quantrill had told his companions earlier, "Any member of [t]his troop who insulted a woman should be shot."[4]

After they resumed the race toward the Thompson farm, their shock turned to anger. The jayhawkers had already set fire to the Thompson place by the time the guerrillas arrived, but they had not as yet ridden away. Many were just mounting their horses when Quantrill and his men boldly charged toward them.

Quantrill was the first to charge into the jayhawkers with his gun blazing. Already known as an unerring shot, he killed the man who had struck the Stone woman. His men wounded two others. The rest of the jayhawkers fled on the Independence and Blue Springs road toward the safety of Independence, five miles away. The fight became a wild horse race as Quantrill's men were in hot pursuit.[5]

When word of the jayhawker's death reached Independence, Unionist citizens clamored for an arrest; this was the first instance of a Federal soldier being killed in Jackson County. The town marshal arrested both Stone and Thompson the next day for the soldier's death.

Not wanting innocent men to be charged for something that he had done, but knowing that he might be putting his life in danger, Quantrill went to Independence and had a justice of the peace assist him in swearing out an affidavit stating that the killing was his responsibility. To Andrew Walker, Quantrill said, "They can't catch me, and I'll save 'em if I can." This affidavit satisfied the authorities, and Stone and Thompson were released. After learning the circumstances of the jayhawker's death, the authorities brought no charges against Quantrill.

This incident, however, led the Unionist militia in Independence to target Quantrill, and for a short time he was forced into hiding. At first he camped in the woods where he and his men could find cover and concealment and water for their horses. Areas like this were abundant in and around the Blue Springs area, and Quantrill's small band brought some relief from jayhawker injustices.

Still, Jayhawker raids left the pro-Southern farmers stunned. In October 1861 they raided the Brooking Township eight miles south of Independence. On October 27 they burned the home of Martin Flanery, who then joined Quantrill. Flanery reported that Charles Jennison's jayhawkers had burned a church and twenty-seven other homes in the neighborhood and had pillaged the home of Reuben Harris in the middle of the night. Harris's wife, Laura, their daughter Nancy, and their other small children were home at the time. Laura's nephew was Thomas Coleman Younger. Daughter Nancy (also known as Nannie) had married Jabez McCorkle, a brother of John McCorkle, Quantrill's chief of scouts. The attack by the jayhawkers on the Harris home was recorded as following:

One night while the family was asleep, the door of Mrs. McCorkle's room on the first floor was broken open and a squad of noisy [jayhawkers] rushed into the apartment. The alarmed lady entreated them to retire until she could put on her clothes, but they cursed her and told her to get up pretty damn quick or they would prod her with their sabers. A bright fire was burning in the open hearth; the wretches took blazing brands and carried them about as they ransacked the closets, dresser drawers and trunks. A little girl [either three-year-old Virginia or six-year-old Eliza], who was sleeping with her mother, was awakened by the unusual noise and began to cry, and one of the men went to her and, holding a saber against her face, told her if she uttered another sound he would cut her head off. The poor little thing was so frightened and subdued that she did not speak a word for days. The young girls who were sleeping upstairs were aroused by the disturbance below, hastily dressed and ran to their mother's room. The outlaws then turned their attention to the girls, using insulting terms, searched their persons for valuables, all the while singing ribald songs or telling obscene jokes. They took from a pocket in the housemaid's petticoat forty dollars, tearing her apparel from her person. The creatures made the girls go before them as they searched every apartment in the house, from which they purloined every article of value they could carry. Then returning downstairs three of the wretches took by force three of the girls into the yard and marched back and forth in the moonlight, making most vicious threats and insinuations. After several hours of this atrocious conduct the creatures started away.

Nannie recounted other depredations committed by Jennison:

He ordered the execution of wounded Confederate soldiers on parole; he murdered men in the presence of their families. The silverplate and jewelry Jennison and his men stole and carried into Kansas would have stocked many jewelry stores; the bedding, wearing apparel and furniture they carted over into their beloved commonwealth was ample to supply the homes of the whole horde; the cattle, horses and mules these thrifty thieves drove to their State from Missouri were enough to stock the farms of any of the "Emigrant Aiders" in Kansas. Jennison's command hauled from the graveyard near Harrisonville a number of tombstones, this was a gruesome kind of highway robbery, but they doubtless reasoned that the smooth side of the marble slabs would make substantial doorsteps. They took the patchwork quilts from the negro cabins as eagerly as they pulled from the beds of the invalid among the aristocrats the downy silken comforts and costly counterpanes. They tore up the hearths to seek hidden treasure; they took the family carriages and drove as their occupants; they packed in wagons all wearing apparel, household articles, harness, plows or whatever they wanted and could make room for. They left not a horse, mule or any cattle they could manage to drive away; they robbed hen roosts, took children's toys, even compelling one gentleman to take off his coat, pants and shoes and give them; they broke dishes they could not carry away; handsome party finery that did not appeal to their pilfering proclivities they wiped their muddy boots on; one Sunday afternoon I counted in the Sni Hills seven dwellings burning at once, two homes of poor widows.[6]

Actions such as these induced many new recruits to swarm to Quantrill's camp to avenge the wrongs that were being done to their homes and families.

One was Thomas B. Harris, whose family had just been assaulted. Harris's brother-in-law Jabez and his brother John also hurried to join Quantrill. Another neighbor, John Jarrette, later rose to the rank of captain in Quantrill's partisan company. Accompanying Jarrette was his brother-in-law Thomas Coleman Younger, known as Cole.

Younger was only eighteen when he met Quantrill. He was about five feet ten inches tall, had a fair complexion, and was heavyset with light hair. Younger's father, Henry Washington Younger, married Bursheba Fristoe of Brooking Township. Her father, Richard Marshal Fristoe, fought alongside Andrew Jackson at the battle of New Orleans, and it was through his efforts that Jackson County was named after his commander. Cole's great-grandmother on his father's side was a daughter of Lighthorse Harry Lee of Revolutionary War fame. His grandfather Fristoe was a grandnephew of Chief Justice John Marshall of Virginia and was the first presiding county court judge of Jackson County.[7]

The Younger family supported the idea of Missouri neutrality, and the parents had been encouraging Cole toward a ministerial career. Both ideas were radically changed after a birthday party.

A neighbor, Cuthbert Mockbee, hosted the party for his daughter's sixteenth birthday. Sally and Caroline Younger attended, along with brothers Cole and Jim. Also present at the party, although unannounced and uninvited, was an arrogant and boisterous militia captain, Irvin Walley, from the Enrolled Missouri Militia garrisoned near the county seat of Harrisonville.

At one time Federal soldiers were welcomed and graciously received by the Southern families of Missouri's border counties, but now the young ladies spurned them. Walley tried to dance with the girls, but none would accept his offers. Embarrassment turned to irritation. The last girl he asked to dance was one of the Younger sisters. When she also rebuffed him, Walley rebuked her with some unkind words. Cole Younger stepped in to defend his sister.

Rather than address the matter of dancing, Walley changed the subject of the confrontation to Quantrill. He demanded that Cole tell him where Quantrill was. When Younger claimed not to know, Walley called him a lair, and Cole knocked him to the floor. The doubly embarrassed Yankee drew his pistol, but other young men stepped in immediately and ended the fight.

After the party, when Henry Younger learned what had happened from his children, he sent his son away to one of his other farms. Almost immediately, Walley arrived at the Younger house that night, accused Cole of spying for Quantrill, and demanded the father surrender his son.

As soon as Cole heard Walley's accusation, he realized he could not return home. Instead, he sought out his brother-in-law, Jarrette, who had earlier joined Quantrill's company.[8] Jarrette and Younger rode with Quantrill for several months before Federal authorities had any proof of the identities of the men who rode with Quantrill.

MISSOURIANS DREADED to see former slaves used as guides for the jayhawkers' plunder raids. In August 1861 the *Emporia (Kans.) News* reported that James Lane had enlisted hundreds of blacks "for immediate service in Missouri under Colonel Montgomery who will have a battalion of Indians, negroes, and white men under his command." By September 14, 1861, Lane had directed Jennison to raise a regiment of black fugitives. While enticing the slaves to run off from their masters, the jayhawkers also encouraged the fugitives to steal whatever they could from their owners. By mid-September prominent Missourians complained to Lincoln about the depredations of armed companies of black jayhawkers raiding their farms.

To fight for the freedom and civil rights of the slaves, the Northerners stripped the Southerners of their civil rights and freedom. Southern possessions were seized and robbed, their presses censored, their crops destroyed, their homes torched, their women and children banished, their men murdered, and their right to vote was ignored. The troops invading Missouri from Kansas considered all Missourians as disloyal. This justified plundering. In the meantime, farmers safeguarded their livestock by keeping them in "timber" stables at night and in some instances in their homes.

In Kansas, James Lane craved political as well as military power. He was greatly disappointed when David Hunter was named to head the new Department of Kansas—encompassing the Indian Territory, Colorado, and Nebraska. Missouri's provisional governor, Hamilton Gamble, had cautioned Lincoln that the border area would only get worse if Lane were put in charge. Lane was not only angered by not receiving the office, he was also not inclined to subordinate himself to another. Instead, he tried to get Lincoln to rescind the nomination of Hunter. When that failed, he turned on the president, calling him a "damned liar, a demagogue, and a scoundrel."[9]

Lane continued to oversee punitive jayhawker incursions into Missouri. As soon as sufficient men were mustered to form a company, Lane sent them into action. Three companies of Jennison's jayhawkers, one of which was black troops, marched on Kansas City, burning homes and fields. From Kansas City, Companies A, B, and H of the Seventh Kansas Jayhawker Regiment marched toward Independence. Five miles east of Kansas City, Company H (commanded by Marshall Cleveland) came upon Pitcher's Mill near the junction of the Independence and Westport roads.[10]

Fifty-six-year-old Col. Thomas Pitcher owned the mill and had gained fame during the Mexican War and as a sheriff in Jackson County. He had joined Sterling Price's army and served in Company C, First Regimental Cavalry, Eighth Division, Missouri State Guard. In addition to owning a large home and plantation, Pitcher operated the gristmill in the region. As soon as Jennison discovered that a Confederate soldier owned the property, he burned it to the ground.

When Company D arrived in the area, the men saw women and children fleeing to the woods while Company H smashed in the windows of Pitcher's home and set it ablaze. Stacks of wheat and oats were also fired. While the jayhawkers were in the area they shot one farmer for refusing to give them liquor and killed another for trying to escape with his mules.[11]

As soon as word reached Quantrill of these events, he gathered his eleven men and linked forces with Upton Hays's twenty-two men. On Sunday, November 10, 1861, the guerrillas attacked a detachment from Jennison's Seventh Kansas. The Federals were encamped on the Charles Younger farm, four miles south of Independence along the Independence to Harrisonville road. Charles Younger was an uncle of Cole Younger and a captain in the Federal militia.

At 4:30 P.M. the guerrillas struck the camp. They were sure shots, and the enemy broke in confusion after the first volley. Five Federals fell during the initial fire, and seven more were killed during the chase. Thirty-two were wounded. The remaining jayhawkers fell back to Independence, avoiding annihilation.

Cole Younger was with Quantrill that day and killed his first man. His persistent pistol practice paid off when he shot one of the Federals at a distance of seventy-one yards.[12]

Hays had been an outspoken Unionist at the start of the war. He was the youngest in a family of thirteen children. At the age of eighteen he led a wagon train to Santa Fe, New Mexico. Before the war Hays formed a company with Henry Clay Chiles, a member of the Christian church in eastern Jackson County, and the venture secured government contracts to carry freight to western government outposts. Hays turned guerrilla after Jennison's jayhawkers captured one of his wagon trains, burned his home, and took his cattle, horses, carriages, and slaves. Jennison soon returned and also burned the home of Sam Hays, Upton's brother.[13]

To avenge his embarrassment by Hays's and Quantrill's meager force, Jennison attacked Independence with his remaining 450 men. The men of the town were collected and confined to the town square. Then the jayhawkers pillaged the homes. Several men were murdered, and sixty-five houses were torched. In addition to the loot, the Kansas troops also stole several thousand head of the finest stock from the surrounding farms and drove off 250 slaves.[14] On the way back through Kansas City, Jennison's men stopped and killed elderly farmer Joseph Williams for expressing pro-Southern sentiments.

For years Missourians had known there was a sizable element in Kansas that, out of economic and moral poverty, willingly plundered the farmers of western Missouri who had "a dangerous reputation for wealth."[15] Eyewitnesses in Kansas City reported that many of the freed slaves rode back later as part of further raids on Missouri towns and farms. On November 17 thirty-five black soldiers arrived in Leavenworth, and most of them went on to Lawrence.[16] During November jayhawkers H. H. Moore and H. D. Fisher gathered all the Missouri slaves they could confiscate and took them back into Kansas for cheap labor for Kansas farms and towns as no more than indentured servants.[17]

At the end of December, after learning of the atrocities committed by the Seventh Kansas, Henry W. Halleck wired the following telegram to Gen. George B. McClellan, commander of all Federal forces:

> The conduct of the forces under Lane and Jennison has done more for the enemy in this State than could have been accomplished by 20,000 of his own army. I receive almost daily complaints of outrages committed by these men in the name of the United States, and the evidence is so conclusive as to leave no doubt of their correctness. It is rumored that Lane has been made a brigadier general. I cannot conceive of a more injudicious appointment. It will take 20,000 men to counteract its effect in this State, and, moreover, is offering a premium for rascality and robbing generally.[18]

While Jennison had been occupied with looting Independence, on November 16 Marshall Cleveland's company robbed the Northrup and the Union Banks of Kansas City of $3,850. In Buchanan County, Cleveland's troops stole slaves, thirty horses, and a great amount of plunder.

The following month Halleck ordered Gen. John Pope to drive Lane's brigade and Jennison's jayhawkers from the border. He told his troops:

> Jennison's men do not belong in this department. . . . I have directed General Pope to drive them out, or, if they resist, to disarm them and hold them

prisoners. They are no better than a band of robbers; they cross the line, rob, steal, plunder, and burn whatever they can lay their hands upon. They disgrace the name and uniform of American soldiers and are driving good Union men into the ranks of the secession army. The course pursued by those under Lane and Jennison has turned against us many thousands who were formerly Union men. A few more such raids will make [Missouri] as unanimous against us as is eastern Virginia. Their conduct within the last six months has caused a change of 20,000 votes in the State. If the government countenances such acts by screening the perpetrators from justice and by rewarding with office their leaders and abettors it may resign all hopes of a pacification of Missouri.[19]

As soon as McClellan received Halleck's message, he relayed the information to Secretary of War Edwin M. Stanton.[20] By March 1962 Halleck was replaced as the military commander in Missouri. Before leaving office, Halleck wrote to McClellan again and condemned Lane's men.[21] Despite Halleck's protestations, the atrocities continued.

Nor was Halleck alone in condemning the actions of the jayhawkers. Nearly every Unionist and Southerner in Missouri expressed his complaint to the authorities in Washington. Gen. George Caleb Bingham wrote to Missouri Congressman Rollins, "Jennison should be executed, for if he were hung [Confederate Gen. Sterling] Price would lose thereby the best recruiting officer he has ever had."[22] Union Gen. Richard C. Vaughn wrote to U.S. Attorney General Edward Bates: "It is a fact well known to me that hundreds of people in Jackson and Cass Counties are true and loyal men; they have already been robbed of their property, insulted and in many cases murdered by these troops from Kansas. The policy has caused hundreds of good men to leave their homes and fly to the bushes for protection, while others have actually joined the guerrillas as a measure of safety, believing they would be less liable to danger there than at their homes."[23]

Throughout the months of January and February 1862, in the wake of Lane's and Jennison's jayhawking raids in Jackson County, Quantrill's band rode into Kansas and recovered cattle and horses stolen by the jayhawkers. Quantrill's initial mission was to to drive off any jayhawkers he found.

Martin Ismert's grandfather had a farm along the Missouri River, and he remembered his grandfather's telling him one day that he discovered five jayhawkers in a camp on his farm while he was rounding up his cows. The men told him not to reveal their whereabouts. Later that day and on several days after their discovery, the wild-looking men came to the house and demanded food. On the last evening the men came to the house and slapped around the cook and then demanded the farmer's best riding horse. When Ismert went to fetch the horse, one of the jayhawkers ran into the barn shouting, "Boys, it's Quantrill's men!" Before they could escape, two of the jayhawkers were shot dead in the barn; the others managed to run away. Quantrill's men then gathered up the bodies, loaded them in a wagon, and dumped them in the river. Ismert remembered, "Quantrill was a quiet, well-mannered man and was no more cruel during his life than any other leader would have been who was engaged in border warfare."[24]

Union Gen. John M. Schofield was appointed to take over the vacated office of Halleck. His chief plan was to employ militia forces against the increasing guerrilla activity. By April 1862 he had recruited fourteen thousand men into the Enrolled Missouri Militia. Unfortunately, the militiamen often proved to be as guilty of vicious outrages as their Kansas counterparts.

In the meantime, Lane gathered around himself a coterie of abolitionists and friends of old John Brown and jayhawkers. They were as careless with their personal loyalties as they were in their dress and habits. Closest to Lane were Jennison and Montgomery, each fighting the other for personal advancement and neither demonstrating any more loyalty to Lane than the expediency of the moment dictated.[25]

Both men competed to command the black refugees being enlisted in Kansas. In the end it fell to neither. Jennison's candidacy was tainted by his brutal reputation, and Montgomery's criminal background finally worked against him. Command went to radical abolitionist James Williams.

By December 1862 rivalries sundered the rapport between the jayhawker bands. Montgomery came to hate Jennison. When he departed in disgust from the border, he called Jennison "an unmitigated liar, blackleg and robber."[26] Montgomery became colonel of the Second South Carolina Colored Volunteers and gained distasteful notoriety for burning the town of Darian, Georgia. The archenemies of Lane in Kansas were Governor Robinson and Senator Pomeroy. Pomeroy lined up solidly behind Montgomery, and as a result Lane was reportedly doing all he could to discredit him.

In late November and early December 1861, while other units of the Seventh Kansas Jayhawker Regiment were terrorizing the towns of Jackson County, a part of the regiment marched into Cass County and plundered the Henry Younger farm of wagons and forty horses. At the time Cole Younger, with a team of horses nearby, was working on a fence. One of the jayhawkers told him, "That's too good a team for a boy your age. We'll take them." The men stripped the harness off and rode away with the horses.[27]

After this raid, Lt. Col. Daniel Anthony led eight companies of jayhawkers to Pleasant Hill to plunder the town. Along the way the expedition had to run a gauntlet of guerrillas. Four jayhawkers were captured, and eleven guerrillas were killed.[28] George Miller of Pleasant Hill reported that Anthony stole ten thousand dollars' worth of livestock and fifty-five slaves.

From Pleasant Hill the marauders rode to West Point and stole more than 150 mules, 40 horses, and 129 slaves and burned every house but one along their line of march. They also nabbed every wagon and carriage they found to haul everything back into Kansas. Their plunder train was over a mile long.[29]

Returning to Kansas City on November 22, the Seventh Kansas Jayhawkers continued their depredations even while being garrisoned in the Union enclave of Kansas City. On the night they returned, forty men from companies C and H broke into a dry goods store and stole several thousand dollars' worth of goods as well as an amount of money.[30] Jayhawker regiments allegedly recruited men from jails and prisons.

Their nonexistent discipline showed its wantonness on November 23. Lt. Isaac J. Hughes of Company D shot Pvt. James C. Murphy of Company B for disobeying orders. Murphy reportedly drew his weapon on Hughes, and Hughes killed him.[31] That same night, Joseph Raymond of Company C raped a woman; he later faced a firing squad.

Jennison led his men toward Independence for another raid. There he detailed a fifteen-man squad under Lt. Francis M. Ray of Company C to a nearby area known as Crackers Neck with a list of a dozen farmhouses to be burned. A Unionist who had been forced from his home led the patrol to his old neighborhood and pointed out which houses were to be destroyed.[32] Yet the atrocities committed there by the jayhawkers were only one reason for peaceful citizens to switch their allegiance to the pro-Southern cause.

During his term as head of the Union Department of the West, Halleck himself provided the other provocation when he issued orders compelling citizens to serve as forced labor in repairing railroads and telegraph lines damaged by the partisan bands. Halleck's predecessor, Hunter, had issued earlier orders assessing wealthy citizens in St. Louis for the cost of feeding and clothing Unionist refugees. Those who had no money lost their property.[33] In short, civil rights were nonexistent in Missouri after martial law was declared.

The wanton destruction wreaked by the Seventh Kansas eventually resulted in the arrest of Jennison and his second in command, Lt. Col. Daniel R. Anthony. Gen. William S. Rosecrans, commander of the Department of Missouri, directed the *Cincinnati Gazette* to correct its reporting of the arrests. Anthony had been arrested, Rosecrans noted, "for allowing his men to rob and steal from private families, and for allowing his men to break into private houses and break open wardrobes, closets, etc. You will confer a favor on this army by not allowing a set of worthless, lying officers to lead you astray. These fight not for love of their country, but to rob and steal from citizens."[34]

On December 12 the Third Kansas Jayhawker Regiment pillaged the towns of Butler and Papinsville in Bates County and stole any slaves they could find and a large amount of livestock.[35] The *Lawrence Republican* proudly recorded the raid: "Our eagles first pounced upon Papinsville, and the town went up in smoke and flame. As we passed through the country, the houses, barns, mills, and other property of Rebels were brought to the altar and full atonement made. Captain [John E.] Stewart paid his compliments to Butler and the business part of that once thriving and pleasant village was burned to the ground. General Lane's expedition in comparison with this were visitations of mercy."

North of the Missouri River, in Platte County, jayhawkers went to the home of Clinton Cockrell and stole five hundred dollars and five horses.[36] In Buchanan County on January 22, 1862, William L. Irvine of Rushville, Missouri, lost slaves and mules to Marshall Cleveland's jayhawkers. In Weston, local Unionist regiments were raised in the border counties to protect against jayhawking. Recruits received twenty-five dollars a month and were clothed and fed by the U.S. government.

After the jayhawking raids of the winter of 1861–62, many Jackson County youths flocked to Quantrill's camp. They were desperate to defend their homes and property, and they realized they could stave off the raids only by banding together in a Home Guard unit. The first to seek out Quantrill during the fall of 1861 was nineteen-year-old William Haller; he became the first recruit. Then twenty-two-year-old John Little joined Quantrill. His younger brother, sixteen-year-old James, became Quantrill's closest follower. James Little later served as a second lieutenant to Quantrill and went with him to Kentucky at the close of the war. Also listed among Quantrill's first recruits was Andrew Walker, the twenty-four-year-old son of Morgan Walker. John Hampton was a member of the first band; he was ambushed and killed eighteen months later by a Federal patrol from Independence. James Kelly, twenty-one-year-old Solomon Basham, and Ed Koger also sought out Quantrill.

In December 1861 the Fourth Kansas Jayhawker Regiment robbed the Morgan Walker farm of all its stock and equipment. Thus the jayhawkers increased the number of raids into Missouri, and as a result, Quantrill attacked them whenever or wherever they could be found and forced to fight.

Guerrilla Harrison Trow reported that Quantrill's little command ambushed a portion of Jennison's regiment in the vicinity of Morgan Walker's farm. They killed five of the thieves and confiscated their horses, saddles, bridles, and weapons.

The next fight occurred on the property of Volney Ryan with a company of Missouri militia. This particular militia company was notorious for three things: robbing henhouses, stealing horses, and fleeing the enemy. Eight guerrillas struck at daylight, charging through the militia camp and back again. When Quantrill's people returned from the pursuit that followed, they counted fifteen dead, the fruits of a running battle.[37] Even Lane's adjutant, Marcus J. Parrot, admitted the jayhawkers were highway robbers and urged Kansas Governor Charles Robinson to prefer charges against him so that he might be put down.[38]

Shortly before Christmas 1861, Quantrill's band was alerted to the presence of George Searcy, a Confederate deserter from Price's army. Searcy had fought under Price for six months then deserted and returned to the Blue Springs area. There he gained a reputation as a thief and robber who made no distinctions between his victims. Andrew Walker noted that Searcy had robbed a fifteen-year-old boy of fifteen dollars. Now Searcy was mainly interested in fine horses, and many believed he planned to go to Texas after he had collected enough horses.

Quantrill determined to rid the neighborhood of Searcy and his criminal deeds. In the absence of civil law, someone needed to bring a sense of justice to the countryside. Walker related: "It proved a difficult matter to locate his corral, but they finally discovered it on the bank of the Missouri River. We beleaguered him, forcing him to surrender, and took charge of his booty; he had twenty-two fine mares, a valuable Kentucky jack and a blooded stallion."[39]

Another of Quantrill's men, Jack Liddil, remembered events this way:

The thief we held court on, I acting as judge advocate, and we condemned him to death and executed the sentence. The horses and cattle were returned to their owners, those who could afford it being required to pay $10 a head for the return of the horses. . . . [T]he Quantrill band was called into existence because some measure was absolutely necessary against horse thieving, plundering and other depredations, which were then running rife in Jackson and other counties bordering Kansas. We captured and punished horse thieves. We meted out justice to them because there was no other justice to be had, for the average criminal was beyond the pale of the courts. Naturally we gained many recruits until we became several hundred strong.

We were all Southern men, in spirit and sympathy, and naturally our band became a fighting machine with a purpose.[40]

Quantrill and his men decided that Searcy was too much of a nuisance to be turned loose. They caught him in the afternoon, tried him that night, and hanged him up along the banks of the Little Blue River the next morning. Harrison Trow commented, "The execution acted as a thunderstorm. It restored the equilibrium of the moral atmosphere. The border warfare had found a chief."

Quantrill then returned the horses, mules, and other property to their owners, some of whom were Union men.[41] This gesture proved Quantrill's integrity. Ordinary citizens could now sleep comfortably in their beds at night. Quantrill's Home Guards provided them with a sense of law and order. Many residents came to view the guerrillas and their leader as some-one who could deal with the injustices being perpetrated on the farmers of Jackson County.

Shortly after Christmas 1861, Quantrill added three recruits to his origi-nal band of eight: James A. Hendricks, John W. Koger, and William H. Gregg. Accounts of how Quantrill's guerrillas started are many. One of the men recorded it this way:

Some of the most desperate men in guerrilla warfare were those who tried to stay at home during the Civil War to care for helpless ones, or who, having gone to the front, returned from time to time to look after their homes. Some times they found ashes where their homes stood. The people of the home were not to be found, or if found, they were naked and hungry, and now and then one would be found whose reason had been overthrown. Then the returned soldier lay in wait in the woods. He skulked by night. When the weather permitted he lay down to sleep by day in the tall grass of the prairie. After he had lived in this way for a little while, after he had comforted his feeling of revenge by the results of some unerring shots, and would have been willing to call it even, he found that he was proscribed. He knew he was hunted. He knew that whatever he had of kin, wherever it was found, would be made to suffer for his sake. And he knew, God help him, that he had no country, and no flag. And then he fought to the death. Now when you find a dozen, twenty-five, fifty or one hundred men whose lives have came together in this way, you can understand how they come to be terrors. You can understand the portent of the "Black Flag." There is no mounting of guard, or dress parade, or hope of reward from Congress, or of degrees by colleges, or of florid descriptions of the fight, with pictures, for men who are guerrillas. Two stand sentinel somewhere in the thicket while the others get a little sleep. And sometimes there is no sentinel, but the guerrilla's faithful horse.[42]

Quantrill's band grew to thirty. Joseph Gilchrist would die in battle only a few short months later. Twenty-four-year-old Perry Hoy was captured in March 1862 and shot by a Federal firing squad the following July. Twenty-two-year-old Joe Vaughn fought with Quantrill for one year then joined the regular Confederate army and died in 1862 at the battle of Pea Ridge, Arkansas. Twenty-two-year-old James B. Kelly joined with twenty-three-year-old James A. Hendricks, an experienced soldier who had seen action with the regular army. William Gregg joined the Missouri State Guard on June 1, 1861, before returning and joining Quantrill. He took part in the first battle in Missouri at Rock Creek and was in sixty-five battles all told. Tall, handsome Harrison Trow joined Quantrill after jayhawkers stole everything he had. He had also served for six months with the regular Confederate service.

Twenty-year-old Canadian George Todd was six feet tall with a dark complexion, dark straight hair, and high cheekbones. He was a stonemason and a bridge builder with his father before the war. Todd first joined the Missouri State Guard before returning to Jackson County and joining Quantrill in January 1862. The Federals in Independence imprisoned Todd's father in a cellar without heat during the coldest part of the winter to try to make him tell where his son was. Others say the elder Todd was kept there to force him to help build Fort Union in Kansas City. When he was released, he was so frozen he could not feed himself. Later it was said that he was pressed into service and sent east. The Federals paid a terrible price for their treatment of Todd's father. The young man became a captain in Quantrill's company and later rose to second in command. Some said that he:

> was the incarnate devil of battle. He thought of fighting when awake, dreamed of it at night, mingled talk of it in relaxation, and went hungry many a day and shelterless many a night that he might find his enemy and have his fill of fight. Quantrill always had to hold him back, and yet he was his thunderbolt. He discussed nothing in the shape of orders. A soldier who discusses is like a hand which would think. He only charged. Were he attacked in front—a charge; were he attacked in the rear—a charge; on either flank—a charge.[43]

Quantrill relied heavily upon him.

Other young men, too young for the regular army, joined Quantrill that first winter. Fifteen-year-old Morgan T. Mattox rode with Quantrill in the battle of Independence, the Lawrence raid, and the Fayette fight. Twelve-year-old Dick Liddel was with Quantrill's band at the Centralia fight. Fifteen-year-old Allen Parmer went to Kentucky with Quantrill at the end of the war and after the war married Frank and Jesse James's sister. John Barbee was fifteen years old when he joined Quantrill's company in 1864.

Not all the men came from Jackson County. John and Joseph Hall were from Cass County. They arrived in Quantrill's camp in early 1862. Their sisters had been raped by jayhawkers and their home burned down. David Poole also came from Cass County; he later became a captain in the partisan rangers. He joined Quantrill after his uncle's home was sacked by jayhawkers. Even young men from Lafayette County, like Mack Poisel from Waverly, joined Quantrill after three Unionists murdered his father.[44]

A few days after the hanging of George Searcy, Quantrill and his ten recruits clashed with Union troops at Manasseth Gap overlooking the Little Blue River just east of Brooking Township. They ambushed a Federal patrol on the Independence and Harrisonville road.[45] The sudden ambush resulted in the wounding of several Federals while the rest quickly surrendered. They could offer no resistance to the accurate pistol fire and wild charge of the guerrillas. After seizing the much-needed Federal arms and ammunition, Quantrill paroled them and sent them back to Independence.

Word of the ambush quickly came to the attention of Halleck. On December 22, 1861, the Federal commander issued a general order outlawing all guerrillas and irregulars. "Such men," he declared, "were to be immediately shot whenever captured." This was the first sign of the "black flag"—no quarter would be given. On January 1, 1862, Halleck published an order on the treatment of captured guerrillas. Its ninth paragraph reads:

[W]hile the code of war gives certain exemptions to a soldier regularly in the military service of an enemy, it is a well established principle that insurgents, not militarily organized under the laws of the State, predatory partisans, and guerrilla bands are not entitled to such exemptions; such men are not legitimately in arms, and the military name and garb, which they have assumed cannot give a military exemption to the crimes, which they may commit. They are, in a legal sense, mere freebooters and banditti, and are liable to the same punishment, which was imposed upon guerrilla bands by Napoleon in Spain and by Scott in Mexico.[46]

Halleck foolishly believed he would eliminate guerrilla actions by these orders. When Sterling Price heard on January 12 of Halleck's general order, he sent a letter through the Union lines demanding that Halleck explain his actions, which were contrary to the rules of war that stipulated irregular soldiers were to be treated as prisoners of war.[47] Price inquired why discharged State Guardsmen, who were not in active military service, were being imprisoned. Even recruiting officers whom Price had ordered back to their home counties were executed when captured.

The popularity and size of Quantrill's command made Union officials nervous. Inclement weather on Christmas Day 1861 induced Quantrill to temporarily disband. Jayhawker activity continued unabated, however.

The Union commander in Independence found a willing ally in twenty-eight-year-old Riley Alley, a Blue Springs teamster from Tennessee and a neighbor of Morgan Walker. Together they worked out an elaborate scheme to catch Quantrill and his guerrillas. Alley hosted a ball in January and invited all the youth of the area to attend, including a special invitation to Quantrill and his men. Wary that the ball was a trap, Quantrill did not attend but observed the party from cover near the farmhouse.

A company of Union soldiers arrived a short time after the ball had begun and charged into the house. Immediately they sent the men and boys upstairs and kept the women downstairs. When they realized they did not have Quantrill or any of his men in custody, they sequestered everyone in the house for the rest of the night and into the next day. Later, additional Federal infantry arrived. The soldiers became "beastly drunk" on peach brandy acquired from the nearby home of fifty-nine-year-old Rhoda Harris.[48] When they realized their plan had failed, the Federals released the women and loaded the men and boys into wagons and took them to Independence.

Fifteen-year-old Frank Smith was abused and threatened by the Federal commander himself. The Yankee told him: "You damn little Rebel. I'm going to let you go, but if I hear of you getting into anything down there at Blue Springs, or taking any part in assisting the Rebel cause, I'll send down and have you brought in here and will cut your damn head off." These threats convinced Frank to flee the area. He traveled to Wyandotte, Kansas, to find work.

Jim Tatum and Solomon Basham were the only guerrillas captured that night at Alley's ball. Basham was sent to the Rock Island Penitentiary in Illinois, where he spent the rest of the war. Alley was also arrested so as not to reveal his complicity. He soon returned home but shortly after heard that Quantrill and Todd were looking for him. Realizing that his collusion was known—and aware of Quantrill's reputation for avenging wrongs—he fled to

Kansas City and never returned. George Todd found partial revenge by chopping the spokes out of one of Alley's wagons.

Ed Koger wrote a song about the episode and sang it, accompanying himself on the banjo, to Todd's wife, whom he named in the lyrics:

> Old Rile Alley gave a ball,
> The Feds came down and took us all
> Over the ice and over the snow—
> Sing-Song Kitty, won't you kiss-me-o!
> Old Rile Alley gave a ball,
> Planned to catch Quantrill and bushwhack all,
> But Quant was smart and didn't go—
> Sing-Song Kitty, won't you kiss-me-o!

While the Southerners were questioned in Independence, Quantrill gathered some men and attacked a Union patrol just west of Blue Springs. He killed two or three and wounded four to five more during the skirmish.

At the beginning of the hostilities in Jackson County, Quantrill and the pro-Southerners were willing to accept and endure the presence of Unionists who lived among them. Whenever Quantrill's company recovered stolen property, it was returned to its rightful owners regardless of whether they were Southern sympathizers or Unionists. That changed, however, when neighbors with traitorous intentions—like Riley Alley—actively aided the Federals. Toleration ebbed. Yet regardless of the brutal and vicious treatment of the Southern sympathizers, Quantrill did not allow his men to perpetrate transgressions in kind on the Unionist population. At worst, his command evicted people from their homes, and the refugees found comfort in Kansas. Harsher treatment was reserved for anyone who participated in harassing the people of Jackson County.[49]

Jayhawking activities in Bates, Cass, and Jackson County reached their height in early 1862. Lane attacked Rose Hill, burning forty-two homes, driving off livestock, and stealing more than seven thousand dollars. Plundered goods fueled a lucrative market at Fort Scott, Lawrence, and Leavenworth. So much was sold at public street auctions in Lawrence that the city achieved the nickname the "Citadel of Stolen Goods."

A more colorful nickname came about with the capture of Independence in 1861. When jayhawkers captured Independence, they snatched a large cache of red calfskins and made leggings for themselves. Thereafter they were also called "Redlegs."[50]

Since before the war jayhawkers justified their Missouri raids under the guise of being Unionists who were only "confiscating" Confederate property.[51] Now jayhawkers were sought out, engaged, and destroyed. Jayhawkers were summarily executed regardless of which side of the Kansas-Missouri border they were encountered. Seldom was mercy extended to them, but occasionally it was.

Quantrill did not tolerate treachery in his command. He dealt with it quickly and remorselessly. When two spies managed to join the command, one was discovered immediately. George Todd shot and killed the known spy that night, while the men were clustered around a campfire. The execution startled the others, and Todd explained the situation. That night the other spy slipped away.

In October 1862 Quantrill's men seized Stephen B. Elkins of Cass County on suspicion that he was a spy. Regarding his captors, Elkins described them many years later as "perfect daredevils": "The moment they were called to halt they were down with their horses tied, singing, dancing, playing cards, reviving the sports of buccaneers. . . . [Quantrill] was not a large man, but you could tell that he was a leader." Recounting his experience on July 4, 1898, Elkins wrote:

> I knew Cole Younger when we were boys and also his parents. They were good people and among the pioneers on the western border of Missouri. The Youngers maintained a good reputation in the community where they lived and were well esteemed, as were their parents, for their good conduct and character. On reaching the camp the first person I saw I knew was Cole Younger. When I was taken prisoner, I expected to be shot without ceremony. As soon as I saw Cole Younger I felt a sense of relief because I had known him and his parents long and favorably, and as soon as I got a chance I told him frankly what I feared and that I hoped he would manage to take care of me and save me from being killed. He assured me he would do all he could do to protect me.

Younger did plead for Quantrill to release Elkins. In his recollection of the affair, Cole commented:

> Quantrill received me courteously and kindly, as he always did, and after a little desultory chat, I carelessly remarked, "I am surprised to find that you have my old friend and teacher, Steve Elkins, in camp as a prisoner." "What! Do you know him?" asked Quantrill in astonishment. Cole replied,

"Yes, and I understand you're going to have him shot." "We shoot all spies," Quantrill said. Colonel Parker's men who were with Quantrill at the time were upset at their leader's recent death and had arrested Elkins in Cass County because he had just returned from enlisting in the Union army in Kansas City. Cole tried to convince Quantrill that Elkins was a Southerner because his brothers were in the Confederate army. Quantrill replied, "My men say he's a spy." "Well, they'll have to fight me," said Cole hotly. "I know him and they don't." "If he's a Southerner, why isn't he in uniform?" asked Quantrill. Cole replied that Elkins mother was an invalid and he was staying home to take care of her. Quantrill finally looked at his watch and remarked, "I will be on the move in fifteen minutes. I will release Elkins, since you feel so deeply about it. I will leave him in your hands. Be careful, for Parker's men are rather bitter against him."

On Younger's insistence, Elkins was saved, but Elkins was afterward a marked man when he entered the Union army. Quantrill ordered he should be shot on sight.[52]

At dawn on January 1, 1862, Lt. Col. Daniel R. Anthony led the hated Seventh Kansas Jayhawker Cavalry on a raid into Cass County and sacked the sleepy town of Dayton. After looting the village, all forty-seven houses of the community were put to the torch. A week later similar treatment befell the village of Columbus. At one home two little children were set out in the snow while their home was burned.[53] Before the end of that day, the jayhawkers descended on Pleasant Hill. There Jennison led the raid and took ten thousand dollars' worth of stock and seized fifty-five slaves. The small town of West Point was likewise plundered. Not even a steady snow hindered the Seventh Kansas Jayhawker Cavalry that next sacked Morristown and Rose Hill. The regiment experienced three casualties at the last site, where ten inches of snow and twilight were factors.[54]

Regimental chaplains continued to participate in the raids so they could enhance their churches in Kansas with the plunder from Missouri churches, including even steeples and other ecclesiastical aids. At Harrisonburg, they stole all the Bibles from the depository of the American Bible Society.

To the jayhawkers their operations were so far removed from the center of government as to be independent. Thus they disregarded administration policy and War Department orders with impunity. James Lane continued to direct his men like a border chieftain of the feudal past.

One resident of Kingsville recounted seeing 160 houses on fire.[55] Here Daniel Anthony apprehended nine men prisoners and had them shot down in cold blood. He cut off the ears of the ninth one. Besides stolen money and stock, Anthony also seized slaves and armed them and put them in uniform.

In late January 1862 Jennison raided two hundred homes in Lexington and set them afire. Next he struck at Chapel Hill and burned a number of homes. Lizzie Brannock remembered:

> Jennison and his gang came upon us stripped us of nearly everything and would have burned us out, but for proving that we were Union and had never done anything against the government. They burned 150 houses, helpless women and young children sick were taken out and left standing in the snow while all they owned on earth save the land was destroyed before their eyes. Later they came upon us while going a few miles from home and put me and my two children off in the mud a good distance from my house. It was well known that the plunder stolen from Missouri by Jennison was sold at his residence near Squiresville, Kansas.[56]

Halleck reported to Lincoln: "The operations of Lane and Jennison had so enraged the people of Missouri that about 80,000 of them had joined the Confederate side."[57] When Gen. George B. McClellan was informed of what Lane and the jayhawkers were doing to the Union cause along the western border, he wrote to Secretary of War Edwin Stanton: "The only way to prevent the seizure and confiscation of property by Lane's brigade was to remove the Kansas troops to some other field of action."[58] Halleck thus found himself trying to control Missouri guerrillas and Kansas jayhawkers. To Stanton on March 25, 1862, he wrote:

> The Kansas Jayhawkers, or robbers, were organized under the auspices of Senator Lane. They wear the uniform of, and it is believed receive pay from the United States. Their principal occupation for the last six months seems to have been the stealing of negroes, the robbery of houses, and the burning of barns, grain and forage. The evidence of their crimes is unquestionable. They have not heretofore been under my orders. I will now keep them out of Missouri, or have them shot.

While Jennison's jayhawkers were ravaging Cass County, another group of jayhawkers scoured the Blue Springs area thinking that Quantrill would be found around his home base. Yet a third group of Federals focused their hunt for Quantrill on southern Jackson County near Brooking Township. Meanwhile, Quantrill shifted his operations to the rugged Blue Hills surrounding the Big and Little Blue Rivers south of Independence. To keep Quantrill from interfering with him, Lane sent another group, a company led by Capt. Albert P. Peabody, to search out the guerrilla leader.

Quantrill and a small band of men spent the last week of December 1861 in Kansas, trying to recover horses and livestock stolen from Henry Younger. After a day or two, and failing to find the animals, Quantrill returned to the hills of the Little Blue and camped at the farm of a friend, John Flanery. There on January 3, 1862, Peabody's company found him and a handful of followers. Even though Halleck had given his men license to treat all guerrillas harshly, the Federals were ill prepared for the type of fighting they encountered from Quantrill.

The shootout at the Flanery farm was Quantrill's first large-scale encounter. His first mistake was the failure to post pickets. Thus Peabody's company surrounded the farmhouse while the guerrillas slept inside. With his men in position, the Union captain boldly rapped on the heavy wooden door and demanded that Quantrill surrender.

Leaping from his bed, Quantrill rushed to a window, astonished at the sight of so many blue uniforms. "Damn!" he muttered. "We certainly messed up here." In answer to Peabody's command, Quantrill replied, "I must consult with my men. Give me a few minutes." Peabody granted him ten minutes.

During that time, Quantrill deployed his men on all sides of the house covering all the windows and doors so they could effectively fire into the Union ranks. Cole Younger was assigned to the attic window in the loft.

Quantrill then strode to the front door, opened it, and yelled defiantly, "Quantrill and his men never surrender!" At the same time a blast from his double-barreled shotgun almost tore Peabody's first lieutenant in two. The entire house erupted with rapid gunfire. Before the soldiers could gather their wits many were killed or wounded.

For several hours the fighting raged. Finally Peabody decided to set the house on fire. The fire was first noticed by Cole Younger, who alerted Quantrill, but the blaze spread quickly. Part of the house collapsed.

Quantrill ordered his men to place pillows and hats in the windows to draw fire. When the Federals were forced to reload, they would run out of the house. Not all his men obliged; two hid under a bed and subsequently burned to death. When the time was right, Quantrill threw open the door and charged out of the house. George Shepherd was right behind him, and Cole Younger was the last in line. The guerrillas formed a flying wedge and charged directly into the Union force; the forward men cleared a path with their shotguns.[59]

After blasting a gap in the Federal line, the guerrillas fought their way out. They lost only their horses and managed to escape into the brush. Peabody had eighteen casualties; Quantrill only two—the two who refused to follow.

Safely in the timber of the country, Quantrill and his men lacked horses and ammunition. So Quantrill sent them out to find these: "Don't come back until you've got a horse. Don't steal any. I won't have a horse thief among my men. We'll meet near Blue Cut in three days."

While the guerrillas were regrouping and rearming, the jayhawkers continued to raid. No Southerner was left unaffected. Everyone seemed to know of a respected neighbor or friend who had been killed or lost a home. In Kansas City, on the night of January 28, men from the First Kansas Jayhawker Regiment, commanded by Col. George W. Deitzler of Lawrence, broke into a warehouse belonging to William Jarboe and stole or destroyed everything there.[60]

The jayhawkers were everywhere now. George Barnett joined Quantrill early in 1862 and summed up the feelings of most of the guerrillas: "It was certain, I thought, that I should go into battle and fight until I was killed. I saw our farm home in ashes and my mother left desolate, robbed of all the livestock and provisions we had gotten together to keep her." John Brinker, later a captain with Quantrill, joined in February 1862 after the Federals imprisoned his sister and younger brother for conveying information to the guerrillas.[61] With so many recruits flooding into his camp, Quantrill assumed the task of organizing and training them. He had not only the authority to do so but also the responsibility of leadership.[62] New recruits were required to take a simple oath to "follow orders, be true to your fellows, and kill those who serve and support the Union."

Frank James described how the guerrillas equipped themselves: "We captured from the Federals, clothes, horses and ammunition. We generally carried our coats and overcoats fastened on our saddles. Most of our clothing was the blue uniform of the Yankees. We wore vests cut low in the front and trimmed in gold lace. Each guerrilla carried two or four pistols."

The guerrillas soon gained the respect of their Federal counterparts. One Union officer remarked:

His [Quantrill's] men were braver and more dangerous than the Apache or Comanche Indians and were better riders. They were industrious, bloodthirsty devils, who apparently never slept; today they would attack with a mad rush of twenty or forty men against a hundred, if they could see a chance of surprise, and in one night's ride they would be fifty miles away. They were familiar with every cow path, knew every farmer, ninety-five percent of whom would give his all to help a bushwhacker fighting the Northern invader.

Quantrill had already seen plenty of action while serving in Price's army and had distinguished himself in every battle he had been in. From the battle of Carthage, the battle of Dry Forks, Wilson's Creek, and the battle of Lexington, he had ridden in the forefront and courageously attacked the enemy on every occasion.

With the experience gleaned from his previous service, he organized his men into squads, and they fought as a light cavalry unit. Horses were the guerrillas' chief concern. They were the lifeblood of the guerrillas, and so Quantrill's men rode the best horses in the country. These were either captured Federal mounts or were loaned or given to them by their neighbors. To many Missouri farmers, a pound of horseflesh was a small price to pay to defend their homes and property.

These horses were shod, fed well, and treated well. The military mission came first, but if no action was imminent, the horses were not overworked. Saddlebags carried small sundry items, but none too large or heavy to burden the horse. Usually the saddlebags carried enough lead, powder, and caps to supply the rider for an aggressive attack or a siege. The saddle and tack were Federal government issue. For sustained fire, extra revolver cylinders were attached to the saddle horn on a string for a quick exchange during a firefight. Some guerrilla horses were guided by the bridle bit, some were guided by "neck reining," but the most experienced and best-trained horses were guided by "knee reining." This method was first used by the Indians who guided their horses by applying pressure with their knees, allowing them to have both hands free during battle.

Guerrilla horses were so keenly trained that even a slight movement of the rider's spurs would automatically launch an animal into a dead run. It was said that guerrillas would do without so their horses might have corn, and they frequently took all the chances at being shot so their horses might not be hurt.[63] Quantrill and his guerrillas have been called the greatest light cavalry command that ever existed. His men were mostly Missouri farm boys who had been born and raised in the saddle. When mounted they became one with the horse, and there was not one man among them who could not outride or outshoot any Federal soldier in the state. They scouted out the most likely avenue of approach to their camps then hid their horses close at hand but out of view. If a skirmish broke out, the horses would not be in the line of fire. One of Quantrill's men summed up the guerrilla's relationship to his horses this way:

> I have heard that a horse has no sense; but I think very much depends upon the man who owns him. I never stopped to study it, but there was some sort of affinity between a guerrilla and his horse. I have slept in my saddle and trusted my faithful horse to keep out of danger. I have sometimes, when alone and tired, dismounted, lay down in the grass or thicket, and left my horse on guard. I always found him there when I awoke. Yes, once my horse called me. I had been in the saddle nearly thirty hours. In that time the rain was incessant. I went to sleep under some branches on the ground. Under such conditions a man will sleep the sleep of the just. I was awakened by the shaking and breaking of the brush. My horse was pulling it from me. I was barely in the saddle when a lot of jayhawkers were upon me. But for my knowledge of the country I would not have escaped. I think I owe my life to my horse. I remember I spoke of this once to Quantrill, and he said it showed a horse appreciated a low voice. For the guerrilla was never known to speak otherwise; at least, not after he had been a guerrilla very long. The American guerrilla's voice was musical. An old cavalryman once told me that he broke a horse with kindness, and I believe it can be done. I reckon you remember what an old French marshal once said, at least he is credited with it, that the best cuirassiers were those who embraced their horses before they did their mistresses.[64]

Cavalry in the Civil War was important not just for tactical duties but also for strategic operations. The use of mounted troops for raiding purposes was something new in warfare. In no war before 1860 had cavalry operated as an independent force to strike the enemy behind the lines. The main objective of the cavalry raid was to damage the enemy's nexus of transportation and supply. Other important objectives were to acquire information and to force the enemy to weaken his armies at the front by increasing precautions behind the lines. A raid was also calculated to lower the morale of the opposing army and thus destroy confidence in its commanders. In its strategic role, cavalry attained objectives less by force than by secrecy, celerity, and surprise. The leader had, therefore, to be bold, resourceful, and capable of accurately judging the potential of his horses and men. The troops themselves had to be well disciplined and strong enough to endure strenuous riding. Because it was next to impossible to provide raiding cavalry with any supply trains beyond pack animals, the troops had to live off the country, each soldier carrying only a minimum of clothing and equipment.[65]

Quantrill never carried a flag or was known to have one of his own except when traveling with his troops across open prairie in enemy territory. Then he would carry a Federal flag at the head of his column to avoid detection and to deceive the enemy. Quantrill's military accouterments included items of a civilian nature turned into a military necessity. His most prized possession was a hand-held telescope. When he lost it in an early engagement, he quickly sought out a replacement. Pocket watches were no mere personal decoration but were very much needed for the synchronization between his subordinate commands to coordinate patrols and offensive actions.

His guerrillas owed their extraordinary victories to various other factors, such as their extremely practical approach to dress and armament, their organization, and their method of fighting. Quantrill gleaned much of his knowledge and style of fighting from the great guerrilla chieftains who had preceded him. American schoolchildren had grown up on stories of their patriot ancestors in the Revolutionary War. With Quantrill's precocity he was familiar with such notable American guerrillas as Francis Marion and the Green Mountain Boys.

The nature of the warfare along the border made the regular gray Confederate uniform unrealistic. So Quantrill adopted the uniform of the great Italian freedom fighter Giuseppe Garibaldi, who had spent a lifetime fighting tyrants in Italy and in South America. Garibaldi's lifelong battle for liberty fired the imagination of the American people at the time, and his customary red shirt probably inspired young Quantrill to adopt it as an early uniform of his own. Quantrill reportedly wore a bright red shirt on the front lines at the battles of Lexington and Wilson's Creek and inspired his comrades during the hottest parts of those battles.

Out of necessity the guerrillas adopted a "uniform" consisting of a large and comfortable blouse that usually had two broad breast pockets. They were immediately recognizable, a distinguishing mark of these men. These "guerrilla shirts" also demonstrated a kind of flamboyance, pride, and esprit de corps. In battle the soldiers would open their jackets to reveal the bright-colored shirts and dare the enemy by presenting themselves as a more recognizable target. Given the practicality of wearing scavenged Union uniforms to be able to operate behind the lines, the flaunting of the bright shirt in combat revealed who was friend or foe amid the dust and smoke of close combat.

Guerrilla shirts were collarless and worn over homespun banded-collared shirts. They all had the same general pattern and cut. Long-waisted, they were gathered about the waist with either a pistol or knife belt. Where a collar would have been, many adoring mothers and sweethearts added patterns and designs of the individual's choosing. The shirts were also highly functional and practical. Designed for close pistol combat on horseback, they were made large enough to be nonbinding. The two large breast pockets were sewed at an angle, without pocket flaps, so the wearer could extract or dispose of extra pistol cylinders without difficulty. Hampton Watts recalled:

> The prescribed uniform of the guerrilla was a black felt hat, the left brim of which was cocked and fastened to crown by a gold or silver crescent pin to which was suspended by a small cross; this pin also held in place a large black plume, which hung gracefully over the back rim; a black velvet overshirt, the breast cut 'V' shape and embroidered in colored flowers; the pants worn were of any dark material, the bottoms being stuffed inside cavalry boots; on the heel of each boot was buckled a Mexican spur. The hair of each man was allowed to grow six to eight inches in length, being brushed straight back from the forehead, the ends reaching the top of the shoulders. The arms carried were usually four 'Colt's Navy' revolvers on the belt and two holster (raised-sight dragoon) revolvers at the horn of the saddle. When in line, mounted on the finest of horses, the band certainly gave a 'Knightly' appearance.[66]

No man was without a hat for long. The regulation Union army headgear known as the kepi was never found among guerrillas. They were, however, used by the leaders to deceive the enemy behind the lines. If a battle were imminent, a commander such as Quantrill would tuck his hat into his jacket to keep from being attacked by his own men during close quarters combat.

In the winter many guerrillas wore Union army greatcoats. Almost all guerrillas wore the regulation Union army jacket, and their officers wore insignia. The clothing was either acquired from victims or pillaged from army wagons. Boots and shoes of various styles were worn, depending on what could be acquired. Because of the irregular warfare waged on the border and the inadequate supply system provided to the state militias, any item of military clothing automatically established the wearer as a combatant. For this reason, likewise, guerrillas wore Union blue jackets so they could travel unnoticed and unchallenged in close observation of the enemy.

Until late in the war, the Union army was only issued single-shot rifles and, for reasons of uniformity, not allowed to carry additional weapons. This single requirement probably caused more Union deaths than any other factor.

Similarly, Quantrill chose the type of armament for his men. The .36-caliber Navy Colt was probably the most admired of all revolvers and proved to be one of the better weapons available. His men, however, were not restricted to a single weapon or type of weapon. Practicality also won out over procedure, thus when a man cleaned his weapons, only one could be disassembled at a time, leaving him with other loaded pistols if a need arose.

Quantrill's men were never known to carry canteens. They made too much noise and attracted too much attention. His men needed to move stealthily. So, to maintain noise discipline, they wore loose-fitting clothing. They also kept their load-bearing equipment tied securely to their saddles.

To combat the jayhawker's intrusions into Missouri, Quantrill developed a strategy that served him well throughout the war. To ensure that his men were motivated, he recruited fighters from plundered neighborhoods. To counter superior numbers, he developed hit-and-run tactics. He made sure his guerrillas were outdoorsmen who were marksmen, hunters, and horsemen. He developed passwords and signals that only the guerrillas understood and recognized.

In the field, they approached oncoming horsemen with suspicion. They knew most of the Federal soldiers by name and even knew the Federal regiments by the shoes of their horses. One Kansas jayhawker said that the Rebels had their own way of shoeing. They had three nails on a side instead of four, as was the case of ordinary shoeing.[67] They could even tell the nationality of troops by the manner that the twigs were broken on their line of march. They were so adept in the woods that they could determine their direction in the dark by noting the moss on the trees. To elude pursuers the guerrillas placed their saddle blankets over the roads then rode their horses over them to mask their trail.

With scouts in every neighborhood and spies among the locals, Quantrill's intelligence network was vast and extensive. Signs and countersigns quickly propelled important messages from one county to another. With friends on virtually every farm, jaded horses could be traded for fresh mounts at a moment's notice. Practicality also influenced residents to realize they had no protection from the law, thus they gladly aided the partisan ranger bands like Quantrill's.

A military axiom summarizes Quantrill's leadership style: To ensure victory, the troops must have confidence in themselves as well as in their commanders.[68] Ahead of their time, Quantrill's men were comparable to today's soldier. In combat, each guerrilla depended on the fighting abilities of the man next to him. If the guerrillas found themselves in a tight spot, they depended as much on their comrades' marksmanship and horsemanship as they did their own. In the din of battle, which is now commonly referred to as the "fog of war," amid the smoke and noise of personal combat, that which enabled victory was individual training and discipline.

Quantrill's company was rarely idle. He continually trained his men on the open prairie, close to the timber, in horsemanship and pistol practice. Since each man depended on the abilities of others as much as his own, training was paramount. The only impediment a recruit might encounter in joining Quantrill was being too young, a poor horseman, or a poor marksman.

Constant training and practice made Quantrill's guerrillas adept at hitting a moving target on horseback with either hand. The tactics were simple: to force or entice the enemy upon terrain advantageous to the guerrilla's mode of fighting.

The most successful of all tactics was to fight the enemy in an expanse of open prairie where he would have to take a volley from a Sharps carbine, usually strapped to the guerrillas' backs, at a distance equal to maximum rifle range. Then the guerrillas would charge on horseback at a full run and be upon the enemy with fire superiority from their blazing pistols before the enemy had time to reload his single-shot weapon. The faster the horses could run resulted in the most steady and accurate pistol fire.

After the initial volley was given and received, the guerrillas bent over their horses' necks, gaining the most speed they could from their mounts. In charging the enemy, the guerrillas would have both their pistols drawn but would hold their fire until they were on top of their adversaries, then they would unleash well-aimed shots at individual targets. Before the enemy could recover from being overrun by the charging horses, the fire superiority, and the accurate pistol fire, the guerrillas would wheel and charge again to complete the engagement. If the enemy broke and ran, the guerrillas rode them down and shot them from their saddles.

These tactics enabled four thousand guerrillas to tie up more than sixty thousand Union soldiers in Missouri.

As each new man made his way into Quantrill's camp, Quantrill himself escorted him to a secluded spot in the woods, far away from all interruptions, and instructed him in pistol marksmanship. By shielding the new man from any potential embarrassment or playful taunts from the other men, Quantrill could give individual attention to each man. He taught every one of them to fire with either hand, how to draw quickly, and how to "point their target" with the end of the barrel. Because they would be mostly fighting from horseback, Quantrill showed each man to wear his pistols reversed, high on his waist so his hands could be both close to the reins and to his pistol butts. He made sure his men wore open holsters so their pistols were easily accessible. Thus they did not use the standard-issue closed-flap holster, which kept the weapon dry but hindered a man from drawing his weapon quickly.

At first, many of the farm youths carried shotguns. Over time, a brace of revolvers became the standard armament. Almost all guerrillas carried at least four revolvers. Some were known to carry six, and some as many as eight. The maximum firepower of four to six pistols, along with a carbine, made the guerrillas into a formidable foe.

In addition to their hardware, the guerrillas had a unique wild, frightening Rebel Yell. No two descriptions of the yell are alike; one soldier described it as "a mingling of Indian whoop and wild-howl."[69] The Rebel Yell was not like the deep-breasted Northern cheer, which was given in unison to signify an advantage gained. The guerrillas' Rebel Yell was a high, shrill yelp, uttered without concert, and maintained continually at a point when a fight was approaching its climax. It was a corporate cry to evoke further effort from everyone.[70]

In many instances the path of Southern guerrilla pursuit was marked with a trail of corpses, leaving the enemy a broken, demoralized foe. In close hand-to-hand combat, the large, heavy Navy dragoon pistol was also used as a club.

It has been said that Quantrill's band was not a "band of brothers," although its members were famous for their loyalty to each other. "A wounded comrade was never deserted; his friends in defending him might die with him, but they would never leave him. They shared with each other every hardship, every danger, and every fortune. They even divided honors among themselves, which was a test of generosity.[71]

In short, Quantrill taught his men well. He taught them that their lives depended upon each other, and he molded them into a crack organization. For this, they were ready to follow him to hell. Quantrill's wife, Kate King, observed that he "seemed to have a hypnotic influence over them and they were ready to lay down their lives for him." She believed that his personal supervision was responsible for this. "He was known to go among them at night to see if all went well and at times even to stand guard over the sleeping men. Such faithfulness endeared him greatly."[72]

The desperate character of the guerrillas was due much to their youth. Frank James noted:

If you ever want to pick a company to do desperate work or to lead a forlorn hope, select young men from seventeen to twenty-one years old. They will go anywhere in the world you will lead them. When men grow older they grow more cautious, but at that age they are regular daredevils. Take our company and there had never been a more reckless lot of men. Only one or two were over twenty-five. Most of them were under twenty-one. Scarcely a dozen boasted a mustache.

Next came the tactics needed for a guerrilla campaign against overwhelming numbers of men and materiel. It was not much of a problem to carry out Sterling Price's orders to disrupt the mails. The guerrillas easily swooped down on stagecoaches and mail couriers. At the same time, this tactic served a twofold purpose for the guerrillas: (1) it kept the Federals uninformed and isolated and (2) with the newspapers being carried on the stagecoaches, the guerrillas could find valuable information about troop displacements, other Union activities, and the latest orders and intent of the Federal commanders.

The guerrilla trademark, however, was a straightforward charge that served well when used in conjunction with an ambush. Because of the military benefit afforded by ambushes, Quantrill resorted to ambushing to his advantage.

Quantrill's ambush tactics are still taught today. If an ambush is well planned and executed with the desirable degree of surprise, the victims are not killed in a "fair fight"; in fact they do not have the chance to fight at all. The first criterion in planning an ambush is a thorough knowledge of the enemy's tactics. The second requirement is a thorough knowledge of the terrain. Knowing how and where the enemy operates offers a good idea of where and how he can be found and surprised. Quantrill knew when the enemy was likely to be in various portions of his terrain. Knowledge of the enemy and terrain let him pick the time and location of the ambush. His own resources and imagination determined how each of his ambushes was conducted.

Some positive characteristics of ambushes always apply, notably, surprise and intensive firepower. Quantrill's well-armed men accomplished this with two to eight revolvers apiece. The flanks of the ambush were anchored to discourage maneuver, reinforcement, or counterattack. Ambushes were always triggered by a prearranged signal. Every man in Quantrill's band also knew the withdrawal route and the rallying point, and everyone wore a distinct mark of recognition. The guerrillas were also adept at noise discipline. Everyone knew what to do once the ambush began, and every guerrilla fired according to the rehearsed plan. They fired at different rates so everyone did not run out of ammunition at the same time, and they had a plan for changing revolver cylinders. They knew if any survivors got out of the kill zone, they had to be pursued by fire and maneuver.

Before searching bodies for documents, arms, and ammunition, the guerrillas made sure all the enemy were dead. They poured fire into the bodies after they were all down, and they put a bullet into every head. They were careful that this part of the ambush strategy was not ignored. Soldiers pretending to be wounded could suddenly return fire when the guerrillas' guard was down. Enemy weapons not taken were destroyed.

Guerrillas never withdrew from an ambush site in the same way they had withdrawn from earlier ambushes. They made sure they took a different route out of the ambush site to their rallying point.

One of their first priorities was to take care of their own wounded. When they got back to their rallying point, they also checked their weapons before they ate, slept, or did anything else.

Ambushing was a tremendous force multiplier and one of the best psychological weapons used in guerrilla warfare. The keys to a perfect ambush were surprise, overwhelming firepower, shock, and the will to kill an unsuspecting stranger without giving him a chance to fight back. When executed by well-trained soldiers, ambushes are the safest of all offensive combat techniques.[73]

After Quantrill taught his men tactics, he divided them into ten-man squads and appointed a captain over each squad. A squad operated within a specified area and was supported by the local residents. The guerrillas were given aid in the form of food, shelter, and clothing, not to mention intelligence about Federal movements. The partisan bands relied heavily upon this kind of information to stay alive and as the basis for both defensive and offensive plans.

From his service in Price's Missouri State Guard, Quantrill had met many soldiers from the Jackson County area. At the same time, several guerrillas wanted to maintain contact with relatives, but this was highly dangerous. Treacherous neighbors might report any visits, which could result in either death or imprisonment for the guerrilla's relatives as well as the destruction of their homes.

The record plainly shows that Quantrill allowed no dishonesty within his ranks. Numerous guerrilla bands roamed through Jackson County during the border wars, and many instances of looting by these bands not associated directly with the defenders of Jackson County have been attributed to Quantrill's band.

Since local papers were not censored at the time, Quantrill obtained most of his information from the numerous daily and weekly newspapers in the area. What spies could not find out, newspapers on both sides printed without the least concern for military security.

The mail run between Independence and Pleasant Hill ran down the old Independence to Harrisonville road, near where Cole Younger had camped on the east fork of the Little Blue River. The mail run was a dangerous mission. On June 11, 1862, Younger shot Isaac Shoat, a Federal mail guard, because Shoat had deserted Quantrill's command just a few months earlier. Frank Tierney, a stagecoach driver on the Independence to Pleasant Hill run, related how a band of guerrillas stopped his stage and robbed him and the passengers of money and other possessions. Drivers soon learned to hide their money in the horses' harness, where the robbers were never able to find it. On one occasion, Cole Younger, then an officer in Quantrill's band, offered to recover his money for him, but Tierney, fearing reprisal if he let the identity of the perpetrator be known, refused to divulge the information. Tierney recalled: "The leader of the guerrillas, Cole Younger, would never allow his men to molest mail carried on the stage."[74]

Quantrill's raiders ambushed many Union patrols on the Independence to Harrisonville road. One of the ways the guerrillas coaxed the Federals out of their camp in Independence, eight miles to the north, was to cut the telegraph wires along the road. This proved to serve a twofold objective. First, it isolated the Union garrisons, and second, when the Federals realized that the lines had been cut, they sent out a patrol to find and repair the broken wire. The guerrillas, after cutting the wires, simply waited in ambush for the patrol to arrive, which they would attack and annihilate. If the conditions were favorable, the guerrillas offered battle. They needed no bugle. Their wild, rousing Rebel Yell followed by murderous pistol fire disheartened any opposing enemy and usually resulted in Federals tumbling from their saddles while the rest tried to race back to the safety of their garrisons. For those of the enemy who decided to stand and fight, the end came quickly. Using their mounts in mass formation, the guerrillas simply rode over their enemies, firing unerringly as they passed. Once past the enemy's line, the guerrillas wheeled and charged through the remaining soldiers, firing the balance of their four to six revolvers until all resistance ended. For those who were mounted and fled, the guerrillas easily rode them down and shot them out of their saddles.

If confronting the enemy in vastly superior numbers and little chance of success in open combat, the partisans would wait in ambush along the heavy brush and use their carbines and shotguns. After the first volley and before the enemy had time to reorganize, the guerrillas simply withdrew back into the thick heavy brush. There they split up into smaller squads and dispersed along tangled trails until they could rendezvous at a predetermined rallying point.

With the Federals sending constant patrols to his initial haunts around the village of Blue Springs and the hills of the Sni, Quantrill decided to make his headquarters at Brooking Township. The valley of the Little Blue was spread along the western banks of the river by the same name. The area most favored by the guerrillas was the high ground on the east side, overlooking the valley.

The Independence to Harrisonville road ran north to south and offered two prime ambush sites. The first was six miles south of Independence and known as the Blue Cut. The second was called the Manasseth Gap and was situated eight miles south of Independence. The Little Blue River ran parallel to the road on the west. A telegraph line was strung along the roadway between the two towns, and the road also served to connect the stage lines, which brought the local news from as far away as St. Louis. The surrounding terrain was wild, but some cultivation had begun in the bottomland, and here and there were some gristmills. Situated in the narrow valley was the picturesque hamlet of Little Blue.

The fertile valley and rolling hills marked an area that was superbly suited for hideaways and ambushes. Dense vegetation lay all along the riverbanks. To the southwest was White Oak Creek, one of the Little Blue's tributaries, in a long, narrow valley running east and west and surrounded by heavy timber and a long ridge of rock outcroppings. Here on the plateau above the ridge lived some of the earliest settlers of Jackson County. The area now known as Raytown was not even a town then, and Brooking Township was not formally established until 1872.

This township was named for Alvin Brooking at the suggestion of Baptist minister J. J. Robinson, a community leader of note. Alvin's son was Capt. Henry Clay Brooking, who served with Sterling Price. Brooking Township had little besides a store, a post office, and a blacksmith shop. The Little Blue supplied water to the area farmers and divided the higher area of Brooking Township to the west from the bottomland surrounding the Little Blue River from the opposite bank toward Lee's Summit.

Quantrill's guerrillas established several camps, used throughout 1862, within two miles of the open fields surrounded by the rocky bluffs. The area had no formal designation other than "lying close to Independence"; farther south it was known as Hickman's Mill.

Brooking Township had two villages: Raytown and Little Blue. Raytown was centrally situated on what was called the Blue Prairie—the ridge between the Big and Little Blue Rivers, eight miles from Independence and ten miles from Kansas City. It was prosperous farming country, having good land, water, and good timber, three qualities not always found together. Many claimed there were more good springs in this township than in any other comparable community in the state. An early settler boasted that the farmers here had not had to drive their stock off their farms to get water for them in the last twenty-five years.[75]

Early Raytown's blacksmith shop was owned by Absolom Wray, one of its earliest citizens. The community offered a last chance to westward-bound settlers for refitting and resupply before setting out for the Santa Fe Trail. Wray repaired wagons and had a reputation for making ox shoes and fitting them securely. Raytown was supposedly named for him.

Here also were many churches, the most notable being the West Fork of the Little Blue Baptist Church, which was established in 1842. In 1799 Daniel Boone, the famous pioneer, had followed his son Daniel Morgan Boone to Missouri. Boone's grandsons—Daniel and Morgan—built the first church building from native stone on two acres of land. The construction expense was borne by Alvin Brooking, J. Mickleborough, and Archibald Rice.[76] Members of this church formed the backbone of Quantrill's partisan ranger company. Most notable among them was Thomas B. Harris, son of Reuben Harris, and John Flanery, son of Zion Flanery. Also a member of the church and in Quantrill's company was John T. House, whose father, Eli, was killed by Jennison. Other members who rode with Quantrill were Randolph Venable; Job Crabtree (on whose farm Quantrill regrouped his band immediately after the Tate house fight near Hickman's Mill on March 22, 1862); twenty-four-year-old Boone T. Muir; and Muir's father, William, a great-great-grandson of Daniel Boone. Benjamin Rice was a church member, later a deacon, and served as a local guard for the area against jayhawker raids; he also fought at the August 18, 1862, battle of White Oak Creek. Rice lost his slaves and much of his property during the war. After fighting alongside Quantrill, Rice joined Price's army.[77]

Even after the war began in earnest, many guerrillas courted or married their sweethearts. Marietta Allen, whose parents lived about two blocks from George Todd's family in Kansas City, recalled that Todd used to slip into town to see his wife, Kitty, in their home, running the risk of being strung up for aiding the guerrillas. Allen stated that Todd's family was "kindness itself" to her family, although all of the family except two was in the Union army.[78] George married Kitty on December 9, 1861, during the height of jayhawking activity and just prior to the Federal occupation in Jackson County.[79]

Twenty-one-year-old Dick Yeager wrote many letters to his wife when he was in winter quarters with Shelby's Brigade in Texas. Other guerrillas also married early in the war. Noah Estes, who served with Quantrill, married Elizabeth Adams on January 3, 1861. On March 12, the day before Halleck declared all guerrillas to be outlaws, Richard Maddox married Martha W. Sanders. Two months later, Ferdinand Scott married Josephine P. Vance on May 20. Even the tumult of war couldn't dim the light of romance for these young cavaliers along the border. Later William Gregg donned a Confederate officer's uniform for his marriage. The men who witnessed the wedding served not only as his best men but also as a personal bodyguard. After the ceremony, these same soldiers fanned out into the surrounding woods to form a protective cordon, enabling their leader to enjoy at least one night of wedded bliss before the war beckoned him with the coming of dawn.[80]

In 1862 few suspected the war would last four years; many rather believed it would last only a few months. So people tried to carry on their lives despite the risks and dangers. Some guerrillas even helped their families put in crops despite engaging the enemy on an almost daily basis. If they thought the military situation was settling down, 1862 proved to be the hardest-fought year of the war. During this time Quantrill lost some of his best men, many of whom were the first to join him. Those who took their places, however, had even more reason for vengeance.

In their ardor to crush out partisan warfare, Federal cruelty and brutality increased. As the jayhawkers resorted to terrorism, the guerrillas practiced the old dispensation over the new: Instead of turning the other cheek, it was now an eye for an eye and a tooth for a tooth.

4

The Making of a Guerrilla

"Steady boys, follow me!"

WILLIAM CLARKE QUANTRILL

S THE WINTER OF 1861–62 ended, sad forebodings filled the hearts of the people. The rich promise of the state had been swept away. Desolation had taken the place of prospering peace. Hordes of armed men filled the land. Trade was no longer, and commerce was paralyzed. Education had ceased, and the culture of the past century seemed fading.[1]

The year 1862 would prove to be the most definitive of the war in terms of battles and skirmishes between the newly formed guerrillas and the Federals. At the first of the year only two dozen men gathered around Quantrill, but his numbers doubled during the first weeks of the new year. Cruel treatment of civilians along the Missouri border fueled the fires of determined resistance, and many chose to fight back in their own way.

Noncombatants contributed to the Confederate war effort by aiding the local guerrillas with food, shelter, medical assistance, and information about the enemy. In the absence of civil law, Quantrill offered the only justice in the area. Many felt relieved when they heard that Quantrill had hanged George Searcy and another man along the Little Blue for horse stealing. In the face of Quantrill's justice, the only mentionable crimes being committed were those by armed militia or jayhawkers.[2]

When the guerrillas tried to protect their neighborhoods, the Federals fought back. On February 3, 1862, Capt. William S. Oliver, commander of the Federal garrison in Independence, reported to Gen. John Pope:

I have just returned from an expedition, which I was compelled to undertake
in search of the notorious Quantrill and his gang of robbers in the vicinity of
Blue Springs. Without mounted men at my disposal, despite numerous
applications to various points, I have seen this infamous scoundrel rob mails,
steal the coaches and horses, and commit other similar outrages upon society
even within sight of this city. Mounted on the best horses of the country, he
has defied pursuit, making his camp in the bottoms of the Sni and Blue, and
roving over a circuit of thirty miles. I mounted a company of my command
and went to Blue Springs. The first night there, myself, with five men, were
ambushed by him and fired upon. We killed two of his men, of which he had
eighteen or twenty, and wounded a third. The next day we killed four more
of the worst of the gang, and before we left succeeded in dispersing them. . . .
Quantrill will not leave this section unless he is chastised and driven from it.
I hear of him tonight fifteen miles from here, with new recruits, committing
outrages on Union men, a large body of whom have come in tonight, driven
out by him. Families of Union men are coming into the city tonight asking
of me escorts to bring in their goods and chattels, which I duly furnished. I
had one man killed and two wounded, during the expedition.[3]

A few weeks later, on February 21, Quantrill and fifteen men camped on
the outskirts of Independence, planning to resupply the next morning.
Quantrill's operations were still centered around Independence, mostly from
the Blue Springs region. Recently he had met with Col. Benjamin Franklin
Parker, head of the First Regiment of Missouri Rangers, the most notable partisan ranger group in the area at that time. What Quantrill did not know was
that an invading army from Ohio was stationed in Platte City with orders to
report to Fort Scott, Kansas. On its way there, the Second Ohio Cavalry
passed through Kansas City and on February 21 camped southeast of town.

Hearing that Parker and Quantrill were regularly seen near Independence, Maj. George A. Purington of the Second Ohio dispatched Lt. Allured
B. Nettleton to capture both men. Nettleton took forty men and marched
twelve miles to Independence, arriving at dawn. According to Nettleton's
sources, Quantrill and Parker were staying with friends. His men surrounded
the town, searched for the two guerrilla chieftains, then discovered that both
had left the night before. Nettleton posted guards on the square and took the
remaining men a half-mile west of town to eat and feed their horses.

While the soldiers were eating, Parker, Quantrill, and fifteen men
entered Independence in pairs from the east. According to one account, a
Federal squad was getting breakfast at Uhlinger's Bakery on the south side of

the square when Quantrill and his men rode in. It was a cool morning with slush on the ground and a heavy fog in the air. Visibility was so poor that neither side could tell friend from foe beyond fifty feet. Still, Quantrill's men came up quickly and surprised the Union troops.

As soon as the guerrillas saw the Federals, they opened a deadly fire with revolvers, shotguns, and rifles. When Nettleton heard the firing, he rushed all his men to aid the men in town.

After a brief skirmish, Quantrill ordered his men to withdraw in the same direction from which they came. Since the Federals had only single-shot carbines, as soon as their rounds were fired, they pursued the guerrillas with their sabers. As a result, Quantrill's men took a heavy toll with their pistols. One count reported seventeen Ohioans killed.

The fog was so thick when guerrilla William Gregg rode out of town that a Union soldier riding next to him believed he was a fellow Federal—until Gregg pointed his pistol at him. After three misfires, the Federal slashed at him with his saber, which only resulted in blackening Gregg's arm. The guerrilla managed to escape in the fog.

Two of Quantrill's men—eighteen-year-old Gabriel George and Hop Wood—were killed in the town. Guerrilla Harrison Trow noted that Gabriel George was in the lead of Quantrill's column, and as the guerrillas chased the Federals into the brick courthouse, George was killed so close to the fence surrounding the building that it was only with great difficulty that his comrades were able to drag his body away under the point-blank fire. Parker's command lost one man killed and several captured.

While attempting to escape down the Spring Branch road, a half-mile east of town, Quantrill's horse was shot out from under him, and the guerrilla leader suffered a leg wound. He escaped on foot by climbing through the protection of some rock outcroppings above the road.[4]

After the skirmish the bodies of the slain guerrillas were picked up by their relatives and prepared for burial. Gabriel George's home was in Oak Grove, sixteen miles east of Independence. Two days after the battle, although wounded, Quantrill attended the funeral.[5] Showing the loyalty and comradeship inherent in his command, Quantrill comforted the family members and spoke at the graveside services of the bravery of the slain guerrilla and for the patriotic cause for which he gave his life. After the funeral Quantrill remained in the Oak Grove neighborhood to recuperate from his wound.

In the wake of the skirmish Quantrill briefly disbanded his men. "Scattered soldiers," he argued, "make a scattered trail. The regiment that has but one man to hunt can never find him."

Soon Quantrill was making plans for a bold strike to counter the jay-hawker raids. He decided to launch a raid of his own on Aubry, Kansas. Around March 1 forty men assembled in Oak Grove. At 5 A.M. on March 7, a Friday, Quantrill led his men into the main street of Aubry. Raising the Rebel Yell and firing their revolvers into the air to quell any resistance, the town was quickly overrun and secured. Quantrill, accompanied by several of his men, rode to the general store and two-story hotel in the center of town.

Five men had been sleeping upstairs in the hotel, two of whom ran to the window. Both were dressed in blue uniforms. One was 2d Lt. Reuben A. Randlett of Company A, Fifth Kansas Jayhawker Regiment. The other was forty-seven-year-old Union quartermaster Abraham Ellis, serving as a teamster with a Kansas jayhawker regiment. Ellis had stopped overnight to rest from carrying supplies from Fort Scott to Fort Leavenworth.

Quantrill saw the two soldiers peering down at him, one brandishing a pistol. He fired at the window. The bullet went through the top of one sash and the bottom of the other, catching Ellis squarely in the middle of the fore-head and knocking him unconscious. Randlett, seeing Ellis on the floor, bleeding profusely and apparently dead, hurriedly ran downstairs, surrendered his weapon, and asked to be treated as a prisoner of war.

Guerrilla Joseph Young approached Randlett and thrust his pistol barrel into Randlett's mouth while another guerrilla stuck his pistol in the Union soldier's ear. They were not inclined to offer any Yankee soldier any hospital-ity, but William H. Gregg intervened, saying that Quantrill wanted the offi-cer unharmed and protected.

The remaining Federal soldiers sleeping on the downstairs floor refused to surrender and attempted to escape into a nearby field. Three of them were shot down as they fled.

Quantrill entered the hotel and questioned Randlett. He asked if he had a horse available, and Randlett replied that his horse was in the stable. Quantrill was ordering a man to saddle the animal and bring it to the front door when two more men carried the supposedly dead Ellis into the room.

Staring intently at the wounded man covered with blood, Quantrill noticed something familiar. Years ago in Stanton, Kansas, when the guerrilla captain had been a schoolteacher, Abraham Ellis had been the school superin-tendent, and the two men had been close friends. In a letter after the war, Ellis remarked on his acquaintance with Quantrill: "I visited his school and put up, at his boarding house. . . . I found him an interesting, well educated man."

Quantrill fetched some water and washed Ellis's face. He apologized, stat-ing that Ellis was one of the Kansas men he did not want to hurt. When Ellis finally replied, he said that he had a team of horses and about fifty dollars' worth of groceries. Afterward Ellis recalled that Quantrill:

> talked kindly to me a few minutes after he recognized me and promised not to disturb any more of my property and when he was about to leave, he discovered that one of my horses had been taken and he inquired who took it and was told, he immediately ordered one of his men to go and tell him to bring that horse back immediately or it would be the last time that he would disobey orders.

After their brief reunion, Ellis faded into unconsciousness and appeared dead. Quantrill left behind the team of horses, the wagon, and the groceries. At the same time, he captured then paroled seven soldiers. After the guerrillas looted all the money they could find, only one house was burned. For his part, Ellis recovered and lived for many years after the war with the grim reminder of Quantrill's marksmanship deeply embedded in the middle of his forehead. For the remainder of his life he was known as "Bullet Hole Ellis."

Quantrill's men returned to Missouri with Reuben Randlett still a prisoner; the guerrilla leader hoped to exchange him for one of Parker's men who had been taken prisoner during the February 22 skirmish at Independence. They did not stop to camp until they had crossed the state line. The next day, Sunday, March 9, a man came to the camp and reported the Redlegs were raiding Cass County. Quantrill immediately ordered the men to saddle up, and the whole band took to the road.

Three houses were found on fire. The Redlegs retreated when they saw Quantrill coming, and a long chase to the Kansas line followed. At a point near the border, east of Paola, but still in Missouri, Quantrill overtook the marauders. Randlett's guard escorted him to a high place where he could see the engagement. A brisk skirmish followed in which some of the Redlegs were wounded, but none killed.

If the jayhawkers had not retreated, Quantrill's men were prepared to give battle as they had been trained. Most of the enemy were armed with only rifles, which had a maximum range of about three hundred yards. The guerrillas' carbines and pistols gave them superior firepower. Quantrill trained his men to give and receive a volley with their carbines then charge full speed on horseback, before the jayhawkers could reload, and use their pistols with deadly effect at close range. The enemy's defenses usually fell apart.

Three days after Quantrill's raid on Aubry, Kansas, a company from the Eighth Kansas Jayhawker Regiment in Olathe went to Aubry to investigate the raid.[6] Southern sympathizers were sought out and accused of aiding the raiders. William Anderson's father and uncle were named as such. When the jayhawker company arrived at the Anderson farm on March 11, William and younger brother Jim were delivering fifteen head of cattle to the U.S. commissary agent at Fort Leavenworth. When the brothers returned to the farm they found their father and uncle hanged. Before the day was done, Bill Anderson killed a Union picket in revenge. The next night he killed two more pickets then fled to Missouri. Two nights later, on March 15, as Anderson made his way through Jackson County, he bedded down in the hayloft of farmer George Reed, whose farm was between the Big Blue River and Lee's Summit. During the night he was discovered by John McCorkle, Quantrill's chief scout, who took Anderson to join Quantrill's band.[7]

Two days later, amid a cold winter rainstorm, Quantrill brought Reuben Randlett to Independence and secured him in a hotel on the northeast corner of the square. Afterward the guerrilla leader headed south to camp in Brooking Township at the vacant church building of the West Fork of the Little Blue Baptist Church, one of the most famous early pioneer churches. Not only was it the center of religious life for the settlers here, it was also the hub of the community's social life.

The West Fork of the Little Blue Baptist Church was the first permanent organization of any denomination in central Jackson County. At first the church had no meetinghouse but met in homes or in groves. On December 10, 1842, a formal church building was erected one mile east of the present town. The site was only one mile west of the Blue Cut, where numerous ambushes and skirmishes occurred between Quantrill's band and the Federals from Independence, eleven miles to the northeast. The church was also only a few miles north of the White Oak Creek, a tributary of the Little Blue River.[8]

When the church was first established, it had 17 members: 7 families and 2 individuals. By 1880 there were more than 170 members. Like most small rural communities in this part of Missouri, the citizens were Southern sympathizers, and because of the early predatory jayhawker raids, the church members of these communities were united in sentiment and support against the invasion of Union troops from Kansas.

In 1859 a second church building was built of brick on the same ground, replacing the original stone structure. Alvin Brooking and Archibald Rice donated most of the construction funds. The two main doors of the building were built not to segregate the races but to segregate the sexes. Slaves were eligible for membership and attended services alongside their masters. Of the handful of church members at the start of the war, twenty-five were slaves.

The original members of the first church were all prominent citizens of the area:

- Reuben Harris, father of guerrilla Thomas Harris
- Nathan Kerr, son-in-law of Reuben Harris
- Richard Marshal Fristoe, a church deacon, one of the county's first court judges, and an uncle of Cole Younger
- guerrilla Benjamin Rice, a deacon in the church
- John S. Muir, uncle of guerrilla Boone Muir
- Job Crabtree, who often sheltered Quantrill's men
- guerrilla John T. House
- William Hagan, whose brother was killed by Federal soldiers
- guerrilla Randolph Venable
- John McCorkle, Quantrill's chief scout
- guerrilla Nathaniel Teague

Along with Richard Marshal Fristoe, two other of Jackson County's first court judges were charter members in the church:

- Alvin Brooking
- John Davis

Fristoe, Brooking, and Davis served alongside other notable judges, such as fifty-year-old James B. Yeager, whose son, Richard Yeager, was one of Quantrill's guerrillas.

The church was situated in a cleared grove of timber with level ground on the north and abruptly sloping land to the south, just a hundred yards from a branch fed by the west fork of the Little Blue River. Quantrill's guerrillas liked this topography. Fresh spring water was everywhere. The fields were surrounded with stone walls, and the river bottoms were covered with trees of every variety. The gently rolling prairies were carpeted with luxuriant grasses and surrounded by thick belts of timber.[9] A correspondent for the *New York Daily Times* visited the area with a Federal patrol and commented:

All of the valleys are broken and densely wooded. In our late ride I rode through timbered hollows and ravines covered with thicket almost as dense as a Mexican chaparral, places in which five thousand men might hide, and an army march by the roads without knowing of their presence. Our troops follow the roads mainly. The guerrillas follow the hog paths through the woods, knowing every foot of ground, and able to evade us at every mile they traverse.

The fabric of Missouri society at the time of the Civil War was comprised of hard-working, God-fearing men and women who came to the state as pioneers and developed the land into prosperous farms. They built fine homes and started businesses. Their Bibles represented their moral code, a standard with which to judge themselves and their neighbors. As soon as they raised a roof over their heads their thoughts quickly turned to building a church for worship. They looked forward to expressing their freedom of religion established by the Founding Fathers and guaranteed in the Constitution that they loved so dear. During this time of strife and unrest, churches provided bedrock foundations for their communities. They were the safe harbors during troubled times. They assured their members that, despite the uncertainty and upheaval around them, there was still a God who comforted and cared for them.

Quantrill derived much of his support and strength from these local churches. Jeremiah Farmer, from Westport, was pastor of the West Fork of the Little Blue Baptist Church at the beginning of the war. He was a well-known circuit-riding preacher who held two meetings a month in this tiny church besides other churches in Westport and Oak Grove.[10] When Farmer asked Quantrill the age-old question—Son, do you know where you're going when you die?—the guerrilla chieftain felt a genuine concern and compassion that he had never known before. It was here that Quantrill found a group of people who genuinely cared for him. They were not trying to defraud him or steal his property, like his former friends in Kansas, but they were actually concerned about his physical and spiritual well-being. It was here that he finally found a home.

Missouri churchgoers were not at all akin to the Kansas settlers just a few miles across the border. Their faith was their anchor in the storm. During the war, when they were able to meet, they held protracted meetings lasting several days. Such meetings were held at the Oak Grove Primitive Baptist Church just south of the Jose White farm one mile south of Oak Grove. Quantrill attended these meetings, commonly referred to as revival meetings. Here he worshiped and made friends of his fellow worshipers.

Sarah E. Farmer, whose father was pastor of the Baptist church in Brooking Township, married Nathan George, a Confederate soldier from Oak Grove. Nathan was the brother of Gabriel George, who was killed while riding with Quantrill in Independence on February 22. The entire George family of Oak Grove attended this church, and many came to ride with Quantrill.

The church's pastor, sixty-three-year-old Hiram Bowman, became the father-in-law of John Koger, one of Quantrill's bravest soldiers. Koger joined Quantrill's Rangers in December 1861. He was most noted for his participation at the battle of Independence, the Lawrence raid, and the fighting at Baxter Springs and Centralia. He went south with Quantrill toward the end of the war and only parted company when Quantrill went to Kentucky.

Southern churches had many problems to contend with during the war. Most tried to remain neutral, but when Abraham Lincoln called for a day of fasting and prayer on behalf of the Union cause, the request was considered a coercion by many in Missouri. The animosity aroused by the presidential proclamation caused many congregations to split or disband. Like many church pastors in the area, Jeremiah Farmer was Southern in his sympathies. When Lincoln asked church leaders to recite designed prayers for divine supplication to the continued unity of the Federal government and to the health of the president of the United States, this Missouri church decided to close its doors for the duration of the hostilities. From August 1862, following the battle of Independence, to June 1866, there are no church records for the West Fork of the Little Blue Baptist Church.[11]

Many well-known and respected citizens in the early Brooking Township and of Jackson County were original members of the West Fork Baptist Church. Because they were outspoken Southern sympathizers, they were targeted by the Federal authorities. Zion Flanery, one of the earliest members of the church, had a son, John, also known as M. V. B. Flanery, who rode with Quantrill. John's house was burned down along with twenty-five other homes on October 27, 1861, by Jennison's jayhawkers. John then joined the regular Confederate army and later joined Quantrill after returning home in 1863. He was killed in Texas when the guerrillas wintered there. Rebecca Jane Flanery, daughter of Zion Flanery, became a Southern heroine when she was imprisoned for several weeks because she had tended Dick Yeager, one of Quantrill's officers, who was wounded at the battle of Arrow Rock on July 19, 1864. Such longstanding bitterness toward jayhawkers in general influenced areas like this to rise up in arms against the cruel injustices endorsed by the Federal occupation army. Although once neutral, these communities became enclaves of Southern support.[12]

Jayhawkers had been very active since early 1862. To counter the enemy's activity, Quantrill attacked every Federal outpost over a five-county area, virtually tying up Jackson County. The mails were stopped and travel was risky at best. Federal troops, for their own safety, were garrisoned only within the larger towns and only ventured out in very large numbers to burn, plunder, and kill. Their harsh measures took a toll on the civilian population. In response, twenty men from Cass County rode into Quantrill's camp on Wednesday, March 19, to join him and avenge these wrongs. Frank Smith commented: "Any new recruits coming into the organization were aware of the type of warfare that Quantrill's followers waged and they just naturally adapted themselves to this method of fighting."[13] These twenty men had previously met Quantrill when he helped them defend their neighborhood during his return from the Aubry raid.

Always waiting for the cover of darkness before settling in for the night, Quantrill led sixty men to the vacant brick building of the West Fork of the Little Blue Baptist Church to set up quarters. Fresh water from the Little Blue River coursed through a branch just a short southerly walk down the hill. Pickets searched for signs of approaching enemy soldiers. The remaining men were split into small bands and visited the area farms for home-cooked meals; at first light they were to reassemble at the church. Those remaining with Quantrill secured their horses in the thick underbrush behind the building.

Whenever Quantrill's men camped for the night, their primary concern was for their mounts. The most dangerous situation a guerrilla could face was to be on foot when he encountered a mounted foe. Therefore the guerrillas' mounts were usually hidden in the thick brush but within easy access. If the guerrillas decided to fight on foot, they kept their mounts over a hillock or behind a building for fear that a stray shot might endanger the animals.

Quantrill and his chief lieutenants occupied the vacant brick church; the others slept outside, watched over by a roving guard assigned by the commander. Contrary to the belief that Quantrill and his men rarely slept indoors, facts prove otherwise, but there were clear restrictions to these occasions. The dwelling had to be made of brick, stone, or logs; a simple clapboard house offered little protection if the enemy caught the guerrillas inside. The house also had to have a commanding view of the surrounding countryside.

To keep himself informed of the enemy's dispositions, Quantrill collected newspapers. Federal orders concerning martial law, promotions, and even troop movements were all covered by the local papers. To obtain this information, Quantrill stopped stagecoaches and retrieved the newspapers they routinely carried. In this manner he obtained a copy of the *St. Louis Republican* with a report of Henry W. Halleck's General Orders No. 2, which warned: "Every man who enlists [as a guerrilla fighter] in such an organization forfeits his life and becomes an outlaw. All persons are hereby warned that if they join any guerrilla band they will not, if captured, be treated as ordinary prisoners-of-war, but will be hung as robbers and murderers."[14]

Few guerrillas complained that the Federals would shoot them on sight or if captured. A bullet was a soldier's death and expected. Halleck's order, however, took the hostilities into another direction. Cold-blooded executions were seen as cowardly and dishonorable. Many Southerners went to war with an ideal "Southern code of honor."

Given this situation, Quantrill lay awake most of that night as he pondered plans for the next few days. He was going to try one last time to negotiate with the authorities as an honorable Confederate officer. He would send his prisoner, Reuben Randlett, into Kansas City to offer a prisoner exchange.

At about the same time that Quantrill weighed his next act, an elderly postmaster named Perry rode into Independence with a letter from the military authorities in Kansas City to Randlett. It announced a black flag policy: no prisoners, no quarter. Perry knew that this meant death for Randlett. Although Perry was a Unionist, he was an old friend of Quantrill's and carried letters to Kansas City for Quantrill. He shared the contents of the black flag letter with the guerrilla chieftain.

Quantrill confronted Randlett with Halleck's order, asking, "What do you think of that, Lieutenant?"

Randlett replied, "I could not blame you for shooting me now."

Instead Quantrill promised, "Not a hair of your head shall be harmed."[15]

His decision was in line with his rules of war. Quantrill remained with Perry into the night, and the old man's wife prepared supper for the three men. The guerrilla leader left at about ten o'clock and rode out of town.

At 3 A.M. the next morning Randlett was awakened and found breakfast ready and his mare saddled. He and Perry rode to Kansas City together. There Perry left him and returned to Independence.

Quantrill wrote a note on the back of Halleck's order and sent it to him, vowing, "For every man of mine you kill, I will kill ten of yours."

The same morning that Randlett rode into Kansas City, Quantrill and forty men launched a raid against Liberty, Missouri. The band crossed the Missouri River in skiffs, swimming their horses beside them, then remounted and rode fourteen miles into Liberty. On the outskirts of town they seized Pvt. Owen Grimshaw and interrogated him for information about the other Federals in town. Grimshaw was shot when he refused to indicate which building housed the Union headquarters.

The guerrillas then charged into town while the small Federal detachment sought safety in their headquarters. The fight raged for nearly three hours. Afraid of being burned out, the eight soldiers finally surrendered after their commander was severely wounded. Quantrill promised to parole them.

After raising the Confederate flag, the guerrillas left town as quickly as they had appeared. There was no looting or burning, because most of the residents were Southern sympathizers. Union cavalry pursued the guerrillas, but Quantrill was already back in the safety of the hills along the valley of the Little Blue.

During Quantrill's attack on Liberty, Reuben Randlett approached Col. John McNeil to negotiate his exchange for B. F. Parker's man captured during the February 22 skirmish at Independence. The colonel dismissed him out of hand, ordering him to return at 8 A.M. When Randlett returned, he found McNeil reviewing a wall map with another officer. Seeing Randlett, the colonel informed him that a company was being ordered out to destroy Quantrill and Randlett was to accompany the unit as guide. Randlett explained that he could not do that because he was honor bound by his agreement with Quantrill to not act under arms until officially exchanged. An argument ensued, and Randlett stormed out of the office and collided with Col. William Weir of the Fourth Kansas Jayhawker Regiment, whom he had decided he must find to appeal McNeil's orders. Weir indicated that McNeil had just been relieved of command, thus the issue was somewhat moot.

Randlett took the matter to Gen. Samuel D. Sturgis in Leavenworth, but the general did not disagree with McNeil's action. Randlett was ordered to have nothing to do with Quantrill and to not communicate with him because he was considered an outlaw. The lieutenant, however, continued to view the matter as a point of honor, thus he was obliged to return and report to Quantrill.

When Randlett returned to Independence, he found hundreds of Union troops in the town. No one would tell him where he could find Quantrill. So the lieutenant approached Perry, who took him to Quantrill. After he had informed the guerrilla leader of his failure to negotiate the exchange, Quantrill asked Perry to see Randlett safely back to Kansas City. In parting, Quantrill said to Randlett: "Go back to your people. I like you very much, but between them and me there can never be peace."[16] Randlett replied that he would stay home because he would not fight for a government that would not exchange a private for a lieutenant. He never saw Quantrill again.[17]

At 6 A.M. on Saturday, March 22, Quantrill addressed his men in the churchyard. Realizing that the concept of partisan warfare and the Federal government's treatment of irregular cavalry had been changed by Halleck's order, Quantrill drew a line on the ground and read aloud the order and explained what it meant. Then he told them: "Now boys, you hear, he said those of you who wish can quit and go home. Those who stay will know what to expect. I'll accept the challenge. All of you who wish to remain and fight with me ride over on this side of the line. All of you who wish to leave the outfit go ahead and nothing will be held against you. Every man will now make his choice."[18] The twenty new recruits from Cass County decided to ride off. William H. Gregg commented:

> At this date we had sixty men, twenty of whom had come to us only the day before, and when the no-quarter order was read and explained to them, these recruits left us. They were disgusted at the idea of being outlawed and the hoisting of the Black Flag by the enemy. All except these twenty rode over the line, but the men that left soon rejoined the band after they realized that they could never go home again in peace. They did not stay away long however, as the Federal troops began murdering by wholesale, old men and boys and, were so insulting to the women that they too, often hid out on their approach.[19]

Matthew Houx initially rode away. On March 25 he inquired at a Federal headquarters what terms he and his friends would receive if they returned to their homes and lived in peace. No terms were offered, so they returned to Quantrill's company.[20]

After his men had made their decision, Quantrill addressed them: "Boys, Halleck issued the order, but we will spill the first blood. Everybody look to your weapons and saddle up." John Newman Edwards reported:

> What they did in self-defense any Anglo-Saxon would have done who did not have in his veins the blood of a slave. The peaceful pursuits of life were denied to them. The law, which should have protected them, was overridden. Indeed, there was no law. The courts were instruments of plunder. The civil officers were cutthroats. Instead of a legal process, there was a vigilance committee. Men were hung because of a very natural desire to keep hold of their own property. To the cruel vigor of actual war, there had succeeded the irresponsible despotism of greedy highwaymen, buttressed upon assassination. The border countries were overrun with bands of predatory plunderers.[21]

Before this date the guerrillas' hatred was directed toward the Federals because of actions aimed at their relatives and friends. After Quantrill read Halleck's order to them, the war took on a new and different meaning. It no longer mattered if Quantrill's men held commissions as officers or if their organization followed the military structure of officers, noncommissioned officers, orderly sergeants, quartermasters, and medical personnel. Halleck's order labeled them all as outlaws. William H. Gregg explained:

> Quantrill never killed a prisoner or robbed anyone until after the order was issued by General Halleck in March, 1862, outlawing him and his men. Even after that he'd let prisoners go if there was any chance to do so. He often did let them go. We captured many of the enemy whom we universally paroled, Quantrill and his men vying with each other who should be most magnanimous toward prisoners.[22]

For the guerrillas, there would be no turning back. To stay and fight honorably or to turn their backs on the wrongs being done to them and their relatives and neighbors and flee south was an option not even considered. With his proclamation, Halleck brought a new type of warfare to the border. There would be no exchange of prisoners. In fact, no prisoners would be taken. The cruelty and harsh conditions imposed by the Federals during the first twelve months of the war were naturally despised but accepted by the partisan rangers in Missouri as part of the stock and trade of civil war. Both sides knew the harshness of combat. Now no quarter would be asked and none would be given. If captured, Quantrill's men expected to be killed.

Angered by this latest attempt to eradicate guerrilla warfare, Quantrill's plans to attack the garrison at Independence were put into action. In the early morning hours the forty-man band left Brooking Township, riding down the West Ridge road and moving straight north three miles to John Deering's farm, four miles south of Independence. Deering had just returned home from Independence and informed Quantrill that the garrison had been reinforced by three hundred men of Charles Jennison's jayhawkers.

Even though he wanted desperately to get at his old rival, Quantrill knew that the odds were too great now. So, flanking Independence to the west, Quantrill decided to run a patrol through Jackson County toward Kansas City then swing south toward Little Santa Fe in the southwestern portion of the county, next to the state line, presumably intent on raiding into Kansas. Riding due west for seven miles from Deering's farm, the guerrillas made for the old Westport road between Kansas City and Independence. Two days previously Jennison's men had come this way, and by all accounts a detachment of thirteen Federals remained here to guard the bridge over the Big Blue River for the jayhawkers' return to Kansas. The bridge was the joining structure along the old Independence to Kansas City and Westport road.

Easing down from the crest of the ridge road that separated the valleys of the Big and Little Blue Rivers, Quantrill's men rode past all that remained of Pitcher's Mill. Col. Thomas Pitcher had already gone south to join Price's army, leaving behind his wife and young son. Only months before, Jennison had burned the mill to the ground, and Pitcher's fourteen-year-old son, Thomas, headed south to join his father. Pitcher's wife, Nancy, wrote to friends in Lexington, Missouri, that several of her relations had lost their homes to the torches of Jennison's jayhawkers; their slaves, horses, and every-thing they owned were taken from them. She reported that the jayhawkers had killed boys as young as ten years old.[23]

Leaving the ridge road, the guerrillas moved a quarter of a mile westward, down the narrow trails through the thick woods and heavy underbrush that covered the rocky bluffs overlooking the river. Here was the bridge that ran over the Big Blue River. To the west of the bridge the road wound up a gently rolling hillside toward Westport and Kansas City. Four hundred yards to the east were heavily wooded bluffs inundated with small caves. As he made his way to the edge of the timber, Quantrill noted the fortified bridgehead and the thirteen soldiers as they milled around, unsuspectingly going about their duties in the mist that rose from the river in the early morning hours. Com-manding the Union detail was a German sergeant. His accent gave him away as a hated "Dutch," which soon cost him his life.

Advancing as close as possible, Quantrill maneuvered his men on a line adjacent to the bridge. When he gave the word, the raiders appeared out of the underbrush like phantoms charging full speed upon the unfortunate sol-diers. The Federals never had a chance to react; they were mercilessly shot down before any resistance could be made. The bridge was then completely destroyed. Cole Younger was present that day and noted: "Thirteen soldiers who guarded the bridge at the Big Blue found their number unlucky."

Before the smoke had cleared his barrel, Quantrill yelled to his men: "They issued the order, but we draw first blood."[24]

The guerrillas rode from there southwest toward Westport, hoping to find a cluster of Union soldiers at a favorite rest area, the Alexander Majors plan-tation, ten miles south of Kansas City. Majors had formerly employed Quantrill as a bull whacker for Utah-bound wagon trains. Although Majors was a Southern sympathizer, Federals frequently stopped at his property to rest and water their horses at his residence. None were in the area, however, when Quantrill's band arrived.

After lunch Quantrill headed his company eight miles farther south to the Little Santa Fe area and rested until 8 P.M. He then divided his men into groups and sought shelter. George Todd, William Haller, and eighteen men went to one house four miles distant while Quantrill and twenty-one men stayed with David Tate, a local minister.

Tate's house was a two-story structure fourteen miles south of Kansas City and only a short distance from the state line. Quantrill spread his men out on both floors and posted a picket in the woods along the road. The guerrillas were to rendezvous shortly after daylight the next morning.

Word of the burning of the Big Blue bridge and the deaths of the jay-hawkers spread quickly. In Independence a Federal officer declared that the staunchest Rebel woman in town should make the shroud for the slain ser-geant. That lot fell to Nellie Wallace, wife of a Methodist preacher, who lived only a mile northeast of the bridge. In answer to the officer's demand that she have the shroud ready by a given hour, she said that she would be most happy "to make shrouds for his whole command."[25]

From Independence word was telegraphed to Kansas City, and a unit was quickly dispatched to pick up Quantrill's trail. Maj. Charles Banzhaf of the First Battalion, Missouri Cavalry, was first on the scene and notified Col. Robert B. Mitchell, whose Second Kansas Jayhawker Regiment was stationed in Kansas City. Banzhaf apprised him of Quantrill's movements and requested his assistance along with that of Col. William Weir of the Fourth Kansas Jayhawker Regiment.

Mitchell left Kansas City at 6:30 P.M. on March 22 and arrived at Little Santa Fe about 10 P.M. the same evening. He immediately assembled a detail from Company D, commanded by Capt. Amaziah Moore, and one from Company E, commanded by Lt. Elias S. Stover, and placed them under the command of Maj. James M. Pomeroy with the task of capturing Quantrill.

Close to midnight Pomeroy's men approached the Tate house.[26] As the Federals moved in, it started to rain. Stover remained with the horses and a sixth of the men to support Pomeroy if necessary. With the assistance of a guide, Pomeroy approached the house by a trail through some woods and, anticipating that pickets might have been posted, got behind the pickets. His men successfully surrounded the house without disturbing anything except the dogs, which heralded Union presence with an uproar. John McCorkle recalled, "Around one o'clock in the morning the Rebel picket dashed by the house, firing his pistol and calling for us to get out as we were surrounded by Federals.[27]

Tate's log house was two stories high with a one-story extension in the rear. The logs were sixty feet long and covered with clapboard siding, making it appear less formidable. Mitchell had ordered Pomeroy to surround the house and wait for reinforcements, but Pomeroy decided to capture Quantrill single-handedly. He sent an officer to the front door to demand the guerrillas' surrender.

Quantrill jumped from his bed, raced to the front door, and listened while his men anxiously crowded around him. He quietly ordered his men back[28] and fired his revolver through the wooden door. The bullet struck the officer, and the man fell to the porch. As soon as he was dragged away, a heavy fusillade commenced upon the structure.

The incessant dull thudding of bullets against the log walls was unnerving, but most shots were inaccurately aimed and caused little damage except to throw shards of broken window glass and wooden splinters throughout the interior of the room. Quantrill's men quickly regained their composure. Over the noise of the firing, they heard him order them to "Bar the doors and barricade the windows."[29]

Manning every window and opening, the guerrillas stacked furniture and bedding in front of the windows and returned fire at the muzzle flashes in the outside darkness. Most of the Federals were standing close together in front of the house.

The women in the house were terrified, and Tate told Quantrill he would fight it out with the Federals but asked him to help him get his family out. Instead Quantrill told Tate that his place was with his family, not the guerrillas. So Quantrill requested a short truce to allow the women and noncombatants to leave. They were escorted to the safety of a large smokehouse behind the main house.

As soon as Tate's family was safe, the fight began again. Guerrilla John McCorkle recalled that they all "could hear the officers on the outside telling their men to shoot low, that we were lying on the floor, but their bullets had no effect on the heavy weatherboarding and logs."[30] Seeing that their firearms were ineffective against the log building, the Federals gathered fence rails, straw, and all kinds of combustibles and piled them up against the two sides of the house that lacked windows, planning to set it afire.

Two of the new guerrilla recruits crawled out and surrendered. Several Federals ran toward them in a bunch. Ten guerrillas—including James Little, Cole Younger, William Hoy, and Stephen Shores—fired at the crowd from the upper story and brought down six.

Quantrill was said to be everywhere the firing was hottest, encouraging his men with his cool demeanor. Running upstairs to assist his men there, Quantrill saw two Union men standing together and shouted, "Is there a shotgun here?" Cole Younger brought him one loaded with buckshot. Thrusting half his body out the nearest window and receiving heavy fire, he discharged the two barrels of his gun so quickly they sounded as one barrel. Both Federals fell, one dead, the other—Pomeroy—mortally wounded.[31]

Command fell to Amaziah Moore. With so deadly a fire now coming from the house, the Federals and their two prisoners took cover behind the smokehouse but maintained a constant fire on the guerrillas. Quantrill had two choices—surrender or die. With Halleck's recent order to summarily execute irregular troops, surrender was not a real option. He asked for a brief truce and called his men together.

Cole Younger remembered that Quantrill said: "Boys, we're in a tight place. We can't stay here and I do not mean to surrender. All who want to follow me out can say so; all who prefer to give up without a rush can also say so. I will do the best I can for them."[32] All the guerrillas agreed to make a dash through the Federal lines. Quantrill then coached them: "Now boys, we are in a desperate situation. Don't anyone lose his head, but listen to me. We are in a tight place and our only chance is to bolt out the door and cut right through them. They are all bunched up and they won't be able to keep shooting or they'll kill one another. Now follow me in single file. Shoot right and left and stay right in line."[33]

Some of the guerrillas prepared themselves by tightening their pistol belts; others knelt in prayer. Quantrill called out, "Shotguns to the front." Those with pistols were arranged behind them, and the men armed with rifles and muskets made up the rear.

Quantrill, armed with a shotgun, took his place at the head of the file. Behind him were John Jarrette, George Shepherd, Perry Hoy, William Toler, James Little, and Cole Younger, still in his stocking feet. Behind them came Morgan T. Mattox, John McCorkle, and the rest of the men armed with revolvers. By now the burning house lit up the inside like daylight. Quantrill shouted for them to follow him and threw open the front door. So quickly did the guerrillas appear with a shout and muzzles blazing, and so furiously did they assault the Federal line, they quickly made their way into the darkness through a patch of gooseberry bushes and into the safety of the heavy timber about fifty yards away.

John McCorkle recalled, "The Federals were drawn up on both sides of the door. Quantrill opened the door, shooting the Federal who was standing near it and we all sprang after him, shooting with both hands. The Federals opened fire on us from both sides, killing their own men."[34] The Union men were armed with large unwieldy muskets known as Belgian carbines. Once the guerrillas were in the timber, the Federals threw down their carbines and opened fire with their French revolvers. Twelve hundred to fifteen hundred rounds chased after the vanishing guerrillas.[35]

Quantrill's men left behind eighteen Federals killed and twenty-nine badly wounded. Andrew Walker reported that the two men who stayed behind were brothers by the name of Rollins; they were shot later that night. Frank Smith claimed that only one man who fought his way out was taken prisoner—Perry Hoy. He was the fourth man in line with a shotgun and fired both barrels so close to the Federals that one of them was able to knock him over the head with his musket and render him unconscious.

Recovering from the dash after reaching the heavy timber, Quantrill built a fire, and his men reloaded. Then he tried to meet up with the remainder of his command. At the same time, Quantrill needed to rest and reorganize his men. Shoeless, hatless, and coatless, the guerrillas melted into the surrounding countryside and made their way back to their former camp on the morning of March 23. After an exhausting fourteen-mile march, they reached the home of David Wilson near the Little Blue River in Brooking Township, evading Federal patrols as they did so.

George Todd had heard the fighting at the Tate house and had his men in the saddle, heading straight to Quantrill's assistance. En route they encountered a one-hundred-man Union patrol. The guerrillas fought savagely for more than an hour but broke off the engagement and headed to the pre-arranged rendezvous on the headwaters of the Little Blue River in Jackson County. From March 25 to 30 Quantrill disbanded his men to secure new mounts and ammunition and reassemble at Samuel Clark's farm on the Sni-A-Bar Creek in eastern Jackson County near Pink Hill.

News of the Tate house fight made its way to the Federal command posts, and numerous patrols scoured the countryside for Quantrill and his men but also burned homes and outbuildings on farms near the site of the fight. Six suspicious men were arrested and sent to Fort Leavenworth, and more than twenty-five horses were stolen.

Back along the Little Blue the guerrillas stayed at Wilson's home for only a short while. About March 25 Quantrill took some men who had escaped the Tate house and moved to John Flanery's farm just south of White Oak Creek. From here they moved toward their prearranged rendezvous at the Clark farm. Of the forty men he had two weeks before, Quantrill was only able to muster seventeen.

On Sunday morning, March 30, Capt. Albert P. Peabody led a sixty-five-man patrol from the First Missouri Cavalry into Quantrill's camp. Clark's farm was nineteen miles southeast of Independence and three miles southeast of

Stony Point. John Koger had just ridden up and was hitching his horse to the rail fence in front of Clark's house when the Federals opened fire. He was slightly wounded in the first volley. William Gregg was cutting a comrade's hair in the front yard when the firing commenced. They immediately took cover and returned fire.

The Federals dismounted and engaged the guerrillas on foot. Feeling that the odds were in their favor, even if they were outnumbered, the guerrillas held their ground. Quantrill realized that, to hold his position, he had to divide his forces. With nine men he secured the house and ordered Gregg to take the remaining eight and secure the smokehouse and slave cabins.

The outbuildings were made of logs, and the chinking was knocked out from between them to make firing ports. The Clark house was about one hundred yards back from a stand of timber, and from here Peabody began a long-distance assault on the dwellings. Finding this to be ineffective, Peabody ordered his men to mount their horses and charge the house.

Quantrill ordered George Todd to hold the house while he and Gregg tried to get their horses from the barn. After the two men began to move toward the horses, Todd feared that he could not hold his position and called for Quantrill to come back. Gregg later blamed Todd for causing them to have to abandon their horses.

When the Federals charged, they found the guerrillas scattered among the outbuildings. Quantrill assigned Todd and some men to the upper floor of the house while he and the rest fought from the lower. Gregg was fighting from the slave cabins in the rear of the house, and another group fought from behind a corner of the main house. The guerrillas held their fire until the charging enemy was within thirty feet. Then, according to Harrison Trow, "A quick, sure volley, and twenty-seven men and horses went down together."

Samuel Clark, fighting from the upper story, was known to be an expert deer hunter. With a shotgun he managed to kill several Federals and later saved Quantrill's life when they were forced to abandon the house.

After the failure of this charge, Peabody rallied his men back into the timber and continued to snipe at the guerrillas at long range.

Feeling emboldened by his success so far, Quantrill gathered his men and made a mad rush at the Federals. His charge carried him into the Union line, where, seizing the opportunity, he captured nine horses. The guerrillas then withdrew to the safety of the dwellings with the captured animals.

The battle had been going on for well over an hour. A second Federal company rode in, attracted by the firing, and linked up with Peabody's command. The 17 guerrillas now faced 160 Union soldiers.

Because of the intense firing, Quantrill's men were cut off from their horses in the barn two hundred feet from the house. The safety of the timber was more than a hundred yards away. The Federals were slowly surrounding the house in overpowering numbers. They had in fact renewed their attack with the recently arrived reinforcements and had crawled up close enough to find cover behind the log fences near to the house.

In utter disregard for his own safety, Quantrill decided to sacrifice himself by drawing the Federal fire away from his men. He ordered the guerrillas to hold their fire. When the Federals exposed themselves to fire at him, they were to pick their targets and fire. He then dashed from the house to the smokehouse. The Federals, seeing such an exciting opportunity rush by, recklessly exposed themselves, allowing the expert fire of the guerrillas to do their deadly duty. Harrison Trow noted that, owing to the short range, the guerrillas managed to kill at least twenty Federals and as many more were wounded and disabled. It was thirty paces from the house to the smokehouse, and Quantrill made the dangerous dash more than eight times with more than one hundred men firing at him as he came and went.

The Federals had initially engaged the guerrillas with revolvers, but once their pistols ran out of ammunition, they turned to their rifles. Sensing this change in the battle, Quantrill decided to lead his men on a wild dash into the timber as soon as the Federals fired their next volley. One last time he made the dash from the house to the smokehouse. Immediately after the Federals emptied their rifles, Quantrill led his men into the safety of the nearby timber. The Federals could do nothing but watch them go. Peabody, counting up the vast number of dead and wounded about him, decided against further pursuit.

After the battle Gregg reproved Quantrill for having lost their horses. The guerrilla leader replied: "I had rather lose a thousand horses, than a single man like those who have fought with me this day. Heroes are scarce; horses are everywhere."[36] Six guerrillas were killed in and around the house; the wounded were taken away by the others. Quantrill also lost a valuable spyglass given to him by Sam Clark's son, John. It was a valuable asset because Quantrill had used it to watch Federal troop movements in Independence from Blue Springs. The battle, however, aroused many people in the area, and more than a hundred of Clark's neighbors converged on the Union force and sniped at them from long range.[37]

The guerrillas retreated but were not routed. As the fight was going on, Peabody had sent to Pink Hill for reinforcements. Quickly rallying in the nearby brush, Quantrill gathered his men and proceeded to nearby Ball Ford, a shallow spot in the creek, where he knew that the Federal relief party would have to cross. Cleverly assessing the situation, Quantrill deployed his men in a counterambush on the relief column summoned from Pink Hill. He knew that if he were successful, he could gain mounts for his men.

The crossing had a perpendicular bluff, inaccessible to horsemen. Here the guerrillas waited unseen, hidden behind rocks and trees. When fifty-one Federals came dashing up to the ford, the patrol commander allowed his men to let their horses drink from the stream. The Union men crowded together until the ford was thick with men and animals.

Quantrill directed his men to open fire. Todd, armed with a shotgun, set off the ambush for the guerrillas. The remaining men fired unerringly. Rearing horses threw off their riders and trampled them underfoot. The surviving Federals sought to escape the killing zone as quickly as possible. The captain of the patrol managed to rally his remaining men in a charge up the steep banks of the creek, but Quantrill's men easily repulsed them. The Federal commander led another charge on foot. He came as close as fifty paces to Quantrill's line when Todd shot him down with his shotgun. The rest of the guerrillas joined in with their pistols, driving the Federals once again from the hill.

After the surviving Union troops had withdrawn, Quantrill's men captured the horses, scavenged firearms from the dead, and scattered into the countryside. The Federals' frustration, however, was not yet over. The retreating Union patrol approached Peabody's mauled command, and the latter mistook the former for guerrillas. Several volleys were exchanged between the two groups, resulting in several killed or wounded before Peabody discovered his mistake.

Quantrill ordered his men to reassemble at Reuben Harris's farm along the Little Blue on April 4. By operating in small bands of ten men and usually not more than forty, he lessened the burden of finding sustenance for his men. Instead, they were fed and their animals given forage by individual farmers. When operations warranted and a mission called for a larger number of soldiers, Quantrill's muster call reached the designated men, and within a few days he had all the well-armed and well-mounted soldiers he desired.

After the fights at the Tate and Clark home, the Federals believed that Quantrill and his men were left on foot. They considered themselves the hounds with the fox at bay. Peabody circulated a report that Quantrill's guerrillas were disorganized and on the run. He called for assistance from the other area outposts to bring in Quantrill and the remainder of his band. For this reason, the Federals concentrated on Jackson County with a vengeance. Plunder, however, was not an issue.

Given carte blanche to operate at will against the civilian community, jayhawkers and state militia alike scoured the countryside and exhibited a cruelty toward noncombatants unparalleled in history. Old men and young boys were murdered, women were raped, and homes went up in flames.

Feeling frustrated at being outgunned and outfoxed by the wily guerrilla chief, Peabody satisfied himself by burning everything on the Clark farm. Three days later, still looking for Quantrill, Union troops burned Frank Smith's home in Blue Springs. As they were leaving the Smith home, they were fired on by the two Smith boys, who managed to kill at least two Federals. Half a mile away, Warren Welch and another guerrilla also fired on the Federals and killed six of them and one of their horses.[38]

Amos Blythe, a local farmer and a close friend of Cole Younger, owned a farm ten miles south of Independence on the old Independence to Harrisonville road. Here Younger had a camp on the east fork of the Little Blue River just across the valley of the Little Blue from the Reuben Harris farm. Albert P. Peabody, now the commander at Independence, sent a scouting party of more than thirty men to find Younger or to get the residents to reveal where he might be found.

Blythe was warned that the Federals were coming. He kept away from his house that day, but the Union troops did find twelve-year-old Theodore at home. They took the boy to the barn and threatened to hang him if he did not tell them what they wanted to know. Young Blythe was not intimidated. He occupied them with conversation for several minutes until he saw an opportunity to escape back to the house. When he made a dash for the house, the Federals fired at him. Once inside he grabbed a pistol and made a mad run through the back door to the safety of some nearby timber. Theodore was mortally wounded before he could get through the yard and past the garden fence. He rolled himself over as the jayhawkers rushed toward him, and he killed the first one to come near him. His second shot mortally wounded a second man, and his third severely wounded another. Before he could fire a fourth time, seventeen bullets pierced his body.[39]

The jayhawkers headed back to Independence. An old black man belonging to neighbor William Moore was on an errand at Blythe's house at the time and witnessed the bloody deed. Afraid for his life, he ran into the brush. There he came unawares upon Younger, Quantrill, Haller, Todd, and eleven other men. Noticing the great excitement of the black man, they coaxed the story from him. There was yet time for an ambuscade.

On the road back to Independence was a pass between two embankments—the Blue Cut. It was about fifty yards wide and thirty feet high, offering both good observation and a good field of fire. The enemy would be helpless in the killing zone, but the guerrillas would be protected behind the terrain features. Quantrill stationed some men at each end of the passageway and some atop either side to guard the likely avenues of approach. The guerrillas lay on their bellies, behind bushes or small trees with their weapons held at the ready.

It seemed like an eternity before the enemy appeared. The anticipation was almost past enduring. After a few minutes, tense, nervous muscles began to tighten. Weapons once locked firmly on target now began to weave perceptibly. Quantrill, sensing their anxiousness, spoke low in an almost inaudible whisper, "Steady boys! Get ready." Quantrill's calm, soothing voice brought them back on task.

Steel muzzles inched forward and firmly locked on the arriving targets. On command, more than a dozen pistols, rifles, and shotguns belched leaden death on the unsuspecting soldiers in the bushy defile. Of the thirty-eight Federals sent after Cole Younger, seventeen were killed. Five barely managed to escape back to Independence. This fatal point of the Blue Cut was afterward known as the "Slaughter Pen."[40]

Following the ambush in the Blue Cut, Quantrill crossed the narrow valley of the Little Blue and camped at Reuben Harris's house, eight miles south of Independence. Keeping always on the move, the next night Quantrill's men camped at the farm of Job Crabtree in Brooking Township, just a mile southwest of the Harris home. Crabtree lived on high ground surrounded by timber and a well-fed stream and overlooking the bottoms on the west side of the Little Blue River. The trail was hilly and narrow, burrowing its way along the winding path that led beside the valley. Every now and then an opening in the dense timber exposed a few acres of tilled soil and a house.

After only one night at Crabtree's, Quantrill headed another mile south to another camp. At each house in which he stayed, Quantrill managed to gather news of Federal movements. On the evening of April 15, Quantrill's men were camped close to the abandoned farmhouse of Jordon Lowe. Concealed in the thick timber, his men tried to get some much needed sleep. About ten o'clock that night the sky suddenly became overcast, a fresh wind blew from the east, and rain fell in torrents. The rain continued until around 4 A.M.[41]

The guerrillas were forced to seek shelter in the house. They hitched their horses to a fence behind it. The building, however, had only one door, which faced south and had a bar across it for safety. Quantrill failed to post a picket on this unpleasant night and soon faced the consequences.

Albert P. Peabody continued to track Quantrill. Lt. Col. Egbert B. Brown of the Seventh Missouri Cavalry was also in on the hunt. Under Brown's command, Lt. G. W. Nash and two hundred mounted men followed Quantrill into Brooking Township. Spies in the neighborhood of the Lowe house had informed Nash that Quantrill was staying in the timber but had gone into the abandoned house during the night.

Unlike the guerrillas, Nash and his men were well equipped for the weather. They waited for the guerrillas to settle down then surrounded the house and captured the guerrillas' horses. At approximately 5:30 A.M. Nash ordered his men to open fire on the one-story log structure's only exit—the front door. In the loft of the house slept George Todd, Andy Blunt, William Kerr, and Joseph Gilchrist.[42]

The first volley startled the guerrillas out of their sleep, but they quickly managed to return fire. Quantrill called out to his men, "Boys, the Red Legs have got us completely surrounded." After his two previous shootouts with the jayhawkers, Quantrill knew it was fruitless to engage the enemy. The Federal commander ceased firing to call for the guerrillas' surrender, and Quantrill asked for three minutes. Quantrill told his men: "Boys, we must charge through them, and as soon as we get safe in the saddle open fire on them."[43]

With the morning being overcast and visibility poor, he ordered his men to abandon the house. The men in the loft, however, failed to hear the order. The guerrillas on the main floor escaped through the mud in their stocking feet. Yet when Quantrill noticed that all of his men had not made it out of the house, they all turned back. Four guerrillas made their way to the corners of the house and returned fire. Above the din of battle they hollered for their comrades in the loft to get out. Only Todd managed to escape. Gilchrist was wounded, and he and Andy Blunt and William Kerr were taken prisoner.

It was four hundred yards from the house to the next closest shelter. One guerrilla was killed, a young Irish boy who was a new recruit. Five Federals were killed in the fight. Even though Quantrill's loses were light, the casualties continued to reduce his command.

Immediately after the fight the Federals shot Blunt and Gilchrist. Gilchrist was killed, but Blunt suffered only a broken arm.

Quantrill and the survivors made for the Little Blue River over a mile away. Because it had been raining so hard, the banks were soon overflowing. Unmounted, out of ammunition, and with Federal troops swarming all around him, Quantrill knew that he and his men were lucky to be alive. G. W. Nash guessed that Quantrill would head for the Little Blue, so within an hour his patrol moved in that direction, too.

On the swollen banks of the river, Quantrill wondered how he and his men would get across. Just then he saw one of his men, William Toler, in a canoe on the opposite bank. Within minutes Quantrill's small band was on the other bank and waiting for the Federals to catch up. When Nash's command approached the river, they expected to find Quantrill's stranded band, but instead they received a deadly volley from the opposite shore.

Being without horses and lacking arms and ammunition, Quantrill ordered his men to disband for a month to find new mounts and rearm themselves. To resupply their dwindling supply of pistol caps, Quantrill and Todd ventured to Hannibal and St. Louis disguised as Federal officers. In Quantrill's absence, William Gregg led the guerrillas, operating in small bands to disrupt the mail and hinder communication in western Missouri.

Quantrill and Todd would travel to St. Louis by railroad. First, they rode to Hamilton, a short distance north of Kansas City. In Hamilton they secured a place to stay in the principal hotel then made the acquaintance of the town's Union commander. A Federal regiment was stationed in Hamilton, and when Quantrill was asked to account for himself, he claimed to be a major with the Ninth Missouri Cavalry and Todd a major with the Sixth Missouri Cavalry. Intrigued by their postings, the commander inquired if they were acquainted with Quantrill and if there was any truth to the stories he had heard about him. In response, Quantrill described his exploits in detail. At the close of their conversation, the disguised guerrilla leader concluded: "If you were here, Colonel, surrounded as you are by a thousand soldiers, and they wanted you, they would come and get you."[44] Two days later, Quantrill and Todd took the train to St. Louis.

Cautiously the two guerrillas purchased fifty thousand revolver caps, spreading their acquisitions over several days and several stores. With their task complete they traveled back by the same route but detoured to spend the night in St. Joseph.

St. Joseph was garrisoned by hundreds of Federal soldiers, but Quantrill and Todd were nothing if not determined. Cautiously they extended their purchases to several more thousand revolver caps as well as revolvers. As the two guerrillas discovered in Hamilton, the regimental colonel in Hannibal was also anxious to swap stories with the two majors. For his part, Quantrill added to his information about the other officers in this area. One in particular, William Penick, from St. Joseph, would soon be a noted rival. Sending their purchases into Jackson County with a trusted friend, Quantrill and Todd made the last leg of their return in a hired hack until they came to the Missouri River.[45]

During Quantrill's absence, attacks on the mail coaches forced the authorities to detach an entire company of Federal cavalry to escort the mail. These troops traveled along known routes and on set schedules, giving the guerrillas valuable targets of opportunity to ambush.

On April 18, only two days after the Lowe house fight, the *Kansas City Journal* reported that a cavalry company would be escorting the mail to Pleasant Hill. The guerrillas resorted to a favorite ruse to lure the Federals into an ambush. Riding nonchalantly in the open, a few guerrillas would show themselves; when the Federals gave chase, the guerrillas would lead them into an ambush.

As usual the guerrillas operated in the area most noted for ambushes along the old Independence to Harrisonville road, six miles south of Independence. Bordering the road was heavy timber. Southern sympathizers owned the farms in the region, and it was here that Quantrill and his lieutenants made their camps. The hills were covered with rock outcroppings, the valley floor ran plentiful with water, and the timber gave ample cover and concealment. Within a short time, the vicinity became synonymous with the word *ambush*.

If properly planned and executed, ambushes are the most effective military encounter in which a small force can engage. The attacking party risks little but gains much in terms of hurting and demoralizing an enemy. Many self-taught leaders made their reputations with the military tactics of the time. Guerrilla tactics developed during the eighteenth century were still studied and used at the beginning of the Civil War. The most notable of these was Maj. Robert Rogers's standing orders for the guerrilla unit known as Rogers's Rangers during the French and Indian War. Seventeen of the nineteen orders were applicable in the mid-nineteenth century:

1. Don't forget nothing.
2. Have your musket clean as a whistle, hatchet scoured, sixty rounds powder and ball, and be ready to march at a minute's warning.
3. When you're on the march, act the way you would if you was sneaking up on a deer. See the enemy first.
4. Tell the truth about what you see and do. There is an army depending on us for correct information. You can tell all you like when you tell folks about the Rangers, but don't never lie to a Ranger or an officer.
5. Don't never take a chance you don't have to.
6. When we're on the march we march single file, far enough apart so one shot can't go through two men.

7. If we strike swamps or soft ground, we spread out abreast, so it's hard to track us.
8. When we march, we keep moving till dark, so as to give the enemy the least possible chance at us.
9. When we camp, half the party stays awake while the other half sleeps.
10. If we take prisoners, we keep 'em separate till we have time to examine them, so they can't cook up a story between 'em.
11. Don't ever march home the same way. Take a different route so you won't be ambushed.
12. No matter whether we travel in big parties or small ones, each party has to keep a scout about 20 yards ahead, 20 yards on each flank, and 20 yards in the rear, so the main body can't be surprised and wiped out.
13. Every night you'll be told where to meet if surrounded by a superior force.
14. Don't sit down to eat without posting sentries.
15. Don't sleep beyond dawn. Dawn's when the French and Indians attack.
16. Don't cross a river by a regular ford.
17. If somebody's trailing you, make a circle, come back onto your own track, and ambush the folks that aim to ambush you.[46]

Such tactics enabled Quantrill's company to terrorize the Federals stationed along the border.

Back in Jackson County, Quantrill maintained the mail raids and exacted a heavy toll on the Union cavalry escorts. To protect themselves and the mail, the Federals forced civilians to ride with them as human shields. For guerrilla John McCorkle, a former Missouri State Guardsman who tried to renounce the war and return to farming, this matter of human shields swung him back in the saddle and riding with Quantrill:

I fully intended, when I started in to raise this crop with my uncle [John Fristoe] to remain a quiet, law-abiding citizen. I had taken the oath of allegiance at Springfield and had been given a passport, showing to the world that I was a law-abiding American citizen and still entitled to protection under the law, but before the ink was hardly dry on that passport, I had been robbed of all I had, and that by men who claimed to be in the service of the United States government. I tried to forget these outrages and work on the farm, but before I had gotten my crop planted, a squad of Federal soldiers came by and compelled me twice a week to accompany them with a mail carrier twelve or fifteen miles then to walk back.[47]

As part of McCorkle's oath of allegiance, he was required to post a five-thousand-dollar bond guaranteeing that he would not take up arms against the United States. To coerce him to fight for the Union, the Federals threatened to imprison his cousin Mollie if he did not enlist in the loyal militia.

To combat the guerrilla activities around the state, Gen. John M. Schofield issued General Orders No. 18 on May 29, 1862: "The time is passed when insurrection and rebellion in Missouri can cloak itself under the guise of honorable warfare. The utmost vigilance and energy are enjoined upon all the troops of the State in hunting down and destroying these robbers and assassins. When caught in arms, engaged in their unlawful warfare, they will be shot down upon the spot."[48]

In Jackson County, Schofield's order did not perceptibly affect Quantrill's activities. Shortly afterward Schofield was granted authority from Missouri's provisional governor, Hamilton Gamble, to draft "every able-bodied man in Missouri capable of bearing arms and subject to military duty to report to the nearest military post." These efforts did nothing to curb guerrilla warfare. In fact, they drove many draftable men into the guerrilla ranks, because they would rather defend their homes than fight in the Federal service.[49]

For his part, Quantrill wreaked havoc in western Missouri, controlling 2,500 square miles in Jackson, Cass, Johnson, and Lafayette Counties. He did this with usually less than one hundred men at his command. In comparison, the well-known Confederate partisan John Singleton Mosby of Virginia, in command of eight hundred men, only maintained control over parts of Loudoun and Fauquier Counties, covering 125 square miles. The people of Virginia looked upon Mosby's men just as Missourians looked on Quantrill's. One Southerner wrote, "They had for us all the glamour of Robin Hood and his merry men, all the courage and bravery of the ancient crusaders, the unexpectedness of benevolent pirates and the stealth of Indians."

Quantrill became the hero of Jackson County. He had attacked the Federal garrison in Independence and survived numerous deadly engagements like the actions at the David Tate house, the Samuel Clark farm, and the Jordon Lowe property in Brooking Township. He had fought his way out of every one of these engagements unscathed while confronting an overwhelming force of the enemy. In May he had even ridden boldly into the Federals' own camp in Hannibal and purchased weapons and ammunition.

Throughout June and July 1862, Quantrill's men continued to operate all over western Missouri. Their numbers increased each day. They ambushed mail escorts and patrols in Jackson, Johnson, and Cass Counties. On June 22 they ambushed a Missouri River steamboat, the *Little Blue*, which they caught by surprise at a landing near Sibley. Forty sick and wounded Union soldiers were terrorized, and large quantities of military supplies were carried away.[50] During this time Col. John T. Burris skirmished with the guerrillas in southeastern Jackson County. He brought with him several pieces of artillery but found it was useless against the fast-moving light cavalry tactics of the guerrillas.

During this time great strides had been made in the recognition of partisan warfare. On April 21, 1862, the Confederate Congress passed an act authorizing Jefferson Davis to commission officers with authority to form bands of partisan rangers. An interpretation of the act by the Confederate War Department on April 28 authorized the commanders of military departments in which partisan units operated to recruit and muster all applications for irregular service. Partisan units were to be entitled to the same pay, rations, and quarters as regular army soldiers.[51]

Gen. Thomas Hindman was in charge of the district of the Trans-Mississippi Department, which included Missouri. Relying on the original wording of the partisan service act, on July 17 Hindman issued orders covering irregular service:

> For the more effectual annoyance of the enemy upon our rivers and in our mountains and woods, all citizens of this district who are not subject to conscription are called upon to organize themselves into independent companies of mounted men or infantry, as they prefer, arming and equipping themselves, and to serve in that part of the district to which they belong.
>
> When as many as ten men come together for this purpose, they may organize by electing a captain, one sergeant, one corporal, and will at once commence operations against the enemy without waiting for special instructions. Their duty will be to cut off Federal pickets, scouts, foraging parties, and trains, and to kill pilots and others on gunboats and transports, attacking them day and night, and using the greatest vigor in their movements. As soon as the company attains the strength required by law it will proceed to elect the other officers to which it is entitled. All such organizations will be reported to these headquarters as soon as practicable. They will receive pay and allowances for subsistence and forage for the time actually in the field, as established by the affidavits of their captains.

These companies will be governed in all respects by the same regulations as other troops. Captains will be held responsible for the good conduct and efficiency of their men, and will report to these headquarters from time to time.[52]

As soon as Quantrill learned of Hindman's order, he organized his band accordingly and set about to execute the general's directives.

By early July, Quantrill's band was organized into an independent partisan military unit according to the laws of the Confederate government. The *Richmond Dispatch* described partisan warfare as "beyond doubt, the most attractive branch of the service" and predicted it would attract the attention "of all young men of daring and adventurous natures."

In mid-1862 Quantrill's ranks had swollen to more than a hundred men. Quantrill was ranked a captain, William Haller was listed as first lieutenant, George Todd was second lieutenant, William H. Gregg was the first sergeant, John Jarrette was the second sergeant, James L. Tucker was third sergeant, Andrew Blunt was fourth sergeant, Ferdinand (a.k.a. Fernando) M. Scott was the commissary, and Richard Maddox was the quartermaster.

While riding through southern Jackson County on July 6, Quantrill's company came across Capt. Henry J. Stieslin's Company A, First Missouri Cavalry. A brief skirmish ensued with the result of one of Quantrill's orderly sergeants being killed. Found upon his body was a muster roll listing ninety-three members of Quantrill's command by name. The list was quickly sent to Federal headquarters in Jefferson City then on to departmental headquarters in St. Louis. Obtaining a list of Quantrill's men by name was a stroke of luck to the Union commanders. Now there was no guesswork about who were Southern sympathizers and whose sons or relatives rode with Quantrill. Over the following weeks the men whose names were on the list were hunted down and killed wherever and whenever they were found. The guerrillas' only protection was to stay together.

Many of the names on the list were a revelation to the Federal authorities. Prior to this many of these men were not viewed as being disloyal. When the Federals could not find the men whose names were on the list, they turned their attention to the men's families and accused them of giving aid and comfort to the enemy.

Cole Younger's name was on the list, and the Federals had never considered him a guerrilla. Younger's father, Henry, tried to be neutral in the conflict. His horses were in great demand, and he sold them to both Unionists and Southerners. Yet jayhawkers continued to raid his five farms.

On July 20, exactly two weeks after the guerrillas' skirmish with Stieslin, according to Cole, Henry Younger traveled from Harrisonville to Kansas City to meet with someone at Federal headquarters to see what could be done about the plundering jayhawker raids that plagued his farms. His mission accomplished, Henry headed back home with fifteen hundred dollars tucked in his money belt. Several miles from Independence he was killed by ten Union soldiers. They took his watch and a diamond stud but did not find his money belt.[53] The body was immediately discovered by Mrs. Washington Wells and her son, Samuel. She guarded the body while her son ran back to Kansas City and reported the murder.

Cole Younger noted that the body was undisturbed until claimed by the Federal authorities, who returned the body to Harrisonville along with the money belt. Within hours of the murder, the soldiers responsible bragged of killing "Cole Younger's pappy."[54] The murder was a direct result of Cole's name being found on the muster roll of Quantrill's rangers. In his memoirs, Cole reported that Capt. Irvin Walley of the Fifth Missouri State Militia from Harrisonville was arrested for the murder of Henry Younger; he was released when fellow soldiers provided an alibi for him.[55]

The muster list became a death list because so many of Quantrill's men were related to one another. Hiram George's name was on the list. As a result, George recalled, "They burned and took everything I had. Killed my father. Hung my brother."[56] The Federals often murdered all the men of a guerrilla's family, burned down their homes, confiscated their property, and stole their livestock. These cruelties did not, however, weaken the resolve of Quantrill's men. As John McCorkle had learned, even if a man wanted to put down his weapons and live in peace, the Federals would not allow it. By threatening and bullying and harassing and killing members of the guerrillas' families, the Federal authorities drove six men into the ranks of the guerrillas for every one they tried to eradicate. The Union army also learned that these vengeful men were much more ferocious and effective fighters than those who fought only for a cause.

5

Band of Brothers

> But we . . . shall be remember'd;
> We few, we happy few, we band of brothers,
> For he to-day that sheds his blood with me
> Shall be my brother.

HENRY V, ACT 4

UANTRILL DID NOT PICK his men; they were delivered to him by fate. They gave one another their complete trust. They were willing to guard something more precious than life. Their feats and accomplishments were known throughout the country. They carried by reputation the memory of one another. It was one of the reasons they were willing to die for one another. They were ordinary young Americans from all walks of life who answered their country's call to arms, endured unimaginable hardships, and accomplished extraordinary feats. They fought for no personal gain, with no aspirations other than to protect their families and win their country's freedom and survive and come home.

Most of them were farm boys. Their families had come mainly from Kentucky, Tennessee, and Virginia. They were hardworking, God-fearing people who worked the land, built new homes and churches, ran for office and became financially comfortable, some even well-to-do. When the border troubles started in the 1850s, most were too young to take part. The Missourians who had traveled across the state line to vote in territorial Kansas were older men by the start of the war, but their sons held to their fathers' views on government and justice. The border war in Missouri was a war of revenge, unlike the eastern theater where principles for an ideal inspired many to choose loyalty to their state over the dictates of the central government.

Those who first gathered around Quantrill had their own stories. John Newman Edwards described why these young men became guerrillas:

As strange as it may seem the perilous fascination of fighting under a "Black Flag" where the wounded could have neither surgeon nor hospital, and where all that remained to the prisoners was the absolute certainty of speedy death, attracted a number of young men to the various guerrilla bands, gently nurtured, born to high destinies, capable of sustained exertion in any scheme or enterprise, and fit for callings high up in their scale of science or philosophy. Others came who had deadly wrongs to avenge, and these gave to all their combats that sanguinary hue, which still remains a part of the guerrilla's legacy. Almost from the first a large majority of Quantrill's original command had over them the shadow of some terrible crime. This one recalled a father murdered, this one a brother waylaid and shot, this one a house pillaged and burnt, this one a relative assassinated, this one a grievous insult while at peace at home, this one a robbery of all his earthly possessions, this one the force, which compelled him to witness the brutal treatment of a mother or sister, this one was driven away from his own like a thief in the night, this one was threatened with death for opinion's sake, this one was proscribed at the instance of some designing neighbor, this one was arrested wantonly and forced to do the degrading work of a menial; while all had more or less of wrath laid up against the day when they were to meet face to face and hand to hand those whom they had good cause to regard as the living embodiment of unnumbered wrongs. Honorable soldiers in the Confederate army, amenable to every generous impulse and exact in the performance of every manly duty, deserted even the ranks, which they had adorned and became desperate guerrillas because the home they had left had been given to the flames, or a gray-haired father shot upon his own hearth-stone. . . . The war had then passed into its fever heat, and thereafter the gentle and the merciful, equally with the harsh and the revengeful, spared nothing clad in blue that could be captured.[1]

One by one they came into Quantrill's camp already touched by the horrors of war. William M. Haller was twenty years old when Quantrill enlisted him as his first recruit. Known for his bravery and daring, Haller was elected as the company's first lieutenant. He fought in all the skirmishes and battles up to the winter of 1862 then had a falling out with brash George Todd, by then Quantrill's second in command. Haller left the guerrillas and joined the regular Confederate army.

Soon after Haller joined Quantrill, his brother, George Washington Haller, joined the guerrillas. George had been educated at Chapel Hill College and was a schoolmate of Confederate Gen. Francis M. Cockrell.[2]

Another of Quantrill's first recruits was Andrew "Andy" Walker, a son of Morgan Walker. Andy was twenty-five years old when he married Elizabeth Bradin on April 12, 1860, just before the war started. Born in Jackson County, he lived just east of his father's two-thousand-acre farm in Blue Springs. In December 1861 four hundred jayhawkers robbed Andrew Walker of his stock and equipment and burned his farm to the ground. The raid turned him against anyone who wore a Federal uniform. He joined Quantrill to avenge his loss. After the war, because he belonged to Quantrill's company, he could not return to Missouri but settled in Texas, where he died around 1910.

George Todd rose to the rank of captain under Quantrill. His father was from Scotland and had served in the British navy. Like his father, Todd was an engineer and built railroad trestles in England. When he was eighteen, he killed a man and fled with his father to Canada then to the United States. They ended up working as stonemasons in Kansas City. Because of his father's occupation, the Federals wanted the elder Todd to enlist as a Union engineer to design and build fortifications. In particular, the Federal authorities wanted his help with the construction of Fort Union on the Coates House Hotel foundation in Kansas City. When he refused he was imprisoned and given skimpy rations. Confined in a cold, damp cell, Todd's father became somewhat incapacitated, and a neighbor came to the prison to help feed him.[3] When Todd's father finally surrendered to his captors' demands, he was sent to Virginia to work on Union fortifications there.

On December 9, 1861, George Todd married Hannah Catherine Todd, who stayed in Kansas City and lived in the house belonging to her father-in-law.[4] Todd told his comrades that he had married his brother's widow to keep her from marrying a Union officer. Todd was described as a smooth-faced young man of twenty, six feet tall, blue eyes, dark straight hair, dark complexion, and high cheekbones. He was known to be a formidable fighter and brave but also overbearing, quick tempered, and strong willed. Consequently, he was not personally popular among the other guerrillas—except for his fighting qualities.[5] Some even described him as being tyrannical even though he was known to be popular with children. Children would run to him because he brought them candy to exchange for any lead they might find, which the guerrillas could use to make bullets. Harrison Trow described Todd:

In repose a little stern . . . and a circumspect regard for his word made him a very true, but sometimes a very blunt man. . . . By and by the guerrillas themselves felt confidence in such a name, reliance in such an arm, favor for such a face. It was sufficient for Todd to order a march to be implicitly followed; to plan an expedition to have it immediately carried out; to indicate a spot on which to assemble to cause an organization sometimes widely scattered or dispersed to come together as the jaws of a steel trap. If one word could be used to describe George Todd it can be said that he was courageous. There were only two of the guerrillas who would fight in a battle just like in a personal difficulty: George Todd and Dick Kinney. They would get mad in a battle just like in a fistfight.

Kate King, Quantrill's wife, said that she had known George Todd as a small child, and that he was her best friend among Quantrill's men.

Joseph Gilchrist was recruited in Blue Springs and joined Quantrill because of the jayhawker raids upon his neighborhood. His valiant fight against Federal despotism ended less than six months later, however. William H. Gregg wrote that he was killed during the April 12, 1862, fight at the Jordon Lowe house in Brooking Township.[6]

In 1860 Perry Hoy was twenty-three years old and living in Johnson County, Kansas. Apparently he was driven from Kansas at the start of the war because of his Southern sympathies. Hoy was with Quantrill up until the Tate house fight in March 1862, when he was knocked unconscious and taken prisoner while the guerrillas were making their escape. Hoy was later hanged at Fort Leavenworth. After reading of Hoy's death in the newspaper, Quantrill launched a retaliatory raid into Kansas and killed ten Union soldiers because the Federal authorities refused to exchange Hoy for one of their own held by Quantrill.

John Little was from Blue Springs, Missouri, living in the Sni-A-Bar Township of Jackson County. Little was twenty-three when he first joined Quantrill at the beginning of the war, but he too was with Quantrill for only a little more than six months. He was killed in an ambush on July 31, 1862, by a patrol from Independence, shot down while he was crossing the Little Blue River. Two other guerrillas were with him at the time: George Todd and Ed Koger. Koger was also killed. Todd escaped and avenged his ambushed colleagues in the August 11, 1862, attack on Independence. There he rushed to the jail and found Sheriff James Knowles, who had led the Federals to the ambush site, behind bars in his own jail. Todd shot him in his cell.

Jim Little was John's seventeen-year-old brother. He joined up with his other brother, Thomas. Jim Little was best known as Quantrill's closest friend. They looked out for each other throughout the entire war, and Jim was always by Quantrill's side during battle. The youth also rode with Quantrill on the Lawrence raid. He was wounded at Fayette, Missouri, on September 20, 1864. Quantrill helped to keep him in the saddle and later tended his wounds. Jim Little recuperated sufficiently to participate in the Centralia battle a week later on September 27. By this time he was a second lieutenant. At the close of the war, he went to Kentucky with Quantrill.

Joseph Vaughn stayed in Quantrill's band for approximately one year before joining the regular Confederate army. He was killed at the 1862 battle of Pea Ridge, Arkansas.

James Vaughn was listed in Quantrill's company as early as July 6, 1862. He was captured and hanged in Kansas City on May 29, 1863, at Fort Union. Confederate Col. Benjamin F. Parker hanged four Union soldiers to avenge Vaughn's death.[7] Vaughn's brother Daniel also rode with Quantrill.

Another of the seven to join Quantrill in Blue Springs was William H. Gregg. He was twenty-two when he joined Quantrill on January 11, 1862, and was elected first sergeant. Soon he became Quantrill's third lieutenant but often commanded a company. Gregg was tall, sober faced, easygoing, shy, never boastful, and conscientious. He had long black hair.[8] His first action was at the first battle in Missouri, the June 13, 1861, battle of Rock Creek.[9] Afterward Gregg was a captain in the Missouri State Guard attached to Rosser's regiment in Rains's division.

He returned home after his enlistment expired and found that his uncle, David Gregg, had been killed for being a Southern sympathizer. Accounts state that Jennison personally executed Gregg's uncle. Gregg's fiancée, Elizabeth Hook, to whom he had been engaged for more than two years, also drew the enmity of the Northerners. They jailed her father, stole every horse, slaughtered every pig, and seized the family's slaves, money, jewelry, and even the bedclothes. After the war Gregg wrote several articles that came to be known as the William Gregg manuscripts. His writings offer excellent descriptions of Quantrill and the Quantrillians, giving great insight into their lives and actions.

As Quantrill's adjutant, Gregg was often the man closest to the guerrilla leader. He noted, "Quantrill was very mild in his manner. He was well informed, and was not given to profanity, nor was he brutal." When comparing Quantrill to other guerrilla leaders, Gregg remarked, "[George] Todd and [Bill] Anderson were much alike. They were both brave to a fault and maniacs in battle. They had no regard for the lives of their men. I have often seen them cry and froth at the mouth in battle simply because they could not kill a whole regiment of the enemy in a few minutes. Not so with Quantrill, who had the greatest care for the lives of his men." In return, Gregg was described by his fellow soldiers as "never being known to decline an opportunity to engage in battle. He was a dashing, fearless, enterprising soldier."[10]

Gregg had a sixteen-year-old brother, Jacob Franklin Gregg, who rode with Quantrill for some time. Jacob served in John Jarrette's company and later under George Todd as a lieutenant until Todd was killed just before the October 23, 1864, battle of Westport. At the start of the war, Jacob was imprisoned because his brother was with Quantrill. After his release, Jacob joined the Missouri State Guard under Sterling Price before joining Andrew Blunt's company of guerrillas under Quantrill.

According to Quantrill's July 6, 1862, muster roll, James A. Hendricks was a third deputy sergeant. He later rose in rank to serve as a lieutenant under William H. Gregg. Hendricks was killed on July 11, 1862, in Pleasant Hill, at the Battle of the Ravines.

John William Koger was born near Independence on March 23, 1834, and joined Quantrill in December 1861. He later became a captain. Koger fought in all the major engagements with Quantrill's raiders, including the August 11, 1862, battle of Independence and probably at White Oak Creek in southern Jackson County a week later. He was also on the Lawrence raid and at the battles of Fayette and Centralia in September 1864.

Gregg referred to Koger as one of the most fearless men in the band, and the man had the injuries to prove it. Koger was wounded in twelve different engagements during the war, including the October 1863 action at Baxter Springs. At the time of his death, he still had five bullets in his body. At one time he bore eight wounds after a fight and removed three of the bullets himself with a knife.

After the war, Koger married Elizabeth Bowman, daughter of the Reverend Hiram Bowman, the Baptist minister in Oak Grove, Missouri. John's twenty-three-year-old brother, Edward, was killed at the same time as John Little in the July 31, 1862, ambush at the Little Blue River.

Morgan T. Mattox was only fifteen years old when he claimed to have witnessed the killing of the first Federal soldier in Jackson County. Charles Jennison had seized Mattox during one of his raids in the county, and so he observed firsthand as the jayhawkers looted Missouri homesteads. Mattox reported the jayhawkers had thousands of dollars' worth of goods they had stolen from several families of the Six-Mile Township of Jackson County. He saw three of Jennison's drunken soldiers kill prisoner Sel Stark. Mattox escaped his captors, quickly found Quantrill, and became a guerrilla. In August 1861 Quantrill invited him to ride with him to thwart a raid in the Blue Springs neighborhood. Mattox said that Quantrill would not accept anyone into his band that was not "moved by injury to selves or family, imbued with malice and bent on revenge."[11] Mattox was also at the August 1862 battle of Independence.

A Kansas City paper commented on the guerrillas and the effectiveness of the warfare they waged:

> They were welded together by the hammer strokes of adversity. When danger was too great they scattered; when there was no danger they broke into squads. These squads became the nuclei of companies, which elected captains. Each man aligned himself under the leader whom he believed would give the greatest opportunity for quick and desperate action.[12]

Quantrill's recruits were mainly from the Blue Springs area of Jackson County, having farms in the Sni-A-Bar Township . They all knew each other, and because of the jayhawker raids on their neighborhoods and the barbarity directed toward their families and neighbors, they were among the first to join Quantrill. In the beginning the band was a neighborhood protection organization. The guerrillas patrolled the roadways and camped in the woods until they heard that jayhawkers were coming. Then they came together to give battle and drive the invaders back to Kansas.

After the October 27, 1861, raid on the Brooking and Big Cedar Townships in which twenty-seven homes were put to the torch, young men saddled their horses, grabbed whatever arms they had, and went in search of Quantrill's camp. There were other guerrilla groups in the county, but Quantrill's was known to have tangible results.

Never before had cavalry been used as an independent command. Quantrill's innovations in light cavalry tactics are still practiced today. His mode of warfare heavily damaged the enemy's lines of communication and supply. He also weakened the Federal armies in the East by draining off much needed men to garrison the western border. He never had more than four hundred men at one time under his command, but Quantrill and sixty other partisan companies in Missouri—numbering only four thousand guerrillas— kept twenty thousand Federals from joining the Union Army of the Potomac.

Quantrill did much to lower morale in the Federal commands in Missouri and Kansas. His audacity and success destroyed the confidence of Union commanders as much as his battlefield victories. To achieve this success, Quantrill had to be bold and resourceful. His men had to be well-disciplined, excellent horsemen, able woodsmen, and expert shots. His troops lived off the land, carrying only the minimum amount of clothing and equipment.

After Charles Jennison's jayhawking expedition in the fall of 1861, many young men left their burned-out homes and found whatever horses that hadn't been stolen and made their way to Quantrill's camp. They were men like H. C. Cogswell from Vernon County, Missouri, who joined Quantrill after Jennison plundered his property, and like Howard Bragg, whose father's house was burned and his cattle stolen.

Guerrilla John Brinker's sister and younger brother were imprisoned for aiding Quantrill's men. Mattie Brinker was seized in the spring of 1862, along with other Southern girls, and used as human shields while the Federals scoured the bush looking for guerrillas.

Federals burned down the home of William McCoy's mother. Seventeen-year-old William "Buck" Fields from Independence joined Quantrill in 1862. Kansas Redlegs had killed his father in 1861, so his twenty-one-year-old brother Rip and his nineteen-year-old brother Kip joined Quantrill. Buck first joined Jo Shelby's army in August 1861 then joined Quantrill the following year after Federals reportedly raped two of his cousins. Fields was at the battle of Lone Jack in August 1862, following in the footsteps of his grandfathers, both of whom were veterans of the War of 1812.

William Halley was born in Frankfort, Kentucky, and came to Missouri in 1850. He was nineteen years old in 1861 when he was jailed in Independence by Jennison's men for killing two jayhawkers who had invaded his mother's home. Then Quantrill's band raided the jail, scattering the Union soldiers and freeing the prisoners—all of whom were jailed because they were Southern sympathizers. Any who wanted to join Sterling Price's army were furnished with horses and equipped for the journey, but many—including Halley—threw in their lot with Quantrill. To avoid reprisals, Halley's family fled Independence for Weston, Missouri, where they remained for twenty years.[13]

In contrast to the harsh realities around them, the guerrillas, rather than being morose or sullen, were often gregarious and cheerful in camp. Frank James had this first recollection of his leader and colleagues: "I will never forget the first time I saw Quantrill. He was nearly six feet in height, rather thin, his hair and moustache was sandy and he was full of life and a jolly fellow. He had none of the air of the bravado or the desperado about him. We all loved him at first sight and every man under his command was tried and true. He was a demon in battle and did not know what it was to be afraid." Andrew Jack Liddil was only twelve years old when he joined Quantrill's band. After the war he became a judge in Independence and remembered that Quantrill "was a young man, dashing, handsome and full of spirit."

Whenever a squad of guerrillas visited an isolated farmhouse and stepped down from their saddles, the farmers would cast a cautious eye about for any Federals before apprising their friends of any known enemy troop dispositions. After exchanging pleasant courtesies, the women would hurry to the kitchen to prepare a meal for their guests. The young awestruck children would stand about silently. Here before them stood dashing young men; handsome and gaily dressed, heavily armed, with a sweeping plume in their hats and high black boots adorned with large Mexican spurs.

New recruits stood out because they tended to be quiet and reticent. Most carried some token from a loved one or a memento from a home no longer standing. For some it was a lock of hair, for others a picture of a relative. Each remembrance kindled the fire of hate that burned within every man and fueled his fighting spirit. The war was personal for these men. Thus combat was not some large-scale encounter between anonymous armies, but a vendetta against a malicious foe.

Fighting under the black flag governed their actions: no prisoners. Quantrill also coached his men to leave no wounded foes behind. On occasion he chastised his subordinates when their reports showed they had left wounded Federals at the end of an encounter. A guerrilla recalled that his lieutenant had reported all but one killed. "It should be all killed, none wounded," said Quantrill. "Let it be so hereafter." The lieutenant acknowledged and rode away.[14]

John Thomas House lived in Brooking Township before the war. He was twenty-three years old when jayhawkers rampaged through his neighborhood. His father, Ephriam Eli House, lived on a farm close by. They were both God-fearing pioneers, being charter members of the West Fork of the Little Blue Baptist Church. When Charles Jennison saw the farmer working in a wooded area, he asked where his sympathies lay. The farmer told him he favored the South, so Jennison killed him then burned the house and drove away his livestock. John Thomas House was on duty with the Missouri State Guard. When he found that his father had been murdered by jayhawkers, he joined Quantrill.[15] John House had been in the first battle along the border at the Rock Creek fight. House reported that he and Randolph Venable never abandoned their homes in Brooking Township when Thomas Ewing's 1863 General Orders No. 11 evicted homeowners from four counties on the border with Kansas. Instead, House indicated, "We hid all up and down the Big and Little Blue, and folks sneaked food to us."[16]

Brothers John and Jabez McCorkle lived along the hills above the Little Blue River just a few miles south of Independence. Jabez, whose biblical name means "honor," was nineteen years old at the start of the war; John was twenty. Jabez worked as a farmhand on his uncle John Fristoe's farm in the Big Cedar Township just two miles east of the Brooking Township. Sometime in late May 1863, Jabez was leading a squad of guerrillas along the southern end of the valley of the Little Blue when he dropped his rifle and shot himself in the leg. The bullet struck him just below the right knee. He died from the wound on June 2 and was buried in Brooking Township in the old Smith Cemetery.

John McCorkle became Quantrill's chief scout. His primary duty was to be the advance guard whenever the guerrilla column made regular patrols through Jackson County. John joined Sterling Price's army early in the war and returned home after his enlistment expired. He tried to return to farming and put the war behind him, but Union authorities demanded he offer a five-thousand-dollar bond as a guarantee he would not take up arms against the North. Not satisfied with that, they then threatened to imprison his cousin, Mollie Wigginton, if he did not enlist in the Union army. McCorkle instead decided to join Quantrill. He was in every major battle and skirmish involving Quantrill's guerrillas. In 1863 his sister was imprisoned then killed when the building in which she and several other women were being held collapsed. After the war McCorkle recorded his wartime experiences in a book, *Three Years with Quantrill.*

McCorkle's best friend and cousin was twenty-year-old Thomas Harris, son of Reuben Harris. Reuben owned a farm and gristmill over the Little Blue River eight miles south of Independence. The Harrises also worshiped at the West Fork of the Little Blue Baptist Church. Their farm served as a rendezvous for Quantrill's men during the war. When Jennison raided Jackson County in 1861, his men plundered Tom's home and assaulted his sisters. Tom was also a cousin of Cole Younger. Tom's sister, Nannie, was imprisoned during the summer of 1863. Cousin Charity McCorkle Kerr was killed in the jail collapse that also killed John McCorkle's sister. Tom rode with Quantrill throughout the war.

Nathan Kerr became a guerrilla after Federal troops hanged his father. On January 26, 1860, he married Charity McCorkle, who was killed in the jail collapse.

George W. "Bud" Wigginton was a cousin of Tom Harris and John McCorkle. Frank James remembered seventeen-year-old Bud as the man who never swore and remarked, "He was a Christian if there ever was one." Bud originally joined Quantrill with his cousin, John McCorkle, after jayhawkers looted his parent's home then burned down the house. Bud's sixty-eight-year-old father, John Wigginton, was killed in front of his wife and daughter by Federals because his son was a guerrilla. Bud's two brothers fought in the Confederate army; all of the brothers were severely wounded during the war. George was one of Quantrill's closest followers and asked to go with him to Kentucky at the end of the war.[17]

Alexander Franklin James was born in Missouri on January 10, 1843. His brother, Jesse Woodson James, was born September 5, 1847, and a sister, Susan Lavenia, was born on November 25, 1849. The James family never owned slaves, but the family was outspoken regarding their Southern sympathies. Frank James was eighteen years old when he enlisted in the Confederate army at Centerville, Missouri, on May 4, 1861. Shortly after fighting at the August 10, 1861, battle of Wilson's Creek, Frank became ill with measles and was hospitalized in Springfield. Union forces then captured the hospital. Forced to pledge allegiance to the Union on April 26, 1862, Frank was released and returned home. Back home he spoke out in favor of the South and was jailed in Liberty. He signed an oath of allegiance then left home and joined Quantrill's guerrillas. Frank was a studious reader and carried the classics in his saddlebags. He was fond of quoting Shakespeare. Frank was serious and straightforward. Neither he nor his brother, Jesse, was ever known to drink. "A man's a fool to drink," he said. "It takes away his money and his brains and does him no good in any way." Frank began riding with the guerrillas under the leadership of Ferdinand Scott before both joined up with Quantrill.

Jesse James was only fourteen years old when the war began. While plowing in a cornfield behind his home in late May 1863, Jesse was suddenly surrounded by a mounted militia detail. Because he refused to disclose any information about his brother or Quantrill's camp, the soldiers whipped him with a rope and left him bleeding in the field. When he returned to his house he found his stepfather hanging from a tree and his mother desperately trying to cut him down. The Federals had ridden to the front door proclaiming: "You have been entirely too loud in your disloyal expressions and so has your wife. Furthermore, you folks are friendly to that damn cutthroat Quantrill, and you harbor his men. We've come to teach you a lesson."[18] Dr. Reuben Samuel's hands were tied behind his back, and a rope was tied around his neck then thrown over a coffee-bean tree in the yard. The soldiers yanked him off the ground several times as he gasped for breath. Finally he was hoisted off his feet, and the soldiers tied the rope to the tree and rode off. Dr. Samuel was left hanging by the Federal patrol after several unsuccessful attempts to get information from him about his stepson's whereabouts. He did not die from the hanging, but oxygen had been deprived from his brain for so long that he remained mentally incapacitated the rest of his life.

The troops also abused Zerelda Samuel, Frank and Jesse's mother, who was pregnant at the time. Her rough treatment caused her to miscarry. When Jesse saw all this, he said, "Mother, I'm going to join Quantrill." After Jesse joined the guerrillas, the Federal militia arrested and imprisoned his mother and sister for two weeks in St. Joseph.[19]

Supposedly Quantrill was reluctant to accept the sixteen-year-old, but he finally agreed when Frank assured Quantrill that he would be responsible for him. Jesse's horsemanship, weapons handling, fearlessness, and natural leadership soon earned him a prominent place in Quantrill's command. Jesse emulated his brother's reading habits, but instead of Shakespeare his favorite book was the Bible, which he memorized and quoted frequently. Jesse was a member of the Baptist church and even sang in the church choir. He was a devout believer and was never known to swear or use foul language. His favorite religious hymn was "What a Friend We Have in Jesus."

William Wyeth James was a cousin of Frank and Jesse James. He was four-teen years old and living with relatives in Independence early in 1862 when jayhawkers attacked his family. He killed eight of the men who attacked them then ran away and joined Quantrill in July 1862. Federal officers put out the word that he should be hanged or shot as soon as he was captured.[20]

Guerrilla J. T. Keller often remarked on Quantrill's intelligence and noted, "Quantrill was a quiet spoken man and his men all liked him. He was not at all tyrannical." Charles Fletcher Taylor from Clay County said almost the same thing: "Quantrill was always well liked by his men. He always treated them well."

Sixteen-year-old William Gaugh was among the earliest of Quantrill's recruits. He had tried to enlist in Sterling Price's army, but the general sent him home, saying, "As badly as I need men, I cannot take a boy of sixteen from his parents."

Joseph Gibson rode up from Bates County to join Quantrill after Kansas jayhawkers burned down his home. Quantrill personally invited Gibson to accompany him to Kentucky at the end of the war.

Randolph Venable was twenty-four years old when he joined Quantrill after Jennison's 1861 jayhawking raid through Brooking Township. Venable was another member of the West Fork of the Little Blue Baptist Church to cast his lot with Quantrill. He was one of the Brooking youths, along with Dave Hilton, who went to Kentucky with Quantrill at the end of the war. Hilton first served in Price's army when he was only seventeen years old. He was captured at the battle of Wilson's Creek and later exchanged. When he returned home, Hilton joined Quantrill after his mother's house had been burned to the ground.

Francis Marion David "Dave" Poole was named after the famous Revolutionary War guerrilla, Francis Marion, known as the Swamp Fox. Poole was quite short with small hands and feet but a long beard and mustache and piercing gray eyes. Poole joined Quantrill after his uncle, Archibald Poole, was killed and his home sacked by jayhawkers and another member of his family shot. Poole was listed as a member of Quantrill's company from the muster roll dated July 6, 1862.[21]

Mack Poisal also joined Quantrill to correct the wrongs done to his family. Three Union men killed his father, Thomas, near Waverly, Missouri, while he was driving a team of oxen. A young boy of the neighborhood witnessed the murder and rushed the information to the Poisal home. Mack and two other men rode after and overtook the killers after dark. The Federals were killed as they sat around a campfire laughing about the murder.

James Poisal and Simeon Whitsett were arrested in retaliation for a Federal defeat near Odessa, Missouri. In 1863 Union soldiers killed James's father. Afterward he too joined Quantrill. Just after his release, Whitsett joined up with Upton Hays's cavalry. He participated in the battles of Lone Jack and Centralia and the Lawrence raid.

Another Quantrillian was named John Brown. He joined the guerrillas after soldiers killed his father while he was hunting his cattle after a jayhawker raid. The Brown home was burned down and his family scattered.

William Reynolds from the Lone Jack area was with Quantrill, but he was one of the few who did not participate in the Lawrence raid. Kansas jayhawkers killed his father and burned his home. He joined Quantrill when he was sixteen years old.[22]

Jayhawkers torched Martin V. B. Flanery's home and twenty-five others on October 29, 1861. Initially, Flanery served under Col. Upton Hays. After Hays's death, he fought under Price, then he tried to leave the war and return to farming. Flanery had protection papers from the local authorities, but he was continually shot at and almost killed. In March 1863 he decided to join Quantrill. After his neighbors pleaded with him not to go, his wife told them, "If it were me, I would go, as he cannot live in peace here, and I would sell my life as dearly as possible." After joining Quantrill, he was shot on June 29,

1864, while in Texas.[23] The Flanerys were all members of the West Fork of the Little Blue Baptist Church.

Boone Muir was twenty-five years old when he started riding with Quantrill early in the war. He was listed on the muster on July 6, 1862. Muir was killed during a raid near Kansas City exactly one year later, June 16, 1863, and buried in Brooking Township's old Smith Cemetery. Muir's father, William Muir, was a descendant of Daniel Boone through his mother, Lavinia Evans Muir, who was Daniel Boone's great-granddaughter. Boone Muir's uncle, John Sylvester Muir Jr., had accompanied Upton Hays on a wagon train to California before the war.[24] The Muir families were all members of the West Fork of the Little Blue Baptist Church.

After finishing his initial enlistment with the Missouri State Guard, Warren Welch returned home to find that the Federals had looted and burned his home, leaving his mother and her five children with nothing but the clothes on their backs. Gen. Jo Shelby provided a home for them for the rest of the war. During the winter of 1863, after the Federals had undermined the women's prison, Warren Welch was shot three times and was cared for by William Anderson's surviving sisters. Even though Molly Anderson was still using a crutch and Jenny Anderson's arm was still bound up, they tended the wounded Welch for more than five weeks.

Harrison Trow was born on October 18, 1843, and had supported himself since he was eleven years old. He rode with Quantrill from the beginning to the end of the war. When he was only sixteen years old, Trow was captured by jayhawkers. He recalled: "They took my old mule from me, my clothes and everything else I had and then set me loose. It angered me then as a boy, I was angry all over. I ran with Quantrill then, stayed with him for some time."[25] In describing Quantrill, Trow said:

[He] had a Roman nose. In height he was five feet eleven inches, and his form was well knit, graceful and sinewy. His constitution was vigorous and his physical endurance equal to an Indian. Quantrill counted the cost of everything. Watched every way lest an advantage should be taken of him, sought to shield and save his men; strove by much strategy to have the odds with rather than against him; traveled a multitude of long roads rather than one short one once too often; took upon himself many disguises to prevent an embarrassing familiarity; retreat often rather than fight and be worsted; kept scouts everywhere; had the faculty of divination to an almost occult degree; believed in young men; paid attention to small things; listened to every man's advice and then took his own; stood by his soldiers; obeyed strictly the laws of retaliation; preferred the old dispensation to the new, that is to say the code of Moses to that of Jesus Christ.

Trow summarized his experience with Quantrill: "Based on skill, energy, perspicacity and unusual presence of mind, his fame as a guerrilla will endure for generations." With the aid of writer J. P. Burch, after the war Trow wrote a book about his Quantrillian exploits, *Charles W. Quantrell*. He admired Quantrill mostly for his devotion to his comrades, his self-denial, and his fearlessness. In describing his leader, Trow remarked: "[Quantrill] snapped his fingers at death; was something of a fatalist; rarely drank; trusted few women; but these with his life; played high at cards; believed in religion; respected its ordinances; went at intervals to church; understood human nature thoroughly; never quarreled; was generally taciturn and one of the coolest and deadliest men in a personal combat known to the border. . . . In personal intrepidity he was inferior to no man."

Four Kimberlin brothers rode with Quantrill: eighteen-year-old William, sixteen-year-old Richard, fourteen-year-old Robert, and twelve-year-old Julian. They joined the guerrillas after Federals killed their fifty-one-year-old father, Samuel Kimberlin, of Blue Springs on November 28, 1862. Their father was hanged from the rafters of his own barn.

Brothers Dick, James, and Isaac Berry were from Callaway County. Their fifty-nine-year-old father remained at home to look after their sisters. Federals from the neighboring town of Danville reportedly raped the girls: twenty-year-old Catherine, eighteen-year-old Nancy, fourteen-year-old Elizabeth, and eleven-year-old Sallie Ann. As a consequence, when the Berry brothers were riding with Bill Anderson near Boonville in the fall of 1864, they convinced their leader to make a raid on Danville. They burned it to the ground after killing many of the men responsible for the outrages committed against their sisters.

George T. Maddox, in referring to the Southern guerrillas, remarked:

A great many of them were made bad men by the cruel treatment they received at the hands of the "hogskin" militia and Kansas jayhawkers. When they had a father, brother or some old friend murdered by them, or a family robbed, they went in for revenge, and if it had not been for the class of men I have mentioned the war would have been conducted in a different manner from what it was. The men left the main army, went to the brush, and fought as guerrillas for the balance of the war. They would have stayed in the regular army if it had not been that their friends had been so cruelly treated as they had; that was the quickest way they had of getting revenge. The Southern people in this country say that the Kansas troops committed the most horrible crimes ever committed by American citizens. It seems to be their main forte to kill old men and make war on women and children.[26]

Dave, Gabriel, John Hicks "Hix," and Hiram James "Hi" George were all brothers from Oak Grove, Missouri, and members of the Oak Grove Baptist Church. The brothers recalled when Quantrill stayed with them in Oak Grove and that "he was an admirer of many of the beautiful girls in that vicinity. To one of these girls he gave the first photograph he ever had made of himself." Gabriel George was killed in the Independence raid of February 22, 1862. John Hicks George recalled how he joined Quantrill's band at the start of the war:

> I had an experience along about the first part of the war that took my breath away. I don't mean that just as an expression, but I mean literally. My breath was taken away and I was extremely lucky to get it back again. It was at the outbreak of the war and I was twenty-three years old. I was at work on my farm one morning when a troop of Federal cavalry came up the road leading to my house. They asked me the whereabouts of Quantrill and I refused to answer. In truth, Charlie and his men were camped about a half-mile over the hill. When I refused to answer, the Federal leader ordered his men to hang me to the most convenient limb. And they did. After several minutes of choking and gasping they cut me down and asked about the guerrilla chieftain again. Again I refused to answer, so up I went. When I was almost dead, they let me to the ground and repeated the questioning and again met with refusal.

In June 1862, Hix George joined Quantrill's command to seek safety and avenge the Federal outrages.[27] Union troops killed his father in February 1863.[28] Hi George explained that he followed Quantrill because "they burned and took everything I had. Killed my father, hung my brother." In remembering Quantrill, Hi noted, "He was a man of few words. . . . I remember him as a man of about five feet nine inches, having light blue eyes and very light hair. His moustache was a small imperial, for that was the way he wore what hair he permitted on his face, and red. There was nothing striking about the appearance of this man of twenty-four. His aspect had nothing of fierceness or magnetism about it. . . . He usually restrained the ardor of his followers and never sacrificed a man needlessly." Both Hix and Hi were at the October

6, 1863, battle of Baxter Springs, and both rose to the rank of corporal in Quantrill's company.

Frank Dalton claimed that he joined Quantrill's band when he was fifteen years old. Dalton remembered:

> Jennison's Jayhawkers, visiting the home of the James brothers and taking the women, Aunt Zerelda, the mother of Frank and Jesse, their sister, and my mother and sisters, and after stripping them to the waist they tied them to trees and taking a blacksnake whip that they found in the stable they whipped them until they got tired and then they rode away, leaving the women and girls to be cut down and carried into the house by our negro slaves, who washed and bandaged their bleeding backs and bodies and put them to bed.

Dalton also asserted that he then "exacted a terrible revenge for this inhuman treatment of our mothers and sisters. We surrounded Jennison's men when they were in camp one night shortly after that and shot into them from the brush until we ran out of ammunition." In remembering Quantrill, Dalton noted: "General Lee once made the remark that, given a half-dozen leaders like Quantrill, he could whip the North in less than six months."[29]

Riley Crawford's sisters, Susan Crawford Vandever and Armenia Crawford Selvey, were killed in 1863 when Federals collapsed the building in which they were being held. Riley Crawford was as efficient at killing as was William "Bloody Bill" Anderson. Both men's fathers and sisters were killed by Union troops, but Riley was only fourteen when he joined Quantrill and too young for a leadership position like Anderson's. Riley allegedly killed every Federal soldier who fell into his hands. He was killed in an ambush while riding into Howard County in support of Price's last raid. Three older brothers also rode with Quantrill: William, Marshall, and Marion.

As was noted earlier, in chapter 3, Coleman and James Younger were sons of Henry Washington Younger. The Youngers were well respected and extremely influential during the prewar years. Ancestors had fought under George Washington and endured the ordeal of Valley Forge; their mother was related to Lighthorse Harry Lee of Revolutionary War fame. Henry at one time owned three farms totaling twenty thousand acres. One farm was in Jackson County on a portion of what was called the Powell farm in the Big Cedar district on the southern end of the valley of the Little Blue and just east of Brooking Township. It was here on adjoining farms along the Independence to Harrisonville road that Cole and Jim's parents and William

Hagan's parents established the Big Cedar Missionary Baptist Church. Frank and Jesse James's parents, the Reverend Robert and Zerelda James, came from Clay County on occasion to visit and preach in the newly built church.

During the 1850s the Younger family sold their farm and moved to Harrisonville. Henry moved his family into town and entered the mercantile business, owned a livery stable, and maintained his farming interests.[30] Federal troops murdered Cole's father, arrested his sister, and forced his mother at bayonet point to set fire to her own home in the middle of winter. Cole was known throughout his life as never having touched liquor or to have used harsh language. In his later years he was described as having a high regard for ministers, was baptized, became a member of the Christian Church in Lee's Summit, and attended services on a regular basis. After the murder of his father, he allegedly said, "The knowledge that my father had been killed in cold blood filled my heart with the lust for vengeance."

Cole Younger had a camp on the Talley farm, which was on the east fork of the Little Blue River on the Big Cedar Creek in Jackson County, four miles south of Independence. Brothers George and Tom Talley were guerrillas in Quantrill's company. At the Talley farm, while in camp with forty men, Cole Younger received a dispatch from Quantrill to prepare to attack Independence in conjunction with the forces of Cols. John T. Hughes, Gideon W. Thompson, Vard Cockrell, and Upton Hays.

Cole's uncle, John Fristoe, also lost his mansion to fire and his stock to Kansas jayhawkers. Cole's brother-in-law, George M. Clayton, who married Cole's sister Caroline, also rode with Quantrill. Both Cole Younger and Quantrill had a mutual friend in Dr. Pleasant Lea, who lived in a colonial home along the Independence to Harrisonville road along the east fork of the Little Blue River. The doctor's sons and nephews were serving in Price's army, but the doctor took no part in the conflict himself. One day the doctor went to the home of his neighbor, Washington Wells, to get news of his sons from the newspapers. He was seized by Federal troops from Iowa serving under Thomas Ewing and William Penick at Independence. The soldiers took him to his yard and executed him in front of his family. On the same raid the Federals killed an elderly farmer and burned fourteen houses in the area.[31]

William Hagan had married a cousin of the Flanerys, and his brother John had been killed by Federals along the Independence to Harrisonville road as he was riding in a wagon with his wife and children. A Union patrol stopped him and took him from the wagon into the woods and shot him as a reprisal for a recently cut telegraph line.

Federal militiamen killed the brother of Archie Clements, and a Federal militiaman burned down his mother's home. Described as short, only five feet tall, blond, beardless, and having blue gray eyes, Archie Clements in one short year eclipsed the record of every known guerrilla by killing fifty-four men. Like Bill Anderson, at Archie's death, a black silken cord was found on his body with fifty-four knots representing the number of soldiers he had killed.

Clay County's Allen H. Parmer was fourteen years old when he joined Quantrill. He was born in Liberty, Missouri, on May 6, 1848. One day in 1863 he stopped by the James farmhouse and met Susie James, Frank and Jesse's sister, and a romance developed. After the war Allen and Susie were married. Parmer joined Quantrill before the Lawrence raid and was in the many battles that followed, including the October 23, 1864, battle of Westport. Under Quantrill's various commands, Parmer served mostly under George Todd. Parmer accompanied Quantrill to Kentucky at the end of the war and was one of the last men to see Quantrill alive.

Guerrilla Dick Yeager came from a prominent and wealthy family. His father, Judge James Yeager, presided over the Jackson County Court, and his family were members of the Cumberland Presbyterian Church in Westport. Judge Yeager was elected to the Missouri legislature for two years in 1858. While he served in the legislature, his son Dick was in charge of one of his father's wagon trains. Upon returning from one of these journeys, Dick found that Charles Jennison had pillaged his father's farm. During the war the Federals arrested James Yeager and imprisoned him in St. Louis. On one occasion when Dick was wounded, Rebecca Jane Flanery, the daughter of Zion Flanery, carried water to him and was caught and incarcerated for two weeks on a diet of bread and water for doing so.

Twenty-two-year-old Dick Yeager was five feet ten inches tall with a fair complexion, dark hair, and dark blue eyes. Dick married Martha J. Muir, the sister of Boone Muir, on November 22, 1860. Both Boone Muir and Dick Yeager were riding with Quantrill as early as July 6, 1862. During Quantrill's first winter in Texas, Yeager was attached to Company K, Missouri Volunteers of Q. C. Shank's regiment in Jo Shelby's brigade of Gen. John S. Marmaduke's division in Sterling Price's army of the Missouri State Guard.

Ferdinand Scott was a captain in Quantrill's company and listed as a member as early as July 6, 1862. On May 19, 1863, he led twelve guerrillas on a raid near Missouri City and ambushed an entire company of Federals. After killing and wounding thirty-three Union soldiers in ambush south of Kansas City on June 16, 1863, Scott was killed by a sniper. His body was taken back to Brooking Township and buried in the Smith Cemetery. After the war a fellow soldier described him:

> Perhaps both by nature and temperament no man was better fitted for the life of a guerrilla than Fernando Scott. Of a highly nervous and sensitive disposition, he slept little; it was not believed that he ever experienced an emotion of physical fear; under fire no soldier could be cooler; he won the love of his men first, later, their adoration; thinking a great deal he did not talk much; gentle, he scarcely ever spoke harshly; tender-hearted, he very rarely ever killed save in open battle. Above everything else he was true. Nothing deterred him in the line of his duty, and if he had been ordered to blow up a powder magazine he would have blown it up and himself with it.[32]

Because of the notoriety that he attained in such a short amount of time, Scott would have gone down in the history of the Border Wars as one of the most famous guerrilla leaders of his time if he had not died an untimely death.

Dick Liddel was a native Missourian from Jackson County and joined Quantrill when he was only twelve years old. He stood five feet eight inches tall and had blond hair, a large blond mustache, pale blue eyes, and a short nose. He was described as dashing with dreamy eyes and having a way with women. He joined the guerrillas after Federals killed two relatives.[33]

George Barnett was seventeen years old when he witnessed Federal soldiers kill his brother after burning their farm and rustling their livestock. After these depredations, he joined the Missouri forces. Two years later he was riding with Quantrill's company. Barnett allegedly said: "It was certain, I thought, that I should go into battle and fight until I was killed. It all seemed hopeless, the odds were great, but there was no choice. I saw my brother killed. I saw our farm home in ashes and my mother left desolate, robbed of all the livestock and provisions we had gotten together to keep her." When asked about why he rode along on the Lawrence raid, Barnett replied, "Redlegs had come into Missouri a short time before and swept a wide swath for miles, clean of livestock, slaves, food, wagons and horses. They even had loaded their wagons and those they had stolen, with furniture and harvest crops. They took the small amount of Federal money they found."[34] When describing Quantrill, Barnett recalled, "What a man, what a leader! Never once did he say, 'Go boys.' He always was at the front and his order always was, 'Come boys, let's get 'em.'"

James Campbell rode with Quantrill for more than two years. He remembered Quantrill's prowess as a military leader in analyzing situations and sorting things out. Campbell said that Quantrill had few standing orders but one, which all the men remembered and respected. "Quantrill's men did not fear him, but there was only one offense for which he said he would have a man shot: "No matter how much a woman may abuse you, take her abuse. Let her talk and scold, but say nothing to her in resentment. We are fighting men, not women. No provocation will excuse an insult or back talk to a woman." Campbell stated, "You will find that no member of Quantrill's command was ever accused of insulting a woman. There were men on the other side who were different."[35]

Jim Cummins rode under Quantrill's command almost the entire length of the war. He was from Clay County and had attended the Baptist church with Frank and Jesse James before the war and lived in the same neighborhood. His ancestors had fought in the Revolutionary War and in the War of 1812. Jim said that his father was a God-fearing man and that his mother was a wonderful woman and deeply religious. During the war a Federal patrol visited the Cummins's home. Jim remembered:

> There were five of Captain Bigelow's men in militia uniform, cursing and abusing my mother because she had nothing left for them to steal, because she had two sons in the Confederate army and for being a Rebel herself. One of them, whose name I have never learned, drew back his fist to hit mother, cursing and abusing her all the time. I think I first began to carry a gun when I was about thirteen years old. Anyway, I carried it for many years. I loved it, practiced with it and was a good shot. After the border troubles started I carried it always with me. I had it when I turned the corner that evening, and I am thankful to God that I did have it, because it enabled me to send that fellow to hell in a hurry who was threatening to strike my mother. That was one of the good acts of my life. When he fell to the ground the others with him reached for their revolvers. I killed three of them altogether and broke the arm of a fourth. I found an order on one of the three I had killed, signed by Bigelow, directing them to go to the home of a Samuel R. Cummins, my father, and commandeer livestock and provisions.

Afterward, Jim Cummins was mustered into the Confederate service at the house of his uncle. This cost his uncle his life: "[They hanged] him and, to show their contempt of him, would not allow his body to be buried, but left it hanging. . . . However I had the supreme pleasure of being one of a party that went to the home of Captain Bigelow, in 1864, to arrest him and his brother, and as they resisted arrest, we killed them both, shot them, which was a shame, as they should have been hung."[36]

Jim Cummins later joined Bill Anderson to seek revenge. He said, "Having looked the situation over I determined to join the worst devil in the bunch. Frank James had joined Quantrill's band. While he was fierce, he was nothing to compare with that terrible Bill Anderson, so I decided it was Anderson for me as I wanted to see blood flow in revenge for the outrages the Jayhawkers had committed."[37]

Peyton Long, like Jim Cummins and the James brothers, was from Clay County. He lived in Liberty when the war started and in May 1861 enlisted in Col. John T. Hughes's regiment. Long fought at the battles of Carthage, Wilson's Creek, Dry Wood, Lexington, Pea Ridge, Iuka, and Corinth. Not until the summer of 1863 did he join Quantrill's command. It was reported that Peyton Long was responsible for killing more Union soldiers while in Lawrence than any of Quantrill's other men. Long stayed with Quantrill after Price's withdrawal into Arkansas and went to Kentucky with him and was killed there.

Isaac "Ike" Hall joined Quantrill's band in the spring of 1862 after his twenty-two-year-old brother Joseph had joined up in 1861. Their eighteen-year-old brother Bob joined Ike later that same year along with their twenty-three-year-old brother John. During the winter of 1862 Jennison's jayhawkers forced the Halls' mother to set fire to her own home then watch it burn. They allowed her to try to save some things, but then they made her throw some of it back into the fire. The jayhawkers stole their slaves and burned the houses of four neighbors the same day.[38] It was alleged that the Federals raped their sixteen-year-old sister Margaret and twenty-year-old sister Ann. Because of this, the four brothers were known to fight like demons in battle. Isaac Hall rose to captain in Quantrill's command.

Another man who rose to prominence as a captain in Quantrill's guerrilla company was twenty-three-year-old Charles A. Longacre from Tennessee. His mother and sister were both arrested and imprisoned in St. Louis. Jayhawkers raped their slaves in the presence of their owners, and neighboring women and children were driven from their homes. Longacre also claimed that soldiers raped his sister. These Federal atrocities started soon after Longacre's name was discovered on Quantrill's muster list on July 6, 1862.[39]

William Anderson and his three sisters—Mary, Josephine, and Martha—his older brother, Ellis, and younger brother, James, were born in Randolph County, Missouri. Seeking farmland at a moderate price, the family moved to Johnson County, Kansas, before the war and settled on a farm. They lived a quiet life and were hard workers and respectable people. The maternal grand-parents, William and Mahala Tomason, also lived with them. The Andersons were not slaveholders; their sympathies were pro-Southern, but they took no active part in politics or agitations.[40]

In the early spring of 1862 Anderson was doing business in Fort Leaven-worth, selling forage to the government, when his father and uncle were hanged as Southern sympathizers by Federals on March 7 in retaliation for Quantrill's raid on Aubry, Kansas. Shortly after his father's murder, Anderson took his homeless and destitute sisters to Westport. With his brother, Jim, he stole some horses, but they were caught by Quantrill and warned not to do it again. The Anderson brothers joined Quantrill on March 12, 1862.

Anderson was five feet ten inches tall. His men said that he was lithe as a greyhound, and as he galloped he could swing himself to the ground and pick up a pistol. Frank James observed, "Anderson always made us keep our horses in good condition. If a man did not keep a good horse and good pistols he sent him to the infantry." The only prisoner that Anderson was ever known to have taken recalled that Anderson's dealings with his men always seemed to be cordial and pleasant.[41] When Anderson was asked why he took up guerrilla warfare he replied: "I have chosen guerrilla warfare to revenge myself for wrongs that I could not honorably revenge otherwise."[42]

Clifton D. Holtzclaw was a guerrilla officer from Howard County, Missouri. Four or five Federal scouting parties came to his house, insulted his parents, abused his sisters, and made all kinds of threats against his life. Later a Federal militia officer went to Holtzclaw's house, seized his aged father, and murdered him.[43] Holtzclaw accompanied Quantrill at the battle of Fayette along with Capt. Thomas Todd, also of Howard County. Holtz-claw was part of between five hundred and seven hundred soldiers in Howard County that joined Sterling Price as he swept through the state on his last raid.

Twenty-two-year-old John Thrailkill, a good friend of Jesse James, was from Holt County. He was of Russian descent and known as a quiet, unassuming painter from northwest Missouri. When the war broke out, twenty militiamen invaded the home of his fiancée and killed her invalid father. As a result of this brutal assault, she went insane and died shortly afterward. To avenge her, Thrailkill joined Quantrill, and he made a solemn vow at his sweetheart's grave: "Blood for blood; every hair in her head shall have a sacrifice!" Thrailkill killed eighteen of the twenty men who murdered his prospective father-in-law and caused his fiancée's death. Similar circumstances also influenced John McKeene to join Quantrill's irregulars.

Bud Pence joined Quantrill late in 1863, following in his friend Frank James's footsteps. Pence's younger brother Donnie, the same age as Jesse James, joined six months later. After Bud had joined Quantrill, Federals came to his father's house in Clay County and threatened to hang him if he did not reveal where Bud was. He did not know. They broke a fiddle over his head and also the stock of a gun in their persuasions before hanging. He miraculously survived and moved to Liberty to prevent his youngest son from joining Quantrill, but Donnie joined his brother anyway.[44] Donnie Pence went with Quantrill to Kentucky and was with him when Quantrill was mortally wounded.

Gooley Robinson's widowed aunt lived in Johnson County and lost her house and cattle to Federal raids. Gooley joined Bill Anderson's company to avenge her loss.

James Mundy was already riding with Quantrill when his sisters, Susan Womacks and Mattie Mundy, were arrested and imprisoned in the deathtrap prison that killed or injured seven women related to Quantrillians. Mundy's sisters survived the plot, but the Federal atrocity drove their brother to seek bloody revenge on the streets of Lawrence weeks later.

Quantrill visited the home of George M. Noland early in the war, and soon after Noland's father and older brother left to join Price's army. When things worsened with the jayhawker raids, Noland's older brother, Morgan, returned to join Quantrill. Morgan was mortally wounded by Federals and lingered for eight days before he died. Afterward fifteen-year-old George joined Quantrill.[45] Once he described how James Lane tried to burn his house down around him:

> I was in a little four room frame and brick house surrounded by Lane's band, waiting for me to come out. They knew I was in there, and they all had their guns pointed in my direction, so as to get me when I appeared. I was in the brick portion of the house, listening to the rafters crackle and fall. I knew I had to get out some time soon. There was a lot of dense smoke drifting in one direction. It came down to the ground and was about as high as the house. There was hardly anyone over there. Seeing that it was my only chance, I climbed through a window and risked it. It was like diving and I had to hold my breath, but I got away, and not one of them saw me.

For the brutality the Federals showed toward his family, Noland said, "I was more in a revengeful spirit than anything else when I joined Quantrill in his attack on Lawrence. Lane had spoiled our home, killed our men, and we wanted him to get what was coming to him."

Levi Potts and his brother, Martin, were from the Blue Springs area of Jackson County. Both men rode with Quantrill during the 1863 Lawrence raid after having joined the guerrillas in 1862. Their fifteen-year-old neighbor, Frank Smith, was one of the first to become acquainted with Quantrill when he came to Jackson County and later joined his guerrilla band. Smith was also a neighbor to Quantrill's wife, Kate King, and a neighbor of Andy Walker. Smith admired Quantrill's intelligence, judgment, and his ability to analyze situations. He noted: "He planned every operation, always keeping in mind just how and where he was going to retreat. Quantrill did the planning." Smith envied Quantrill for his calm in stressful situations. He died in Blue Springs at the age of eighty-six years old, having been a member of the Blue Springs Baptist Church for more than sixty-two years, more than fifty years as a deacon.

Sylvester "Ves" Akers was a twenty-six-year-old farmer from Kentucky at the beginning of the war and a member of the Christian Church in Buckner, Missouri. He left his wife and three children to ride with Quantrill and was with him in Kentucky when he died. Sylvester's brother, Henry H. Akers, also rode with Quantrill and was listed on Quantrill's July 6, 1862, company muster list.

Sam Hildebrand operated with Quantrill in southern Missouri. Hildebrand had two other brothers, one of which was in the Union army. Federal militia hanged his thirteen-year-old brother. Union troops also burned down his house. Hildebrand received a major's commission from Gen. Jeff Thompson in late 1861.

John Newman Edwards described the common thread that bound these men into a motivated fighting force:

> He saw that he was hunted and proscribed; that he had neither a flag nor a government; that the rights and the amenities of civilized warfare were not to be his; that a dog's death was certain if he surrendered even in the extremest agony of battle; that the house which sheltered him had to be burnt; the father who succored him had to be butchered; the mother who prayed for him had to be insulted; the sister who carried food to him had to be imprisoned; the neighborhood, which witnessed his combats had to be laid waste; the comrade shot down by his side had to be put to death as a wild beast, and he lifted up the Black Flag in self-defense and fought as became a free man and a hero.[46]

Yet Quantrill kept more than just combatants in his company. He needed a myriad of support for his fighters. Projectiles from the weapons of the time were low velocity and fired bullets of pure lead. Many times, if they did not kill the victim outright, they would leave a horrible wound. Oftentimes the lead remained in the body, and after the wound closed it would leave no permanent harmful effects. For wounds of this sort, Quantrill needed medical support. He found it in willing doctors who had also suffered at the hand of the jayhawkers.

Men like Dr. John W. Benson served Quantrill as a surgeon. He had belonged to other military units before joining Quantrill's company. He rode along on the Lawrence raid but was talked into surrendering in September 1863 with guarantees that he would be treated as a prisoner. Within a month he was executed by firing squad.

Dr. M. C. Jacobs rode with Quantrill, as did a doctor named Campbell who accompanied the guerrillas on the Lawrence raid. Dr. P. H. Henry also assisted. He was captured but returned home in time to assist Quantrill in treating the wounded of the August 11, 1862, battle of Independence. He helped Andy Blunt to escape when Blunt was a prisoner in Independence. Dr. J. M. Angel served both as a surgeon with the regular Confederate army and also rode with George Todd's company in Jackson County. After the war the Federal Third Cavalry Missouri State Militia killed him on July 7, 1865.

Thirty-three-year-old Dr. Thomas B. Hale rode with Cole Younger in Jackson County. On February 10, 1863, he was with a squad of twelve guerrillas when they were surrounded by Kansas Redlegs and captured. They were murdered in cold blood.

Dr. H. F. Hereford assisted many wounded guerrillas around Westport, Missouri. He was accused of being a guerrilla himself, which caused him to flee for his life. He went to California until the war ended then returned home to continue his practice.

Dr. W. M. Doores was listed as a doctor on Quantrill's muster role as early as July 6, 1862, when he participated in a skirmish against troops of the Missouri State Militia just south of Lee's Summit. A doctor named Herndon assisted Quantrill following the April 1862 Lowe house battle.[47]

Many slaves and freedmen took up arms on both sides during the border war. The usual practice was for the jayhawkers to seize slaves from Missouri slave owners and force them into Union service. The reason James Lane was an advocate of recruiting black troops during the Civil War was that he had very early sensed that the first Federal commander to enlist black troops would be a hero of the radicals and abolitionists, whose support might well carry him to the White House.[48] There were many blacks in the Confederate army doing duty not only as cooks, servants, and laborers but also as soldiers.

Henry Wilson was black and served as Quantrill's bodyguard. Wilson explained that he did not want to be free. He ran from Union troops for miles without stopping and joined Quantrill's band. He also served as the company's cook in camp. Wilson was also one of Quantrill's best spies, because he could slip into a village without alarming the occupants and secure significant information.[49] Wilson was offered a chance by the jayhawkers to go to Kansas: "When they asked me if I wished to go, I said, Hell, no! I don't want to have nothing to do with such robbers and thieves. I joined Quantrill when Master Wilson moved to Texas and I carried supplies to [Quantrill] and his men. I took an oath that I would stick to the end, and Quantrill trusted me because I didn't drink whiskey and because I was dependable and could shoot."

John Noland was a black soldier who also served Quantrill as his hostler. Federals once offered him ten thousand dollars to betray Quantrill and his men, but Noland only replied with scorn. When Noland was with Quantrill during the battle of Lamar, he was reported to have shouted more orders than any other of Quantrill's men trying to make the Federals inside the brick courthouse surrender by thinking they were surrounded. For years after the war Noland attended Quantrillian reunions. When he died he had all white pallbearers at his funeral. His comrades referred to him as "a man among men."

A black man by the name of John Lobb also served Quantrill and reportedly spied on Lawrence prior to the raid. Quantrill also had a Cherokee Indian, Adam Wilson, riding with him.

Quantrill's ranks were filled with a diversity of race and talent, but those on whom his men most depended were Southern women. One guerrilla said:

The Southern women, no matter how cold it was or how much it rained or snowed, would get up at the dead hour of midnight to let us know that Mr. Yankee was coming, and I must say they were truer and better than the men. There were Southern ladies of the South, especially in the scope of country where I ranged, who never knew what want was, and had plenty of slaves to wait on them, brought down to poverty by having their wearing apparel, and even their beds and bedclothes carried off, forcing them to work at spinning and weaving and making their own dresses and clothes at home. Sometimes they [jayhawkers] would come to a house where a lady had a piece of cloth in the loom weaving it, and cut it out and tear it up, break up their cards and spinning wheel, and perhaps rob them of the last bite to eat on the place, when they really had no use for it but did it out of pure meanness. Sometimes the ladies would go from Northwest Arkansas clean down to the Little River country, a distance of about 250 miles, with an old pony to get some salt, and then sometimes they would be robbed of it and their pony before they could get back home. Notwithstanding all this, they were always hopeful and had a cheering word to say to a Southern soldier. Many women and children I have seen who were once stout, healthy and fine looking, reduced down almost to skeletons for want of something to eat that had been taken away from them by the robbers. They managed to live on wheat bran and parched corn, or anything they could get. Southern women were the best women that the Lord ever let the sun shine on. All of them who were in the war and are living now have a crown laid up for them in Heaven, to reward them for what they endured during the war.[50]

At the beginning of the war, the womenfolk at home spun socks, made homespun shirts and pants for their husbands and sons, and sewed uniforms for their men. For all their patriotic support the women probably suffered the most. Frances Fristoe Twyman recalled: "To me it was a most cruel and unjust war, a war in which innocent women and children suffered most. Our homes were invaded and ransacked by the Federal soldiers and women and children were dragged off to prison." Another Southern woman remembered: "The home of my mother, seventy years old, was burned. She had neither husband nor son. She was an invalid, confined to her bed. She was accused of sending a ham of meat to Quantrill's camp. It was a false accusation, but she owned slaves and had to suffer for it although innocent of the charge against her."[51]

With so much devotion to the cause—which was reflected in their devotion to the men in the field—young Southern men were naturally attracted to these heroines. Records abound with the names of many of Quantrill's followers who married such women during the war or immediately preceding it.

Besides the women who supported the guerrillas there were other women associated with Quantrill's company. One of these was Kate King, the daughter of Robert and Malinda King of Blue Springs, Missouri. The Kings owned an eighty-acre farm a half-mile east of Andy Walker. It was a pretty farm situated in the rugged Sni Hills with a branch of Prairie Creek running along its border. One day Quantrill and one hundred men encamped near Blue Springs. As he was riding along the Owen's Schoolhouse road just north of town, he stopped to talk to Robert King.

As Quantrill was standing on the front porch, King's daughter, Sarah Catherine, was returning from school with her younger brothers, Marion and

Samuel. Kate, as she was called, was only fourteen but very beautiful and older looking than her years. The stranger gave her an encouraging smile. Kate remarked that she "was struck by the young man's straight and graceful stature." She remembered, "[H]e had clear features and a complexion inclined to be pale, which was beginning to show an outdoor color." Quantrill was twenty-four but looked younger. Kate described him as "extremely handsome, with a clear complexion and a scraggly mustache." She said, "He was almost six feet tall and carried himself well."

It was easily love at first sight for both of them, but especially so for this country girl attracted to a handsome man unlike the local boys in that he was polished, debonair, and polite. Quantrill complimented her on her looks, and the flattery took hold with an easy infatuation. Finding excuses over the next several months to visit the Kings, Quantrill brought Kate trinkets and souvenirs to win her favor.

In a later newspaper article, Kate claimed that after their first meeting Quantrill became a regular visitor to their farm, stopping by every few days when he knew she would be home. They began to take rides together, and it was natural to see that the two were quite taken with each other. Quantrill sometimes met her down the hill from her house, next to a spring. Here they talked for hours and made plans for the future.

When Quantrill returned to Missouri after the Lawrence raid, he headed for Kate's house and picked her up by the well. She was then fifteen years old, but she could ride a horse as well as any man. Her horsemanship made Quantrill apprehensive, enough that he would grab the reins of her horse to get her to slow down.

One day Quantrill borrowed a gray mare from Fletcher Taylor, and together he and Kate rode to a preacher's house and were secretly married. The preacher was probably Hiram Bowman, pastor of the Primitive Baptist Church in Oak Grove, approximately six miles from Quantrill's camp in Blue Springs. Bowman had conducted other marriages for Quantrill's men during the war, and Quantrill became acquainted with him when the guerrilla leader was a regular attendant during protracted church meetings.

After the 1863 collapse of the women's prison in Kansas City, Quantrill realized what the Federals were capable of doing to anyone related to any of his men. So he was naturally nervous concerning the safety of his wife's life. In those days, country preachers simply recorded marriage ceremonies in private logbooks. B. J. George Sr. of Oak Grove wrote after the war: "Hiram Bowman kept a small private book of marriages that he performed. This was the only official record."

To keep Kate safe, Quantrill persuaded the preacher not to make a record of his marriage. She did take the last name Clarke, Quantrill's middle name, so that if she were ever questioned, the name would throw off suspicion as to their relationship.

IN A speech at a Quantrillian reunion, William H. Gregg said of the women of the South:

> The part played by the women of the South exceeds in self sacrificing glory that of the men. From the war sounded the appeal to arms, and the sweet and bright light of Confederate victory burst forth and spread over the plains of Manassas and continued through alternate epochs of cloud and sunshine, to that awful night in Appomattox, the women of the South, with a devotion, a heroism and a patriotism, unexampled and unparalleled in sublimity, stood by the altars of the Confederate States and kept the fires of patriotism aglow in the hearts of the men.[52]

Elvira Scott recorded in her diary the admiration that many Southern women had for Quantrill: "Quantrill has held his own. He is exemplifying what one desperate, fearless man can do."

6

Fields of Glory

I would rather die on my feet than live on my knees.

USMC SAYING

CONFEDERATE PRESIDENT JEFFERSON DAVIS did not personally approve of partisan warfare, but he knew he needed all the support he could muster from every sector of the country. On April 21, 1862, he approved an act authorizing commissioned officers to form companies of partisan ranger bands. In Missouri, Confederate Gen. Thomas C. Hindman, commander of the Trans-Mississippi Department, enthusiastically believed in guerrilla warfare. Soon after the Confederate Congress approved partisan warfare, on July 17 Hindman issued the Confederate Partisan Act in Missouri from his headquarters in Little Rock, Arkansas. In part, it read:

1. For the more effectual annoyance of the enemy upon our rivers and in our mountains and woods all citizens of this district who are not conscripted are called upon to organize themselves into independent companies of mounted men or infantry, as they prefer, arming themselves and to serve in that part of the district to which they belong.

2. When as many as ten men come together for this purpose they may organize by electing a captain, one sergeant, one corporal, and will at once commence operations against the enemy without waiting for special instructions. Their duty will be to cut off Federal pickets, scouts, foraging parties and trains and to kill pilots and others on

gunboats and transports, attacking them day and night and using the greatest vigor in their movements. As soon as the company attains the strength required by law it will proceed to elect the other officers to which it is entitled. All such organizations will be reported to their headquarters as soon as practicable. They will receive pay and allowances for subsistence and forage for the time actually in the field, as established by the affidavits of their captains.

3. These companies will be governed in all respects by the same regulations as other troops. Captains will be held responsible for the good conduct and efficiency of their men and will report to these headquarters from time to time.

Gen. Robert E. Lee also favored mustering a force of men for partisan service, but with the understanding that they were only to be mustered for local service and to be subject to the orders of the general commanding their military departments.[1] Along the western border in a departmental report, Hindman wrote to T. H. Holmes on November 3, 1862:

With the view to revive the hopes of loyal men in Missouri and to get troops from that State I gave authority to various persons to raise companies and regiments there and to operate as guerrillas. They soon became exceedingly active and rendered important services, destroying wagontrains and transports, tearing up railways, breaking telegraph lines, capturing towns, and thus compelling the enemy to keep there a large force that might have been employed elsewhere.[2]

The Confederate government attempted to make an exchange of information with Federal authorities regarding an agreement on the acceptance of partisan warfare. The Confederates were displeased that Union military leaders would not exchange partisan soldiers as they did other regular soldiers when captured. Robert Ould, Confederate commissioner of exchange, on behalf of the Confederate government, stated, "Partisan Rangers were not persons making war without authority, but were in all respects like the rest of the army except that they were not brigaded and acted generally on detached service. They are not irregulars who come and go at pleasure," he said, "but are organized troops whose muster rolls are returned and whose officers are commissioned as in other branches of the service. They are subject to the Articles of War and Army Regulations and are held responsible for violations of the usages of war in like manner with regular troops."[3]

Comment from Washington seemed to agree with the Confederate ideals on partisan service. The adjutant general of the Union army told Secretary of War Edwin M. Stanton that Ould was correct in maintaining that partisan rangers and independent companies, properly authorized and commissioned, should be placed on the same footing as other Confederate troops. It was pointed out that in Virginia the North had such a company, called the Loudoun County Rangers, operating around Leesburg as well as Unionist "Buffalos" who bedeviled coastal North Carolina.[4]

In Missouri the Union command had its own opinions on how to address partisan warfare. When Gen. John M. Schofield, the Federal commander in St. Louis, heard about the Confederate Congress's new act concerning partisan warfare, he hurriedly issued the following general order on May 29: "The time is passed when insurrection and rebellion in Missouri can cloak itself under the guise of honorable warfare. The utmost vigilance and energy are enjoined upon all the troops of the State in hunting down and destroying these robbers and assassins. When caught in arms, engaged in their unlawful warfare, they will be shot down upon the spot." Even President Davis's regularly commissioned army officers appointed as recruitment officers were to be killed when captured and not treated as prisoners of war.[5]

Schofield's order had little deterrence on Quantrill's activities. On June 28 a Federal patrol riding down the Independence to Harrisonville road at Manasseth Gap was ambushed. Twenty-eight were killed and routed with only a handful making it back to the safety of the garrison in Independence.

Recruiting officers on orders from Hindman took to the field quickly, and the men they recruited immediately wreaked havoc on the Federal outposts between Kansas City and St. Louis. Col. Benjamin Franklin Parker had already made a raid with Quantrill on the Federal outpost of Independence earlier in February.

Col. Joseph C. Porter recruited up to two hundred men from counties in north Missouri. In Marion County, on July 13, Porter captured a unit of the state militia. Maj. John Y. Clopper, with a detachment of the Third Iowa Cavalry, held the town of Florida in Monroe County. When Porter attacked, the Iowans retreated, leaving behind twenty-six killed or wounded. The Federals called upon Schofield in St. Louis for help. He wired the Federal commander in the area, Gen. John McNeil to gather all the troops he could rally and send them toward Porter. On July 18, McNeil found Porter in Scotland County and without caution immediately attacked Porter's rear guard. Porter arranged a feint attack then a withdrawal, making McNeil believe he was winning the battle when in fact Porter was drawing

McNeil's men into an ambush. In the battle that followed, the Federals lost eighty-three men killed or wounded.

Schofield knew he had to strike another blow at the partisan units, so on July 22, 1862, in cooperation with the provisional governor of Missouri, Hamilton Gamble, he put into effect a conscription act for all Missouri men. Schofield's General Orders No. 19 requested, "Every able-bodied man capable of bearing arms and subject to military duty is hereby ordered to repair without delay to the nearest military post and report for duty to the commanding officer. Every man will bring with him whatever arms he may have or can procure and a good horse if he has one . . . for the purpose of exterminating the guerrillas that infest our State."

The order seemed a logical way to bolster the state's forces and combat the guerrillas at the same time, but it was an ill-fated plan. Instead, it forced every military-aged man to decide either to fight with the Federals against their relatives and friends or join the regular Confederate forces. Most simply took their fighting experiences and joined local partisan units, like Quantrill's and other like-minded bands. Also the order countermanded an understanding that any paroled Confederate would be allowed to return home to his normal occupation and would not be required to join the Union army.

Because of Quantrill's influence in Jackson County, Southern recruiting officers believed they could enlist large numbers of recruits. Many of the recruiters converged on Jackson County while Quantrill was defeating one Federal force after another.

Union Brig. Gen. James Totten, commanding the Central Military District that included Independence, assigned Lt. Col. James T. Buel to the command of the Federal post at Independence. After the battle of Pea Ridge, Arkansas, where the Confederates suffered a narrow but demoralizing defeat, the Missouri State Guard was reorganized and reassigned to duty east of the Mississippi River. Those Missouri soldiers who felt it was their first duty to protect their state returned to their homes to serve in partisan units.

After their recent battles, Quantrill and George Todd were gone for a month securing revolvers and a supply of pistol and rifle caps for their men. Upon his return, Quantrill found that he had almost a hundred men in his command. These men were as brave as men could be and true comrades. And if any man faltered, he was disowned and jeered out of the ranks.

About the middle of June, Quantrill's old friend, Upton Hays, now a Confederate colonel, came north to recruit a regiment. Quantrill led his men into the northwestern part of Henry County to meet Hays and escort him back to Jackson County. The ability to recruit successfully in Jackson County was hampered by the large number of Federal troops stationed there. Quantrill contemplated a maneuver that, if successful, would allow Hays to complete his mission without resistance.

Sgt. William H. Gregg was present when Quantrill proposed the idea to Hays and recalled that his captain said, "The best thing for me to do to help you is for me to take my command, go away from Jackson County, and draw the enemy away."[6] So acting in conjunction with Hays, Quantrill moved his company into the southeast corner of Cass County near Pleasant Hill, camping at the abandoned farm of Brinkley Hornsby on the west side of Big Creek.

At about 5 o'clock on the morning on July 8, the First Iowa Cavalry stationed in Clinton and acting as an army of occupation, learned where Quantrill was camped. Maj. James O. Gower, in command of the Iowa troops, detached a scout under Lts. R. M. Reynolds, Foster, Bishop, and Wisenand to find the guerrilla leader and attack him at first light. As the guerrillas had just finished their breakfast, Bishop initiated the engagement without waiting for support. His ninety-six-man detachment drove in the Rebel pickets, but once the Federals came upon the main body of the guerrillas, they were easily beaten back. While the remainder of the Iowans regrouped for another charge, they found themselves heavily engaged in their front while a second group of guerrillas began encircling them with fire and maneuver. Even though their forces were evenly numbered, the Union troops were outmatched against the deadly firepower of the guerrillas. The Iowans quickly pulled back and retreated to Clinton. As the badly mauled patrol limped into town, Gower sent dispatches for all available cavalry from nearby Harrisonville and Warrensburg to come to his aid.

A noteworthy incident of war occurred when the guerrillas captured a wounded Federal and, after treating his wounds, tenderly carried him to a nearby house after borrowing a wagon and team of oxen to transport him. The Federals reciprocated by treating the Confederate wounded with kindness and exchanged the one unhurt prisoner they had for one of their own. This was the only guerrilla soldier of Quantrill's ever exchanged by the Federal government.

Before the next engagement that was sure to come, Quantrill assigned George Todd to take Dick Yeager, Boone Muir, and twenty-eight men to accompany Upton Hays as a personal bodyguard and escort him into Jackson County. On July 10, 1862, Quantrill and his remaining sixty-five men marched all night through a heavy rainstorm, passing within a half-mile of several hundred Federal troops garrisoned in Pleasant Hill. Recrossing Big Creek four to five miles west of Pleasant Hill, he halted his company at a house owned by a man named Searcy. Here they bivouacked in the open prairie, close to a wooded area.

By now Gower had personally taken to the field with seventy-nine men of the First Iowa. While Quantrill had been marching all night, Gower had been reinforced with sixty-five additional men from the First Iowa under Capt. William H. Ankeny along with sixty-five men of the Seventh Missouri Cavalry under Capt. William A. Martin. They were joined by sixty-three men of the First Missouri Cavalry under Capt. Martin Kehoe. Gower split his force to ascertain Quantrill's line of march so as to close with him and give battle.

Information reached Gower that Quantrill was camped for the night along the Big Creek bottom on the edge of Cass County, six miles west of Pleasant Hill. Gower decided to rest his horses and men and attack the guerrilla camp at first light. Quantrill knew that more Federals would soon be on his trail, but he did not attempt to move his camp. The next day, just as Quantrill expected, the Federal commander marched 260 men against him.

Kehoe, with the First Missouri Cavalry, disobeyed Gower's orders to attack Quantrill's position in a coordinated attack combining the entire force. Instead, at first light, Kehoe saddled up his men and led a peremptory attack against Quantrill's position. Complying with Upton Hays's request, Quantrill left his men in their defensive position, expertly decoying the large number of Federal troops in the area to him and away from Jackson County.

Kehoe found the guerrillas camped in a horse lot on top of a hill at the Searcy farm. He had followed their trail left on the muddy road. Quantrill's men were soaked to the skin and had only three or four hours' sleep, but they were wide awake and ready and eager for the upcoming battle. The morning was bright after the night's rain, and the men could hear the birds caroling in the woods. Hicks George and Bob Houx were posted in the rear as pickets. Early that morning one of the pickets came running in to report that the Federal cavalry was coming up beyond the hill. Quantrill asked how many were in sight. The picket estimated seventy cavalrymen. Quantrill then ordered the picket back to his post to take a shot at the horsemen when they were close enough and then fall back. "Draw them down here and we'll unsaddle them," he said.

Quantrill had already formed a plan for an ambush when he heard his pickets firing at Kehoe's troops. He had his men saddle their horses and move them to safety behind the house. As soon as Kehoe spied the guerrillas' camp, two guerrillas ran wildly in the front yard, acting confused and frightened, decoying the Federals into believing they were unprepared for an assault.

With sabers drawn, Kehoe ordered a charge. The Federals came on at a fast run, down the dirt road toward Searcy's yard, which was bordered by a rail fence. Because of the previous night's rain, the guerrillas had draped their saddle blankets over the rail fence. The unsuspecting Union horsemen did not realize that well-armed guerrillas were hiding in ambush behind the cover of this fence. Quantrill himself stood by the front gate, in one hand a pistol and the other on the latch, waiting the charge.

When the Federals were within forty to sixty feet, Quantrill yelled out, "Let 'em have it, boys!" His men rose up from behind their blankets and poured a withering fire into the charging column. A Federal sergeant and six of his men fell dead, falling backward over their horses. Nine others immediately behind them were wounded as well as Kehoe, who received a bullet wound in the shoulder.

All the riderless horses of the Federals continued to charge forward. William H. Gregg shouted to Quantrill to open the gate and let them into the yard. Quantrill stood and calmly did so. The riderless horses ran past him and were captured. Meanwhile, Kehoe and his wounded men retreated as fast as they could to the safety of the timber. Quantrill quickly arranged his men on line and led them in an attack on the Union position, killing two more of Kehoe's men. George W. Maddox, John Jarrette, Cole Younger, George Morrow, William H. Gregg, Andy Blunt, David Poole, and William Haller relentlessly followed the Federals into the timber before withdrawing. Returning to the house, Quantrill and his men picked up the arms and ammunition of the slain Federals lying in the lane. They captured seven six-round Colt carbines, seven Navy Colt revolvers, and six canteens filled with whiskey.

The remaining Federals began a long-range assault from one hundred yards away, wounding George W. Maddox and William Tucker and killing twenty-four-year-old John Hampton. Quantrill determined to withdraw and take his dead and wounded with him. William Tucker was carried away by his brother, who was also in the fight that day. The only conveyance that could be found was a yoke of oxen and an old lumber wagon without a bed. Gregg reported that he and the other guerrillas made a floor of rails on the wagon, borrowed two featherbeds, and laid the wounded and dead side by side. The slowness of the oxen made hurried flight impossible. The wounded Maddox was carried away along with the slain John Hampton, taken to a farmhouse near the Kansas line, and placed in the care of friends.[7]

Unable to match their pistol fire with the range of the Federal musketry, Quantrill withdrew his men to the rear of Searcy's house to a ravine where they had tied their horses. There he awaited another Federal charge.

Kehoe mounted three charges and saw each expend itself before it became a concerted effort. Even though they outnumbered the guerrillas, the soldiers of the First Iowa refused to make another charge. Realizing that any further attempts to overrun the guerrillas' position would result in his defeat, Kehoe pulled his men back one mile south of where Quantrill was positioned.

Quantrill then dispatched Cole Younger, David Poole, John Brinker, and William Haller with orders to "Lay up close to [Col. Everett] Peabody" and keep the Federal movements in view. During the interval, Quantrill gathered his men at the rear of the dwelling and deployed them in a more defensible position bordering the deep ravine where the guerrillas had hidden their horses in relative safety.[8]

It was eleven o'clock before Gower arrived to assist Kehoe. He immediately sent a detachment of the First Iowa to flank Quantrill's position. Gower dismounted his troops, now numbering 250, and began an advance toward the guerrillas. Quantrill took advantage of the natural cover of the ravine's heavy underbrush and tangled bushes to conceal and protect his men. The banks of the ravine were five to seven feet high and from thirty to sixty feet apart.[9]

Capt. William A. Martin of the First Missouri Militia was the first to lead a small squad of Federals who rushed toward the ravine. It was impossible to see more than ten feet in any direction. When they were close enough to engage the enemy with pistols and shotguns, the guerrillas rose up with their weapons blazing and mowed them down. The overpowering Federal numbers forced the guerrillas to the other side of the ravine, where Gower sent forward another group to engage them there. Here again the guerrillas waited in the tall brush of the ravine until the Union line came in range, and again they fired another deadly volley and retired to the other side of the ravine.

This seesaw battle continued until the guerrillas' ammunition began to run low. Both sides turned to sabers, Bowie knives, and even rocks and clubs.

The Federals were dismounted and charging Quantrill's position on foot. Quantrill's men desperately tried to keep their horses safely tied in the bottom of the ravine and away from the murderous rifle fire of the Federals, but many animals had become uncontrollable and had escaped.

Twice Quantrill's defensive line around the ravine was pushed back upon his interior perimeter. With ever failing numbers, the guerrillas began falling back into the ravine. The fiercely fought battle had been going on for more than two hours, and only now did the tempo quicken.

A Federal who had lay hidden in the heavy brush suddenly raised himself to his knees and fired point blank at Quantrill. The bullet, intended for the chest, struck the guerrilla leader in the right leg, below the knee, and cut clean through, narrowly missing the bone. Quantrill fell but leaped up so quickly to his feet that his men imagined he had only stumbled. Gregg, fighting alongside of Quantrill, shot the Union trooper before he could fire again. "Say nothing of my wound," Quantrill said to Gregg, so low that none heard him, "and tell the men to mount rapidly and at once."[10]

One of Quantrill's men recalled:

A terrible melee ensued. Both bushwhackers and soldiers battled desperately. No quarter was asked and none was given. The only sounds heard were the bark of pistols and carbines, the groans of the wounded and dying, and the heavy breathing of men locked in mortal combat. Most of the guerrillas were forced to abandon their horses and some even fought with rocks and clubs when their ammunition ran out. The vicious struggle raged for over an hour. It was here in the ravine that Quantrill was wounded. Bleeding from a bullet wound in his thigh, he realized that the ravine would become a grave for his men unless they escaped soon. Therefore, on his orders, Captain Gregg led all the men who still had horses—about twenty-one in all—in a wild charge, which broke through the Union lines on one side. At the same time Quantrill and the dismounted men cut their way out in the opposite direction. Then they scattered into the timber in small parties, carrying their wounded with them.

As guerrilla Otho Offutt was making for his horse, he saw his friend Al Cunningham standing with his arm all bloody and tied up in a handkerchief. Cunningham's horse had been killed. Showing a common devotion displayed by all of Quantrill's men, Offutt raced to Cunningham's side and asked, "How are you fixed, Al?"

Cunningham replied, "Well, you see, I am shot in the arm and my horse has been killed."

Offutt told him, "Get up here, quick, and I will take you as far as I can."

With the wounded Cunningham behind him, they both made their escape through the Federal lines. Offutt's horse managed to jump over three fences with both men still astride.[11] What made this so remarkable was that Offutt was distinguished as being the tallest and most powerful man among Quantrill's men. He was six feet three inches tall and weighed 210 pounds.

William H. Gregg said that the Federals were "brave soldiers, but [they] were loaded up on whiskey and continually rushed upon us, the very thing we wanted them to do, for our men were armed with pistols and shotguns and could do little execution at long range."

Several of the Southerners' horses were either killed or scattered. Quantrill saw many of his men lying dead or wounded upon the battlefield.

In the initial engagement with the Federals, one of his best soldiers, John Hampton, had been killed, and George W. Maddox and William Tucker had been wounded. After two hours of hand-to-hand fighting, Quantrill's casualties added up to five men killed and ten to twelve wounded. Ezra Moore was shot from his horse and killed. Jerry Doors was shot through the knee and afterward died from his wound.

As the battle drew to a close, Quantrill shouted a final order: "Cut through! And it's every man for himself and the devil take the hindmost." So after ordering Gregg to mount on one side as many of the wounded men who could still ride and escape through the enemy lines, Quantrill, John Koger, and the rest of the dismounted men charged through and escaped through the enemy lines on the opposite side of the ravine, closest to the timber.

The men commonly paired up, each one helping the other. Frank Ogden and John Jarrette rushed out together. Andy Blunt paired up with Joe Hart, and William Haller accompanied David Poole. In a close hand-to-hand encounter, Jim Cunningham was shot in the groin. His weapons were empty, but he managed to kill his attacker by clubbing him with his pistol. Even though he was wounded seriously, Cunningham escaped on horseback with James Campbell.

Before leaving, Quantrill gave the men orders to rendezvous at a point southeast of Pleasant Hill. Gregg led out about twenty men while Quantrill sacrificed himself by letting another more seriously wounded comrade have his horse.

Regarding the battle itself, Quantrill's bold maneuver of attacking in two different directions stunned the Federals and completely threw the enemy off balance. As they reeled back in confusion, Quantrill's men miraculously cut their way out. Frank James cut his way through on foot until he found a nearby farm where he found a horse and saddle and rejoined his comrades. Quantrill was forced to abandon his personal gear, which included his captain's coat and his saddle as well as a valuable spyglass that he had just replaced after the Clark house fight.

This fight would afterward be known as the Battle of the Ravines, and Quantrill's guerrillas long remembered it as the hardest fought battle of their careers. On the other side, Maj. James O. Gower had never fought a fight so desperately as this. He reported Quantrill's strength at 250 men. It contributed to Quantrill's reputation in that he was known to hold his own in a standup fight against superior numbers, even when fighting as dismounted cavalry.

This is the first instance of Quantrill's guerrillas fighting a large-scale static battle. Generally, historians have said that guerrillas only fought using hit-and-run tactics. They claimed that guerrillas waited in ambush then ran away to avoid open fights and casualties. As the Battle of the Ravines demonstrates, this distinction is hardly the truth. Throughout the wartime history of Missouri, Quantrill's guerrillas openly attacked garrisons and strongholds. They made three separate attacks upon the garrison in Independence and saw battles at Baxter Springs, Centralia, White Oak Creek, Lone Jack, Lamar, Carthage, Wellington, Fayette, Liberty, the Wagner fight, Shawneetown, Olathe, Lawrence, and many more noted elsewhere in this book. Most of the above-mentioned battles were based on cavalry charges, but the guerrillas could not bring their horsemanship to bear in such a battle as that which occurred in the ravines of Big Creek. Only expert marksmanship and individual bravery proved to be their salvation, plus the knowledge that fighting under the black flag would bring them no quarter if taken prisoner.

Although the guerrillas suffered heavy losses, the mission proved a success. Decoying the Federals into Cass County gave Upton Hays the time he needed to accomplish his recruitment mission. Even though half of the guerrillas were wounded, with many escaping on foot through the surrounding woods to safety, the numerically superior Federals declined to pursue them.[12] Union losses amounted to twenty-six killed and thirty-five wounded. If it had been necessary to prove the courage and discipline of Quantrill's soldiers, the Battle of the Ravines proved it abundantly.

It took Quantrill more than three weeks to recover from his wound, which was complicated by a case of erysipelas. The wound caused him to suffer from a severe rash accompanied by fever and chills. His men used the time to obtain fresh mounts and resupply their ammunition. Quantrill spent some time resting in the brush along the Sni-A-Bar Creek around Wellington. A new and bolder plan was taking shape in his mind.

Independence had officially become a Federal post on June 7, 1862, commanded by Col. James T. Buel of the Seventh Missouri Cavalry. Even though he knew of Hays's recruiting efforts within sight of Independence, Buel had kept his men garrisoned close to town. To combat Hays's efforts, Buel issued an order on August 10 that all Jackson County citizens should be disarmed. His men were prepared to carry out his order the following day.

Knowing this, Quantrill wanted to catch all the Federals together in garrison. Buel had his headquarters in the southwest corner of the town square in the Southern Bank building while the bulk of his garrison was quartered in tents a half-mile west of the town.

Buel's troops consisted of three companies of the Seventh Missouri Cavalry commanded by Capt. James Breckinridge; two companies of Maj. Andrew G. Nugent's Second Battalion, Enrolled Missouri Militia, commanded by Capt. Jacob Axline; and Capt. Aaron Thomas with a company of the Sixth Enrolled Missouri Militia, under the command of Capt. W. H. Rodewald, which was attached to the Seventh Missouri.[13] Rodewald's men were quartered across the street from Buel's command post and served as guards for the headquarters. The company provost guard was quartered in the city jail one block north. With these troops, Buel commanded more than six hundred men. The disjointed command structure resulted in poor communication, which served to hinder Buel's defense of the town.

While the Federals were stationed in Independence, City Marshal James Knowles informed Buel that he knew the location of a ford over the Little Blue frequently used by Quantrill's men. It was west of the old Independence to Harrisonville road, eight miles south of Independence, at the southeastern end of the Little Blue Valley. Here lay the small hamlet of Little Blue, consisting of a store, a schoolhouse, and several houses.

Buel sent a small militia detachment under Capt. Aaron Thomas to sit in wait along this ford in hopes of ambushing some guerrillas. The ford was a few hundred yards east of the town of Little Blue. It wasn't long before three guerrillas rode up: George Todd, John Little, and Ed Koger. They had just returned from escorting Hays through Jackson County.

The guerrillas were at ease in familiar territory with close Southern friends living nearby. Forgetting the usual vigilance known of guerrilla fighters, these three soldiers carelessly rode too close together into the ford. They should have entered the ford cautiously, one at a time, but their guard was down. As they entered the ford, they stopped to let their horses drink from the stream.

At this opportunity, Thomas led his men from their hiding places in the heavy underbrush and poured a deadly volley into the group. Little and Koger were killed instantly. Todd miraculously escaped unhurt. He spurred his horse up the hill into the safety of the timber. In his fright to get away, his horse became wedged between two large boulders, which forced him to escape on foot. The Federals did not attempt to follow. It was said that from this day on, Todd became one of the most daring and desperate guerrillas to ever sit astride a horse. He feared no man and took orders from very few. The killing of his two friends heightened his hatred for any man who wore a Federal uniform.

The Federals had previously captured two other of Quantrill's men: Harrison Trow and twenty-four-year-old Preston Webb. While spending the night at Trow's father's farm in Blue Springs, both Webb and Trow were surrounded by a Union regiment. They were taken to the Independence jail and kept as prisoners. Webb was convicted and sent to the Alton, Illinois, military prison; Trow was kept in Independence to be executed.

Trow's father, however, was a Union sympathizer, and after interceding with Buel, he was allowed to post a fifty-thousand-dollar bond for his son's release with the stipulation that Harrison would report to Federal headquarters every two hours and return at night to be locked up. Three days after giving bond, Trow escaped to a friend's house and got a horse. He then returned to Preston Webb's house and retrieved his pistols, which he had hidden, and returned to Quantrill's camp. Soon afterward, jayhawkers from Kansas burned down Webb's father's home and drove off all his livestock. In the meantime, Trow gave Quantrill a complete description of all troop dispositions in and around Independence.

Around August 1, 1862, regular Confederate officers converged in large numbers in Jackson County. Confederate Col. John T. Hughes arrived from Arkansas with about seventy-five men. Hughes had obtained military experience with Alexander Doniphan's celebrated exploits during the Mexican War and had fought alongside Gen. Sterling Price. He was also the editor of the *Plattsburg Clinton County News* and served in the Missouri General Assembly, where he ardently opposed Missouri's secession. When radical abolitionists forced the governor and the state leaders from office, Hughes gathered the troops under his command as an officer in the Missouri State Guard and resisted the Federal government's attempts at coercion. Following the battle of Pea Ridge, Arkansas, he was directed by the Confederate government to return to Missouri and recruit a brigade of volunteers from north of the Missouri River. He knew he could not get them south to Arkansas with such a large Federal force stationed in Independence to intervene.

Charles Coward, an elder in the Lee's Summit Christian Church, invited Hughes to camp on his farm south of Independence and just east of the Little Blue Valley. If Hughes could quickly gather enough men to attack and defeat Buel at Independence, then the victory would encourage young men to enlist in his new brigade. He also knew that he had to act before the Federals could muster enough men to oppose him if his plan was to be successful. Yet Hughes managed to recruit only about one hundred men. Failing to garner enough men by himself for an attack on Independence, Hughes turned to Upton Hays and Quantrill for assistance.

On Saturday, August 9, Quantrill, still suffering from a leg wound that was only partially healed from the recent Battle of the Ravines, joined Hughes at Blue Springs. Only two days before, Quantrill had met Hughes for the first time and learned of his intention to attack Independence. Hughes wanted as much up-to-date information as he could get. Knowing that Quantrill had a vast network of friends and spies, he asked him to reconnoiter the town.

Independence was built around a courthouse square. There were approximately seven businesses on each block that surrounded the stately southern-style courthouse.

Morgan T. Mattox entered the town on August 10 disguised as a farmer selling his produce; he returned with accurate information on the disposition of the Federal troops. Quantrill also sent Cole Younger, Dick Yeager, Boone Muir, and another man to gather any useful military information on the Federals in town. Hughes finalized his attack plan on August 11 and called Quantrill in to give him his orders.

Hughes assigned Quantrill the most important part of the mission: spearheading the assault. He would first engage the pickets without raising an alarm then charge on the town and secure the Federal headquarters in the brick bank building across the street from the courthouse. This action would cut the Federal commander off from the rest of his command. Quantrill was then to post a picket throughout the town to guard against counterattack. Hughes assured him, "You will be well supported. In fact, I shall be right behind you when you enter the public square."[14]

At ten o'clock Sunday night, three miles north of Blue Springs, Upton Hays and about three hundred men marched to join Hughes. Another Confederate officer, Col. Gideon W. Thompson, was attached to Colonel Hughes, but he did not command any men of his own here. Thompson had been with Price from the start of the war, seeing action at the battles of Lexington, Wilson's Creek, and Pea Ridge.

Sitting snugly in his headquarters in Independence, James T. Buel had been warned repeatedly by concerned citizens that he could expect an attack at any time. But he made no added precautions for the defense of the town.

Tales of Quantrill's previous exploits, however, spread quickly. His company had gained instant fame as formidable fighters in battle even though vastly outnumbered and outgunned by their enemies. Their fame was added to their arsenal of weapons, so much so that many Federal commanders would rather keep their men in garrison than venture too far out patrolling in guerrilla territory and did so only in overwhelming numbers.

It was Hughes's plan to have Quantrill seal Buel and his company of headquarters guards in town then interpose his men between the Federal commander and his troops. Quantrill and sixty men led the column toward Independence from Blue Springs at 4:30 in the morning of August 11.

In the early morning darkness Quantrill's advance scout quietly sneaked in and killed the Federal pickets on the eastern side of town, allowing Quantrill to continue along the Spring Branch road into Independence. Then, just east of the square, he formed his men into platoons. One platoon would help Hughes to attack and defeat the Federals west of town while Quantrill would lead the other platoon against Buel's headquarters.

Quantrill placed Cole Younger, Tom Talley, and Jim Morris right behind him. Pulling their pistols and readying themselves for the charge, Quantrill called out to his men, "Come on, boys!" and spurred his horse at a sharp gait toward the public square west on Lexington Street. Hughes's men followed Quantrill on foot through the square. The guard in front of Buel's headquarters saw the soldiers approaching and yelled out for them to halt. When they ignored his command, he fired a shot in alarm and ran to alert his comrades, who had been awakened by the noise and were already running for their weapons.

Rodewald, in charge of the guards on the second floor, ran to a window and fired at the Confederate soldiers below. In the darkness and confusion a Confederate shouted at the Federals, "For God's sake don't fire; it's your own men!" Not knowing if in fact the moving body of soldiers were indeed Union comrades or not, Rodewald had his men cease fire then led them downstairs to the street below. In the fading darkness, Rodewald recognized a Confederate soldier he knew personally and then ordered his men to fire at the rear of the Confederate column that was moving to the west of town to engage the Federal camp.

In the volley that followed, one of Quantrill's men, Kit Chiles, was killed. The Confederates made no halt until they reached the Federal camp where the soldiers were still asleep. Rodewald realized that he was surrounded by a vastly superior force, but he continued to make a gallant effort at defense. Some of his men were across the street and inside the brick courthouse. These men were able to fire at Quantrill's men from a different angle.

Colonel Buel, awakened from a sound sleep, saw from his window what was transpiring. He hollered at Rodewald to get his men into the headquarters building where they could make a more defensible stand. Rodewald complied immediately but soon learned that it was a mistake. Quantrill's men surrounded the bank building as soon as the Federals were inside and started firing at any soldier they saw in a doorway or window. Buel was cut off and trapped. The Federals inside were pinned down and unable to return fire. While Quantrill had one squad pin down the guards in Buel's headquarters, he ordered the other squad to seize the other posts around town.

George Todd and ten men rushed toward the county jail and quickly subdued the provost guards. Lt. Charles W. Meryhew, in charge of the guards at
the jail, only managed to fire one volley at the charging guerrillas before he
abandoned his post and fled for his life toward Kansas City.

Marshal Jim Knowles, who had previously piloted Buel's men into the
Little Blue Ford, was locked up in his own jail for killing an Irishman in a
brawl just a few days before. Todd found him there. Knowles looked into
Todd's eyes with the look of a doomed man. He confessed to piloting Buel to
the ford where Little and Koger were killed. Todd was said to have smiled as
he raised his pistols and emptied both barrels into Knowles.[15]

Three Southerners were also in the jail: William Basham, Frank Harbaugh, and John Cartmill Wallace. None had taken part in the war, but they
had been arrested as Southern sympathizers and were to be executed the next
day. Basham had been a stage driver on the Santa Fe Trail, but he had quit
and come home to Independence about the time Knowles killed the Irishman. Someone identified him as a Quantrill man, and he was locked up in
the jail.[16] Todd and Gregg took sledgehammers from a blacksmith shop and
proceeded to break open the doors of the jail, setting the three men free.
Basham immediately made for the provost marshal's office where huge supplies of confiscated guns were stored. He grabbed a shotgun and took off to
look for the men responsible for putting him in jail. After his revenge, he
stayed with Quantrill, following him all the way to Kentucky in 1864.

Frank Harbaugh ran away as soon as he was freed. John Wallace escaped
the country and didn't return until after the war.[17]

In the Commercial Hotel, just off the square, another squad of Quantrill's
men captured Capt. Aaron Thomas in his hotel room. Thomas, along with
Marshal Knowles, had led the ambush at the Little Blue Ford. After admitting
that he was also part of a pillaging party that stole from area farmers, Thomas
was shot then kicked down a flight of stairs.

Elsewhere during the attack, John McCorkle had been following right
behind Col. John T. Hughes and had just jumped the fence surrounding the
courthouse when Federals opened fire on them from the bank building and
the courthouse, catching them in a crossfire. In the first volley, Hughes was
shot five times. The fatal shot struck him in the middle of his forehead. Col.
Gideon W. Thompson, riding next to Hughes, was wounded next, a bullet
shattering a bone in his leg. As Thompson was carried from the field, command fell to Upton Hays.

On the west side of town, Hughes's men were already attacking the Federal camp. Many soldiers were killed before they could get out of their tents.

Panic seized others, and they ran away and did not stop until they were in Kansas City, more than eleven miles away. The Federals who did manage to get to their weapons found protection behind a rock wall on a hill facing the town. North of the rock wall was a hedge fence. The senior officer in charge at the camp was Captain Breckinridge. As soon as the Confederates fired their first volley, he was heard to call out to his men, "Boys, we are completely surrounded, and we had better surrender."

Capt. Jacob Axline, Breckinridge's second in command, could not believe that they were going to give up without a fight. Quickly taking charge, Axline shouted above all the noise, "Boys, get your guns and ammunition and rally behind the rock fence." Most of the Federals chose to obey Axline.

Seeing this organized resistance, Hays called upon his men to shoot the Federals' horses to keep them from escaping. He then asked for volunteers from Quantrill's men to try to get behind the hedge fence and force the Federals from behind their rock wall protection.

John McCorkle, his brother Jabez, and their cousin George Wigginton, along with Benjamin Rice and Barney Chambers, a Presbyterian minister, and thirty others volunteered to go. Once the guerrillas were in place, Chambers gave the order to fire. The Federals replied with a devastating hail of bullets that tore the hedge fence to pieces. Chambers was killed in the volley as the others withdrew to safer positions. While attempting to return fire on the Federals, George Wigginton received a wound in the leg, and Ben Rice was shot in the foot.

As McCorkle was taking these wounded men to a stable to load them in a wagon, his brother Jabez went back to the square and observed Quantrill returning from pursuing the fleeing Federals toward Kansas City. Hays relieved Quantrill's men at the stone wall, enabling them to concentrate on Buel at his headquarters. The battle had been raging now for at least an hour. Quantrill was seen bareheaded and coatless upon his black charger in every part of the town where the fighting was progressing. No man fought harder or exposed his life more recklessly. He seemed to be courting death, but he suffered not so much as a scratch.[18]

Quantrill rejoined his men on the square firing at the Federals in the bank building. The men inside realized they were in desperate straits. Every window had been shot out, and the building was completely riddled with bullets. Buel did not even have his flag flying from his headquarters. Trying to rally his men, Rodewald sent two soldiers to the roof to secure their flag to the chimney in hopes that the men west of town would see it and take heart. Both men were quickly shot down by Quantrill's sharpshooters.

Seeing that it was going to be difficult to get Buel out of the bank building, Hays asked Quantrill to make some type of demonstration against the
building. Quantrill replied, "Give me thirty men and plenty of guns and
ammunition and I will take Buel out of that bank."[19] Quantrill realized that it
was going to be nearly impossible to dislodge the Federals with only small
arms, so he decided to set it on fire. He then called for volunteers.

Jabez McCorkle and Cole Younger immediately stepped forward. Both
men ran under a hail of bullets to a nearby carpenter shop and gathered up
armfuls of wood shavings and piled them against the doors. Cole carried his
to the front door, and Jabez went to the rear door, and both managed to set
them on fire while their comrades kept up a constant fire at the windows.
John T. Noland and four other volunteers had to crawl more than two hundred yards. As they passed a stable on the northeast corner of the public
square, each of them gathered up an armful of straw and stuffed it into some
dry goods boxes that were under the eaves of the bank building. They then
placed the boxes in the doorway and set them on fire. As soon as the Federals
saw the smoke, they knew they were doomed. Pvt. John Haskell was ordered
to hoist a flag of truce over the building, but he was shot in the attempt. Buel
then tied a white flag to a bayonet and held it out a second-story window.[20]

Quantrill yelled out to his men, "Cease fire." After the firing died down,
Buel hollered out the window that he would surrender if his men were
treated as prisoners of war. To this Quantrill readily agreed. Buel emerged
from the building with tears in his eyes as he offered his sword to the
wounded Colonel Thompson. As the guerrillas lined up the Federals along
the town square awaiting parole, Buel commented that they would have surrendered earlier, but when they saw that they were fighting Quantrill's men,
they were afraid.

Quantrill had one of his men hoist the Confederate flag above the courthouse. Seeing the Confederate banner and hearing that the firing had ended
in town, the Federals behind the rock wall west of town knew that Buel had
given up. Even though they had an almost impregnable position, they lost
their fighting spirit once they knew their commander had surrendered.

The enemy dead and wounded filled the town. The Federal loss was
twenty-six killed and seventy-four wounded. Eleven of the wounded later
died from their wounds. The Confederates lost twenty-three killed and nine
wounded. Hays paroled Buel and his men. One of the paroled men, Anderson Cowgill, was a neighbor to John McCorkle. McCorkle tried to speak
with him, but Cowgill angrily replied, "I will get even with you yet."[21] They
marched off to Kansas City then were sent to St. Louis where they were mus-

tered out of the service. Only about one hundred of the Federals were present and able to surrender. The remaining Union soldiers had fled rather than face Quantrill's command.

Local women came out and sat with the men who were dying and wrote letters for them to their loved ones. Quantrill's wounded were taken to a nearby house and cared for. Mrs. R. T. Bass, who was a teenager at the time and living at a house in the middle of town, recalled seeing Quantrill as he checked on his men while she assisted Dr. P. H. Henry. She recalled:

> I saw Quantrill that day after the fighting was over, when he rode to the house to look after his wounded. He looked as little like the horrible, blood-thirsty bandit, he is usually described as, as it is possible to imagine. Instead of this, he was a modest, quiet, good-looking man, with blue eyes, light hair, gentle of manner and courteous as well, true as steel to his friends if implacable to his foes. I gave him a little silk flag, which pleased him very much. The Southern victory was short lived, for the same afternoon we were again appalled by the appearance of the dreaded Jennison's Jayhawkers on their horses at every window and doorway with guns leveled at us, shouting, "Let's shoot the damned secesh; they have no right to live."[22]

Where Capt. Aaron Thomas had been in charge of the commissary stores south of the Commercial Hotel, Quantrill's men found more than two hundred pounds of plundered bacon. After the wounded were taken care of, the Southerners destroyed the Federal camp. When they withdrew they took all of the guns, ammunition, and supplies that they could carry. They loaded the military stores into twenty wagons and headed back to the camp near Blue Springs.

The following morning as Quantrill's men were dispensing the spoils of war, a messenger brought them word that the noted Kansas Redleg George Hoyt was burning the houses of Southern people on the east side of the Blue River. Colonel Thompson, still suffering from his wound from the previous day, assumed command and started in pursuit. Hoyt had already started back to Kansas and was so far ahead of the Confederates that he managed to escape. Thompson and Hays left Quantrill outside of Independence and marched the rest of their troops sixteen miles east, toward Lone Jack, to seek reinforcements and recruits.

Quantrill meanwhile led his company to the Morgan Walker farm in Blue Springs, east of Independence. Here he distributed the captured military supplies and confiscated commissary stores among his company to take to neighboring farms and hide them for future use. He deposited several large barrels of gunpowder in a cave on the north side of the Walker farm. When this was accomplished, he marched his men to the George Ingraham farm, six miles west of the tiny hamlet of Lone Jack. Quantrill had recruited many new men who saw his organization as the only way to save their farms and possessions. There were 150 men mustered in his command.

Two and a half miles northwest of Lone Jack, Colonel Thompson, now traveling in an ambulance captured from Buel at Independence, had the authority from the Confederate government to formally swear Quantrill and his men into the Confederate partisan service. With the swearing in, the soldiers in Quantrill's band were henceforth committed to the authority of their officers and were only to obey the orders of Quantrill himself. His discipline was strict enough that his men always quickly and explicitly obeyed his orders without question. After being sworn in by Thompson on August 12, Quantrill was ordered to report his activities to the proper authorities every thirty days. He would be on the payroll of the Confederate government, and when his company found themselves within Confederate lines, he could draw provisions on the regular Confederate army commissary stores for his men and horses.

Quantrill had had his men organized as a military unit for some time now. After being sworn into the partisan service, there was little change he had to make in his company structure. Quantrill, Haller, and Todd all retained their rank and positions. His new structure included William H. Gregg as third lieutenant. Cole Younger was one of those sworn in that day. Cole remembered, "It was within a day or two after the surrender of Buel at Independence that I was elected as first lieutenant in Captain Jarrette's company in Colonel Upton B. Hays' regiment, which was part of the brigade of General Joseph O. Shelby." Quantrill's new company duty roster was reported to regular Confederate authorities the next day.

News of the Confederate victory was splashed across newspapers all over the South. On August 15 the *Richmond Whig* and *Mobile Advertiser and Register* carried the jubilant news of "Quantrill's victory in Missouri."

In Lexington, across the river to the north, Union Col. Emory L. Foster learned of the Federal defeat at Independence and was determined to do something about it. He gathered 985 cavalrymen and two guns of Rabb's Indiana battery and headed south to find the Confederates and offer battle. He felt confident of victory because he had assurances from Gen. Fitz Henry Warren and the First Iowa Cavalry from Clinton that they would meet him on the morning of August 16. Once they joined forces, they were to wait for

Gen. James G. Blunt, commander of the Department of Kansas, who would join them with his Kansas regiment from Fort Scott. It was a sound plan, but one that was not well coordinated. Each commander was unable to join forces with Foster until the anticipated battle was already under way.

Lone Jack, Missouri, was named for a large jack oak tree that stood alone on the prairie. This is where the principle settlement grew and where the township elections were held. The town was on a ridge of prairie between the Osage and Missouri Rivers. Pioneers from North Carolina settled the area in the early 1830s. There were nearly thirteen hundred people, predominately Southern, living in the area.

As Quantrill was resting with his men outside of Lone Jack, word came once again that George Hoyt was returning to burn the town of Independence. At this news, Quantrill divided his men into two platoons. On the morning of August 16 he took ninety men back to Independence to guard the town from the suspected jayhawker attack. The remaining sixty men were left under the charge of 1st Lt. William Haller in camp at the Adams farm, halfway between Independence and Lone Jack. Before leaving, Quantrill left orders for Haller not to abandon his position under any circumstances except by Quantrill's own orders. Quantrill knew numerous Federal patrols would be looking for the victorious Confederates after the Independence fight. After hauling away the remainder of the military supplies from Independence, he would rejoin the rest of his command and assist the Confederate army that was in the vicinity.

Gen. Thomas C. Hindman's other recruiting officers, Cols. Vard Cockrell and John T. Coffee, had already pushed toward Jackson County with more than a thousand men. Poorly armed and equipped, Coffee's men were hoping to obtain arms, ammunition, and additional recruits. While Union Col. Emory Foster's patrol was looking for Quantrill and Hays's Confederates, he stumbled upon Cockrell and Coffee's forces in Lone Jack and opened an engagement the following morning.

On August 15 Foster opened with his Indiana battery on the town where the Confederates were stationed. Cockrell withdrew to the west while Coffee withdrew to the south. Hays and his small command soon marched to the sound of the guns and found the Southerners had all agreed upon a general attack on the Union forces in the morning.

The battle began a little after 5 A.M. on August 16. All morning the fighting raged back and forth. Each time the Confederates attacked and captured the artillery battery, the Federals beat them back and reclaimed the guns. The battle was indecisive for almost five hours.

Maj. Harry J. Vivian, attached to Gideon W. Thompson's command, had his horse shot out from under him during the battle of Independence. At the battle of Lone Jack he was captured with two or three other Confederates. The Federals lined them up and executed them. Vivian only managed to escape death when his executioner's pistol failed to fire. Vivian angrily remarked that such actions would exact a terrible revenge.

Upton Hays knew that Quantrill had left part of his command a few miles away, and knowing how they could easily turn the tide of battle, he sent a courier to seek their aid. When the courier found Lieutenant Haller and relayed Hays's request, Haller refused. He knew the repercussions of disobeying Quantrill's orders. James Campbell, one of Quantrill's men, remembered, "Now, when Quantrill gave orders he was obeyed. No man stopped to parley any further." So the courier returned and informed Hays that Haller was not coming. Hays knew he was in a desperate situation and respected the fighting abilities of Quantrill's men, so he sent a second courier to again ask for assistance. Haller was adamant about refusing to leave his post, but William H. Gregg, John Jarrette, and Cole Younger persuaded him that Quantrill would understand and agree to their cooperation with Hays. Haller issued orders to march toward Lone Jack.

The guerrillas covered the area in short order. When they arrived on the field of battle, the Southerners cheered them on with a hearty welcome. Being told that the Confederates were short on ammunition, Cole Younger was said to have found a ready supply. Disregarding his own safety, Younger rode across the front lines and distributed ammunition by the handfuls to his Confederate comrades. He was the only soldier to have remained mounted during the entire engagement.

Now the Confederates attacked, and the Federals took defensive positions in the town's buildings as the battle turned into a house-to-house fight. During this daring Confederate assault, the Federals lost forty-three men killed and had all their horses killed as Quantrill's men attacked and captured the battery guns.

During the fighting Emory Foster was wounded but did not leave the field. A second time he was wounded but remained in command. The third time he was wounded, he had to be carried from the field to the only hotel in town, which was being used a hospital. Foster's brother, a captain, was mortally wounded. Dr. Summers, a medical doctor in Quantrill's company, was also killed during the battle.[23] Knowing that Quantrill's men were taking part in the battle, Foster was initially fearful of surrendering until he was guaranteed his men would be treated as prisoners of war and paroled.[24]

As the battle was drawing to a close, William H. Gregg, with Quantrill's men, managed to capture about 150 prisoners. Gregg reported, "Cole Younger displayed the greatest of magnanimity, in that he saved the life of Colonel Foster and his brother, and, also saved them some seven or eight hundred dollars in money." While in the hospital having his wounds treated, the Union colonel entrusted his money to Younger, who despite being labeled as a robber by his enemies, carried the treasure to Foster's mother in Warrensburg.

Two hundred Federals shirked their duty during the fighting, and sensing the smell of defeat, they managed to break through the Southern lines to the south, where it was weakest, and ran for the safety of Lexington. William Haller, William H. Gregg, Harrison Trow, Coleman Younger, and the remainder of Quantrill's company pursued them and cut them down whenever they attempted to make a stand. The wounded were so numerous in the countryside around the tiny hamlet of Lone Jack that maneuvering was difficult.

Dr. Minor T. Smith, a doctor from Brooking Township, heard the firing from the cannon when the battle started and hurried in his buggy to offer medical assistance. He was on the battlefield and treated the wounds of Union and Confederate alike all day and all the following night. When he was criticized for tending the Union wounded, he vehemently asserted, "I'm a doctor!"[25] Southern kindness such as this was seldom repaid along the border.

The Federals withdrew after the battle, enabling the Southerners to continue their recruiting efforts. But within a few days, Federals from every corner of the state began converging on Jackson County. The enormous casualties suffered kept the Confederates from remaining in possession of the field following their victory. There were approximately 2,300 soldiers in the battle. The Federals lost 136 dead and more than 550 wounded. The Confederate loss was said to be 118 killed and 134 wounded.[26] Union Brig. Gen. James G. Blunt marched 2,000 cavalrymen across the border and began pressing the Southerners the night after the battle.

Colonels Cockrell and Coffee turned south and withdrew back to Arkansas, closely followed by Blunt. Col. Jo Shelby camped his brigade at Waverly, Missouri, slipped through the Federal lines under the cover of darkness, and rejoined Cockrell. Upton Hays had not finished filling his quota of recruits, so he determined to stay in Jackson County.

Buoyed by their recent victories at the August 11 battle of Independence as well as the battle of Lone Jack five days later, Hays and part of his victorious troops, assisted by Quantrill's partisan rangers, set up a recruiting station in southeast Jackson County along a tributary of the Little Blue

River called White Oak Creek. While other Southern forces withdrew toward Arkansas, Quantrill and Hays alone remained in western Missouri to challenge Yankee domination.

Enlistments were brisk. The men from nearby Brooking Township and other nearby villages flocked to join up. The officers noted that they found "the woods full of men" willing and ready to join the Southern fight. The recent Confederate triumphs had made the local men eager to sign up. An edict from the provisional Missouri government, ordering all able-bodied men to join the "loyal militia" or to "leave the State," nudged formerly reluctant enlistees into the Southern ranks.[27]

Just north of the Missouri River in Platte County was a Confederate militia company commanded by a forty-nine-year-old farmer from Kentucky, Capt. Henry M. Woodsmall. He started out in Southern service early in the war as a private in Col. John H. Winston's regiment from Clay County, and in the spring of 1862 Woodsmall had obtained a commission to recruit a company. Most of his volunteers were from the vicinity of Parkville in Platte County, and he succeeded in collecting enough men to form a company. From the beginning of the war to the end, there were between eighteen hundred and two thousand Southern volunteers from Platte County, not counting reenlistments. In the early part of August 1862, Woodsmall encamped his volunteers about four miles east of Parkville and drilled his men.

Woodsmall's presence was reported to Union Col. William Penick, in command of a regiment at Liberty. Penick moved rapidly into the county and surprised Woodsmall's company, killing two men. The Confederates successfully defended themselves, slipping away from Penick and marched south to join Sterling Price. On Saturday, August 16, Woodsmall crossed the Missouri River with 128 men, looking for Quantrill's camp in southern Jackson County just south of Brooking Township.[28] There he found Quantrill assisting Hays with the recruiting efforts.

Upon receiving news of Hays's recruiting camp, Federal Col. Charles Jennison in Kansas City, along with Colonel Penick, who was still trying to pick up the trail of Woodsmall's company, each set out with a troop of cavalry to find the camp and break it up.[29] On Sunday evening, August 17, the Federal troops arrived twelve miles southeast of Kansas City, at the tiny hamlet of Hickman's Mill, and bivouacked for the night after stabling their horses inside the Hickman's Mill Christian Church.

In 1856 only ten families lived in Hickman's Mill. By 1862 the settlement contained a general store as well as a small Federal outpost.

Around five o'clock on Monday morning, August 18, Jennison's Seventh Kansas Jayhawker Regiment and Penick's Missouri cavalry were mounted and ready to march eastward. Within two miles of Colonel Hays's camp, they passed by the farm of James H. Kemper, a Baptist minister. The Federals interrupted the work of Kemper's eighteen-year-old son George, ordering him to unhitch the team working in the cornfield so he could accompany them and guide them to Hays's recruiting camp. Once there, George Kemper and another young man—David Bryant, whom the Federals had earlier pressed into being a guide—were ordered to hold the cavalrymen's horses. They witnessed the entire action that followed.[30]

Two hours after leaving Hickman's Mill the Federals closed in on their objective. They approached a mile-long valley floor that was only four hundred yards wide, east to west, surrounded by woods and rock outcroppings forty to sixty feet high. At the base of the rock ledge on the south side of the valley ran the tributary of the Little Blue River known as White Oak Creek. Here the Confederates were camped, protected by the rocks above and close to a good supply of water.

The Union commanders decided upon an east-west pincer attack. The company attacking eastward proceeded down a narrow winding trail, through heavy timber, and entered the long, narrow valley.

As soon as the Federals were spotted, Pvt. Ben Estes, one of Quantrill's pickets, tried to alert Hays's camp to the enemy's approach but mistook the force between him and the camp as Confederates. When he yelled, "Boys, they are coming," a barrage of shots was his reply. Although twenty-six bullet holes were afterward counted in his clothing and blankets, he suffered not a scratch. Estes was, however, captured, held for two days, then exchanged for the one Federal soldier captured by the Confederates.

Hearing the Federals firing at the Southern picket, the Confederates quickly withdrew to the rock outcroppings above them. Realizing that they had found the Rebel recruiting camp, the Union commanders immediately ordered a charge. The accuracy of 160 Southern sharpshooters safely nestled in the rocks easily drove the Yankee horsemen to the other side of the valley to regroup. The Federals had no choice but to try to rally and make a stand in the level field across the creek.

The battle raged for more than two hours. Three times the Federals charged, attempting to dislodge the Southerners from their stronghold in the rocks, but each time they were forced back by a galling fire. A nearby farmer, forty-five-year-old George Washington Wells—married and a father of six children—heard the noise of battle and hurried to get a good look. Wells was a cousin of the Flanerys and Shepherds who were fighting in Quantrill's company, and his wife was said to have discovered the body of Cole Younger's father when Federal militia murdered him along the road to Kansas City just a few weeks earlier.

When Wells arrived near the scene, he climbed atop a large bolder and began to hurrah for the Southern forces. In their disgust at being unable to rout the Southerners, the Federals turned their fire on the unarmed civilian and shot him down in cold blood. After the battle the Southerners carried him a mile back through the eastern end of the valley to his home and buried him.

The Northerners suffered seven or eight killed and an unreported number of wounded. After they retreated, their dead were carried by the Southerners to the only farm in the neighborhood, owned by Zion Flanery, and buried in a ravine in hastily dug graves. The Federal wounded were immediately cared for on the battlefield by Hays and Quantrill's men then taken into the Flanery home and cared for by Dr. Caleb Winfrey, a surgeon in Hays's regiment. Winfrey had also seen service at the battles of Wilson's Creek, Lexington, and Lone Jack. Flanery's wife and other local women assisted the doctor. Later Zion Flanery reburied the Federals in a little cemetery surrounded by a slat fence in his own back yard. To repay his kindness, the Federals returned under Gen. Thomas Ewing's General Orders No. 11 a year later and chased the elderly Flanery through his fields, where he was gathering corn for his family, and murdered him. When the Federals were asked why they had killed him, they simply replied, "Because we knew he was a Southern man."

After the battle Jennison and Penick pulled their battered regiments back to their base while Hays gathered up his Jackson County regiment, strengthened now by dozens of new recruits, and moved off to Arkansas to join General Price. Hays lingered ten days in southern Jackson County before he himself headed south, leaving the field exclusively to Quantrill and his partisan ranger company.

Before Hays left, Quantrill demanded that a Federal prisoner, Lt. Levi Copeland of Nugent's regiment, who had been captured at the battle of Lone Jack the week before, be turned over to him. Hays did so. Copeland was from Kansas. According to Quantrill's chief scout, John McCorkle, Copeland had a short time before gone to the house of a very old man who had two sons in Quantrill's company and demanded the surrender of the two boys. After being told that he knew nothing of their whereabouts, Copeland and his men took the old man to a tree within a few feet of his front porch and there, in the presence of his wife and daughters, hanged him. Copeland remarked as he rode off, "This is what I do to all damned Rebel sympathizers." Quantrill wanted Copeland for a hostage for one of his own men, Perry Hoy, who was being held at Fort Leavenworth under sentence of death.

The significance of the battle of White Oak Creek is that it was the third Southern victory in Missouri within a week's time in which the tide of battle turned because of the fighting abilities of Quantrill's partisan rangers. Recruitments were bolstered as many young Missourians joined up to fight in Price's army. Many later joined Gen. Jo Shelby's brigade under Gen. John Sappington Marmaduke while a few stayed behind to join Quantrill's band to guard Southern homes against other Northern incursions.

Cole Younger stayed with Quantrill in Jackson County. He still had his mother and brothers and sisters at home to protect. After the battle of Lone Jack, Cole learned that a Federal officer had raped his eighteen-year-old sister, Sarah Anne "Sally" Younger. When she relayed the story to her shocked brother, he swore to her that the man would never bother her again. Cole recalled: "I had decided that minute to make him pay, and after he paid he would never be able to return to persecute my sister, or any other virtuous girl again."[31] Cole found the Union captain with a squad of men on the open road sometime after this incident. When the smoke had cleared, there were thirteen Federals lying dead in addition to the captain. Cole had kept his word. In retaliation for Cole's revenge in murdering the officer and his men, the Federals continually harassed the remaining Younger family.

While Quantrill and Hays basked in their recent victories, the Federals swarmed over the county and made ordinary life impossible. Lt. John T. Burris, in command of the Fourth Kansas Jayhawker Regiment, followed up in the Southerners' wake by destroying the Southern newspaper the *Border Star* in Independence and burning homes of Southern sympathizers. On August 22 Burris led his troops south to Harrisonville. On the morning of the next day, Burris arrived at the farm of Charles Coward, which was a known guerrilla rendezvous and camp. He burned the house and outbuildings and the immense ricks of grain on the premises.[32] When Quantrill heard of these depredations, he brought up his men and formed a line of battle. Burris confronted the guerrilla force in the valley of the Little Blue with two pieces of artillery, scattering the Confederate force. Burris chose not to pursue Quantrill's command but instead, after seizing forty slaves and a quantity of plunder, headed back to his base at Fort Leavenworth.[33]

On August 28, a week after Hays marched south to Newtonia, Missouri, two farmers, Charles Cowherd and William B. Howard, both with large spreads where Cole Younger had a camp on the East Fork of the Little Blue, brought Quantrill a copy of the newspaper *Missouri Republican*. The guerrilla chieftain read the paper at a table in a cabin at his hideout in Brooking Township, just a mile north of the recent battle of White Oak Creek. William H. Gregg was sitting nearby, waiting to see the paper, and saw a sudden striking change come over his commander's face. Dropping the paper, Quantrill scribbled a note and handed it to Gregg with the curt order, "Give this to Andy Blunt." Gregg was curious, so as soon as he left the cabin he read the note: "Take Lieutenant Copeland out and shoot him. Go to Woodsmall's camp, get two prisoners from his camp, shoot them, and return as quickly as possible."[34]

Quantrill had always tried to exchange prisoners. He naturally did not wish to execute prisoners, but he likewise could not abide not avenging the murder of his own men.

Afterward Gregg picked up the paper and saw that Perry Hoy had been executed on July 28 at Fort Leavenworth. Several shots reverberated through the forest, and Blunt reported that the order had been carried out. Quantrill was livid because the Federals would not negotiate prisoner exchanges with him. Immediately after Blunt reported, Quantrill ordered his men to saddle up and get ready to march. When Gregg asked what Quantrill was planning, he replied, "We are going to Kansas and kill ten more men for poor Perry."

Solomon Perry Hoy had been one of Quantrill's first recruits. After being captured at the fight at Tate's house the previous March, he was taken to Fort Leavenworth and tried for the murder of a man named Allison, a soldier in the First Missouri Cavalry killed during the battle at the Tate house. Even though Hoy was a soldier sworn into a partisan ranger company, the Federals had him executed.[35] A witness reported that Hoy was made to kneel in front of his executioners for a prolonged time as if his killers were intent on torturing him. He was brought before the firing squad, and his sentence was read to him. Then he was taken back, forced upon his knees, and blindfolded. The firing squad was only twenty yards away. After they fired, Hoy fell face forward and died without a struggle. One ball went through his head and two through his body. After examination of the body, it was placed in a coffin and borne to the military burial ground. The soldiers marched off while the band played a lively air.

It was late Friday evening, September 5, when Quantrill and his 150-man company started for Olathe, Kansas. Olathe was becoming an armed camp and a jumping-off point for jayhawker raids into Missouri. The guerrillas first rode as far as Red Bridge, just five miles from Brooking Township, where they camped for the night. Along the way they stopped at several homes belonging to Union militiamen. The men were taken from their homes and shot. Gregg observed that most of the slain were known to them. Dick Maddox and Joe Hall killed three: Frank Cook and brothers John and James Judy. They were recent volunteers in Company A of the new Twelfth Kansas Jayhawker Regiment being organized in Olathe. The Judy brothers' father had formerly lived in Cass County, but he had gone to Kansas after being driven out because of his Unionist sympathies. One of Quantrill's men, John A. Workman, recalled the scene when the guerrillas captured the jay-hawkers: "Don't you know that every mother's son of them denied knowing anything about those deeds? Can soldiers stop to inquire who has wronged them?"[36] Before the guerrillas had reached the outskirts of Olathe, ten men were dead in their wake.

As Quantrill rode into Olathe at midnight, he was trying to remain unnoticed and unobtrusive. He ordered Gregg to take sixty men and throw a cordon around the town and let no one enter or escape. Quantrill took the remaining eighty men and made straight for the center of town. Most of his men wore Federal uniforms.

Even at this late hour, there were a few loafers lounging around the streets. One of the vagabonds thought that Quantrill's men were cavalrymen arriving to join the new jayhawker company. "Is that Captain Harvey's command?" he shouted, and got a whispered "Yes" for an answer.

The raiders found 125 soldiers drawn up on the sidewalk south of the town square. Quantrill immediately planned to capture these men without bloodshed. He ordered his soldiers to hitch their horses close together then form a line to the rear of their horses. Then he shouted out an order: "Halt! Dismount. File right. File left. Take immediate possession and don't let a man escape. Every third man hold the horses, respect women and children. Kill no one unless you are resisted."[37] With this completed, the guerrillas drew their revolvers and ordered the Federals to surrender, which they did without firing a shot.[38]

Once the civilian loafers realized that the guerrillas were not a Federal command, two of them began running to give an alarm. Quantrill's men, with their pistols at the ready, attempted to stop them before the town could be awakened. One sluggard wearing a Federal overcoat, Marion Melhoran, attempted to run and was shot in the foot. Hiram Blanchard, another civilian who had been in the saloon, tried to get to his horse outside. A guerrilla stopped him and seized the horse. Blanchard stepped to the opposite side of the animal, pulled a butcher knife from his boot, and attempted to reclaim his horse. He was shot down by a blast from a double-barrelled shotgun.

There were a number of jayhawker recruits sleeping on the second story of the courthouse. The guerrillas made for the barracks to disarm the Federals before they could offer any resistance. Philip Wiggins, a new recruit, yanked the pistol from the nearest guerrilla at the top of the stairs and snapped it four times in the guerrilla's face, but it did not fire. While the guerrilla wrestled with Wiggins, other guerrillas came to help and shot Wiggins.

In addition to avenging Perry Hoy, the raiders were also there to retaliate against recent raids in Missouri. They confiscated wagons from the nearby farms and stables and loaded up arms, ammunition, and military supplies to take back to the Southern army.

By now the raiders had surrounded the town and disarmed the Federal soldiers. Quantrill herded all the male civilians and Federal militia into a town corral. He recognized Judge Ezra W. Robinson among the prisoners and invited him out of the corral, saying, "Ezra, come out here. I want to see you." They then walked to a nearby bench on the town square and talked in a friendly manner for more than an hour. Quantrill pulled his commission from his pocket and lit a match so Robinson could read it.

In an 1881 letter, Robinson recalled their conversation. "During our conversation I addressed him once as Bill, he very politely requested me to address him as Captain Quantrill, and took from his pocket and showed me what he claimed was a commission from the Confederate government, but I did not read it, being an old acquaintance, and having no grudge against me, he treated me kindly." Judge Robinson inquired if and when Quantrill would be raiding Paola. The guerrilla captain replied, "Ezra, that is uncertain. I will try to make a call there sometime, but must decline to make an appointment for any special time."[39]

The only men killed in the Olathe raid were those who were attempting escape or resisting capture besides the jayhawkers who were killed along the route. In contrast to Henry W. Halleck's order to shoot or hang Quantrill and his men when found, Quantrill promised his prisoners that they would not be harmed. True to his word, early the next morning, Quantrill marched them to a prairie two miles east of town and paroled them. He and his men then continued back to Missouri without burning a single building and managed to avoid the various militia units dispatched to intercept them.[40]

In retaliation for Burris's burning of the Southern newspaper in Independence two weeks earlier, Quantrill ordered his men to destroy the town's newspapers, the *Olathe Mirror* and the *Olathe Herald*. When news of his actions reached Fort Leavenworth, Burris set out in pursuit of Quantrill's company. Burris caught up with him on the morning of September 10 on the north branch of the Grand River in Cass County. Not wanting to give battle, the guerrillas led the pursuing column through three counties before losing it.

After the Olathe raid Quantrill led his men to safety in the heavy timber in Lafayette County, along the banks of the Sni-A-Bar Creek just outside Wellington. On September 18, 1862, Capt. George Summers's Company I of Colonel Neal's Seventy-first Missouri State Militia, under the command of Lt. Matthew Reid, was camped in the town of Wellington. As was their usual practice, small groups of four to five soldiers would take meals at private homes.

On this particular day a Federal patrol from Wellington was searching for guerrillas near the Sni-A-Bar Creek. Quantrill's camp was along the banks of the Big Sni, on the farm of Harvey Gleaves. Quantrill and a small detail were doing exactly what the Federals were doing: eating meals in small groups at private homes. While Quantrill was eating breakfast, he heard distant gunfire. The Union patrol had discovered the camp on the Gleaves farm, and in the attack that followed, the Federal horsemen had chased away the few guerrillas left in camp. The Union troops captured the camp equipment and also one of Quantrill's horses.

On hearing the Yankees firing in his camp, Quantrill immediately rode to the scene. By this time the rest of his men rejoined him, and by noon he had forty guerrillas assembled. At first Quantrill thought the Federals were part of Burris's command but soon discovered it was only a militia unit of seventy-five men from nearby Wellington. Quantrill deployed his men, and in the counterattack that followed, he drove the Federals toward the town. While the Union troops retreated through the main streets, they yelled out warnings to their comrades.

Resident C. M. Bowring reported that the guerrillas came riding down the Independence road at full speed. He remembered Quantrill leading the charge and that each guerrilla had a pistol in either hand and that they had their reins between their teeth. He reported that their long hair was blowing behind them and that their hats, held in place by a cord around their necks, hung down across their backs.

As soon as the guerrillas entered the town, Quantrill divided his men into two platoons and ordered each to cut off the Federal retreat. When they reached the Sni Bridge, some of the Union soldiers attempted to make a stand, but Quantrill's men attacked without making a halt and drove past the bridge, scattering the enemy in every direction and killing many of them. Quantrill's own shooting was superb; he emptied six saddles. Andy Blunt emptied five; William Haller and Cole Younger four each; David Poole, Fletcher

Taylor, and George Shepherd took out three apiece; and George Todd, William Gregg, Simeon Whitsett, John Koger, Hicks George, and Ferdinand Scott each felled two.

Of the seventy-five Federals, ten returned unhurt.[41] One guerrilla went to the home of G. C. Adamson, took a stick of burning wood and burned down the bridge over the Big Sni to keep the rest of the Federals from escaping. Only one guerrilla, Ferdinand Scott, was wounded.

David Poole and six or seven of his men dropped behind the charging column and began searching the houses in town for any trapped Federals. The first home Poole searched belonged to Peter Wolf. Three Federals were eating lunch inside when they heard the firing in town. One quick-thinking soldier managed to slip away quickly out a side door and into the nearby timber.

While Poole kept guard by the front gate, he ordered two of his men to go around back to cut off any Federals left inside. As they entered the dining room, one of the Federals, George Williams, was shot and killed. The other, James Porter, attempted to escape via the front door when he ran into Poole and quietly surrendered. Poole wanted Porter desperately. Not long before, Porter led his gang of militia to the farm of Poole's sister and shot her husband, leaving his body in the field where he was slain. Poole made a solemn vow to avenge the wrong done his sister. As Porter stood before the guerrilla, he anticipated his fate, knowing it was useless to try to run. For a few short moments, Poole aimed his pistol at Porter. After the memories of what Porter had done to his sister had run through his mind, he finally pulled the trigger, killing Porter instantly. Ironically, Poole and his victim were schoolmates and cousins.[42]

Hearing of the devastating Federal defeat at Wellington, Col. Everett Peabody's regiment pursued Quantrill, pushing him back through Wellington and across the Sni. Quantrill burned the bridge in his rear, slowing Peabody's pursuit. Quantrill then marched his command west to Mecklin, in eastern Jackson County, where they stopped for supper. After scattering a local militia unit, the guerrillas learned that Burris was still on their trail. Keeping constantly on the move, Quantrill moved his men three miles to the north then rested until morning. At daybreak they moved to Bone Hill, where they took breakfast. They had barely finished when Burris's men drove in their pickets.

Burris and his Kansas regiment were attempting to cut him off at the Blackwater Ford on the Sni-A-Bar Creek. This time Burris pressed them more vigorously, but the guerrillas did not bring the action to a stand until about four o'clock in the afternoon. The situation looked bad for the guerrillas. They found themselves between two Federal forces, and if they were allowed to come any nearer, Quantrill's company might have been annihilated. Quantrill's only hope was to turn and fight, breaking through the Federal line.

Cole Younger was detailed to fall back with twenty men and act as rear guard for Quantrill's main force. The guerrillas withdrew to the south toward the high prairie north of Pleasant Hill, but before they got halfway across, Younger sent to Quantrill for reinforcements. Quantrill sent word to cross over to a nearby ridge, where he would form the men on line and give battle.

Younger dashed for the ridge with the Federals in close pursuit. As he and his small force reached the ridge, Quantrill appeared with the remainder of the men and charged, momentarily scattering the enemy.

Quantrill gathered his command near Pink Hill and spelled out his plan. "Men," he said, "you see how it is as plainly as I do. It is my business to get you out of this, and I will get you out. Just over the ridge yonder, you can see them from the summit, five hundred Federals, your old friends under Burris, are coming up to hold you in check until Peabody's column arrives. Then, instead of ten to one, there will be thirty to one. We shall strike Burris first, and trust to luck."[43]

Following this brief speech, Quantrill arrayed his men in line. He had to change his tactics somewhat. He did not mean to attack and rout; this time his only thought was to break through the Federals and escape. Quantrill placed his men in two ranks at double intervals, allowing enough room for deadly pistol play. From two hundred yards away, the guerrillas began galloping toward Burris. At thirty yards the guerrillas spurred their horses into a fast charge, pistols blazing and the old Rebel Yell.

The scene was incredible. Dense powder smoke from their pistols seemed to hide the wedge as it broke the Federal line. Instead of wheeling and charging for another pass, Quantrill led his men into the heavy timber beyond. Too many of his men had been wounded in the running battles of the last few days. Ferdinand Scott, Charley Harrison, Hicks George, and George Shepherd were all wounded, as was Quantrill himself. Todd had been wounded twice; Poole was shot and Anderson Scrivener was killed.[44] The Federals lost nine men in this engagement; the Confederates only lost one, a young man named Simmons from Westport.

Before he reached the timber near Pleasant Hill, Quantrill instructed his men to scatter in groups of twos and threes to avoid pursuit and assemble again in four or five days at one of his old rendezvous. Darkness enabled them to escape. The Federals lost their trail the next morning.

The guerrillas had lost two men during the running ten-day battle, and the Federals recovered most of the spoils taken by the guerrillas during the Olathe raid. Burris recovered six wagons, one hundred muskets, ten thousand rounds of ammunition, clothing, and groceries. Not satisfied at retrieving the spoils of war, Burris's jayhawkers plundered the countryside. When they returned to Fort Leavenworth, they brought back a hundred horses, four yoke of oxen, and more than sixty seized slaves.[45]

Although Quantrill disbanded his men on September 21 to rest and resupply, many continued to confront Federal troops. The day after disbanding, Cole Younger, twenty-year-old William Hulse, and a detachment of ten men made a reconnaissance of Independence, which was guarded now by seventy-two Federals. With them were Ferdinand Scott, William Haller, Simeon Whitsett, David Poole, George Wigginton, Frank James, Warren Welch, and Harrison Trow. Outside of town they discovered a Federal picket detail guarding some horses much needed by the guerrillas. Four men formed the picket, but a score more were in reserve on the Blue Springs Road. Waiting until dark, Younger had two men hold the guerrillas' horses while he, Hulse, and the rest of the men snuck up on the unwary Federals. The guerrillas managed to capture the four without alarming the reserve outpost, some of whom were asleep in their blankets while others were sitting at ease around the fire. Suddenly, like a thunderclap, the guerrillas poured a deadly volley into the picket party with their Navy Colt revolvers, killing seventeen Federals and wounding the rest. The guerrillas managed to capture three horses apiece and made their escape back to their camp hidden by the darkness.[46]

The Federal officer who had captured Quantrill's horse at the battle of Wellington was using it as his own. Shortly afterward, Quantrill spied it tied to a hitch in front of Wellington's general store while the officer and another soldier were inside on business. Quantrill walked up to his horse and waited patiently outside the store until the officer came outside. He reclaimed his horse after shooting the man then rode off for Jackson County to gather up the rest of his men in their camps among the hills of the Little Blue Valley.

Once again the Federals were on Quantrill's trail. Col. John T. Burris's Kansas regiment followed Quantrill's command into Columbus, Johnson County, Missouri. There was not much left of Columbus. Only eighteen months earlier Jennison had burned the town to the ground. The guerrillas were attempting to refit themselves, get forage for their horses after the raid, and lay low for a while. Once Burris found them, however, he drove them into Lafayette County just south of Lexington. Col. William Penick, in command of the Fifth Missouri Cavalry at Independence, sent 150 men in Company B, under thirty-two-year-old Capt. Daniel H. David to continue the search for the guerrillas. David "was a blustering, drunken, profane, ill-mannered, brutal character and his administration of affairs gave no great satisfaction to anybody," and the men of Company B were known as "Penick's Thieves." The company was mustered out after only one year due to "the reputation of the command for lawless insubordination, and conduct unworthy of soldiers generally."[47]

David bivouacked his men on the farm of Morgan Walker on the night of October 5, 1862. The next day he learned that Quantrill's camp had been discovered on the outskirts of Sibley, on the banks of the Missouri River. Quantrill's reassembled force now numbered one hundred men. The guerrillas wanted badly to get at David's command for the cruel manner in which the Yankee soldiers treated the local citizens. Quantrill anticipated that the Federals would be coming up the Lexington and Independence road, so he let the Northerners drive his pickets through the town of Sibley, hoping to draw them into an ambush. He broke camp and moved his men to the farm of a Mr. Garrison where they waited the Federals' approach.

Earlier in the day another Southern force, commanded by Confederate Col. Dick Chiles, had found Quantrill's camp and joined in with him. When Chiles was apprised of Quantrill's intended plan, he asked to trigger the ambush. Quantrill replied, "No, I do not know you. I do not know if you would carry out my instructions. Here are my Lieutenants, Gregg and Todd. I know that either of them will do just as I tell them." Still Chiles insisted until both Gregg and Todd said, "Let him have it." Relenting, Quantrill told Chiles, "You must obey these orders. When you meet the enemy, you must not stop, but go right through them. I will be there to support you, now go."[48]

Chiles moved out with an advance of twenty-five men to an old log house situated at a sharp turn in the road. The house was surrounded by a high rail fence enclosing about half an acre. Quantrill's plan was to have Chiles trigger the ambush by surprising the Federal column and charging through it with pistol fire to scatter them, causing as many casualties and as much confusion as possible. Quantrill would follow up the action with the rest of his command, finishing off the remaining opposition when they were disorganized and ill prepared to resist.

When the enemy came down the road, however, Chiles ignored Quantrill's instructions and dismounted his men, which in turn gave the Federal commander time to dismount his men and prepare for an assault. The Southerners were outnumbered, and Chiles's action gave the Federals the opportunity to take possession of the log house and seek cover behind the heavy rail fence. Soon after, Chiles was wounded, and the attack ground to a halt. Seeing that the outcome would not be favorable to his troops, Quantrill withdrew his men. They carried Chiles to the Garrison house, where they left him to be cared for. The Southerners had one other man wounded, Pat O'Donnell. Federal losses were one man killed, one other mortally wounded, and one slightly wounded.

The following day, David continued his pursuit of Quantrill, but the Southerners scattered to avoid being pursued. By the end of the first week of October, Quantrill and his men were reported camped on Big Creek in Cass County. In his report, David noted, "We do not believe that guerrillas can ever be taken by pursuit; we must take them by strategy."[49]

Like his Virginia counterpart, John S. Mosby, Quantrill disregarded established rules and fought upon a principle that his enemies could neither discover nor guard against. He was in their front, in their rear, on their flank, at one place today, and tomorrow in their camps at a point far distant. By his enemies he was thought to be almost ubiquitous. What he lacked in numbers he compensated for with the celerity of his movements and the boldness of his attacks. He generally fought against odds, often great odds, and seldom waited to receive a charge, but nearly always sought to make the attack.[50]

On October 17, 1862, Quantrill, undaunted by the Federal pursuit, led his band across the Kansas border and attacked the small village of Shawnee-town. He decreed that for every house burned in Missouri, one in Kansas would also be burned. Federal units continued to patrol Jackson County for the trail of Quantrill's company. As autumn came to Missouri, Quantrill needed to secure winter clothing for his men and believed that a raid on the small garrison at Shawneetown would net that objective.

The raid was to be a bloodless affair, but just before they arrived on October 20, the guerrillas struck a Federal wagon train along the Santa Fe Trail guarded by a troop of about thirty infantrymen. The infantry command was ill prepared to meet a force such as these guerrillas. The Federals had stopped to rest and most of the men were asleep. They had no flankers for protection and had not posted a guard over the sleeping men. In their usual way, the guerrillas charged with a rousing Rebel Yell and pistols blazing.

"As soon as they awakened," William Gregg recalled, "there was a general scramble to get away and only about half escaped. The others were shot down as they ran."[51] The guerrillas claimed fifteen Federals killed in this encounter before burning the wagons and riding away.

Quantrill had planned the raid on Shawneetown to perfection. His spies had informed him of the number of soldiers stationed in the town and their state of readiness. Using his usual tactics, he detailed part of his command to surround and cordon off the town while he and the remainder of the company rode nonchalantly into the town's center. With their Federal uniforms serving as a subterfuge, they would attempt to get the drop on any of the soldiers. By this method, Quantrill was able to surprise and demoralize his enemy.

It worked as well at Shawneetown. The guerrillas first searched the businesses, taking whatever they wanted, then they set fire to nearly every house in retaliation for the twelve homes burned in Pleasant Hill by Burris on September 19. They burned the hotel owned by B. L. Riggins and pillaged and burned the dry goods store of the noted jayhawker J. A. Walker. J. J. Buffington was killed next to the Riggins Hotel along with another citizen shot down in the street. An eyewitness reported that the guerrillas "had dashed in about midnight, ransacked the town, carried off what they wanted, and destroyed more than they took. They had burned a few houses and killed one or two men. The men of the place were taken prisoners and held during their stay, and then set at liberty. All their arms were taken from them and all the horses that could be found. This was all done in about an hour."[52]

Quantrill tried to limit the amount of bloodshed whenever possible. When he captured a large contingent of Federal soldiers, he intended to parole them from further military service. Only those prisoners found to be dreaded Redlegs or recognized as jayhawkers were summarily executed.

In Shawneetown seven prisoners belonged to Jennison's jayhawkers and were escorted back into Missouri. The sun was just starting to set as they approached the heavy timber along the banks of the Big Blue River in Jackson County. Quantrill glanced back at the prisoners then looked at Andy Blunt and ordered, "Bring ropes; four on one tree, three on another." Realizing their fate, the youngest of the seven gathered enough courage to speak to Quantrill. "Captain, just a word; the pistol before the rope; a soldier's before a dog's death. As for me, I'm ready." The prisoners were arranged in line, the guerrillas opposite them. They had confessed to belonging to Jennison but denied the charge of killing and burning. Quantrill hesitated a moment. His blue eyes searched each face then he said, "Take six men, Blunt, and do the work. Shoot the young man and hang the balance."[53]

Falling leaves brought with it the realization of approaching winter. A denuded countryside denied the guerrillas cover and concealment. Bare trees along the river bottoms would reveal their campfires. Snow on the ground would show hoof- and footprints to any wary Federal patrol. Quantrill thus looked to the security behind the Confederate lines farther south in Arkansas. He began preparations to move his command south to Texas and winter quarters on November 3, 1862. With the level of fighting that had taken place within the last few months, Quantrill knew that he could not long remain undetected in Jackson County.

While he was waiting for his men to rendezvous for the trip south, Quantrill received a report that two of his men, Privates Carlyle and Black, had been taking horses from farmers, telling them that Quantrill had ordered them to take them. They then took the horses to Lexington and sold them for a high price. Quantrill sent out his chief scout, John McCorkle, and six other men to look for them. McCorkle captured them and brought them back, together with eight horses they had stolen. Quantrill made them return the horses and told them that if they ever did this again, he would have them shot.

Two weeks later the citizens again came to Quantrill and asked him what he wanted with so many horses, informing him that these men were still stealing horses. Quantrill took ten men and found Carlyle at his brother-in-law's house. They knocked on the door, and William Hulse discovered Carlyle hiding beneath a trundle bed. Quantrill told Hulse to throw back the top mattress and shoot him through the straw tick. Carlyle immediately jumped out, turning the bed over. Quantrill compelled him to reveal the location of the stolen horses. Carlyle took them to the hiding place, where they discovered sixteen head of horses. Carlyle was placed on a horse, a rope was tied around his neck, and the horse was led from under him. The next day the horses were returned to their owners. This incident proved to the community that Quantrill ruled with his own brand of justice and discipline, and as a result, the community held him in high esteem.[54]

7

Early Skirmishes

War therefore is an act of violence to compel our opponent to fulfill our will.

KARL VON CLAUSEWITZ

LATE IN THE FALL of 1862 the leaves were beginning to turn, giving William C. Quantrill advance knowledge that soon his camps and hideouts would no longer conceal him from enemy patrols. On October 22 he mustered his men along the banks of the Little Blue River. They dressed in line in two ranks. Quantrill counted them front rank to rear. There were seventy-eight men in all. He informed them that on the morrow they had orders to rendezvous on Big Creek, in Cass County, just south of the Jackson County line. Quantrill made it known that any civilians who wished to be escorted behind Confederate lines in Texas would be escorted there in safety. On October 23, 150 men—including civilians and new recruits—were assembled and ready to move to the safety behind Southern lines. Cole Younger, Joseph C. "Joe" Lea, and Dick Yeager remained in Missouri, each with a small detachment of men. William Haller, because of a disagreement with George Todd, had gone into a squad commanded by a Captain Harrison, whose men were also traveling south with Quantrill. As soon as Quantrill rode out of Jackson County, the Federals felt confident that they could ride without fear of being attacked or ambushed.

Heading due south, the guerrillas rode through Cass County. About sundown that evening Quantrill put Gregg and forty men in the advance, striking the Harrisonville and Holden road where Dayton once stood. Dayton had been a quiet town of forty-seven houses before Charles Jennison's Seventh Kansas Jayhawker Regiment burned it to the ground on January 1, 1861. As the guerrilla band rode past, they could only grit their teeth in anger at what was becoming a desolated countryside due to the war.

Soon after getting started, the advance guard spotted a Federal wagon train of fourteen vehicles with a twenty-three-man escort under the command of Lt. W. M. Newby of Company G, Sixth Missouri Cavalry. Quantrill knew that the best tactic would be a wild charge accompanied with the old Rebel Yell. He immediately ordered Gregg to attack and capture the wagons.

Gregg charged the enemy just as they were trying to seek shelter behind the corralled wagons, but Gregg was too quick for them. Many of the Federals immediately took flight, trying to get away as fast as they could. John McCorkle ran one cavalryman down before he surrendered. McCorkle took his weapons then paroled him. Nearly every one of the Union troopers was either killed or captured.

Harrison Trow reported that they ran the retreating Federals down for more than four miles before shooting twenty of them from their saddles. In this engagement George Todd killed six; Boone Scholl killed five; Fletcher Taylor killed three; George Shepherd killed two; and John Koger, Simeon Whitsett, James Little, and George W. Maddox all managed to kill at least one. Newby was captured along with some privates.[1] The guerrillas ransacked the wagons, taking whatever provisions they could carry, then set fire to the vehicles.

The sky was becoming dark and cloudy, so Quantrill marched his men for only about two more miles before camping for the night near Dayton. Here, while the guerrillas kept a silent sentinel among the ruins of the town, a rider, James Williams, came into their camp dressed like a civilian. He said that he wanted to become a guerrilla, but to his misfortune, Quantrill recognized him as a former jayhawker that he had known in Kansas before the war. Quantrill gave Gregg an order to have him disarmed. After admitting who he was and that his intention was to assassinate Quantrill, Williams was hanged.

That same evening Federal Lt. Demuel Campbell reported to Col. Edwin C. Catherwood, in charge of the Sixth Missouri Militia in Warrensburg, that he had seen Quantrill's command marching down the divide between Harrisonville and Rose Hill. Catherwood knew his wagon train was on the guerrillas' line of march, so he immediately started out with 150 men to protect it.

Quantrill had picket posts stationed around the perimeter of his command element. Catherwood found the guerrillas in camp about nine o'clock that night and moved against their rear guard of ten men and a sergeant under the command of Charley Harrison. The rear guard were mostly inexperienced men and fired a volley or two at the enemy then were driven back upon the rest of Harrison's company, which withdrew to the main body of Quantrill's command.

The guerrillas had just arrived at the top of a sharp ridge when Quantrill ordered his veteran commanders—William H. Gregg, George Todd, and William Haller—to form all the veterans in their commands on line and face the enemy's force. Harrison Trow reported that when Haller was holding the rear with his squad, "He fought at the outpost half an hour. Behind huge trees, he would not fall back until his flanks were in danger."

Realizing that the enemy had the superiority in numbers, Gregg, in the diminishing light, ordered his men back from the ridge so he could see the Federals against the sky as they passed over the crest of the hill. As soon as the Union soldiers came into view, Gregg ordered a charge. The enemy was so surprised, and Gregg's charge so impetuous, that the Northerners were hurled back at least half a mile.

The Federals soon recovered enough to charge again, but they were again driven back in disorder. Coming on in increasing numbers, they attempted a third time to charge the guerrillas' rear guard. This time Gregg, Todd, and Haller wished to put an end to the engagement, and when they charged again with their men, it was with such vigor that the enemy broke and ran and did not resume the attack. The guerrillas had not lost a man killed or wounded.

After this, Quantrill's command proceeded their march southward unmolested until they came to the Osage River. It was seven o'clock in the morning when they approached the old town of Papinsville, which was now only a memory. Houses and businesses that once were animated and busy now stood bleak and lifeless. Only darkened timbers and lone chimneys stood as a reminder that on December 12, 1861, the Third Kansas Jayhawker Regiment burned the town to the ground after plundering everything they could carry off. On the same day the jayhawkers destroyed the nearby town of Butler.

In the wake of the guerrillas' march south, the Federals searched the area for Southern sympathizers who might have aided them. They found Charles Duncan, a farmer. Five Federals took him from the arms of his sobbing wife and five small children and carried him about a half-mile from his house before they murdered him. Seemingly, the only charge against him was that he had been a teamster in Sterling Price's march on Lexington the year before.[2]

While riding past what was left of Papinsville, the guerrillas observed a Federal cavalry regiment following them about five miles away. They pressed forward hurriedly all day until about ten o'clock that night, when they stopped to feed their horses and eat. Before daylight the guerrilla band was mounted and on the move, making camp that evening near Lamar.

On November 5 Quantrill's pickets discovered a Southern camp nearby commanded by Col. Warner Lewis, who was also heading south with his men. Quantrill invited them to join him. As they were sitting around the campfire together, Lewis suggested to Quantrill that they attack the Federal garrison in Lamar. To this Quantrill agreed, and together they laid out their plans. Both leaders agreed to attack the town simultaneously at exactly 10 P.M. Lewis was to enter the town from the north; Quantrill would circle around and charge into Lamar from the south.

On nearing the town limits, Quantrill found that he was a few minutes ahead of time, so he halted and waited for the time agreed upon. At the pre-arranged time, he commenced his attack on the darkened town by driving in the enemy's pickets. But before the Confederates got into town, the Federals somehow heard that they were coming. Knowing the reputation of the men that they were up against, the Union soldiers took refuge in the brick court-house, gathering up all the arms and ammunition they could find.

The Federals made a gallant stand. The battle raged for two hours. The Northerners, under the command of Martin Breeden, were fighting for their lives behind the brick walls of the courthouse; the guerrillas had only sidearms and were not able to dislodge the Union men.

Fighting a foe sheltered behind brick walls worked against the guerrillas. Without the use of their horses and having only revolvers, the guerrilla attack was mostly ineffective. John McCorkle and Will Halloran crawled up behind an old frame building and fired into the windows. The Federals turned and poured a concentrated volley into the old shop, and the flying splinters knocked both guerrillas down. McCorkle was wounded above the right eye, and Halloran received a neck wound.

During the fight, John Noland, a black soldier in Quantrill's command who had been with him since Col. Henry Clay Chiles had been wounded in the Sibley fight, crawled up close to the courthouse and gave more com-mands than anyone. Noland served Quantrill as a hostler and was well known for his bravery. He began calling for General Shelby to come up on the south side and General Marmaduke to come on the west and ordering the artillery to advance and blow the courthouse up. But his ruse failed to scare the Federals into surrendering.

Three separate charges were made against the Union stronghold, but the Northerners inside were prepared to sell their lives dearly and were fighting desperately, knowing there would be no quarter if they surrendered to Quantrill's men. They heroically beat back each of the Confederate attacks. The Federals did not lose a single man; the guerrillas lost two men killed, Peter Burton and James Donohue. They carried Donohue's body about two miles south of town and buried him at the mouth of a lane, building a rail fence around the grave before they departed.

The attack netted the guerrillas nothing. They finally withdrew, resuming their journey southward after setting fire to several buildings in town. They arrived in Newton County, and the two commanders parted ways.

Quantrill's men proceeded into the Indian Territory toward Fort Smith, Arkansas. Making their way through southern Missouri, Quantrill's Rangers encountered numerous militia units, but being dressed in Federal uniforms they did not attract attention. Harrison Trow recounted that many militiamen came upon their column and fell in with them, believing they were Federal comrades.

Near Cassville, in Barry County, twenty-two Federal militiamen came upon the guerrilla column. A subterfuge was thought of that would keep them from being discovered and would reduce the chances of suffering numerous casualties in a heated contest. The guerrillas were given orders that each man would move alongside a Federal militiaman, engage him in conversation, then shoot him when a signal was given. Thus an entire patrol was killed without a single loss to the guerrillas.

John McCorkle recalled, "The whole country was swarming with militia and but for the fact that every guerrilla was clad in Federal clothing, the march would have been an incessant battle. As it was, it would never be known how many isolated Federals, mistaking Quantrill's men for comrades of other regiments, not on duty with them, fell into a trap that never gave up their victims alive."

They continued down the old Fort Scott and Fort Gibson road until they arrived at the Confederate lines in Fort Smith, where they remained for ten days.[3] According to war records, while in Fort Smith on November 17 Quantrill requisitioned forage of 2,400 pounds of corn for 211 horses from the quartermaster, Col. John B. Clark, commander of the post. After Quantrill departed for Richmond, his men remained in this camp about a week before the entire Southern command went from there to Cane Hill, Arkansas.

After this brief respite, Quantrill took his command across the Arkansas River at Van Buren, Arkansas. At Dipper Springs the guerrillas joined Gen. John S. Marmaduke with orders to attach themselves as an independent cavalry command to Col. Benjamin Elliott's cavalry battalion. Marmaduke was a

West Point graduate and before the war had been on the Utah expedition with Albert Sidney Johnston. Now that he was formally attached to the army, Quantrill submitted a pay voucher and received a record of payment from the quartermaster for pay for his men starting from August 7, 1862.

When the Confederates made it safely into Van Buren, Arkansas, they set up camp and remained there for four days. Here they awaited the arrival of Sterling Price's infantry. The first units to arrive had many men who were close friends of those in Quantrill's company. Here, far away from home, they were reunited with old friends from Jackson County that they had not seen for many months.

After taking care of his men, Quantrill left his command in charge of his adjutant, William H. Gregg. Because his independent partisan ranger command had grown so rapidly and had won outstanding victories against the Federals, Quantrill obtained a leave of absence and traveled to Richmond to secure from President Davis a commission as a colonel of independent Missouri cavalry. Accompanying him was orderly sergeant Andrew Blunt. Quantrill expressed the conviction that it would be no trouble at all for him to raise a regiment for the Southern cause. He had numerous times in the past assisted other colonels in successfully recruiting new men from Jackson County. Even during past battles and skirmishes along the border, high-ranking officers had subordinated themselves to his leadership.

The Confederate government was fully aware that William C. Quantrill had greatly aided its recruiting efforts and had brought some military equality to the Northern domination within the state of Missouri. Back in August 1862 he had led the vanguard that captured the garrison in Independence and much-needed supplies and arms that went directly to the regular Southern army. Under the leadership of William Haller and Cole Younger, Quantrill's Rangers had arrived at the opportune time at the battle of Lone Jack to turn the battle in favor of the Confederacy. His was the only organization that successfully protected Southern recruiting officers as they made their way into Missouri. Even after the battle of Lone Jack, when Col. Upton Hays set up a recruiting camp on White Oak Creek, it was Quantrill's men who protected and successfully defended Hays against an overpowering Federal onslaught and sent the Federals reeling back to their home base. Quantrill's raids on Federal garrisons inside Kansas also netted much-needed military arms and supplies for the Southern army. Such victories brought men into the Confederate army who would otherwise have avoided regular military service.

Gen. Thomas C. Hindman sent a highly commendable report to the adjutant general describing Quantrill's heroics and usefulness. Hindman congratulated Quantrill for being "extremely zealous and useful . . . and that the victory won at Lone Jack by Colonel [Clinton] Cockrell . . . aided by Captain Quantrill was one of the most brilliant affairs of the war."[4]

After Quantrill left his men in Arkansas, a large Federal force slipped past the Confederate picket line. During the night the jayhawkers started shelling the Southern lines. Scouts reported that the Union force was too strong to engage, so the Confederates withdrew across the Boston Mountains.

Elliott's Battalion, now strengthened by Quantrill's company, distinguished itself by holding the Federals in check until the Confederate baggage train could get up the mountain. John McCorkle, serving as a scout, observed the Federals coming up fast and notified Colonel Elliott, who in turn ordered an immediate retreat. As the Confederates were retreating, the Federals followed them up with cannon fire. Only two of Elliott's men were wounded.

Upon hearing the firing, Gen. Jo Shelby left his command in charge of his adjutant, Maj. John Newman Edwards, and rode to the sound of the guns to judge the tide of battle for himself. He was soon engulfed in the midst of the hottest fighting. Shelby remained with Quantrill's men, holding the rear guard, until he was assured that the baggage train had made it safely across the mountains. During this withdrawal, Shelby had three horses shot out from under him.

This was only one of several battles Quantrill's men participated in while he was in Richmond. These included the battles of Fayetteville and Prairie Grove. At the battle of Fayetteville, Quantrill's men distinguished themselves by their rescue of General Shelby after he had been taken prisoner.

Shelby had been surrounded by an enemy force along the Fayetteville-Prairie Grove road in northern Arkansas. A command of guerrillas that included Frank and Jesse James was pursuing an enemy patrol when it came across Shelby as he was being surrounded. Although the guerrillas had only a few men in their force, they stormed the Union position and scattered the enemy, enabling Shelby to escape. Although Shelby and Quantrill were never good friends, Shelby was forever indebted to Quantrill's men for their outstanding show of bravery. Years after the war Shelby volunteered to act as a character witness at the trial of outlaw Frank James.

After hearing that Quantrill's command had left the Missouri border, Jim Lane's brother-in-law, Col. Charles W. Adams, in command of the Twelfth Kansas Jayhawker Regiment, believed he could make an unchallenged raid into Jackson County and continue to plunder the Missouri countryside. Such raids were justified as military necessities, and Quantrill's absence would allow Adams to proceed unmolested.

Adams raided deep into Missouri and was returning with a plunder train—one hundred horses, eight teams of oxen, mules, cattle, and enough wagons to haul his spoils—when he was overtaken and surrounded by Union Brig. Gen. Richard C. Vaughn, commander of a large militia force in the Central District. Vaughn had to train his cannon on the jayhawkers before they agreed to release their plunder. They were also compelled to liberate up to forty slaves who had been seized from their owners. The jayhawkers were then escorted back to the Kansas border after the two senior officers were arrested and sent to St. Louis for court-martial. These charges, however, were dropped by Gen. Samuel R. Curtis, and the two were restored to full duty.[5] Curtis was not about to antagonize James Lane or the Kansas abolitionists.

After having been routed by Quantrill and Hays's forces at the battle of White Oak Creek in August 1862, Charles Jennison had concentrated his raids on Clay County. Members of the Enrolled Missouri Militia stationed in Clay County managed to capture eight of Jennison's men in possession of stolen property and about twenty-five slaves. Jennison demanded their return or threatened to raid and plunder the Missouri countryside indiscriminately. His threat showed his true character as a border robber and thief more than a military man in the service of his country.

Even the Federally supported provisional governor of Missouri, Hamilton Gamble, became sufficiently alarmed to wire President Lincoln: "If such an invasion is made I will resist it with all the force I can command [and give Kansas] a taste of the evils of war in their own territory." Jayhawkers had already defied the orders of Gen. John M. Schofield that forbade any armed force not in military service from crossing the border. On September 4, following Jennison's raid into Clay County, Schofield assured Gamble: "There will be no invasion of Missouri by the people of Kansas. The Governor and the people of Missouri may be perfectly at ease on that subject."[6]

Frank Smith recalled that the winter of 1863 was very severe in Jackson County after Quantrill's men left. Redleg raids plundered Jackson and Cass Counties, and a great deal of that was conducted by Col. William Penick's men and the jayhawkers stationed in Independence. Penick made it a standard practice to assassinate anyone who was suspected of being in sympathy with the guerrillas. Smith noted that Penick hanged Sam Kimberlin, a fifty-one-year-old farmer with six children, on November 8 from a rafter in Kimberlin's own barn. Smith recalled Kimberlin had taken no side in rebellion and no specific charges had been brought against him.[7]

A month earlier, on Friday, October 4, just across the river in Lexington, Redlegs burned several houses and killed seven men after plundering what they could carry off. The next night, near Lexington, they rode up to John McPhadon's house after sunset and demanded that he accompany them. McPhadon's two daughters were in the house. Redlegs took McPhadon a few yards from his house and murdered him. His "crime" was that he had two sons in the Confederate army. Jayhawkers also raided the newspaper offices of the *Lexington Expositor* and stole its presses. The *Lexington Express* was closed by military order. From a neighboring county, Willard Mendenhall wrote in his diary, "The Redlegs had killed about fifty men in this neighborhood in the last few days."

Meanwhile, Quantrill and Blunt arrived in the Confederate capital. Quantrill was well known in the Deep South. Newspapers had carried the exploits of his victory at the August 11 battle of Independence, noted how his men helped turn the tide during the August 16 battle of Lone Jack, and reported his victory over Jennison and Penick at White Oak Creek on August 18. He also earned recognition for his September 5 raid on Olathe and the October 17 raid on Shawneetown as well as the September 18 battle of Wellington. The Confederate government was also aware that, without Quantrill's assistance, Southern recruiting officers could not possibly do their job in northern Missouri.

Quantrill sought an audience with President Davis, but due to the president's busy schedule, he was only able to meet with Secretary of War James A. Seddon and Sen. Louis T. Wigfall of Texas. There has been some controversy as to what was actually said during this meeting. After reading about Quantrill's exploits along the western border, the sensitivities of the Southern politicians were inclined to be unfavorable to his mode of warfare, but they knew they should reward him in some way for his exploits in aiding the cause. They had heard that the black flag policy toward guerrillas was being observed by Federal authorities, but according to many Southern officers' code of conduct, the no-quarter policy was an unchivalrous way to conduct warfare.

The secretary of war suggested that war had its amenities and its refinements, and in the nineteenth century it was simple barbarism to talk of a black flag. Quantrill allegedly replied:

Barbarism? Barbarism, Mr. Secretary, means war and war means barbarism. Since you have touched upon this subject, let us discuss it a little. Times have their crimes as well as men. For twenty years this cloud has been gathering; for twenty years, inch by inch and little by little those people called the Abolitionists have been on the track of slavery; for twenty years the people of the South have been robbed, here a negro and there a negro; for twenty years hates have been engendered and wrathful things laid up against the day of wrath. The cloud has burst. Do not condemn the thunderbolt. Who are these people you call Confederates? Rebels, unless they succeed, outcasts, traitors, food for hemp and gunpowder. There were no great statesmen in the South, or this war would have happened fifteen years ago. Today the odds are desperate. The world hates slavery; the world is fighting you. The ocean belongs to the Union navy. There is a recruiting officer in every foreign port. I have captured and killed many who did not know the English tongue. Mile by mile the cordon is being drawn about the granaries of the South, Missouri will go first, next Kentucky, next Tennessee, by and by Mississippi and Arkansas, and then what? That we must put gloves on our hands, and honey in our mouths, and fight this war as Christ fought the wickedness of the world?

Seddon then asked him, "What would you do, Captain Quantrill, were yours the power and opportunity?"

Quantrill replied, "Do, Mr. Secretary? Why I would wage such a war and have such a war waged by land and sea as to make surrender forever impossible. I would cover the armies of the Confederacy all over with blood. I would break up foreign enlistments by indiscriminate massacre. I would win the independence of my people or I would find them graves."

Then the secretary of war asked, "And our prisoners, what of them?"

Quantrill finished by stating:

Nothing of them; there would be no prisoners. Do they take any prisoners from me? Surrounded, I do not surrender; surprised, I do not give way to panic; outnumbered, I rely upon common sense and stubborn fighting; proscribed, I answer proclamation with proclamation; outlawed, I feel through it my power, hunted, I hunt my hunters in turn; hated and made blacker than a dozen devils, I add to my hoofs the swiftness of the horse, and to my horns the terrors of a savage following. Kansas should be laid waste at once. Meet the torch with the torch, pillage with pillage, slaughter with slaughter, subjugation with extermination. You have my ideas of war, Mr. Secretary, and I am sorry that they do not accord with your own, nor the ideas of the government you have the honor to represent so well.

Afterward the politicians and Quantrill may have talked about future operations against Kansas. It is well known that after this meeting, his men began referring to him as "Colonel," and one man stated that the guerrilla commander was awarded this rank with the title of "range recruiting officer." He began signing dispatches with the title, and many Confederate officers afterward sent correspondence directed to Colonel Quantrill. He also posed for a photograph in a colonel's uniform.

As Quantrill was returning from Richmond, he stopped by a camp of Missouri troops on the Black River, twelve miles east of Vicksburg. It was here that he met with Gen. Sterling Price, whom many believe at this time may have actually given him his colonel's commission, a common procedure in the Confederate service west of the Mississippi. Because of the conflicting dates referring to Quantrill as a captain signed on pay vouchers following his return from Richmond, it is highly likely that Price himself had granted Quantrill a colonel's commission. Price was authorized to make promotions to soldiers serving in state units, but these informally bestowed ranks were not the same as equivalent ranks in the regular army. Thus regular Confederate army officers likely did not recognize Quantrill's rank as colonel but as a captain of an independent company.

Whether promoted in Richmond or Mississippi, Quantrill's colonel's commission has never been found. Many of his men, including Frank Smith and John McCorkle, referred to him as a colonel on his return to Jackson County. Smith recalled, "Quantrill left his men in camp in Arkansas and with Andy Blunt went to Richmond where he got his colonel's commission and promptly on returning to Missouri waged warfare along the Kansas-Missouri border."[8] Quantrill returned to Arkansas sometime in January 1863.[9]

George Todd had been in charge of one group in Quantrill's company during the commander's absence, but he returned to Jackson County sometime in late November. He took with him James Little, Fletcher Taylor, Andy Walker, Boone Scholl, John Koger, James Reed, John McCorkle, George Wigginton, and others. Several of their comrades, like Cole Younger, had chosen to stay in Jackson County during the winter, living in dugouts, trying to keep their presence hidden from the eyes of Federal scouts.

Much had changed during the time the guerrillas had been out of the state. Federal authorities began to demand loyalty oaths and security bonds from Southern sympathizers to guarantee their good behavior as well as assessments from suspected Secessionists. Loyalty oaths were an important weapon against Missourians. Anyone with an important job was required to sign an oath. In effect, it demanded the signer to vow to support the Constitution and not to take up arms against the Federal government. If a person was found in arms who had previously taken the oath, he was immediately executed.

Missourians were required later to post bonds in conjunction with their oaths. These bonds usually ranged from two thousand to twenty thousand dollars, depending on the property owned by the individual. Yet all it took to revoke the bond and confiscate the money was for a neighbor to accuse the oath taker of disloyalty. The April 23, 1863, *Kansas City Journal* announced that the Federal provost marshal general held bonds of "traitors and secessionists" to the amazing sum of twenty million dollars. This government practice was little more than extortion, because people who did not post the requisite loyalty bond were forced from their homes or imprisoned. Once incarcerated, these people had no legal rights, since the Lincoln administration had rescinded most constitutional rights. Corruption was rife in administering the bonds, and many bond funds were seized with little provocation. The bond subterfuge was essentially an artful program of highway robbery. Union Gen. Clinton Fisk even remarked on the corrupt provost marshals in his district, addressing the following to provost marshal Maj. R. A. DeBolt:

> I have the honor to state that it has come to my knowledge that many persons have been arrested and imprisoned for a long time by some of your subordinates upon evidence insufficient to warrant the military authorities restraining citizens of their liberty. Great care should be exercised in the use of arbitrary power confided to provost marshals, and we cannot be too cautious in receiving as truth the statements of apparently good men who seek through the military power the punishment of neighbors for alleged offenses, old grudges, local animosities, and private griefs, to frequently seek adjustment through the military arm of power, much to the scandal and prejudice of honesty and loyalty.[10]

Provisional Governor Hamilton Gamble wired President Lincoln that he had stopped assessments by state militia officers and urged that they not be made by U.S. forces as "great distress is produced."[11] The Missouri congressional delegation on January 6, 1863, presented the president with a memo asking that the assessments be stopped.[12] Nevertheless, many Union commanders levied assessments because they believed they were a constraint on Southern sympathizers. One Union general who did not condone these assessments was John M. Schofield. He informed the president that in counties along the border Gen. Samuel R. Curtis had confiscated Southern property "without any form of trial known to any law, either civil or military."[13] Furthermore, Curtis's General Orders No. 35 ordered his provost marshals to banish people "though no specific act of disloyalty can be proven against them."[14]

Citizens were considered disloyal simply by letting Confederate soldiers drink from their wells or giving forage to their horses. The steps the Federal government took to put down guerrilla warfare were excessive and intolerant. The list when viewed shows the absence of any kind of respect for civil rights, any compassion for innocent civilians, and a complete lack of disregard for the rules of war. Some are as follows:

1. Hang or shoot all suspected guerrillas or Southern sympathizers on the spot without benefit of trial.
2. Seize all property of guerrilla soldiers or suspected guerrilla sympathizers.
3. Burn and destroy homes, livestock, and property of all guerrillas and their sympathizers.
4. Refuse the right to vote or hold civil office for any Southern sympathizers or those who refuse to take a loyalty oath.
5. Levy loyalty bonds against Southern sympathizers to guarantee their nonsupport of guerrilla activity, then find excuses to accuse them of disloyalty so their property can be seized and sold for profit.
6. Refuse the right of military pardons or paroles or exchanges of guerrilla soldiers as afforded to regular army soldiers.
7. Seize guerrillas' relatives for imprisonment or banishment from the state.
8. Deny all guerrillas and their sympathizers rights when captured as afforded prisoners of war.
9. Seize suspected disloyal citizens and imprison them without benefit of trial or a reading of the charges brought against them in accordance with constitutional law, thus denying the writ of habeas corpus.
10. Deny Southern sympathizers the right to freedom of religion by forcing compulsory prayers in support of the president of the United States and the Federal government.
11. Force citizens in the vicinity of guerrilla activity that results in destruction of property to pay for repairs and to contribute hard labor to repair destroyed property.
12. Use of noncombatants for human shields while on dangerous military operations not in accordance with the rules of war.

During the winter that Quantrill's command was out of the state, the Northerners reinforced their Missouri outposts by stationing a regiment in Pleasant Hill and Harrisonville. They also reestablished a command at

Independence in charge of Col. William Ridgeway Penick, commanding the Fifth Missouri State Militia. Penick was described as rough and uneducated. He was a radical Unionist who placed a price on the heads of the guerrillas. He stated that the guerrilla problem could be wiped out "if hemp, fire, and gunpowder were freely used."

In late January 1863 Penick sent a patrol from Independence to burn down thirteen houses of Southern sympathizers along with the Baptist church in Oak Grove. Penick had been itching to get back at the guerrillas ever since his command suffered humiliating defeats in almost daily skirmishes along the banks of the Little Blue. On November 29 one of his foraging parties from Independence was gathering corn in the vicinity of Daniel Wilson's farm when George Todd and Cole Younger sprang from ambush and shot down five of his men. The very next day, Cole Younger, along with the McCorkle brothers and Tom Talley, met four of Charles Jennison's men near the Blue Cut neighborhood across from Reuben Harris's farm. After a three-mile chase, three of the jayhawkers were shot from their saddles. Near the border, west of Little Santa Fe and just south of Kansas City, George Todd led thirty men against sixty-two jayhawkers on the open prairie. Todd's tactics—the "old yell and the old rush"—swept everything. Every man attacked with a revolver in each hand, firing right and left, and the reins in his teeth, his horse at a full run.[15]

Wanting desperately to drive the guerrillas away, the Federals sent three heavy columns into the countryside to find them. They did find one guerrilla camp, Abe Cunningham's on Big Creek in Cass County. They killed one of his men, Will Freeman, and drove the rest back into Jackson County.

The weather was getting colder as Christmas approached. The Federals seemed to want a reprieve from the incessant patrolling and skirmishing and losses of men, horses, and supplies. Eight hundred Union soldiers garrisoned Kansas City at the time, and a strong picket post guarded every road leading into town. The streets were patrolled continually, and the soldiers' horses were kept saddled and bridled and standing ready in their stalls.[16]

Cole Younger wanted to get even with the militia unit that had killed his father back in June. So he stayed in Jackson County to take care of his family when Quantrill went south. On the morning of December 25 George Todd approached Younger with information that part of the command that had murdered Cole's father was in Kansas City. The soldiers, members of the Fifth Missouri State Militia, had been stationed in Harrisonville until being summoned as witnesses in a court-martial convened by Brig. Gen. Benjamin Loan.

Todd told Younger that, if it was his desire, they would all go into Kansas City and kill a few of them. They quickly made plans. Only six were chosen for the mission: Todd, Younger, Abe Cunningham, Fletcher Taylor, Zachary Traber, and George Clayton. They were to dress themselves in Federal uniforms, but instead of only one pistol, which the Federals were authorized to carry, each man was to carry four.

They rode to the south of town at around 4 P.M., as the sun was setting. They easily made their way unchallenged past the picket post on the Westport to Kansas City road.

As Traber watched their horses a short distance from the picket post, the other five men made their way down the darkened streets. Already the place was filled with revelry. Most of the soldiers had taken to the saloons and were celebrating in small groups. The five guerrillas had only one thought on their minds: revenge. Despite the cold, their heavy Union cavalry coats hung loosely about them, covering up their revolvers. While hunting for the murderers, they frequented one saloon after another, drinking toasts to the death of Quantrill and all of his guerrillas.

It was near midnight when the five guerrillas entered a saloon near the public square. They discovered six soldiers playing cards. Two sat at one table, and four at another. The remaining table in the saloon was unoccupied. A kerosene lamp hung over each table and dimly illuminated the players. There was only one door to the building. The saloon counter ran against the far wall, where a man and boy stood behind it and dispensed drinks when called for.

As the guerrillas entered, Todd spoke low to Younger: "Run to cover at last. Five of the six men before you were in Bailey's crowd that murdered your father." They went up to the bar and called for drinks, inviting the card players to join them. The players asked them if it would be agreeable that the boy would bring the drinks to them while they continued to play.

"Certainly," said Todd. "That's what the boy is here for." At the bar the guerrillas spoke low to each other and formulated a plan. Cunningham and Clayton were to casually approach the table where the two players sat; Todd, Younger, and Taylor would surround the table of the four players. Todd's signal was to be the words, "Come boys, another drink." Then they would pull their pistols from their holsters and hold them under their coats. The next signal would be for Younger to say, "Who said drink?" At this signal each man would shoot the soldier directly to his right. Younger was given the honor of shooting the sixth man.

As they took their places each guerrilla steeled himself as he had in so many such close encounters with death before. There was no wavering. Each man was calm and determined. As the moment of truth approached, the remembrances of past hatreds welled up in their hearts, making them more

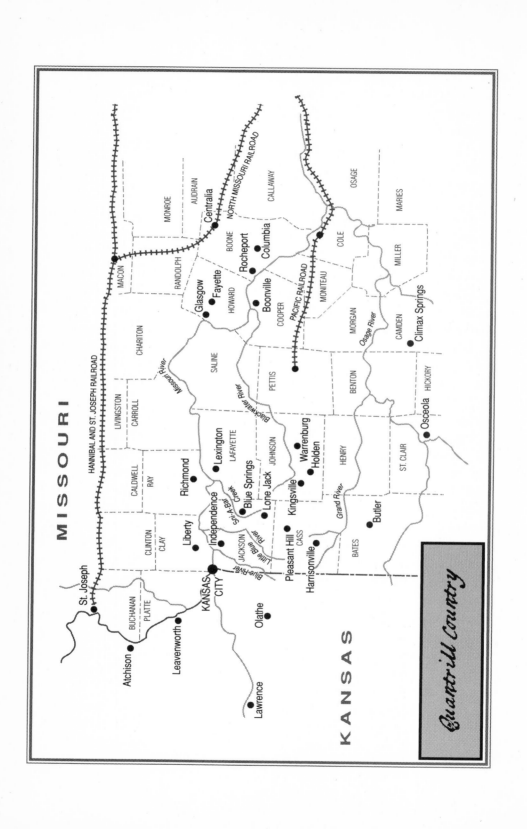

determined than ever. Todd called for another drink. The card-playing soldiers never noticed the slight movement of each man standing behind them. At Younger's final signal, each guerrilla drew his pistol to arm's length.

Five shots rang out as one. Five soldiers fell dead upon the floor. Immediately another shot rang out as Younger finished off the last man.

The barkeeper froze with fear. The boy hid behind the counter. Todd quickly extinguished each light and stepped out onto the street. He whispered to his men, "Do not make haste."

The shots had rung out as an alarm throughout the town. As soon as the dead men were discovered, large groups of soldiers frantically searched for the killers. Soldiers poured out of every dance house and saloon and shouted, "Guerrilla! Guerrilla! The guerrillas are among us in Federal clothing and killing the Kansas men!"[17]

Todd managed to lead his men out of town and back toward the picket post and the safety of their horses just down the road. But by this time a squad of soldiers had reinforced the picket. The picket asked for a countersign to let them pass. Todd replied that they had no countersign, they were only out for a walk. When the picket replied that they would not be allowed to pass, Todd yelled out his familiar command, "Fire and charge, men!"

Four pickets fell dead while the rest ran for cover. Traber, hearing the firing, brought the horses at a run, enabling the guerrillas to make their escape. They rode over the Federal picket on the Independence road and made their way back to the Reuben Harris farm on the banks of the Little Blue. Here they warmed themselves next to a roaring fire.[18] Penick responded by offering a thousand dollars for the head of Cole Younger, five hundred dollars for either of the McCorkle brothers, and one hundred dollars for any of the rest of the guerrillas, dead or alive.

Still wanting desperately to get at Quantrill's men, especially Coleman Younger, the Federals resorted to the worst barbarisms. Because they had just lost more than ten soldiers shot down in the midst of a Union camp in Kansas City on Christmas Day, Penick once again sent a detail to the Younger farm. Arriving at midnight on February 9, 1863, they had orders to burn the house to the ground. They poured lamp oil on the floors and forced Bursheba Fristoe Younger—Cole's mother—to set fire to her own home.

Cole Younger recalled: "My mother had the negroes place a bed in a farm wagon and carry her out of the house. She set it afire with her own hands. She was placed on the bed in the wagon. They drove away, my mother, four children, and two negroes. Seven persons were in that wagon; not one among them had ever done anyone a wrong in their lives."[19]

With the trauma of being widowed at the hands of Federal soldiers and all her earthy goods stolen by the Kansas jayhawkers, Bursheba Younger was now frail and in very poor health. While she lay on a mattress salvaged from the burning home, her old black maid warmed a blanket by hanging it next to the burning building then covered Widow Younger with it to keep her from freezing to death.

Reuben Smith was a member of the Federal patrol that burned the Younger home. He recalled: "Mrs. Younger lived about four miles from Pleasant Hill and she informed me that Cole had been there that day, and that she should feed him or harbor him at any other time he might come. A few days later I found that another of her boys had been there and that she had fitted him out with clean socks and under clothing. She talked as though she were funding the whole Confederacy, and she said she would give aid and comfort to the boys in the brush at any and all times. Reporting this to Captain Pinger, who outranked me, he instructed me to send out a detail to burn the house."[20]

The day after the burning of the Younger home the same band of Federals torched the home of Cole Younger's maternal grandmother, Mary L. "Polly" Fristoe, and that of her neighbor, Mrs. Rucker, both of Brooking Township.

While on patrol six miles south of Independence, Penick sought out and killed Wallace Wigginton, a brother to guerrilla George Wigginton. In the aftermath of the killing, the Federals also took the opportunity to steal. Afterward, Gen. John M. Schofield sent out a general order proclaiming, "The practice of plundering and robbing peaceable citizens and of wantonly destroying private property has become so prevalent in some portions of this command as to require the most vigorous measures for its suppression."[21]

The winter of 1862–63 was unusually cold, and snow covered the ground most of the time. It was a dangerous season for the guerrillas to try to hide. John McBride, a resident and a Union spy, informed Colonel Penick that he could lead Union soldiers to a guerrilla hideout five miles south of Independence. As a result, on February 7 a Federal patrol surrounded a camp of twelve guerrillas in Jackson County and, after a brief skirmish, captured nine of them. The orders from the Union commander were explicit in this matter, and the prisoners were immediately shot.

Penick put every man he had in the saddle to try to bring Quantrill's remaining men to bay. He murdered any Southern sympathizers he could find and burned their homes, forcing them to leave the country and drying up the guerrillas' base of civilian support. He also resorted to spies.

The day after the nine captured guerrillas had been executed, a nineteen-year-old soldier in Cole Younger's command, John McDowell, reported that his wife was sick and asked permission to visit her. Younger granted the request with the proviso that McDowell report back by three o'clock that afternoon. The wife's illness, however, was a sham. Instead of going home, or even in the direction of home, McDowell hastened immediately to Independence and informed Penick of the details of Younger's camp and its surroundings. Echoes of the desperate Christmas Day adventure of Younger and Todd in Kansas City had long ago reached Penick's ears, and he was anxious to act on the traitor's information.[22]

On February 10, 1863, Penick mounted a patrol of eighty cavalrymen and managed to surround Younger's camp, dismounting his men about two hundred yards away. Younger had two houses dug in the ground with a ridgepole to each, and rafters.[23] Occupying it was Younger, George Todd, Tom and Wallace Talley, Otho Hinton, George Wigginton, James Morris, John Koger, John and Jabez McCorkle, Nathan Kerr, William Hulse, Ike Basham, Dr. Thomas B. Hale, Joe Hardin, and a few others.

Tom, George, and Wallace Talley were brothers and cousins of Cole Younger. At the start of the war, their sixty-eight-year-old father, John, was killed by Federal troops. Because of this, the brothers joined Sterling Price's army. Later George returned home and joined Quantrill.

Younger, on hearing a horse snort at someone's approach, hollered out if it was George Todd. The Federals shouted back a reply, "Don't mind us, we're friends." Not hearing the proper response and sensing that there was danger approaching, Younger immediately alerted the rest of the men inside and fired at the attackers. Kerr, Wigginton, Hulse, John McCorkle, and the rest of the guerrillas leaped out of the hut with a revolver in each hand, firing as they made their escape into the timber. Basham was killed just as he came out the door along with Dr. Hale. Hardin was struck and fell dead within ten feet of the entrance. John McCorkle and cousin George Wigginton managed to get away; George suffered a bullet wound to his hand.

Younger, with four revolvers in his belt, tried to hold the enemy off until his men were safely away. He killed a lieutenant and another man and kept fifteen soldiers at bay while Hinton struggled with his heavy cavalry boots. Talley hesitated, also having trouble with his boots—one off and a foot stuck in the leg of the other. Younger stopped to help him amid the hailstorm of bullets.

The Federals came on in a rush, trying to get at Talley. He raised his pistols, but none of the chambers fired, being wet from the snow. Knowing that he was in trouble, Younger yelled at the guerrillas to turn and fight so they could all stand or die together. The guerrillas returned, and in their stocking feet, they held their attackers at bay.

Younger managed to kill two more during the skirmish. Jabez McCorkle, Morris, Koger, and five others were wounded. Talley, fighting like a lion at bay, finally fell mortally wounded. Younger received a bullet to the shoulder.

Yet after gaining fire superiority, the guerrillas managed to drive the Union soldiers back to their horses, giving them time to get away. The guerrillas made their way barefooted, without hats or coats, for more than three miles, running over bluffs where the Federal horsemen could not follow, until they came to the house of Mrs. William Moore, overlooking the valley of the Little Blue. The Federals lost seventeen, and Younger lost four with eight wounded.

While the guerrillas were skirmishing in Jackson County, Quantrill was making his way back north. He combined forces for a while in southwest Missouri with General Marmaduke, who informed him that Union Col. Obediah Smith was murdering Southerners and burning their homes in that region. Quantrill asked, "Why don't you kill him?" Marmaduke replied that he was too sharp and cunning for him. Quantrill replied, "If you will detail one or two of your men to come with me and show me where he lives, I will kill him with his own gun." Marmaduke agreed.

Quantrill made his way along Spring River toward Smith's house. The guerrilla chieftain's command, which wore Federal uniforms, went unnoticed. Quantrill found Smith working in his garden with a rifle close by. Thinking that the men were Federals, Smith came to the fence and shook hands with Quantrill.

"Captain, that is a fine gun you have there," Quantrill commented. "Why don't you furnish us scouts with a gun like that?"

Smith replied that he had killed lots of bushwhackers with it. So Quantrill asked, "Captain, would you mind letting me see that gun?"

In handing the rifle to Quantrill, Smith replied, "Yes, and I've turned many a damned Rebel over with it."

With Smith's rifle now in his hands, Quantrill said, "Ain't that a dandy?" He pointed the rifle at Smith and killed him. Harrison Trow remarked that killing Smith was getting rid of one of the worst men in Cedar County.[24]

As Quantrill's column continued its northward march, small groups of Union militiamen innocently approached and were killed. In one day almost two dozen Federals were killed after they rode up to the column, believing the guerrillas in blue uniforms were comrades.

Quickly the local Federal command learned of the killing of Smith and launched a pursuit of Quantrill's column. The guerrillas were not hard to track—a trail of dead bodies littered the way. Union troops caught up with

Quantrill just south of the Osage River. But they made the mistake of having the advance guard too far in the lead when they came upon Quantrill's rear guard. The guerrilla leader immediately saw the error and turned and ordered a charge. Out of sixty cavalrymen, twenty fell dead from their saddles in the first charge. The Federals regrouped and tried to hold their own as another column attacked Quantrill's flank. The most damage they did, however, was to kill Andrew Blunt's horse before the guerrillas slipped into the heavy timber at nightfall.

Quantrill kept up a forced march until he came to the farm of Judge Russell Hicks on the Sni-A-Bar Creek in Blue Springs. Here he disbanded his company for ten days then sent word to various captains for them to meet with him at the end of that time. Rather than rest, many of the guerrilla chieftains chose to attack whenever they saw targets of opportunity.

Quantrill sought out his old strongholds along the banks of the Sni and the Little Blue River east of the Brooking Township in Jackson County. It was here that he felt at home and relatively safe. The citizens of the area were his friends, and they supported him with news and whatever else they could offer. When he returned to Jackson County, Southerners informed him of the barbarity and cruelty inflicted by the Federals during his absence.

Union spies also reported his presence. A May 5, 1863, dispatch included the information that Quantrill was now a colonel with the power to recruit:

> Quantrill is here; he came from Price to conscript; he came with forty men; he has joined Reid's, Jarrette's, Todd's, Younger's, and Clifton's gangs to his own, which give him from one-hundred twenty-five to one-hundred and fifty men; he disbanded his own force on Sunday night, with orders to rendezvous on Thursday night on the Big Sni, precise place not definitely learned; has orders from Price to stop bushwhacking and horse stealing. Price is to invade Southeast Missouri, and Quantrill is to annoy Kansas and western Missouri; intends to conscript all of military age; has secret notice among Southern men to come to his camp and get property taken by mistake; came here to stay, not to take away any recruits; seems to be rather elevated in his purpose by his six or eight months experience with the regular forces.[25]

Dick Yeager, another of Quantrill's captains, made a daring raid on the interior of Kansas upon Quantrill's return. Yeager had been with Quantrill almost from the beginning. His father, Judge James Yeager of Westport, was in the freighting business and had been the presiding judge of the Jackson County Court in 1840. In 1858 the judge was serving in the state legislature while Dick was traveling the Santa Fe Trail in charge of one of his father's wagon trains. In 1861 he returned to find his father's farm completely stripped and burned by Jennison's jayhawkers.[26] Dick Yeager then sought out Quantrill and joined his partisan ranger company.

Now armed with the names of those who had perpetrated this crime against his family, Yeager, along with William Anderson, led a small force 130 miles into the Kansas interior. Yeager took his company into Council Grove on May 4 but did no damage except to have an aching tooth pulled by the local dentist. The next day, however, Yeager's group rode into the nearby town of Diamond Springs, killed a man, robbed a stagecoach, and burned several farmhouses on the return to Missouri. On their way back, they encountered a hastily thrown together militia unit west of Emporia. The Federals managed to capture at least a dozen of Yeager's men and forced the remainder to scatter across the prairie. Capt. John E. Stewart, the noted jayhawker whom Quantrill had known before the war, executed the twelve prisoners. Once Yeager's column regrouped, they managed to find other Union soldiers, killing one then going on to loot various stores and houses at the stage depot at Rock Springs and at Willow Springs, southeast of Lawrence and Black Jack.

At about the same time in Lafayette County, Missouri, Col. John T. Burris of the Fourth Kansas Jayhawker Regiment led forty Redlegs and two hundred jayhawkers on a jayhawking raid on Missouri farms. Civil liberties were ignored as Burris's men ransacked property, killing more than fifty unarmed men, and burning at least thirty houses.

On May 29, 1863, Federals under the command of Gen. James G. Blunt attempted to strike back at the guerrilla menace by hanging twenty-three-year-old James Vaughn, one of Quantrill's guerrillas. James's brother Dan also rode with Quantrill. James Vaughn was described as large and powerfully built. He had ridden into Wyandotte, Kansas, close to Kansas City. Believing he would not be recognized, he took off his pistols to get a haircut. A squad of Federals rushed in and captured him. He was hanged at Fort Union, in Kansas City, in front of a crowd of three thousand witnesses.

As Vaughn mounted the gallows he moved forward with his head erect and addressed these prophetic words to the crowd below: "You may kill me, but you'll never conquer me, and taking my life today will cost you a hundred lives and this debt my friends will pay in a short time."[27] On the scaffold Vaughn took some trinkets and money from his pockets and gave them to an officer with the request that the Federal deliver them to his sisters who had been imprisoned at Fort Leavenworth.

Left: This was once believed to be a photograph of William Clarke Quantrill in a Federal officer's coat. The image came from Frank James's personal photograph album. Images of Quantrill are rare. As soon as one is identified, the matter is debated among historians and collectors, usually leaving the issue undecided.

Right: There seems to be little doubt that this photograph was made of Quantrill before the war.

Above: Quantrill is flanked by Oliver Shepherd on his right and George Shepherd on his left. Oliver was at the September 27, 1864, battle of Centralia. He was killed by vigilantes on April 4, 1868, at his home near Lee's Summit, Missouri. George fought in the battles of Wilson's Creek, Prairie Grove, and Pea Ridge as a Confederate regular. As one of Quantrill's men he participated in the battles of Independence, Lawrence, Baxter Springs, Fayette, and Centralia.

Left: Capt. George Todd was Quantrill's second in command. He fought as a member of the Missouri State Guard before returning home and joining Quantrill in January 1862. Todd was killed in Independence during the October 22, 1864, battle of Westport. Prior to the battle he had a premonition of his death and told his comrades: "I know I'll be killed, but it is just as fitting for me to die for my country as any other man. All I ask is that you boys stay with me and see that I get a decent burial."

Above: This is the only known photograph of Capt. William Anderson (*left*) with Gen. Joseph O. Shelby (*right*). After Federals murdered one of Anderson's sisters and maimed the other two for life, Anderson became such a determined fighter that his enemies gave him the sobriquet of "Bloody Bill."

Right: Jim Anderson was the brother of "Bloody Bill" Anderson and a first lieutenant under Archie Clements. He joined Quantrill shortly after his brother did, because Federals had hanged his father and uncle on March 7, 1862, for being Southern sympathizers.

The Hudspeth brothers are pictured above. William Napoleon "Babe" Hudspeth (*seated*) and Joel Rufus "Rufe" Hudspeth (*left*) both rode with Quantrill. Lamertine Hudspeth, on the right, was too young to fight during the war, but in 1882 he helped to identify the body of Jesse James. The image comes from the album of Ben Morrow, a cousin of the Hudspeths who also rode with Quantrill. The Hudspeth family was forced from their home by Gen. Thomas Ewing's infamous Order No. 11.

Right: This is the only known photograph of Capt. Richard "Dick" Yeager. In 1861 he was in charge of one of his father's wagon trains when he returned to Jackson County and found that Charles Jennison's jayhawkers had stripped his family's farm of everything they owned.

Left: This is the only known photograph of Jesse James in a Federal uniform. The image was reportedly given to the Mimms family who had cared for him after he had been wounded early in the war and was hiding in Harlem (now known as North Kansas City), Missouri. James joined Quantrill after being beaten on several occasions by Union troops and after seeing his stepfather hanged and his mother and sister beaten and imprisoned.

Above left: Clark Hockensmith died in Kentucky trying to save Quantrill at Wakefield's farm on May 10, 1865. *Above right:* Capt. John Jarrette joined Quantrill at the same time as brother-in-law Cole Younger. After the war, because Jarrette was known to have been with Quantrill, vigilantes killed him on his doorstep. They also shot his wife, Josephine, then set the house afire with his two children inside. *Below left:* Bill Ryan rode with the James-Younger gang after the war. *Below right:* Daniel Boone Scholl was killed on June 16, 1863, in a skirmish with Federal troops in Westport, Missouri. Afterward Quantrill commented that one of his men was worth fifty of the enemy. Frank James reportedly killed the Union soldier who shot Scholl.

Lt. Archie Clements (1), Capt. Dave Poole (2), and William Hendricks (3) posed for the cameraman in 1863 in Sherman, Texas.

The Kansas City building that served in the summer of 1863 as a prison for women is marked with an X in the image above. On August 14 Federal soldiers undermined and collapsed the structure with the women inside, killing five of eleven captives who were relatives of Quantrill's men.

The Lawrence raid was sensationalized with such images as the three reproduced here that originally appeared in *Harper's Weekly*. The scenes are nothing more than fanciful depictions based only on the imaginations of New York artists who had never seen the town of Lawrence. They created what their editors told them to produce.

Virtually all accounts of the Lawrence raid in Northern newspapers were grossly exaggerated. The conflagration pictured above was a wartime vision of hell. Most newspapers reported that every building in town was burned and men, women, and children were wantonly murdered in the street. Nothing could have been further from the truth. While buildings were burned and men were shot down in the street, the raid targeted specific individuals who had wreaked havoc in Missouri over the years. This was payback, and it was less than the jayhawkers and Redlegs had wrought across the river—but that distinction was never made in the coverage given the story.

When he was named the district commander of the Department of Kansas, Gen. James Blunt adopted his predecessor's order raising the black flag, that is, no guerrillas were to be taken prisoner, they were to be executed. Regarding the guerrillas' mode of warfare, Blunt was quoted in the June 28, 1862, *Leavenworth Daily Times:* "They shall not be treated as prisoners of war, but be summarily tried by drum-head court-martial, and if proved guilty, be executed, by hanging or shooting on the spot, as no punishment can be too prompt or severe for such unnatural enemies of the human race."

Col. James Ridgeway Penick posed for this portrait after the war. He was the commander of the Fifth Missouri State Militia stationed in Independence. Because his troops plundered the homes of Unionists as well as Southerners, his soldiers were referred to as "Penick's Thieves." Penick took no prisoners of Quantrill's men, and as a result, Penick's men were summarily executed when they were captured by the guerrillas. Penick asserted that the guerrilla problem could be wiped out "if hemp, fire, and gunpowder were freely used."

James Henry Lane was the senator from Kansas and leader of the Kansas jayhawkers. In a speech Lane vowed, "Missourians are wolves, snakes, devils, and damn their souls, I want to see them cast into a burning hell! We believe in a war of extermination. There is no such thing as Union men in the border of Missouri. I want to see every foot of ground in Jackson, Cass, and Bates Counties [in Missouri] burned over, everything laid waste."

Capt. Francis Malone commanded Company F in the notorious Seventh Kansas Jayhawker Cavalry.

Above: George Scholl (*left*) lost his brother Boone during the war, but he survived and attended Quantrill reunions, like the one where this image was made. Gabe Parr (*right*) was fifteen years old when he joined Quantrill. He later became a deputy sheriff of Jackson County.

Below left: Hugh Cameron, known as "The Hermit," came to Kansas in 1854 to join in the border troubles. He was a captain in the Second Kansas Jayhawker Cavalry. After the war he became a recluse.

Below right: Charles Fletcher "Fletch" Taylor noted, "Quantrill was always well liked by his men. [And] he always treated them well." Taylor lost his right arm in an 1864 ambush. After the war he served in the Missouri legislature.

Above: This cave is on the Morgan Walker farm in the Blue Springs area. Quantrill used it to hide barrels of gunpowder seized during the August 11, 1862, battle of Independence. The powder was used to make ammunition for the Lawrence raid. Before leaving Jackson County in 1864 Quantrill blew up the remaining barrels. The townspeople of Independence—seven miles away—reported hearing the blast.

Right: The members of the West Fork of the Little Blue Baptist Church in Brooking Township elected to close the church during the war because they refused to submit to Federal coercion to pray for Abraham Lincoln. Here on March 19, 1862, Quantrill saw the *St. Louis Republican*'s account of Henry W. Halleck's order to hang all guerrillas when captured and not to treat them as prisoners of war, and he accepted the challenge of the black flag.

Quantrill died in Louisville, Kentucky, on June 6, 1865, and was buried there in the old Portland Catholic Cemetery. In 1887 his mother had his bones brought home to Ohio. Parts of the remains were stolen, and some bones came to be in a private collection. After many years these remains were reinterred in 1992 in the Old Confederate Veterans Home Cemetery in Higginsville, Missouri.

A crowd of more than seven hundred witnessed the 1992 ceremony involving five bones and a vial containing a lock of Quantrill's hair. Among them was Judge James R. Ross, great-grandson of Jesse James. An honor guard was provided by the Fifth Missouri Infantry (CS). All but one of the pallbearers were direct descendants of men who had ridden with Quantrill.

Young Anton Petersen, the author's son, respectfully throws a handful of earth on Quantrill's grave.

A gravestone for Kate King, wife of William Quantrill, was recently placed in the Maple Hill Cemetery in Kansas. An early newspaper article reported that she was buried here in an unmarked grave.

A gravestone for Kate King Quantrill was also placed in the Slaughter Cemetery in Blue Springs, Missouri, just a short distance from her birthplace. It was erected by her nephew, Arthur Dealy, and her neighbor, Fred Ford.

One witness to Vaughn's hanging remembered that the guerrilla addressed the crowd in a tone of mingled defiance and bravado. "He died a Southern man," the witness observed. "And hoped he should go to a better world and threatened vengeance upon the crowd saying that some of them would suffer for his death."

Confederate Col. Benjamin Franklin Parker, an officer operating in northwest Missouri, had written to Blunt seeking to exchange Vaughn for five Federal prisoners. Blunt replied in the most vitriolic manner:

> I have instructed the officers in command of troops in the border counties of Missouri, that every Rebel, or Rebel sympathizer, who gives aid, directly or indirectly, shall be destroyed or expelled from the military district. These instructions will not exempt females from the rule. Therefore all persons known to be in arms against the Federal authorities of this district will be summarily put to death when captured. The only Constitutional right that will be granted them will be the right to make a choice of the quality of rope with which they will be hung.

In reply to Blunt's communiqué, Parker commented: "What, sir, can you expect from a people whose rights are trampled in the dust, whose property is taken ruthlessly, whose families have been outraged and subjected to indignities unbecoming the savage, whose friends and kindred have been shot and hanged for opposing the unwarrantable and unconstitutional invasion of our rights and country? All this has been done, and now you threaten us with extinction. To extirpate our race and reduce to a wilderness the land we once inhabited." Upon learning of Vaughn's death, Parker hanged five Federal prisoners in retaliation.[28]

Only a few days after Vaughan's arrest, Quantrill captured three Union soldiers: a lieutenant, an orderly sergeant, and a private. He sent word to the Union commander in Kansas City that if James Vaughn was hanged, Quantrill would either shoot or hang his three prisoners. When the courier returned, he stated in front of the three prisoners that the commander refused to exchange Vaughn and would hang him as scheduled.

The Federal lieutenant observed the integrity of Quantrill and his men, and out of respect he offered a proposition. John McCorkle recalled the conversation between Quantrill and the prisoner:

> The lieutenant . . . said, "Colonel, I know you intend to execute me and my two companions and, after knowing you have tried to save us, I do not

blame you, but I have a proposition to make to you: if you will let me, I will go to Kansas City and see the authorities and, I believe, that being a lieutenant in the regular army, I may be able to prevail upon them to accept your proposition, and I now promise you, upon my honor, that I will return, whatever may be their decision." Quantrill looked at him a moment and said, "I will trust you; go." On the afternoon of the third day, the lieutenant rode into our camp and, walking straight to our colonel, said: "I have failed; I gave you my word, and I have returned to be executed, and am prepared to die. I do not blame you, Colonel, and I do not believe that if you had fifty of our best men, they would exchange Vaughn for all of them, so, Colonel, we await your orders." Quantrill looked at him a moment, making no reply, turning on his heel, called Cole Younger, Frank James, and myself to him, and taking us to one side, said, "Boys, this man is too honorable and brave to die; he has done all in his power to save Jim Vaughan, and I believe that either one of the others would have done the same thing, and they ought not to suffer for the brutality and meanness of others, and I'll be damned if any of them shall die by my hand." He then sent for the three prisoners and said to them, "Boys, your lieutenant is too honorable and brave a man to die and I believe you are all that way. There is not one man in ten thousand who would have acted as your lieutenant has. Now, if you'll give me your word of honor, and I know your lieutenant is a man of honor, that you will never again take up arms against the South, I am going to let you go. My men and I may be outlaws, but we are honorable and have some heart left and have never yet murdered a brave man."

The three Union soldiers eventually returned to Kansas City and resigned from the service. Jim Vaughn was hanged in Kansas City ten days after his capture.

QUANTRILL HAD not been long in his camp in Jackson County when news of the most cruel and dastardly deed perpetrated on two Blue Spring citizens was brought to his attention. They had not participated in any hostilities, but to callous Union commanders the only thing that mattered was that they were Southerners and therefore enemies. Some Union commanders adopted the thinking that simple proximity to partisan camps was sufficient proof of guilt and male residents could expect no mercy. Wrote Penick: "It is next to impossible to fight these guerrillas on their own ground in the brush, where they have every advantage over us. We must make it unhealthy for the neighborhoods where they harbor them. . . . It is my intention, wherever I find a camp of bushwhackers, to take summary vengeance on those who I have satisfactory reason to believe have knowledge of the existence of such a camp and do not report it."[29]

Thus Federal commanders who believed that guerrillas had camped in a neighborhood were authorized to shoot anyone who failed to report any such contact to the closest Union post within forty-eight hours. In their futile efforts to kill or capture Quantrill's men, Penick ordered atrocities against civilians whom he believed aided or sheltered guerrillas. Earlier in November 1862 a Federal patrol had burned from two to twelve houses in the Little Blue neighborhood, leaving the families homeless.[30]

On January 29, 1863, John Saunders and Jeptha Crawford, two forty-nine-year-old farmers, were seized from their homes in the Blue Springs area by Penick's men. Both men claimed to be neutral during the conflict. Saunders was taken on horseback to the house of John Burris, the Federal commander in Independence. In his front yard, Burris had Saunders shot. Burris then had his men ride back and burn down Saunders's home.

Jeptha Crawford was married to Elizabeth Harris, a sister of Reuben Harris, whose son Thomas rode with Quantrill. Jeptha had nine children, the youngest of which was five years old. A neighbor recounted the murder:

Mr. Crawford, an old man with a large family of children, was a Southern sympathizer, but had never taken up arms against the government. He went to the mill one day with a sack of corn to have it ground to make bread for his wife and children. He left home early in the morning—was to be back by noon. Noon came, the wife had prepared dinner as best she could, but was waiting for her husband's return so she could have bread for their dinner. Two o'clock came and the husband was still absent. The children were hungry, crying for something to eat. The mother would say, "Papa will soon be here, then my darlings shall have something to eat." Three o'clock came, and the mother saw a company of soldiers approaching. They rode up to the door. The mother looked out and saw her husband a prisoner in their midst. He was told to dismount. Then they shot him down before the eyes of his wife and children—shot down like a wild beast. The mother was told to get out of the house with her children, as they were going to burn the house. She asked them to let her give her little children something to eat, as they had had nothing to eat since early morning. In answer to her appeal one of them snatched a brand from the fire and stuck it in the straw bed. Everything was soon in flames. The mother hastened from the house, snatching up a few things as she went. Her husband killed, her house burned, she and her little children turned out in the cold world, homeless and destitute. . . . O, how strange that men, made in the image of God, could be so cruel and heartless.[31]

Being thrust into the harsh winter weather without provisions and shelter, Elizabeth Crawford sought shelter and comfort with some neighbors who had the courage and Christian charity to take her family in. There was nothing she had left but her family—that and a hatred for the kind of men who would do these things to peaceful citizens.

Shortly after Quantrill's return, Elizabeth Crawford learned that he was camped nearby. She took her four sons—twenty-two-year-old William, twin fifteen-year-olds Marshall and Marion, and thirteen-year-old Riley—to the guerrillas' camp. She approached the colonel and said, "These are all I have left. Take them and make soldiers of them." Riley was not only one of the youngest guerrillas, he was also one of the hardest fighters in Quantrill's band. It was said that he killed every Union soldier who fell into his hands.

Like Jeptha Crawford, Samuel Kimberlin also had four young sons who— because of the brutality of Federal troops—left the grave of their father and the smoldering ashes of their homes to join Quantrill.

On March 26 Quantrill took the Crawford brothers and ambushed some unwary Federals. Patiently waiting for a Union patrol from Independence, Quantrill and Todd sprung from ambush along the east fork of the Little Blue, shooting five Federals from their saddles and running down and killing four more as they retreated. After the ambush Quantrill had the bodies loaded into a wagon and taken back to Independence with a message for Colonel Penick that the same fate awaited all of his soldiers who ventured out into "Quantrill Country."[32]

As Quantrill settled back into his old haunts, he mulled over the stories from the Jackson County farmers of the depredations of Penick's troops and the Kansas soldiers. Kansans like James Lane, Eli Snyder, Hugh Fisher, Charles Jennison, Daniel R. Anthony, George Hoyt, and other radical abolitionists were causing all the trouble in Missouri, and Quantrill contemplated how to get at them. Radical Union newspapers that fomented unrest among their readers were also in Kansas, along with the goods stolen from Missouri farmers. These goods were warehoused in Lawrence and guarded by black troops before being auctioned off on the streets of Lawrence. Those residents of Lawrence not actually collaborating with the jayhawkers still gave their tacit approval to the criminal deeds they observed. Soldiers of the Kansas militia were housed there. They may have been proper citizens at home, but when called upon by Lane and Jennison, they donned their uniforms, saddled their horses, and dashed across the border to kill, burn, and plunder. If the districts they attacked had already been plundered of horses and wagons, they brought their own vehicles and took whatever was left. Nothing was overlooked: children's clothes, bedding, women's dresses. Even headstones from the graves of Southerners' honored dead were carried back to Kansas for use as front porch steps. Some jayhawkers limited their activities to plundering only livestock.

A jayhawker private from Kansas named Chandler recorded that he sneaked into Missouri in disguise and made a list of the properties with all the best horses. After nightfall he gathered the horses and made for the Kansas border. Chandler said, "This we did, and upon reassembling it was found that nearly every man had two horses. We immediately struck out and as soon as we had set foot upon Kansas soil we separated with the understanding that we were to meet one week from that day at Leavenworth." He boasted, "We didn't let our consciences trouble us very much. We continued to make similar raids on the Missourians off and on during the summer."[33]

Gen. Egbert Brown from the Central Missouri District informed his departmental headquarters that Kansas jayhawkers were raiding in his district and robbing the people of slaves and whatever property they had left. He said, "If Kansas wants negroes I will send 500 women and children to the State in two days, as they are a great annoyance to me, and everybody wants them removed. But they do not want them; they want the property the negroes carry off and the opportunity of taking it by coming into the State."[34]

On May 2 Missouri provisional governor Hamilton R. Gamble wrote an impassioned plea to President Lincoln to use his influence to stop the Redleg slaughter:

> Sir . . . I wish to call your attention now to the perpetration of murders and arsons and other outrages committed by persons connected with the Army, over which you are Commander-in-Chief, and whose crimes you have the power to restrain. . . . The Kansas officers reports the killing of many bushwhackers. The information coming to me is that these bushwhackers were men shot down on their own farms or in their own houses peaceably pursuing their own occupations. That many of them were what are here called "Southern sympathizers" I think probable, while I am very credibly informed that some were known Union men who were unfortunately in possession of slaves or other property coveted by the *Patriots*. . . . Will you . . . allow butcheries to go on by men whom you have the authority to control?

Lincoln ignored Gamble's pleas and allowed the raids to continue.

John M. Schofield, the Federal district commander stationed in St. Louis, finally moved to reduce the effectiveness of the jayhawkers in western Missouri. On June 9 he divided up the state of Kansas into two districts. One was called the District of the Frontier, and Gen. James G. Blunt was appointed its commander. The other was called the District of the Border and commanded by Gen. Thomas Ewing, who took command on June 17.

Blunt originally had all of the District of Kansas to himself, but he was so closely affiliated with James Lane that Schofield orchestrated this redistricting to lessen both Lane's and Blunt's influence in the area.

Wanting to strike a blow at the Kansans, Quantrill decided on a second raid on Shawneetown. On June 6 the guerrillas made their way from the Little Blue, across the low rugged hills, past numerous abandoned farmhouses, until they crossed over the ridge separating Kansas City and Independence. They turned their horses slightly to the south and proceeded through the narrow trails toward a spot south of Westport. A Federal garrison of fifty Kansas militiamen was in town when the guerrillas arrived. The guerrillas surprised them but did no killing. After checking the identification of the soldiers, they were all paroled. Effecting little damage the guerrillas returned back to their hideouts along the Little Blue.

Both Northern and Southern commanders wondered what made Quantrill's guerrillas better fighters than the Federals they encountered. One reason is that they excelled in horsemanship. Quantrill had his men teach their horses to jump fences, which the Federals would have to let down in order to pursue them. This gave them a great advantage in outdistancing their pursuers when they needed to escape a larger force. The horses were also trained to maintain their composure under fire. Their mounts were usually the best blooded stock that well-established Missouri farms had to offer. Quantrill and his men usually rode their horses at a walk. In this way they conserved their mounts' energy when needed either for a charge or for escape.

Quantrill's men were young, and they joined the partisans seeking a daily adventure rather than the dull routine of regular army life. They were both daring and brave and developed a camaraderie that bonded them into a tightly knit, highly effective fighting unit. Combat welded them together and made them closer than brothers.

Another trait that made them such a dreaded force was their firepower. Almost every guerrilla carried at least two revolvers, but most carried four while some even carried up to eight. This amount of arms gave them vast fire superiority over any enemy. Some pistols were holstered while the rest were stuck in their belts. Many had pistol holsters attached to their saddles. Any man worth his salt kept his weapons and firearms in top shape. Firearms were life supporting not just for hunting but also for protection. Inspections by military officers, whether in the partisan service or the regular army, were frequent and intensive. Officers ensured that everyone's firearms were functional and clean. Dirty or rusty weapons would bring quick punishment and retribution.

The guerrillas relied not only on the dependability of their own arms but also on their fellow soldiers in battle. Frank Smith noted that the guerrillas were armed with all kinds of weapons: derringers, pepperboxes, and often double-barreled rifles and shotguns. These weapons were small and lightweight. Guerrillas carried only what they could transport and thus were never encumbered with heavier articles of war, such as artillery or caissons. Because of the nature of their warfare, they were able to attack or defend whenever they so desired.

The enemy was usually armed with only single-shot rifles. Their first shot was normally fired in a volley at one hundred yards. This volley usually proved ineffective. The normal reloading time for a black-powder rifle was twenty seconds. With a charging guerrilla on horseback, these hundred yards would be covered before the enemy had time to get off another round. Then the guerrillas' deadly pistol fire would tell a ghastly tale.

The only way the guerrillas could survive in the communities where they fought was with the support of the inhabitants. One of Quantrill's disadvantages in fighting a guerrilla war was a susceptibility to heavy casualties simply because he had limited medical support. Realizing this liability, Quantrill sought out sympathetic doctors who, if they didn't actually ride with him on an expedition, could be counted upon to minister to the medical needs of his men when needed.

At the beginning of the border conflict much of the male population was only part-time guerrillas, but due to the constant harassment from government troops, local men quickly joined Quantrill's full-time guerrilla company. Because they were all members of the local culture, they slept, ate, and identified with the residents in the areas in which they operated. In this way the guerrillas obtained most of their supplies. If Southern sympathizers could not feed them, they forced Union families to feed them. Oftentimes local populations provided the guerrillas with munitions by making bullets and bullet molds and confiscating, from under the diverted gaze of the Federals, any article of war that the guerrillas might need. What the locals could not supply, the guerrillas simply obtained from enemies captured or killed in battle.

Weapons and ammunition were precious commodities, and the guerrillas' sympathetic followers were only too happy to hide such goods on their property until they were needed. Barrels of gunpowder and military supplies were reportedly stored in caves and recesses among the numerous rock outcroppings inundating the hilly terrain from which they operated. Eight barrels of gunpowder captured during the battle of Independence were kept in a small cave along a ridge just north of the Morgan Walker farm in Blue Springs.

Another reason the guerrillas excelled is that they had an outstanding leader in William Clarke Quantrill. He was known for studying a mission and determining the enemy's capabilities, characteristics, strengths, and weaknesses. Quantrill was always able to maintain the initiative by making the Federals react to him. Frank Smith observed that his commander carefully planned every maneuver and attack, always keeping in mind just how and where he was going to retreat.

Quantrill was able to constantly throw the Federals off balance by organizing his command into smaller units of ten men each. These units took advantage of the natural cover of ravines, hollows, reverse slopes, trees, and rock outcroppings situated along the hills overlooking the lowlands of the Sni-A-Bar Creek and the Big Blue and Little Blue Rivers. By dividing his command into smaller elements, he could strike at several military targets simultaneously. Quantrill's ambushes on Federal patrols enabled him to harass a larger enemy force by using a smaller one. The loss of the enemy's men killed or captured as well as the loss of captured or destroyed equipment and supplies greatly reduced the combat effectiveness of the Union army in Missouri.

Quantrill's assaults also caused the enemy to divert his forces from combat to guard duty for convoys, mail, and supply trains. This drain of manpower kept the enemy from assembling a large force for offensive combat operations. The Missouri militia, which usually guarded the posts along the border, became apprehensive and cautious and were reluctant to go on patrols or to move in convoys or in small groups.

When on a large expedition, Quantrill would keep out flank security. The soldiers detailed to protect the main body were kept close enough for Quantrill to maintain control and contact. The advance guard kept his troops from inadvertently running into the enemy and being surprised, and the rear guard checked for any signs of pursuing enemy. Quantrill placed himself toward the head of his marching column for the greatest control over his men. If he had any special personnel, like doctors or civilians, riding with him, they were kept in the center of his column for the greatest protection.

While passing through the enemy's territory and over open ground, the guerrillas developed hand and arm signals that enabled them to determine if the enemy was in the area or if it was safe to move through. Southern sympathizers also knew these signals and would signal Quantrill's men from far away. The signals were simple and easily recognized and understood by all the members of the unit.[35] Quantrill was also known to carry with him an Opelousas or Texas steer's horn, which had a peculiar sound and could be heard at a distance of about four miles. All his men were acquainted with its peculiar sound, and whenever a certain blast was given, all hands rallied to the assistance of their commander.[36] Each guerrilla always carried a good pocket watch, and their leaders were known to have a spyglass to observe enemy troop movements from a long distance.

After a raid, Quantrill stressed returning to camp by a different route and a predetermined rallying point. This rallying point was known to all and was suitable for resting, refitting, and rearming.

Oftentimes his men would spread their saddle blankets over the roads then walk their horses over them to hide their tracks. At other times they would drag tree limbs and brush behind them to obliterate their tracks. Another method that was sometimes used was to scatter feed on ground where tracks were visible to the enemy, then hogs and livestock came and covered up the tracks. When being pursued, the guerrillas would often walk in a stream for a short distance. They would also avoid being trailed by moving over rocky or hard ground or by walking backward, or if there was more than one person, they would walk in each other's footprints. The surest way to avoid being pursued was to split into smaller groups.

With jayhawkers plundering Unionists as well as Southerners, it was easy for the guerrillas to gain the support of the populace. Most of the civilians who suffered from jayhawker raids either joined the guerrilla units or supported them. The guerrillas needed little propaganda to support their cause. Virtually every citizen in the border area had been a victim of jayhawker atrocities and brutality at one time or another. Those who managed to escape likely had a relative or neighbor who was abused in some way. They supported the guerrillas by giving them hiding places, food, recruits, and information. Many of those who suffered under Federal rule but continued to claim to be Unionist were more than willing to aid the guerrillas by relaying information they had about the military situation in the area. From this information, Quantrill was able to conduct his raids on the enemy's fortifications, supply routes, and communication links. These raids constantly kept the Federals off balance and made them disperse their forces to protect other key military posts.

Even those people who did not actively support Quantrill out of fear of retaliation from the Federals gave the guerrillas passive support by not giving the Union troops information about the guerrillas' activities and movements. There was scarcely a man or woman who saw the actions of the jayhawkers who did not give Quantrill the information. Even some strong Union men acting as spies became disgusted with the conduct of the Federals. So complete and thorough was the cooperation of the citizens with Quantrill that the slightest demonstration on the part of the Federal forces was duly noted and immediately reported to him.[37]

While the Federals maintained military posts in towns and cities, the guerrillas freely operated in the countryside. In the vastness of the rural countryside Quantrill and his chieftains established sanctuaries and camps. Here their chief advantage was their knowledge of the terrain.

Frank Smith noted that he and many other Jackson County boys joined Quantrill's guerrillas simply out of desperation and a sense of self-preservation because they had little alternative. What attracted so many to Quantrill's camp rather than the other commands or the regular army was the guerrilla leader's charismatic leadership. The men who joined him would readily lay down their lives for him. They would follow him anywhere, and until the day they died, they only had praise for their respected leader.

"Quantrill was the smartest man I ever knew," James Campbell commented. "He had the qualifications of leadership in him. He knew just what to do in every situation." William H. Gregg remembered Quantrill as "a man of few words. He usually restrained the ardor of his followers and never sacrificed a man needlessly." Harrison Trow recalled that Quantrill "had extraordinary resource and cunning" and remarked "Quantrill became a guerrilla because he had prudence, firmness, courage, audacity and common sense." Frank James observed, "Every man was brave and had absolute confidence in the gallant leader."[38]

Quantrill's organization was also known for the discipline he maintained over his men. This discipline was necessary to keep an effective guerrilla force fighting under the conditions they were forced to endure. Twenty-six-year-old Hiram George remarked that Quantrill "was a man of few words, but those few were law." Fletcher Taylor remembered that Quantrill gave an order stating, "If I find any man insulting a woman, I'll hang him to the first limb I come to." Jack Liddil summarized that Quantrill's "men respected and obeyed him."[39]

The guerrillas endured extreme hardships. Those of Quantrill's men who were captured knew they would be executed and even tortured. They usually had little to eat and rarely had any shelter from the weather, choosing to sleep outdoors rather then get surprised by a Union patrol and surrounded indoors. They were continually harassed and pursued around the countryside. The hardships they endured were not for the weak at heart. Quantrill's Italian contemporary, Giuseppe Garibaldi, told his freedom fighters: "I offer neither pay nor quarters, nor provisions; I offer hunger, thirst, forced marches, battles and death. Let him who loves his country in his heart, and not with his lips only, follow me."[40]

Quantrill had no trouble recruiting young men for his cause, but his cause was somewhat different than those fighting with Robert E. Lee in Virginia or Braxton Bragg in Tennessee. Because of the Federal treatment of the civilian population along the Missouri border and the atrocities committed by the men who hid behind the uniform of the Union to perpetuate their crimes, Quantrill's men joined up first to avenge their families and then to fight for the more popular cause of state sovereignty. States' rights took second place as these men defended firsthand their property and rode into battle against the actual aggressors who attacked their homes and families. They were fighting a personal war.

Even though Quantrill was fighting a classic guerrilla war, he tried to adhere strictly to the rules of war. For guerrilla units to be recognized as acceptable combat units, they had to meet certain criteria to be treated as prisoners of war if captured. Quantrill strove to meet each of these points:

1. A guerrilla unit must be commanded by a person who is responsible for his subordinates. Quantrill clearly was.

2. Guerrilla soldiers must wear a fixed, distinctive sign recognizable at a distance. This was the stickiest point of all. Even though Quantrill's men wore captured Federal uniforms to deceive the enemy, and because the Confederate government did not supply partisan units with uniforms, they did have the distinctive apparel called the "guerrilla shirt," which was worn beneath their uniform blouse. Most guerrillas also wore a long black plume in their hats. Another point was that guerrilla units had to bear their arms openly. Quantrill's men usually wore four revolvers each, and some even wore up to eight. They also carried either a carbine or shotgun slung across their backs.

3. Guerrilla units also had to conduct operations in accordance with the laws and customs of war. Quantrill did this explicitly until he was ignored in the taking and exchanging of prisoners and the black flag of no quarter was hoisted upon him and his men by Federal authorities.

When Quantrill first organized his military unit and selected his leaders, he established camps and sanctuaries to bring an enlarged territory under his control. After this Quantrill often had a large enough command to openly challenge Federal forces by conventional warfare. All during his guerrilla activity he tried to establish his military authority. Over and over again he sought to exchange prisoners of war, but in each case his Federal opponents were not interested in acknowledging his organization as purely military in nature. Even when trying to obtain a single guerrilla prisoner release from the Federals by threatening to kill many more enemy soldiers in return, the authorities adamantly refused to negotiate. They would have been better off if they had. The label of being a recognized leader in the conventional pro-fession of arms might have held Quantrill to a higher standard as the summer of 1863 approached.

8

Brutality Unfolds

When war is declared, truth is the first casualty.

ARTHUR PONSONBY

EIGHTEEN SIXTY-THREE WOULD prove to be a devastating year. While Quantrill was seeking a colonel's commission in Richmond, the Federals stationed along the border counties kept the local pro-Southern citizens in turmoil. Col. William R. Penick, commanding the Fifth Missouri State Militia, was stationed in Independence. Penick was a radical Unionist, and during Quantrill's absence, Penick freely pillaged the homes and farms of pro-Southerners. Many said that his men were worse than the jayhawkers from Kansas.

As spring approached, Quantrill spent the next few weeks getting his company ready for the march home to Jackson County. By early spring the guerrilla company had passed Warrensburg, Missouri. Col. Edwin C. Catherwood, the Federal commander at Warrensburg, hurried a telegram to Brig. Gen. Benjamin Loan, commanding the District of Central Missouri, to report that Quantrill had been seen with a force of two hundred to five hundred men near Warrensburg. In Independence, Jacob Hall wrote in his diary on May 6: "They say there are a great many bushwhackers here. I understand Quantrill is here again. Colonel Penick I understand has sent for reinforcements and artillery."[1]

As soon as Quantrill returned to his old haunts along the banks of the Little Blue in southeast Jackson County, his men spread out and began harassing the Union outposts. Traffic all along the Missouri River was stopped by guerrilla attacks. One squad of guerrillas composed of David Poole, William Gregg, Coleman Younger, Ferdinand Scott, John Jarrette, John Ross, William Greenwood, and some others captured the steamboat *Sam Gaty* docked below Sibley. Found on board were twenty-two black Union soldiers, but Younger vowed they should not be harmed. Twelve white Federal soldiers were also discovered. Six belonged to Colonel McFerrin's regiment and six belonged to Penick's. Only Penick's men were killed, because Penick had ordered his command to never take a bushwhacker alive.[2]

While Quantrill was daily battling Union forces in Jackson County, sad news reached the guerrillas from Lt. Gov. Thomas C. Reynolds of Missouri's government-in-exile. Gov. Claiborne Jackson had died. Added to this somber report was the constant news about the suffering inflicted upon both the partisan bands and the local inhabitants. In midwinter, houses had been burned by the hundreds, and whole neighborhoods had been devastated and laid waste.

Aroused as he had never been before, Quantrill devised a terrible vengeance. In the spring of 1863 he issued a proclamation to the Federals in Kansas that if they did not stop pillaging and destroying homes and farms and killing old men and women, he would come to Lawrence at some unexpected time and paint the city blacker than Hades and make its streets run with blood.[3]

Sometime during the spring the Federals raided across the Osage River into Bates County. At a point in the river, Hog Island divided the waterway into two streams, named Double Branches. The island was used as a rendezvous by guerrillas returning from the South. To combat the guerrillas, the Federals burned eleven Southern homes in Bates County on orders from Gen. Thomas Ewing. Elsewhere, Col. Edward Lynde of the Ninth Kansas Jayhawker Regiment boasted that he killed more than one hundred guerrillas between June 18 and 20. Most of the killed were noncombatants, not soldiers.

Guerrilla forces in any theater of operations needed civilian support, and during this time Quantrill relied upon the people more than ever. The greatest aid given to his band came from the vast interwoven association of relatives and neighbors of Quantrill's men.

The guerrillas knew they would take heavy casualties if the Federals ever managed to trap them. One problem was that their casualties would be multiplied by their limited medical support. Wounded guerrillas many times waited days or even weeks to seek proper medical treatment. Knowing this,

Quantrill had several doctors serving within his command. Many women also gave aid. Lucy Nicholson Lindsay, from Boonville, smuggled quinine, morphine, socks, and clothing under her skirts and in the coils of her hair.[4]

The main reason Quantrill's band had such widespread popular support is that they were fighting for a cause the population supported. There was no one in the border counties who had not been affected by the raids of the Kansas jayhawkers. James Lane and Charles Jennison had stripped the counties bare regardless of whether the inhabitants were Northern or Southern in their sentiments. The plunder taken from the Missouri border counties supplied a lucrative market in Fort Scott, Lawrence, and Leavenworth. Kansas Redlegs sold their booty at public auctions on Lawrence streets until that city achieved a distinction of sorts as the "Citadel of Stolen Goods." The *Kansas City Journal of Commerce* on July 25, 1863, reported, "An honest man engaged in some honest business could do well in Ft. Scott for he'd have no competition." The *Journal* also reported on July 20 that Leavenworth had been placed under martial law in July 1863 to combat the ready market offered there for contraband.[5]

It was said that Missouri was more Northern than Southern and that two Missourians enlisted in the Northern army for every one who enlisted for the South. More than half of the population was loyal to the Union, but the havoc spread by the jayhawkers along the state's western border turned probably nine-tenths of the public in favor of the South.[6] As a result, while the Federals established garrisons in the towns and cities of western Missouri, the guerrillas controlled the countryside. Rural areas provided the guerrillas with breathing space. Here they established sanctuaries far from the government's tentacles of power. Because of their many sympathizers, the guerrillas had an easy time gathering intelligence. They had spies in every military and civil organization. The populace often provided them with food, clothing, hiding places, recruits, and other services. The guerrillas obtained all of their material support from the local population. They won the people's active support by fighting for something the people wanted: protection from the thieving incursions of the Kansas jayhawkers and the depredations of the Federal troops stationed in their communities.

On one occasion, Quantrill and three men were invited to supper at a widow's farmhouse in Jackson County. As Quantrill and his companions sat around the kitchen table and exchanged pleasantries they noticed that their hostess was using the last of her flour to make biscuits for them. Her one small child sat in the corner by the fire and watched the soldiers with wide curious eyes. The guerrillas had been acquainted with the widow's husband, who had recently been killed while fighting in Sterling Price's army. At first being gay and jocular, the guerrillas began to lose their appetites as they felt an awkwardness when they realized that they were eating the poor widow's last food in the house. Quantrill was overcome with sadness and politely protested her sacrifice in a gentlemanly way by stating that neither he nor his men could bring themselves to impose in such a manner as to take her last meal. The widow insisted, however, and as she set biscuits in front of each guerrilla, she made a point of gently touching each man on the shoulder and said, "We're all making sacrifices. We're both just trying to survive from day to day, but you all are doing the fighting and that's the most important thing that can be done."

Is it any wonder then that Quantrill and his men made it a practice of sharing with the impoverished citizens of Jackson County? Whenever gold or Federal greenbacks were acquired during a raid, or spoils were captured, including Federal commissary supplies, the guerrillas always made sure they were divided out among the local farmers.

Quantrill's attacks on Union outposts and installations came from knowledge gained from his vast intelligence sources. Before he planned his raids on Kansas towns, he knew the enemy's strengths, weaknesses, capabilities, and characteristics. He knew what he expected to find in the towns in the way of supplies and clothing for his men.[7] Quantrill had received a report that a militia captain named Sessions had been terrorizing and murdering Southerners in Clay Country, north of the Missouri River. Around June 5 Quantrill sent William Gregg, Ferdinand Scott, James Little, Joe Hart, John Jackson, Henry Coward, Fletcher Taylor, James Hendricks, and Frank James into Clay County to mete out justice.

The Federal captain had a troop of militia stationed within one mile of Richfield.[8] Gregg sent a local farmer into the Union camp to report that two drunken bushwhackers were threatening his family. Gregg expected that Sessions would lead a small detail to investigate the situation. The guerrillas planned to ambush the Federals at a wooden bridge along the road. Scott stationed seven men on each side of the road just beyond the bridge. Gregg and Little remained mounted to ride down any survivors. The hoofbeats of the Union horses on the bridge would alert them to Sessions's arrival.

It was not long before Sessions and twelve cavalrymen rode into the ambush. When they came into the killing zone, Scott opened the ambush and killed eight outright and wounded one. Gregg and Little then ran down the remaining three soldiers and shot them out of their saddles.

Gregg then rode into town and seized the Union flag from the courthouse. Citizens informed him that a militia unit was stationed in Plattsburg, only a short distance away. Gregg resolved to attack the town and take possession of it. As the guerrillas rode to Plattsburg they captured Col. James Burch, who was serving as aide de camp to Missouri's provisional governor. When Gregg and Little's men reached the town, they found the militia had barricaded themselves inside the courthouse with more than three hundred muskets. After managing to eliminate the heavy fire from the courthouse windows, the guerrillas forced the militia to surrender after guaranteeing them that they would not be shot. Gregg paroled the militia as well as Colonel Burch then destroyed the three hundred captured muskets.

Meanwhile, Gregg's actions had aroused all of north Missouri. With thousands of militiamen on his trail, Gregg divided his force and crossed the Missouri River on skiffs, managing to get his men safely back across the river near Sibley.

On July 31 Quantrill moved on Westport and planned an attack on a Federal wagon train. Capt. Charles F. Coleman, Company D of the Ninth Kansas Jayhawker Regiment, had been assigned to guard the train. While Coleman was keeping a watch on the wagons from a concealed position, he saw a body of soldiers approaching. Taking them for guerrillas, he ordered a charge. He chased them a considerable distance, leaving the wagon train unprotected until he discovered that his prey was a detachment of Federals from Westport. In the interval that the wagon train was unprotected, the guerrillas attacked and plundered the wagons.

Coleman returned and pursued the guerrillas all the next day to the Taylor farm, situated on the Little Blue River, where the guerrillas turned to counterattack. Forty guerrillas poured a deadly volley into the oncoming Federals, forcing them to dismount and seek cover. The guerrillas then scattered and disappeared in the heavy timber.[9]

Early on in the war it was easy for the guerrillas to purchase what they needed by having friends and relatives travel into towns to buy much-needed supplies. These were then hidden in such things as trunks with false bottoms or even hidden in women's apparel. Knowing that they did not have the ability to destroy or even contain the guerrillas in Jackson County, the Union military issued an order on January 20, 1863, from the headquarters of the Department of Missouri: "All persons who shall knowingly harbor, conceal, aid, or abet, by furnishing food, clothing, information, protection, or any assistance whatever to any emissary, Confederate officer or soldier, partisan ranger, bushwhacker, robber, or thief, shall be promptly executed."[10] This meant that no husband, son, or brother could expect the slightest charity from his own relatives. There could be no comfort to a sick or dying relative or friend, no water for a thirsty horse or rider, no clothing to a needy relative or friend in the harshest of winter. Mainly, the realities of war, in all of its harshness and cruelty had been directed upon soldiers.

In Jackson County, thirteen-year-old John Fox, who had a brother with Quantrill, was shot and killed by Federals while his sister and mother had hold of him and begged for his life. He was charged with feeding his brother.[11] Federals also killed fourteen-year-old James Nicholson because he had two brothers with Price. Thirty-five-year-old Henry Morris was serving with Col. Upton Hays when Federals rode up to his house and killed his eleven-year-old son.[12]

Around April 1 Kansas Redlegs raided Lexington, burning several homes and killing seven men after plundering everything they wanted. Willard Mendenhall reported in his diary that the roads around Lexington were lined with refugees driven from their homes by the Redlegs. He observed: "The Redlegs are desolating the country, they have no respect for any person's political opinions. They appear to be a band of murderers and robbers." Not satisfied with torturing and killing only young boys from families of Southern sympathizers, Federal authorities now turned their attention to the guerrillas' female relatives.

For weeks a few psychotic soldiers in Kansas City planned how best to direct their venomous hatred at their notorious guerrilla foes. On their raids of plunder, the most sought-after articles were family Bibles, because these contained a record of the names and birth dates of family members. Most highly suspicious were the names of any males born of fighting age. When Federal soldiers confiscated these records, their first question to the families involved was, Where are the men whose names are listed here? If the men were in the Confederate army, the home was plundered and burned. Often the head of the house was shot down on his own doorstep in front of his wife and children.[13]

Women were not spared anything. For the women left behind, the Federals knew or suspected that they were actively aiding their loved ones in whatever ways they could. Southern patriotism among the women of the Confederacy was said to be the prime motivation behind the convictions of the Southern soldiers. It was to these women that the Federal command now directed its savagery in trying to eliminate the guerrillas.

The Southern women of Jackson County had indeed demonstrated their patriotism by aiding the guerrillas. Often they hid stray horses in the woods to give to the guerrillas. They carried medical supplies to the wounded and nursed them back to health. Southern women did not give their actions a second thought, because the men they were aiding were husbands, brothers, and sweethearts.

The most frustrating feeling on the part of the Federal commanders in Jackson County was their inability to destroy Quantrill's band outright. Their patrols were ambushed and annihilated. Their spies were found out and either fled the state or were executed by Quantrill's men. Everything seemed to be going in Quantrill's favor. So the Federal commanders slowly tightened their restraints on the civilian population, who turned against them in even greater numbers. Even those who, like most Missourians at the conflict's start, wanted to be neutral began to shift their loyalties. In Jackson County, Quantrill was the embodiment of the only Southern force strong enough or willing enough to protect the lives and property of those remaining on their farms and seeking to carry on normal lives.

Quantrill's efforts brought praise from Confederate officers. A June 29, 1863, report to Maj. Gen. Thomas C. Hindman noted:

> In the enrollment and organization of troops from Missouri . . . Captains Standish, Buchanan, Cravens, Perry, Quantrill and Harrison were especially zealous and useful. In estimating the value of their labors and of the many other devoted men who assisted them, it is to be considered that in order to bring out recruits from their State it was necessary to go within the enemy's lines, taking the risks of detection and punishment as spies, secretly collecting the men in squads and companies, arming, equipping and subsisting them by stealth and then moving them rapidly southward through a country swarming with Federal soldiers and an organized militia, and whose population could only give assistance at the hazard of confiscation of property and even death itself. That they succeeded at all under such circumstances is attributed to a courage and fidelity unsurpassed in the history of the war.[14]

The decision-makers of the North began to look for a military leader who could lead them out of the morass of guerrilla warfare. By midsummer they thought they had found such a man. Brig. Gen. Thomas Ewing took over the command of the District of the Border on June 16, 1863, in Kansas City. Ewing was thirty-four years old. He was described as "a man who believed that he had 'few equals in mental vigor.' He was intensely ambitious and hoped to secure election to the U.S. Senate. With that goal in mind he was at this period seeking the favor of Senator James H. Lane, the 'King' of Kansas politics."[15] Ewing had come to Kansas in the late 1850s and set up a law practice in Leavenworth. He had already projected himself into Republican politics, becoming chief justice of the Kansas Supreme Court. In 1861 he resigned his position to accept a brigadier general's commission from Lane to raise a regiment. Ewing brought with him his Kansas jayhawker cronies and had them garrisoned in Kansas City, even placing some notorious Kansas Redlegs on his headquarters staff. Once he received his promotion, his headquarters were set up in the Pacific House, the finest hotel in the city.

In 1860 Kansas City was a thriving metropolis situated along the south bank of the Missouri River, bordered on the west by the Kansas state line. Twelve miles to the east was the city of Independence with a population of 3,161. To the south lay Westport with a population of 1,195. Many wagon trains started west from Kansas City as soon as it was settled in 1837. In 1860 the population of the community had reached 4,414, and it boasted four railway connections, seven churches, one daily and five weekly newspapers, two banks, several seminaries, numerous companies manufacturing a variety of goods, one hundred retail establishments, and four large hotels.[16]

Gen. John M. Schofield in St. Louis told Ewing that he would have his work cut out for him in Kansas City. He mentioned that the citizens "seem to fear as much from the Kansas troops [militia] as from Lane's lawless rabble." Well-known military men such as Richard C. Vaughn commented on Schofield's advice to Ewing: "It is a fact well known to me that hundreds of the people of Jackson and Cass County are true and loyal men; they have already been robbed of their property, insulted and in many instances murdered by these troops from Kansas." But Schofield gave Ewing contradictory advice, telling him that the large majority of the people in the border area were "open Rebels" and all the inhabitants practically the "friends of the guerrillas."[17] In a speech at Olathe, Kansas, Ewing came down hard on the depredations of the jayhawkers he said were "stealing themselves rich in the name of liberty."

To soothe the opinions on both sides of the border, Ewing called for tough measures. He believed that at the outbreak of war three-fourths of western Missouri was "intensely disloyal." Regarding the guerrillas, he said that he would "drive out or exterminate every band of guerrillas now haunting that region. I will keep a thousand men in the saddle daily in pursuit of them and will redden with their blood every road and bridle path of the border."[18] Referring to the jayhawkers, he promised: "I mean, moreover, to stop with a rough hand all forays for plunder from Kansas to Missouri." But in less than two months he began endorsing such forays himself.[19]

Thomas Ewing was Gen. William T. Sherman's adopted brother as well as his brother-in-law. How similar these two were in military atrocities and civilian brutality became evident to the country in the next few weeks. Sherman had written about his own philosophy on military treatment toward civilians:

> Next year their lands will be taken, for in war we can take them, and rightfully too, and another year they may beg in vain for their lives. A people who will persevere in war beyond a certain limit ought to know the consequences. Many, many people, with less pertinacity than the South, have been wiped out of national existence. To those who submit to the rightful law and authority, all gentleness and forbearance; but to the petulant and persistent secessionist, why, death is mercy, and the quicker he or she is disposed of the better.

Sherman rightfully deserved the eternal scorn of all Southerners as he left a wake of devastation behind his conquering army. Rather than pursue Gen. John Bell Hood's Southern army back into Tennessee, Sherman instead chose to destroy civilian communities wholesale. With sixty thousand soldiers he forced all civilians to evacuate Atlanta, Georgia, then set about plundering more than twenty million dollars' worth of property and destroying other property valued at eighty million dollars. Sherman cut a path sixty miles wide and three hundred miles long across the state, from Atlanta to Savannah. As he displaced 100 percent of the civilian population, Sherman was quoted as saying: "No provision has been made for the families in Savannah and many of them will suffer from want—and I will not undertake to feed them."[20]

William Gregg compared his own feelings when he remembered, "The Bushwhackers did some bad things, but they never devastated and ruined the country. When General Sherman, who the North worships as a great Christian soldier, went on his famous march he issued orders that the country should be made so desolate that to get over it a crow would have to carry his haversack full of rations with him."[21]

Immediately after Ewing took over his new position, he arranged for military posts to be stationed approximately fifteen miles apart along the border, to serve as a blocking force to counter any guerrilla raid into Kansas. If a guerrilla unit was seen approaching, the posts simply had to send for assistance or wire the next station, which would be alerted and ready for an attack. Ewing established this defensive line by putting four companies of Kansas cavalry at Westport, Missouri; three companies of Kansas cavalry at Little Santa Fe in southern Jackson County; two companies of Kansas cavalry in Aubry, Kansas;

one company of Kansas cavalry at Coldwater Grove; and one company of infantry each at Olathe, Paola, and Mound City, Kansas. With these posts in place he was confident that he could thwart any further guerrilla incursions.[22]

On June 17, 1863, Maj. Luin K. Thacher, from Kansas City, then in command at Paola, was ordered by Ewing to move three companies of the Ninth Kansas Jayhawker Regiment to Kansas City. At around the same time Quantrill's second in command, Capt. George Todd, was ordered to make a raid on Kansas City. After receiving his orders from Quantrill, Todd formed his men in line and relayed his orders to them: "It has been settled that we attack Kansas City. The venture is a desperate one; you can only promise yourselves hard fighting and hard riding; the most of us may be killed. If any among you desire to remain behind move two paces to the front." Not a horse stirred; rear rank and front rank, the seventy men were as adamant.[23]

With Capt. Henry Flesher of Company E and a portion of Company K of the Ninth Kansas being absent on a scout, Thacher proceeded to Kansas City with Company A and the remaining portion of Company K, sending orders to Flesher to join him at that point.

With Todd was a newcomer by the name of Alexander Franklin James from Clay County. Andrew Walker recalled seeing Frank James for the first time riding with Ferdinand Scott: "[He was a] blue-eyed, boyish, beardless stripling of eighteen or nineteen." Although Frank had been active in guerrilla activity north of the river, now he was with Todd and facing the Federals in his first fight in Jackson County.

Ferdinand Scott had been with Quantrill for more than a year. He had lived in Liberty, Missouri, and while there had become acquainted with the James brothers. He had fought at the battle of Independence and only a month earlier, on May 19, had led twelve guerrillas—including Frank James—in an ambush.[24] Scott had also shown tremendous bravery leading a charge against the enemy while serving as a lieutenant under Gen. John Sappington Marmaduke on an earlier expedition into Missouri.[25] Seventeen-year-old Frank Smith, a neighbor of Andrew Walker, had also just joined the command. A few months before he had gone to Wyandotte, Kansas, to find a job because it was impossible for him to plant a crop at his home in Blue Springs. While in Kansas, jayhawkers captured him and tried to coerce him to join them, threatening to kill him if he refused. He joined out of desperation as much as self-preservation and because he had no other alternative. As soon as he could, he decided to "take to the bush" and sought out Quantrill's company.

Four miles south of Kansas City, near Westport, on the road leading to Kansas City, Todd saw a column of blue uniforms. On the southeast side of

Westport was a lane bordered by a tall rock fence on either side. As the guerrillas entered the lane, Todd deployed his men into platoons of eight on both sides of the road. Each man knew what was to be done. The column approaching them was led by Captain Flesher and riding toward Kansas City in accordance to Thacher's orders.

Flesher reported that he was surprised by a large force of guerrillas that was concealed behind stone fences, which were half-hidden in thick underbrush and dense foliage and lined either side of the road. Quantrill scout John McCorkle noted: "They came riding very leisurely over the hill, the captain in front, with his leg thrown over his horse's neck."

As soon as Flesher discovered blue-uniformed soldiers on his flanks, he called out and demanded to know who they were. In reply Todd gave the signal to set off the ambush, shouting, "Charge, kill 'em, boys, kill 'em!"

With pistols blazing, the guerrillas attacked. Charging horses kicked up so much dust on the road that it was hard to tell friend from foe. The attack was so sudden, and the first volley so rapidly followed by a charge of mounted guerrillas, that the Federals were forced back until they reached an open space where they could re-form.

Todd had with him many of Quantrill's best men. Besides Scott were John Jarrette, Dick Yeager, Bill Anderson, William Gregg, Richard Berry, Dick and George W. Maddox, Alson Wyatt, Will McGuire, John McCorkle, Boone Muir, George and Boone Scholl, and Fletcher Taylor.

Scholl had killed four of the enemy when he was shot out of the saddle. His horse was new, and in the rush of the charge, he lost control of it, and the animal ran with him through the Federal lines. A Union soldier shot him in the back, and the bullet passed through his body, breaking the buckle of his belt.[26]

Fletcher Taylor toppled five Federals from their horses with five shots. Bill Anderson was seen in the thick of the battle and was described as a tiger unloosed. All of Quantrill's men fought bravely. Jarrette found himself surrounded by three Federals, all shooting at him simultaneously. Untouched by their rounds, he killed all three.

Flesher reported thirty-three men killed or wounded.[27] The rest of his command put spurs to their horses and tried to make it to the safety of Kansas City. A short distance beyond, a regiment of Federal infantry emerged from the shelter of the woods to succor their retreating comrades.

Ferdinand Scott led the pursuit of the fleeing Federals, and because he was gaily dressed, he was singled out by their sharpshooters. While the guerrilla captains were observing the Federals at a safe distance, a Union sniper, more than a mile away and using an Enfield rifle, shot Scott through the neck. He threw up his hands and exclaimed, "I am a dead man," and fell from his horse. This was a great loss to Quantrill's company. Scott was much loved by his men. He talked little, showed little emotion, and never showed any physical fear. Others have added that he was tenderhearted, true to his ideals of patriotism above everything else, and that nothing deterred him in the line of duty.

The other guerrilla losses were Alson Wyatt (killed) and Boone Scholl (mortally wounded). All three casualties were said to be "as three as good men as belonged to Quantrill's command." Quantrill remarked later that this was a "bad fight" and that "One of my men is worth more than fifty of the enemy."[28]

With Flesher's force now reinforced by infantry, Todd knew that it would be useless to continue the battle against such huge odds. In the aftermath, Will McGuire rode up to a dead Federal officer who had assisted in the hanging of Jim Vaughn and wrote upon a slip of paper, "Remember the dying words of Jim Vaughn," and placed it in the teeth of the corpse.[29] The guerrillas slowly pulled back, out of range. Despite his wounds, Boone Scholl rode his horse about nine miles that night; he was taken to the home of a widow and died the next morning. The guerrillas tied the bodies of Scott and Wyatt across their saddles and took them back to Brooking Township. They buried Wyatt in a small cemetery along the Blue Ridge Road. They took Scott and Scholl to the Smith Cemetery, where John McCorkle had buried his brother, Jabez, who had died just two weeks before from an accidental gunshot wound.[30]

The guerrillas uncovered the faces of their dead comrades for one last look before they laid them to rest. At night, amid a tempestuous windstorm, they wrapped the men in their saddle blankets and lowered them into their graves. As the guerrillas stood with torches in their hands, the rain began to beat down heavily. The guerrillas were visibly moved as they stood around the graves of their fallen comrades. It is said that tears are the noble language of the eye. Ferdinand Scott was one of those men whom revolutions cast up sometimes to be Titans and sometimes monsters. Todd said that he did not know the meaning of the word *fear,* and of all the men Todd led or rode with, he wept for Scott alone the night they buried him.[31] After suffering the hardships of a soldier's life, the comradeship that united this band of brothers made their wartime attachments stronger than kin.

Some reported that Federal troops were camped all about, but as the funeral cortege passed within twenty paces of a Union bivouac, the guerrillas were not halted or challenged. The funeral was quickly performed and mostly done in silence.

Afterward, Quantrill took his men to a prearranged rendezvous in the dense woods around Cedar Creek just a mile south of Manasseth Gap in Jackson County. Federal patrols of from ten to twenty men were stationed at all the fords and road crossings to catch Quantrill and his men. The guerrillas had to stay constantly on the move.

Meanwhile, back in Kansas City, when Ewing received the report of the defeat of his troops in Westport, he was angry and upset. He decided to get at the guerrillas in a more circuitous way that he hoped would compel them to leave the border counties for good. Instead of combating the guerrilla problem with troops of the Missouri militia, Ewing instead relied on Kansas troops whose "loyalty was unquestioned."

Ewing knew that the guerrillas were aided by their numerous friends and relatives in the area. On August 13 the *Kansas City Journal* reported that Ewing was at departmental headquarters in St. Louis seeking authorization to banish the families of known guerrillas. From this meeting, five days later, Ewing issued General Orders No. 10. It reads in part:

> Such officers will arrest, and send to the District Provost-Marshal for punishment, all men and all women, not heads of families, who willfully aid and encourage guerrillas with a written statement of the names and residences of such persons and of the proof against them. They will discriminate as carefully as possible between those who were compelled, by threats or fears, to aid the Rebels and those who aid them from disloyal motives. The wives and children of known guerrillas, and also women who are heads of families and are willfully engaged in aiding guerrillas, will be notified by such officers to move out of this district and out of the State of Missouri, forthwith. They will be permitted to take, unmolested, their stock, provisions, and household goods. If they fail to remove promptly, they will be sent by such officers, under escort, to Kansas City for shipment south, with their clothes and such necessary household furniture and provisions as may be worth removing.[32]

Acting upon Ewing's orders, Union troops began to arrest the guerrillas' female relatives living in Jackson County. The Ninth Kansas Jayhawker Regiment was still stationed along the border, and these men had not forgotten the loss of their comrades to Quantrill's forces only two weeks before. Initially the intention was to detain the female relatives until arrangements could be made to transport them out of Kansas City, where they would be tried for "sheltering Union enemies." Shortly afterward, the *Kansas City Daily*

Journal of Commerce printed an editorial supporting the effort to strike at the families of the guerrillas: "It is an utter impossibility to rid the country of these pestilent outlaws, so long as their families remain. . . . One of the greatest difficulties the military authorities have to encounter, is the constant and correct information, which the families of the bushwhackers give of every movement the troops make. . . . With the aid of these spies, dotted all over the country and living in perfect security, a hundred bushwhackers may defy the utmost efforts of five-hundred soldiers to exterminate them."

Harrison Trow recalled that a "body of Federal soldiers, especially enrolled and uniformed to persecute women and prey upon non-combatants, gathered up in half a day's raid a number of demonstrative Southern girls whose only sin had been extravagant talk and pro-Confederacy cheering. They were taken to Kansas City and imprisoned in a dilapidated tenement close upon a steep place."

Nancy "Nannie" Harris McCorkle was one of the women arrested by this special squad. She later told her granddaughter that the Redlegs set fire to her home and mill in the early summer of 1863, wrecking it so that she had to buy flour and supplies in Kansas City. There were bushwhackers in the Sni Hills and all through Jackson County, and the Union men believed that the women were smuggling arms and ammunition to them—but that wasn't so. They did, however, smuggle food under their hoop skirts and buggy seats. The menfolk were always able to get ammunition without help from the women.

Nannie McCorkle recalled going to Kansas City with her sister-in-law, Charity McCorkle Kerr, in July 1863. They made several purchases, which they put into a satchel.[33] While they were in a store, some men approached them and arrested them. They were then taken to a women's prison.

Charity and Nannie were not the only women taken into custody. Others arrested included sisters Susan Crawford Vandever and Armina Crawford Selvey; sisters Lou Mundy Gray, Susan Mundy, and Mattie "Martha" Mundy; sisters Josephine, Mary, and Martha Anderson; Mollie Grinstaff; a Miss Hall, and a Mrs. Wilson. Also arrested was an Alice Van Ness. She had just arrived in Kansas City from visiting the Torreys, Quantrill's prewar friends, when she was seized and charged with spying.

At first the women were imprisoned in the Union Hotel at the southeast corner of Sixth and Main Streets, one block south of Lockridge Hall, the city's first public theater. Then some of the women were separated from the group on the pretext that the prison was becoming overcrowded. All of them happened to be relatives or acquaintances of Quantrill's soldiers. Susan

Crawford Vandever and Armina Crawford Selvey's brothers—William, Marshall, Marion, and Riley Crawford—and Susan's husband, Thomas Vandever, were all in Quantrill's company. Union soldiers had murdered their elderly father and burned their home only six months before. Charity McCorkle Kerr's brothers were John and Jabez McCorkle, and she had married Nathan Kerr, one of Quantrill's men, on January 26, 1860. Nannie Harris McCorkle's husband was Jabez. Her brother, Thomas B. Harris, also rode with the guerrillas. Their father, Reuben M. Harris, owned a farm overlooking the valley of the Little Blue and situated between Brooking Township and Manasseth Gap. Eighteen-year-old Nannie's cousins included the Younger brothers via the marriage of her father, Reuben, to Laura Fristoe, whose sister Bursheba married Henry Younger, Cole and Jim Younger's father, who was murdered by Union soldiers in July 1862. Sixteen-year-old Mary "Molly" Anderson, fourteen-year-old Josephine Anderson, and ten-year-old Martha Anderson's brother was William Anderson, one of Quantrill's captains. Also arrested were Lou Mundy Gray and her orphaned sisters, Susan and Martha Mundy; their brother was in Price's army. Mollie Grinstaff's brother, William, was also in Quantrill's company.

These women were moved into the cellar of the former Mechanics Bank at Delaware and Commercial Streets.[34] The building was infested with rats and vermin and considered uninhabitable. The women were moved again, but only because of the complaints from the guards who had to guard them.

Mattie Lykins described the women's circumstances:

> As a place of imprisonment for such in this city, an old dilapidated brick building on the levee . . . was taken possession of by the military authorities and set apart as a prison for Rebel women. After the building had been occupied as such for some time it became so infested with rats and vermin of all kinds as to render it unfit for human beings to live in. Even the health of the guards, who had access to the river for bathing, suffered so much from the stench and torture of the vermin as to lead them to appeal to headquarters for a change of location.[35]

Almost all of the women had been arrested in town. The Anderson girls, however, were not. Their arrest was ordered by Ewing on or about July 30, and he gave the task to Capt. Henry Flesher, the same Henry Flesher who had so recently suffered a humiliating defeat at the hands of Quantrill's men. He was still vengeful over his battlefield losses. Flesher sent fourteen men to fetch the girls. They found them at home with a boy of twelve or fourteen years old. The girls asked for time to comb their hair and change their clothes and make ready for the journey. After several minutes one of the men—Patrick Reddington—noticed the boy was missing and told Sgt. Maj. Ed Bolson, who was in charge, that the boy had been sent to summon the guerrillas. Sensing that any further delay would likely result with his men being buried nearby, Reddington quickly moved the girls out and placed them on horseback behind three other riders.

North of the home where the Anderson girls were staying, where the roads crossed, was a rock fence and a stone house and timber back of the fence. As Reddington's detail reached this spot, three guerrillas jumped over the stone wall and ran to the middle of the road. A man, possibly William Anderson, raised a double-barreled shotgun and fired over the heads of the squad. The three Anderson girls were on horses in the lead, and this fact probably saved the lives of the Union men, because Anderson did not want to hit his sisters. The three guerrillas fled, jumping over the stone wall and disappearing into the brush. Reddington fired and thought he hit one of them.

The Anderson girls had hindered the men whom they were riding behind from using their handguns during the attack. After Bolson saw that no one was hurt, his detail proceeded to Kansas City.[36] Reddington reported that had any of his men been hit, he would have ordered the girls shot. An account of the arrest of the other women can be found in the Kansas City Star from a statement by Susan Vandever's son (who died in Kansas City in 1933). He said that his mother "had driven a wagonload of produce from Grain Valley to Kansas City, had sold it, and was returning by way of Westport when she and other farm women were captured by Union soldiers."

John McCorkle elaborated: "My sister, Mrs. Charity Kerr and my sister-in-law, Mrs. Nannie McCorkle, the widow of my brother, Jabez, went to Kansas City in a wagon, driving a yoke of oxen, with a load of wheat to exchange it for flour, the women then having all the buying to do. When they had procured their flour and were ready to start home, Anderson Cowgill, a neighbor, who had known these girls all their lives, and the same man who refused to speak to me when we paroled him at Independence, saw these two girls and reported to the authorities that these two women were Rebels and were buying flour to feed the bushwhackers. They were immediately arrested and placed in jail with some other girls who had been arrested and sentenced to be banished."[37]

From the vermin-infested building the women were taken to the home and studio of Gen. George Caleb Bingham. The structure had been vacant for eighteen months since Bingham was serving as the state treasurer in Jefferson City. The house was part of an 1859 addition to a row of identical two-story brick buildings known as McGee's Addition. It was similar to the other buildings within the addition but was built adjoining the house on the north and situated on the same lot. Ewing did not inform Bingham that his home was needed for a prison but simply took possession of it and ordered the women prisoners transferred there.[38]

The first story of Bingham's home, called the Thomas Building after the original owner, was occupied as a grocery run by Jewish tenants. The third-story studio was undisturbed; the women prisoners were kept on the second floor. The only egress was a set of wooden steps and a small balcony built in the rear of the building leading to the second story. The women could effectively be guarded by a minimum of guards who only had to watch the second-story windows and the back stairs leading up from the rear of the building.

After a few days of uncomfortable imprisonment, the women were allowed to send for some of their personal belongings and their bedding. This was a small consolation for their treatment at the hands of the guards. Harrison Trow reported that their "food was flung to them at intervals, and brutal guards sang ribald songs and used indecent language in their presence."[39]

Charles Vincent, working for Elijah McGee, had erected the Thomas Building in 1859. While construction was going on, many people were naturally curious and became well acquainted with its erection. The unusual construction of the building was that it was actually two separate buildings that shared a common wall as well as floor joists that ran the width of both buildings, almost fifty feet, and rested on the outside walls of both buildings. When it was finished, the structure to the north was known as the Cockrell Building, and the portion to the south was called the Thomas Building, both named after their occupants.

The soldiers garrisoned in the adjoining guardhouse had examined the building and realized that it could easily be destroyed. A few days prior to August 13, they began to weaken the structure of the Cockrell Building, which they occupied. The soldiers premeditated their designs, knowing that if they weakened the structural integrity of their own building, it would cause the instability in the adjoining building being used as the female prison.

They began by removing the center posts on the main floor of the guardhouse. This left no support for the roof and floor joists of their own building, thus creating a lever action and causing the adjoining female prison to collapse on top of their own building.

The soldiers gained access to the basement of the Thomas Building and removed the brick pillars that held up the floor joists of the first floor.

Afterward a formal report stated "that the building had been weakened by the removal of the brick pillars, which supported the first floor and further that some of the sleepers of the adjoining buildings on both sides had also been removed, thus weakening the dividing wall beyond safety."

August 14 was typically hot and humid. The destruction of the guard-house was beginning to show signs of damage to both buildings. The grocers on the ground floor of the women's prison noticed cracks along the walls and ceiling of their shop. Sensing danger, they began removing their goods. Earlier that day, Lt. John M. Singer, Company H of the Ninth Kansas Jayhawker Regiment and serving as captain of the provost guard, received word from Capt. Frank Parker, Company C of the Eleventh Kansas Jayhawker Regiment and head of the prison guard, that he was becoming increasingly uneasy about the prison's safety. When Singer arrived at the prison, he noticed that the floor was colored white with mortar dust from the cracks in the ceilings and walls. He immediately reported this to General Ewing, who sent his adjutant general, Maj. Harrison Hannah, to investigate. Upon his return, Hannah reported that he believed the building was safe. Immediately Ewing left the city, which was reported in the *Kansas City Journal*.

At about two o'clock in the afternoon, back at the prison, Charity McCorkle Kerr, was ill in bed. She developed a fever due to exposure and improper diet. Her cousin asked the guard for some water. Charity was being closely cared for by Mollie Grinstaff, who was fixing her hair. Several of the girls sat on the floor and watched. Ten-year-old Martha Anderson had angered the guards the day before, and in retaliation they chained a twelve-pound ball to her ankle.

The girls sitting around the bed of Charity Kerr saw the ceiling begin to crack, sending debris down upon the women. Sensing imminent danger, they tried desperately to get out of the building. Nannie Harris McCorkle and Molly Anderson had just gone into the hallway to wait for the guard to return with the water when they heard the other girls shout that the roof was falling.

Not wanting to injure one of their own men, the assassins next door waited until the lone guard left the prison to fetch the water when they made the final stroke against the supporting column. With the supporting posts and columns in the Cockrell Building finally cut down and removed, the building began to sink. The structure began to fall as the guard was returning. Once the pressure from above started to drive the top stories into the cellar, the Thomas Building, still connected by the common floor joists, sprung from its supports in the outside walls and, following a lever action, collapsed on top of the guardhouse.

All but five of the eleven women imprisoned here escaped death. Four were killed immediately: Susan Crawford Vandever, Armina Crawford Selvey, Josephine Anderson, and Charity McCorkle Kerr. All others sustained various injuries; Mrs. Wilson died as a result of hers. Mollie Grinstaff suffered several broken bones, and her back was hurt in the collapse.

Most of the survivors either ran to the back balcony or climbed out windows. Martha Anderson, restricted by the ball-and-chain, tried desperately to make it to a window; she lived but her legs were horribly crushed. Harrison Trow stated:

> At night and in the darkness [the building] was undermined, and in the morning when a little wind blew upon it and it was shaken, it fell with a crash. Covered up, the faces disfigured, the limp, lifeless bodies were past all pain! Dead to touch, or kiss, or passionate entreaty, Anderson's eldest sister was taken from the ruins a corpse. The younger, badly injured in the spine, with one leg broken and her face bruised and cut painfully, lived to tell the terrible story of it all to a gentle, patient brother kneeling before her at her bedside and looking up above to see if God were there.[40]

Josephine Anderson was buried in the ruins. For a long time her cries were heard calling for anyone to take the bricks off her head. Finally her cries ceased. Charity McCorkle Kerr was also killed in the ruins by falling timber.[41] The other girls who were killed had been at Charity's bedside and refused to leave her helpless.

In a matter of minutes a crowd gathered, and as the evidence of the building's collapse became clear, the people began shouting for justice to be done to the Federal guards who caused the disaster.

General Ewing's personal guard, made up of men from the Kansas jayhawker regiments garrisoned in town, surrounded the building and tried to restore order. The surviving girls became hysterical, screaming that the Federals were murderers, that the building had been a deathtrap. The gathering crowd became angrier and louder. With bayonets fixed, more Federal troops soon arrived. They were jeered and threatened by the mob.[42]

Throughout their imprisonment the women prisoners had been tormented and teased that they were going to be killed. But the sadism of the guards only strengthened the patriotism of the girls. A little less than an hour after the collapse, while helping the survivors, neighbor Mattie Lykins recalled: "I was informed by some of the women prisoners that they had been told repeatedly by their guards that this house was giving away and would

eventually fall. 'But,' they said, 'we had so often been told during our imprisonment equally as alarming stories, which proved false that we paid no attention to this one; yet every few days we heard the building crack, which was
invariably followed by the falling of pieces of plaster from the ceiling.'"

The first inkling that there was a plot afoot came when Mrs. B. F. Duke,
who had a boarding house at Independence Avenue and Oak Street (only
four blocks from the women's prison), overheard some soldiers who were
staying at her house speak of the progress they were making in tearing down a
wall. Mrs. Duke was a cousin of Bill Anderson, but the soldiers did not know
that and told her of their schemes and how they had removed a large section
of the foundation wall of the women's prison. Gen. George Caleb Bingham,
the owner of the building, had protested, they said, but it did not stop them.

The building did not fall the first day, so more of the wall was removed,
and it was at this time that Mrs. Duke learned of it. She was beside herself
with rage and ordered all the soldiers out of the house. With a number of
friends she hurried to the Union headquarters and begged that the girls be
taken from the building before they were killed. The pleadings were in vain,
and an hour later the building fell.

Another account reported that the girls had been uneasy over hearing the
people on the floor below moving out their stock of groceries and whiskey.
The plaster had been falling all day, and the girls were in a panic. According
to this version of the story, when Nannie Harris McCorkle and Molly Anderson were in the hallway awaiting the return of the guard and heard the cries
from the other girls that the roof was falling, the guard evidently repented at
the last moment and returned and carried these two girls to safety.[43]

Ewing's headquarters had to have been abuzz during the days before the
building's collapse. Not only had Lt. John M. Singer and Capt. Frank Parker
expressed concerns over the prisoners' safety, but Dr. Joshua Thorne, chief
surgeon of the Kansas City hospital and the military post surgeon, also notified headquarters that the building was unsafe.[44]

Standing at the ruins of the collapsed building immediately afterward,
Mattie Lykins was standing next to Dr. Thorne, watching the removal of the
living and the dead from the debris, when she heard someone remark that
surely there would also be soldiers buried in the rubble since it was the soldiers' guardhouse that the women's prison had collapsed upon. "No," replied
Dr. Thorne, "not a bluecoat will be found; every man who has been detailed
to stand guard at this prison for the last few days and weeks knew the house
to be unsafe and have kept themselves at a safe distance from the trembling
walls. I knew the building to be unsafe," he continued, "and notified the mili-

tary authorities of the fact, and suggested the removal of the women prisoners, but my suggestion was not heeded and before you is the result."[45]

Years later, after Thomas Ewing had left the border and returned to his home state of Ohio, Dr. Thorne changed his story to say that some women who were drunks and prostitutes cut through the cellar wall and weakened it so that they caused it to fall. His story refutes all other eyewitness explanations. If there had been women in the cellar causing the building to collapse, then the building would have naturally collapsed upon itself and not on the Cockrell Building. The fact is that there is no record of any prisoners other than the guerrillas' relatives, who were incarcerated only on the second floor. There were never any women prisoners in the basement.

Most of the survivors carried emotional scars for the rest of their lives. It was not long before their stories were carried back to their loved ones in Quantrill's company, and shortly afterward came the counterclaims and alibis of the Federal soldiers and the military authorities in charge.

After the massacre a new name was heard along the border: "Who is this Anderson? He kills them all. Quantrell spares now and then . . . but Anderson never does."[46]

In Jefferson City, General Bingham became outraged when he heard the news. He did not condone the Union strategy toward the guerrilla movement; he knew that the brutality of the Kansas jayhawkers was the main reason for the anti-Union sentiment along the border. He was also well aware of General Ewing's inability or unwillingness to stop it due to the political favor he wished to curry with James Lane.

Federal authorities were quick to deny any wrongdoing. The contradictions and inconsistencies in these alibis bordered on fantasy and the absurd. Still, the Northern and Eastern press printed these unbelievable stories as fact, and these explanations and interpretations were subsequently accepted and incorporated into the record of the war and into subsequent studies of Quantrill and the border conflict. One such amazing excuse was that the building was blown down by a strong wind. Another was that the women themselves caused the collapse by trying to dig an escape tunnel through the cellar walls. Another blamed soldiers for tearing out the basement walls to get to some prostitutes imprisoned in the basement. Yet another claimed that the women used an ax to chop through a supporting post, which made the building gave way. No official inquiry was ever initiated by Gen. Thomas Ewing, the person most responsible for an investigation.

Statements were taken soon after the collapse and duly recorded by Philip Brown, a notary public in Kansas City at the time of the jail collapse.

These statements by informed and expert witnesses exposed the alibis of the soldiers as false and fabricated. On September 10, 1863, Solomon S. Smith, who had been a workman during the building's construction, made a statement notarized by Philip Brown:

> Smith, brick mason, that he built walls of Thomas building and also the walls of Cockrell building. Erected in 1857, outer foundation walls of Reverend Thomas building was 18" thick and partition walls 13" thick. Entire Metropolitan block was built in same manner. Said that foundations of Thomas building were firm and on solid clay bottom, foundation 7' deep. There was one common partition wall, these joists went in the partition wall between Mrs. Cockrell's house and the house belonging to the estate of Reverend Thomas and the other ends rested upon girders extending the entire length of each house running east and west 60' the length of the buildings. These girders were supported by wooden posts or columns placed in first story, after these posts or columns should be removed then the girders of course would bend or sink until the ends would come off the wall, which then would be their only support and then the joists having been securely nailed and fastened to the floor would operate as a lever extending the entire length of the wall dividing the two houses and necessarily cut the wall half in two the entire length and that would force the wall the entire length beneath the joists into the basement of the adjoining house and cause the upper walls to fall over into the house from whence the posts or columns had been removed and the girder and joists give way in. Said walls of Thomas building sufficiently thick to withstand six stories. Could only have given way by removing the columns aforesaid or by cutting the walls or undermining the foundation in some way.

On September 7 Charles H. Vincent also made a notarized statement to Philip Brown. He stated:

> Mrs. Cockrell who owned the north half of house said the soldiers cut away and removed the center posts or columns and partitions leaving no support for the roof and joists of the Cockrell building. That some time after said posts or columns and partitions had been removed by the soldiers as aforesaid the affiant noticed that the girder in the center of the Cockrell building on which the joists rested had given way and that the building was about to fall. That this affiant then named to Colonel E. M. McGee, that the building was about to fall that when the Cockrell building finally fell and the

weight of the Cockrell house roof falling on the center of the second floor of the same building and the joists remaining firmly tied in the wall common to both said buildings caused the partition or common wall between the two said building to fall into the Cockrell building and of course caused the female prison building, the building belonging to the heirs of said Reverend Thomas, deceased, also to fall. That he is satisfied that the cause aforesaid as stated alone caused the said female prison building to fall that he has examined the ruins of both buildings since they fell and found that the materials composing the female prison building had fallen on top of the materials composing the Mrs. Cockrell building. That the second and third stories of Thomas building (the female prison) had fallen completely over on the ruins of the Cockrell building, bottom side up. Showing conclusively that the fall of the Thomas building was caused through the falling of the partition wall between the two buildings. This affiant further states that said building used as a female prison and belonging to the heirs of said Reverend R.S. Thomas, deceased, was in good condition and repairs at the time the United States military authorities took possession of same, as aforesaid, this affiant further states that he has heard from hearsay that the soldiers *cut* away or removed the center posts or columns and leaving no support for the roof and joists of the Cockrell building that this affiant noticed that the girders in the center of the Cockrell building on which the joist rested had given away and the building was about to fall. (This affiant on a personal examination has found the foundations of said Reverend R.S. Thomas building are now yet standing perfect solid and sound without a crack.)

On September 10 Col. Elijah M. McGee also made a statement for Philip Brown. He claimed that he was:

Well acquainted with building. That Mr. Charles Vincent, two or three days before said house fell, directed this officer's attention to the condition of the Mrs. Cockrell house that consequently this affiant the second morning before said house fell entered the Mrs. Cockrell house and found the posts or columns had been cut away from the girders on center beams and that the girders on center beams had already sunk some two or three feet and this affiant feeling that the house was unsafe immediately left and went to the meat market stand and there told three or four bystanders that the Mrs. Cockrell house on account of the said posts or columns having been cut away must certainly fall and that when it fell the house belonging to the estate or heirs of Reverend Thomas must also fall with it in consequence.

This affiant says that he has been an extensive builder in Kansas City, Missouri, and that he saw said building daily when in progress of erection being near his residence and that he considered said building erected of substantial and of good material.

These statements given by the builder Elijah M. McGee, the bricklayer Solomon Smith, and eyewitness Charles H. Vincent, who had been in the Cockrell Building the day before the collapse, demonstrate that the posts or columns had been cut away by the soldiers and that the building was sinking and on the verge of collapse. In addition, other statements show the criminal intent of the collapse.

The survivors' reports after the collapse reveal that the girls had heard the nighttime excavation work in the lower basement. The cowardly individuals who carried out this deed believed that the cover of darkness, when the women prisoners were asleep, would hide their crime. Not wanting to accept blame for causing harm to women, the Federal soldiers sought to kill them wholesale and make it look like an accident. Their subsequent alibis, even though widely repeated, could easily be disproved.

Alibis were still being conjured up years after the affair. One excuse given was that the women were moved because of overcrowding of the women prisoners at the Union Hotel, but why was the excuse of overcrowding due to only eleven women prisoners? When the excuse for the building's collapse was blamed on women in the cellar cutting down a supporting post with an ax, it could easily be disproved because the female prison fell onto the adjoining building and not upon itself. This also contradicted the public record that plainly stated the women prisoners were kept on the second floor of the Thomas Building and were not allowed access to the basement.

After the war General Bingham sought redress for the cost of the destroyed building caused by the soldiers under Ewing's command. No reports were ever filed about the jail collapse by Ewing to his immediate superior, Gen. John M. Schofield. If it had not been for Bingham's diligence in seeking a monetary claim against the government, there would be no record to understand why and how this crime was committed.

In a claim filed in the U.S. Senate and the House of Representatives after the war, John P. Thomas, the son of the original owner, stated that the building was requisitioned by military authority on July 30, 1863: "That building was well built and was substantial when taken possession of by the United States and its destruction resulted from cutting away the supports of one of the walls of said building by the soldiers doing guard duty in the adjoining building. . . . [T]he same was occupied and used by order of Brigadier General Ewing as a military prison."

Most false accounts claim that the building was dilapidated, and one cause attributed to its destruction was a combination of faulty structure and high winds. Yet the building was only five years old, and no records exist that mention any unusually high winds at that time.

The walls were eighteen inches thick with the common wall measuring thirteen inches thick. Solomon S. Smith claimed that the building could have held up to six stories on its foundation. William Elsey Connelley even tried to claim in *Quantrill and the Border Wars* that the building collapsed due to a high wind. Yet it was impossible that high winds could have affected this one building and no others. The fact that the first-floor merchants moved out before the collapse testifies to the building's unsafe condition, contrary to Ewing's adjutant, Maj. Harrison Hannah, and his findings. Hannah, who would have been high enough in command to share complicity in the crime, reported to Ewing the building was safe. If General Ewing had previously stated that he did not intend for any harm to come to female relatives of any known guerrillas, then why was Sgt. Ed Bolson of the Ninth Kansas Jayhawker Regiment—serving under Ewing's orders—so willing to shoot Bill Anderson's sisters (according to Patrick Reddington's report) when they were being arrested and brought to Kansas City?

One alibi claimed that the soldiers were trying to make a large open barracks room when they were removing the middle girders in their building. If the soldiers were trying to make a large barracks room, why did they not move the women when they saw the building being damaged and weakened? And why were there no soldier fatalities?

Records also show that an inspector reported that the building was unsafe. Shortly afterward General Ewing sent another inspector, who agreed with Ewing's contentions that the building was indeed safe.

Bingham's postwar claim reported that no inquiry was ever instituted by Ewing and no soldier was ever punished. There seemed to be an overwhelming collusion to keep the facts quiet and cover up any type of responsibility. When Ewing was asked to make a statement so that Bingham could recover the value of the property, he declined. Even after evidence was furnished to him that showed the building was a good and substantial one when taken over by his troops as well as other statements about the condition of the building, Ewing only signed his name to a report stating, "This certifies that a certain house in McGee's Addition in Kansas City, Missouri, known as 'No. 13 in Metropolitan Block' was occupied by my order from some day in the

latter part of July, 1863, until the 13th day of August last when it fell."[47] Bingham asked Schofield to get a further statement from Ewing, but "[Schofield]
did not endeavor to get any further statement from General Ewing or from
any other parties."[48]

Bingham wrote an article for the *Washington Sentinel* in early 1877 and
stated:

> These females were arrested and confined under the pretext of holding
> them as hostages for the good behavior of their brothers, husbands or rela-
> tives, who were supposed to be in sympathy with, or actually engaged in,
> the Confederate cause. . . . Explaining as we proceed, we will state that in
> the lower story of the building in which they were incarcerated, and also in
> the lower story of the adjoining building, occupied by soldiers who guarded
> them, large girders, supported by wooden pillars, extended from the front to
> the extreme rear of each. From these girders, joists firmly held together by
> flooring securely nailed thereon, extended into and met each other in the
> dividing wall, which formed a part of each building. It will thus be readily
> seen that the removal of the wooden pillars, which supported the girders in
> either building would force it to yield to the great pressure from above, and
> cause the joists resting thereon, and firmly held together by flooring, to
> operate as a lever the entire length of this dividing wall, with a force suffi-
> cient to cut it in two, and thus effect the certain destruction of both build-
> ings. The soldiers on guard had greatly weakened this wall by cutting large
> holes through the cellar portion thereof, but as it still stood firm, they found
> it necessary to the most certain method of accomplishment in the diaboli-
> cal work required. Not having access to the pillars, which supported the
> girder in the building in which the helpless females were confined, they
> removed those supporting the girder in the building occupied by them-
> selves. As soon as this was done, as was clearly foreseen, the girder began
> and continued to yield, until, losing its support at each end, it suddenly
> gave way, and by leverage of the joists resting upon it, cut the dividing line
> in two, forcing the lower portion into the cellar of the prison and causing
> the super-structure thereof to fall over with a force of a mountain avalanche
> upon the ruins of the adjoining buildings thus producing a scene of horror
> in the death groans and shrieks of mangled women, which fiends could only
> contemplate without a shudder. In vain, had they, upon the first discovery
> of the danger, begged in piteous accents to be released. Their earnest
> appeals were to hearts as callous as that of the general by whose authority
> they were confined. While their prison walls were trembling, its doors

remained closed, and they were allowed no hope for release except through the portals of a horrible death into that eternity where, in the great day, which is to right all wrongs, they will stand as witnesses against the human monster, who to promote his selfish aspirations, could cruelly plan, with satanic coolness, the desolation of a large district of country and the utter ruin of its defenseless inhabitants. That the death of these poor women crushed beneath the ruins of their prison was a deliberately planned murder, all the facts connected therewith sufficiently established.[49]

An operation of this magnitude could not have been carried out without the knowledge and approval of the commanding officer. This was not a single premeditated act on the part of a few revenge-crazed soldiers acting alone. The Ninth as well as the Eleventh Kansas Jayhawker Regiments were stationed in Kansas City at the time. The Ninth Kansas had just been humiliated by an ambush by Quantrill's command on June 16, and noted Redlegs were on Ewing's staff in Kansas City. Reports that the building was unsafe were brought to Ewing's attention but ignored. The plot to murder the girls was overheard and recorded by eyewitnesses. A Federal surgeon admitted that he knew what the outcome of the collapse would reveal before the bodies were pulled from the ruins. The building was proved to be a safe structure prior to its collapse. Ewing never opened an investigation or indicted anyone because to do so would have placed the crime squarely on his shoulders. He never spoke a word of explanation about the crime because to do so would have incriminated him. Only after being brought before a congressional inquiry over the loss of property involved in the building collapse did he make an evasive statement that he authorized the use of the building as a guardhouse until its collapse, offering only the barest minimum of responsibility for the murders.

The fact that some survivors lived to tell the truth about the premeditated act to their relatives changed forever the course of the border war. Where prisoners were once captured and paroled, after the jail collapse, no quarter became the rule rather than the exception. Characters of individual soldiers also changed. Riley Crawford, whose two sisters were killed in the collapse, gained a reputation afterward for killing every Union soldier who fell into his hands. Little-known William Anderson had three sisters in the collapsed building; one died in the collapse and another was horribly mangled and died shortly afterward. Anderson soon gained the sobriquet of "Bloody Bill" after the jail collapse and began carrying a silken cord with a knot for every Union soldier that he killed. Even Quantrill, who was known to take and parole prisoners, usually killed captured soldiers after the jail collapse.

Over the course of time the coverup stories in subsequent historical accounts caused the truth to vanish like the wind. In undermining the building the jayhawkers believed they could strike a blow against the guerrilla bands that they were unable to do militarily. But from the accounts of the survivors themselves, the truth was told to those who could fight back.

The only claimant to make a contradictory report was Dr. Peter Arnold. To notary Philip Brown he reported that he had been in the Thomas Building the same day that Charles H. Vincent had been next door in the Cockrell Building and noticed damage. "This affiant in his professional capacity was called upon to visit one of the female prisoners in said Thomas building the evening before the said building fell and that he then did not see anything wrong with the building before the said building fell or that any part of it in the least given way." Dr. Arnold was on official business in a professional capacity and would not have been looking for structural dangers to the building; he was only looking after the physical care of his patients.

Union authorities ignored Philip Brown's affidavits as well as the accounts given by Mrs. Duke, Lieutenant Singer, and Captain Parker when they reported to Ewing's headquarters the unsafe condition of the building. Every witness who made a statement or testified about the jail collapse offered no other explanation than the Federal soldiers' intent to cause the collapse of the female prison for the purpose of murdering the relatives of Quantrill's men.

The collapse of the makeshift women's prison at 1425 Grand in Kansas City on August 13, 1863, was possibly the worst case of Northern butchery on record during the Civil War. Due to the efforts of the Northern and Eastern press, the facts and details of the tragedy were minimized and obscured.

THE VICTIMS were removed from the rubble of the prison collapse, and family members carried the bodies to local cemeteries for burial. Four graves were dug in the Union Cemetery in Kansas City, but Josephine Anderson was the only one buried there. The other bodies were carried to the Little Blue and buried in the Smith Cemetery in Brooking Township.

In this small cemetery, in the heart of a country that had seen the most vicious fighting for the past two years, they buried the bodies of the victims. It was also the burial ground for fallen comrades over whom the guerrillas had wept just a few days before. Now the guerrillas stood side by side with their friends from Brooking Township as they buried the young girls who had been murdered in the most cowardly manner of the war.

As family and friends gathered around the grave sites of the murdered girls, Federal officials were accused of their murders. John McCorkle commented:

This foul murder was the direct cause of the famous raid on Lawrence, Kansas. We could stand no more. Imagine, if you can, my feelings. A loved sister foully murdered and the widow of a dead brother seriously hurt by a set of men to whom the name assassins, murderers and cutthroats would be a compliment. People abuse us, but, by God, did we not have enough to make us desperate and thirst for revenge? We tried to fight like soldiers, but were declared outlaws, hunted under a "Black Flag" and murdered like beasts. The homes of our friends burned, our aged sires, who dared sympathize with us had been either hung or shot in the presence of their families and all their furniture and provisions loaded in wagons and with our livestock taken to the State of Kansas. The beautiful farming country of Jackson County, Cass County and Johnson County were worse than desert, and on every hillside stood lone blackened chimneys, sad sentinels and monuments to the memory of our once happy homes. And these outrages had been done by Kansas troops, calling themselves soldiers, but a disgrace to the name soldier. And now our innocent and beautiful girls had been murdered in a most foul, brutal, savage and damnable manner.[50]

Here they stood over the graves of women who had fed and clothed them. No more would they visit the wounded guerrillas in their hideouts to tend their wounds. William H. Gregg observed: "Heaven bless the women, they were friends in need and indeed, no braver and truer women lived than the Southern ladies of Missouri, we often owed our lives to them."[51]

Over the past two months old men and young boys had been shot down and murdered. Kansas troops had raped the guerrillas' mothers and sisters, and now, in a premeditated act, the Federals had coldly murdered their wives and sisters. A short poem by James C. Edwards entitled "Lawrence Massacre" reveals the feelings of most of the guerrillas:

Men at war never war with women, but women from the South
    they take,
To an ancient cell which killed as it fell, with the aid of the
    Union's weight
We're gonna ride and track you down. We're gonna burn
    Lawrence to the ground.

Life was not worth living if these deeds were not avenged. The guerrillas would have unhesitatingly ridden into the jaws of death as soon as the last shovelful of dirt was placed upon the graves. Standing there with bowed heads, grief made them unreasonable, and in a blind fury they would have charged any outpost. But Colonel Quantrill maintained control over his men and assured them that they would soon get revenge. He had been working on a plan. If they were to risk all, let it be a blow against the instigators and the perpetrators of the hatred that caused all this evil.

Quantrill ordered his bands to a rendezvous away from any Federal observation. The men were told to report far to the east in Johnson County, along the banks of the Blackwater River at the home of a friend named Perdee.

9

From Lawrence to Legend

For the strength of the pack is the wolf,
And the strength of the wolf is the pack.

RUDYARD KIPLING

UANTRILL'S MEN WERE SHOCKED over the barbarity shown by Union troops toward Southern women and children. And for that reason alone, they were ready to charge the very gates of hell to avenge them. In this portion of the country, it was still part of an unwritten code that all wrongs had to be avenged; to do nothing was the way of cowards. Quantrill's men had proven themselves many times in combat against Northern troops, but the premeditated murder of women catapulted the border war into a personal conflict. Enemies were not faceless; their names were known as well as the names of their victims. Around the campfires of the guerrillas, past horrors were recalled in rapid succession.

Among their recollections was the execution of an elderly man named Laws in Kansas City. His crime, according to Union Maj. W. C. Ransom of Kansas, was that he fed a squad of Federals who were disguised as guerrillas to root out Southern sympathizers. Redleg George Hoyt recently rode into Westport, took Philip Bucher from his wife and children, marched him onto the commons, made him kneel down, and shot him. Another man, Henry Rout, was hanged. One of Col. William R. Penick's men, calling himself Jim Lane, murdered a doctor named Triggs for his money. Sam Jones and an old man named Doty were hanged. In Cass County, George Tyler and men named Hedrick and Somers were shot. Other murders included a Bates

County resident named Samuels; in Vernon County, men known only as Peters, Monroe, Farwell, and Lowers were killed; and Jackson Countians named Givens, Manchester, Bolling, Newton, Beamish, Parker, and Ralls died at the hands of jayhawkers and Redlegs. More than two hundred others were killed during the summer of 1863.[1]

With the passing of time, Federal atrocities increased in scale. William H. Gregg recorded many in his memoirs, including the hanging of Samuel Kimberlin from the rafters in his own barn while the barn was burned down around him. Moses Karr was arrested, taken to Independence and sent back to his home, but before he could get there, he was tied to a tree and shot to pieces. Gregg reported and his fellow guerrillas recalled how they felt when they learned of the murders of Jeptha Crawford and John Saunders, three men of the Cummings family, the eleven-year-old son of Henry Morris, eighty-year-old Howell Lewis, David Gregg (William Gregg's uncle, shot by Jennison himself), and many others too numerous to catalog here. The guerrillas had often discussed how to punish the Kansans, and now the opportunity and the target had been selected.[2]

To better strike back at the Federal menace, separate companies under Quantrill had recently been reorganized. Along Big Creek in Cass County, in the area that he knew best, Capt. John Jarrette restructured his company by electing brother-in-law Coleman Younger to be first lieutenant as his second in command. Joseph C. Lea was chosen as second lieutenant. Lon Railey was elected third lieutenant, and John Webster was elected orderly sergeant.

Just a few miles south of Independence, at the farm of blacksmith William Hopkins, where numerous skirmishes had formally taken place, Capt. George Todd also reorganized his company. Fletcher Taylor was elected first lieutenant, James Little was made second lieutenant, William Anderson became third lieutenant, and Isaac Berry was elected orderly sergeant.

Capt. Dick Yeager was at the time patrolling along the Big Blue River at the farm of his father, near Westport, when he received a message from Quantrill to gather for an assembly. Harrison Trow recalled:

Originally, the Jayhawkers in Kansas had been very poor. They coveted the goods of their Missouri neighbors, made wealthy or well-to-do by prosperous years of peace and African slavery. Before they became soldiers they had been brigands, and before they destroyed houses in the name of retaliation they had plundered them at the instance of personal greed. The first Federal officers operating in Kansas; that is to say, those who belonged to the State, were land pirates or pilferers. . . . Houses gave up their furniture; women, their jewels; children, their wearing apparel; store-rooms, their contents; the land, their crops, and the banks, their deposits. To robbery was added murder; to murder, arson, and to arson, depopulation. Is it any wonder, then, that the Missourian whose father was killed should kill in return, whose house was burnt should burn in return, whose property was plundered, should pillage in return, whose life was made miserable, should hunt as a wild beast and rend accordingly? Many such were in Quantrell's command—many whose lives were blighted; who in a night were made orphans and paupers; who saw the labor and accumulation of years swept away in an hour of wanton destruction; who for no reason on earth save that they were Missourians, were hunted from hiding place to hiding place; who were preyed upon while not a single cow remained or a single shock of grain; who were shot at, bedeviled and proscribed, and who, no matter whether Union or disunion, were permitted to have neither flag or country.[3]

To this was added the observation of John Newman Edwards: "The militia and the Jayhawkers preyed upon the citizens and the non-combatants, and the guerrillas preyed upon the militia and the Jayhawkers. To the sword the torch had been added. Two hundred houses in Jackson County had been burnt; Vernon County was a desert; a day's ride in Bates brought no sight of a habitation; Cass was well nigh ruined; a black swathe had been mowed through Lafayette; Butler was in ashes; Harrisonville was in ashes."[4] To combat these abuses by the Federals, the guerrillas fought back with a vengeance, so much so that there was a price upon the head of Quantrill and every one of his men.[5]

As always, Quantrill was one step ahead of the Federals. He had contingency plans for every occasion, and as he now desperately tried to control his men's emotions, he assured them that they would avenge this latest atrocity, but they must think with their heads and not with their hearts. Quantrill had already sent spies into Lawrence, Kansas, anticipating some future foray against the headquarters of the hated Redlegs. He knew that if he was to strike, he must do it now or forever lose the advantage. Information had reached him that a bridge was being built over the Kaw River above Lawrence that would enable military aid to be quickly brought to bear if Lawrence was in need of assistance. Quantrill also knew that the telegraph line would be up and running in just a few more weeks, and this he feared more than anything. He knew if he was caught behind enemy lines, with the communication wires shouting his whereabouts, he could never get his men safely back into Missouri, much less from such a distance as Lawrence. This mission would be a masterstroke, a way to repay the jayhawkers for the murder, plunder, and rape of Missouri farms and families.

For the first time he needed to assemble his companies away from the watchful eyes of Union spies and Federal patrols. In the vicinity of Blue Springs, Quantrill had his men make as many cartridges as they could from captured barrels of powder taken from a previous raid on Independence a year earlier. The barrels of gunpowder had been hidden in a cave in the woods just north of Morgan Walker's farm.

After he issued orders for a muster, Quantrill disappeared for several days at a time, presumably going into Kansas on a reconnaissance patrol as far as Eudora and assessing the routes to and from Lawrence and estimating how long the raid would take. He knew Lawrence was home to twelve hundred people. Every able-bodied man belonged to the militia. Exceptions were few.[6] It was a brilliant maneuver for a commander of Quantrill's caliber. He carefully rehearsed the route of march so he would not be confronted with any surprises.

When he returned, his men broke camp and moved south to the farm of Edmund Coward, northeast of Lee's Summit, where he was joined by Yeager, Jarrette, and Todd. The men knew something big must be up. Word was sent to the various units to assemble on the Little Sni Creek in the Cummings settlement, twenty-four miles southwest of Independence, Missouri. As the guerrillas moved to their appointed rendezvous, they passed by the farm of a man named Wallace, who was suspected of relaying information to the Federals about guerrilla activity. George Todd took several men to Wallace's house and confronted the suspected spy. Fearing for his life, Wallace denied the allegations. Todd pistol-whipped Wallace and warned him that if he heard that Wallace passed any more information to the Federals, he would kill him.

By now many small groups of guerrillas arrived at the rendezvous point. Those men who were not sure what was going on realized there was no small raid in front of them. They noticed that Colonel Quantrill had also recruited two doctors, John W. Benson and a man named Campbell, for this mission. Under cover of darkness they then rode to the Perdee farm on Blackwater Creek, nine miles east of Lone Jack, Missouri. Various small guerrilla bands arrived on August 18.

Bill Anderson rode in with thirty to forty men, and Andrew Blunt rode in with around one hundred men. Many others filtered into camp that night.

Riding with Quantrill was a trusted black man, John T. Noland. Andrew Walker described him as "a brave, resourceful fellow. No negro ever fought with us as a regular member of the band, but John would have done so had Quantrill consented." Again Quantrill held Noland back: "John, if I let you go with us once, your usefulness will be gone. I want you for another purpose." While the guerrillas continued to assemble at Oak Grove, where the water was good and the hiding excellent, Quantrill sent Noland into Lawrence to spy out the situation.[7]

Quantrill had studied the contingencies and laid his plans well. He knew that the Federals had garrisoned troops in Westport, Little Santa Fe, Aubry, Harrisonville, Coldwater Grove, Rockville, and the Trading Post. These troops formed a virtual barrier to any raid toward Kansas. There were more than one hundred men in each of the seven different posts along the border. Quantrill knew that he had to get his expedition past these outposts unnoticed and unaware of his purpose and destination as well as his withdrawal back into Missouri. He calculated how long the march would take and when would be the best time to start. He also calculated how long the actual attack on the town should last and how long their trip back into Missouri would take. He predicted that if they surprised the town just before daylight, a vigorous assault would capture the town's arsenal and paralyze any resistance. But the guerrillas could only spend so much time in actual possession of the town. Their withdrawal through hostile enemy territory would be perilous, and he predicted their arrival back into the heavy timber of Jackson County around sundown where nightfall would guarantee their escape.

Noland was delayed in his mission twice and did not report to Quantrill until almost the last moment before the raid started. His second delay was caused when some soldiers stopped him because he was riding a horse with a government saddle and because he was carrying a large sum of money.

Because of Noland's delay, Quantrill sent Fletcher Taylor to spy on Lawrence by posing as a land speculator. Taylor lodged at the Free State Hotel. He liberally spent a lot of cash to play the part of a hospitable gentleman and uncovered many erstwhile details. Finally, Noland arrived in camp a little before Taylor. Noland reported that the shanties by the river were stuffed to the ceilings with plunder and tended by former slaves from Missouri.

Only at this time did Quantrill reveal his plans to his captains. Secrecy had been his main concern, especially with Union spies close by. He assembled the captains and gave them his plan of attack for Lawrence. Those present included George Todd, Bill Anderson, Andy Blunt, Dick Yeager, William H. Gregg, Oliver Shepherd, John Jarrette, Coleman Younger, Harrison Trow, and Ben Estes. Around the campfire, Quantrill laid out his plans.

He first let the spies give their reports. Taylor revealed that Lawrence was weakly garrisoned and not many soldiers were in town. He described the layout of the settlement and pointed out George Hoyt's headquarters at the

Johnson House Hotel, where the hated Redlegs were quartered. Other points of concern were the homes of the abolition leaders, the stores that sold stolen goods, and the newspaper offices that printed virulent words against the Southern people. Taylor drew a map showing the locations of the men most troublesome to the Missourians. Marked off were the residences of Gov. Charles Robinson, influential leader of the hated Eastern Emigrant Aid Society; and Mayor George Washington Collamore, quartermaster general of the state who was responsible for organizing and arming the companies in and around Lawrence; and the home of James Lane. Taylor mentioned that there was a Federal company across the river at the ferry.

It was agreed that when the guerrillas attacked, a patrol would rush toward the river and cut the ferry line, thus isolating the soldiers and keeping them from aiding the town. Taylor added that Lawrence was an ideal battlefield for the guerrillas' style of fighting. Its streets were wide and could accommodate a large column of charging cavalrymen. He reported that none of the residents thought it plausible that Quantrill would attack their town. Taylor reported their boasting and overstating their defensive readiness. He also noticed how many useful horses could be found in town, knowing that the guerrillas would need fresh mounts to escape back into Missouri.

Mayor Collamore had also recently ordered all the local militia weapons to be kept in a central arsenal in the middle of town. The only arms the individual militiamen carried were personal weapons. If Quantrill's men acted fast enough and just before dawn, when the town would be least ready, the guerrillas could seize the arsenal and cut off any organized resistance. In addition to the arsenal, weapons were also stored in the warehouse of Ridenour and Baker, well-known citizens of Lawrence.

After hearing Taylor's and Noland's reports, Quantrill said to his captains: "You have heard the report, but before you decide[,] it is proper that you should know it all. The march to Lawrence is a long one; in every little town there are soldiers; we attack the town garrisoned by soldiers; we retreat through soldiers, and when we would rest and refit after the exhaustive expedition, we have to do the best we can in the midst of a multitude of soldiers."[8]

He then turned to each officer individually and said, "Let's go to Lawrence!" After passing each man and looking each in the eyes, Quantrill continued. "The Kansan has been murdering and robbing our people for two years or more, and burned their houses by districts, hauled their household plunder, farming implements . . . to Kansas, driven off their cattle . . . until forbearance has ceased to be a virtue. Lawrence is the great hotbed of abolitionism in Kansas. All the plunder, or the bulk of it, stolen from Missouri, will be found stored away in Lawrence. And we can get more revenge and more money there than anywhere else."[9]

The officers knew it would be the most dangerous mission they had participated in to date. They had suspected the raid on Lawrence for some time but had kept silent about it. The gathering of so many guerrillas gave them an added boldness when they replied.

Gregg reported the discussion over the raid lasted for twenty-four hours. Each officer had questions. What about the border guards? Quantrill replied that they were far apart and weakly manned. What if they were seen along the way? Quantrill said that they would make their way cautiously toward the Kansas border then rest and prepare for the final assault. They would start for Kansas after dark, making their way toward Lawrence along well-known trails and striking the town before daybreak. They would attack and accomplish their mission, take fresh horses for the return trip, then withdraw into Missouri as fast as they could, reaching their old camps and haunts at sundown and then splitting up to avoid their pursuers.

After all the questions had been answered, there was still some slight hesitation by some of the captains. Quantrill replied to their objections by stating, "I consider it almost a forlorn hope, for if we go, I don't know if anyone of us will get back to tell the story. . . . But, if you never risk, you never gain."

When the time came to make a decision, Quantrill turned to each leader and asked for his vote. The men who sat before him now were hardened by years of fighting. Most had waged personal vendettas against the Federals. This latest brutality of the female prison collapse perpetrated against the guerrillas' relatives made them realize they were fighting an inhuman enemy who would stop at nothing to satisfy a desire for blood.

Knowing Bill Anderson's feelings about losing a sister only days before, Quantrill turned to him first and asked his opinion. Anderson replied, "Lawrence or hell, but with one proviso, that we kill every male thing." Quantrill next turned to Todd, whose father had been tortured. He replied, "Lawrence, if I knew not a man would get back alive." Turning to Gregg, whose uncle had been killed by the Federals, Gregg said: "Lawrence, it is the home of Jim Lane; the foster mother of the Red Legs; the nurse of the Jayhawkers." Oliver Shepherd replied, "Lawrence. I know it of old; niggers and white men are just the same there; it's a Boston colony and it should be wiped out." John Jarrette said: "Lawrence, by all means. I've had my eye on it for a long time. The head devil of all this killing and burning in Jackson County is in Lawrence; I vote to fight it with fire, to burn it before we leave it." Dick Maddox added: "Lawrence; and an eye-for-an-eye and a tooth-for-a-tooth; God understands better than we do the equilibrium of Civil War." Col. John D. Holt tersely answered, "Lawrence, and be quick about it." Dick Yeager added: "Where my house once stood there is a heap of ruins. I haven't a neighbor that's got a house. Lawrence, and the torch." Andy Blunt replied, "Count me in whenever there is killing. Lawrence first and then some other Kansas town; the name is nothing."

After going around the campfire, Quantrill asked, "Have you all voted?" They all answered yes. Quantrill stood and gave the order: "Then Lawrence it is; saddle up, men!"

Another factor in this decision to attack Lawrence was another brash decision passed down from Federal headquarters. The same day that the guerrilla bands assembled on the banks of the Blackwater, Gen. John M. Schofield concurred with Gen. Thomas Ewing's plan to banish guerrilla families from the border counties.

For the guerrillas, only one measure for retaliation would satisfy their already troubled souls: a strike at the heart of the hatred headquartered in Lawrence. An attack on Lawrence had long been in the back of everyone's mind. Lawrence's newspapers incited the citizens to raid into Missouri. John Speer, editor of the *Lawrence Republican*, invited the townspeople to enlist just to "fight for fun."[10] With their incendiary propaganda spreading excitement everywhere, Kansas adventurers dashed off to "spread terror, free slaves, and lay claim to Missouri loot."[11] Since the beginning of Jennison's early raids into Missouri, Lawrence had become the mecca for runaway slaves. Many settled along the border towns in Kansas, but most were attracted to the center of abolition, and that center was Lawrence.[12]

Since the start of the war, when the first jayhawkers swept across the border, Lawrence had been a prime recipient of loot from Missouri. Early in the war returning raiders brought back carriages, pianos, furniture, silverware, linens, and anything they could carry. Kansas homes were suddenly and lavishly furnished.[13] Ladies appeared on the streets in silk finery, farms were outfitted, even churches were adorned with the booty. Later, however, most of the plunder came on the hoof.[14]

Although Lawrence was selected as the object of the raid, no one but Quantrill knew every aspect of the plan. He would allow no one to jeopardize the mission. Every detail of the attack had been worked out and rehearsed. Now it was time to launch the operation. The different commanders had made their decision to face the most dangerous mission of their careers. Honor was long past gone. The dashing cavaliers were now vengeful-minded young men who carried small mementos of loved ones close to their chests.

Others rode with visions of family members slain on their own doorsteps and of their homes and their neighbors' homes lying in ruins. Now was the time for revenge. They had lived for this moment, and now they must prepare themselves as soldiers. None had at first expected to get back alive, but by now their feelings did not matter, and they faced the reality that they were prepared to give their lives in defense of their country and their beliefs.

Before the raid Richard Cordley of Lawrence stated, "The men [of the town] were organized into military companies, and had regular times for drill. There were five companies, one of which was composed of men beyond the age of military service."[15] Back in November 1862 the town had experienced a false alarm concerning a raid by Missouri guerrillas. Within an hour of the alert, thirteen militia companies were assembled and ready to fight. They had mustered every man and boy, replete with bayoneted rifles and ready to fire their cannon.[16] After easing back into their normal routines, the citizens were again aroused on July 31, 1863, when the armory bell pealed a call to arms. Within minutes the militia again wheeled the cannon into place and readied it with shot and shell. Several hundred soldiers were at their posts with rifles leveled at an enemy who never came.

After Robert E. Lee's defeat at Gettysburg and Ulysses S. Grant's victory at Vicksburg in early July 1863, many in Lawrence believed the war was coming to a close. They felt a great sense of relief at not having to continue their taxing military exercises along with the nightly patrols, but the townspeople of Lawrence continued to brag about their military efficiency; the *Lawrence Journal*, referring to the Missouri guerrillas, reported, "Lawrence had ready for any emergency over five hundred fighting men, everyone of whom would like to see [some Rebels]."[17]

Three months before, in April, the greatest plunderer along the border, Charles Jennison, was given a "grand military ball" sponsored by the ladies of Lawrence at the Free State Hotel. Newspapers carried word of the occasion, and it was quickly circulated how many toasts were offered to the little officer of the Seventh Kansas Jayhawkers for the outstanding job he had been doing in plundering the farms of Missouri farmers. These instances were still fresh in the Missourians' minds as they made plans of attack.

After addressing his officers, Quantrill next addressed the rank and file of his company: "Now boys, you will have to go through a lot. There are great dangers ahead of us. There will be troops behind us and troops in front of us. There may be very few of us that get back alive. Now if there is any men in the outfit that don't want to go, now is the time to fall out, for after we leave here there will be no falling out or turning back."[18] The guerrillas now knew for certain that their destination was Lawrence. Some were deeply troubled, knowing how arduous it would be to get there and back, but they also knew Quantrill's character and his leadership abilities. After they put their trust and faith in him, there would be no change of heart.

Gregg reported that Quantrill addressed the men: "You one and all, will understand that the undertaking we are about to commence is one of extreme hazard. It might be that the entire command will be overwhelmed, the ranks decimated, as they have never been before. Hence, I say to one and all, if any refuse to go they will not be censured."[19]

While they had been waiting for the reports from the spies from Lawrence, Quantrill had given the order to secure as many pistol caps as could be found and for the men to make as many cartridges as possible. His captains also passed down orders for the men to look to their weapons and mounts. An inspection was coming, and each man must pass with distinction if he was to call himself a guerrilla. For this trip each man was mounted on the best horse he could find.

Frank Smith observed: "I doubt if there was ever in the history of this country or have been at any time since a like number of horsemen who were as good of riders and pistol shots and were mounted on as good horseflesh as Quantrill's command was when it rode across the Kansas line on its way to Lawrence to sack and burn the town. Many of the guerrillas' horses were thoroughbreds of pure Kentucky strain. Each of Quantrill's men had one object in mind and that was to possess the best steed and arms available."[20]

When the guerrillas began the march on Lawrence on August 19, as usual William H. Gregg was a quarter of a mile in front of the advance. He was well ahead of the main column and zigzagged along the general route that Quantrill told him to go. He maintained visibility with the main column while checking out any danger areas as they proceeded. They moved slowly at first, with flankers and vedettes surrounding the main force as they made their way from one camp to the next. The scouts from the vedettes reported back every few minutes. If they were discovered by a Union patrol this early in the operation, the raid would have to be called off and the element of surprise would be lost.

George Todd was in command of the rear guard, but once Quantrill sensed there was no danger, he ordered Todd to take over Gregg's position. Riding two abreast in close cavalry formation, the guerrilla column spread out over the prairie for more than a mile.

At approximately five o'clock that afternoon Quantrill stopped at Benjamin Potter's house near Lone Jack and purchased meat from Potter's smokehouse. While Quantrill was making the purchase, Potter called out to his daughter Martha and his granddaughter Amanda, "Girls, here's Quantrill." Quantrill's embarrassment greatly amused his men because they knew he was always bashful around women.

The men cooked their supper over campfires. The surrounding neighbors were asked to contribute half a bushel of bread to go with the meal. Potter had a reputation of Southern hospitality and graciousness at his table. Keeping with this tradition, Potter served Quantrill and his officers at his own table.

While they were eating, Potter asked one of the enlisted soldiers, "Where are you boys going?" They answered that the only ones who might know would be the officers. "We think we're going to Kansas."

In addition to the horses they rode, each man led a horse, which were all fed from Potter's supply of oats. At eight o'clock that night the march began again and continued throughout the evening. The entire march was through smoking ruins and blackened fields left from previous jayhawker raids.

On the night of August 19 the guerrillas passed through the burned-out remains of Chapel Hill on the head of the Middle Fork of the Grand River, eight miles northwest of Harrisonville and fifteen miles southeast of Aubry, the nearest Union post in Kansas.

Quantrill's men arrived at the headwaters of the Grand River at five o'clock on the morning of August 20 and stay concealed in the timber. By prearrangement about fifty guerrillas from Cass County joined them. The plan that Quantrill had envisioned for so long was working perfectly.

Confederate Col. John D. Holt had camped with Quantrill and was under the protection of his command. He was an officer of the regular army and had been sent to Clay County, north of the Missouri River, to recruit. Quantrill had suggested to Holt that he continue on to Clay County to pick up his new recruits then meet him at a prearranged time and place along the Missouri border as Quantrill made his way toward Lawrence. Many times regular officers deferred to his authority while in joint operations in the field. Holt's recruits could bolster his forces and serve as lookouts and guards to cordon off the town once they got there. To this Holt readily agreed. Holt had his own reasons for revenge. Before the war he had owned a large hardware store in Vernon County, which was put to the torch by Charles Jennison. Holt rendezvoused here with Quantrill, bringing with him about a hundred new recruits from Clay County.

Quantrill's initial concern was to make it into Kansas without being observed. He knew that if his force could make it undetected as far as the Kansas border, he had a good chance of making it all the way to his objective, forty-five miles away. If the guerrillas were not reported before reaching the

Kansas border, with most of his men wearing Federal uniforms and probably carrying a Union flag, he just might carry out the operation successfully. To avoid detection he concealed his movement by screening his column behind hills and in the timber along the creek bottoms. If he was noticed with such a large force moving toward Kansas, he knew he would be immediately reported to the authorities in Kansas City. In turn the telegraph wires would carry the warning to all Federal posts and stations in Missouri and Kansas, and it would be impossible to proceed with his plans. If the guerrillas were detected, Quantrill's only hope would be to scatter and tell every man to take care of himself. The mere size of his force was an audacious undertaking, being the largest partisan ranger band ever assembled. Its size would probably throw off suspicion if they were spotted. At last the order to mount up was given around noon of August 20, and the men started out in a southwesterly direction toward their destination.

Federal Lt. Col. Bazel F. Lazear commanded two companies of the First Missouri Militia at Warrensburg and heard on the morning of August 20 that Quantrill's force had passed the day before twelve miles north of him and going west. He moved promptly after the guerrillas, sending orders to Maj. A. W. Mullins, commanding two companies of the same regiment at Pleasant Hill, to move against the guerrillas from that point, but Quantrill quietly and quickly slipped past them both. To deceive the enemy of his intentions, Quantrill detailed Andrew Blunt and fifteen men into Johnson County to attract the attention of the Federals.

As Quantrill led his command into Kansas, at a point about ten miles south of Little Santa Fe, he turned directly west toward Lawrence. On the evening of August 20 Quantrill led approximately four hundred men across the state line a half-mile from Aubry, Kansas. Almost half of the guerrillas wore Federal uniforms. Quantrill placed these men up front. Their coats were buttoned to hide the guerrilla shirts underneath. At Aubry there were two hundred men from the Ninth Kansas Jayhawker Company under the command of Capt. Joshua A. Pike. At 7 P.M. one of Pike's scouts reported the guerrilla column approaching. In the fading sunlight Pike's men came into view on the prairie and formed on line. From a quarter of a mile away, the Federals simply watched Quantrill's men pass before them in a northwesterly direction. Pike made no attempt to engage the guerrillas but did report their presence to the other border posts north and south of him, although he failed to notify any of the towns farther to the west—the direction in which the column was moving. Pike also notified Ewing's headquarters in Kansas City, but Ewing was spending the night at Fort Leavenworth, and the telegraph office was closed.

Ewing did not receive Pike's message until 10:45 the next morning. Ewing then gathered three hundred men and started in the direction of Lawrence.

Quantrill had given orders that not a man should break ranks and not a shot should be fired. The guerrillas were well disciplined and obeyed his orders explicitly.

Pike did send the information along about the unidentified column to his commander, Lt. Col. Charles S. Clark, in Little Santa Fe, Missouri, about twelve miles north of Aubry. Clark, like Pike, did nothing to stop or pass along any information about the strange column entering Kansas.

Quantrill halted his column at dusk to graze the horses and for his men to eat. They were one-half mile south of Squiresville, which was ten miles inside Kansas. Two miles farther on they stopped at the home of a colonel named Sims, whose name was on their death list. Sims had formerly lived in Missouri but had been chased out. He often led jayhawker patrols back into Missouri seeking revenge on those who had forced him from his home. Quantrill sent a patrol to capture him, but fortunately for Sims, he was not at home.

This portion of Kansas was open prairie and sparsely settled, and no one was around to report the presence of the guerrillas. The night was warm, and some of the men rode with their hats off, enjoying the night breeze. The guerrillas resumed their march once darkness had set in.

They crossed the Santa Fe Trail at Spring Hill, now Gardner, Kansas, between ten and eleven o'clock in the evening. One Kansas farmer watched the guerrilla column ride by and noticed many of the riders had tied themselves in their saddles in case they fell asleep during the night march. Quantrill knew that Federals would be stationed in the town. The people of Spring Hill were not yet in bed as there were lights still on in the houses. He gave the command to his men: "Make no attack unless fired upon." There they saw several Federal soldiers in uniform on the streets, but the guerrillas did not molest them or attempt to stop in this place. The Federals they encountered along the way did not suspect anything. When one of the soldiers asked them where they were going, they replied that they were a scout on their way to Lawrence to get their horses shod.

Three miles farther west the column turned north toward the German town of Hesper. Most of the men were familiar with the area just beyond the state line, but now the land around them was unfamiliar, so they procured farmers along the way to act as guides. One guide was seized outside Spring Hill then killed after Quantrill and Todd recognized him as a jayhawker. In fact, whenever guides were found, many of the guerrillas recognized them as jayhawkers who had plundered Missouri. Cole Younger recalled that Quantrill would order a farmer to serve as a guide, and after a while the farmer's directions would get hazy. "Is this as far as you know the country?" Quantrill would ask. When they replied that it was, Quantrill would send them back home.[21]

When the column was only twelve or thirteen miles from Lawrence, two quick pistol shots rang out. The column had stopped at the house of Pvt. William Bentley of the Twelfth Kansas Jayhawker Regiment. Bentley was not at home, but two other jayhawkers were discovered there asleep. One saw the danger and escaped into the brush; the other surrendered and was shot. George Todd rode up to where the sound came from and found Fletcher Taylor standing over the dead Federal. Taylor insisted the shooting was in self-defense, but Todd was angry.

The column marched until making a planned stop at the home of Capt. Andrew J. Jennings of Company E, Twelfth Kansas—the company commanded by James Lane's son-in-law—but Jennings was not home. The next planned halt was the home of Joseph Stone. George Todd recognized Stone as the man who had caused his arrest at the beginning of the war; Stone's son was a private in the Eleventh Kansas Jayhawker Regiment. The guerrillas seized the elder Stone, but the son escaped by the back door. Also at Stone's house a boy, Jacob Rote, was acquired to act as a guide as far as the Wakarusa River. About a half-mile from the house, Joseph Stone was shot in the head.[22]

Having reached the Wakarusa timbers, Quantrill recognized the country and so led the way himself to within four or five miles of Franklin. The cocks were starting to crow at sunrise, and Quantrill gave the order, "Push on! It will be daylight before we get there. We ought to have been there an hour ago." Quantrill knew that being spotted at daylight on the open prairie near Lawrence would raise an alarm for the militia companies in the town. The guerrillas hurried along at a long trot as they reached Franklin just at dawn. They passed through the town without stopping.

Quantrill turned to Gregg and told him to "take five men and go ahead to see if there is anything in the way."[23] With five miles left to cover and wanting to reach Lawrence before sunrise, Quantrill shouted to the rest of the column, "Form fours." The men quickly shuffled their horses and maneuvered into a column of fours and were put into a gallop.

Up until this time Quantrill had ridden in the rear of the command to limit straggling and ensure that everyone was keeping in line. Just before daylight he rode to the front of the command; the sleeping town of Lawrence was over the next ridge.

In the August 6 edition of the *Lawrence State Journal*, editor Harvey Lowman bragged: "The martial spirit of the people is fully aroused. All around, the eye meets the gleam of the freshly burnished Sharps rifle, and the ear catches the significant click of the newly oiled revolver."[24] He taunted the guerrillas: "We invite any number of Border Ruffians to visit any part of our State. The nearer they come to Lawrence the better." Other Kansans boasted that if Quantrill's gang came into their state, the guerrillas would be "welcomed with bloody hands to hospitable graves."

Before entering Lawrence, Quantrill wanted to question one last citizen. Cole Younger awakened a farmer and brought him to the colonel. Quantrill wanted to know about the soldiers in town and if Sen. Jim Lane was there. As the farmer stood before him, Quantrill said, "If you tell us the truth we'll spare you, if not you will die." The trembling farmer said, "[T]here [are] three hundred regular Federal troops in Lawrence and three hundred militiamen."

Harrison Trow remembered that the farmer said there were probably four hundred soldiers in camp across the Kansas River, and about seventy-five Redlegs on the Lawrence side. Younger explained, "These 'Redlegs' were particularly hated by us for they had robbed and plundered and murdered and raped in a hundred Southern homes on the Missouri side. They were really brigands." Even a Kansan remarked, "The [Redlegs] contained men of the most desperate and hardened character, and a full recital of their deeds would sound like the biography of devils. Either the people of Lawrence could not drive out the freebooters, or they thought it mattered little what might happen to Missouri disloyalists. Governor Robinson made a determined, but unsuccessful effort to break up the organization. The Redlegs repaid the interference by plots for his assassination, which barely miscarried."

When Quantrill heard the farmer's statement, he reportedly laughed and said, "They outnumber us two to one, but we will whip them and as for those Redlegs we will exterminate them. Not a man of them is to escape." The farmer reported that one company was camped on the road into town. Quantrill asked, "What time did you leave?" The farmer replied about four o'clock. Regarding Lane, he reported that the senator was not in town at four o'clock; the three companies were the only soldiers in town.

Quantrill had plans to send a picket to Lane's house to capture him but not injure him. "I would like to meet him," he said. "But then there would be no honor in whipping him. He is a coward. I believe I would cowhide him."[25]

Finally Quantrill asked, "Where does Colonel Sam Walker live?" Walker was an early Free Soil advocate and a militia officer who, along with James Lane and old John Brown, was responsible for numerous destructive and murderous jayhawking raids. Walker had also tried to arrest Quantrill on spurious charges when the guerrilla leader lived in Lawrence before the war.

Quantrill ordered one of his men to take charge of the farmer until he could determine if the man was telling the truth.[26]

And so Quantrill led his men toward their final objective and expected to encounter a large body of Federal troops. He had often attacked the enemy when the odds were as high as ten to one, so with the odds in Lawrence at two to one, he did not give a second thought about turning back.

Quantrill detailed two men northwest to the home of Lt. Samuel S. Snyder. Snyder had been with Lane at the destruction of Osceola, Missouri, and was responsible for looting a number of Missouri churches. Presently he was in charge of recruiting a regiment of blacks in Lawrence. The guerrillas found Snyder in his yard, milking his cow, and shot him there.

Five hundred feet east of Snyder's, Quantrill stopped at the house of Josiah Miller of the Eleventh Kansas Jayhawker Regiment. The occupants at first believed the command to be Federal soldiers because of their uniforms. The guerrillas asked numerous questions until a young woman blurted out, "You are not soldiers, you are Quantrill's." At this, Quantrill leaned forward across his horse and replied. "You have guessed right, I am Quantrill and these are my men." They had planned to take William Miller, the young woman's brother, prisoner, but so earnest was her plea that Quantrill recanted with the threat for him to stay in the house or his life would be forfeited.

Just before the guerrillas made for the camps in town, they came upon a couple of riders. The man was around eighteen years old and wearing a uniform; he was instantly shot. His lady companion quickly rode back into town.

On the outskirts of Lawrence, Quantrill's heart beat faster. Before him lay the hated one-mile-square town of twelve hundred. The guerrillas came into the western precincts of the city, where the wealthiest homes stood and few people lived. To the east was the older section of the town, running to the river. A narrow ravine near the center of town divided it east and west. Lining the banks of the ravine were the only trees in the city. The streets were very wide, and there was a great deal of open space between houses. The only areas that offered any cover were fence rows and areas of tall grass and brush. Unharvested cornfields covered many areas around the town.

Events unfolded rapidly and according to plan. Quantrill turned to his men and said, "Boys, this is the home of Jim Lane and Jennison; remember that in hunting us they gave no-quarter. Shoot every soldier you see, but in no way harm a woman or child." Frank Smith recalled that Quantrill shouted out, "Molest no women or children. Kill every man in Federal uniform."[27]

Quantrill's lieutenants briefly hesitated to consider the consequences. Noting this, he shouted, "You can do as you please, I am going to Lawrence." He unbuttoned his Federal blouse and threw it on the ground, exposing his elaborate guerrilla shirt. The rest of the men followed his example rather than tie their uniforms to their saddles. They knew that in the fog of war they needed to be instantly recognizable to their comrades, and the guerrilla shirt was their unmistakable uniform. They also expected to die on the streets of Lawrence, and they wanted to be dressed as the partisan rangers they were.

Each man had three to four revolvers in addition to a carbine. The battle plan was simple: fire their pistols, give the wild Rebel Yell, force everyone off the streets, then go house to house to find the men on their lists.

And so turning his horse toward the east, Quantrill drew his pistols and, with a yell, charged toward the town. Meeting up with William H. Gregg, Quantrill and he rode together until they encountered a company of troops quartered in about forty tents along the main road.[28] As he dashed past the tents, Quantrill pointed to the camp, and part of his command broke ranks and charged through them. Scarcely any resistance was made.[29]

Andy Walker was riding in the van of the column when he reported, "We didn't see any pickets, and hence rode up the main street unannounced and unmolested. There was a bunch of tents upon the right of the main street. Soon the sleeping Federal soldiers were aroused, and the bullets came at us from every direction."[30]

In this camp were twenty-one recruits of the Fourteenth Kansas Jay-hawker Regiment, all uniformed and armed. Eighteen were killed during the first wild charge.[31] One guerrilla recalled that a sentry discharged his rifle to give alarm and shouted, "Corporal of the Guard! Post 6!" then fell riddled with bullets. He said that the Federals came swarming out like bees and tried to rally and form a square with their rifles and bayonets, but bayonets were useless against the deadly pistol fire of the guerrillas.[32]

Edward and Sarah Fitch awoke to the noise of the firing. Edward assumed that the shots were coming from the recruits and was not alarmed. He told his wife, "Oh, it's the boys having some fun."

On reaching the ground on which the recruits' tents stood, Quantrill's command deployed right and left and then charged. In three minutes not a recruit or a tent was left standing.[33] Surprised, ridden over, shot in their blankets, some paralyzed with terror, others running frantically—what could raw recruits do against the deadliest pistol shots along the border?[34] The officer in charge hid beneath his office, which was later set on fire. When the flames became too intense, he stripped off his uniform and ran until he came to a house that permitted him to dress as a woman; he escaped further detection.[35]

The farmer the guerrillas had seized just outside of town had told them that one of the companies of soldiers was in a store building. Fletcher Taylor was sent after them with twenty men. They surrendered, were led out, and promptly shot.[36] A little way off a camp of black recruits under the command of Capt. Leroy J. Beam was encountered. After the first shot was fired the black soldiers immediately rushed out of their tents. The majority of them started toward the direction of the river, while some tried to make it into town. A few of the blacks reached the river, plunging into it, but none succeeded in reaching the opposite shore. The guerrillas dashed back up into town and shot at every blue coat that came into sight.[37]

Quantrill's next order was, "Rush on to the town!" Instantly his guerrillas rushed forward, yelling like demons. They rode five or six abreast and were splendid horsemen. They were desperate-looking men. One eyewitness recalled: "I can still see the raiders as they stormed into town with their broad-brimmed hats, much like those which cowboys wear on the plains, with their unshaven beards and long hair, their dirty, greasy flannel shirts, coatless, and carrying no weapons except side-arms."[38] Another eyewitness said, "Their horses seemed to be in the secret of the hour, and their feet scarcely seemed to touch the ground. Their riders sat upon them with bodies erect, and arms free, some with a revolver in each hand, shooting at each house or person they passed, and yelling at every bound."[39]

With William H. Gregg at his side, Quantrill turned toward town and charged up Massachusetts Street. Gregg remembered Quantrill's order: "Kill, kill, and you will make no mistake. Lawrence is the hotbed and should be thoroughly cleansed and the only way to cleanse it is to kill."

The attack was perfectly executed; every man knew his place. Quantrill's first objective was to secure the town from any resistance. The guerrillas flowed into every street and lane like water poured upon a rock. Holt's recruits broke off from the main column and set up pickets on the east side of town. Andy Blunt separated with eleven men and rode off to guard the west side of town, immediately racing toward Mount Oread to set up an observation post to watch for approaching Federals. The Kansas militia had previously covered Mount Oread with breastworks and rifle pits.[40]

Meanwhile, the main column raced through town and divided into three columns, each riding up one of Lawrence's main streets, and quickly surrounded the buildings quartering soldiers and any other houses that looked like they could offer any resistance. Robert Gaston Elliott of Lawrence recalled, "The people were awakened from their slumber by the cracking of pistols and the tramping of horses, and as they ran out to form companies or to find a place of security, they were shot down in cold blood."

Many of the guerrillas shouted a battle cry at the top of their voices to "Remember the girls!" and "Osceola!" These shouts underscored the kind of war they were fighting. The girls were the victims of the Kansas City jail collapse, and the town of Osceola, Missouri, had been destroyed in 1861 by jayhawkers. A portion of the raiders raced toward the river to cover the ferry crossing to block any assistance coming from the other side.

Quantrill, Andy Walker, William H. Gregg, and one or two others galloped from one side of town to the other, shooting right and left and drawing fire. As they rode opposite the Free State Hotel near the river, a man wearing a major's uniform darted across the street. Quantrill shouted, "Get that major!" Gregg chased him into a stable down Winthrop Street where the officer barricaded himself. Gregg shot out his pistols, and while he was reloading, the main body of guerrillas rode up and surrounded the Free State Hotel.

Quantrill and Walker continued on the length of the main street until they reined up on the riverbank and peered across. A shower of bullets came whistling from the other side. Capt. Edmund Ross's company of the Eleventh Kansas Jayhawker Regiment and a squad of the Ninth Kansas Jayhawker Regiment occupied the ground directly opposite; they had camped overnight on the north bank on their way to Fort Leavenworth. John Newman Edwards reported there were four hundred soldiers in this camp across the river.

Walker shouted to his commander, "Good God, Quantrill! Let's get away from here, or they'll kill us."

There was a livery stable close to the river, but because of the fire from the Federals on the opposite bank, the guerrillas were prevented from getting the horses out of the stable. The ferry over the river was a flatboat drawn by a rope. Quantrill detailed fifteen men to prevent the soldiers from using the ferry to cross the river. At the same time, the militia on the north side of the river feared that the guerrillas would cross over and annihilate them, so one or two of them snuck up to the edge of the river and cut the ferry's cable, thus saving the guerrillas the trouble. Edwards asserted that the Union troops across the river made scarcely any attempt to cross to the rescue of their butchered comrades; a few skirmishers held them in check.

Yet fire from the militia wounded two of Holt's recruits and one of Quantrill's veterans: Josiah L. Bledsoe. Under fire, Hicks and Hi George, two brothers and friends of Bledsoe, after taking possession of a carriage, carried him away. The brothers' father had been murdered, the home of their mother burned three times, each of them had been wounded, a brother had been killed, and they lived solely to fight and avenge the family.[41]

One bystander in Lawrence, the Reverend Richard Cordley, watched the guerrillas pass by his house and recounted their appearance: "The horsemanship of the guerrillas was perfect. They rode with that ease and abandon, which are acquired only by a life spent in the saddle, amid desperate scenes."[42]

One of the key points of resistance was expected at the city armory in the middle of town. Here were kept the muskets that were supposed to be used for the defense of Lawrence. Shortly before Quantrill's attack, the muskets had been issued to individual militia members, but then Gen. George Washington Collamore, the town's mayor, had them collected and stored at a central site for immediate use. Statements made by Lawrence citizens to a congressional investigation years later were found to be false and deliberately misleading. Allegations were made then that the muskets were old and rusty and of no practical military use. The truth was that Collamore had petitioned Gen. Thomas Ewing for new guns and cannon and had received them only a few months before the raid. Even a few days following the raid, when word was spread of another attack on the town, the citizens ran to the armory and grabbed up these weapons to defend themselves.

The armory was next to Gov. Charles Robinson's house, and a squad of guerrillas guarded it to keep the militia from rallying to arms. Cole Younger reported, "We shot the soldiers down as they ran out of the houses on the way to the rendezvous their officers had given them."[43]

Pvt. Levi Gates lived a mile from town. As soon as he heard the firing, he picked up his gun and rushed into town to join his company. Seeing the guerrillas in possession of the streets, he shouldered his rifle and fired at one of the riders. His first shot made one soldier jump in his saddle but did not kill him. Gates managed to fire only one more shot before other guerrilla soldiers rode him down and killed him.

Capt. George W. Bell lived on the side hill overlooking the town and saw the Rebels before they made their charge. He grabbed his gun, as he had practiced in the past, and attempted to make his way to the armory. His family endeavored to dissuade him, telling him he would certainly be killed. To their entreaties, Bell replied: "They may kill me, but they cannot kill the principles I fight for. If they take Lawrence, they must do it over my dead body." Bell's brave words were greatly exaggerated, because as soon as he discovered there was no chance of resistance, he threw his gun away and tried to make his way back home.[44] Discovered by some guerrillas, he was chased into the home of Pvt. Josiah Miller of the Eleventh Kansas Jayhawker Regiment. Miller's home therefore was no sanctuary. The guerrillas ordered the men to surrender. While they were being led outside, another group of guerrillas fired a volley at the two men. Bell was killed, and Miller was wounded.

Quantrill's spies had informed him that the area of greatest resistance would be the four-story brick Free State Hotel, also known as the Eldridge House. Iron grills protected the ground windows, parapets had been built into the roofline, and portholes for firing had been built into the façade. The hotel had been built and paid for with funds from the New England Emigrant Aid Society and was run by Shalor W. Eldridge, a field officer in the Second Kansas Jayhawker Regiment. Room 7 in the Eldridge House had a reputation throughout the territory as a favorite place for carousals, where the uproar usually continued all night as one party of roisterers succeeded another.[45]

By now a large contingent of Quantrill's company had surrounded the famous building. The guerrillas were sitting their horses, waiting for some type of resistance to come from within the structure. Suddenly a gong began ringing from inside the hotel. Startled, the raiders scurried for cover, thinking that this might be a signal for those inside to open fire, but the occupants of the hotel possessed neither the will nor the means to defend the place. After a short interval, one of the guests, Capt. Alexander Banks, appeared at a window and waved a white bed sheet.

Banks was a regular army officer and served as the provost marshal of Kansas. He recalled that he was sleeping on the third floor of the hotel with his wife when:

I was awakened by the rapid discharge of firearms on Massachusetts Street, and when I arose and looked from the window, I saw a body of horsemen riding rapidly up the street toward the hotel. I told my wife that the guerrillas had taken the town and we began to dress hastily. Soon the hotel gong sounded loudly and the guests hastened into the corridors from their rooms. Many of them were scantily attired. Their first idea was to escape by the rear, but just then a revolver cracked and, looking from a window into the back yard, I saw Joseph Eldridge, the landlord's brother, lying at the foot of the high fence with which the yard was enclosed. He was evidently wounded. I saw also that [the adjoining streets] were crowded with men and knew that escape was impossible in that quarter and that the building was surrounded. Resistance was then suggested but that was soon found to be out of the question as upon investigation we could only muster three or four weapons and I was urged to surrender the house as speedily as possible. Re-entering my room, I took a pillowslip from the bed and waved it from the window. Until this time a steady fusillade had been kept up on the windows at the front of the house, but when I appeared an order was given to cease firing and one of the raiders stepped from the street to the sidewalk and asked if we surrendered. I replied that we would upon condition that the men should be held as prisoners and protected, and that the women should not be molested. He shouted back: "All right. Come down. Your people won't be hurt." Going to the clerk's room on the next floor, I found the stairway leading to the street crowded with men, and asked one of them to bring one of their officers to me. By this time Quantrill had returned from the river and rode up to the hotel. Soon, a slightly built, but tall young man rode up on a magnificent brown gelding. Before I knew it the notorious and dreaded Terror of the Border stood facing me.

Eyewitnesses reported that Quantrill wore a black slouch hat with a gold neck cord and gold tassels along the brim, gray pants, and black high-topped cavalry boots. He also wore a highly decorated brown guerrilla shirt and had four .36-caliber Colt Navy revolvers in his belt. A rifle and other weapons hung from his saddlebow. The people of Lawrence also noted his bluish-gray eyes, sandy brown hair and imperial moustache, and reddish sideburns, His face was sun-beaten and unshaven.

A description of Quantrill appeared in the August 31, 1863, *New York Daily Tribune:* "Quantrill would pass anywhere for a well-looking man and exhibits in his countenance no traces of native ferocity. He is of medium height, well-built, very quiet, and even deliberate in speech and motion. His hair is brown, his complexion fresh, and his cunning, but pleasant blue eyes and aquiline nose give to his countenance its chief expression."

When Quantrill saw the white sheet waving from the window, he rode forward to accept the surrender. Banks asked what his intention was in coming to Lawrence, and Quantrill replied, "To plunder and destroy the town in retaliation for Osceola."[46] Banks responded, "We are defenseless and at your mercy. The house is surrendered, but we demand protection for the inmates." Quantrill paused for a moment then told Banks, "I will be back in a minute."

A cheer went up when Quantrill's men discovered that the hotel had surrendered. The town was theirs. Quantrill assigned George Todd the task of conveying prisoners from the Free State Hotel to the Whitney House Hotel.

Several Catholic priests, including the bishop of the area, were given their freedom when they informed the guerrillas of their professions. Quantrill also gave his word that they would not be harmed. They milled about the streets for several hours and witnessed the raiders' actions. Realizing that he could now release most of his men from the mission of securing the Free State Hotel, Quantrill divided his men into squads of six to eight and sent them throughout the town to search for the men on their death lists.

Approximately sixty occupants of the hotel were led from their rooms as prisoners. As they began to file through the lobby, Quantrill dismounted from his horse and entered the hotel. He climbed the stairs and walked out onto the first-floor landing that overlooked the street. He watched for a long time as his men methodically went about their business. When he came downstairs, some of the prisoners tried to talk with him.

One of these was Judge Lawrence Dudley Bailey, who had awakened to a commotion outside his room. He had hurriedly dressed and stepped outside in time to see the other occupants milling in the hallways and being robbed of their possessions and money by the guerrillas. As he was being escorted from the hotel, he encountered Quantrill on the steps of the landing. Judge Bailey refused to believe that Quantrill was going to order the burning of the hotel.

"Yes, it will be burnt," Quantrill replied. Bailey remarked that it was a pretty rough thing to do. "Yes, it is pretty rough," agreed the guerrilla colonel, "but we have had our houses burnt, and we will burn also." Bailey recalled that Quantrill "was not a man whom I should have been frightened at meeting in a lonely place, in ordinary times. He did not look more formidable or ferocious than many a man I have met at other times and passed without fear. I should not have known him to be the dreaded Quantrill, but for the fact that a youngish man, whose name I think was Spicer, was leaning over the banister talking to him."

Arthur Spicer recognized Quantrill from his earlier days and tried to start a conversation. "Remember me, Charley? We use to have good times over on the ferry landing, you were called Charley Hart then!" Quantrill gave him an unfriendly look and replied, "It doesn't make any difference what I was called." Spicer quickly drew back with the other prisoners and did not attempt to make further conversation.

While the prisoners were being assembled in front of the hotel, a passing guerrilla fired at a man he recognized as a Redleg. Quantrill quickly took charge of the situation and prevented any further bloodshed toward the prisoners. After speaking with lawyer Robert S. Stevens, whom Quantrill had known previously, he told the guerrillas nearby that these people were under his protection and "I will put bullets in anyone who harms these prisoners."

One Lawrence resident said, "[The] treatment of the prisoners of the Eldridge House show that they expected resistance from that point and were relieved by the offer of surrender. They not only promised protection, but were as good as their word."[47]

Quantrill informed the prisoners they were being taken to the Whitney House Hotel, which was owned by Nathan Stone, an old friend of Quantrill's. The guerrilla leader explained, "I once boarded there years ago and the Stones were kind to me. Nothing will happen to their property so long as I am in Lawrence. One man was kind to me years ago and I have promised to protect him and his family and house. All of you go over to the City Hotel and stay in it, and you will be safe. But don't attempt to go into the streets."

Stone's wife and daughter had nursed Quantrill through a difficult illness when he had stayed at their hotel, and for this kindness Quantrill repaid them by guarding them and their property. His orders had been to not burn Stone's hotel, but afterward it caught fire from the other buildings around it after the guerrillas had pulled out of Lawrence.

Quantrill now turned his attention to the main part of town, where he expected resistance. He knew that the men in the streets would be militiamen running to join their companies to defend the city. With all the wild yelling and pistol shots going on, Quantrill was an exception, giving off a calm, even pleasant attitude. He stood out from the other guerrillas in his manner and his appearance.

One of the prisoners from the hotel ventured a compliment to the effect that this raid was by far his greatest exploit. Another prisoner posed a question as to why Quantrill had not come a few weeks earlier, when the rumors were the greatest. To this Quantrill calmly replied. "You were expecting me then, but I have caught you napping now."[48]

After making sure the prisoners were safe, George Todd and John Jarrette returned to the Free State Hotel to ensure the hotel was empty of any occupants before setting it afire. They came upon a locked door, and Todd knocked and cried out that the building was in flames and it was time to get away. "Let it burn and be damned," a deep voice answered, and the voices of three men were heard in conversation. Jarrette threw his whole weight against the door, bursting it open. As he did so, Todd fired and killed the first one of the three hiding there, Jarrette took care of the second, and Todd killed the third. The three were soldiers who had escaped the morning's massacre and had not made an effort to defend themselves.[49]

While the Free State Hotel was being emptied and torched, the majority of the guerrillas were busy hunting down men in blue uniforms.[50] After leaving the Free State Hotel, Quantrill walked across the street to the Whitney Hotel and joined his friend Stone. This is where he set up his headquarters. While his men were accomplishing their mission, the Stones prepared a breakfast for Quantrill as they sat and talked over old times. When Quantrill finished eating, he said, "Ladies, I now bid you good morning. I hope when we meet again it will be under more favorable circumstance."

Another objective of the attack was the Johnson House Hotel, the second largest hotel in Lawrence. George Hoyt and his band of Redlegs were known to stay there between their many plunder trips into Missouri. Someone familiar with the Redlegs said, "At intervals the gang would dash into Missouri, seize horses and cattle, not omitting other and worse outrages on occasion, then repair with their booty to Lawrence, where it was defiantly sold at auction. Redlegs were accustomed to brag in Lawrence that nobody dared to interfere with them. They did not hesitate to shoot inquisitive and troublesome people. At Lawrence the livery stables were full of their stolen horses."[51]

The guerrillas hoped to catch the notable leader of the gang, but most of the Redlegs were not in town on this day. Some of them gained notoriety afterward, men like James Butler "Wild Bill" Hickok, Kit Carson, and William "Buffalo Bill" Cody. Cody at one time had proudly boasted, "We were the biggest gang of thieves on record."[52.]

A squad of guerrillas surrounded the hotel and demanded the surrender of the occupants. This was the same hotel where two years earlier proprietor Ben Johnson, a radical abolitionist, had discovered that some of his paying guests were Missourians in search of their stolen property. He unceremoniously booted them from his hotel with a warning not to come back to Lawrence if they valued their lives. Even John Speer thought it amusing when he advised Missourians to "give the Johnson House a wide berth."[53]

Because the hotel had the notoriety as a Redleg hangout, the fourteen men inside knew they were in imminent danger when the guerrillas surrounded it. Hiram George wrote: "The officers in the hotel begged to be taken prisoner, but Quantrill reminded them of General Halleck's order, and of the hundreds of old men they had killed in Missouri."[54] Some attempted to escape and were spared. Others stayed, thinking they would be safe.

Eyewitness Getta Dix recounted seeing the cowardly way the Redlegs were "jumping from windows and fleeing for their lives. Several were killed as they ran." Even after telling her husband, Ralph, and his brother Steven and several others that the occupants were being killed, these men still tried to reach their friends in the Johnson House by crawling over an adjoining rooftop. Surely they thought the Redlegs would at least offer some sort of resistance.

After reaching the hotel, the men were taken prisoner. Along with Ralph Dix were the notorious Redleg Joe Finley, George Kallmer, John Cornell, and three men known only by their last names: Hanson, White, and Goldman. Finley was recognized and immediately shot. Realizing the gravity of his situation, Dix had his wife plead for his life. The guerrillas, realizing that the men in their possession were either Redlegs or their allies, herded the men into an alley and shot them. A Lawrence resident noted: "They pursued the Redlegs with particular earnestness, and showed them no mercy when captured."[55]

The last main objective of the raid was Sen. Jim Lane's house. One of the reasons for the timing of the Lawrence raid was that Quantrill knew Congress was not in session and that Senator Lane should be at home.[56] After learning that Lane was not in town the previous day, the guerrillas did not expect to find him, but a detail accompanied Quantrill to his house to make sure. Lane was also a brigadier general in the state militia as well as the leader of all Kansas jayhawker units. The atrocities he committed in Missouri marked him and his house for destruction.

What the guerrillas did not know was that Lane had been home since a little after midnight on August 21. Only two years earlier he had been penniless, but through political influence and graft and by plundering Missouri homes, he now had the finest house in town. It was well known that when he was elected senator of Kansas in 1858, he had a very small amount of money. As soon as he arrived in Washington, he tried to get an advance on his salary.

Quantrill, followed by scout John McCorkle and several men, rode to Lane's house. When Lane saw the guerrillas approaching, he quickly leaped out a window in his nightshirt and hid in a nearby cornfield. Quantrill strode up to the front door and knocked. Lane's wife opened the door and looked into the eyes of her husband's determined enemy. With gentlemanly politeness, Quantrill asked if the senator was at home: "Give your husband my compliments, Madam, and tell him I should be most happy to meet him."[57] When she replied that the senator was not at home to receive visitors, Quantrill did not bother to search the house but gave orders to burn it down.

Before they applied the torch, McCorkle saw three pianos inside that he recognized as having been stolen from Southern families in Jackson County. The guerrillas were amazed at the amount of plunder that furnished the house and recognized as being stolen from Missouri homes. Over the mantle was a handsome sword and gold-plated scabbard presented to Lane from Gen. Winfield Scott for his service in the Mexican War. Also found was a black flag representing no quarter in battle with the inscription: "Presented to General James H. Lane by the women of Leavenworth."[58]

Lawrence had often been described as a peaceful Kansas town. William H. Gregg observed, "Since before the war Missouri had been infested with thieving bands from Kansas, who, justifying their actions under the guise of being loyal Unionists, made frequent trips into Missouri and 'confiscated' what they held to be Confederate property."[59] As Gregg made his way toward Lawrence's commercial district, he recalled:

> [There] was a ravine across Massachusetts Street. Near the ravine was a collection of about forty shanties, made in part of boards and in part of hay. These shacks were filled with household goods stolen from Jackson County by the Kansans on their raids into Missouri. There were featherbeds, quilts, blankets, etc. stacked in there higher than I could reach. Five bedsteads, bureaus, sideboards, bookcases and pianos, which had cost $1,000 apiece. . . . I recognized some from my own neighborhood . . . many of these shacks were in charge of negro women, many of whom we recognized. One negro woman I recollect distinctly was the property of Colonel Steele who lived near Sibley, Jackson County, Missouri. . . . We went among the shacks touching matches to the hay. It is stated that we destroyed property in Lawrence worth $150,000. I don't know about that; I have always contended that the fires we started that morning destroyed as much property that had belonged to Jackson County people as that belonging to the citizens of Lawrence.

Cole Younger, Hiram George, and John Koger collaborated Gregg's account. They added: "The camp contained thousands and thousands of dollars worth of pianos and carpets and old mahogany furniture and silverplate that had been stripped from the homes of Southern sympathizers. Even for

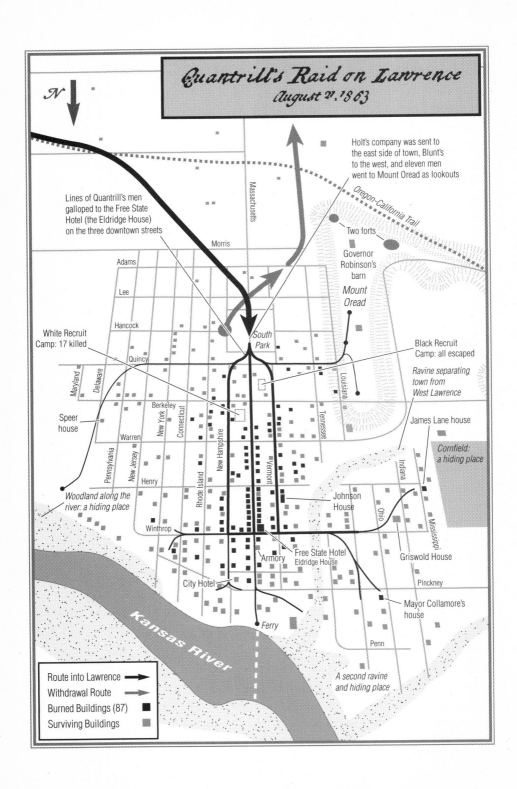

Quantrill's Raid on Lawrence
August 21, 1863

N

Holt's company was sent to the east side of town, Blunt's to the west, and eleven men went to Mount Oread as lookouts

Oregon-California Trail

Lines of Quantrill's men galloped to the Free State Hotel (the Eldridge House) on the three downtown streets

Two forts

Governor Robinson's barn

Mount Oread

Massachusetts

Morris

Adams

Lee

Hancock

Quincy

White Recruit Camp: 17 killed

South Park

Black Recruit Camp: all escaped

Louisiana

Ravine separating town from West Lawrence

Maryland

Delaware

Berkeley

New York

Connecticut

Tennessee

James Lane house

Speer house

Warren

Cornfield: a hiding place

Pennsylvania

New Jersey

Henry

Rhode Island

New Hampshire

Vermont

Indiana

Johnson House

Ohio

Mississippi

Woodland along the river: a hiding place

Winthrop

Armory

Free State Hotel
Eldridge House

Griswold House

City Hotel

Pinckney

Mayor Collamore's house

Ferry

Penn

Kansas River

A second ravine and hiding place

Route into Lawrence →
Withdrawal Route →
Burned Buildings (87) ■
Surviving Buildings ▧

those citizens who did not actually participate in the jayhawking raids themselves, when the stolen loot made its way to their town and was stored and auctioned off on Lawrence's street corners it was heartily condoned by both the men and women of Lawrence."

The guerrillas recalled how only a year earlier Lane had followed in Sterling Price's wake at the Southern victory at the battle of Lexington. Lane journeyed as far as Osceola, a beautiful town of two thousand along the banks of the Osage. The people fled as Lane's army of fifteen hundred jayhawkers approached. Lane's men looted everything in sight, from the stores to private homes. The senator's share of the spoils included more than thirteen thousand dollars in cash, silk dresses for his mistresses, and a grand piano for his home. When the rabble of jayhawkers finally pulled out of town in a drunken stupor, many were too drunk to ride and had to be carried back in wagons. They left the town in flames, and not more than a half-dozen homes survived. After the war Lane introduced Hugh D. Fisher in the U.S. Senate chamber as having saved his brigade from destruction at Osceola. Fisher claimed he had repelled a large force of Confederates and that the Rebels burned the town afterward. The truth is that only a handful of defenders fired on the advance party of Lane's battalion, and the jayhawkers themselves applied the torch.

Bragging about the destruction of Osceola, Lane's neighbor John Speer— owner and editor of a newspaper launched with funds provided by Lane— wrote that what Lane had done at Osceola was but an inkling of what Missourians could expect in the future. Because he endorsed Lane's activities, and because of the way he had often described the guerrillas in his newspaper, Speer was a marked man as well when Quantrill's men attacked Lawrence.

Gov. Charles Robinson, a Lawrence resident but a political enemy of Lane, wrote in the local papers that Lane's method of warfare was "pouncing upon little, unprotected towns and villages and portraying their capture as splendid victories." Robinson knew that someday Lane's activities in Missouri would exact a heavy revenge. "If our towns and settlements are laid waste by fire and sword," Robinson wrote, "we will have General Lane to thank for it."[60]

Meanwhile, the vast majority of the guerrillas executed house-to-house searches for the individuals named on their death lists. One Lawrence citizen observed, "There were men in Lawrence whom they naturally would look for." The raiders were not seeking the blood of innocent men that day. Every name on the death list in some way or other had been marked as enemies of Missouri. One of these was Edward P. Fitch, an abolitionist from Massachusetts. His wife, Sarah, reported, "Many guerrillas carried pieces of paper on which were long rows of names, indicating those men in Lawrence most wanted. In the house-to-house searches that now followed, these Death Lists were referred to again and again."[61]

The hunted men were soldiers, militiamen, jayhawkers, and Redlegs as well as individuals who had aided jayhawkers, notably individuals who had trafficked in the property stolen from Missourians. Also included were newspapermen who for years had expounded virulent, caustic, and inflammatory articles. No small example of this was John Speer Sr. He had once written of the guerrillas: "Of all the mean, miserable creatures that infest the earth, these canine wretches in human form are the most despicable."

Quantrill's men carried maps that noted the houses marked for destruction. Once a house had been put to the torch, guerrillas surrounded it to ensure the flames were not extinguished and that the house was completely destroyed. According to Frank Smith, Quantrill told his men to set the house fires by applying a match to window curtains or bedclothes.

In addition to the execution of the death lists and the house burnings, men were shot down in the streets, in their yards, or wherever they were encountered if they wore Federal uniforms or were known to have worn the uniform or openly advocated abolitionism. They were shown no mercy nor given a chance to defend themselves.[62]

And Union soldiers were running everywhere by now. Some would have liked to have offered any kind of organized resistance, but grasping the futility of it, they fled for their lives. If they were spotted, they were chased down and shot by the guerrillas. Two cousins, Capt. William A. Rankin and Lt. John K. Rankin of the Second Kansas Jayhawker Regiment, encountered six guerrillas on the street. They fired on them and managed to escape after emptying their guns at their pursuers.

Lt. George Ellis was in charge of the Union troops across the river, but the lieutenant was staying in Lawrence at the Eastern House Hotel. When the attack began, he was unarmed. Dodging guerrilla bullets, Ellis tried to make his way into the livery stable to get a horse. Chased by guerrillas, the Federal lieutenant climbed to the loft of the stable and escaped out a rear window and into some weeds.

A militiaman known only as Paul attempted to get to the armory with his rifle and join his company when he encountered men from his company running for their lives into a cornfield. They convinced him to do likewise. Paul threw down his rifle and escaped with the others. When the guerrillas came to Paul's house, the building was undisturbed since his name was not on their list.

Jayhawker Capt. John R. Wilder lived in a stone house close to the intersection of Kentucky and Winthrop Streets. When he heard the firing, he immediately closed his shutters and curtains and cowered inside. The guerrillas left his house alone.

Two brothers, Pvts. John and William Laurie, were trying to escape when they were recognized as militiamen and shot.

Among the agitators known to the guerrillas, Francis B. Swift was a printer, a member of the New England Emigrant Aid Society, and a captain in the First Jayhawker Regiment. He was killed as soon as he was discovered.[63]

Newspaperman John Speer Sr. was a Kansas militiaman and employed his entire family in his newspaper offices. When he first heard the shooting in Lawrence, Speer fled his house, leaving his wife unprotected, and hid in a nearby cornfield. Because the Speer house was marked for destruction on the raiders' maps, the structure was soon in flames.

John Speer Jr. worked and slept in the office of the *Lawrence Journal*, which was around the corner from the *Kansas Tribune* office. When he heard the firing, he ran from the *Journal* office and, with his friend Marcellus M. Murdock, hid in the cellar of a nearby building. There they would have been safe except John Jr. ran into the street and was shot down by the guerrillas.

Seventeen-year-old Robert Speer was a printer for the *Lawrence Republican* and a private in the militia. The *Lawrence Republican* building was marked for destruction and torched, and Robert was presumed to have perished in the flames along with David Purinton, but their bodies were never recovered. The *Kansas Tribune* office, across the street from the Free State Hotel, was also destroyed.[64]

Fifteen-year-old William Speer was stopped in the street by guerrillas who checked to see if his name was on their list. Because William gave them a false name, he was allowed to go his way unharmed.

Any house with porch steps made from gravestones stolen from Missouri cemeteries as well as any house where any property was recognized as stolen from Missouri raised the guerrillas' wrath and indignation. They felt compelled to use the torch freely in such instances.

At the corner of Indiana and Winthrop Streets the guerrillas came to the home of Dr. Jerome F. Griswold, the town druggist. Griswold had three families boarding with him. They included Josiah C. Trask and his wife, Simeon M. Thorpe and his family, and Harlow W. Baker and his wife. Trask was editor of the *Lawrence Journal* and a drillmaster for Lawrence's militia.[65] Thorpe was a state senator and a marked man, as was Baker, who belonged to the Seventh Kansas Jayhawker Regiment. Baker was also the partner of Peter Ridenour, who ran a general merchandise business. Supposedly many stolen goods from Missouri were bought at auction then sold in Ridenour and Baker's store.

Griswold, Trask, Thorpe, and Baker were armed with revolvers but afraid to use them. When the guerrillas demanded their surrender, they meekly dropped their weapons and held up their hands. As soon as they recognized the four men, the guerrillas marched them a short distance from the house and shot them in the street. Griswold and Trask were killed immediately, but Thorpe and Baker were so badly wounded that the guerrillas left them for dead. Thorpe later succumbed from his wounds, but Baker recovered.

Mayor George Washington Collamore lived just to the north of the Griswold place. Collamore's house was well known and quickly surrounded because it was expected to be a place of resistance. Collamore knew that he would find no mercy from the guerrillas. So he and a hired man, Patrick Keith, hid from the invaders by lowering themselves into a well behind the house. The house was soon engulfed in flames, and the smoke from the fire swept over the mouth of the well and suffocated the two men. After the guerrillas abandoned Lawrence, a friend of Collamore's, Capt. Joseph G. Lowe of the Seventh Kansas Jayhawker Regiment, tried to rescue the two men by lowering himself into the well. The rope broke, killing Lowe. Thus three men perished in this one hiding place.

Many of Lawrence's militiamen were caught unawares due to the swift arrival of Quantrill's company. Many ran away at the first sound of gunfire while some hid themselves and others tried to find their companies.

When the attack first started, Kansas militiaman Henry S. Clarke grabbed his gun and ran to seek his company. He was an eyewitness to the early attack on the group of recruits bivouacked in the middle of town as the guerrillas made their initial charge. Clarke owned a furniture store in the eight hundred block of Massachusetts Street. He quickly gave his wife the bulk of his money, and when the guerrillas came to his door, he tried to use this to bargain for his life. They took the money and spared him but informed Clarke that his house was to be burned. After allowing the Clarkes to remove their possessions, the raiders applied the torch to their house.

One old score to settle in Lawrence was with Solon O. Thacher. He was the presiding judge who pronounced the death sentence on William Griffith, one of the men who participated in the shooting of the jayhawkers along the banks of the Marais des Cygnes River before the war.

Another notorious jayhawker that the guerrillas wanted badly to arrest was Lt. Hugh D. Fisher. Fisher served as a tobacco-chewing chaplain in James Lane's Fifth Kansas Jayhawker Regiment. He was well known and hated for being a party to the 1861 destruction of Osceola. Fisher was also responsible for being the first to arm black soldiers during the war, but most of all, Fisher had gained a nefarious reputation for his plundering of the furniture and assets of Missouri churches. One Kansan remembered that Fisher "succumbed to the rampant spirit of thievery, and plundered Confederate alt[a]rs in the interest of his unfinished church at home."[66] As a Lawrence pastor, Fisher was accused of mishandling or stealing church funds.[67] He had bravely helped to shell the defenseless town of Osceola, but now he ran in cowardly fashion to the cellar of his substantial brick house and hid behind a pile of dirt.

Fisher had been ill but had awakened around four o'clock on the morning of the raid by the sound of horse hoofs directly in front of his home. He quickly ran to his barn and released the horses there because his life and property were sure to be forfeited if the guerrillas recognized them. Soon four guerrillas came to the door of the Fisher home and demanded his surrender. When Fisher's wife told them that he had left, they knew he had not had sufficient time to escape, so they brushed past her and searched the house. After not finding their man, the guerrillas informed the woman that the house was to be destroyed. The guerrillas soon put the building to the torch. One man remained behind to prevent anyone from extinguishing the blaze. The guard left as soon as he determined that nothing could save the house. Fisher's wife ran back into the house and yelled to him through the floorboards to lie down and she would roll him up in a carpet and drag him out of the house. In this way she saved his life.

Fisher's two sons ran from the house and made for a nearby hazel grove. There Willie Fisher found Robert Martin, a teenager in a blue uniform, carrying a musket and a cartridge box slung over his shoulder. When the guerrillas spotted them, they were chased down, and Martin was shot. Willie Fisher was not harmed.

Another man the guerrillas wanted desperately to find was former governor Charles Robinson. He had been the agent responsible for bringing the first contingents of the radical abolitionist organization, the New England Emigrant Aid Society, to Lawrence. Robinson likewise served as the commander in chief of the antislavery forces in Kansas. He had also thwarted the territorial laws and caused much bloodshed between the early settlers. Staying with Robinson that day was another notorious jayhawker, Gen. George W. Deitzler, head of the First Kansas Jayhawker Regiment. The general had just returned from a jayhawking expedition into Missouri where he had ransacked the store of a Kansas City Unionist.

A detachment of guerrillas was sent to capture Robinson, but because his house was near the riverbank, fire from a Federal contingent on the opposite riverbank prevented the guerrillas from approaching the house.

George Holt and John Lewis Crane were partners in a shoe store in Lawrence. They were arrested and detained when another guerrilla rode up and
recognized them. He shouted, "They have been in Missouri killing our
people." The two men were immediately shot down.

Many of the soldiers killed during the raid were either former jayhawkers
or militiamen on active duty who were home on furlough.

The name of Frederick Kimball, an early member of the New England
Emigrant Aid Society and a private in Company B of Jennison's dreaded Seventh Kansas Jayhawking Cavalry, was on the guerrillas' list. He was killed. In
fact, the criminal careers of many jayhawkers were ended in the dust of Lawrence's streets or in the parlors of their homes. Cpl. John Green and Pvt.
James Woods from Company H of the Seventh Kansas Jayhawker Cavalry
were killed, as was Charles Smith of the same regiment. Pvt. John Read had
long since run away by the time the guerrillas broke into his house searching
for him, but the guerrillas did find Pvt. Christopher Leonard of Company E,
Eighth Kansas Jayhawker Regiment, and Rich Loomis and James O'Neil
both of Company I of the Second Kansas Jayhawker Regiment; all were
killed. Sgt. Jacob McFadden of the Kansas militia was killed, as was Sgt.
Michael Martin and Nathan McFarland. Also killed was Pvt. Jacob Pollock
of Company D of the Fourteenth Kansas Jayhawker Regiment. Samuel
Reynolds of the Sixteenth Kansas Jayhawker Regiment was killed, as was
Pvt. Louis Wise of the Eighth Kansas Jayhawker Regiment.[68]

In contrast to the cowardly way the men of Lawrence behaved, the
women of the town offered the most resistance. Guerrilla Frank Smith noted:
"The heroic devotion of the women shone out amid the black wreck of things,
a star. Many a husband was saved by his wife; many a lover by his sweetheart.
Something about most of the guerrillas was human, if the way to reach that
something was only hit upon. During the fighting many of the women were
brave enough to bring out cakes and pies to offer to the guerrillas, but few of
them touched them out of fear that they were poisoned." After the raid,
Quantrill similarly remarked: "The women of Lawrence were the bravest lot I
have ever encountered, but the men were a damn set of cowards."[69]

One of the women noted: "The universal testimony of all the ladies and
others who talked with the butchers of the 21st . . . is that these demons
claimed they were here to revenge the wrongs done their families by our men
under Lane, Jennison, Anthony and Co. They said they would be more merciful than were these men when they went into Missouri."[70]

With the killing finished, and with William H. Gregg by his side,
Quantrill turned to his men and said, "Give the Kansas people a taste of what

the Missourian has suffered at the hands of the Kansas Jayhawker."[71] Soon much of Lawrence was in flames. Three hundred buildings comprised the town; the guerrillas singled out around forty for destruction, mostly in the commercial district that housed or made their business by dealing in plundered goods. Because other buildings caught fire and suffered collateral damage due to their proximity to the condemned buildings, more than eighty buildings were eventually destroyed in the flames.[72]

Despite the attack and the execution of the men whose names were on the death lists, the guerrillas also showed many kindnesses and acts of mercy. A judge was killed in the yard of Henry S. Clarke, but Col. John D. Holt, one of the Confederate officers with the expedition, saved the lives of Clarke and many others. Samuel A. Riggs was saved by his heroic wife from Peyton Long, one of the best pistol shots in Quantrill's command. Riggs's wife seized the guerrilla's horse by the bridle, causing it, a high-spirited animal, to rear up suddenly. Long relented when she explained that she wished to save her husband. Gregg saved the house of Frederick Reed from destruction, and in saving it, he saved Reed's life, because the man was hiding in the garret.

On another instance, a man known as Savage and his wife, Mary, were fleeing the burning town in a buggy accompanied by a German immigrant-soldier in a blue uniform. When spotted by the guerrillas, Savage jumped down and escaped into a field of corn. When the buggy was stopped, the German was ordered to step down. Mary Savage pleaded with the guerrillas to spare the German's life. After looking the man over carefully and seeing him trembling for his life, they decided to release him.

Contrary to what others have written, Quantrill ordered the bloodshed at Lawrence to be minimal. The refugee Savage noted: "It would have been much worse for Lawrence if Quantrill had not been along."[73] John Newman Edwards added: "Quantrill, during the entire occupation, did not fire his pistol. He saw everything, directed everything, was the one iron man, watchful and vigilant through everything; but he did not kill. He saved many."[74]

Years after the war, an article from the *Cincinnati Enquirer*, reprinted in the April 22, 1898, *Topeka Mail and Breezem*, asserted: "As a matter of fact investigation has shown that Quantrill's methods of warfare were not looked upon with favor by some. He was too humane, and generally shrank from the needless taking of human life. He led the 300 guerrillas against Lawrence, Kansas, and helped sack the town of Olathe, but those living today, who were under his command on those memorable occasions have testified that Quantrill's horror of needless blood-spilling held his men very much in check and minimized the slaughter."

In one instance, Cole Younger dragged a very large man with asthma out of his hiding place in a closet. Out of fright and in a hurry, the poor fellow could not articulate his pleas. Younger's pistol was against his heart when the man's wife cried out, "For God's sake do not shoot him; he hasn't slept in a bed for nine years!" This appeal and the asthma made Younger roar out, "I never intended to harm a hair in his head."

Younger saved at least a dozen other lives. Indeed, he killed none save in open battle. At one house he captured five men over whom he put a guard, and at another three, whom he likewise defended and protected.

John Jarrette, not given to tenderness or compassion when Kansans were to be killed, yielded sufficiently to the requirements of his order to save five prisoners who gave him the Masonic sign of recognition. James Little took a wounded man away from a fellow guerrilla because the wounded man, in pleading for his life, had the accent of a Southerner. Andrew Blunt saved a man's life because the man's daughter gave him a cup of coffee. Twenty-year-old George Shepherd rescued a wounded man and two children from a burning house because one of the children had given him a rose. According to John Newman Edwards, Jesse James refrained from shooting a soldier in uniform who had just been smoked out of a cellar by the entreaties of a young girl.[75]

Many have written that Quantrill gave orders to kill every man in Lawrence, but this is not true. Accounts by his lieutenants assert that their orders were to search and shoot only soldiers. John McCorkle reported that Quantrill's orders were to shoot every soldier they saw but in no way harm a woman or child. He emphatically stated that, while in Lawrence, the command was occupied with hunting down men with blue uniforms.[76]

All during the raid the Confederates exhibited their exuberance for revenge. In the midst of the smoke and pillage, all honor was gone and men focused on why they had come to this place. Their revenge was sated on the male population of Lawrence. Those who were found in uniforms and those who were known to further the abolitionist cause were hunted down and killed. The guerrillas carried death lists with only the names of those they were after. Only they and those who resisted were killed.

The facts about the killing at Lawrence prove that many men were saved by Quantrill's own intervention. Most of the guerrillas did no killing at all. Many residents were saved by Quantrill's men, including soldiers in uniform. Richard Cordley of Lawrence reported: "In some instances they advised men to get out of the way. They burned houses, but were not unnecessarily harsh."[77]

The fury of many guerrillas was mistakenly attributed to drunkenness. But Quantrill had never before allowed his soldiers to drink before a raid, and he was not inclined to do so at Lawrence since the risks in getting back to Missouri were higher than they were in getting to Lawrence. In battle, Quantrill did not permit his men to be anything but of "keen mind and body." Subsequent eyewitness reports after the raid note that the raiders approached the many houses not marked for destruction and asked for water, not whiskey. Only sick and wounded soldiers used whiskey for medicinal purposes. Its value was inestimable for that purpose. Because each man's success depended on the other, stories of drunkenness during the Lawrence raid should be attributed to sensationalism and to the effect of hatred and revenge that the guerrillas elicited. At the same time, their "fighting blood was up," which made them appear less than rational in their blind fury for revenge. To divert scrutiny from the motives for the Lawrence raid, the townspeople of Lawrence went to extensive pains to portray the guerrillas as inhuman.

Stories that surfaced after the raid were embellished to show that the citizens often outwitted the stupid guerrillas by ingenious actions. Preposterous stories—many more than those just described—surfaced of men disguising themselves as women to escape the guerrillas' attentions. Questions on how a woman's shoes would fit a man or why a woman would be wearing a bonnet indoors at five o'clock in the morning have never been explained.

Other wild stories include the allegation that a young boy was killed because he wore a blue suit made from his father's old uniform, and the guerrillas mistook him for a soldier. As was mentioned earlier, the rifles in the armory were reported afterward to be useless and rusty, even though they had just been received from the Federal government and confidently stored in the city armory for an emergency of this kind.

Lawrence was home to twelve hundred citizens in 1863. There were approximately three hundred buildings in a one-square-mile area making up the town.[78] Some accounts after the war claimed that all the men in town were killed and every building was burned down, but this was not even close to the truth. In an account of the pursuit of the guerrillas from Lawrence to Missouri, Pvt. Albert Greene reported that a rider approached him and exclaimed, "Lawrence is in ashes and every man, woman and child in the town is dead."[79] In fact, 148 men were killed and 87 buildings were destroyed.[80]

After the raid, the people of Lawrence protested their innocence of any wrongdoing or involvement in the looting and plundering of Missouri farms. Subsequent accounts of the attack on Lawrence omitted all military titles in conjunction with the names of the dead.

Accounts of brutality and the statements of dying men were recorded by individuals who were not present to witness their deaths. John Speer's account includes pictures of his slain sons as preadolescents when in fact they were fifteen and seventeen years old at the time of the raid, which was comparable to the ages of many of Quantrill's men. The ages of Speer's sons have been falsely listed by most historians as being much younger than they were in order to discredit the actions of the raiders. Many of Quantrill's men were teenagers during the raid, some being as young as fourteen and fifteen years old.

Sensationalism dominated the reporting of the raid. Even the Eastern press ran stories of and woodcuts depicted Quantrill's men killing women and children, although no such deaths were reported. It is true that many of the town's stores were plundered, mostly for hard U.S. currency. There was no small need for the money. Prior to the raid, Quantrill confided to Gregg: "I want to compensate the people who have divided their last biscuit with us and are still willing to do so." Since so many Missourians were made destitute by Lane's jayhawking raids, Quantrill's men distributed the funds they gathered in Lawrence to these needy families. John Jarrette allegedly toted more than eight thousand dollars in his saddlebags from a Lawrence bank. Afterward Quantrill said, "My plan is that whatever money may be gotten in Lawrence shall be divided among the men with instructions to give to these needy people very liberally."[81]

After four hours of killing and plundering, the guerrillas drifted slowly back down Massachusetts Street. Behind them a large portion of Lawrence was in flames. Evidence that Lawrence was an armed camp was realized as stocks of gunpowder that had been stored for the defense of the town intermittently exploded, giving off the smell of powder mixed with the scent of burning merchandise and stores.

By nine o'clock that morning, Quantrill issued orders to his lieutenants to form their men and take account of all those present. He did not intend to leave anyone behind to fall into the hands of the enemy. As the muster took place, lookouts on Mount Oread noticed a distant blue line approaching from the east. When they rode off, they looked back. Lawrence and all it stood for was behind them. Jayhawkers and hated enemies lay in the blood and dust of the streets. With an almost perfect blend of nerve, stealth, and timing, the expedition to Lawrence was one of the most remarkable cavalry raids of the war.

10

After Lawrence

The essence of war is violence. Moderation in war is imbecility.

JOHN A. FISHER

HE PICKETS ON Mount Oread, the high hill a half-mile south of Lawrence, spotted dust raised by approaching Federals more than ten miles away. The hill was 150 feet high and overlooked a treeless prairie, making it an ideal lookout point. When the pickets reported this news to Quantrill, he asked how many there were. The pickets replied that the whole country was alive with them. With this news Quantrill gave the order to begin a slow pullback onto Massachusetts Street. The rest of the pickets were called in from Mount Oread to lead the column southward and out of Lawrence. Quantrill passed the word to his lieutenants: "All right now. Four hours of this is all any man can stand. 'Formation mount!' We all ride to Missouri in a body."

Many of the guerrillas were still in a fighting mood and voted to continue the fight. Quantrill turned to them and replied, "No, we will not fight them." The guerrillas shouting for a fight demanded to know why. "There's more than one reason," Quantrill replied. "In the first place, we haven't got enough ammunition to make a stand; in the second place, our horses are not able to make a charge."

Quantrill, turning to George Todd, said: "George, get your company and fall into the rear. Check them and hold them back as long as you can till I can get the men strung out to moving."[1]

Even though the pickets had reported seeing a Federal relief party approaching the city, Quantrill believed he had enough time to make his withdrawal a path of destruction by spreading out his column and putting anything to the torch that his men came across.

At about 9 o'clock the raiders gathered to the south of the area where the first action had taken place: the camps of the recruits. Here they collected what they were taking with them and secured it to their saddles. When that was completed, Quantrill gave the order to move south along the Fort Scott road toward the Wakarusa River.

Before the column had had a chance to cross, Frank James approached Quantrill and reported that about sixty Redlegs had entered Lawrence after their departure. He asked if the colonel wanted him to take some men back and clean them out since they were only a mile back to town. Quantrill knew that it was too late. It was time to get his command out of Kansas as best he could. He replied, "No. Look to the east, look to the northwest. Boys, you'll get all you want of it before the day is over. It's going to be a running fight all the way back and I'm going to need every one of you."[2]

Before leaving Lawrence, William H. Gregg was given orders to take twenty men and scour the place to see that every man was withdrawing. One man, Larkin Skaggs, however, escaped the vigilance of the guard and remained in town, where he soon met a horrible fate. Skaggs was a Cass County guerrilla who had joined Quantrill just before the raid on Lawrence.

James C. Horton of Lawrence described the guerrilla's demise: "Skaggs rode near a squad of armed men, who shot him off his horse. One of these men got a rope tied about Skaggs neck and about the pummel of his saddle, dragged the dead body through the streets, until the body was nude and terribly mutilated. Then hanged the body and further mutilated it by cutting it with knives, shooting and throwing rocks, clubs, etc."[3]

The citizens also scalped him. They then made an unsuccessful attempt to burn the body, and it was later thrown into a ravine and left exposed all winter. The blacks sawed rings off Skaggs's fingers, and the body was never buried.[4] The scalping was the first instance recorded by the pro-Union forces.

When asked, "Did Quantrill's men do anything that mean in Lawrence?" Horton answered, "They did not." He had been captured at the Eldridge Hotel and by chance was part of a group of captives under Quantrill's protection; otherwise he might have been killed also. Horton added that if there was a woman or child harmed by Quantrill's men at Lawrence, "I never heard of it."[5]

Knowing it would slow down his pursuers, Quantrill ordered the destruction of Blanton's Bridge on the Fort Scott road across the Wakarusa River.

He detailed Gregg, with twenty men, to a place to the right of the column, and Bill Anderson, with twenty men, to a place to the left of the column, to burn a wide swath as they marched back parallel with the main body. Gregg's group included Frank James, Arch Clements, Jim Little, Ben Morrow, and Harrison Trow. Anderson's detail included Clark Hockensmith, Peyton Long, Andy McGuire, Allen Parmer, Hicks George, Hi George, and Doc Campbell. The mission of destruction covered twelve miles from Lawrence and was over a mile wide. When Quantrill was pressed too heavily in the rear by the Federals, he recalled his detachments to look after the safety of his aggregate columns.[6]

Dick Yeager, with twenty men, was in charge of the advance; Gregg held the rear with sixty. Tom Hamilton and another guerrilla had been wounded while in Lawrence. They were placed in an ambulance and brought up with the advance guard.

The pursuing Federals recovered many guns the citizens in Lawrence had thrown away. James Lane regained his composure from the indignity of running away in his nightshirt, leaving his home defenseless, and rallied around him more than one hundred of the townspeople, armed and with enough horses to follow the raiders south. Joining him were several Union soldiers who had returned after running away during the destruction in Lawrence.

At a spot along their withdrawal from Lawrence, the raiders stopped and clustered around the residence of Lathrop Bullene. John C. Shea recollected that George Todd ordered that the house should not be burned. Food was brought out and given to the raiders. The guerrillas also took from the stable three horses. One of the men asked the woman of the house for something to eat. The woman, Shea noted, was from Wisconsin, and she waited on the young man then voiced her opinion that it was outrageous for the guerrillas to have shot down unarmed men in the streets of Lawrence.

Said the bushwhacker in reply, almost fiercely: "I had two sisters arrested in Kansas City by Union men for entertaining Southern sentiments. They were imprisoned in a dilapidated building used as a guardhouse. The building was known to be unsafe, and besides it was undermined. One night that building fell, and my two sisters, with three other ladies were crushed to death." The young man paused for a moment, and then continued excitedly: "Jennison had laid waste our homes, and your 'Redlegs' have perpetrated unheard of crimes, I am here for revenge, and I have got it."[7]

Other writers have tried to identify the young man as William Anderson. But the evidence points instead to fourteen-year-old Riley Crawford, who lost two sisters in the collapse.

As the raiders withdrew through the tiny hamlet of Brooklyn, they burned the village behind them. Attempting to follow the Santa Fe Trail eastward, the raiders were alerted to Federal troops closing in on them from that direction.

Gregg was ordered to remain stationary until the main command could manage to get to the nearby timber. After Gregg guarded the column into the timber, he and his sixty men slowly withdrew, rejoining the main column, until he found Quantrill waiting for him with these orders: "Form your sixty men in skirmish line and hold the rear, fall back on me whenever it may be necessary, but whatever you do, don't let them break your line." Before Gregg had completed his skirmish line, the enemy, now twelve hundred strong, was upon him and the battle was on.[8]

Quantrill rode at the head of the column. Falling back on his alternate route of withdrawal, he doubled back and headed southward toward Paola.

In command of the troops closing in on Quantrill's rear was Maj. Preston B. Plumb, Thomas Ewing's chief of staff. Plumb had only received word about a large body of guerrillas crossing the border at half-past midnight. He hurriedly passed the word to Ewing, who was at Fort Leavenworth, then gathered up fifty Redlegs from Ewing's headquarters in Kansas City and started out in pursuit. Since Plumb did not know the objective of the raiders, he led the column to the garrison in Olathe. After reaching Olathe at dawn, Plumb was told that the raiders had headed toward Lawrence, so he turned his troops in that direction. When he was within six miles of Lawrence, Plumb ran into 180 cavalrymen led by Capt. Charles F. Coleman and added them to his command. Looking toward the south, Plumb saw smoke rising from the wake of Quantrill's forces. He swung his forces toward the tiny hamlet of Baldwin in hopes of overtaking the guerrillas before they could get across the border.

For ten miles farther the guerrillas rode with their pursuers warily out of reach and refusing to charge, even though the Federals had overwhelming numbers and were capable of overwhelming everything in opposition to them. Instead, the Union troops contented themselves with firing on Quantrill's men at long range.

The guerrillas, relying principally upon dash and their revolvers, felt the need of a charge. Quantrill halted the column to charge, turned about quickly, and quickly dressed up in line. As soon as George Todd trotted up, he fell into line on the left, and Quantrill gave the word.

Plumb's men hardly had time to fire a volley before they were rent to shreds and scattered over the prairie.[9] One of the pursuers, Pvt. Albert R. Greene, recalled the scene:

We got a few shots but did no execution. Their rear guard was commanded by a daring fellow, and the horsemanship of the dozen men who covered the retreat was superb. These men carried no plunder and their horses were guided entirely by the legs of the rider, leaving both hands free to use [their] revolvers. When they finally turned to race after their command the riders bent far forward, almost to the necks of their horses, and seemed to be a part of them. . . . The Rebels had invited us to come on and made a number of uncomplimentary remarks reflecting on our courage and scandalizing our ancestry when they saw we were disinclined to accept a challenge on the basis of 25 to 1, all of which had a nettling effect and made us impatient of delay.[10]

Later that evening, when Quantrill's column was within five or six miles of the town of Aubry, Dick Yeager, leading the advance, suddenly turned to the left. Quantrill remarked, "Boys, there's something wrong, or Dick Yeager would not have turned off." When the guerrillas reached the top of a ridge, they discovered a Federal regiment formed in line of battle. The Union men stayed in line until Quantrill's entire command had passed; the Federals never made a move or fired a shot. If they had charged, with Plumb's column in Quantrill's rear, none of the guerrillas would likely have escaped.[11] The

Federals only grouped and continued to close in. Quantrill's rear guard, however, began firing, signaling how close the Northerners were to them.

Quantrill's command went west, through a lane, until the colonel ordered his men to form in line. When the following Federals came into sight, riding through a cornfield, Quantrill ordered a charge. But this action only pushed the Union troops back a short distance. After the guerrillas fell back, the Federals soon closed up.

Some of Quantrill's men, becoming excited, broke ranks and rushed to the advance guard. The colonel immediately formed the rest of his men into line and ordered them to shoot anyone who attempted to pass. When the men had been quieted and reformed, he said to them, "Now if any of you intend to break ranks again, do it now; if you stay with me and act like men, I can get you out of this, but if you are going to run, go now, but do not come back to me." After this not a man broke ranks again. The command withdrew in line of battle, and each time the Federals approached too close, Quantrill ordered his men to face about, causing the Northerners to stop, expecting a charge.[12]

At one point, as the Federals were coming dangerously close to the rear of Quantrill's column, a rider reported this situation to Quantrill. "How do they look?" the guerrilla chieftain asked. The man replied, "Like thirsty buffaloes making for a water course." Quantrill asked, "Can't the rear guard check them?" The rider answered, "Can a grasshopper throw a locomotive off the track?"

William H. Gregg had been holding the rear against a larger force for more than five hours. He later commented that the Kansans "accuse us of killing their citizens, which is not true, for in that day Kansas had no citizens. They were all soldiers, armed, equipped and ready for the fray. As evidence of this fact, they had 5,000 men at our heels in two hours after we left Lawrence, whom we kept at bay with sixty men." Gregg's voice, hoarse from shouting orders for five hours, was beginning to fail him, and when he reported his condition to Quantrill, the colonel ordered George Todd to take over the rear guard.

The guerrillas had just entered a lane running south through a large cornfield. They scattered in all directions after riding out the lane into the open prairie. Frank Smith observed that the men became panicky and added, "This was the most excited I ever saw Quantrill's outfit."

Todd realized that the enemy must be checked or the column would be in danger. As a result, his bravery and quick thinking saved the guerrillas from the most hazardous situation they were in at any time during the raid. Todd dismounted at the mouth of the lane and stood there holding his horse's bridle and swearing at the top of his voice to the remaining guerrillas as they came to him. "Boys!" he commanded, "let down those rail fences. Part of you go up one side through the corn and part of you follow me right up to the lane and by God we'll charge them. We've got to check them or the whole outfit is lost."

With only twenty men, Todd charged the enemy, firing pistols almost in the faces of their foe. Todd's horse Sam Gaty, which he had captured off the riverboat by the same name, was shot out from under him. Todd jumped clear and threw off his short Union officer's coat, which also held four thousand dollars he had taken from Lawrence. The enemy's front rank went down in a tangle of wounded horses and cursing men.

Upon Todd's return to the main column, Quantrill rode up to him and shouted, "Todd, if there is a man that can hold the rear, you can. Cut out fifty or sixty of the best men for a rear guard. Throw out a skirmish line. I know the country and will take the main body and lead the outfit out. If I run into any Federals in front of me I'm going to cut right through them."[13]

Todd immediately set about organizing the rear guard. For this important mission he selected the best men from Anderson's, Blunt's, Yeager's, and Quantrill's companies.

On the whole, the guerrillas were worn down and dead tired. Even though most of them had taken extra horses with them, many of these animals were laden with plunder. At various points, the guerrillas discarded what they had and left the loot on the open prairie. Albert Greene noted, "Packages of plunder lined the way. Piles of felt hats nested together, bolts of broadcloth, of silk, of calico, shoes tied in bundles; clothing of all sorts and description; shelf hardware and cutlery, table war, etc."[14] Adding to the men's misery was the intense August heat. But the heat also overcame the Federal pursuers.

After such a long ride, it was nearly impossible for the Union pursuers to keep up with the magnificent horsemen they were following. The horses that the guerrillas had taken from Lawrence as extra mounts were not able to take the strain and were shot when they gave out.

All morning and late into the afternoon the guerrillas maintained the withdrawal from Lawrence, and all the way the Federals persistently dogged their trail. Heading southward and toward evening, Quantrill suddenly swung his men eastward. Close to seven o'clock, as the sun was setting, the raiders found themselves outside the Federal outpost at Paola, Kansas. Quantrill surveyed the tiny hamlet through his spyglass and saw a hundred Union soldiers milling about the town.

Maj. Preston B. Plumb had just received a company of fresh troops from the Kansas militia when the raiders entered the timbered heights of Bull

Creek. Emboldened by fresh troops, Plumb made a determined charge on
Quantrill's rear guard, driving it into the main body.

"Halt!" ordered Quantrill. "Face about!" The guerrillas turned. Hiram
George remembered that Plumb "was the only man I ever saw carry a black
flag and this was the first black flag I ever saw. It was near Osawatomie. There
were about 290 Quantrill men and about 300 with Plumb."[15] William H.
Gregg recalled:

> Quantrill quickly deployed his entire command into line of battle, con-
> fronted the Federal troops and hollered out. 'Steady men.' 'Charge!' The
> Federals were only sixty yards away. The men charged, the enemy stood.
> Our men were thinning their ranks, the enemy were falling thick and fast.
> Their line began to break. Quantrill ordered another charge, our boys went
> at them again and drove them pell-mell like a drove of sheep, for half a mile
> or more. Seeing an enemy so emboldened and with the reputation that
> Quantrill's guerrillas shared along the border the Federals quickly halted
> and simply stood watching the guerrillas as they deployed back into column
> and resumed their march, this time turning back north to bypass the town
> of Paola. In all this fighting covering a distance of more than twenty-five
> miles, the fighting never ceased for a single moment, yet this little band of
> heroes, came out of it all unscathed. Not a man of them being touched.[16]

After this Plumb lacked either the heart or the stomach for further battle
with Quantrill's men. So instead of continuing his pursuit, he turned his
company toward Paola and turned over his command to Lt. Col. Charles S.
Clark, who had just arrived from Spring Hill with thirty men.

As darkness fell, other companies of Federals angled their way toward
Quantrill's command. In Kansas City a hundred Union troops were mustered
and pushed south toward the border. From Spring Hill two hundred Federals
with artillery were on the move. Behind them another fifty soldiers were
riding to join them. Three miles south of Kansas City, in Westport, Maj.
Luin K. Thacher of the Ninth Kansas Jayhawker Regiment was busy assembling men from the area. He managed to mount eighty soldiers and sent
them west, toward Lawrence. With the alarm being spread by couriers and
civilian riders, all of Kansas was alerted within hours. The civilian population
dropped the pretense of innocent shopkeepers and farmers and raced into
uniform to join their militia units.

It was getting dark, and in the faint light Quantrill took his main column
over the summit of Big Hill, two miles northwest of Paola. He rode to the

front of the column and halted until the rear guard under Todd came up. Once they arrived, Quantrill formed his men again into line of battle and informed them, "I'm going to charge them again and I want every man that's got a horse able to gallop to come with me."[17] He seized the opportunity for the greatest military advantage. Quantrill knew an all-out charge with the wild Rebel Yell and blazing pistols would finally scatter his pursuers and enable his command to scatter into the darkness of the nearby timber.

Lt. Cyrus Leland was at the head of forty militiamen in the advance of hundreds of Union soldiers. They drew rein to decipher the growing noise coming from behind the crest of the hill to their front. Halfway up the hill Leland and his men saw what they feared most: two hundred screaming Rebels charging down the hill toward them. Forgetting military discipline, the Federals ran for their lives. Quantrill had struck at precisely this moment knowing that the demoralized and fearful Federals would take so much time to regroup that he could lead his command to safety as darkness fell, making further pursuit almost impossible.

To justify the inability of his soldiers to bring Quantrill to bay, Gen. Thomas Ewing stated, "Quantrill skillfully kept . . . his best mounted and best trained men in the rear, and often formed line of battle, to delay pursuit and give time and rest to the most wearied of his forces. By the time our scattered soldiers and citizens could get up and form line, the guerrilla's rear guard would, after a volley, break into column, and move off at a speed that defied pursuit."[18]

The raiders had been in the saddle for three days without sleep. They had had very little water or food, and now that their resistance was low, the only thing that held them together was the discipline and training they had learned under their capable leader. No other commander could have maintained unit cohesion under such circumstances. On their way to Lawrence, when they were fresh in the saddle and eager for the fray, the guerrillas wanted no more than to fight and avenge the wrongs done by the Kansas jayhawkers. They knew in all probability that they would be killed in this daring raid on Lawrence. Now that the raid had been completed, and they had headed their mounts toward the Missouri border, they thought they might have at least a slim chance of escape. Behind them the countryside looked black with Federal soldiers closing upon their rear. They trusted their own horsemanship and knowledge of the terrain to outdistance their pursuers. With the Missouri border in view, many of the raiders wanted nothing more than to spur their mounts and escape individually into the brush of familiar territory. Here was the true test of Quantrill's leadership. Only by the discipline he held over his men and the faith they had in his tactics did they rally to his leadership. Quantrill knew his command was a potent fighting unit as long as he could keep his men together. His powerful and forceful orders were reassuring to the tired and anxious raiders.

At ten o'clock that night Quantrill marched his command another five miles to a branch of Bull Creek. There he let the men rest and water their horses. Around eleven o'clock he issued orders for the men to remove their horse's saddles and let them graze on the grass, but the men were not yet allowed to sleep. After only an hour's respite, scouts reported an approaching Federal column. Quantrill and his officers forced their groggy soldiers to their feet and back into their saddles, and the command continued the ride into the night. They entered Missouri a little south of where they had exited the state.

At midnight Maj. Luin K. Thacher reached Olathe with more than a hundred men. Only miles away two hundred more Union troops were riding hard and fast for Paola. Close to Osawatomie a Federal company was also riding toward Paola. By nightfall more than five hundred Northern soldiers had gathered in Paola to block Quantrill's escape to Missouri.

Along the border, Lt. Col. Walter King and the Fourth Missouri Militia were in the saddle and also heading for Paola. During the night Paola hosted more than a thousand Union soldiers and Kansas militia. As the guerrilla column made its way toward the heavy timber in Missouri, King saw the shadows of a large body of riders heading east. He immediately threw out his skirmishers and ordered a slow movement forward, expecting at any time the staccato sound of gunfire.

Sensing the enemy to his front, Quantrill knew that to stand and fight would allow more pursuing Federals to catch up, and the noise of battle would give away his position. He wisely slid around the enemy's flank and melted into the darkness. After a long delay, King's men finally realized their prey had slipped from their grasp and escaped into the night.

Getting close to home now, Quantrill was forced to abandon the ambulance with Jim Bledsoe and two of Colonel Holt's wounded recruits. Placing them in the woods close to a sympathetic farmer, he believed this would offer them their best chance of survival.

But it was not long before Redlegs under George Hoyt tracked down the wounded men. While preparing to shoot them, the recruits pleaded for mercy. Bledsoe bravely scolded them, "Stop it! We are not entitled to mercy! We spare none and do not expect to be spared!" With this the Redlegs killed all three men and introduced a new atrocity to the border war: They scalped all three corpses. After this they continued to track down any guerrillas they found as well as any farmers who they believed might have aided them. Cold-blooded murder was rampant as the jayhawkers tried to find any trace of the Lawrence raiders. Farmers who did not have adequate explanations were shot down on their doorsteps.[19]

At sunup on August 22, a little after five o'clock, Quantrill's command reached the headwaters of the Grand River in Cass County. As the guerrillas climbed a ridge, they could look back and see that the whole face of the earth behind them was darkened with pursuing Federals. Quantrill turned to those around him and proudly remarked, "Boys, we are back home. Not all the troops in Kansas can catch us now. Now every man who thinks his horse is able, follow me to Big Creek; those not able, take care of yourselves in the timber of the Grand River." The guerrillas rested their horses until the Federals were within a half-mile of them, then they started off across the prairie toward Big Creek.

Later that evening, as they were making their way back toward Missouri, chief scout John McCorkle saw some men to the right of the road in the edge of the timber. He told Quantrill that they were Federals, but the colonel disagreed saying, "No, it's Andy Blunt returning from Johnson County." Blunt had been ordered into Johnson County to the south to lure the Federals away from Jackson and Cass Counties so Quantrill could get his command unnoticed across the border toward Lawrence. Blunt had been instructed, if he could give the Federals the slip, to rendezvous at this point in case Quantrill needed his assistance in making his withdrawal out of Lawrence.

McCorkle, still insisting that the men in the timber were Federals, said to Quantrill, "I reckon you can see their uniforms now and tell who they are."

The colonel replied, "If you are so damned certain of it, ride out and see."

McCorkle started toward the horsemen at a gallop, and two rode out to meet him and started firing.

Quantrill remarked, "That'll do, John; you are right. Come back."

The Federals made a rush at the guerrilla command and fired only one volley, inflicting no damage.

After another mile the command found itself in the Big Creek timber. Halting his command, Quantrill sent small details into the surrounding neighborhoods to search for food. He was scanning the Kansas border with his spyglass when a farmer approached and told him there was a large force of Missouri State Militia just over the next ridge.

Once more the gallant colonel mounted his horse and encouraged his men, "Boys, saddle up, we've got to get going." His men, more hungry than scared, grumbled that they had not yet had time to eat. Quantrill pointed out, "See those Kansans coming across the line?" His men shouted back,

"Damn the Kansans! We whipped them yesterday and can whip them today."
The colonel replied, "Yes, I know you can whip the Kansans, but what will
you do with the twelve hundred Missouri troops just over the divide?"

Quantrill's chief concern was to get his main body into the heavy timber.
Only there could he be certain that the Federals would never catch him. By
this time Andy Blunt and his fresh command joined Quantrill's column.
Andy Walker and George Todd were helping themselves to some plums from
a fruit tree when one of the men rode up and reported that five hundred of the
enemy were close by. When Quantrill rejoined the group, he found that Blunt
had his men drawn up in line ready to charge. The colonel rose up in his stirrups and hollered out, "Andy, what are you going to do?" Blunt replied that he
was going to charge. Quantrill yelled back. "No, you're not. Our horses are not
able to make a charge. Follow me and every man take care of himself."

The men agreed that continuing the march was the best thing to do.
Those whose horses were too jaded to continue were ordered to hide themselves in the timber and wait until the Federals followed the main body, then
they could slip back to friends in the Blue and Sni Hills of Jackson County.

The great Lawrence raid was over. Asked afterward to name those who
fought bravest and best during the withdrawal from Lawrence, Quantrill's
simple answer was: "They all fought. No one ever had men to exhibit more
coolness and daring."[20]

Back in Lawrence the citizens were quickly laying out the dead for
burial. Once the newspapers began to carry the story of the raid, sensationalized accounts dominated the news. The *Leavenworth Daily Conservative*
reported 182 buildings were destroyed. The *American Cyclopaedia* for 1863
included this comment on the raid: "The most atrocious outrage of the war
was the attack of Colonel Quantrill and his band of Confederate guerrillas
upon the thriving city of Lawrence on the 21st of August."

Even though he now had two thousand soldiers in his command, Lt. Col.
Charles S. Clark was unable to find any of Quantrill's men. Thinking he could
catch the guerrillas if he divided his force, Clark sent Majs. Preston B. Plumb
and Luin K. Thacher to the north, toward Jackson County, while he searched
to the east.

As darkness set in on August 21, Clark returned to headquarters in
Kansas City and found Gen. Thomas Ewing and George Hoyt with his
Redlegs. They were tired, discouraged, and simply worn out, but one man
there was shrieking and cursing at everyone in sight: Sen. James Lane. Ewing
and Lane withdrew to private quarters and argued into the night about what
the general should do next. Ewing had already issued orders to banish the

families of the disloyal from the border counties, and it had backfired on him when the guerrillas accused him of cold-blooded murder in the collapse of the Kansas City prison. The Kansans were reminded of their crime as the guerrillas shouted down Lawrence's streets during the raid: "Remember the murdered girls!"

While strict measures were being dealt in retaliation, Lane called for something more sinister. He proposed the wholesale banishment of all citizens along the border in a four-county area. Lane envisioned the entire border depopulated of anyone, especially those who could feed and support the guerrillas. Ewing was in a quandary. He was a political general. His position depended on the support of powerful politicians like Lane, and Unionists were clamoring for Ewing's head for his inability to control the guerrilla menace.

On the night of August 21, Ewing and Lane laid out plans to retaliate for the Lawrence raid. Ewing knew he was going to be blamed for the raid and for letting the guerrillas penetrate his defenses. Since his future depended on Lane's patronage, Ewing agreed to depopulate the border counties. Even Gen. John M. Schofield in St. Louis was anxious when he heard that Lane threatened to thwart his confirmation as a major general by the Senate if he did not endorse Ewing's order.

Lane pointedly insisted that Ewing proclaim the banishment edict immediately: "You are a dead dog if you fail to issue that order." Seeking approval from the Union population, Ewing gathered his staff and a few prominent citizens into his headquarters and informed them of his intentions. Some approved, many did not, but the naysayers were too afraid to disagree in the light of what had transpired in Lawrence.

Ewing summoned Maj. Harrison Hannah, his adjutant general, to write out the order from his original draft. After the decree had been officially recorded, Judge William Stevenson observed to Ewing that "it was a very tough order." John Newman Edwards commented: "Some reported that General Order No. 11 was known to have come from district headquarters at St. Louis where Schofield commanded, and through Schofield from Washington City direct. Ewing had neither choice nor discretion in the matter. It is said that he did not originate it, but that he gave it form and as a soldier he had but to obey and to execute."[21]

Gen. George Caleb Bingham was enraged that no aid or protection was afforded the banished inhabitants under Ewing's order. The citizens of the affected area, disarmed by Federal edict, were thrown into an indefensible position.[22] The order itself was a deathblow to the people living in the affected areas. The final edict read:

First. All persons living in Cass, Jackson and Bates counties, Missouri, and in that part of Vernon including in this district, except those living within one mile of the limits of Independence, Hickman's Mills, Pleasant Hill and Harrisonville, and except those in that part of Kaw Township, Jackson County, north of Brush Creek and west of the Big Blue, embracing Kansas City and Westport, are hereby ordered to remove from their present places of residence within fifteen days from the date hereof [August 25, 1863].

Second. All grain and hay in the field, or under shelter, in the district from which the inhabitants are required to remove within reach of military stations, after the 9th day of September next, will be taken to such stations and turned over to the proper officer there, and report of the amount so turned over made to district headquarters, specifying the names of all loyal owners and the amount of such produce taken from them. All grain and hay found in such district after the 9th day of September next, not convenient to such station, will be destroyed. Third: The provisions of General Order No. 10, from these headquarters, will at once be vigorously executed by officers commanding in the parts of the district, and at the stations not subject to the operations of paragraph First of this order—and especially in the towns of Independence, Westport and Kansas City.

Fourth: Paragraph 3, General Order No. 10, is revoked as to all who have borne arms against the government in the district since August 20, 1863.

General Orders No. 11 gave the populace until September 9 to relocate to the Union outposts or leave the area. The population of Cass County before Ewing's order was 9,794; after the order was executed, fewer than 600 were allowed to remain. Supposedly, six thousand soldiers were assigned to implement the order. To Ewing and all the military men in the area, the edict was another blow at fighting the guerrillas. If they could not beat them on the battlefield, they would defeat them by removing the support of the civilian community. General Orders No. 11 was the harshest military measure directed toward a civilian population in American history.

To James Lane and the vengeful Kansans, the order meant that Kansas troops would be used to enforce it. Schofield had earlier prohibited the two state militias from entering the other state without orders from the district commander.[23] Not only did Ewing's order require that Kansas troops enforce the edict in Missouri, he also authorized specific Kansas units to operate in Missouri at the discretion of their commanders.[24] Pressure from political figures—especially Lane—undoubtedly led to this unwise decision to use Kansas troops in Missouri. No small factor in enforcing the edict was the continued looting of the counties. Lane knew that by forcing defenseless civilians to abandon their homes with little notice, all their possessions would have to be left behind, which he could then claim as spoils of war.

During the pursuit of Quantrill's column, many civilian homes were destroyed by Federal troops if even the slightest hint of complicity was brought to mind. Many Union soldiers took this opportunity to settle old scores and murder anyone they had a mind to, covering up the fact by claiming the victims were guerrillas.

But the greatest disappointment of the Federals was that the man who planned and led the raid lived to savor his triumph and bask in its glory. And glory it was. For his role that morning in Lawrence, Quantrill gained the eternal respect and admiration of thousands who had long since given up hope; thousands who felt that, though it had come ever so slowly, justice had finally been done. There was a deep, quiet sense of satisfaction for some; there was a lifting, hardly contained elation for others upon learning that their old foe had been paid back for Osceola, Kansas City, General Orders No. 10, and a slate of other wounds.

And although it was the most punishing ride of their lives, Quantrill had also won the undying allegiance of his men. Indeed, the march to and retreat back had few equals in the war, and it was a feat many in the North might have secretly envied had circumstances been different. Five grueling days in the saddle—more than two hundred miles—across much of occupied western Missouri, through four counties of the most warlike state in the nation, where he had "dodged," "bewildered," and "baffled his pursuers," all with the loss of only a handful of men.[25] Newspapers across the South trumpeted Quantrill's expedition. The *Charleston Mercury* reported, "The whole town swept. A perfect success." In the Confederate capital, the *Richmond Examiner* wrote, "The expedition to Lawrence was a gallant and perfectly fair blow at the enemy, as the population of Kansas is malignant and scoundrelly beyond description."[26]

The Federals accomplished little in their search for the Lawrence raiders. Only a few were found and executed, but most seemed to vanish into thin air. Harrison Trow reported that even with the vast numbers of Federal troops after them, Quantrill still managed to evade capture and oftentimes turned the tables on the Union patrols by ambushes along the dusty roads. To make it impossible for Ewing to engage him in any significant way, Quantrill divided his company up into ten-man patrols. Only rarely did the Federals manage to kill one of his men, and none was ever captured alive.

Abraham Haller, brother to William Haller and a guerrilla of great courage and prowess, was wounded and hiding in some timber near the Texas prairie at the extreme eastern edge of Jackson County. He was alone when a seventy-two-man Federal patrol discovered him. Before they brought him down with rifle fire, he had managed to wound or kill five of his attackers before dying. When they rushed him, they found eleven bullets in his body and both of his pistols empty. The Union men then scalped him and cut off his ears.

An hour later, Andy Blunt found Haller's mutilated body and remarked to his companions: "We have something to learn yet, boys, and we have learned it. Scalp for scalp hereafter!" The next day Blunt, along with Peyton Long, Archie Clements, Bill Anderson, and Andy McGuire, captured four militiamen from northern Missouri then shot them. Afterward Blunt returned the Federals' brutal gesture by scalping all four.

Most of the guerrillas allegedly killed by Union forces were actually civilians or regular Confederate army soldiers on furlough or medical leave. On October 1 Kebil Stovall and two other Southern soldiers home on furlough were killed after surrendering when Kansas jayhawkers raided Wellington.[27]

The rest of the guerrillas had melted into the heavy timber of the Sni and the Blue Hills of Jackson County. Six thousand Federals combed the countryside for Quantrill and his raiders, but despite this threat, Quantrill maintained a tight grip on Bates, Cass, Clay, Jackson, Lafayette, and Vernon Counties.

Back on the Little Blue, Dick Yeager and ten men laid in ambush among the rock outcroppings of a ford along the river when a Missouri militia lieutenant named Blackstone began to cross the water with his troops. Oblivious of any danger, the lieutenant paused in midstream to fill his canteen when Yeager set off the ambush with a deadly volley. Fourteen soldiers fell dead from their horses before the rest realized what had happened. Farther east in Lafayette County, John Jarrette and David Poole, each with ten men, made a raid that resulted in the deaths or wounding of many German-immigrant militiamen. In Jackson County, Quantrill's men crossed back and forth at various places in Blue Springs. Along the Little Blue the Federals hardly ever left the main roads. If they found themselves ambushed by the guerrillas, they would break out and head back to Independence.

Society offered no collective outcry when Lane and his drunken army of scavengers leveled the town of Osceola, Missouri, in September 1861. No army stopped him. Only a handful of women and children ran screaming from their homes as artillery shells rained down on their town. Because of military censorship in Kansas City, the public did not protest the premeditated murders of young girls whose only crime was their relation to men engaged in a partisan war. No John Greenleaf Whittier put his pen to paper when Federal authorities rounded up these women, confined them to a three-story brick building, then undermined the building, causing its collapse and the deaths of five of the women. The banishment of the families of suspected guerrillas was claimed to be a military necessity, but no cry of concern was lifted to bring these injustices to light. Southern sympathizers in western Missouri could only grit their teeth and endure what was to come next.

In mid-1863 there was no Southern press in Missouri, but word of the Lawrence raid made the pages of most of the newspapers in both the North and the South. Northerners decried it as a massacre. Southern papers carried a different story. The *Richmond Daily Dispatch* commented, "Let the guerrilla system . . . be thoroughly carried out and if the barbarous retaliate . . . let the guerrillas, without waiting for orders, exact an eye-for-an-eye and a-life-for-a-life." Only Gen. John M. Schofield was somewhat sympathetic to the plight of Missourians and he wrote to Abraham Lincoln asserting that the guerrillas "all sought vengeance for the radical measures the Union had initiated against them and their friends and relatives."[28]

Since before the war, Missourians had constantly guarded against jayhawking marauders. Now they attempted to checkmate the jayhawkers by retaliating in kind. Jayhawkers had burned Butler, Chapel Hill, Columbus, Dayton, Kingsville, Morristown, Osceola, Papinsville, Pleasant Hill, and West Point in Missouri—and in return, the Missourians burned Lawrence.

Quantrill's sympathizers were too far away to offer anything more than verbal assistance. James Lane, however, was inciting everyone around him to invade Missouri and punish the guerrillas and their abettors once and for all. Gov. Thomas Carney of Kansas immediately reacted to the raid by calling up the jayhawkers. Forgetting the past jayhawker invasions of Missouri, Carney issued a proclamation addressed to Charles Jennison in the *Leavenworth Daily Conservative*: "The State of Kansas is invaded. To meet the invasion, you are hereby authorized to raise all the effective men you can. I call upon all loyal Kansans to aid you. Kansas must be protected at all hazards! The people of Leavenworth, and of every county in the State, will rally to avenge the lawless sacking of Lawrence, and to punish the Rebel invaders of the State."[29]

In the August 23 *Daily Conservative*, Jennison published his own proclamation vowing to march into guerrilla territory and punish anyone who helped the guerrillas.[30] Kansans went rabid attempting to find anyone who did not subscribe to their politics. Some of the townspeople of Lawrence, men and women, were accused of having spied for Quantrill. One man was hanged, and two women were incarcerated at Fort Leavenworth and later released when military and prominent citizens vouched for their actions during the raid. Kansans rushed from their homes and joined their militia units. Governor Carney issued General Orders No. 1, calling the state militia into active service and using inflammatory statements about murders and rapes. An example of the sensationalism accorded the Lawrence raid by the Northern press appeared in the notable *Frank Leslie's Illustrated Newspaper*, which carried lurid images of the raiders killing men and women in Lawrence.

Gen. George Caleb Bingham, Missouri state treasurer and owner of the collapsed building in which the women prisoners died, became Ewing's harshest critic. When Bingham learned of General Orders No. 11, he immediately confronted Ewing in his headquarters and demanded that he rescind the order. Bingham saw no need or cause for the edict. In his eyes, the real bandits of the border were not Quantrill's bushwhackers but Kansas Redlegs who carried on their "nefarious operations under the protection and patronage of General Ewing."[31] Bingham's pleadings went unheeded.

As he left Ewing's office, Bingham promised: "If you persist in executing that order, I will make you infamous with pen and brush as far as I am able." Bingham was an artist of no small renown, and he painted a picture titled *Order No. 11, Martial Law*, which portrayed a likeness of Ewing in red leggings commanding a jayhawker raid on a Missouri farm. The painting shows a contingent of soldiers who have just shot down a man's young son and are threatening to shoot the aged father while crying women plead for mercy. In the background, Kansans loot the house while refugees carry whatever belongings they can down the road to exile amid burning farms and fields.

According to Bingham, General Orders No. 11 was "an act of purely arbitrary power, directed against a disarmed and defenseless population in violation of every principal of justice." He claimed the order was inspired by vengeance and issued by Ewing to curry favor with the Kansas "mob" and advance his political ambitions. Bingham said, "Scarcely was the ink dry upon the paper, when like a pack of infuriated and starved bloodhounds they were unleashed and turned loose upon the horror stricken communities. Never was a robbery so stupendous, more cunningly devised or successfully accomplished, with less personal risk to the robbers."[32] Months later, Bingham wrote on February 22 from Jefferson City:

General Ewing has doubtless discovered that his crowning military achievement of 1863, was not of a nature as well calculated to secure the favor of the Democracy with whom he is now associated, as it was to win to his support the "Jayhawkers" and corrupt rabble of Kansas, through whose aid, there is reason to believe, he then looked for political preferment, and thence his effort arising from necessities of his shifted aspirations, to secure for it a gloss, which his associate in responsibility therefore has endeavored to put upon it, at the sacrifice alike of justice and truth.

After the Lawrence raid, all Kansas chafed at the bit to retaliate and plunder Missouri. Turned down by General Schofield, who came from St. Louis to talk to him, Lane was told that no mob force would be allowed to raid the border counties. Not to be deterred, Lane and the Kansas militia entered Missouri under the guise of Federal troops to supposedly carry out the terms of Ewing's General Orders No. 11. Under this pretext, the Kansans executed the edict with such effectiveness and thoroughness that the region was later referred to as "the Burnt District."

Many Southerners believed that Lincoln himself endorsed Ewing's General Orders No. 11. The president took an involved stance on most major military decisions along the border. When Gen. John C. Frémont issued an emancipation proclamation to Missouri slaves early in the war, the president believed it to be too radical at the time and had Frémont rescind the order.

Gen. John M. Schofield ultimately approved the banishment edict and submitted an explanation to the War Department: "The evil which exists upon the border of Kansas and Missouri is somewhat different in kind and far greater in degree than in other parts of Missouri. It is the old border hatred intensified by the rebellion and by the murders, robberies, and arson, which have characterized the irregular warfare carried on during the early period of the rebellion, not only by the Rebels, but by our own troops and people."[33]

Ewing, in defending himself, then quoted one of the biggest lies during the war to explain General Orders No. 11: "The order was an act of wisdom, courage and humanity, by which hundreds of innocent lives were saved and a disgraceful and barbarous warfare brought to a summary close. Not a life was sacrificed, nor any great discomfort inflicted in executing it. The necessities of all the poor people were provided for, and none were permitted to suffer." To this George Caleb Bingham responded:

Never did an equal number of words embody a greater amount of error. Never was robbery so stupendous more cunningly devised or successfully accomplished, with less personal risk to the robbers. As an act of purely arbitrary power, directed against a disarmed and defenseless population, it was an exhibition of cowardice in its most odious and repulsive form. As outraging every principle of justice and doing violence to every generous and manly sentiment of the human heart, its title to be regarded as an act of humanity can only be recognized by wretches destitute of every quality usually embraced under that appellation. It did not bring a "disgraceful conflict to a summary close." It, indeed, put an end to the predatory raids of Kansas "Redlegs and Jayhawkers," by surrendering to them all that they coveted, leaving nothing that could further excite their cupidity.

It did not take long for Kansans to swarm across the border to help enforce the edict. In an August 26 letter to the *Missouri Democrat*, Schofield warned that a thousand Kansans would be in Missouri within a week. Regardless of the intent of the order to banish Southern sympathizers from the border area, Kansans seized the opportunity to murder and burn. The first to suffer were the people whose homes were along the path of Quantrill's route to Lawrence.

George Hoyt and his Redlegs had been prowling the Missouri border since the Lawrence raid. It took very little for a man to lose his life. If he was wearing a new hat or clothes or had a good horse, he was either hanged or shot on the spot. Nor were women and children exempt from the barbarities. One woman wrote:

> They piled all the bedding, barrels of molasses, sugar, all clothing and provisions in the yard and started a fire, which destroyed everything, including the house and mill. The commanding officer drew a gun in Grandma's face. They tried to force her to tell where Quantrill was, but she would not say a word. They left, taking all the horses, and cattle with them, leaving a pair of old oxen and a surrey they thought useless. My grandfather was a cripple, walked with one crutch, so he and my grandmother with five small grandchildren they were caring for rode and the rest walked.[34]

What could not be quickly carried off had to be left behind. William Gregg observed, "All of this wealth left by these people, was either burned, appropriated by the Federal government or the Kansans and for which these people never received a single cent from any source, and yet, in the eyes of the people of the North, there were no demons, but Quantrill and his men."

Quantrill was camped back in his old haunts roughly three miles north of Blue Springs. On September 3 he attacked the Federal steamboats *Mars*, *Marcella*, and the *Fannie Ogden* on the Missouri River. In retaliation, Union soldiers burned about a dozen buildings, including a large warehouse and a church.[35] A Federal scouting party was on his trail and getting too close for comfort. Quantrill gathered forty to fifty men to give battle but suddenly changed his mind. Frank Smith claimed that they did not want the North-erners to know they were in Jackson County. If they knew where he was, they would have destroyed every farm in the vicinity. The Federals had already taken a toll on the people of Blue Springs. Elderly men and young boys had been killed, farms were burned to the ground, and every provision that could be carried off had been stolen.

When Quantrill returned from Lawrence, he returned to the Blue Springs area and picked up his wife, Kate. She asked why he had attacked Lawrence, and he replied, "I wanted to kill Jim Lane, the chief of all the Jay-hawkers, and the worst man that was ever born into the world."[36]

Whenever he had an opportunity, Quantrill and Kate would ride together through the Sni Hills, but he was concerned for her safety above everything else. After the brutal murders of the girls in the Kansas City jail, he was more concerned about Kate's safety than ever before. He had her use the name Kate Clarke to throw off suspicion of her identity in case Federals learned of her relationship to him.

Keenly concerned with Kate's well-being, Quantrill made sure there were no written records for the Federals to find and track down her and her family to murder them. Union soldiers regularly examined family Bibles for the genealogies recorded in them. With this information they could identify the men of military age. In this way they tracked down Southern soldiers and sympathizers and killed them. Since orders had been given to round up all relatives of guerrillas, including women, for imprisonment or banishment, Quantrill was naturally concerned about his bride. He kept her hidden in the most isolated and heavy timber for her safety. In past instances, jayhawkers like Jennison murdered Unionists in cold blood who only shared the same name as members of Quantrill's band.

In Lone Jack, early on Sunday morning, September 6, Col. Charles S. Clark and his Kansans came upon several Jackson County families as they were fleeing their homes in accordance with General Orders No. 11. They were detained until their identities could be verified. Clark directed Capt. Charles F. Coleman and a squad of the Ninth Kansas Jayhawker Regiment to separate the prisoners. One was Martin Rice—a farmer, dairyman, and a Unionist—traveling with his son and his son-in-law, William C. Tate. Rice was the only one with a certificate of loyalty. They were traveling with their neighbors: brothers David and William Hunter, one of their young sons, Andrew Ousley, John S. Cave, and seventy-five-year-old Benjamin Potter. The men and their families were attempting to move their bedding and clothing into Johnson County, near Basin Knob.

Coleman instructed Rice to resume his trip with his son-in-law. Rice said that he "immediately left as commanded, leaving our friends and neighbors behind. In a very short time after reaching home, the report of several guns, in quick succession, alarmed us still more. I however persuaded myself, and tried to persuade the alarmed and distressed families that it might be the soldiers shooting fowls for their breakfast. They would not, however, be so persuaded, and Miss Jane Cave heroically repaired to the spot and found the company gone, and the six prisoners all dead, some of them pierced with many balls."[37]

The youngest of the murdered men was seventeen years old. Because of the hurried necessity in evacuating their homes under Ewing's edict, John Hunter had to bury his sons without shroud or coffin, merely covering them with quilts and placing them in the ground.[38] Marion Potter joined Quantrill the day after his father had been murdered by Coleman's jayhawkers. In the spring of 1865 Marion was wounded and staying with friends in Waverly, Missouri, when he was captured by Federal soldiers. They took him to Marshall, Missouri, where he was taken, still unconscious, to the cemetery on his casket and shot.[39]

In Brooking Township, six miles south of Independence, along the valley of the Little Blue, jayhawkers paid a visit to the home of Reuben M. Harris, an uncle of Coleman Younger. They had raided the property before, but this time they wanted to complete the destruction. Only a month earlier they had tried to murder one of Reuben's daughters, eighteen-year-old Nannie Harris, in the collapse of the Kansas City prison. Now they stole everything of value and burned the house. One daughter asleep upstairs was rescued from the flames by her sister. As the raiders left, one of them shouted, "Now, old lady, call on your protectors. Why don't you call on Cole Younger now?"[40]

South of Brooking Township, Zion Flanery had already moved his family farther east. He returned to gather up the crops he had left. While he was working in his field, a squad of Kansas jayhawkers chased him down and shot him because they knew he was a Southerner. They also torched the Flanery home. Immediately after the murder, Zion's son Si joined Quantrill's band.

The guerrillas retaliated against their enemies like a firestorm in the night. As the Federals and Kansas jayhawkers were busy depopulating the border counties and plundering the homes, they still had to contend with guerrilla ambushes and attacks. Union soldiers only rarely dared to stray off the main roads. The guerrillas knew all the paths through the dense brush and timber, but with so many Federal patrols in the neighborhoods, they mostly stayed in the brush except at night. Union troops chased the guerrillas out of one of their camps along the Little Blue River and into Lafayette County.

William H. Gregg, Fletcher Taylor, William Noland, James Little, and Frank James captured six of William Penick's men near Napoleon, held court over them, then shot them. The next day John Jarrette, Richard Kinney, Jesse James, and Simeon Whitsett attacked a picket post of eight Federals a mile from Wellington, completely annihilating them as the Union men tried to escape across the prairie. Two days afterward Ben Morrow, Pat O'Donnell, and Frank James prepared an ambush on a Federal column along the Lexington Road. They fought eighty men for nearly an hour, killing seven of them and wounding thirteen. O'Donnell was wounded three times during the fighting, and Morrow and James were each wounded slightly.

All of Quantrill's men were actively swarming over Jackson County and striking the Federals incessantly. The majority of the activity was being drawn eastward as the majority of Union soldiers was in the process of carrying out General Orders No. 11.

In a bold maneuver, George Todd gathered thirty Quantrill veterans and, evading Federal patrols, flanked Kansas City and deployed his men in ambush along the Shawneetown road. He had information that a Kansas militia battalion was headed to Kansas City, and he intended to intercept them. He did not have long to wait. Twenty wagons, with twenty soldiers in each, soon rolled into sight. The wagons were not closed up, and an interval of fifty yards separated them. Todd waited until all but the last three had passed the point of his ambush, then with a rousing Rebel Yell the guerrillas sprang out of the brush and poured a deadly volley into the crowded and helpless mass of screaming soldiers. Sixty Federals lay dead in and around the ambushed wagons. Even after the killing was over, Todd and his men continued their attack, chasing the rest of the column into Kansas City.

Even though the Federals had forced all the border inhabitants to leave the area, every smokehouse held a huge supply of ham and bacon. And with their owners gone, the country was full of stray hogs, cattle, and chickens. At night the guerrillas would gather food for themselves and forage for their horses. Quantrill was in no hurry to leave Jackson County, but the presence of so many Federal patrols caused him to break camp and head for a camp near Wellington.[41] His next camp was at the farm of a judge named Stanley.

The judge was a Southerner and hated the Federals for what they had done to his family. A year before, a Redleg in the guise of a Methodist minister had traveled around the county and robbed Southerners. He would go to their homes and hold family prayers with them then charge them for divine service.

If they had no money, he would take their bedding, silverware, or anything else of value. The minister and the Redlegs had come to the house of Judge Stanley and demanded money from him. Upon failure to comply with their demands, they burned his feet, pulled his fingernails out, and pistol-whipped him. They then stole a roll of blankets, two silk dresses, and silverware.

A year later, guerrillas in Federal uniforms came upon the minister, who thought they were Union soldiers. James Little recognized the minister and confronted him: "You are the old devil we have been looking for. You have been going around this country praying with Southern people and in every one of your pretended prayers you would offer an insult to the South, and demanding pay, and when you were refused, you would rob defenseless women and children by taking what little property they had and you now have blankets and dresses belonging to Judge Stanley's wife and now we've got you."[42] Little then shot the Redleg, ridding the country of one of the worst jayhawkers known.

A Federal scout discovered Quantrill's hiding place at the Stanley farm. They were quartered indoors when Union soldiers arrived. Quantrill, his wife, and Todd shared one room of the log house, and other guerrillas shared the rest of the house. When they saw the Federals approaching, they sent Kate off on horseback and escorted her quickly out of camp.

Quantrill led the Federal patrol south along the Little Blue River until he came to the East Fork near Joe Dillingham's farm, then he turned west toward Brooking Township. Here one of their best camps was situated. It could only be approached by one route, and a single picket could guard it. Enemy patrols could be seen at a great distance. The guerrillas stayed here for several days and were never discovered. When they left camp for provisions, they spread their saddle blankets over the road to avoid leaving any trace of their movements.

In enforcing General Orders No. 11, the jayhawkers devastated the countryside. Arson was rampant. The people living in Jackson, Henry, and Lafayette Counties were so abused by Ewing's soldiers that Schofield was forced to remove them from the border. The Redlegs whose official job was to aid in carrying out the edict made their primary mission the looting of Missouri farms. Elvira Scott described the Redlegs as "the lowest, most desperate looking specimens of humanity it has ever been my lot to witness." Elsewhere Kansas troops broke into the home of an elderly man named Lawrence. They hanged him from a tree in his yard to get him to tell where his money was hidden. His wife had just died, and her casket was sitting on chairs in the parlor when the jayhawkers broke open the lid and cut off her finger to steal her wedding ring. Two daughters were forced to drag the coffin into the yard while the house burned down around them. They then cut down their father and nursed him back to health.

The Kansans were very proud of the work they were doing. One officer boasted that a squad of his men were responsible for burning more than 110 houses, "some of them worth, it is said, as high as $20,000." One Kansan crowed: "The border counties of Missouri have almost as desolate an appearance as before the soil was trod by the white man. Not a man, woman or child is to be seen in the country to which Order No. 11 applies. . . . Chimneys mark the spot where once stood costly farm houses, cattle and hogs are fast destroying large fields of corn, prairie fires are burning up miles of good fencing every day or two, and turn which way you will, everything denotes a state of utter desolation and ruin."

In late September Quantrill called for his men to gather at their Lawrence raid rendezvous—Pardee's place on the Blackwater Ford—for the march south. He issued orders that every man who wanted to make the trip was to have a fresh, newly shod horse. Every man had a blue overcoat, blue pants, and a Federal cavalry hat. As the guerrillas gathered, Bill Anderson's men and Col. John D. Holt's company joined them. Some new recruits were among the men, but many old faces were missing. Most of the recruits were simply being escorted south to join the regular Confederate army. Andy Blunt and a number of the old men decided to stay in Jackson County during the winter, but four hundred men joined Quantrill for the march south. Some of the guerrillas, like William Gregg, James A. Hendricks, and Dick Maddox, brought their wives. The rest of the guerrillas vowed to stand by them.

Quantrill's command was organized as the First Regiment, First Brigade, Army of the South, and composed of four companies of approximately thirty to eighty men. The companies were led by George Todd, Bill Anderson, David Poole, and William H. Gregg.[43]

In Quantrill's absence a Confederate lieutenant named Wedington, operating in Harrisonville in Cass County, sent a dispatch to Col. Charles S. Clark of the Ninth Kansas Jayhawker Regiment to report that he had captured two jayhawkers. Instead of shooting them, as was customary, he planned to release them because they were only boys. He hoped the Federals would reciprocate in kind.[44]

There were relatively few incidents as Quantrill's command traveled south. His regiment stored their provisions in a Federal army ambulance until it broke down. They had to carry provisions with them because the country had been denuded by jayhawkers. Every town had been sacked and burned.

The countryside was vacant, depopulated. Jacob Hall remarked, "But we might say that we still 'dwell in the midst of alarms.' The whole three counties of Jackson, Bates and Cass are depopulated and a mass of smoldering ruins."[45]

By luck the guerrillas came upon a hundred Federal militia with several wagons as they emerged from the woods. The guerrillas made a mad dash for them, and the Federals ran, leaving their wagons behind. Quantrill's men simply changed the wagon teams and continued on their way. When they reached the Indian Territory south of the Grand River, Gregg skirmished with a Union lieutenant and six soldiers. They were carrying dispatches from Springfield to Kansas City. Six of the Federal soldiers were killed, and Gregg chased the remaining man down, until he came in sight of Union cavalry numbering more than four hundred men. The guerrillas withdrew back across the Grand River. After a few brief skirmishes with black Union soldiers and Indians, the guerrillas counted more than forty-five enemy dead.

At the Osage River the guerrillas attacked a ferry guarded by a Home Guard company of thirty men, only three of whom managed to escape. Beyond the Osage, sixteen cavalrymen from Fort Scott had been jayhawking cattle in Vernon County when they were confronted and killed by the guerrilla column.

Within a few days Quantrill's company reached the outskirts of Carthage, Missouri. While they were in camp they heard of a large Federal wagon train traveling north. When Quantrill sent out a scout, they found that the Union men greatly outnumbered them, so they let them pass undisturbed. The scouts returned with two men who claimed to be Southerners. Quantrill detained one of them to use as a guide.

The column traveled mostly at night. After leading Quantrill's command for a ways, John McCorkle asked Bill Anderson where Quantrill was headed. Anderson said they were headed south. McCorkle knew that the guide was leading them to Fort Scott and a large body of Federals. It was ten o'clock that night before he was able to tell Quantrill that the guide was taking him in the wrong direction. Quantrill was incensed at being duped. He told McCorkle to get him and his men safely out and headed back south or he would have him shot. McCorkle had the command countermarch until they came to a place at around three o'clock in the morning that they all recognized. Quantrill felt relieved and rode up to McCorkle. He playfully exclaimed, "John, you do know this country and I will not have to shoot you." He then directed McCorkle and Allen Parmer to scout the area and report back.

The scouts found a mill owned by a Southern sympathizer who told them to take whatever they needed. By morning the entire command was settling down to a breakfast of bread, bacon, and coffee. By October 6 they were at the edge of the Indian Territory and headed for the Fort Scott road in Kansas that would take them to winter quarters in Texas.

David Poole was in charge of the advance scout of thirty men while Gregg made up the rear guard with twenty men. The women and families traveling with the guerrillas were kept as far away from the action as practical. The guerrillas came upon ten to fifteen Federals in mule-drawn wagons. Poole's men quickly captured the soldiers. Innocently thinking that their cooperation would save them, they told Poole that they were on their way to Fort Blair near Baxter Springs, Kansas. After shooting the Federals, Poole sent John McCorkle back to inform Quantrill that he was headed for the fort. It was the first time anyone had heard about a Federal outpost in this area.

Fort Baxter, officially known as Fort Blair, was in southeast Kansas in what was known as the Cherokee Neutral Lands. Both Union and Confederate forces claimed this land and sent constant patrols into the area.

After hearing Poole's report, Quantrill shouted out hurried orders to Gregg: "Support Poole. I will come in on the north and support both of you." Quantrill then turned to Andy Walker: "Lope back and tell the boys to hurry up." Once his company had caught up with him, Quantrill left the main road and headed through the timber.

It was noon at the fort when Lt. James Pond and approximately 155 soldiers were preparing their lunch. Pond was a renowned abolitionist who had fought alongside John Brown in Kansas and aided in the Underground Railroad. He had also served as a printer of the *Kansas Herald of Freedom*. His command included two companies of the Third Wisconsin Cavalry and one company of the Second Kansas Colored Infantry.

The fort was yet not finished. It was simply a three-sided earthwork of dirt and few logs, standing four feet high with one-hundred-foot-long sides. The wall at the west end had been taken down to lengthen the sides. Mission-wise, the fort was intended to protect wagon trains traveling along the Fort Scott to Fort Gibson military road.

Among the first victims at Baxter Springs were three men who were target shooting. One of the victims was Johnny Fry, an army scout who had gained some notoriety before the war as one of the first Pony Express riders. The soldiers did not have an opportunity to defend themselves before they were shot down.

Gregg and Poole began the attack on the fort before Quantrill had time to come up with the main command. The Federals were in the midst of their lunch, about fifty yards from the fort, when the guerrillas attacked. Pond had failed to post pickets. His undisciplined, unwary soldiers had left their rifles inside the fort. Post surgeon W. H. Warner described the scene:

> At 12 P.M., the enemy suddenly advanced upon us at double-quick and opened fire. Riding at full gallop, they passed on the south between the men at dinner and the camp, discharging their revolvers right and left as they advanced. The colored soldiers and the cavalry seizing their carbines and revolvers and the infantry their muskets, all commenced a return fire. . . . While this attack was being made, the main body of the enemy galloped from the woods skirting Spring River on the east, forming in line sixty or eighty rods north of the camp, on the ridge, apparently with the purpose of making a charge upon us in full force.

The guerrillas wisely calculated their attack by charging between the soldiers and the fort. Pond's command tent was about two hundred feet from the camp. As he exited his tent and saw what was transpiring, he made his way to the fort and was shot at by the guerrillas the entire route. Pond hollered at some men to man the only howitzer inside the fort, but none would undertake the dangerous mission.

Pond made it over the embankment of the fort and single-handedly manned the howitzer, loading and aiming it before bringing it to bear on the attacking guerrilla cavalry. His fire managed to bring down one of the guerrillas, Dave Woods, who was decapitated.

After the initial dash, the guerrillas withdrew to the nearby timber and commenced an incessant fire on the soldiers for twenty to thirty minutes. Poole's quick-thinking charge scattered most of the soldiers away from their fort. About seventy-five of them ran about two hundred yards and sought refuge in the tall grass and willows. Gregg cut out a few of his men and began capturing these scattered remnants.

After noticing that the firing from the fort had ceased, Gregg rode to the crest of a nearby ridge and noticed that Quantrill had his men in line and ready for a charge. Gregg and his men abandoned their prisoners and rode to join Quantrill's line. Quantrill turned to John McCorkle and said: "Get the boys away from the fort and form in line."

What the Federals did not know was that Quantrill had just received word that a Union column was approaching from the north. It was Maj. Gen. James G. Blunt and one hundred men of the Fourteenth Kansas Jayhawker Regiment along with a company of the Third Wisconsin Cavalry. The approaching Federals were unaware that the fort was under attack. In addition to the soldiers, Blunt had at his command eight baggage wagons, two ambulances, two buggies, and a bandwagon with fourteen players of his brigade's brass band.

Blunt had enlisted in the war as a private but soon rose to become a lieutenant colonel in James Montgomery's jayhawker regiment. He had no prior military experience and was described as coarse and unscrupulous. Equaling James Lane in licentiousness, Blunt oftentimes took "female servants" with him on his expeditions. Lane used the overweight general to get kickbacks by awarding government contracts to his friends for military supplies sent to Kansas. These contracts were let out by the officers in the quartermaster and commissary departments under the control of the different commanding generals.

In addition to these flaws of Blunt, the guerrillas had a special reason to hate the man. Even though he was considered a hard fighter, he had as his chief of scouts the noted Redleg Capt. William S. Tough, a ruthless killer and one of the original Redlegs known for "stealing himself rich in the name of liberty."

Blunt, as commander of the District of the Frontier, was on his way to Fort Smith, Arkansas, to engage the Confederates there. Knowing that he was nearing the fort, he waited for his column to close up in sharp military order before continuing on and ordered his band to the forefront to play a martial air and display a new flag he had just received. Then something caught his eye.

Looking up, he observed about one hundred cavalrymen in blue uniforms forming in line about five hundred yards to his front. Blunt's suspicious were aroused. Riders, supposedly officers, were frantically riding back and forth along the length of the line. A black soldier overheard Blunt comment, "Oh, it's just a few of [Capt. Samuel D.] Jackman's guerrillas from south Missouri. Give them a few rounds and they will all run off to cover."

More than a year earlier, in March 1862, Blunt had adopted Henry W. Halleck's order to raise the black flag on the border when he was named as the district commander of the Department of Kansas. In response to the guerrillas' mode of warfare, he said: "They shall not be treated as prisoners of war, but be summarily tried by drum-head court-martial, and if proved guilty, be executed, by hanging or shooting on the spot, as no punishment can be too prompt or severe for such unnatural enemies of the human race."[46]

Quantrill quickly ascertained that Pond had around one hundred men in his command, so he only permitted one hundred of his men to ride out to receive Blunt's column, knowing that Blunt would naturally think that they

were Federal soldiers riding out to escort the general into the fort. The guerrillas' horses became skittish, anticipating the upcoming danger.

Blunt then ordered his men to dress in a line opposite the opposing
column as he ventured forward to ascertain who these horsemen were. He
positioned Company A of the Fourteenth Kansas on his right and Company I
of the Third Wisconsin about forty yards to the left and ordered the band and
the rest of the noncombatants to the rear.

As he closed to within fifty yards of the enemy, he could hear sporadic
firing from the direction of the fort. Realizing finally that the cavalrymen
facing him were indeed Confederates, Blunt immediately turned and
ordered his men to fire. But they were too afraid to fire accurately, and many
of them had already started to run. Maj. Henry Z. Curtis managed to overtake two of the soldiers fleeing from Company A and return them to the line
when the rest of the command realized there was no hope for them. They all
started a wild stampede across the prairie and were closely pursued by the
screaming guerrillas.

As Gregg and Poole came thundering down on the frightened Federals,
Quantrill emerged from the woods one hundred yards north of the fort with
the rest of his command. The guerrillas fired a volley from their carbines then
pulled their pistols and closed with the fleeing enemy. Quantrill shouted,
"Hold your fire, until you are within fifty yards." At this range, riding at a fast
charge, the guerrillas would be upon the enemy before they could reload and
fire a second volley from their carbines.

Quantrill took his customary place in the center of the line then
removed his hat and placed it inside his coat. He spurred his horse forward
and yelled out the command, "Come on, boys!" Quantrill led his men forward. As they came across a little branch, they were within seventy-five yards
of Blunt's line. They charged with the wild Rebel Yell and pistols ready.

The ground on which the fight occurred was rolling prairie that extended
far to the west. It was covered with grass and intersected with deep ravines and
gullies, the banks of which were filled with willow bushes sufficient to conceal
any difficulty in crossing but not to protect from observation.[47]

Blunt had been riding in a buggy with a beautiful twenty-two-year-old
woman, Mrs. Chester Thomas, when the guerrillas began their charge.
Horses were tied behind the buggy, and this attracted attention. Seeing a
Federal officer with excellent horses, John Jarrette, Dick Yeager, and Frank
Smith turned and charged him. Fearing for the woman's safety as well as his
own, Blunt and Mrs. Thomas abandoned the buggy and escaped on horseback. Jesse James allegedly followed Blunt for several miles, firing at him

four times without effect before finally being outdistanced by Blunt's superior horse.

The Federals running in all directions were chased down by the guerrillas and shot out of their saddles. Blunt's musicians were riding in a specially made wagon pulled by four mules. When they saw their fellow soldiers running by them in sheer panic, Henry Pellage, the bandleader and driver, turned the wagon in a southwesterly course, different from what the others were taking.

William M. Bledsoe, one of Quantrill's best-loved men, rode up to the wagon and demanded its surrender. Frank Smith said that a black soldier in the bandwagon pulled a revolver and shot Bledsoe out of the saddle. Todd and Gregg saw Bledsoe fall. As a result, about twenty guerrillas descended on the fleeing wagon. Fletcher Taylor immediately rode to Bledsoe's side. As Bledsoe handed him his pistols, his dying words were, "Fletch, that outfit have shot and killed me; take my two pistols and kill all of them."

After fifty yards the left front wheel of the wagon fell off, throwing the passengers to the ground. As the guerrillas rode up, all the occupants pulled out white handkerchiefs and waved them in surrender. Todd angrily demanded why they had not waved their handkerchiefs at Bledsoe. The musicians were mostly Germans, and among them were a newspaper reporter and a twelve-year-old drummer boy. The musicians wore splendid uniforms with new swords and pistols. The guerrillas remorselessly shot them down.

The civilian in the bandwagon was a reporter named James O'Neil, an artist and writer for *Frank Leslie's Illustrated Newspaper*. Someone among the guerrillas may have seen the newspaper's September 12 issue and read its inaccurate account of the Lawrence raid. A half-page drawing depicted Quantrill's men burning buildings and killing men and women. O'Neil had previously been assigned to cover Blunt's victory at Honey Springs, Oklahoma. Back in July he did a pen-and-ink drawing of a charge by the Sixth Kansas Jayhawker Regiment against the Confederates, showing a highly imaginative scene of the battle. Todd had the correspondent killed along with the musicians. The bandwagon was then set on fire. Of the one hundred cavalrymen in Blunt's column, seventy-nine were killed.

Maj. Henry Z. Curtis, son of Gen. Samuel R. Curtis, commander of the Central Military District in Missouri, sought to flee alongside Blunt, but he became separated from the general during the retreating stampede. Curtis was riding a fine horse and wore a conspicuous uniform. As he was attempting to jump a ravine, his horse was struck in the hip with a ball, which so stung or frightened him that he missed his leap. Falling short, the animal threw the major over his head. The horse gathered himself almost instantly and galloped wildly over the prairie.

Peyton Long was the first to reach Curtis and took him prisoner. Long searched him and found an order signed by General Curtis commanding the soldiers of his division to take no prisoners among the guerrillas, especially among the guerrillas commanded by Quantrill. Long asked Curtis if he had written the order, and the major replied, "Yes, by the orders of my superior officer." Long then asked him, "Would you have obeyed it?" Curtis replied unhesitatingly, "Most certainly." He spoke his own death sentence; Long shot him down where he stood.

Curtis had served in Arkansas at the battle of Pea Ridge as an aide to his father. When General Curtis took command of the Department of Missouri, his son remained with him as assistant adjutant general, and when the general was relieved of that command in May 1863, his son sought and obtained a position with Blunt as his assistant adjutant general.[48] The major carried out his father's hatred for the guerrillas and their mode of warfare.

Only five months before, in his capacity as commander of the Department of Missouri, General Curtis issued General Orders No. 30, which defined what a guerrilla was and specified how Federal troops should deal with captured guerrillas. The general stated: "Whoever shall be convicted as a guerrilla shall suffer death. They deserve no-quarters; no terms of civilized warfare. Pursue, strike, and destroy the reptiles."[49]

The Union soldiers who could not flee from the guerrillas fast enough tried to surrender. Most were shot down. Sgt. Jack Splane of Company I, Third Wisconsin Cavalry, attempted to surrender. He was shot five times: in the head, the chest, the stomach, an arm, and a leg. Despite all this lead, Splane lived to tell the tale. Quantrill allegedly said to him just before Splane was shot the last time: "Tell old God that the last man you saw on earth was Quantrill."[50]

From Blunt's command, eight wounded men managed to escape and five were finally listed as missing; the rest were killed. At the fort, Pond lost six men killed and ten wounded. Blunt was briefly relieved of command because of his humiliating defeat suffered at the hand of Quantrill's guerrillas.

George W. Maddox was about to shoot a black soldier when the fellow threw up his hands and begged to be taken to George Todd. When Maddox delivered his prisoner, Todd ran to him like a long-lost brother and turning to his fellow guerrillas remarked, "The first man that hurts this nigger, I will kill!" He explained that during the winter of 1862, when he had returned from serving with Sterling Price, he would sneak into Kansas City to see his wife. The black man's name was Rube, and he was a freed slave who owned a barbershop in town. One day Rube overheard a Federal plot to kill Todd. Rube sent word to Todd to come to his house and hid him in the cellar for ten days, watching out for him and feeding him. That afternoon Rube joined the guerrillas on their march south.

Brothers George and Dick Maddox were from Cass County, and their solemn mission of the war was to kill every black soldier they encountered. They had a special reason for revenge. A slave named Jack Mann had run away from his owner in Jackson County, joined the Redlegs, then guided jay-hawking raids back into the county. John McCorkle remembered Mann as exceedingly insulting to Southerners and especially old men and women. One day Mann led a squad of Redlegs to the home of Dick Maddox. Finding only Dick's wife, Martha, at home, he cursed and abused her. As he was tearing through the house searching for valuables, Mann found Dick's wedding suit. He undressed in front of her and put on the husband's clothes. Then he strode before her, exclaiming, "How do you like my looks with this wedding suit on?" In an ironical twist of fate, the guerrillas at Baxter Springs captured Mann alive. Dick Maddox begged to shoot Mann, but Quantrill told him to wait.

The guerrillas found that the canteens of most of the Federals were full of whiskey, and more whiskey was found in the wagons. The only time anyone ever saw Quantrill drink liquor was while he searched through Blunt's belongings and discovered a jug of brandy, which he slung over his saddle-horn. As he sat astride his horse, he saw John McCorkle riding up and wanted to play a joke on him. He called out, "John, I thought you always knew that whenever a pilot led me into trouble, I always shoot him." McCorkle, remembering Quantrill's words from a few days before, pulled his revolver and remarked in earnest, "If you can shoot quicker than I can, shoot." Quantrill laughed and said, "Put that thing up, you damned fool; I'm going to 'shoot you in the neck,'" then handed the brandy jug to McCorkle.

The guerrillas were jubilant after the battle. Baxter Springs proved that they had not lost any of their zest for fighting. They had just killed more than eighty Federals in a matter of minutes and lost only three of their own killed and four wounded. Anderson's men did not take part in the battle but busied themselves searching the ten wagons of supplies and taking what they needed. They burned the rest.

While John Koger searched one of the wagons, a Federal ran out of the fort, shot him in the back, then ran back into the fort. Koger already had five Yankee slugs in his body. Quantrill placed the wounded Koger with Bledsoe's body in an ambulance.

In another wagon McCorkle found a colonel's uniform, a pair of cavalry boots, six white shirts, and a pair of Colt revolvers. He also found Blunt's sword and saddle. Quantrill confiscated all of Blunt's personal correspondence along with his general's commission. They also found his personal silk flag sewn with an American eagle surrounded with a black border, meaning no quarter. It was inscribed, "Presented to Major General James G. Blunt by the ladies of Leavenworth Oct. 2, 1863."

As the guerrillas searched the rest of the wagons and gathered weapons from dead soldiers, fifteen-year-old Riley Crawford, whose father and two sisters had recently been murdered and his home burned down, was playfully shouting commands at the corpses lying around him. To one prostrate soldier he yelled, "Get up you Federal S.O.B." To everyone's amazement the Federal stood up, believing that Riley had discovered him feigning death. Riley immediately killed him. Neglectfulness was contrary to the guerrillas' rules of war. They did not need an enemy soldier rising up and playing the hero while they were relaxing after a battle. This incident caused the rest of the men to mount up and finish their work by putting a bullet into the head of every fallen Federal.

Quantrill triumphantly rode around the battlefield and watched his men collect useful supplies. He rode up to Todd and Anderson and shouted, "By God, [Jo] Shelby could not whip Blunt. Neither could [John S.] Marmaduke. But I whipped him." Quantrill had reason to be proud. Three months before, Col. James Williams, in command of the First Kansas Colored Regiment, marched south and took up a position at nearby Honey Springs. Along with Blunt's troops, they engaged a strong Confederate force of Indian and Texas troops under Gen. Douglas Cooper. After two hours of constant volleys the Rebels turned and withdrew from the field, leaving Blunt's troops victorious. Other Confederate leaders had not bested Blunt in their best tries, but now Quantrill's men had come close to destroying his entire command.

Both Todd and Anderson insisted that Quantrill attack the fort. Quantrill quickly surmised that he had just experienced the lightest casualties he had ever suffered in a battle of this size. He knew another attack on the fort, with the Federals now armed and ready behind breastworks and Pond manning his howitzer, would cause numerous casualties.[51] He replied, "No, there is nothing to be gained by it; besides, we would probably lose fifteen or twenty men, and I would not give the life of one of my men for the whole business."

This statement angered the impetuous Anderson and Todd, who believed Quantrill lacked the nerve for another battle. His concern for his men, however, only endeared him to his troops as a great leader. Statements by his men after the battle attest to his common military sense. Hiram George and his brother remarked after the battle, "He usually restrained the ardor of his followers and never sacrificed a man needlessly."

While Quantrill gathered his men and resumed the trip south, one of his men left a note behind for Blunt, knowing he would return after the fighting was over: "Hello, Jim Blunt! Do you recollect the letter you wrote to Colonel Parker, last Spring, and the execution of James Vaughn? Stop and turn your eyes to Lawrence and Baxter Springs, and see what your amiable policy has brought you to . . . see what you have done for your fellow soldiers . . . and then remember the dying words of James Vaughn."

Following the October 24 battle, Blunt was relieved of his command. Gen. John McNeil replaced him.

After they had traveled about ten miles south, the guerrillas stopped to bury Bill Bledsoe. Jack Mann was made to dig two graves: one for Bledsoe and one for himself. While the guerrillas were burying their friend, Mann began making insulting remarks to his guard, Andy McGuire. Suddenly McGuire pulled out his pistol and shot the gravedigger between the eyes. Dick Maddox had wanted the honor of killing Mann and was so incensed at McGuire that he drew his revolver and started to shoot his comrade. Only the actions of the guerrillas standing nearby kept the two men from shooting one another.

In the week following the battle of Baxter Springs the guerrillas killed 150 Indians in the Federal service along with some black soldiers who were known to have killed and scalped a number of women and children.[52] When they were encountered, the guerrillas charged them and destroyed their command. Quantrill put out a detachment of twenty-five guerrillas in Federal uniforms and carrying a Federal flag a quarter of a mile ahead of his main column.

The guerrillas had advanced into the Cherokee Indian Nation. The Cherokees were the most civilized tribe in the territory and opposed to the South. Each day ten to twenty Indians in Federal service would ride up to join them, and each night they were shot.[53]

A few days' ride later, the guerrilla company came to a small stream at the bottom of a ravine. The ambulance could not be gotten easily across, so Quantrill prepared to camp there for the night and get the ambulance across in the morning. It was a good site for a camp. They were near a stand of timber and close to a farm with a cornfield, fine hogs, and water. Quantrill deployed his men in a horseshoe-shaped perimeter around the ambulance, fanning out to the north and leaving his position on the south unguarded, as he expected no danger from that direction.

Quantrill and Todd slept near Koger in the ambulance. The weary guerrillas removed the saddles from their horses then settled down for the night. Around 5:30 the next morning they were suddenly awakened by a bugle blast from the south. Quantrill quickly called out, "Mount and form line!" He scrambled coatless, hatless and barefoot across the ravine, gave the alarm, and mounted his horse with only a halter to rally his men. Todd was right behind him, shouting orders for everyone to get mounted.

The approaching soldiers rode to within shouting distance of the ambulance when John Koger, rising on his elbow and poking his pistol through the ambulance curtains halted the approaching soldiers and demanded to know who they were. Their colonel answered that they were Confederates. Koger hollered back. "Then if you are Confederates, for God's sake stop, for you'll be torn all to pieces in a minute." The colonel demanded, "Who are you?" Koger called out, "It's Quantrill!"

The approaching force belonged to Col. Daniel McIntosh of Gen. Douglas H. Cooper's command leading a battalion composed of two companies of Cherokee, Choctaw, and Chickasaw Indians and one company of white soldiers. The Confederacy had made a treaty with some of the tribes in the Indian Territory and had taken more than four thousand into its service. Quantrill rode with some of these same Cherokee soldiers while he was a private in Joel Mayes's company at the beginning of the war.

One of the soldiers at the colonel's side who had ridden with Quantrill was sent toward the ambulance with a white handkerchief tied to his ramrod to ascertain the situation. When they discovered that Koger was one of Quantrill's men, McIntosh sent this soldier across the ravine with a message.[54] Quantrill already had his men mounted and was ready to charge when the soldier rode into sight and yelled out, "Don't fire boys; we are friends."

McIntosh's fifteen hundred soldiers had been scouting for Quantrill's command after they discovered guerrillas dressed in blue uniforms and using James G. Blunt's ambulance. McIntosh then escorted Quantrill to his camp fifteen miles away. They made it past the Confederate lines on October 12 and joined Gen. Douglas Cooper in command of Indian troops along the Canadian River at a place called Boggy Depot on the southern border of Oklahoma. The general treated Quantrill's men well and provided them with everything they needed, especially rations for the men and horses. Quantrill stayed with McIntosh for several days before continuing on across the Red River at Colbert's Ferry, fifty miles from Sherman, Texas.

The next day was Tuesday as Quantrill sat down and wrote Sterling Price a dispatch describing his recent campaigns. In the last six weeks Quantrill's command had accounted for more than five hundred Union soldiers and jayhawkers killed. He recounted that his losses were three men killed during the march south. As he notified Price about his encounter with the 150 Federals that belonged to the First Indian Home Guard, he simply stated their fate as, "We brought none of them through." He ended the report by saying, "At some future day I will send you a complete report of my summer's campaign on the Missouri River." He signed the dispatch as a colonel.

Shortly after Price received Quantrill's dispatch, he sent him a message expressing his interest in how the Federals treated Confederate prisoners of war. Price's adjutant dictated the following message to Quantrill on November 2:

Colonel: I am desired by Major-General Price to acknowledge the receipt of your report of your march from the Missouri River to the Canadian, and that he takes pleasure in congratulating you and your gallant command upon the success attending it. General Price is very anxious that you prepare the report of your summer campaign, alluded to by you, at as early a date as practicable, and forward it without delay, more particularly so as he is desirous that your acts should appear in their true light before the world. In it he wishes you to incorporate particularly the treatment to which the prisoners belonging to your command received from the Federal authorities; also the orders issued by General Blunt or other Federal officers regarding the disposition to be made of you or your men if taken or vanquished. He has been informed that orders of a most inhuman character were issued. Indeed, he has some emanating from those holding subordinate commands, but wants to have all the facts clearly portrayed, so that the Confederacy and the world may learn the murderous and uncivilized warfare, which they themselves inaugurated, and thus be able to appreciate their cowardly shrieks and howls when with a just retaliation the same "measure is meted out to them." He desires me to convey to you, and through you to your command, his high appreciation of the hardships you have so nobly endured and the gallant struggle you have made against despotism and the oppression of our State, with the confident hope that success will soon crown our efforts.

On the same day Price wrote to the new Missouri governor, Thomas C. Reynolds, who had been sworn in after the death of Claiborne Jackson:

"Colonel Quantrill has now with him some three-hundred and fifty men of that daring and dashing character, which has made the name of Quantrill so feared by our enemies, and have aided so much to keep Missouri, though overrun by Federals, identified with the Confederacy."[55]

All of Missouri and the South were proud of what Quantrill had accomplished. He was the only Southern military leader who achieved any victories won by the Confederacy in the West in 1863. Glowing reports preceded his command as he made his way to the safety of Texas.

The guerrillas made their winter quarters about twenty miles northwest of Sherman. Here they could rest and relax with their friends and family without fear of constant Federal patrols or ambushes. Most took to building winter quarters while others rode into the nearby towns in search of old friends and a bit of fun. Gen. Henry E. McCulloch's quartermaster in the district, together with the commissary, made themselves thoroughly acquainted with the circumstances under which the guerrillas operated and informed themselves intelligently of the condition of those Missourians who were driven penniless from their homes at the commencement of a rigorous winter. As a consequence, they furnished them bountifully with supplies and provided comfortable shelter for the wives and the children of the refugees.[56]

11

Hallowed Ground

War means fighting; and the soldier's cardinal sin is timidity.

THEODORE ROOSEVELT

HE GUERRILLAS COULD BREATHE easier now that they were behind Southern lines. They stayed with Gen. Douglas Cooper for several days. After reporting to Gen. Sterling Price about his summer activities along the western border, Quantrill moved his command across the Red River at Colbert's Ferry into Texas. Once across the river they were in the district under the jurisdiction of Gen. Henry E. McCulloch.

McCulloch was egotistical and brash. His haughty airs kept him from making friends among his allies in Missouri. He also did not care for Quantrill's style of efficient fighting.[1] In short, McCulloch looked down on all other military organizations but his own. He knew nothing about the hardships the Missourians had suffered at the hands of the Kansas jayhawkers, nor did he seem to care. When he heard about the Lawrence raid, he said: "We cannot, as a Christian people, sanction a savage, inhuman warfare, in which men are to be shot down like dogs."

Other Confederate generals were less judgmental of the Missouri guerrillas. Maj. Gen. John Bankhead "Prince John" Magruder, commanding the District of Texas, issued a general order congratulating Col. William C. Quantrill for his victory at Baxter Springs.[2] Although General McCulloch expressed his concerns over Quantrill's tactics in a letter to the assistant adjutant general of the Trans-Mississippi Department, he also stated, "I appreciate his services, and am anxious to have them." McCulloch received his information about Quantrill secondhand and failed to weigh its veracity.

Gen. Edmund Kirby Smith, commander of the Trans-Mississippi Department, disagreed with McCulloch. Based on the information he had received about Quantrill's men, he expressed his views in a letter to McCulloch: "They are bold, fearless men, and, moreover, from all representations, are under very fair discipline. They are composed, I understand, in a measure of the very best class of Missourians. They have suffered every outrage in their person and families at the hands of the Federals, and being outlawed, and their lives forfeited, have waged a war of no-quarter whenever they have come in contact with the enemy."[3]

Quantrill, commissioned by President Jefferson Davis to lead an independent command, was instructed to follow orders given by higher authority, placing him outside the chain of command of regular Confederate army officers. His partisan command served as a detachment to regular Confederate forces. But for now the guerrillas only wanted to rest. Every inch of Missouri soil had been their battlefield. They had stood in the presence of death so often that they felt little trepidation for their lives. When not in battle, they enjoyed the presence of friends and each other. As a result, they lived life to the fullest, filling every day with meaningful experiences. The time spent in Texas was to be a time of relative rest and security.

The Missouri guerrillas made camp three miles south of the river on Mineral Creek, twenty miles from Sherman. Most built homes for themselves and their families while others looked up old friends from the year before and stayed with them.

Quantrill sold the ambulance captured at Baxter Springs, and with the money he purchased a hundred-pound sack of coffee for his men. His men also ate well. Frank Smith noted that deer were plentiful, and the guerrillas hunted them for food. They also traded with the farmers in the area, especially since the coffee Quantrill had purchased proved to be highly desirable to the farmers around Sherman. Quantrill tried to purchase more, but he found that coffee was a very scarce commodity.[4]

The guerrillas expected this winter would be as uneventful as previous winter bivouacs in Texas; however, General McCulloch had other ideas for the daring men on horseback. A Federal raiding party had come through the Indian Territory and struck at the Southern lines as far as the Texas border. McCulloch issued orders for Quantrill to pursue and destroy them.

The guerrillas quickly gave battle, and the Federals turned and ran, trying to make it safely back into Kansas. Quantrill's command caught up with them near Coffeyville after having chased them for more than 270 miles. The Missourians rode more than 40 miles a day before finally bringing the enemy to bay just across the Kansas border. A brief skirmish took place, and the guerrillas killed six Union soldiers before the others escaped. Quantrill's men returned to their Mineral Springs camp after being gone for two weeks.

The respite was short lived. McCulloch ordered the guerrillas to chase down a Comanche party in Texas. The guerrillas pursued them for more than a week but never managed to catch up with them.

When they returned, McCulloch had another assignment for them. To the north, Gen. Douglas Cooper commanded a regiment of Indians. His men had been getting drunk on whiskey distilled along the Red River Valley. Because Cooper's men were frequently drunk, they were little more than useless. Thus McCulloch ordered Quantrill to destroy all the stills his men could find. The guerrillas managed to destroy only one of the stills after killing its three operators.

When McCulloch did not have the guerrillas out on special assignment, the Missourians did manage to have a little fun. Small groups found time to visit nearby Sherman during the day. There was a racetrack just outside of town, and racing their horses against each other became a chief form of amusement. Dick Maddox was one of the best riders among the guerrillas. He gave exhibitions of his riding skills in bronco busting and was also known as an expert rope thrower. John McCorkle reported that Quantrill's men spent much of the winter hunting, fishing, and going to dances. It was a period of relaxation from all the stress and horror of war and from the many battles and skirmishes of the preceding year.

Christmas week was full of activity around Sherman. The town's young people invited Quantrill's men to a large ball, and most of them attended. McCulloch also invited Quantrill's men to celebrate Christmas with him at his headquarters in Bonham, twenty-five miles from Sherman.

One evening before Christmas, Anderson took his men into town for some fun. They stole a demijohn of whiskey from a drugstore and proceeded to get gloriously drunk. The next morning after breakfast, Anderson formed his men into platoons and made a systematic sweep of the streets and the public square, during which they shattered every doorknob amid peals of laughter. The merriment was no less when they rode their horses into the lobby of a hotel. They perforated the clock with a number of bullets, then two troopers urged their steeds over a lounge on which Dick Maddox lay. They succeeded in reducing the couch to kindling wood. Then various

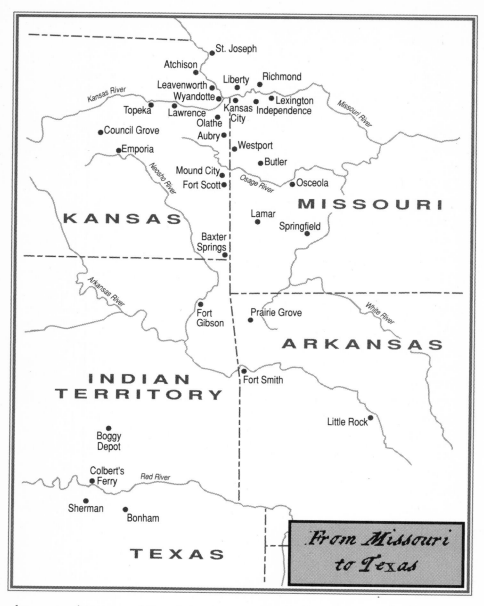

St. Joseph
Atchison
Liberty   Richmond
Leavenworth
Wyandotte   Lexington
Kansas River
Topeka   Lawrence   Kansas   Independence
City
Olathe
Aubry
Council Grove
Missouri River
Emporia   Westport

Butler
Neosho River
Mound City
Fort Scott   *Osage River*   Osceola

KANSAS   MISSOURI

Lamar
Baxter   Springfield
Springs

Arkansas River

Fort   Prairie Grove   *White River*
Gibson

ARKANSAS

INDIAN
TERRITORY   Fort Smith

Little Rock

Boggy
Depot

Colbert's
Ferry   *Red River*

Sherman
Bonham   *From Missouri
to Texas*

TEXAS

objects in the room claimed their attention. Bullets passed to either side of
Oliver Johnson, who was sprawled on the floor upstairs.[5]

Benjamin Christian, the proprietor of the hotel and a close friend of
Quantrill, sent word to the Mineral Springs camp that he would like the
guerrilla leaders to stop his men from tearing up the town. Quantrill gathered
Todd and a few men and started toward Sherman. There they collected their

drunken comrades and escorted them back to camp. After Anderson's men had sobered up, Quantrill ordered them back into Sherman to pay for the damages they had caused.

With so much attention bestowed on Quantrill's command, petty jealousies arose. Shortly after Christmas a select group of guerrillas was invited to attend a dance at the home of Jim Crow Chiles. Twenty guerrillas who had not been invited took the slight very personally. They rode into Sherman and tried to break up the dance at Chiles's. Several fistfights broke out, but no shooting occurred even though the guerrillas were all heavily armed.

Word came to Quantrill and Todd at the Mineral Springs camp that their assistance was needed again to quell the disturbance in town. By the time they arrived, however, all the troublemakers had gone, and the guerrilla leaders could find no trace of them until the next morning when they showed up for morning muster.

On March 2 Bill Anderson invited all the guerrillas to attend his marriage in Sherman to Bush Smith. She ostensibly got her name for riding with the guerrillas through their many haunts in Missouri as bushwhackers.[6] Previous writers have asserted that Quantrill was upset that Anderson had married against his advice, but this was not so. Many of his men had married amid the carnage of war, including Quantrill himself. Twenty-five-year-old John Jarrette married Cole Younger's nineteen-year-old sister Josephine. Richard Maddox married Martha Sanders on March 12, 1861. Noah Estes married Elizabeth Adams on January 3, 1861, and Ferdinand M. Scott had married Josephine P. Vance on May 20, 1861.

Critics of Quantrill's second in command, George Todd, have claimed that he kept a mistress, but a letter by Marietta Allen indicates that he had married Catherine "Kitty" Todd, his brother's widow, to prevent her having to marry a Union officer. Allen, a neighbor of Todd's family, asserted that George would often slip into Kansas City to meet his wife, running the risk of being strung up.[7]

Sterling Price and the Missouri State Guard were also wintering in Texas. Quantrill received a message from Price to report for a conference. The guerrillas had been effective fighting the Federals in Missouri, but many questions were being asked during the war as to their legal status. The general informed him that his partisan ranger command was to be limited to eighty-four cavalrymen, thus comprising a brigade of irregulars.

Up until this time small bands of guerrillas operated under the commands of captains, which had anywhere from ten to one hundred men. The articles of the Confederacy's Partisan Ranger Act authorized and governed their size and leadership structure: "When as many as ten men come together for this purpose they may organize by electing a captain. As soon as the company attains the strength required by law it will proceed to elect the other officers to which it is entitled."[8] When up to eighty men were formed together they were put under command of a colonel. Many historians believe that it was after this reorganization that Price awarded Quantrill with a colonel's commission.

Upon his return to camp, Quantrill met with Todd and Anderson, and together they handpicked the men for their brigade. The remaining men were mustered into the regular army.

Up until this point William H. Gregg had been Quantrill's adjutant and had normally been in command whenever Quantrill was absent, but when Quantrill conferred with Price, he left Todd in charge. Gregg and Todd had a serious disagreement over this, and upon Quantrill's return, Gregg was released to join Gen. Jo Shelby's army. When Gregg told Quantrill he was leaving, Quantrill praised him for being a "good soldier and a good officer and an honest man" and was saddened to think that Todd had caused another of his most trusted men to leave (William Haller and Hi and Hicks George had left the company after disagreements with Todd). In this instance, Todd had allowed an old animosity to fester and had never forgotten Gregg's criticism of his conduct at the Sam Clark fight. Jim Chiles also left with Gregg.

After the reorganization, officers were selected. Todd was chosen as captain, William Anderson as first lieutenant, Fletcher Taylor as second lieutenant, James Little as third lieutenant, and Ike Berry as orderly sergeant.[9]

Part of Quantrill's command, including a company each under the command of John Jarrette and David Poole, were ordered to report to General McCulloch at Bonham. These companies had decided to join the regular army. From here McCulloch ordered Poole's and Jarrette's cavalrymen to report to Shelby, whose command was under Gen. Edmund Kirby Smith at Shreveport, Louisiana. These two companies were given a special mission to curtail cotton speculation along the Mississippi River.

The North allowed commerce in cotton speculation with the South by issuing special permits and licenses through the Treasury Department at the insistence of President Lincoln, who understood cotton's importance to the North. Northern speculators were buying cotton from Southern plantations along the river, and cotton shipments were escorted by Federal cavalry and protected by Federal gunboats. Southern cotton speculators accepted much-needed medical supplies, gun caps, clothing, and a few luxuries for their product, but along with them also came Union spies.

What came to be called the Red River campaign by the North was an operation to invade Louisiana with thirty thousand troops and the goal of capturing the cotton plantations, thus gaining the product and eliminating the need to do business with the enemy. General Smith ordered the two former guerrilla commands, now united under the leadership of Jarrette, to attack and make quick work of the illegal cotton trading. Owing to the guerrillas' efforts, western Louisiana and east Texas remained in Confederate hands. Jarrette received the thanks of General Smith in a special order.[10] When the winter of 1863–64 was over, most of the guerrillas who had joined the regular army returned to their former area of operations in Jackson County and took up guerrilla fighting again.

After conferring with Quantrill, McCulloch offered the guerrilla's services to Gen. Hamilton P. Bee on the Texas coast:

There is no doubt about [the guerrillas] being true Southern men, and, no odds what happens, will fight only on our side. They have been bad behaved in some instances, but have not been guilty of a fourth of what has been charged against them. They are in a country filled with the very worst character of men, numbers of whom are hid in the bush and come out at night and rob and steal, and there are plenty of enemies in the country who would have been glad to get up a conflict by telling bad tales upon them besides those that were true, and I really think the people are to a great extent unnecessarily uneasy about them. If these men are not kept on partisan service they will disband and scatter through the country, where, if bad men, they will do us great harm, if kept together under Quantrill they can be controlled. They are superbly armed and well mounted, and there is no reason that they should not do good service. They have not been paid for months, this should be done immediately, and let them see that they are to be treated properly, and required to behave themselves.[11]

The guerrillas who stayed in Quantrill's command had much attention and admiration directed toward them while they were in Texas. Fighting against the Federals in Missouri, the guerrillas had proved themselves demons in battle. Most had shown such bravery that they had become icons of individual courage, but as a result of their individual prowess in battle, they had also become hard to discipline as a fighting unit.

George Todd, whose fighting style was always the Rebel Yell and wild charge, drew to him the same caliber of men who reacted instinctively to the sound of the guns by charging pell-mell into the heat of battle, regardless of the danger or the odds.

William Anderson gained the nickname "Bloody Bill" after the Kansas City jail collapse that took the life of his sister and changed his tactics to not taking prisoners. He killed every Union soldier who fell into his hands. The word passed along the border, "Quantrill pardons rarely, but Anderson never does." Anderson's talisman was a black silken cord tied with a knot for every Federal he killed. In addition to the murder of his sister, he carried with him the memory of his father and uncle murdered in Kansas by Federals.

The motivating elements behind each of Anderson's men were similarly personal: revenge. Anderson and his men were resigned to the fact that they would probably die in battle, so they determined to take as many Union soldiers with them before they fell. Ike, James, and Richard Berry were brothers from Danville, Missouri, and all rode with Anderson. They had reason enough to hate the Federals; Union soldiers had reportedly raped their sisters.

Archie Clements was as vengeful as Anderson himself. Federal militiamen had burned the home of Clement's mother, leaving her destitute. Blue-eyed, nineteen years old, and not yet sporting a beard, Clements gained notoriety by personally killing fifty-four Federals in one year.

Sixteen-year-old Jesse James also rode with Anderson. Jesse still felt the cruel beating he took when he was fifteen years old and recalled the hanging of his stepfather when the Federals came to his house looking for his brother Frank. He could still feel the stripes across his back and the cut of the rope that the Federals put around his neck when they hanged him to get him to tell where his brother was. These experiences and the imprisonment of his mother and sister drove him into the ranks of the guerrillas.

Others were just as vengeful and motivated to ride with Anderson. The full catalog of atrocities committed against them have been forgotten to history, but a few stories survive. Before he joined the guerrillas, John Hicks George was hanged until almost dead to make him reveal Quantrill's location. Isaac Hall, Joseph Gibson, and Warren Welch all joined Quantrill after the Federals burned down their homes.

Quantrill's closest circle of men all had some horrible crime or dishonor perpetrated against their families by the Federals along the border. As a result they fought without mercy. Such fighters were hard to tame.

Invariably in all such circumstances, a few unsavory characters found their way into the ranks of the guerrillas. A soldier by the name of Morgan in Anderson's company stole a bolt of cloth belonging to one of Quantrill's men and had a pair of pants made from it. Quantrill could never sanction thievery among his men. When he found out about it, he had Morgan taken across the Red River, disarmed, and turned loose with the warning never to come back or he would be killed.

Shortly afterward Morgan did return and reportedly robbed and murdered an elderly farmer nearby the guerrilla's camp. Quantrill sent four of his men to arrest and execute him.

But Quantrill had not consulted Anderson before his decision. When Anderson found out, he became furious. Quantrill was known for the discipline that he maintained over his men while Anderson's men, although brave and relentless fighters in battle, were lacking in military discipline. Normally no one dared to stand up to Bill Anderson, especially when his fighting blood was up. Anderson knew that neither Quantrill nor his men were afraid of him, and he also knew that he could not start anything in camp. So Anderson stated that he would not belong to such a "damn outfit," and he took twenty men and rode off to Sherman to fetch his bride prior to setting out to establish a camp.

Losing Anderson was not a concern to Quantrill, but he was not going to let him take any men of his command with him. He ordered George Todd to round up the rest of the command for a muster. He then had Todd send ten men into Sherman to round up the deserters and bring them back.

Anderson received word of Quantrill's intentions and immediately rode to McCulloch's headquarters in Bonham. Anderson might have been angry, but he was still wary of Quantrill. He believed that Quantrill might have been out searching for him in the same way that he had searched for Morgan.

The ride into Bonham did nothing to quell Anderson's temper. Before Christmas two of Quantrill's men had been playing cards with Maj. George N. Butts, a local farmer and father-in-law to Benjamin Christian, Quantrill's friend and proprietor of a hotel in Sherman. Butts was later found dead along the road a few miles above Sherman. No one was ever accused of the murder, but the suspicion lay on the men who had been gambling with the man last: Fletcher Taylor and Andy McGuire. When Anderson appeared in Bonham, he told McCulloch that Quantrill and his men had been committing all sorts of crimes, including robbery and murder.

After Quantrill and Todd rode into Sherman to search for the deserters, they found their orderly sergeant, Ike Berry. They disarmed him and sent him back to camp under guard. After returning to camp they found Fletcher Taylor, who had just returned, and after disarming him, put him under an armed guard. Quantrill wanted Taylor to be tried and hanged for the murder of Butts. Quantrill sent a dispatch to McCulloch at Bonham requesting permission to hold a court-martial.[12]

The deserters were naturally upset. They remembered what Quantrill had done to Morgan for his infractions, and they worried that they would suffer the same fate. Taylor secured a weapon and joined Anderson in Bonham.

McCulloch had never fully appreciated the rough-and-tumble guerrillas from Missouri. They had attracted too much attention in Texas, and being an independent unit, they were impossible to put under anyone else's command.

The Confederate camp in Texas drew many unsavory characters. Deserters from the regular army congregated there, seeking fortune by preying on anyone and everyone they found. Many committed crimes then threw off suspicion by claiming to belong to the guerrilla bands from Missouri. In most cases, whenever a murder or robbery took place, the blame was directed toward Quantrill's command. Accusations began to mount against him. Andy Walker reported,

> It was during this time that a lot of fellows, claiming to be Quantrill's men, fell to robbing and killing in the country about McKinney and Dallas. Any mischief or atrocities committed within miles of Sherman, while Quantrill was there, were ostensibly blamed on Quantrill's men. General McCulloch brought Quantrill to task about them. Whenever Quantrill made a personal account of his men and their actions the accuser's opinion was always changed toward him and his men. Quantrill insisted that they were not his men, but declared that, if the general would commission him to do so, he would undertake to arrest them. The general agreed, and Quantrill sent George Todd with twenty men, of whom I was one, to try to apprehend the robbers. They got wind of us though, and had deserted those parts by the time we arrived.[13]

To divert attention away from his men, Anderson placed the blame for every alleged crime on Quantrill's command. After his escape to Bonham, Taylor also lay the blame on Quantrill. When Anderson's accusations were reported to McCulloch, the general sent for Quantrill's entire command. He intended to arrest them all without benefit of giving their colonel a chance to respond to the allegations or explain.

When he received the summons, Quantrill left George Todd and ten men behind to guard the camp while he and the rest of the command, fully armed and ready for the unexpected, rode toward Bonham. They arrived at McCulloch's headquarters in the city hotel around noon. As Colonel

Quantrill tied his horse to the hitch in front of the building, he ordered his men to stay with their mounts, keeping their bridles in their hands and alert for any trouble while he went inside.

As soon as he entered McCulloch's office at the top of the stairs, the general stood from behind his desk and said, "Quantrill, you are under arrest. Remove your side arms and throw them on the bed."

Quantrill was calm but furious as he did as the general ordered. When he threw his pistol belt on the bed in the corner, two guards stepped into the room. Quantrill protested and asked, "What's the meaning of this?"

McCulloch replied, "Well it's dinner time. Come and go down and have dinner with me and I will discuss it with you after dinner."

Quantrill refused, "No sir! I will not go to dinner."

When McCulloch invited him again to eat with him, Quantrill answered, "I consider this a strange way of doing business, General McCulloch. I have preferred a criminal charge against one of my officers. I placed him under guard. He made his escape from my camp, and now you place me under arrest on his word. No sir! I'll never eat another bite in Texas."

McCulloch left the room, leaving the two guards to watch Quantrill until his return.

Quantrill got up from his chair to get a drink of water from the cooler in the corner of the room. He drew the dipper of water from the jar, and just as he was putting it to his lips, he jumped to the bed and grabbed his pistols. To the two surprised guards, he said, "If you make a move, I'll kill you." He disarmed them then backed through the doorway, locking the door behind him.

As he made his way out he came upon two more guards at the bottom of the stairs. He surprised them also and, after disarming them, backed out into the street. Quantrill called out to his men, "Boys! The outfit is under arrest. Get on your horses and let's get out of here!" They rushed down the street and back to their camp at Mineral Springs.

When McCulloch was informed of Quantrill's escape, he ordered his troops to follow the guerrillas and bring back Quantrill. Bill Anderson was ordered to attach himself to these troops and follow Quantrill's band. They occasionally got close enough to fire some shots, but reportedly no one was hit. The pursuit was abandoned around five o'clock as darkness set in.

As soon as Quantrill arrived back in camp, he ordered his men to gather up their belongings. He ordered Todd on a night patrol to sweep around the camp to guard the men while they were packing. Todd's men rode up on a group of soldiers standing around a campfire. Todd called out, "Who are you?" They replied that they were Confederate militia. At that moment a

pistol from one of Todd's men accidentally went off, striking James Little in
the arm. The startled militia thought they were being shot at and took off
into the darkness. Todd chased them until they escaped into some timber.

As he was returning to his own camp, Todd encountered Anderson's men
hiding in the woods on the side of the trail. Todd arranged his men in the
woods opposite the trail where Anderson was hiding. Discovering it was
Todd, Anderson called out to him, "If you are not a damn set of cowards,
come on out and fight." Todd hollered back, "You have the most men with
you. If you are not a damn set of cowards, come on in and take us out." Some
fifty shots were exchanged in the darkness, but no one was hurt. Todd and his
men then made their way back to camp.

After getting a few hours sleep, Todd's men were again in the saddle on
another scout. In the morning Todd encountered a militia company sent out
to find Quantrill's command. Todd rode up within range of the militia captain
and asked the commander what he was doing. He replied, "We have been
sent down by General McCulloch's orders to get Quantrill." Todd emphatically told him, "Well, don't you know that you are not going to get him? Now,
you listen to me, Captain. You had better get your men together and go back
to Bonham. You tell General McCulloch that Quantrill said that if he was
molested any further he would turn his bushwhackers loose on Texas and he
would not be responsible for anything that might happen for what his men
did." Quantrill's message was, "I'm not fighting Confederates, but if you try to
arrest us I'll certainly fight you. If you or your command follow me any further,
I will fight you as long as I have one man alive with a cartridge to burst and
the strength to pull the trigger." The militia captain turned his men around
and rode back to Bonham. He reported to McCulloch, "It wouldn't do to fool
with that man."

After that the guerrillas weren't harassed any further.[14] They took their
time packing their belongings, and after two days they broke camp and
headed to the north side of the Red River, out of McCulloch's jurisdiction.
Once they crossed the river they were once again in the department of their
old friend Gen. Douglas Cooper. He provided them with provisions until
they could return to Missouri in the spring. McCulloch left them undisturbed
and unmolested, apparently thankful that they had removed themselves from
his jurisdiction.

On or about March 10, 1864, Quantrill broke camp and his First Regi-
ment, First Brigade, Army of the South began the trip back to Missouri.
There were only sixty-four members remaining after Anderson's departure.
Col. Vard Cockrell, a brother of Gen. Francis M. Cockrell, who for many

years was a U.S. senator from Missouri, accompanied Quantrill for part of his journey, as far as Neosho, Missouri. Here the advance was ambushed, and Cockrell was wounded.

On their way north, the guerrillas met Gen. Stand Watie and stayed with him for two days. Col. Daniel McIntosh, who had helped escort them into Texas, joined them and rode with them as far as the Canadian River. They followed the same path back that they had taken months before on their way to Texas. Near Baxter Springs they came across the grave of their old comrade Bill Bledsoe and the black jayhawker Jack Mann. Because the graves had been shallow, the corpses were now exposed.

From the Canadian River to the Arkansas River, early spring rains were an impediment almost their entire trip. All of the rivers they had to cross were swollen from flooding. They traveled both day and night. Quantrill and Todd always led in the van. They never asked their men to do anything they were not willing to do themselves. When a swollen river was reached, Quantrill and Todd swam their horses across first then lit fires to guide the rest of the company.

On one such occasion, Quantrill came upon two abandoned log cabins with hogs rummaging around inside. He ran to each of them, closing the doors and trapping the hogs inside. Riding back to the riverbank, he called out to the men, "Hurry up, boys. I've got a good supper for you over here."[15]

Quantrill next led his men into Carthage, Missouri, on May 18, hoping to force the small Federal garrison there to surrender. He sent a message to the commander, Capt. Philip Roher, to bring out the Seventh Missouri Cavalry to fight. Roher decided he could conduct a better defense within the walls of the town's brick buildings, so he declined Quantrill's invitation. The guerrillas decided not to attack and continued their journey northward.

At dawn on May 20 they launched an attack on Lamar, Missouri. The season before they had failed to take the town. This time they caught the Federals by surprise. The forty Union soldiers were busy in the early morning hours feeding their horses and making their breakfast over small fires.

When the guerrillas attacked, Sgt. Jefferson Cavender and a small detachment of the Seventh Missouri Cavalry ran into the brick ruins made by Quantrill's raid the preceding fall and grabbed the rifles they had prepared for such an emergency. Many of the Federal soldiers were militiamen who stayed in their own homes. When they heard the battle begin they hid rather than help their comrades in town. Most of them ran and scattered while some fled on horseback all the way to Fort Scott. Some fled on foot to the timber along Moody Creek. Only nine Federal soldiers stayed to fight.

As the guerrillas swirled around the entrenchments, the Union troops managed to shoot several attackers out of their saddles. Numerous times Quantrill sent in a message to Cavender seeking his surrender, but each time it was denied. The Federals used the lapse in the fighting for their men to reload their empty weapons. Cavender and his men had decided to sell their lives as dearly as possible and knew that their chances for survival were greater by fighting than by surrendering. In this they were correct, because Quantrill eventually pulled his men out of town and withdrew to the north.

As the guerrilla band rode away, they took with them thirty casualties; none of the defenders were reported hurt.[16] The guerrillas managed to cross the Osage and Grand Rivers and make their way into Cass County toward their old camps in Jackson County. They still wore Federal uniforms and managed to capture several Union soldiers along the way whom they shot on Quantrill's orders. The company then swung east into Johnson County, where the guerrillas stopped at a large farmhouse near Chapel Hill.

Quantrill and Todd intended to ride into Jackson County to assess the situation, but before they could get started, they learned that two hundred troopers of the Second Colorado Cavalry were waiting for them just six miles south of Warrensburg. After breakfast Quantrill scattered his men in groups of three and four to requisition horses and equipment and to rest. He intended to take all the men who had serviceable mounts and attack the first Federal command he encountered then withdraw toward Warrensburg. This would draw the Federals away from Jackson County and allow the men who needed new mounts and supplies to seek them out from Southern sympathizers. Horses and men were worn from the long march through the muck and mire of barely passable roads and lack of forage and food, but through it all, Quantrill was able to hold his men together and grapple with every Federal unit he met.

John McCorkle, accompanied by George Wigginton, Dave Hilton, and George Langdon, ventured into Lafayette County. Three of them were barefooted. They searched out friends who could supply them with new clothes, weapons, food, and mounts. They headed for Hilton's mother's house by the Missouri River. She had been living there with her two daughters and youngest son since soldiers had burned down their house. McCorkle left Hilton there while the rest of them went to the home of John Wigginton near Waverly. Wigginton's former house, like Hilton's, had been destroyed by the Federals.

Meanwhile, while drawing the Colorado troops away from Jackson County, Quantrill spied a smaller detail of eight militia cavalrymen heading toward Warrensburg. When the two groups confronted each other, each halted then sent out a detachment to ascertain the other's identity. Quantrill spoke first: "We are Colorado troops going west on special duty. And you?" The reply was, "Missouri militia under Lieutenant Nash, en route to Warrensburg." Facing the eight Federals were Quantrill and twelve guerrillas. All of them rode forward after this exchange, except for one militiaman who held back and remained wary. There was no further need for parley.

The guerrillas' sudden charge struck like a thunderclap. Quantrill shot Nash and one other militiaman. Jesse James, William Hulse, George T. Maddox, George Shepherd, and John Ross each shot one. The one wary militiaman turned and fled unpursued.

After this skirmish, Quantrill turned back to probe the Federal defenses in Jackson County. On his trail were the Colorado troops from Warrensburg. These soldiers were quite different from the Kansas units or the Home Guard militia. John Edwards Newman described them as:

> slashing fellows, fond of a grapple and fond of a *melee*. They were grave, quiet, middle-aged men, the most of them, rarely influenced by sentiment and not at all by romantic folly. They volunteered to fight, and they did it as they would follow an Indian trail or develop a silver mine. They could be whipped, and they were whipped; but such fighting as would do for the militia would not do for them. Man to man, the best of the border knew that to drive them required close work and steady work.[17]

It had rained almost incessantly since the little band of guerrillas had left Texas. Pursued by the Colorado troops while heading toward Jackson County, Quantrill discovered two companies of Federal infantry lying in ambush along the road, waiting for his arrival. Caught between two overpowering forces, he decided to countermarch and attack the Colorado troops to his rear.

When he began the attack, he found to his favor that the Colorado column was not closed up. He hurled his little force at the Federals with everything he could muster. The guerrillas charged the enemy down a narrow lane before attempting to turn off into some heavy timber beside the road. But before they could reach the safety of the timber, one man, William McGuire, was thrown from his horse. While McGuire tried to remount, Quantrill held his men in a hasty defense until McGuire could get away.

Reeling from Quantrill's initial charge, the Coloradans rushed up as the guerrillas stopped to protect their downed comrade. The guerrillas killed nine Federals in their wild charge. McGuire had shot down three before he was thrown from his horse. All the guerrillas who protected McGuire as he remounted his horse received wounds except Quantrill and Todd, who were the closest to the enemy.

The word was carried on every breath and every telegraph wire. Quantrill was back! Historians have suggested that, after the Lawrence raid, Quantrill's men were ashamed of their deed and of Quantrill's leadership. But evidence shows just the opposite: Quantrill's band came back into the border area in the spring of 1864 to wreak more havoc with the Union forces than ever before. Yet after this date the Missouri guerrillas showed little military discipline except for the men who were directly under Quantrill's command. The separate commands led by Todd and Anderson committed the most horrendous retaliatory measures known along the border.

As a result Jackson Country swarmed with Federal cavalry. The border warriors in blue had suffered too much in the past to allow another season of their blood to flow on Missouri soil. Every Federal soldier available was assigned to a detachment, and every detachment was hurried into Jackson County to hunt down Quantrill and destroy him. Guerrilla Hampton Watts recalled "a large force of the enemy had concentrated, who made too frequent reconnaissance into territory almost rurally depopulated, making it difficult to obtain food for either man or steed."[18]

Where once there were hundreds of Federals stationed in Jackson County, now there were thousands. In fact, seven thousand Union soldiers were assigned to Jackson County with the sole purpose of hunting down the guerrillas and destroying them. Their constant patrolling through the timber along the Sni and Little Blue made the lack of detection impossible. Several of Quantrill's men were discovered and died singly or in small groups.

The area became unstable for any concentrated guerrilla operations. The guerrillas' main source of strength—a sympathetic populace—had either been killed or driven from the area. Without the sustenance and shelter provided by Southern sympathizers, the guerrillas' means to resist had eroded. Continuing the fight meant shifting their base of operations elsewhere. Many of the refugees from Jackson County had fled east into Howard, Lafayette, and Saline Counties in the heart of Missouri, and the guerrillas followed close behind.

Quantrill realized that the time was not right to commence large-scale operations. It was still too early in the season for the trees to be in full foliage, which was necessary to hide his men and movements. The rain had made travel almost impossible. Roads were washed out. Rivers were overflowing and too swift for crossing. The bottomlands were nothing more than bogs and swamps.

The Federal commander of the Department of Missouri, Gen. William S. Rosecrans, decided to launch a major campaign to search out and destroy Quantrill's company. He called upon Col. Thomas Moonlight and a force composed of the Fifth, Eleventh, and Fifteenth Kansas Jayhawker Regiments. They were joined by Col. James H. Ford and the Second Colorado. These combined units combed through the tangled lairs and heavy underbrush of the Blue and the Sni regions looking for Quantrill and his men. The Union troops force-marched and countermarched until June 20 but could claim few dead guerrillas.

Two who did not escape the Union patrols were William McGuire and Theodore Sanders. Both were surprised while recovering from wounds in one of their old hiding places along the bank of the Sni Creek in Blue Springs. Surrounded and outnumbered by a patrol of eighty Federals, McGuire killed three and Sanders two while wounding five others before they were shot down in a hail of bullets. In the fight McGuire suffered sixteen bullet wounds, Sanders was shot eleven times.

At midnight on June 22 George Shepherd came into camp with the remnants of the band that had been left in Johnson County. He also brought news that a force of seven hundred Federal cavalry were behind him and would likely attack at daylight the next day. With this news Quantrill led his men to an area of timber along the Little Blue that showed the most growth of the season. Here he rested and sent out scouting parties for forage and food. He was unable to venture far with a large body of men, so he split up his company into small groups that rode out on their own to seek targets of opportunity.

Eight guerrillas crossed the Missouri River on a raft and attacked a Federal garrison in Camden, Ray County. The little band was composed of Frank and Jesse James, Allen Parmer, Ben Morrow, James Noland, Joel Chiles, William Gaugh, and Sylvester Akers. This group, all wearing Federal uniforms, next rode into Claytonville, in Clay County. They surprised and captured a Federal militiaman named Bradley Bond. A few years earlier Bond had headed the scouting party that killed four Clay County citizens and hanged the Jameses' stepfather and insulted their mother. Bond pleaded for his life, but Jesse coolly repeated his past crimes to him then shot him.

The following day the same group of guerrillas caught Alvas Dailey on the road. Dailey had been part of the scouting party with Bond when they visited the Jameses' home. Frank James shot Dailey. They left him unburied in the road. Before withdrawing across the river, the guerrillas left ten Federals killed and seven wounded.

David Poole gathered forty men along the Tabo Creek in Lafayette County and raided Concordia. All wore Federal uniforms. Poole wanted to capture the militia without raising an alarm, so he had one of his men carry a Union flag at the head of his column. A militiamen, however, recognized the guerrillas before they reached the town and alerted the garrison. The militiamen made it to the protection of their blockhouse before they were attacked. The guerrillas did little damage except to rob some Unionists before heading back to Jackson County and linking up with George Todd.

At this time Quantrill made one of the most important decisions of his career: He decided to end military operations in Jackson County. John Newman Edwards, Shelby's adjutant who knew Quantrill in Texas, reported that Quantrill "was sick, wounded, barely able to ride, and worn [out] from long pain and exposure." Edwards commented that the decision to abandon Jackson County was necessitated because "Quantrill, suffering somewhat from old wounds, and indisposed generally, took with him into Howard County sixteen tried men altogether. His object was not so much to fight as to rest, not so much to seek adventure as to recuperate. He found what he sought for, respite and inactivity."[19]

Quantrill had suffered either a saber or a pistol wound to his face that left a scar. With a group of handpicked men, he left for Howard County in the heart of Little Dixie. He knew that Price would soon be making another campaign into Missouri in the fall of 1864, so he decided to rest for a while and then meet with the general at a prearranged point and time in Howard County. Those who accompanied him were his wife, Kate, and Jim Little, John Barker, Tom Harris, Dave Hilton, Tom Evans, George Shepherd, John Ross, and Bill Toler.

He had been contemplating this move and a year earlier had discussed the idea with Andy Walker. "It's a lost cause," he confided to his friend. "We'd better make preparations to get out of the country; they'll hang every one of us. We ought to get some money together to take us out of the country. Don't say a word about this." He had no doubt that surrender was not an option and that the Federals would hang him. While in Texas Quantrill asked Gen. John Magruder, commander of the Trans-Mississippi Department, for a pass for himself and five others to get across the Mississippi and into Canada. As it turned out, Magruder was willing to issue passes for only two. Quantrill, unwilling to leave his men behind, decided to return to Missouri.

When Quantrill shared his plans with George Todd, Todd became furious and uncontrollable. He called Quantrill a coward and accused him of running away. Numerous reports followed of a falling out between the two guerrilla leaders. Some of the guerrillas claimed it was a quarrel over a card game. One account surfaced that Todd had pulled his pistol on Quantrill and forced him to admit in front of his men that he was afraid of Todd. This seems impractical, as Todd's life would have been forfeit after such a daring act. Another account claimed that Quantrill shot at Todd. Other guerrillas, however, said it would be highly unlikely that Quantrill would have missed or that Todd would not have killed Quantrill afterward.

Todd's quarrelsome attitude was well known. Harrison Trow remembered him as "sometimes a very blunt man," and William H. Gregg added that Todd had no regard for the lives of his men. Joe Vaughn stated, "Quantrill was always well liked by his men. He always treated them well. But Captain George Todd was a tyrant. Quantrill and he didn't agree."

Todd's abrasive attitude had already caused the departure of some of Quantrill's best men. His disposition had indeed been the cause at one time or another of the withdrawal of several of Quantrill's oldest and best men from the command, among them Bill Haller and brothers Hicks and Hiram George, who eventually went to the Confederate army. Andy Walker noted that Todd was a formidable fighter and as brave a man as ever went into battle, but he was overbearing among the men, quick tempered, and bent on having things his own way, even to the disregard of Quantrill. Quantrill told Walker it was distasteful to him to operate with a man with whom he could not get along. Quantrill admitted, "I have had to give way to him too often."

Consequently, Todd was not respected except for his fighting abilities, while Quantrill, tactful and companionable, was a favorite with the men. Walker described an earlier incident concerning Todd's character:

One morning Quantrill, Todd and I were in camp alone, currying our horses. Quantrill and I, on finishing, stood at a little distance from Todd, and Quantrill, in a playful way, flipped a twig at George, taking him on the cheek. Stung for the moment [with] unthinking resentment, George threw a hard clod, striking Quantrill with stunning force in the ear. Both whipped out their guns and would have fired in another breath; but I was quickly between them, shouting, "Hold on here! You don't know what you are doing, what do you mean? You ought to be ashamed of yourselves." Todd, realizing that he had acted with undue heat, turned on his heel, and walked off in the direction of the trees. Quantrill went to his tent, and I joined him presently. He declared that he would kill George, but stated, "It would be a pity to kill such a good fighter." I put as good a face on the matter as I could for George, knowing his weakness.

That same afternoon Quantrill said to Walker, "Andy, saddle up, and ride out with me. I can see that George is offended at you for siding with me. I believe that you'd better part company with him while you are still on good terms. You can't tell what might happen if he was to lose his temper some day." Walker claims that he left the command later because of Todd's continuing grudge against him.[20]

While in Texas, Sterling Price had apprised Quantrill of his plans for another Missouri campaign. He would be heading straight through the middle of the state, stopping only at the Missouri River, before making a westward turn toward Kansas City and destroying all the Federal forces he encountered. Price knew he would need all the partisan rangers he could muster to support his raid by drawing off Federal resistance until he made his final assault on Kansas City. The upheaval resulting from the guerrillas' activities would force the Union command to muster its forces closer to home, thus preventing it from concentrating in strength against Price.

The first stage in this mission was to be a successful assault as far north as Howard and Cooper Counties, which lay along the Missouri River. Here Price would meet up with the partisan ranger bands after they had disrupted the Federals, thus making a clear path for the army's final objective.

By early summer 1864 Quantrill gathered his most trusted, tried, and true men and prepared to march to Howard County. He met Warren Welch near the Blackwater Ford and asked him to pilot them through since Welch was familiar with the territory. They traveled two days and nights until they came to a place close to Arrow Rock in Saline County, where they made camp.

Quantrill recognized the area as the home of some friends who were refugees from Jackson County. He left Little and Barker in camp while he went to find his old friends. When he appeared at their door, they greeted him warmly and invited Quantrill and Welch to stay for supper. Afterward Quantrill returned to camp with a large basket of food for his men.

Quantrill told Welch that he had decided to stay here for two weeks unless the Federals found him. He instructed Welch to return after that time and they would secure a skiff and cross the river, but when Welch returned, he found Quantrill and his men had already crossed the stream.[21]

Back in Jackson County, Quantrill had left George Todd in charge of his remaining forty guerrillas. During the month of May the Federals had chased the guerrilla band from place to place, giving them no peace or rest. By now most of the guerrillas had made their way back into Jackson County after friends provided them with supplies and mounts. Todd passed the word for the guerrillas to assemble at Bone Hill in eastern Jackson County.

Troops of the Second Colorado Cavalry, commanded by Col. James H. Ford, were stationed in Independence and had been actively on Todd's trail. They had made repeated threats that, if they ever met up with the guerrillas, they would exterminate the entire command. Todd decided to lure them out of the garrison and into an ambush.

Eight miles south of Independence, on the Independence to Harrisonville road, the guerrillas gathered at an old rendezvous at the Howard farm. From here they rode to the nearby farm of the widow Moore, and in the early morning hours they cut the telegraph wires along the road, knowing that it would bring the Federals out to reconnoiter. The guerrillas took up positions in the woods opposite the Moore farm and waited.

Just down the road and only a quarter of a mile from the Moore farm was an open field in the half-mile-wide valley of the Little Blue. It was here the guerrillas planned to pounce on the anticipated Federal patrol. The ambush was set up along a long hill on the south of the Little Blue, where the road led up from the bottomland to higher land on the south. Commonly referred to by the guerrillas as Manasseth Gap, it followed up a branch between hills on either side and was covered with brush. Todd stationed pickets at either end of the ambush site to give the alarm when the Federals approached.

Manasseth Gap was an ideal place for an ambush. The ridge on either side was high enough that the attacking party could fire down on the road, and the sides were so steep it was almost impossible for a man on horseback to climb up. One of the guerrillas stated, "Most of our men were in the edge of the brush on the east side of the road. South of the cut, on the opposite side, was an open field that looked as though it had been in wheat for the last crop that had been raised on it."

The guerrillas waited patiently until two o'clock that afternoon. Their patience lasted only another two hours. Todd and Lee McMurtry crossed the road and went into the widow Moore's house after hitching their horses out front. Almost immediately the pickets gave the alarm that about twenty Federals were coming down the road. Todd and McMurtry ran out of the house and made their way down the road, closely followed by the Federal cavalry.

Springing to the aid of his comrades, Dick Yeager ordered the rest of the guerrillas to charge. Seeing guerrillas gaining on them from the rear, the Federals guided their horses off the road and into the timber, where they tried to escape on foot. Yeager commanded his men to dismount and follow the fleeing Federals.

Just as they dismounted, they heard someone yell, "Charge!" and looked back to see the rest of the Colorado cavalry, numbering around forty-two men under the command of Capt. Seymour W. Wagner, charging down on them. Yeager immediately commanded the guerrillas to remount, face about, and charge. The guerrillas were still able to attack in the open field just as they had planned. One guerrilla remembered, "None of our men had less than two, and some of them three and four Colt's six-shooters, while the Federals only had one, with carbine and saber."

Amid the rearing and plunging of horses, carbines were useless. The smoke and the dust raised by the animals soon got so thick that it was almost impossible to distinguish friend from foe, and men had to be careful to identify their targets for fear it would be one of their own men.[22]

The guerrillas charged through the Federal line with pistols blazing. Then they wheeled their horses and charged again with the same deadly effect. Seven times they charged and wheeled about until the Federals were out of ammunition with no time to reload. The Federals then attempted to charge the guerrillas with sabers. Armed with a double brace of revolvers apiece, the guerrillas had just begun to fight. When they discovered that the Federal guns were empty, they got as close to them as possible and used their revolvers to the best advantage.

Every man on both sides knew that it was a fight to the death; no quarter was asked or given. At the first rush, Yeager rode straight at Wagner. The Union captain shot off half of Yeager's mustache in the melee before he himself fell from his horse, shot through the body. They then had a hand-to-hand fight. Wagner was wounded but kept advancing on foot with a pistol in each hand. Some of the Coloradans' horses became unmanageable, so they dismounted to fight on foot. These men perished where they stood. One guerrilla remembered:

I saw a man draw his saber and start for me. I waited until he got nearly close enough to hit me with it, then I aimed a shot at his body. The shot must have struck a vital part for the saber immediately dropped from his hand. As quick as I possibly could, I fired two more shots. When I fired the last shot my pistol was not three feet from his body. His horse went on past me and the rider did not fall from him until he had gotten 15 or 20 paces beyond. The Coloradoans were credited with fighting fearlessly and desperately, but without effect. They had shot their pistols too low, which resulted in only wounding three guerrillas; Ike Flanery, Henry Potter and Warren Welch, and killing five of the guerrillas' horses and wounding six or seven more. When the ghastly toll was taken, thirty-seven Federals lay dead in the open field including Captain Wagner. The rest retreated into the timber or back towards Independence with the guerrillas in hot pursuit. Some of the Federals at this engagement were mounted on better horses and managed to escape. Dick Kinney, Frank James and Ike Flanery followed the routed enemy in sight of Independence, James killing his fourth man within fifty steps of the picket post. Afterwards the Coloradoans were very cautious when they saw any of Quantrill's men and managed to keep their distance.[23]

Todd took muster after this brief but hotly contested skirmish, and all his men answered up.

The guerrillas managed to disrupt all modes of transportation and communication in and out of Jackson County. Mail service was stopped because the mail agent could not get enough escorts to deliver the mail. The guerrillas cut the telegraph lines and destroyed the poles. General Rosecrans ordered all riverboats to cease their trips on the Missouri River beyond Jefferson City because, due to the guerrilla attacks along the shore, the trip was too hazardous.

All during the hot summer months Todd kept the Federals busy patrolling every road and path in the county and looking for any sign of him or his men. In the first three weeks of July, Colonel Ford sent out more than a hundred patrols, engaged the guerrillas more than twenty-eight times, and claimed to have killed more than a hundred of them. Ford also claimed to have ridden over ten thousand miles in his efforts to bring the guerrillas to bay.[24]

In an August 9 letter Ford informed Rosecrans that he had received word that all the guerrilla leaders with three to five hundred men were in the Sni-A-Bar hills, twelve miles north of Chapel Hill in Lafayette County. Ford's scout, T. C. Kelsy, reported that the guerrillas were waiting for Price to make another raid into Missouri and mount an attack into Kansas.[25]

By late summer Bill Anderson had also returned to Jackson County. He led some of the most desperate guerrilla fighters into Lafayette County, first, to rest after the long trip up from Texas and, second, to secure supplies and additional weapons. Anderson was attacked by a militia company led by a notorious captain named Colly who foolishly underestimated the guerrillas' ferocity. Colly was bested, losing his life and that of twenty-two of his men before the remainder of his command was scattered in every direction.

Anderson's subsequent patrol through Lafayette, Ray, and Carroll Counties became one long skirmish. In one of these battles Fletcher Taylor was caught in an ambush. He was seriously wounded by a shotgun blast to his right arm. His comrades kidnapped a doctor, who amputated Taylor's arm and saved his life.

Anderson moved north of the Missouri River and marched by way of Ray, Carroll, and Saline Counties before crossing into Howard County. Like Todd and Poole, Anderson headed his command toward Howard County, where Quantrill was waiting.

Throughout the summer Anderson kept the Federals worried about where he would strike next. On June 12, near Kingsville, Anderson and forty guerrillas in Federal uniforms attacked Cpl. John V. Parman and fourteen men of the First Cavalry, Missouri State Militia. Only Parman and two other men escaped. Two days later, north of Lexington, Anderson attacked a wagon train and twelve Federals. The guerrillas killed eight then burned the wagons and shot the twelve mules. A month later, on July 11, Anderson and twenty of his men were reported to be in Carroll County.

Newspapers in Lexington, Missouri, printed an article urging the public to take up arms against Anderson's band. In reply Anderson submitted an editorial to the Federal commanders and the citizens at large:

> In reading both your papers I see you urge the policy of the citizens taking up arms to defend their persons and property. You are only asking them to sign their death warrants. Do you not know, sirs, that you have some of Missouri's proudest, best, and noblest sons to cope with? Sirs, ask the people of Missouri, who are acquainted with me, if Anderson ever robbed them or mistreated them in any manner. All those that speak the truth will say never. Then what protection do they want? It is from thieves, not such men as I profess to have under my command. My command can give them more protection than all the Federals in the State against such enemies. There are thieves and robbers in the community, but they do not belong to any organized band; they do not fight for principles; they are for self-interest; they are just as afraid of me as they are of the Federals. I will help the citizens rid the country of them. They are not friends of mine. I have used all that language can do to stop their thefts. I will now see what I can do by force. But listen to me, fellow-citizens; do not obey this last order. Do not take up arms if you value your lives and property. It is not in my power to save your lives if you do. If you proclaim to be in arms against the guerrillas I will kill you. I will hunt you down like wolves and murder you. You cannot escape. It will not be the Federals after you. Your arms will be no protection to you. Twenty-five of my men can whip all that can get together. It will not be militia such as [Col. James] McFerran's, but regulars that have been in the field for three years, that are armed with from two to four pistols and Sharps rifles. I commenced at the first of this war to fight for my country, not to steal from it. I

have chosen guerrilla warfare to revenge myself for wrongs that I could not honorably avenge otherwise. I lived in Kansas when this war commenced. Because I would not fight the people of Missouri, my native State, the Yankees sought my life, but failed to get me. Revenged themselves by murdering my father, destroying all my property, and have since that time murdered one of my sisters and kept the other two in jail twelve months. But I have fully glutted my vengeance. I have killed many. I am a guerrilla. I have never belonged to the Confederate Army, nor do my men. A good many of them are from Kansas. I have tried to war with the Federals honorably, but for retaliation I have done things, and am fearful will have to do that I would shrink from if possible to avoid. I have tried to teach the people of Missouri that I am their friend, but if you think that I am wrong, then it is your duty to fight. Take up arms against me and you are Federals. Your doctrine is an absurdity and I will kill you for being fools. Beware, men, before you make this fearful leap. I feel for you. You are in a critical situation. But remember there is a Southern army headed by the best men in the nation. Many of their homes are in Missouri and they will have the State or die in the attempt. You that sacrifice your principles for fear of losing your property will, I fear, forfeit your right to a citizenship in Missouri. Young men, leave your mothers and fight for your principles. Let the Federals know that Missouri's sons will not be trampled on. I have no time to say anything more to you. Be careful how you act, for my eyes are upon you.[26]

Anderson's men killed nine Federals before turning on July 15 toward Huntsville in Randolph County. Anderson had been raised in Huntsville and had attended school there. Union Capt. W. R. Samuel was in the city hotel when he was awakened. "About daylight," he reported, "I heard a clatter of horses up the main street and looked out and saw somewhere between sixty and one hundred men riding down in martial array, like trained soldiers. They all had on the blue coats of the United States army, and I felt no apprehension. I never dreamed for a minute it was Anderson's gang until I saw them dismount and break in the doors of the stores."

The guerrillas took forty thousand dollars from the bank and another sixty thousand dollars from businesses and citizens. They broke into the stores by backing their horses to the front doors of the buildings then spurring the animals, which kicked in the doors with ease.

By July 22 Anderson was in Allen, Missouri. When a party of Federals attacked him, he shot twenty of their horses before making his escape. On the same day he attacked another force and managed to kill six of them. On the next day he attacked a company of forty men of the Seventeenth Illinois Cavalry. The next day he moved against Huntsville and killed another two Federals. On July 25 Anderson was in Middle Grove, Missouri. The following day, as he slowly made his way toward Howard County, he burned a 150-foot span of the Shelbina and Salt River Bridge on the Hannibal and St. Joseph Railroad and torched the depots at Lakenan and Shelbina.

George Todd sent couriers to his detached squads with orders to make their way to Lafayette County and join up with David Poole. He would join them there. Once together the two guerrilla leaders decided to strike eastward and attack a Federal company stationed at Arrow Rock in Saline County. Todd was assigned to surround the town and prevent any Federals from escaping while Poole's men attacked the town itself.

Using the same tactics as he had at Concordia, Poole sent a man forward with a Union flag, but a Federal recognized the man and sounded the alarm. The Federals raced to their horses and fled the town. As they were firing back on the pursuing guerrillas, they managed to wound Dick Yeager. The guerrillas carried Yeager to the nearby home of Isaac Flanery's father, who was a refugee from Jackson County. While Yeager was recovering from his wounds, Federals learned of his location, and a company of cavalry from Marshall killed him.

North of the Missouri River, Anderson passed through Richmond in Ray County and made camp. Before morning he was ambushed and attacked by 300 militiamen and 150 Kansas Redlegs under Col. Edwin C. Catherwood. Displaying excellent battlefield tactics, Anderson hollered out when the ambush commenced for half of his men to lay down a field of fire while the other half quickly saddled their horses. Amidst a shower of minie balls that kicked up the dust around them and cut limbs from nearby trees, the guerrillas managed to mount and counterattack. The guerrillas made a mad dash through the Federal lines but lost several men in the process.

Anderson's horse was shot out from under him. Archie Clements took him up behind him as they escaped. Leading the charge, seventeen-year-old Dock Rupe was shot from his saddle. Riding next to him was Jesse James, who was wounded during the attack. Woot Hill rode up to assist Rupe and realized that the young man was breathing his last. Before Rupe died he handed his pistols to Hill along with a final message for his mother.

The Federal fire took a devastating toll and wounded several more of Anderson's men. Cave Wyatt was shot through the chest, and Patrick McMacane was shot in the left side. Peyton Long's pistol was shot from his hand. William Reynolds fell with a broken arm alongside Jesse James. Frank

James, attempting to come to his brother's aid, was wounded in the face and leg. Anderson himself was wounded in the thigh. Other wounded guerrillas included Archie Clements, Hiram Guess, and Theodore Cassell.

Finally arriving in Howard County and searching for Quantrill, Anderson disbanded his company until September 2 to rest and resupply. They scattered in small groups across the county, stopping at friendly farmhouses to seek food and shelter.

Union Maj. Austin King from Fayette reported that his men on September 12 killed five of Anderson's men and captured seven horses and twelve pistols. One captive was seventeen-year-old Al Carter, who had moved his family to Howard County from Kansas City because of General Orders No. 11. The other was seventeen-year-old Buck Collins, who was foraging for food with Carter when they were cut off and surrounded at a farmhouse by twenty-five Federals looking for Anderson. They shot the two men from their saddles. After killing Carter, the Federals shot out his eyes then scalped him. Carter had long black curly hair, and the Federals believed they had killed Anderson. The atrocity only showed the deep hatred of the Union troops toward the guerrillas and the brutal deeds of which they were capable.[27]

Mustering his men on September 15, Anderson's first mission was to search out a Union commander in Boonville who was robbing Southern families and killing old men. In the meantime, Capt. Joseph Parks had crossed the river and boldly announced: "I'm here to capture or to kill Bill Anderson." Anderson found Parks leading seventy-six cavalrymen of the Fourth Missouri Cavalry the following day. Here the guerrillas waited in the thick brush along a narrow lane five miles east of New Franklin, along the Fayette to Rocheport road.

Anderson sent Arch Clements with eleven men to make a feint upon the Federal company to draw them back to the waiting guerrillas. Instead, the twelve guerrillas charged the shocked Federals, who turned to flee without firing a shot. Clements chased the retreating Union troops for four miles, managing to shoot twenty-two out of the saddle and capture forty of their horses.

Shortly after this engagement, a Federal scouting party of two hundred men found James Bissett and four others of Anderson's men while they were at breakfast at a farmhouse in eastern Howard County. Bissett was described as "an educated gentleman, with a courtesy that was displayed in both address and manner; a superb horseman, a born soldier, with a valor and boldness devoid of fear." It was nine o'clock in the morning, and a strong rain began falling when the five guerrillas turned their horses from the road to seek shelter in a nearby barn. The guerrillas had removed their saddle blankets to dry and were busy oiling their pistols when a Federal patrol discovered their tracks and followed them to the barn.

With no picket on watch, James Bissett, James Wilson, Harvey Brown, Thomas Fulton, and Patrick McMacane were taken by surprise. Firing their pistols with both hands while trying to get to their horses, Bissett and Brown were shot down at the first charge. The rest lay wounded against a tree trunk. Each man had a pistol in his hand, ready to take a few Federals with them. Fulton tried to rally the men. A round to the head killed Wilson. Fulton, wounded numerous times, hollered out a last good-bye to his comrades before he fell. McMacane was the last to fall. The Federals rushed at them still firing, riddling their bodies until they were unrecognizable.

One of the attacking officers recalled, "They fought desperately before we succeeded in their killing." The five guerrillas managed to kill thirteen Federals and wound twenty-one before being overpowered. Official reports failed to mention that the Federals scalped the dead guerrillas.[28]

When Anderson was notified of the deaths of his men, he was visibly affected. Guerrilla Hampton Watts was present and recalled that "great tears coursed down his cheeks, his breast heaved and his body shook with vehement agitation."[29] Watts noted that Anderson was morose for several days afterward, planning an equitable revenge for the men he lost.

George Todd made his way across the Missouri River on September 13 and three days later engaged a militia company in Ray County. In the advance of Todd's column was a company under regular army Capt. Thomas Todd of Fayette and a newcomer by the name of John Thrailkill who brought with him sixteen men.

Thrailkill was by occupation a painter in northwest Missouri when the war started. He was engaged, but on the eve of his wedding, a militia patrol rode to the bride's home and killed her fifty-year-old father on the doorstep in front of his daughter. She suffered an emotional breakdown and later died. Thereafter Thrailkill became known as a ruthless killer all over northern Missouri.

Leading George Todd's advance, Thrailkill's company often skirmished with Federal militia. Todd's forty men and Poole's thirty men made a long-range patrol through the counties east of Kansas City and toward Howard County, where they knew Quantrill was staying. Together they attacked the Federal garrison in Tipton and killed its garrison of forty militiamen. Leaving Moniteau County, the guerrillas next raided the town of Boonville in Cooper County.

Here Riley Crawford was shot from his saddle by a load of "buck and ball" fired by a militiaman in ambush from a fence corner.[30] Not yet seventeen years old, Riley had witnessed the hanging of his father and the murder of his two sisters by Federal troops. Thereafter he killed every Union soldier who fell into his hands. Because of his youth, Riley's death was much lamented by his fellow guerrillas. In revenge, they fought ferociously, and the result of their raiding soon claimed 114 Federal militiamen killed and 80 horses captured, 50 recruits gathered up, and half a million dollars of Federal property destroyed.[31]

Quantrill and his small band arrived in Howard County around July 10, 1864. He and his wife, Kate, secured a safe hideout in the dense woods just north of the Missouri River. Their camp was in a secluded, heavily wooded hollow about three miles south of Boonsboro and about four miles from the Arrow Rock ferry. They pitched a tent with a kitchen built onto it. Quantrill chose this area because the residents were overwhelmingly sympathetic to the South.[32] Here they remained in relative safety and comfort for most of the summer.

Only once was Quantrill surprised in his secluded hideaway. One day Kate was preparing a meal outside the tent when she saw Redlegs coming up the road. Quantrill was inside when she informed him. He was fully armed at all times and was prepared to fight his way out of any trap. He yelled to the approaching riders, asking them what they wanted.

"Who are you?" one of them shouted back.

"I'll show you who I am," Quantrill replied and fired a volley into them. He wounded two, then taking to his horse, which was tied to a nearby pole, he held the others at bay and escaped into the woods. He found more Redlegs farther back on the road. The Kansans questioned Kate, but she gave them no useful information. She did learn that they were out to get Quantrill and had heard he was in the region.[33]

George Todd reached the eastern portion of Howard County by September 18. He halted his men on the Rocheport to Sturgeon road, resting both men and horses after a long and grueling ride. While encamped, Todd was attacked by fifteen hundred Federal cavalry. They drove him into the heavy timber, where he found concealment and escape.

The next day started out cold and wet. A blustery east wind blew sporadic rain all morning. While moving his camp across the Sturgeon road, Todd's scouts brought word of a Federal wagon train of seventeen wagons escorted by seventy-five cavalrymen and seventy-five infantry. Moving as swiftly as possible along the muddy roads, Todd's command caught up with the Union column within thirty minutes. Todd was in the lead of fifty-three screaming guerrillas when they charged. He shot down the Federal commander while his men routed the remainder of the soldiers. Ninety-two Union troops were killed along the muddy road. All the wagons were burned after they were looted. They found uniforms and much-needed ammunition as well as plunder taken from neighboring farms.

By September 18 George Todd managed to find his old commander just across the Missouri River from Arrow Rock where he had crossed with his small band two months before. John McCorkle recalled that all the men were "delighted" to see Quantrill and their old friends once again.[34] Together Quantrill and Todd rode east toward Rocheport, looking to join with Anderson's company.

In Boone County they came upon a foraging party of twenty-one Federals camped in Goslin's Lane. The guerrillas immediately attacked, killing all of the Federals except two. Unable to find Anderson or any members of his command, they turned back toward Fayette in Howard County.

Bright and early Tuesday morning, September 20, as if by some invisible hand, the separate bands of Missouri's greatest guerrilla fighters were riding out of the rugged hills in southern Howard County toward a momentous meeting six miles south of Fayette. Anderson had mustered his company the day before along the banks of Bonne de Femme Creek in Howard County. Before this he had been encamped in the Perche Hills of Boone County to the south. Anderson supposedly chose this spot because the surviving members of his family were brought to Howard County for protection against further Federal brutality.[35]

As daylight approached, Anderson ordered his men to mount up. They made their way toward the Franklin road, riding in a column of twos. Coming to a farm gate along the road, Anderson halted his men and rode out alone toward another column of horsemen waiting patiently in the middle of the lane. The separate guerrilla commands were now rejoined, gathered together like the spokes of a wheel with their commanders in the hub. Anderson's column numbered sixty-seven men. George Todd had fifty-three. David Poole commanded fifty-two. Quantrill had sixteen. And regular army Capts. Thomas Todd and Caleb Perkins commanded forty-two and forty-seven respectively.

Thomas Todd lived in Fayette. He stood out from the others with his long red beard, and he wore a black plume in his hat. The guerrilla leaders were questioning him at length about Fayette's defensive fortifications. As Anderson rode up, Quantrill and the other officers greeted him. To most of the guerrillas in the ranks, the presence of the other guerrilla commands was a complete surprise. Many believed they had been operating independently throughout the surrounding region, but now seeing so many mounted men together, they sensed that something important was soon to take place. Most of them suspected the operation would be a part of another raid by Gen. Sterling Price, but no one knew exactly where he would strike.

The guerrilla leaders stayed on their horses in the middle of the road and discussed the merits of attacking Fayette, the county seat of Howard County and a Federal garrison. Quantrill knew the country well and argued against the attack. John McCorkle reported that he heard Quantrill say to the other officers, "There's no use in attacking men in brick houses and log cabins with only side arms; if we do, we'll only succeed in getting some of our men killed and wounded. . . . Fayette is too strongly garrisoned. Nothing will be gained. It will cost the lives of many men."[36]

The only other officer to vote against the attack was Caleb Perkins. Anderson and George Todd insisted on attacking Fayette. Anderson argued that the town would be easy prey; only that morning Col. Reeves Leonard led a large patrol out of Fayette to the south to search for Quantrill, Anderson, and Todd. This left only a handful of soldiers in town. The guerrillas believed with such a reduced garrison the town could easily be overrun.

Still smarting from Quantrill's decision to leave them in Jackson County three months before, and not understanding full well his motives for it, Anderson and Todd taunted Quantrill, telling him that they were going to Fayette. He could come along if he wanted, but if not, he could go back into the woods with the rest of the cowards. Even after being offered command of the attack, Quantrill continued to protest. Finally he told Anderson to lead and he'd fight in the ranks as a private.[37] Anderson told George Todd that after he cleaned up the pickets, all Todd had to do was to follow behind him and take possession of the town.

Anderson anxiously wanted to avenge the loss of the five guerrillas and the mutilation of their bodies. His actions demonstrated he was fighting with his heart and not his head. After the votes were taken, the attack on Fayette was finally decided. Anderson would take the lead with George Todd following behind him, then Quantrill's men would follow, and Thomas Todd would bring up the rear.

As soon as Anderson returned to his men, he gave the order, "Forward men," then the other guerrilla companies fell into column behind him. They moved north along the New Franklin road, one and a half miles, turning east through the farm of Col. William Hocker, and coming into the Fayette and

Maxwell Mill road seven and a half miles south of their destination. Up to this time none of the rank and file knew the target nor the purpose of their leaders, but word was passed down the line: "Boys, we're going into Fayette."[38]

At 10:00 A.M. on September 20 the guerrilla column emerged from the timber just a quarter of a mile south of Fayette and made its way up Church Street west of the city cemetery. All the guerrillas at the head of the column wore Federal uniforms so the soldiers in town would assume they were the returning patrol.[39] Less than a hundred yards away from the town square the column broke into a gallop. One of Anderson's less disciplined guerrillas noticed a black soldier in a Federal uniform standing on the street corner and shot at him as he passed. This ended any chance for a surprise attack.

Immediately the guerrillas charged toward the courthouse, where by now the Union troops had rushed to take refuge behind its brick walls. Shooting at anything that moved as they rode past, the guerrillas were surprised to find thirty soldiers from the Ninth Missouri Cavalry barricaded in railroad-tie blockhouses just past the courthouse. As they came charging toward the fortification, a picket shot Thad Jackman, the first guerrilla to be killed in the action.

Lts. Joseph M. Street and Thomas H. Smith commanded the troops left in town. They directed their men to fight for their lives, and they easily picked off Anderson's and Todd's men as they charged the courthouse. Todd's men tried to dislodge the Federals from the courthouse while Anderson attacked the blockhouses just north of the city square. Todd was furious that his men were being shot out of their saddles without being able to effectively fire back at the enemy inside the brick building. Meanwhile, Anderson made three bloody assaults on the blockhouses. Not more than 75 guerrillas out of a force of 250 engaged in any one of the three charges made upon the stronghold.[40]

Both Anderson and Todd sent messengers to Quantrill to send reinforcements, but each time he refused. Quantrill was said to be furious at seeing so many lives wasted. He knew the attack was a useless venture, so he refused to join it, thus keeping many more men from being killed or wounded.

Almost immediately Garrett M. Groomer and George McMurtry were killed in the first charge on the blockhouse. Guerrillas Dick Kinney and Jesse James volunteered to bring McMurtry's body out from under the hail of fire. Before they could accomplish this feat, Bill Akin was mortally wounded, and Thomas F. Maupin and Silas King were hit and slightly wounded.

In the second assault, Younger Grubbs was killed alongside Plunk Murry. Twenty-five-year-old Oliver Johnson, who stood six feet two, was wounded six times; a seventh wound later proved fatal. Johnson, shot through the hips, fell on a slight rise only a short distance from the blockhouse. The guerrillas were well known for not leaving their wounded on the battlefield, so Simeon Whitsett, Dick Kinney, and Frank James volunteered to go after Johnson's body. They were in plain view of the Federals, who peppered them with bullets. They got as close to the ground as they could and finally managed to get Johnson's body rolled up in a blanket then brought back to the rear. After getting Johnson to safety, his friends placed him on a pillow on a saddle and led his horse to a nearby house where he received treatment. Johnson lived five days before succumbing from his wounds.

Lee McMurtry, whose brother George had just been killed, was struck beneath his left eye, temporarily blinding him and knocking him from his horse. John McCorkle grabbed the reins of McMurtry's horse and led it back to him. Anderson sent word for George Todd to help him because he and his men, atypically dismounted, were caught up in a desperate battle.

Todd's command, however, was fighting dismounted as well. He ordered a headlong attack on the fort and tried to get his men close enough to the rifle ports to pick off a few defenders, but the effort was to no avail. Todd led the attack himself and drew the entire fire of the Federals, but he was never hit. Each time he led a charge, his men were repulsed with numerous casualties.

Frank James recalled, "We charged up to a blockhouse made of railroad ties filled with port holes and then charged back again. The blockhouse was filled with Federal troops and it was like charging a stone wall only this stone wall belched forth lead."

Quantrill's closest friend, James Little, was hit in the hip and arm and also lost a finger. Quantrill rode to his aid and took him from the field to dress his wounds. To his men he said, "Boys, I will take Jimmy to cover. He is all shot to hell." Quantrill led Little to a pasture just west of the town square.

McCorkle brought Lee McMurtry to Quantrill. When he headed back to the battle, Quantrill called out to him, "Where are you going?" McCorkle replied, "To help the boys." Quantrill responded, "Come on back. There's no use trying to shoot through brick walls and logs with pistols." McCorkle turned back, followed by the rest of the command who had failed to dislodge the defenders.[41]

Recalling the fight, Frank James said, "I was mightily scared. It was the worst fight I ever had." Peyton Long's horse was shot out from under him. He made a desperate, mad rush under a heavy fire to the corral where the Federals kept their horses, selected a good one, and rode bareback to rejoin the fight.

Harrison Trow, armed with a shotgun, kept up a steady fusillade against the windows of the female academy where other Federals had opened a deadly barrage of fire. The accurate fire from his shotgun silenced a dozen rifles. Trow was known to be calm and cool in the midst of danger, and his comrades nicknamed him "Iceberg."[42]

The guerrillas had numerous men killed and many severely wounded. Among the wounded were Tom Maupin, Bill Stewart, William Stone, and Lawrence Wilcox. Despite desperate circumstances, their compatriots rescued the wounded guerrillas on the battlefield. Some grabbed blankets and carried away their wounded friends under a hail of bullets.

Will Hayes of Anderson's company was standing in the road, preparing to leave town, when a sniper from the east tower of the female academy shot him. Hayes died a few hours later.

Finally the guerrillas pulled north of town, toward the Roanoke road, leaving thirteen dead behind. Following the battle, fifteen-year-old Hampton Watts of Anderson's company and a resident of Howard County reported that two of the townspeople, Dr. J. T. Bailey and Joseph McGraw, witnessed Federal soldiers place the bodies of five dead guerrillas in the street and ride their horses roughshod over them.[43] One report after the battle listed Caleb Perkins as losing ten men, Thomas Todd seven, and Poole eight, but did not mention the losses of either Anderson's or George Todd's companies.

Some thirty guerrillas were seriously wounded but still able to ride with the retreating column. Many were left with sympathetic farmers to be cared for and nursed back to health.

George Todd was furious at the losses incurred. He initially blamed Quantrill for the defeat because Quantrill did not reinforce him during the battle. He wanted his men to kill Quantrill, and those who were around him reported that he was acting like a madman. His men defended Quantrill and asserted that he was not to blame; Quantrill had always treated them well. Furthermore, Todd's men threatened to quit his company before they would harm their leader. Still furious, Todd said that he would kill Quantrill himself. But his men stood in his way and told him that Quantrill's death would accomplish nothing, that Todd would likely wind up getting himself killed and leaving them without a leader.[44]

Quantrill took his men and part of the wounded from the battle back into Boonslick Township to nurse their wounds. John McCorkle recalled that, after a few days, Quantrill was still looking after James Little's wounds, and Little was not yet well enough to ride. Quantrill sent McCorkle to a prearranged rendezvous at Rocheport to tell George Todd to take command.[45]

On the Friday following the battle, Todd and Anderson pulled their forces south of Fayette and along the road leading from Sturgeon to Rocheport. A government wagon train of fourteen wagons escorted by 70 soldiers of the Third Missouri Militia was moving along the road at the same time. The guerrillas, 115 strong, attacked, killing 11 Union soldiers and 3 black teamsters and taking 30 prisoners. The wagon train was filled with plunder from the surrounding farmhouses as well as items of military clothing, camp equipment, ammunition, and medical supplies.[46] After taking what they needed from the wagons, Todd ordered the wagons burned.

After the battle of Fayette, Southerners soon learned that Quantrill was making his headquarters in Howard County. Plagued by depredations at the hands of Federals, others acting ostensibly as their military protectors, and neighbors who preyed on the weak, several refugees and residents of Howard County sought retribution from Quantrill toward specific individuals who had wronged them.

One such person was Capt. Richard M. Kimsey, a twenty-two-year-old resident of Howard County. He had been a guerrilla fighter of little renown, but in the second half of the war he began to rob the residents, many of whom were his neighbors. Kimsey would approach a neighborhood with a large number of refugees with news that Quantrill told him to secure money and horses from them. If anyone was bold enough to resist Kimsey, the unfortunate offender paid with his life. Forcing his way into people's homes, he took whatever he wanted. He had a penchant for robbing women of dress material, hair ribbons, and jewelry. Frequently Kimsey would enter homes, take what he wanted, then go to barns and pastures and do the same.

The people complained to Quantrill about Kimsey's manner. Quantrill had sent warnings to the renegade in the past, but he had been ignored. Quantrill was known by North and South alike not to tolerate harassment of women, regardless of their political beliefs. Thus when Kimsey began stealing personal items from the women of Howard County, Quantrill decided that it was time to hunt him down.

On Saturday, October 8, 1864, Quantrill, accompanied by Thomas Harris, began the search for Kimsey. It was not long before the two found their man riding with an accomplice, Robert Montgomery. On the high road west of Clark's Chapel, the four men met in the middle of the road. After confronting Kimsey with his crimes, angry words were exchanged, and Quantrill attempted to arrest Kimsey. He ordered Kimsey to surrender his pistols, but Kimsey went to draw his gun. Quantrill was faster, and Kimsey fell dead from his horse.[47]

The Union garrison in Paris, Missouri, soon learned the direction the guerrillas took after the battle of Fayette. After the battle the Federals believed the guerrillas were vulnerable and, furthermore, that a concerted effort to track them down would finally destroy their command.

Maj. A. V. E. Johnson, in command of the Thirty-ninth Missouri Militia, mounted around 175 men and gave pursuit. Johnson's advance scouts ran into Anderson's company around noon on September 26, 1864. Anderson, not wanting to bring on an attack, slipped into the darkness just outside Centralia. He rejoined George Todd's command along with John Thrailkill's and other small guerrilla units camped on the Singleton farm four miles south of Centralia. Here they gathered with a combined strength of more than 225 men. It was here that the guerrillas received word of Sterling Price's reentry into Missouri with twelve thousand men.

The next day, September 27, Todd's men remained in camp. At first light, Anderson took Arch Clements and thirty men on a foray into the nearby town to verify the information about Price's movements and get a St. Louis newspaper. Anderson and his men dressed in Federal uniforms.

At the time Centralia was a small village with about a dozen houses, only two with more than one story. There were two hotels in town; the other buildings were a saloon and commercial stores. Centralia was also a stop on the rail line with a depot and a water tower.

The guerrillas found several crates of much-needed boots inside the depot. The town was on a wide-open prairie. From the roof of any of the houses a person could see for miles in every direction. On the morning of Anderson's mission, he and his men rudely awakened the people with shouts and pistol shots, demanding breakfast at Sneed's Hotel. Others searched for Unionists to rob. Anderson allegedly rescued a number of civilians who were being roughly handled by his men. The railroad depot was set on fire, which was the usual practice of the guerrillas.

When Anderson assembled his men after three hours of brazenly riding about the town, the eastbound stage from Columbia arrived. The passengers were robbed. Any conscription-aged men not in Southern service were considered suspect. After taking their time while going through the belongings of the passengers, the guerrillas heard a distant whistle announce the westbound North Missouri train from St. Charles. Anderson ordered his men to quickly pile ties on the track to halt the passing train.

When the train pulled into the burning station, the guerrillas surrounded the cars, firing their pistols into the air to discourage any resistance. There were twenty-five Union soldiers on board. Some were going up the road on duty and some to their homes on furlough. The Federals on board with rifles crowded the windows and the platforms and fired briskly at the guerrillas.[48] Before the firing stopped, Anderson's men overran the train. One of the guerrillas discovered a man who had once testified against him. They dragged him from the crowd and shot him alongside the tracks.

The twenty-five soldiers, most of whom were on furlough from Gen. William T. Sherman's army, were taken from the train and lined up alongside the platform. Anderson questioned the soldiers and told them how Union troops had recently killed and scalped a number of men from his command. A sergeant was separated from the rest to use for a prisoner exchange.

Anderson, still reeling from the recent loss of his closest men, announced, "You Federals have just killed six of my men, scalped them, and left them on the prairie. I will show you that I can kill men with as much skill and rapidity as anybody. From this time on I ask no quarter and give none."

When the soldiers protested, Anderson replied, "You are Federals, and Federals scalped my men, and carry their scalps at their saddle bows."[49] He then ordered Clements to "muster out" the remaining soldiers. After the soldiers were shot down, Anderson gathered up his men and rode back to rejoin the rest of the guerrilla band.

Riding into Centralia just after Anderson left was Major A. V. E. Johnson and the Thirty-ninth Missouri Militia. His men were mostly farm boys from Monroe County who had only recently been enrolled. Johnson detailed them as mounted infantry on old farm horses. They were armed with new Enfield rifles equipped with a bayonet and firing a one-ounce lead ball. They felt confident and superior to any foe. Johnson had been on the guerrillas' trail ever since Middlegrove, saw the smoke from the burning depot at Centralia, and hurried to the scene. The scene of destruction was like nothing he had encountered before.

The Union commander climbed to the top of Sneed's Hotel and surveyed the open prairie in the direction of the guerrillas' camp. He saw Anderson's small group riding over the prairie, quickly descended the stairs, mounted his men, and started off in pursuit.

Dr. A. E. Sneed told him before he left that besides the men who had raided the town, the guerrillas had four hundred men in camp not far away. Johnson haughtily replied, "They may have the advantage over me in numbers, but I will have the advantage of them in arms. My guns are of long range and I can fight them from a distance." Sneed insisted that the guerrillas were well-trained and desperate men. Johnson hesitated for only a moment then retorted, "I will fight them anyhow."

Before Johnson left town he mounted a black flag at the head of his column and boasted that no quarter would be given or asked. Yet Johnson also suspected the townspeople had aided the slaughter in Centralia. On his return he swore "to devastate the country and leave the habitations of the Southern men not one stone upon another. Extermination, in fact, was what they all needed."[50]

Johnson called his officers together and ordered Capt. Adam Thiess and some thirty-five men to remain in town with the unit's supplies. What Johnson did not know was that the guerrillas had spotted him, too.

George Todd sent a twenty-five-man patrol toward Johnson's command to lure the Federals into the open prairie. Three miles across the prairie the rest of the guerrillas waited.

The sky was blue with the chill of early fall in the air. The ground was covered with prairie grass, long and coarse, bending in the afternoon breeze. Todd ordered his men to saddle up. The outcome of the battle was determined before the action began. The guerrilla warriors sat their horses, armed to the teeth. Many were only teenagers but still veterans of numerous battles the North called massacres because of the overwhelming death toll the guerrillas inflicted on the enemy. The men under Capts. Thomas Todd and John Thrailkill threw down a fence and advanced along a small creek branch to the west of their camp. To the left of the little branch rode the commands of George Todd and Silas Gordon. Bill Anderson was assigned the center of the battlefield. David Poole arranged his men behind Anderson, slightly overlapping his line.

Major Johnson and his 125-man command advanced to the guerrillas' front. At five hundred yards Johnson marched at a slow walk in a column of twos toward the trap, not seeing or aware of the separate guerrilla commands on his flanks. Anderson's men dismounted only to tighten their saddle girths and pistol belts before mounting up again.

Discovering the guerrillas to his front, Johnson halted his men and arrayed them on line. He called out to the guerrillas, "We are ready, come on!" When the guerrillas made no reply, he called out again, "Wait for us, you damned cowards!" Johnson closed the gap between the lines until he was within two hundred yards of the Southerners. He needed this distance to fire his long-range guns and reload for a second volley.

Frank James recalled, "We dismounted to tighten the belts on the horses and then at the word of command started on our charge."

As a result, Johnson dismounted his men, leaving every fifth man to hold the horses of the rest, apparently expecting the guerrillas were going to fight on foot also. Once his men were dismounted, Johnson, riding on a fine gray horse and holding a Colt dragoon revolver in his right hand, ordered his men to fix bayonets.

John Koger watched from his saddle in disbelief as he saw the Yankee troopers dismount. He commented, "Why the fools are going to fight us on foot. God help them."

The only guerrillas visible to Johnson were Anderson's company. When Anderson saw that the others were in place, he waved his hat three times as a signal. Poole's and Thrailkill's forces soon appeared. Anderson's company was on line and began a slow walk toward the enemy. It was four o'clock in the afternoon. The sun was beginning to set, and the guerrillas knew that they must make short work of the fight ahead of them.

When Anderson's men came into range, Johnson gave the order to fire, believing his long-range rifles would do much damage. Frank James reported the guerrillas were lying low on their horses, a trick learned from Comanches that had saved their lives many times. James said, "For a moment we moved slowly. Our line was nearly a quarter of a mile long, theirs much closer together. We were still some 600 yards away, our speed increasing and our ranks closing up."

Most of the Federal fire was over the guerrillas' heads, and this initial volley killed three of Anderson's men and wounded three others. One of the dead, Richard Kinney, had been one of the most desperate fighters among the guerrillas. His pistol, which he gave to Frank James just before he died, had forty-eight notches on the handle, one for each Federal he killed. Kinney was Frank James's closest friend, and James said that it hurt him when he heard Kinney cry out, "Frank, I'm shot!" He added, "He kept on riding for a time and I thought his wound wasn't serious." James reported that Frank Shepherd was riding next to him on his right when Shepherd was struck in the head. "The blood and brains from Shepherd splashed on my pants' leg as he fell from his horse." Frank's brother Jesse was riding on his left.

From a fast walk the guerrillas spurred their horses into a dead run, trying to catch the Federals before they could reload and fire another volley. Once the charge was ordered nothing could stop the killing until the last enemy soldier drew his last breath or some fortunate cavalryman managed to escape. Frank James reported:

> We couldn't stop in that terrible charge for anything. Up the hill we went yelling like wild Indians. Such shrieks, you will never hear as broke the stillness of that September afternoon. On we went up the hill. Almost in

a twinkling of an eye we were on the Yankee line. They seemed terrorized. Some of the Yankees were at "fix bayonets," some were biting off their car-tridges, preparing [to] reload. Yelling, shooting our pistols upon them we went. The tremendous impetus of horses at full speed broke through and scattered their line like chaff before the wind. The guerrillas dug their spurs into their mounts just before they reached the Federal line. The horses worked up to a frenzy during the charge, made an impregnable solid mass of flesh, which when they struck the Federal line knocked most of the terrified soldiers down. The guerrillas then wheeled their horses and made another pass, this time with pistols and unerring shots. Not a single man of the line escaped. The few who attempted to escape we followed into Centralia and on to Sturgeon. There a Federal blockhouse stopped further pursuit. All along the road we killed them. Arch Clements killed the last man and the first man. He had the best horse and got a little on the start.[51]

Harrison Trow remembered that "probably sixty of Johnson's command gained their horses before the fierce wave of the charge broke over them, and these were pursued by five guerrillas; Ben Morrow, Frank James, Peyton Long, Arch Clements and Harrison Trow, for six miles at a dead run. Of the sixty, fifty-two were killed on the road from Centralia to Sturgeon."

Darkness ended the guerrillas' pursuit. At the conclusion of the running battle, Clements was credited with killing fourteen of the fleeing Federals while Trow killed ten, Long nine, Morrow eight, and Frank James managed to overtake and kill eleven.[52] Frank James claimed that his brother Jesse killed Maj. A. V. E. Johnson. Jesse was wounded during the battle then car-ried off by William Gaugh and taken to safety. During the brief battle the Federals broke ranks in confusion. Some clubbed with their muskets, some tried to reload, some used their bayonets, while others tried to surrender and were shot down without mercy.

In a matter of seconds the guerrillas rode over the soldiers who chose to stand and fight. Those less terrified after the first volley had their lips black from tearing the paper off their powder cartridges with their teeth while attempting to reload. During the fight one Federal slashed at George Todd with his bayonet but missed. Frank Smith then killed the soldier.[53]

The guerrillas fired with both hands as they passed the Federal line. There were very few Union troops left standing once the guerrillas wheeled their horses for another pass. Those left standing had nowhere to run. They were unmounted and held empty rifles—and they were completely surrounded.

They stood dumbfounded, shocked at finding themselves so suddenly in this predicament. One more pass and all resistance ended. To keep any Federal soldier from feigning death, the guerrillas fired an extra bullet into each soldier's head.

Poole led a guerrilla company to attack the remaining Federals back in town. He shot two of Federals off their horses as they were starting out to Paris to spread the news of the defeat. Dr. Sneed and Lt. John E. Stafford, standing in the attic of the hotel, saw the smoke of the battle and witnessed the Federals on horseback coming toward town. Stafford hastily descended to the ground and joined his company as one of the survivors came riding into town and shouted to Thiess's men, "Get out of here! Every one of you will be killed if you don't run!" The men mounted and started to run for Sturgeon, but in a few minutes Archie Clements, Frank James, Harrison Trow, Ben Morrow, Peyton Long, and others ran down most of them and shot them from their saddles.[54]

After the battle was over and the mad dash after the fleeing Federals had ended, the guerrillas rejoined their commands on the battlefield. Poole counted the dead and reported 130 bodies were lying within the space of a city block and that the others were strewn along the prairie for a distance of ten miles or more. The actual number of dead was 123. Only 11 men from Thiess's company managed to escape. The guerrillas shot the wounded Federal horses that ran wild on the battlefield. They also captured the black flag that Johnson had carried into the battle. According to Frank James, "It was apparently a black apron tied to a stick."[55]

Many stories of guerrilla atrocities on the bodies of the slain Federals were spread in the Northern newspapers, but there is no basis for these allegations. They can be ascribed to the sensationalism that accompanied the reporting of any guerrilla victory. No such record can be found in the *Official Records of the Rebellion* from reports made by the Federal officers involved.[56] One of the guerrillas allegedly said, "We burned towns; we pillaged homes when there were no women and children in them; we slew in the face of prayer . . . and we never mutilated the dead."[57]

Harvey Silver and his father lived near the battlefield and helped to load the corpses into nine wagons. The bodies were piled in like logs. Some of the dead were taken to Mexico, Missouri, for burial while seventy-nine were interred in a single trench near the railroad in the eastern part of Centralia. On December 17, 1873, the trench was opened and the remains removed to Jefferson City, where the soldiers were reinterred in a common grave in the national cemetery.

When the guerrillas withdrew from the battlefield, orders were given not to break ranks. They traveled all night. In the morning they broke into small groups and approached farmhouses in search of food. The guerrillas were vulnerable now, short on ammunition after the fight. Six hundred Federals were on their trail and discovered them the next day. The Federals were afraid to get too close, so they opened up with their artillery, but the guns fired too high. The Federals continued to follow them at a safe distance until nightfall, when the guerrillas slipped away and the Union troops broke off further pursuit.[58]

Both Todd and Anderson turned their companies toward Boonville to link their forces with Price's army arriving from Arkansas. Every man had a Federal uniform tied on the back of his saddle. When the enemy was sighted, the guerrillas put on the uniforms, rode right up to them, and shot it out at close range.

One Federal company came into contact with David Poole's lead scouts. When the scouts came riding back, chased by thirty to forty Federals, Todd brought up his men on line and immediately charged, wiping out nearly the entire command. Only those Federals who were able to outrun the guerrillas managed to escape.

The mad pursuit conducted by the Federals desperately looking for Todd's trail kept the guerrilla commander constantly moving and skirmishing and dodging enemy patrols. On October 5 Todd disbanded his command to avoid further pursuit. He gathered eight of his most trusted men around him and turned back into Howard County, looking for Quantrill. Unable to find him, Todd joined Poole, and together they crossed to the south side of the Missouri River into Cooper County.

12

Last Raid——Last Hope

Not for fame, not for place or rank, not lured by ambition or goaded by necessity, but in simple obedience to duty as they understood it, these men suffered all, sacrificed all, dared all, and died.

DAVID W. GRIFFITH

N AUGUST 29 GEN. Sterling Price was put in charge of the Confederate Expeditionary Force being organized in Princeton, Arkansas, for another raid into Missouri. Price had recently gained authority from the Confederate government to launch the expedition to draw Union troops away from the beleaguered Rebel forces in the Deep South. He also had hopes that, if he could muster enough volunteers on his way north, he could drive out the Federals from Missouri and regain the state for the Confederacy. Price counted heavily on guerrilla forces to disrupt enemy concentrations from forming before his arrival.

Quantrill received orders from Missouri Gov. Thomas C. Reynolds, living in Arkansas, to send him ten scouts with up-to-date information on Federal troop strengths, how many militia were on duty, and what posts had been fortified along the western border. Quantrill chose his ten men well. They were to ride day and night, fighting their way through the Union lines, stopping for nothing. At their head was the indomitable George W. Maddox. Riding with him were William Strother, John Koger, Patrick Nagel, Silas Woodruff, Henry Hockensmith, Sam Jessup, Newt Majors, James Whitsett, and Preston Webb. Before they reached their destination, five were dead and three were seriously wounded. Only Maddox and Webb delivered their dispatches.

Thus Price was well informed as he planned the campaign. He entered Missouri on September 19 with three divisions, twelve thousand men, commanded by Gens. John Sappington Marmaduke, Jo Shelby, and James Fleming Fagan. Each division followed a different route north. After advancing as far as Fredericktown, Price's army turned west toward the Federal garrison at Fort Davidson, situated at Pilot Knob, eighty-five miles south of St. Louis. With the Union Sixteenth Corps campaigning with William Tecumseh Sherman in Georgia, Gen. Thomas Ewing had only a thousand men at the garrison.

Federal authorities did not know for certain what military objective Price had in mind. Some believed he planned to attack St. Louis, which was vulnerable. Union troops could have been rushed to the city's aid from various parts of the North within a very short time, however, because St. Louis was the hub of a vast transportation network.

Shelby encouraged Price to bypass Fort Davidson and continue on to St. Louis, but Price did not want a strong enemy force left in his rear. Price believed his superior numbers could easily overtake Ewing's smaller force. Yet Ewing's men managed to hold two-thirds of Price's army at bay for twenty-four hours. Only after Price hauled his artillery to the top of two mountains overlooking the fort did the Federals realize how untenable their position was. Waiting for the first light of dawn to open fire, the Confederates discovered that Ewing had abandoned the fort during the night and fled north to join other Union forces at Rolla. In this brief encounter at Fort Davidson, Price suffered the loss of more than fifteen hundred irreplaceable men.

The Federals fearfully awaited Price's next move. Which way was he going to strike?

Shifting his objective farther west, Price moved toward the capital at Jefferson City on the southern bank of the Missouri River. Waiting for Price behind hastily prepared defensive positions were more than seven thousand defenders. Gen. William S. Rosecrans, commander of the Department of the Missouri, ordered more than ninety-five hundred troops under Gen. A. J. Smith to reinforce the city. Among the units ordered to defend Jefferson City was the notorious Seventh Kansas Jayhawker Regiment.

With his huge losses at Pilot Knob, Price could no longer consider an attack upon St. Louis. On October 7 Price struck with a feint attack upon Jefferson City, which allowed his troops to cross the Osage River. He then slipped around the city's flank and headed for Boonville, his next objective. After Pilot Knob, Price's army now numbered only nine thousand men.

Finally ascertaining his objective, the Federals began a pursuit. Led by Gen. Alfred Pleasonton, the Federals converged on Price's rear.

With Price moving his main army through the middle of the state, the guerrillas sensed that their rendezvous with him at Boonville was fast approaching. So far they had been successful in disrupting the enemy's lines of communication along Price's intended line of march.

After the Southern victory at Centralia, the guerrilla leaders turned their forces west, riding along the north side of the Missouri River to affect a passage. Along the way William Anderson's men tore down telegraph wires, silencing communication between the Federal outposts. As a result, Union authorities were forced to depend upon dispatch riders to carry messages, which was a hazardous proposition.

In early October Anderson camped for several days close to Rocheport, waiting for other independent commands to join him. His camp was close enough to the town that his men could see Federal soldiers putting the torch to a large portion of the commercial district.

Various guerrilla bands were wreaking havoc on the Union outposts in Price's advance. George Todd and David Poole, after having crossed the Missouri River, killed fifteen militiamen eight miles south of Boonville. Next they attacked Syracuse, tearing up the railroad track and burning the depot after killing twenty militiamen. Guerrilla Peyton Long killed a Union courier disguised as a mule driver. Along with the courier's dispatches, the guerrillas found that the man was also carrying a pair of human ears recently cut from a victim. Todd and Poole then struck Otterville, destroying and scattering the militia there. Over and over they attacked, first at Brownsville, then in Lafayette County, where they destroyed the German-immigrant militia settlement. During a hard-fought battle in which many of his men were wounded, Todd's forces managed to kill 117 immigrant militiamen and burn 35 buildings in town.

Meanwhile, Ben Morrow, William Hulse, and Harrison Trow rode back to Howard County and rejoined Quantrill. Hidden away in the rugged hills of Boonslick Township, it did not take long for Jim Little's wounds from the Fayette fight to heal. Quantrill and Kate had cared for him, and in less than two weeks he was again able to ride.

Leaving the safety of his lair, Quantrill gathered his trusted men around him and started toward Boonville for a rendezvous with Price. On October 11 Quantrill, joined by Anderson, met with Price in Boonville. Price was apparently pleased to hear of their victory at Centralia. He needed a fast, mobile cavalry force to destroy the railroads and bridges north of the river to prevent their use by the enemy to rush supplies and reinforcements to the west. There was only one group of men able and more than willing to carry out his orders—Quantrill's guerrillas. Price intended to use the partisans as an advance striking force once they had destroyed the railroad lines in his rear and disorganized any Union effort to gather along his line of march. Capt. T. J. Mackey of Price's staff remarked that the guerrillas "were the terror of the enemy in that section and accustomed to operating on railroads."[1]

When Anderson reported to Price, he presented the general with a pair of silver mounted revolvers. John Pringle, a large redheaded guerrilla leader with his own group of partisans, accompanied Anderson into Boonville. Pringle and some of his men reportedly had Federal scalps hanging from their horses' bridle bits. Price ordered the scalps removed before he would talk to the guerrilla leaders. Afterward Price received Anderson's report of his summer activities along the Missouri River and in reply stated that if he had fifty thousand men such as Anderson he could hold Missouri for the South indefinitely.[2] But in his official report, Price stated:

> Captain Anderson, who reported to me that day with a company of about one hundred men, was immediately sent to destroy the North Missouri Railroad. At the same time, Quantrill was sent with the men under his command to destroy the Hannibal and St. Joseph Railroad, to prevent the enemy, if possible, from throwing their forces in my front from St. Louis. These officers I was informed afterwards did effect some damage to the roads, but none of any material damage, and totally failed in the main object proposed, which was to destroy the large railroad bridge that was in the end of Saint Charles County.[3]

George Todd finally reported to Price on October 18 when Price's army crossed into Lafayette County. The general assigned Todd to cross south of Boonville and cut the Pacific Railroad then to rejoin him and accompany Jo Shelby as his advance scout. Todd managed to burn the bridge on the Pacific Railroad, along with the depot, water tanks and a few houses at Otterville, in Cooper County.

After destroying the Hannibal and St. Joseph Railroad, Quantrill and his company were to serve as advance scouts for Price's main column. General Marmaduke was responsible for holding the rear, keeping Pleasonton at bay. Price planned to move west along the south side of the Missouri River, toward Kansas City, while the guerrilla forces advanced north of the river and destroyed the enemy's transportation and communication links along the way.

When Anderson's company was delayed while waiting for Price to move with his army, Anderson detached a small platoon toward Danville in Montgomery County. Danville was garrisoned by a small detachment of Federals. Three brothers—Richard, Isaac, and James Berry—had been riding with Anderson's company since the raid on Lawrence. They left behind their father and four sisters—twenty-year-old Catherine, eighteen-year-old Nancy, fourteen-year-old Elizabeth, and eleven-year-old Sallie Ann—all living in Callaway County across the county line from Danville. Union soldiers had allegedly raped the girls. The brothers persuaded Anderson to allow them to avenge their sisters. Anderson agreed. He assigned Archie Clements to lead the three Berry brothers along with brothers Tuck, Tom, and Woot Hill, Richard West, Theodore Cassell, John Maupin, Moses Huffaker, Ben Broomfield, Gooley Robinson, Bill Stuart, and a handful of volunteers.

On the evening of October 14, while the Federals were preparing to post evening sentries, thirty-five guerrillas led by the three Berry brothers charged into Danville. They killed the five soldiers believed to have raped their sisters. Only eight Union troops managed to escape. The remainder took refuge in the houses, and it was only with great difficulty that the guerrillas managed to get them out.

The guerrillas split up to set fire to the houses occupied by the soldiers. Dick and Ike Berry set fire to one house while Clements and Dick West put fire to another. Theodore Cassell, John Maupin, and Moses Huffaker set fire to a third building while Ben Broomfield and the Hill brothers set fire to a fourth.[4] In the surreal specter of fire and smoke, the screaming Federals ran from the burning buildings and were shot down by the vengeful guerrillas waiting in the darkness.

Only one guerrilla, Gooley Robinson, was killed. The guerrillas then burned eighteen buildings and looted several others in the business district, including the post office. The next day they burned the railroad depots in New Florence and High Hill before riding seventy miles to rejoin their company.

In the tiny town of Glasgow, just thirty miles northwest of Boonville, the Federals kept a large amount of arms and supplies guarded by an eight-hundred-man garrison commanded by Col. Chester Harding. Price ordered Brig. Gens. John B. Clark and Jo Shelby to seize these supplies. Quantrill and his independent command were attached to Shelby's brigade. The combined mounted infantry, cavalry, and artillery force advanced on Glasgow and laid siege to the town beginning at dawn on October 15.

The Confederates moved on Glasgow by various routes after opening up on the defenders occupying the vacated town. The Federals soon fell back to prepared fortifications on Hereford Hill and quickly formed a defensive perimeter, but the Confederate onslaught was overpowering. Realizing that he was unable to hold back the assault, Harding destroyed some of the Federal stores then surrendered his command at 1:30 P.M.

As soon as the battle ended Quantrill rode up to Clark and notified him that he was the first man to enter the Federal rifle pits. From here Quantrill rode to the home of W. F. Dunnica, a Unionist banker, and commanded him to turn over to him all the money in his bank. Dunnica opened the bank vault and handed over twenty-one thousand dollars. Quantrill then escorted the banker back to his home so his men would not harm him.[5] One wealthy Unionist in Glasgow, William B. Lewis, was robbed of one thousand dollars and forced to borrow another five thousand dollars from his neighbors before he was released unharmed.[6]

Despite unfounded reports to the contrary, neither the guerrillas nor the regular Confederate forces perpetrated any atrocities on the people of Glasgow. Bill Anderson allegedly abused several townspeople the night after the Federal surrender, including the mother of Confederate Gen. John B. Clark and a brother-in-law of Gen. Sterling Price. This would not have been possible because Clark was present and on the scene. As Federal Capt. G. A. Holloway commented after the battle: "I must testify to the uniform kind and gentlemanly treatment we received at the hands of the Confederate officers among whom were General J. B. Clark, Brigadier General Joseph Shelby, Colonels Green, Quantrill, [Sidney D.] Jackman, [Dick?] Kitchen, [William L.] Jeffers, [John Q.] Burbridge, [W. O.] Coleman, and Nichols; all Missourians and most of the subordinates to Major General Marmaduke."[7]

Price's men captured 1,200 rifles, a large supply of much-needed overcoats, and a large quantity of underclothing. They also captured 150 horses. In comparison to the Southern losses, the Federals suffered horrendously. Union casualties amounted to more than 450 men while the Confederates only suffered around 50 casualties. The Union prisoners were paroled. After the horrendous casualties at Pilot Knob, the Confederate victory at Glasgow was a much-needed morale boost for the Southern army. Following the surrender, Southern officers extended their magnanimity toward their defeated foes with a generosity rarely practiced or reciprocated by the Federals in Missouri.

The Confederates remained in Glasgow for three days before rejoining Price's main column and the advance toward Kansas City. While Price traveled west, the large cavalry force under Maj. Gen. Alfred Pleasonton relentlessly pursued him.

Price's next stop was Lexington, Missouri. Quantrill was leading the advance when Price moved into the town, which quickly surrendered before the onslaught. Harrison Trow was riding with Quantrill and remarked, "We then went on to intercept Price at Waverly, Saline County, Missouri, where arrangements were made for Quantrill's men to take the advance clear on up through Fayette and Jackson Counties, and up through Kansas City. We were in advance all of the way from that time until Price started south."

As Price continued on from Lexington toward Independence, Quantrill turned south and headed into eastern Jackson County to his old haunts. George Todd stayed with Price as Shelby's advance scout.

To oppose Price's advance, Union Gen. Samuel R. Curtis was summoned from western Kansas to Union headquarters in Kansas City. He commanded twenty thousand men of the Army of the Border and moved now to intercept Price. Federal authorities placed both Kansas and Missouri under martial law and called for every able-bodied man to bear arms. Curtis commanded two divisions: one of four thousand men under Gen. James G. Blunt from Kansas, and the other of sixteen thousand Kansas militia under the command of the noted jayhawker Gen. George W. Deitzler of Lawrence. Also present was Quantrill's old enemy, Col. William R. Penick, commanding the Tenth Kansas Jayhawker Regiment.

After engaging Price's army on the outskirts of Lexington, Kansas militia quickly fell back to Independence, where they attempted to make a stand on the banks of the Little Blue River. Here they joined two regiments of the Second Colorado Cavalry, which were stationed in Independence and commanded by Col. James H. Ford. Like his men, Ford had a reputation of splendid fighting. Col. Thomas Moonlight from Kansas joined Ford with orders to make a strong resistance along the Little Blue River.

When Shelby's "Iron Brigade" advanced upon Independence, the Federals stubbornly held the western bank of the Little Blue River, taking defensive positions behind stone fences and walls along the bank. All morning individual units of the Colorado regiment tried desperately to stop the Confederates from routing their retreating army. On October 21, after brisk fighting all day, the Confederates finally drove the Federals from their positions and back toward Independence, but the Northerners had savagely contested every foot of ground before finally giving way.

While trying to slow the Confederate assault, the Federals burned the bridges behind them. The Little Blue, however, was shallow at that time of the year, and the Southerners forded the river in a number of places and swept across.

As the day was ending, Maj. Nelson Smith drew his half of a Colorado regiment onto the crest of a hill and turned to make another stand just two and a half miles northeast of Independence. Shelby's skirmishers were out in force, and every time the enemy attempted to make a stand, the skirmishers broke them up with unerring fire. Shelby, as was his practice, was at the front, where the firing was hottest. He rode to where his advance had slowed to see what was the problem. On his left rode Capt. Arthur C. McCoy, and on his right rode George Todd.

The Second Colorado had gathered themselves to fire a volley before abandoning their positions and fleeing to the streets of Independence. This last volley killed the gallant Todd, fulfilling his premonition of several nights past when he told his men: "I know I'll be killed, but it is just as fitting for me to die for my country as any other man. All I ask is that you boys stay with me and see that I get a decent burial."[8]

Sitting on a slight rise on the side of the road, he had just raised himself in his stirrups when a Spencer rifle ball entered his neck in front, passed through and out near his spine, paralyzing him.[9] Surrounded as he normally was by his most trusted men, Todd was carried from the field to a home in Independence. Realizing that he was dying and having great difficulty in speaking, Todd tried to relay last messages to his closest friends. He sent Dan Vaughn to find John McCorkle and the other guerrillas of his command so he could see them one last time. After struggling for two hours, the brave guerrilla fighter died. He was remembered as a brilliant fighter who always charged the enemy, no matter what the circumstances. Known as a desperate fighter, he drew other desperate fighters to him.

While the Federals were evacuating Independence, Todd's men carried their leader's body to the city cemetery for burial. Around the grave stood David Poole, Ike Flanery, Dick Burns, Andrew McGuire, Ben Morrow, Press Webb, Harrison Trow, Lafe Privin, George Shepherd, George W. Maddox, Allen Parmer, Dan Vaughn, Frank and Jesse James, and John Ross. After a hasty funeral, the guerrillas united themselves under Poole and continued for the next three days as Shelby's advance scouts.

By October 21 Price's army pushed Curtis's Federals back across the Little Blue River as far as the Big Blue River, east of Kansas City. Skirting Independence and heading past Brooking Township in southern Jackson County, Price marched his army toward Westport, south of Kansas City. His division commanders captured numerous Federal supplies along the route, and he desperately tried to protect his many unarmed men and supply trains, reported to be more than five miles long.

Fording the Blue River at a place called Byram's Ford, two miles west of Brooking Township, Price attempted to cross his army and supply train toward Westport. Marmaduke joined Shelby in taking the lead in the attack. Fagan led Price's third division, and he was responsible for guarding the rear.

On October 23, at Westport, Price came up against overwhelming odds. The Union troops numbered around twenty-three thousand while Price only had around eight thousand effective fighting men. The Southerners fought valiantly, but the tide of victory that had carried Price through the state subsided as he fought along the Missouri state line. Finally, sensing that the day was lost, Price turned his worn army south in a desperate retreat that resulted in the capture of Marmaduke and much of his brigade. Shelby and his Iron Brigade fought a constant rear-guard action almost all the way back into Arkansas. During the three-day battle, afterward dubbed the "Gettysburg of the West," thirty-five hundred men died or suffered wounds.

Following Price's retreat, the guerrillas under David Poole returned to Jackson County. Some decided to follow Quantrill to Kentucky, but the remainder elected to follow George Shepherd to Texas.

Exploiting this opportunity, Charles Jennison made one last mad raid through Brooking Township in Jackson Country. Capt. Green C. Stotts of the Seventh Missouri Militia wired a dispatch to Gen. John B. Sanborn outlining Jennison's depredations: "Jennison has just passed through this vicinity on his return from the Arkansas River. Where he passed the people are almost ruined." According to Stotts, the jayhawkers stole clothes, bedding, animals and equipment, and he noted: "There are cases where the men tore the clothing off of women in search of money, and threatening to burn houses in order to get money is the common practice."[10] Kansan George W. Martin overheard Jennison remark, "I have grown stoop-shouldered carrying plunder out of Missouri in the name of Liberty."

Yet Jennison did not stop at robbery. In August 1864, as he made an excursion through Platte, Clay, and Ray Counties, all north of the Missouri River, a stranger came into his camp who was known by most of Jennison's men. When Jennison saw him, he walked up to him and, learning that he was a Missourian, murdered him in cold blood. The following day, while Jennison and his command were marching along a road near Parkville, Missouri, they came upon an old white-bearded farmer who was mending his fence. When the farmer mentioned that his name was Gregg, Jennison said nothing but shot him dead. One of Jennison's men, Pvt. H. C. Dryden, reported, "The United States Government printed 'Death Lists,'" and he recalled seeing many of them with names marked off. He surmised the men had been killed.[11]

While Price was fighting near Kansas City, William Anderson crossed back into north Missouri from Boonville on orders from the general. As Price advanced, Anderson paralleled his movements north of the Missouri River. Each day Anderson picked up new recruits, swelling his ranks to several hundred. And along the way Anderson struck at anything or anyone who appeared to support the Union. In response, every Federal unit north of the river was ordered to pursue Anderson and bring him to bay. Five hundred Union troops were reported to be on his trail as he left Monroe County heading toward Chariton County.

In late October, in Ray County, Anderson saw the report that Price had been defeated and that George Todd had been killed. On October 24 he determined to punish the Federals for the Southern defeat at Westport. With Anderson was a detachment of regular Confederate soldiers, and among them was Capt. A. E. Ashbury in charge of fifty recruits and traveling with Cols. John Holt and James Condiff along with Capt. John Rains.

As Anderson made his way into Mound City, he discovered three hundred Federals to his front commanded by Maj. Samuel P. Cox in charge of the Thirty-third and Fifty-first Missouri Infantry from Ray, Davies, and Caldwell Counties. Anderson determined to attack them in the morning, despite advice from his other officers. Ashbury knew his new recruits could not execute the type of desperate charge Anderson would demand, but Anderson would not be deterred.

The Federals were encamped along the north side of the Missouri River between Richmond and present-day Orrick. Cox reported that Anderson charged his line with twenty men. The guerrilla leader had a revolver in each hand and rode a fine gray mare. When the Federals opened fire, many of Anderson's command went down and others turned and fled. Wearing a white hat with a large black feather in it, Anderson went right through the line, shooting and yelling.[12]

Harrison Trow recalled that William Smith, a veteran guerrilla with four years' experience, rode next to Anderson. Trow claimed that five bullets struck Smith and three struck Anderson, and at the end of the fight, both men were dead.

The company suffered other casualties in the initial volley: John Maupin was wounded twice, Condiff once, and Ashbury four times. Guerrillas John Holt, Jim Crow Chiles, and Peyton Long all lost their horses. While the rest of the guerrilla company drew rein and exchanged fire with the Federals, they realized their leader had fallen. Knowing the history of brutality practiced by the Federals toward captured guerrillas, Anderson's men tried desperately to recover his body. Richard West and the Hill brothers fought their way up to Anderson and tried to carry him away. They managed to throw the body across a horse, but before they could escape, the horse was killed, pinning Anderson beneath it. For their effort Tuck and Woot Hill and West were seriously wounded. Others also made valiant efforts to rescue the body of their slain leader, but they too were shot down. Henry Patterson fell dead next to Anderson. Anson Tolliver, Paul Debonhorst, Smith Jobson, John McIlvaine, Jasper Moody, Hodge Reynolds, William Tarkington, and two other men remembered only as Luckett and Simmons all died trying to recover Anderson's remains.

Also killed was John Rains, son of James S. Rains, a Missouri state senator and a general in Price's army. Guerrilla John Pringle, a veteran of the Mexican War, was the last man killed. Pringle attempted to tie a rope around Anderson's leg so he could pull him from beneath the horse, but before he could get away, Pringle's own horse was killed. Pringle was shot four times while he emptied three revolvers at the enemy.

Even the recruits proved their mettle. Joseph and Archibald Nicholson, William James, and Clell Miller were wounded once. John Warren was shot four times before he managed to crawl away. All these men were either killed or wounded trying to regain Anderson's body.[13]

But the odds were simply too great. With the Federals standing their ground, the guerrillas had no choice but to withdraw. Union bugler Adolph Vogel found Anderson's body. He recalled: "I saw the body of a man in front of me who looked like he might be an officer. He was dressed well and in his big wide brimmed hat there was a long feather. I told Major Cox about him and he ordered me to take everything off him. We took his pistols, his hat and papers he had on him that told who he was. We took the body of Anderson to Richmond, and I held it up while they took a picture of it."[14] Cox gave Vogel six of Anderson's pistols and kept one for himself.

Anderson also carried a picture of him and his wife along with a small Confederate flag on which these words were inscribed: "Presented to W. L. Anderson by his friend F. M. R. Let it not be contaminated by Federal hands." He had letters from his wife, written from Texas, and a lock of her hair, as well as a letter from Cox, the Union commander of the group that killed Anderson, to Brig. Gen. James Craig. The Federals also found orders from Price, which the authorities used to confirm the identify of the body.

Not satisfied at simply conquering the enemy and killing him, Cox had a rope tied around Anderson's neck, affixed it to the back of a wagon, and dragged the body through the streets of Richmond. There Cox had pictures taken of the slain guerrilla leader. By this time the Federals had already cut off Anderson's finger to steal his wedding ring.

One of Anderson's cousins lived near Richmond. When she heard that his body was in town, she drove to Richmond and attempted to persuade the Federal commander not to take a picture of Anderson until she had combed his matted hair and washed the blood from his face. Cox refused. After taking Anderson's picture, Cox had Anderson's head removed and attached to a telegraph pole in town as a warning to other guerrillas. His body was then buried in an unmarked grave.[15] Cox was promoted for these barbarities.

Meanwhile, the leadership of Anderson's company fell on his second in command, eighteen-year-old Archie Clements. Anderson's company continued to raid Unionist outposts and settlements north of the Missouri River for the next several weeks. Eventually the band separated into smaller units of twenty to one hundred men and scattered throughout the counties of northern Missouri.

Quantrill had accompanied Price's assault from Boonville to Kansas City and as far as Lexington. Then he left Price and headed southwest into Jackson County. Only one month after Todd's death at Independence and Anderson's at Richmond, the guerrilla bands were starting to break up. Price made a hasty retreat south along the border of Kansas and Missouri with Jo Shelby's brigade holding the rear guard. Price was desperately trying to keep his army from disintegrating into a frenzied rabble.

Heading south with Price to Texas was not an option for Quantrill. His disagreements with Gen. Henry E. McCulloch the previous winter had made him unwanted in Texas, and he could plainly see that Price did not have much of an army left. It was evident to him that the end of the war was near. Quantrill was convinced that neither he nor his men would be permitted to surrender in Missouri or the West. If he stayed in Missouri, he and his men would eventually be caught and hanged.

Quantrill had known for some time that the best option for him and his men was to head east to join with Robert E. Lee's army or another Southern general and seek reasonable surrender terms when the end of the war came. Allen Parmer recalled that Quantrill "told us, though, the day we started from Missouri that the game was up, that he expected Lee would have to surrender soon and that he was going to try to get in touch with Lee or some other Southern commander and get terms for the boys when the end came." Sylvester Akers added "that it was not the original intention of Quantrill to go to Kentucky. He started from Missouri to Virginia to the army of Lee, and intended to go through Tennessee. At the Mississippi he was told that he would not be able to pass through the Federal lines in east Tennessee. Then he turned aside to go through Kentucky."[16]

Before heading south with his closest men, Quantrill arranged for his wife, Kate, to stay with friends in St. Louis until things were settled enough for her to join him. He told her he would return in two months. Kate reported that she was provided with sufficient cash to tide her over. In addition, she had her jewels.[17]

Men from George Todd's old command, now under David Poole, retreated with Price as far as Mine Creek and served as scouts and skirmishers. Parmer remembered that Quantrill met the survivors of the Westport battle at Harrisonville: "He ordered us to round up all the boys for a rendezvous at the farm of Mrs. Dupree, a few miles over in Lafayette County. He gave us a list of the names he wanted to be there. Quantrill had John Barker and James Little to pass the word to the rest of his command to meet him on the 4th of December. Some of the guerrillas grew impatient for Quantrill's arrival and so elected George Shepherd commander and started south to Texas on November 13, 1864."

Among the twenty-six guerrillas who accompanied Shepherd to Texas were Matt Wayman, John Maupin, Theodore Cassell, Jack Rupe, Silas King, James and Alfred Corum, Bud Story, Perry Smith, Jack Williams, Jesse James, James and Arthur Devers, Press Webb, James Cummins, and John Norfolk. Most of them traveled with their wives, and out of concern for the safety of their families, they left as soon as possible.

When Quantrill finally returned, he gathered his men together. John McCorkle remembered that he told them he intended to cross the Missouri River at Arrow Rock, go across Missouri to Illinois to Kentucky then into Virginia. "We were all to wear Federal uniforms," McCorkle added, "and to pass ourselves as Union soldiers, and his name was to be Colonel Clark, in command of a Colorado regiment."[18] Quantrill cautioned: "Many will never come back and it may be my lot to fall among the first; but those who do not mean to die if the need come ever in the future for them to die, can ride now two paces to the front. They shall lose nothing in name, or fame or comradeship." Not a man moved but instead cast their fate with their able leader.[19]

At Arrow Rock the Missouri River was running too heavily for the guerrillas to cross, so after waiting four days at Saline City, Quantrill on December 9 abandoned his intention of marching through Illinois and Ohio and chose Kentucky as the next best route to Virginia. Quantrill had started his small command at Dover, going through Lafayette, Saline, Cooper, Moniteau, and Miller Counties during extremely cold weather.

At Tuscumbia on the Osage River, Quantrill rode into town accompanied by William "Babe" Hudspeth to mete out justice to a notorious Federal militiaman there. The Union commander asked him if he could help him. "Yes," replied Quantrill. "Some food and forage will be very acceptable indeed. We have ridden far and fast, and have still great need to make haste. I have a special mission to perform under special orders." While warming themselves at the Federal's fireplace, the guerrillas overpowered the soldiers and took them prisoner. The commander, after realizing that Quantrill had captured his entire command, offered Quantrill his sword. "I do not want your sword," Quantrill replied. "My duties are imperative. You have permitted your soldiers to steal with impunity, to rob the citizens right and left, to occasionally kill some so-called Southern residents who may have become obnoxious to this or that personal enemy; and because of all these things, and in pursuance of direct and positive order, I have disarmed you."

A private managed to escape, and twenty guerrillas started to shoot at him. "No shooting here!" Quantrill remonstrated. "Not a single drop of blood. Take him, some of you, but take him alive."[20] The guerrillas confiscated a supply of blankets and clothing before Quantrill paroled his prisoners.

Making their way across the Osage River by ferryboat, Quantrill's command crossed the Current River into Arkansas. Here one of the Hall brothers was taken with smallpox, and Quantrill, leaving one of Hall's brothers to take care of him, proceeded on to the Black River through the swamps to Crawley's Ridge. While encamped near this place, some of the guerrillas decided to leave the command and headed south to join the Southern army. They traveled as far as Tennessee, serving their leader as a close-knit bodyguard and making sure he was escorted as far as possible to a safer area of operations. Those who left were Jesse James, Oliver Shepherd, John Koger, Ben Morrow, Bob Rufus, William "Babe" Hudspeth, and a man named Baker. Some wept as the men said good-bye to each other, and Quantrill himself was sensibly affected. They never met again.[21]

After their comrades had departed, Quantrill moved toward the Mississippi River and tried to make arrangements for a crossing. When they were unable to secure a crossing they traveled twenty-five miles upriver to a place called Shawnee Village on Devil's Bend. Quantrill attempted to hail a passing Federal steamboat coming up the river, but the boat captain hollered back that he had orders not to land under any circumstances.

On January 2, 1865, Quantrill managed to get his forty-seven men across the river fifteen miles above Memphis after repairing a boat given to him by a nearby citizen. Quantrill advised his men to "steer boldly."

The small band rode northward reaching Brownsville, Tennessee, after being fired upon several times for being in Federal clothing. No one in this part of the country had recognition signs or countersigns like the guerrillas had used in Missouri. But dressed as Federals they managed to obtain food and forage from military posts along the way. Quantrill represented himself as Captain Clark in command of the Fourth Missouri Cavalry.

By mid-January Quantrill's company had managed to cross Tennessee and enter Kentucky near the little town of Canton. Here Quantrill's favorite horse, Old Charley, developed a loose shoe. The horse would not permit anyone but Quantrill to control him, becoming vicious if anyone else approached it. When Quantrill took Old Charley to a blacksmith to get the loose shoe repaired, the horse jerked and severed its tendon, rendering itself useless.

Quantrill was badly shaken in losing his favorite horse. A guerrilla fighter was as close to his horse as to his fellow guerrillas. The loss of Old Charley, like the losses of Todd and Anderson before him, gave Quantrill a premonition of death. He told his men: "It is fate. My career is run and now for me the long lane of a successful career is about to have a turn. So be it."[22]

John McCorkle reported that Quantrill felt so bad at losing his horse that he wanted to stay where he was. But after obtaining another animal he told McCorkle, Thomas Harris, and George Wigginton that he would join them and they would continue on their way to Virginia.[23]

The guerrillas were slowly being run to ground in Kentucky, and blow by blow their numbers and effectiveness were reduced. Just a few days after Quantrill lost his horse, the guerrillas encountered a small Union cavalry force and gave battle. The Federals retreated as fast as they could, but twelve of them took refuge in a farmhouse that the guerrillas quickly surrounded.

John McCorkle and Jim Little were maneuvering themselves to get a better shot at the house when a bullet caught Little in the leg and shattered the bone in his right thigh. Little called out for help. Under intense fire McCorkle and his comrades managed to carry Little away on a blanket. Then a bullet tore the heel off of McCorkle's boot. In anger he turned to attack the house single-handedly. Quantrill tried to save him from a certain death, hollering at him, "John, you are a damned fool. Come back from there!"

Unable to silence the guns, Quantrill ordered Chat Renick, Peyton Long, William Hulse, and Frank James to set the house afire. The Federals quickly surrendered.

When only three Federals came out of the house, Quantrill demanded to know where the remaining soldiers were. "Where are the balance? In the stable I have counted twelve horses; that would be four horses for each of you; not thus do cavalrymen ride in the country I came from."[24] They reported that the nine others fled into the woods when they saw Quantrill's men dismounting to attack the house. Quantrill paroled the Federals on condition that they take care of the seriously wounded Little. A few days later Quantrill learned that the young guerrilla who had always ridden into battle at his side was dead.

After moving all night Quantrill led his men to a farmhouse to get some breakfast. Even though the guerrillas were still wearing Federal uniforms, the two young women who lived there with their father ascertained that the men were Southerners. But Quantrill insisted that his men keep up the ruse that they were Union soldiers on patrol. As they were mounting and starting to ride away after breakfast, McCorkle reported that the women came to the fence and denounced them if they were Union soldiers but told them that they wished them well if they happened to be Southern soldiers. To this Quantrill's men waved their hats and gave a boisterous cheer. Quantrill, in a very stern manner, commanded, "Silence in ranks; forward gallop." Then taking off his hat, he bade the ladies good-bye.[25]

On January 22 Quantrill sought out Capt. Jasper W. Benedict, commander of the garrison in Greenville, Muhlenburg County, and inquired about the guerrilla problem in the area. Quantrill presented himself as a scout seeking guerrillas and their abettors. The captain saw this as an opportunity to rid the country of some nuisances and readily agreed to send a captain named Barnett and thirty men to accompany Quantrill's band.

As the guerrillas rode along with the Federals, Barnett pointed out to Quantrill the farms of Southern sympathizers and suggested what plunder might be carried away. Quantrill summoned William Hulse, Richard Burns, Richard Glasscock, and Frank James and gave them silent instructions. These four men dropped to the rear of the column and, one by one, enticed the last Federal in line to fall out and do a little plundering at a farmhouse they were passing. Not a shot was fired to alert the forward column, but every quarter of a mile or so a Union horseman was hanged from a tree.

When Barnett noticed his men were missing, Quantrill assured him: "They are scouting behind us and if anything happens you will hear of it. Do not be uneasy."

Twenty minutes later he observed: "I see the most of your men, Captain Clark, but I do not see any of mine. Can it be that they have not returned?"

Quantrill replied, "Of course not, Captain Barnett. Are you not in command of them?" Then Quantrill turned and rode back along the column of his soldiers. When he saw that none of the thirty Federals remained with his company, he returned to the front of the column and signaled Frank James to shoot the captain from his saddle.[26]

The guerrillas rode on to Houstonville, where about thirty soldiers were garrisoned under the command of a major named Houston. Quantrill distracted Houston at his headquarters in the local hotel while his men traded their horses for the fresh mounts kept in the town stable. As Quantrill was talking with the major, a private ran and informed the officers of the guerrillas' actions. Houston grabbed his pistols and ran to the livery stable.

Just as he arrived, Allen Parmer rode out of the stable on a magnificent mare. The major grabbed the reins and ordered Parmer to dismount. Parmer informed him that he was operating under his commander's instructions.

Major Houston shouted back, "Damn you, and damn your instructions. Dismount!"

Parmer, who had been in many close situations such as this before, calmly looked at the major and remarked, "Ah! Has it really come to this?"

Both men started to draw their revolvers. The major's pistol was inside his military-issue flap holster, which had to be opened before the wearer could draw his weapon. Parmer's pistol, however, was exposed and stuck inside his belt. Before Houston realized what was about to happen, Parmer leveled his pistol at his head and pulled the trigger.

By this time a dozen Federals had followed their leader to the stable and had leveled their rifles at Parmer. Quantrill, following close behind them with twenty guerrillas, yelled out a warning: "Hold hard! Hold for your lives! For if so be it that one of you fires a gun in anger I swear by the God above us all to murder you in mass!"

The Federals lowered their rifles and surrendered. After this, the guerrillas could no longer conceal their true identities. As the Missourians rode out of town, the story seemed to fly before them. Whenever they visited a Southern sympathizer's home for food or shelter, it seemed that they had already heard that Quantrill was in Kentucky and they welcomed him as his true self and not as one in disguise. Union authorities also learned who he was and began pursuing him through the state.

From Houstonville, Quantrill rode toward Danville. John Newman Edwards reported that by this time Quantrill's exploits had preceded him. Riding into Danville, the guerrilla band initially did not raise suspicion since they were still clothed in Federal uniforms.

One lieutenant, however, took particular notice of the newly arrived captain and followed him into the local saloon. While Quantrill was having a drink at the bar, he looked up in the mirror and saw the lieutenant not three feet away with a rifle aimed at his back. Quantrill's overcoat was buttoned to his chin, thus he could not reach his revolvers. Knowing that his only salvation would be in keeping a cool head, he leaned back across the bar and inquired, "How now, comrade? What are you going to do with that gun?"

The lieutenant replied, "Shoot you like a dog if you stir! You are Quantrill. You have played it for a long time, but you have about played the farce out at last. March into that room to the right of you there!"

Quantrill knew that he would be defenseless if he were separated from his men, so he tried another ploy to throw off any suspicion. "You take me for Quantrill, but you do wrong. Permit me to call my orderly sergeant, who has all my papers, and a glance at them will convince you in a moment that I am as true to the cause of the Union as you are."

The lieutenant was taken aback at the guerrilla's cool demeanor, and not absolutely certain of Quantrill's identity, his resolve seemed to weaken.

Quantrill recognized the opportunity and said, "I have heard, perhaps, the same stories you have heard about the whereabouts of the famous Missouri guerrilla, and if I had not been officially informed to the contrary, equally with yourself I might have believed them. He is not in Kentucky, to my certain knowledge, and you are making a damned fool of yourself. Put down your gun, pull off your pistols, and as long as we are comrades let us be friends."

The lieutenant was not entirely convinced, but Quantrill turned his back on him and moved to the doorway and called to the orderly sergeant. Several of his men started toward him, but he stopped them. "Go back, all of you! I only want John Barker."

The nineteen-year-old sergeant entered the room and pulled his pistol before the lieutenant had time to divert his eyes from Quantrill. But Quantrill quickly stopped him:

You are too fast. Put back your pistol. There need to be no killing here. Our friend, the lieutenant, yonder, has heard much of Quantrill of late, had made up his mind to the fact that I am Quantrill, has armed himself like an arsenal to capture Quantrill, has followed me here and got the drop on me here, and to convince him of his mistake and to show him how absurd and ungenerous he has been; I have called you here as my orderly sergeant to show him our special orders, and to put into his hands the authority of no less a person than the Secretary of War himself, Edwin M. Stanton, per A. J. Smith. Show him these papers, Barker, and then we will go to dinner.

Barker rummaged inside his coat pocket for something that sounded like the rustle of papers then swiftly sprung upon the dazed lieutenant, knocking the rifle out of the way while Quantrill drew his own revolver and held it on the lieutenant.

"Here are my papers," he said. "Now drop that gun!"

The lieutenant's mother happened to be watching and rushed up to Quantrill and pleaded, "He is my boy; for my sake do not kill him."

Quantrill replied, "Well, madam, for your sake I will not. Take him and make him behave himself, but if he bothers me any more, I may kill him."

Climbing up in his saddle, Quantrill told the soldiers and the men with them to go home and that he intended to hurt no one.[27]

Leaving Danville, they rode to a point five miles west of Harrodsburg, where they stopped for the night. In their usual manner the guerrillas split up to seek food and shelter from the farmers in the area.

A company of Kentucky militia commanded by Capt. James H. Bridgewater had pursued Quantrill's men from Danville and managed to surround a group of guerrillas in a farmhouse. According to Allen Parmer, seventeen guerrillas went to a house a few miles from Harrodsburg. "We hadn't had a good meal in a week," he recalled. "And we didn't think there was a Federal within a good many miles of us. After supper, we were sitting around listening to the girls playing the piano, even our two pickets, and I was one of them, came in to listen to the music. Bridgewater came up and surrounded the house."

The trapped guerrillas tried to fight their way out, and Henry Noland, John Barker, and Foss Key were killed. The remaining guerrillas, after running out of ammunition, fought the Federals with clubbed muskets but were eventually captured.

Sylvester Akers knelt next to Barker's body and paid tribute to his fallen comrade: "Boys, if I knew a prayer I would say it here for John Barker. He was true, he was brave, he never went back on his word, he never left a comrade when it was touch and go and the devil a grabbing for the hindmost, he never faltered because it was dark in the South and the men many days had neither rations nor cartridges; but he's gone. God take care of you, John."[28]

Those captured with Akers were James Younger, Andy McGuire, Jack Graham, George Robinson, William Gaugh, and Tom Evans. Parmer, however, escaped and told Quantrill the news. Parmer later recalled: "Most of the boys that were killed were from Independence. Quantrill flew into a terrible rage when we told him about it and he wouldn't believe it. He sent Chat Renick, Frank James, Peyton Long and myself back to see if we could get any of the wounded boys out. They killed Chat Renick on the way back."

The captured guerrillas were taken to a prison in Lexington and threatened with hanging. On three different occasions their captors took the

stalwart guerrillas from their cells and marched them up to the gallows to
scare and intimidate them. Each time they were brought before the gallows,
Quantrill's men marched out cheering for Jefferson Davis and daring the Federals to hang them. They warned that if they were hanged their deaths would
be avenged many times over. The following April the jailed guerrillas were
transported to another prison in Louisville but quickly escaped.

After losing a third of his band, Quantrill headed for Nelson County,
where many refugees from Missouri, including several guerrillas' relatives,
reportedly fled after being forced from their homes by General Orders No. 11.
One day his men noticed a company of Federals was following them. Quantrill
ordered McCorkle to ride ahead and let a fence down to a nearby pasture.

When the band reached the fence, Quantrill commanded, "Rush, boys,
those fellows are coming like the devil." As the guerrillas raced through the
gate, they crested a hill where Quantrill arranged them in line of battle. As
soon as the Union cavalry cleared the top of the hill, Quantrill ordered his
men to charge, driving the Federals back through the fence. The Union
horsemen refused to follow the guerrillas farther.

John McCorkle recalled that the guerrillas heard of a deserter from the
Union army who roamed Nelson County and robbed various farmhouses. In
one instance, he tortured an old man to learn where the man had hidden his
money. As he was leaving, he told the old man he was from Missouri, and if
the old man reported him, he would kill him and his wife. McCorkle learned
the story from the old man's neighbor and finally convinced the old man to
tell him who had abused him. When McCorkle shared the tale with
Quantrill, his commander replied, "Well, why didn't you go get him? Go
back, catch him, and make short work of him. We do not rob people and I
swear no man can accuse us of such hellish acts as this and live." Within two
days McCorkle found and executed the deserter and terrorist.

Recognizing the reduced effectiveness of his depleted force, Quantrill
joined the remainder of his band to the guerrilla band of Jerome Clarke, alias
Sue Mundy. They attacked all Federal outposts in their new area of operations. On February 2 they burned a railroad depot at Midway, northwest of
Lexington, then six days later captured a wagon train at New Market, killing
the seven guards.

Meanwhile, Capt. James H. Bridgewater continued to dog the tracks of
the guerrillas. The day after their New Market raid, Bridgewater caught up
with Quantrill and Clarke's joint command west of Houstonville. He killed
four of the guerrillas, captured four more, and ran the remainder into the
woods barefooted and horseless. For the next several weeks the guerrillas

were scattered across the countryside, seeking food, shelter, clothing, and new mounts. They were entirely dependent upon the residents to support them just as they had been in Missouri.

The going was slow and treacherous, but Quantrill continued to move his small command through the countryside toward Lee's Army of Northern Virginia. And there seemed to be more Union troops and patrols in Kentucky than there had been in Missouri. The guerrillas had to familiarize themselves with the terrain and gain new friends. By April the band had only occasional encounters with Union patrols.

And the war had taken a turn that made Quantrill reevaluate his intentions. On March 29 the siege of Petersburg went badly for the Confederates. After a three-day struggle, Lee's army was forced to abandon the city. And after the collapse of the Petersburg defenses, on April 2 the Confederate government was forced to flee Richmond.

Quantrill could no longer plan on joining Lee's army to seek honorable surrender terms. He proceeded as far east as Spencer County, an area south of Louisville predominantly inhabited by Southern sympathizers. There he waited to see what would happen. Shortly after April 9 Quantrill received news that Lee had surrendered at Appomattox Court House. John Newman Edwards wrote: "While Lee stood everything stood, erect, hopeful, defiant. When Lee fell, the fabric which four years of heroic fighting had erected and the blood of half a million of men had been poured out to make its foundations immutable, fell with him and with a great crash."[29]

The war was over, although many still endeavored to carry on. Joseph E. Johnston continued to fight in North Carolina, and many in the South looked to him for salvation. After abandoning Richmond, President Davis fled to the south. Some still held out hope that a Southern victory could be won. On April 15 news arrived that Abraham Lincoln had been killed, which encouraged all Southerners to further hope for victory despite Lee's surrender.

Many Southern military units had refused to surrender, continuing their offensive campaigns. Price, Shelby, and E. Kirby Smith headed their forces in Missouri south toward Mexico rather than accept defeat. Quantrill and Mundy in Kentucky continued to carry on raids of Union outposts. Federal forces attempted to strike back with local militia, but it became apparent that a different style of aggression would have to be employed.

Quantrill led his men to southern Spencer County. In the early part of May, knowing that the war was over, Quantrill held a conference with his men to determine what they should do. There they decided to separate and seek the best terms of surrender individually. McCorkle reported:

Colonel Quantrill had one last act to perform before his band entirely split up. Quantrill had just been told that a man, claiming to be a Missourian and one of our men, robbed an old citizen by the name of Jones, and that the description given of the robber fitted one of our men, telling me the name of the man. He said he was going to take the man described to old man Jones and if the old man identified him he would have him killed, that he never had permitted, nor never would permit any of his men to commit robbery.

McCorkle told Quantrill that the suspected robber had ridden with him in a number of close places. He considered the man a brave soldier, and so he decided not to hunt him down with Quantrill.

Quantrill told McCorkle to meet him in a day or two. Quantrill intended to surrender to Federal authorities at Louisville.[30] McCorkle and his cousins, George Wigginton and Thomas Harris, turned back with John Barnhill to their former camp.

Quantrill led the remainder of his men along the pike from Taylorsville to Bloomfield. Those who accompanied him were John Ross, William Hulse, Payne Jones, Clark Hockensmith, Isaac Hall, Richard Glasscock, Robert Hall, Bud Pence, Allen Parmer, Dave Hilton, and Lee McMurtry. It had been raining for three days, and the guerrillas were looking for shelter and relief from the weather. They had passed the James H. Wakefield farm several times before and found him to be a friendly and supportive Southern sympathizer. They assumed the rain would prevent any enemy patrols and did not believe there were any Federals for miles.

Quantrill turned his company down the lane and toward the barn a short distance behind Wakefield's large farmhouse. Richard Glasscock was stationed as a picket at the house and stood on the front porch conversing with Wakefield. Inside the barn the guerrillas turned their horses loose and settled back to dry out. Some gathered in small groups and played cards while others picked up stray corncobs and threw them at one another in a sham battle. Quantrill was soon asleep in the hayloft. Only two days before his horse had kicked him, and he found it extremely painful to walk.

Nineteen-year-old Edwin Terrill and a guerrilla patrol had been on Quantrill's trail for more than a month. Terrill had reportedly been in the Confederate army for a brief time, but he had killed his superior officer and was imprisoned and sentenced to be executed. He escaped and joined the Union army. Terrill became a bully, a thief, and a murderer of civilians, Confederate and Union. In a letter R. T. Owen observed, "[Terrill's] reputation was the worst imaginable and his fighting qualities were only developed when under the influence of whiskey."[31] Recently, Terrill had been commissioned by Federal authorities to fight guerrillas.

On the morning of May 10, while Quantrill was asleep in Wakefield's hayloft, Terrill and fifty members of his patrol tracked Quantrill's muddy trail. Around noon they halted at the mouth of the lane from Wakefield's house and inquired from a local black man if he had seen any guerrillas lately. The man pointed toward Wakefield's house. Terrill ordered his men to look to their weapons while he sent a man to reconnoiter the area. The scout reported that the Confederates were lounging around the barn and that their horses were tied to nearby fences. Terrill then gave the order to charge. His men spurred their horses down the lane, unslinging their carbines, shooting, and yelling at the top of their voices.[32]

Glasscock was still talking to Wakefield when he saw the Federals charge. Clark Hockensmith was standing in the barn when he turned to look down the lane as the Federal yell caught his attention. At once the pickets gave the alarm, and every man grabbed his pistols.

Quantrill jumped down from his place in the loft and shouted an order to his men: "Mount, about face and charge. Cut through, boys; cut through somehow. Don't surrender while there is a chance to get out!" Unfortunately, the guerrillas' horses were unsaddled and loose about the barn. The guerrillas quickly realized that they could not be caught in the barn and expect to get out alive. All of the men leaped for their horses and tried to escape. Some found their animals unmanageable and tried to escape on foot to the nearby timber.

Quantrill shouted out one last command as his men opened fire on the Federals: "Take care of yourselves, everybody!" His horse, not accustomed to battle, reared in terror and could not be mounted.

While their comrades were attempting to flee, Glasscock and Hockensmith, both mounted, fired their pistols as fast as they could to check the charge. But their efforts were to no avail. Terrill's men also knew the advantage of a quick charge and accurate pistol fire.

Some of Quantrill's men who were fortunate enough to reach their horses begged Quantrill to mount in their place, but he refused. He made sure all of his men escaped before attempting to flee himself. Most jumped their horses over the fence in the southwest corner of the lot and made it to the nearby timber. Quantrill was the last to leave the barn.

As the first men to notice Terrill's attack, Glasscock and Hockensmith could have been the first to escape, but instead they stayed to serve as a rear

guard and lay down a steady fusillade to cover the hasty retreat of their comrades. Without a horse and limping badly, Quantrill was in desperate straits.
Hockensmith saw his predicament and reined back his horse to help him.
Quantrill yelled at him to go back, but Hockensmith ignored the order. After
he had emptied his pistols at the oncoming Federals, Quantrill held out his
arm to leap up behind Hockensmith, but Hockensmith dismounted so that
Quantrill was in the saddle, then Hockensmith sprang up behind him. While
the two guerrillas were attempting to mount the horse, Glasscock placed
himself between them and the enemy to shield them.

The Federals chased the guerrillas from the barn then rested their carbines along a top fence rail to steady their aim and poured a deadly volley
toward the fleeing men. Glasscock, Hockensmith, and Quantrill were only a
few hundred yards from Wakefield's barn. A volley cut down Hockensmith,
killing him and his horse and pinning Quantrill underneath. Glasscock's
horse was struck in the hip and became unmanageable. As Quantrill tried to
pull himself from beneath Hockensmith's horse, a bullet struck him at the
shoulder blade, ranged downward, struck his spine, and left him paralyzed
below the arms. The same volley killed Glasscock's horse.

After Quantrill fell, the Federals, continuing to fire, ran toward him. The
unhorsed Glasscock stood like an immovable object, firing his pistols over
the body of his wounded leader. He managed to kill two of Terrill's men and
wound three others. The charging Federals turned their fire on the last guerrilla standing. A bullet tore through his shirt, another his hat, two tore
through his trousers, and one tore off a lock of his hair, but none drew blood.

After emptying his revolvers, Glasscock stooped to take a pistol from
Quantrill's belt, and a Federal bullet struck him, causing him to fall next to
Hockensmith and Quantrill. As Terrill's men rushed up, they continued
firing. Another bullet struck Quantrill, tearing off the tip of the ring finger on
his left hand.

To the soldiers rushing upon him, Quantrill said, "It is useless to shoot me
any more; I am now a dying man."

The rest of Quantrill's men managed to escape. Hockensmith and Glasscock were steadfast in their loyalty and died striving to save their chief. Even
during his childhood, Clark Hockensmith had a reputation of being singu-
larly devoted in his friendships and unfaltering in the discharge of his duties.[33]

Quantrill was helpless as the Federals converged on him and unceremoniously pulled off his boots and took his pistols. And with the fighting ended,
they turned to looting. After a while some of Terrill's men fetched a blanket
from the Wakefield house and used it to carry Quantrill into the house. At no

time did he complain or moan. His endurance remained unimpaired to the end. His mind, always clear in danger, seemed to recognize that his last battle had been fought. He spoke very little.[34]

Terrill asked who he was, and he automatically replied that he was Captain Clark of the Fourth Missouri Cavalry. When he was made as comfortable as possible, Terrill asked Quantrill if there was anything he could do for him. He replied, "Yes, have Clark Hockensmith buried like a soldier." He added, "While I live let me stay here. It is useless to haul a dying man about in a wagon, jolting out what little life is left in him." Quantrill then gave Terrill his gold watch and five hundred dollars. Terrill gave his word that Quantrill would not be removed if Quantrill would give his word that he would not try to leave Wakefield's. Quantrill agreed, then Terrill hurriedly left to pursue the other guerrillas.

Some of the escaped guerrillas made their way twenty-three miles to another Southern sympathizer's house, the home of Alexander Sayers, where the rest of Quantrill's men were staying. When they heard the news of Quantrill's plight, Frank James spoke up immediately, "Volunteers to go back? Who will follow me to see our chief, living or dead?" Allen Parmer, John Ross, and William Hulse agreed to accompany him. Within twenty minutes the four stalwart guerrillas were on their way to Wakefield's.

John Newman Edwards related that it was two o'clock in the morning by the time the guerrillas knocked at Wakefield's door. Wakefield's wife opened the door and led them to the room where their leader was lying, partially propped up with pillows, on a trundle bed. Frank James stood over the bed, but seeing his beloved leader prostrate, he was unable to speak and had tears in his eyes.

James then went to the bedroom door and motioned for Parmer, Ross, and Hulse. With tears in their eyes they entreated Quantrill to let them take him into hiding, but Quantrill told them he had pledged his word to stay or Wakefield's farm would be destroyed.

Parmer pressed close to his wounded chieftain, bending low over his body as Quantrill said, "Allen, my boy. What made you come back? The enemy is thick around us and you are liable to be killed at any moment. Why did you come back?"

Amid choking sobs, Parmer replied: "I came back to get you if alive and to bury you if you were dead." Quantrill smiled and spoke in return, "I thank you Allen, but why not let me alone for I am already dead. Put your hands on me. I am as cold as ice and can not move let alone ride or walk. I am comfortable here and here let me die."

The three guerrillas wept for their fallen leader, but Quantrill told them to dry their tears. Frank James enjoined his entreaties to those of his comrades and pleaded with Quantrill for permission to carry him to the mountains of Nelson County. Each man swore to guard him hour by hour until he recovered or die over his body.

Quantrill knew that every pledge would be kept to the death, every word was golden and meant absolute devotion. His faith in their affection was as steadfast and abiding as of old. He listened with the staid courtesy of the old victorious guerrilla days till they had done, then he silenced them with his answer: "I cannot live. I have run a long time; I have fought to kill and I have killed; I regret nothing. The end is close at hand. I am resting easy here, and will die so. You do not know how your devotion has touched my heart, nor can you ever understand how grateful I am for the love you have shown for me. Try to get back to your homes, and avoid if you can the perils which beset you and may God bless you and yours."[35]

The four guerrillas stayed together until ten o'clock the next morning. They passed the hours listening to Quantrill's final instructions for their surrender and taking messages for old friends. Then they departed.

Wakefield summoned Dr. Isaac McClaskey from Taylorsville to look at Quantrill's wounds. The doctor had previously treated Quantrill. When Quantrill recognized him, he asked if he was the same man who had treated him before. The doctor replied, "I am the man. I have moved here." Quantrill in a sullenly humorous vein replied, "So have I."

After the examination Dr. McClaskey told him that he would not recover. He left after making Quantrill as comfortable as possible. Wakefield reported that while Quantrill lay wounded in his house he thanked him for his kindness and gave instructions to forward some money to his mother and sister.

The Federals finally discovered that the wounded soldier lying at Wakefield's house was the famous Missouri guerrilla. Even though Terrill had given his word that Quantrill would not be moved, three days later an "ambulance" sent by Gen. John M. Palmer arrived, accompanied by a heavy cavalry escort, and bore Quantrill to the military prison hospital in Louisville. The ambulance was an old Conestoga wagon filled with hay and pillows to make the trip more comfortable for the wounded man.

While en route to the prison, the ambulance stopped along the way so a local doctor named Marshall could check on Quantrill's condition. Quantrill arrived at the hospital around noon on May 13. While he was being carried inside, onlookers noticed Quantrill was holding a bouquet of flowers. An attached card read: "Compliments of Miss Maggie Frederick and Sallie Lovell to Mr. Quantrill." Until his wounds were confirmed as fatal, he was not allowed visitors.

Prior to dying Quantrill gave the Catholic priest at the hospital eight hundred dollars and directed him to use part of the money for his grave. The priest gave a portion of the money to the Reverend Michael Powers of the Portland Cemetery, later called the St. Johns Catholic Cemetery, with instructions for Quantrill's burial. Quantrill requested that no mound be raised over the grave, but that the ground be kept level, and that they should throw their dishwater and other slops over the spot, so as to obliterate it as much as possible to keep his body from being stolen.[36] Quantrill knew that otherwise he would never be allowed to rest in peace.

Some reports say that two Southern women visited him while he was dying in the Louisville hospital. A guerrilla named White added, "Several persons visited him while he was in the hospital. Kate Quantrill said that she arrived from St. Louis three days before her husband died and stood at his bedside as he breathed his last.[37]

While he was in the hospital, Quantrill was visited daily by two Catholic priests. He asked Father Michael Powers to hear his confession and became a Catholic by requesting membership in the Catholic Church. Another Southern woman, Harriet Ross, the mother of John Ross, who accompanied Quantrill to Kentucky, also visited him in the hospital and brought dying messages from him to loved ones in Missouri. She claimed that his passing was hastened if not caused by neglect. The tenacity with which he held to life amazed the doctors.[38]

Harriet Ross left the hospital at one o'clock in the afternoon of June 6. A short while later Quantrill called for a nun to bring him a glass of water. The Sister of Charity put the glass to his lips, but Quantrill did not drink. Instead, she heard him utter his last command: "Boys, get ready!" Then, after a pause, he spoke one last word: "Steady!" At four o'clock in the afternoon of June 6, 1865, the great guerrilla chief William Clarke Quantrill was dead at the age of twenty-seven.[39]

Henry Porter gathered most of the remnants of Quantrill's band, now numbering only eighteen, and surrendered at Samuel's Depot in Nelson County on July 25, 1865, according to Quantrill's dying orders. The group included Frank James, Andy McGuire, Lee McMurtry, Allen Parmer, William Hulse, Bud Pence, Isaac and Bob Hall, Jim Lilly, Dave Hilton, Thomas Harris, John Ross, Randolph Venable, and Payne Jones. John McCorkle and his cousin George Wigginton attached themselves to a regular

Confederate command and surrendered to ensure that they received honorable terms.

Quantrill's seventeen-year-old wife, Kate, returned to St. Louis and opened a boarding house after selling some jewelry that Quantrill had given her. Rumors circulated that she received a large sum of money from Quantrill before he died, but she denied it. Four years after the war, Kate returned to her parents' farm in Blue Springs and built them a new home to replace the one that was burned by jayhawkers during the war. From 1912 to 1920 she kept house for her brother and nephew on the farm where she was born. Kate died on January 9, 1930, at the age of eighty-two. In a newspaper interview shortly before her death, she said, "I never knew a kinder, more considerate a gentleman."[40] Throughout her life, she often remarked that Quantrill was the only man she had ever loved.

13

Vengeance Is Mine, Sayeth the Lord

Though they survived the shells, they became casualties of the war.

ANONYMOUS

I T IS SAID THAT a civil war never truly ends. The surrender at Appomattox Court House did not bring about, as the people had hoped, an end to the hostilities—at least not in the area along the western border of Missouri. Nor did Federal atrocities cease with the formal ending of the war. Everyone looked forward to a return to normality, but nothing changed and uncertainty about the future grew. Everyone knew what war would bring, but no one knew what peace would bring. Where Southern men once fought together, they no longer had the assurance of finding safety in armed force. They found themselves confronting a still-armed enemy in an environment where the justification and legality of being on an opposing force was gone.

Some things changed quickly with Lee's surrender on April 9, 1865. The Confederate army in the East followed Lee's example and gave up their arms. Gen. Joseph E. Johnston tried to make a continued stand in North Carolina but finally surrendered his army on April 26. Along the western border, however, where bloodshed had resulted from the cruelest atrocities against both Confederate soldiers and civilians, surrender was not an option quick in coming.

In Texas the Confederates saw a futile attempt at further military action. On May 16 Gen. John Bankhead Magruder wired Gen. E. Kirby Smith that

411

Confederate soldiers in the Galveston area had mutinied. More than half of the troops in western Texas had deserted. Other Texas cavalry units took a wait-and-see attitude on when their commands would be allowed to surrender. On May 19, without word from higher command, two Texas cavalry regiments met at Hempstead, Texas, and agreed to disband. They committed that each would retain its original organization and return home to protect citizens from "roving bands of thieves and robbers."[1] In only a matter of days all the Confederate armies in Texas had disbanded. E. Kirby Smith found himself a general without an army. On May 26 Gen. Simon Bolivar Buckner surrendered the Confederate Army of the Trans-Mississippi Department to Gen. Edward R. S. Canby.

Many Missourians knew that peace would be long in coming. Refusing to surrender, five hundred Confederates rode together across the Rio Grande into Mexico. Among those determined men were Gens. Sterling Price, Thomas C. Hindman, E. Kirby Smith, and Joseph O. Shelby. The soldiers took their battle flags with them and buried them in the Rio Grande as they crossed. Shelby was quoted as saying: "We are the last of our race. Let us be the best as well." Once in Mexico, Emperor Maximilian, in exchange for their support for his government, gave land to the Confederates. Price went to Cordova, where the emperor proposed the establishment of a colony for ex-Confederate soldiers. After the fall of Maximilian's government, most of the former Confederates returned home. Price returned to Missouri in 1866 and died in St. Louis on September 29, 1867. Shelby returned in 1867 to Lafayette County, Missouri. In 1893 he was appointed U.S. marshal for the western district of Missouri and held that office until his death on February 13, 1897.

For the former Confederate soldiers who remained in Missouri after the war, theirs was the hardest lot. The end of the war may have been the end of military operations, but it signaled the beginning of a civil unrest that the country had never before witnessed. Many Southerners were more than willing to put down their arms and return peaceably to their homes and do the best they could for themselves, but the same radicals who had pushed the country into war were not about to allow their defeated foe any type of voice in the political arena.

Lincoln's postmaster general, Montgomery Blair, and his brother, Col. Francis Blair of Missouri, controlled Republican politics in the state. Before his second inauguration, Lincoln eventually split with the radical Blairs and demanded Montgomery Blair's resignation. He finally discovered what he had suspected all along: The Blairs' political self-interests were the paramount object of the their actions in Missouri. Montgomery's younger brother, Frank

Jr., was the unsuccessful vice presidential nominee on the Democratic ticket in 1868, but he maintained a firm hand on the radical political policies in Missouri for years.

The Unionists in Missouri turned their vehemence toward their former foes by passing laws that subjugated them and subjected them to intolerable conditions. They made it illegal for former Confederates to own guns. This in itself was enough to cause a great hardship since many hunted to feed their families. Unionists transferred their power from military law to civil law. Where recently a Federal militia fought a Confederate foe, now Home Guards united into vigilante bands and took whatever retaliatory actions they deemed appropriate. They requisitioned horses and mules and even unhitched them from the plows of former Confederates while they were plowing in their fields.

After Missouri's elected governor was chased from the state early in the war, radical politicians gained the upper hand in Missouri politics. The radicals set up a provisional government to usurp the authority of the legally elected one that was forced to vacate at bayonet point. The radicals during the war were often kept in check by the military authorities appointed from Washington. Once peace came, however, and the military authority was no longer justified, the radicals pushed their vengeful actions on their defeated foes.

Sensing that their political power was ending with the peace that would bring back fairness to the voting process, the radicals gathered to begin their agenda. They tried to overthrow Gen. John M. Schofield, the military commander, along with Hamilton Gamble, the conservative provisional governor. Schofield discovered a plot by the radicals to kidnap him and the governor so they could take over operations in Missouri. The radical press worked feverishly to persuade the public of their point of view. Their incendiary articles encouraged a regiment of the Missouri Militia to mutiny. As the military authority in Missouri, Schofield was greatly alarmed.

Previously Schofield had backed the ultraradical policies of Gen. Nathaniel Lyon, his former superior, but lately he had come to realize just how disruptive were the policies of the radical party. The radicals openly showed their contempt for Schofield because he opposed their plans on destroying the provisional government and setting up a radical one.

On September 17 Schofield issued an order threatening fines and punishment for anyone trying to sow discord among his troops or who tried to incite citizens to violence. He warned the radical newspapers that further incendiary articles would result in censorship and suppression. To Henry W. Halleck, the general in chief, Schofield wrote:

The revolutionary faction, which has so long been striving to gain the ascendancy in Missouri, particularly in St. Louis, to overthrow the present State government and change the policy of the national administration has at length succeeded, so far as to produce open mutiny of one of the militia regiments and serious difficulties in others. I am thoroughly convinced of the necessity for prompt and decided measures to put down this revolutionary scheme, and my sense of duty will not permit me to delay it longer. It is barely possible that I may not have to enforce the order against the public press. They may yield without the application of force, but I do not expect it. The tone of some of their articles since the publication of the order indicates a determination to wage the war, which they have begun to the bitter end. This determination is based upon the belief that the President will not sustain me in any such measures as those contemplated in the order. A distinct approval of the President of my proposed action, and a knowledge of the fact here, would end the whole matter at once. It is difficult, I am aware, for any one at a distance to believe that such measures can be necessary against men and papers who claim to be "radically loyal." The fact is, they are "loyal" only to their "radical" theories and are so radical that they cannot possibly be loyal to the Government.

In like measure all across the South, radicals were taking over the civil governments and thwarting the fair-election processes in the former Confederacy. Virginia's guerrilla leader, John S. Mosby, knew he and his men would not be afforded an honorable surrender, so Mosby elected to disband his men. After Lee's surrender, Confederate President Jefferson Davis was captured in Georgia and imprisoned in Virginia in chains. And after the war there was no public outcry about the outrages committed along the Missouri-Kansas border, only cries from the radicals against rebellious Southern sympathizers.

With the death of Lincoln, the South lost its only hope of an amicable return into the Federal fold and forgiveness. The radicals were fearful when they heard Lincoln say, "With malice toward none, with charity for all, with firmness in the right as God gives us to see the right, let us strive on to finish the work we are in, to bind up the nation's wounds, to care for him who shall have borne the battle and for his widow and his orphan, to do all which may achieve and cherish a just and lasting peace among ourselves and with all nations."[2] After Lincoln's death the administration was unforgiving and hostile toward any claim of injustice done to Southerners or those who sympathized with them.

In 1866 Lincoln's successor, Andrew Johnson, faced serious opposition from congressional Republicans. They feared that if Johnson restored the Southern states and pardoned the former Rebel leaders, the Democratic Party would regain its prewar strength and frustrate Republican plans for economic and social reform in the South. Many believed that either the South should be declared—like so many conquered provinces—to be under military rule or given back the freedom of the ballot.

Thwarting the Republican vision was precisely what Johnson wanted. He did not welcome the vast acceleration of social and economic changes for which the Civil War was responsible. Few elections in American history were as important as the Congressional race in 1866. The future of constitutional government seemed to rest on its outcome. Since Congress had refused to seat the senators and representatives from the Southern states, Congressional elections in the fall would determine whether the president or the Congress would control the course of Reconstruction.[3]

Woodrow Wilson observed, after the midterm elections of 1866, "Adventurers swarmed out of the North, as much the enemies of the one race as the other, to cozen, beguile, and use the negroes . . . in the villages the negroes were the office holders, men who knew none of the uses of authority, except its insolences. . . . The policy of the Congressional leaders wrought . . . a veritable overthrow of civilization in the South . . . in their determination to put the white South under the heel of the black South."[4]

After calling for a state convention and electing Charles D. Drake, as their leader, the radicals came together to "reform" the Missouri constitution. Early on the radicals in Missouri met in convention in September 1864 and called for the resignation of the provisional government and the appointment of a committee of seventy to take their grievances to Washington to Lincoln. Missouri Sen. Charles Drake, heading the committee, summoned, of all people, James Lane from Kansas to accompany the committee and present their complaints. Lane saw this as a way of gaining influence in Missouri as well as Kansas, and he gladly accepted.

Drake and his radical friends wanted to restrain the returning Secessionists, and Drake especially wanted Lincoln's blessing to do it. When Lincoln was not attentive enough, Drake turned on him. In a subsequent speech he called Lincoln "a tyrant and a dictator." He knew that the basic fundamental right to vote would be the radicals' undoing if the returning Confederates were allowed access to the ballot, so he immediately focused his attention on this issue. An unrelenting vindictiveness emerged among the radicals toward anyone who disagreed with the party and its platform.[5]

The radicals began to take over Missouri politics with the Ironclad Oath. The oath excluded all but those who had been loyal citizens from participating in politics and even some civilian professions. As an indication of the severity of the oath, it excluded anyone who might have given a cup of water to a Confederate soldier or even forage to his horse. Even those who had handed a letter to a soldier in arms against the government were at fault. Uttering any statement of dissatisfaction against the government was enough to mark one as disloyal. And anyone found to be disloyal during the war was not allowed to be an officer of a public or private company or allowed to teach in the public schools or hold a leadership position in a church.[6]

In Jackson County the oath required all voting citizens to travel to the county seat at Independence and swear to eighty conditions and to account for what they did or did not do during the war. Neighbor turned against neighbor and challenged each other's oaths and accounts of their wartime activities.[7] In Boone County, in the heart of "Little Dixie," out of 4,290 qualified white voters, only 410 were allowed to vote.[8] Any persons attempting to practice law, vote, teach, or preach without taking the loyalty oath were to be fined not less than five hundred dollars or be incarcerated for six months or both. If accused of perjury when taking the oath, violators were to stand trial. The only marks of citizenship these rejected men had under the Drake Constitution were "to pay taxes, work the roads, and hold their peace."[9]

The president and officers of the state university were required to take the oath or vacate their office. Presidents and managers of the railroads were put under heavy bond to employ no one but those who professed their wartime loyalty to the Union.

Drake's goal was to disfranchise anyone of questionable loyalty to the Union and to add whatever constitutional amendments might be necessary to further the radicals' establishment of political power over Missouri. The ironic aspect of the Ironclad Oath was that the radical Unionists who had called for the Secessionists to return to the Union all during the war were trying now to keep them from coming back in. Thomas S. Barclay observed: "During the war the Radicals used to say, 'Let the Rebels lay down their arms and submit to the Constitution and law; that is all we ask of them.' They *have* laid down their arms and ask to be permitted to have the Constitution and laws; but the Radicals now reply, 'You shall *not* have the Constitution; and as for the laws, we don't intend to let you have any sort of law, except the tax law, and you shall have *no* voice in making that.'"[10]

The election in November 1864 saw the radicals carry the state in Missouri by electing eight out of nine congressmen. Thomas Fletcher, a former brigade commander under William T. Sherman and a radical of renown, was elected governor.

Fearful that their work might be undone by unsympathetic judges, radical members of the state convention pressed a law through the legislature called the Ousting Ordinance while the state supreme court was in recess. The measure vacated all positions of judges, county clerks, circuit attorneys, sheriffs, and recorders by May 1, 1865, and stipulated that the governor would appoint men to complete any unfinished terms. In effect, the act purged all of Missouri's legally elected officials who had served from the beginning of the war. The ordinance removed more than eight hundred officials throughout the state. When the Missouri supreme court ruled it unconstitutional, the radicals arrested the justices. Militia officers also seized the court records.

In one instance the governor called out a company of black militiamen to quash efforts by some officials to retain their positions. In this way the radicals willfully and corruptly defrauded the citizens of their freedom to vote.

Because the Ironclad Oath covered ministers of the gospel, church doors remained closed to Southern sympathizers. One radical observed, "No class of people between heaven and earth, or outside of heaven or hell deserve the curse of God more than disloyal ministers and no class deserve sympathy less than this class. If they can not take the oath, they should go and seek a home elsewhere." One uncompromising pastor, the Reverend M. M. Modisett, wrote: "I confess that I am placed in a very unpleasant situation, not because of the fear of perjury or of doing violence to my feelings for any act of my life, by taking said oath, but on account of the seeming unreasonableness of the thing, and, as I now view it, as being an infringement of religious liberty, as well as a species of tyranny to which I dislike to submit."

The Baptists were split over the issue. Their general association met in Boonville in August 1865 and adopted a resolution declaring the oath to be a violation of the U.S. Constitution, an unjust attempt to punish ministers for crimes not committed, and a breach of the longstanding principle of separation of church and state.

In reply to the church's outcry, Gov. Thomas Fletcher responded: "Religious liberty is a political right." Hundreds of priests and preachers were indicted, arrested, and tried in civil courts for preaching the gospel.[11]

As the Rebels began filtering back into Missouri, they were met with animosity on every side. Many Unionists believed that all Rebel property should be seized and all Rebels should be hanged. The radicals, however, feared Lincoln's Reconstruction policies. They believed that his conciliatory program toward former Rebels was too lenient and feared the political consequences. When Quantrill left Missouri he perceived that the radical's political machinations would prevent any former guerrillas from returning to take up their former peaceful occupations. The Test Oath in 1861 had already disenfranchised more than fifty-two thousand voters, most of whom were Democratic voters who took a counterstand against the Radicals.

On April 8, 1865, Drake's new constitution granted amnesty to all Union soldiers for any acts since January 1, 1861, but held former Confederate personnel responsible for all they had done as soldiers or civilians. Section 4, Article 11 of the new Missouri constitution stated, "All persons in the military service of the United States or who acted under the authority thereof in this State, are relieved from all civil liability and all criminal punishment for all acts done by them since the 1st day of January, 1861."

Yet when Andrew Johnson assumed the presidency at Lincoln's death, he offered amnesty to the defeated Confederates. Many accepted Johnson's amnesty and returned home believing they had been absolved of all past crimes, but the radicals soon set up grand juries and indicted some of these men for so-called wartime crimes. With the results of the war in their favor, most Unionists sought to rid the country of any returning Confederate soldiers and made those who did return feel unwelcome.

In subsequent elections, Governor Fletcher established all-black regiments throughout the state to "guard the polls." The defeated Rebels saw themselves locked out of the country they had fought for and knew they had nowhere else to go. The Southerners saw the political winds shift sharply against them.

Now that former Confederates were excluded from the ballot box, Drake sought to amend the constitution to give African Americans the right to vote in the upcoming 1866 election. A small minority of conservative politicians continued to try to work toward a political compromise to keep the state from boiling over into turmoil. After they failed, the leader of the conservatives explained his disappointment: "We have worked with a determination to create harmony, but we have failed; there was a party of men who had such a greed for office, such a determination to have the spoils, that they would not listen to reason."[12]

With their political future well established and the civil law firmly in their grasp at all levels, the radicals at last turned their vehemence on the returning Confederates. After fighting during the war as one of Capt. Clifton Holtzclaw's lieutenants, Howard Bragg returned to his home to find a price had been put on his head. When he learned that he was not eligible for the amnesty offered to Confederate soldiers, he went to Mexico, fought under Benito Juarez, and received a land grant for his service.[13]

Col. Gideon W. Thompson, a Confederate from Clay County, fought at the battle of Lexington in 1861 and alongside Quantrill at the battles of Independence and Lone Jack in August 1862. When he returned home after the war, his property and belongings were confiscated by the U.S. District Court of the Western District in November 1865 for siding with the enemy or assisting in the rebellion.[14] Col. John D. Holt had ridden with Quantrill on the Lawrence raid in August 1863. His property and personal effects were confiscated for the same reasons as Thompson's.[15] Many other returning Confederates experienced the same confiscations.

Those men who had ridden with Quantrill were especially harassed. Union newspapers throughout the state urged the establishment of "vigilance committees" to seek out and destroy any returning Southerner who did not keep his place.[16] The former Confederates were usually without funds or property, and the ruined state of affairs made it difficult for them to make a new start. When they showed any opposition to radical rule in Missouri, they were suppressed in a heavy-handed fashion. Governor Fletcher called on the state militia, whose members were composed mainly of radicals and served the governor, to serve as unofficial posses to put down any disturbances caused by disgruntled former Rebels.

Still Quantrill's guerrillas slowly filtered back to Missouri and surrendered. Those who had gone to Kentucky with him had already surrendered, and some of these gained recognition as the last Confederate soldiers to lay down their arms.

In March 1865 Archie Clements, now leading William Anderson's old company, marched from Sherman, Texas, to Mount Pleasant, Arkansas. Starting out on April 14 and reinforced by ten men under David Poole, the guerrillas made their last march into Missouri. They resisted everything in their path. The advance element of David Poole, John Poole, John Maupin, Jack Bishop, Theodore Cassell, Jesse James, and Press Webb killed more than twenty militiamen as they pushed toward Jackson County. At Kingsville in Johnson County, Missouri, they killed another ten Federals in a small skirmish. Among the dead was a militiaman named Duncan who had a reputation as a highwayman and house burner.

The guerrillas settled back into their old haunts along the banks of the Sni and Little Blue Rivers in Jackson County and heard about Lee's surrender. A council was held to discuss the pros and cons of surrendering. All during the war the Federals insisted that the guerrillas were not regular Confederate soldiers, but after Appomattox they ordered all guerrillas to report to the nearest Union post and officially accept the terms of surrender.

Clements agreed to find out what terms he could get for his men. On April 15, with Jesse James, Jesse Hamlet, Jack Rupe, Willis King, and John Vanmeter, Clements entered Lexington under a flag of truce. Maj. J. B. Rogers, the provost marshal, told them that they would have to relinquish their horses and weapons and submit to the laws of the state. Such terms meant the unhorsed and unarmed guerrillas would have been as sheep among wolves. After convincing Rogers that there were men who would kill them on sight to settle old scores from the war, the guerrillas were allowed to keep their horses and weapons. After agreeing to return the next day to formally accept the surrender terms, Clements and his companions mounted and rode off.

In town that day were men who would change the course of history. As Clements's group was riding out of Lexington, they encountered eight Union soldiers. The Federals were the advance guard of a unit of sixty men, half from the Johnson County militia, the rest from the Second Wisconsin Cavalry. The eight fired point-blank at the guerrillas, who returned fire and charged, killing four and wounding two.

When the larger Union force was encountered, the guerrillas attempted to escape. Vanmeter's horse was killed, and Rupe stopped under fire to carry him to safety. Clements and Jesse James rode away swiftly, side by side, turning and firing at their pursuers. One Wisconsin trooper on a swift black horse advanced ahead of the rest and closed in on James. When they were within ten feet of each other, both fired. James killed the trooper with a bullet through the heart. Before he knew it, another Wisconsin trooper was upon him. James managed to kill his horse, but the trooper shot Jesse through the right lung. The rest of the Federals rushed upon him, killing his horse, then pursued Clements. While James lay wounded in the middle of the road, other Federals rode past him and fired at him as he lay bleeding under his horse.

Clements looked back and saw his colleague fall. He also saw sixty Federals firing at the prostrate body and believed that Jesse James had been killed. Yet James managed to pull himself from under his horse and crawled into the nearby woods. Five Johnson County militiamen pursued him, maintaining a constant fire. He killed the foremost Federal before firing and shattering the pistol arm of a second soldier. The wounded guerrilla kicked off his heavy cavalry boots and tried to escape. But the three remaining soldiers kept after him relentlessly.

With a bullet in his right side, James had trouble raising his pistol. As the Federals came closer, he reinforced his right hand with his left and shot the trooper closest to him out of the saddle. The remaining two soldiers soon gave up the chase.

James managed to stagger four or five hundred yards before he collapsed and fainted at the edge of a nearby creek. Here he lay for two days, bathing his wound and burning with fever. Harrison Trow reported that on the evening of April 17 James crawled into a field where a man was plowing.[17] That night the farmer put him on a horse and rode with him fifteen miles to the house of John Koger's father-in-law, Hiram Bowman, the Baptist preacher in Oak Grove. Here James rejoined Clements and Rupe. Jesse's condition was thought to be mortal. He was sent to be cared for by his mother in Nebraska, where she was living as a fugitive. Three years later, through her efforts, he was back in the saddle.

Jesse's brother Frank was at first not permitted to return to Missouri. When he did finally return to his home in Clay County, he was challenged by four soldiers. Daring him into some provocation, Frank forced the issue by killing two of the Federals instantly. The third was wounded seriously while the fourth managed to shoot Frank in the hip, causing a grievous wound. Friends carried him into hiding and summoned a doctor who saved his life.

The brothers eventually returned to their old home place, and Jesse's wounds improved even more. Homer Croy noted: "Frank had been farming it, but they were postwar sufferers. Their horses had been stolen. Prices were at starvation levels; it took hard scratching to make a living. Meanwhile, Jesse had good days and bad days. Sometimes he would be up and around; then his wound would open and he would have to go back to bed. As he got better he began to go the Baptist church in Kearney; not only that, but he sang in the choir."[18]

The hunt for the guerrilla brothers continued. On February 18, 1867, five militiamen rode to the James farm in Kearny, Missouri, looking for the former guerrillas. The weather was bitterly cold, and Jesse was in bed with a fever. His stepfather, Dr. Reuben Samuel, heard the militiamen on the front porch and inquired what they wanted. When they demanded he open the door, Dr. Samuel asked Jesse what he should do. His stepson replied, "Help me to the window that I may look out."

There was snow on the ground, and the moon was shining. He saw that all the horses hitched to the fence had cavalry saddles. Jesse decided either to drive them away or die. While a militiaman was hammering on the door with the butt of his pistol, Jesse placed his pistol up to the inside of the door and fired. When the soldier cried out and fell dying, Jesse threw open the door with a pistol in each hand and fired rapidly.

A second man was killed as he tried to run, and two more were seriously wounded. A fifth soldier escaped in the darkness. With this act, Jesse and his brother were forced to take to the bush as outlaws.[19]

John Blue, a guerrilla under William Anderson, was captured and jailed in Illinois when he was killed "trying to escape." This was a convenient way to rid the state of the guerrilla problem by vengeful-minded individuals.[20] David Poole finally surrendered with forty men on May 21, 1865, in Lexington, Missouri. But because of the attack on Archie Clements, the remaining guerrillas were leery of Federal intentions. Union authorities told Poole he would received a full pardon if he would help bring in the rest of the guerrillas. It took him more than a week to dig them out of their camps along the banks of the Sni and Little Blue.

Poole and his men agreed to surrender, but they were trying to arrange terms so they would be treated as prisoners of war.[21] Poole told Col. Chester Harding in Lexington that he believed Archie Clements and James Anderson would surrender if they were treated properly, but Harding believed the guerrillas would leave the country before giving themselves up. Clements was reportedly in Saline County at the end of May, and Anderson was in Howard County. A militia company there reported having a fight with eleven guerrillas supposedly commanded by Anderson. The militia claimed they killed four of the guerrillas and captured some of their pistols after losing a man.

During June 1865 Clements and Anderson were supposedly together in Howard County. They were rounding up their men and having them surrender, although they were asking for special terms for themselves, believing that they would be arrested and charged with crimes if they turned themselves in.

On June 9 Capt. Warren Harris, in Fayette, accepted the surrender of eight of Anderson's and Clement's men and had them in Rocheport under armed guard. The two leaders agreed to hunt up the rest of their men and have them report to Rocheport in Howard County on June 11. On June 10 nine more of Anderson's and Clements' men surrendered in Glasgow in Howard County. While Clements and Anderson were still seeking surrender terms, Asst. Adj. Gen. William Clarke was ordered to hold no more talks with the guerrilla leaders but to bring them in dead or alive.[22]

Anderson and Clements escaped to Texas with a price on their heads, but Clements returned a few months later. After an altercation in Texas, Anderson was allegedly killed by William Poole, a brother of David Poole.[23]

To bring further charges against the former guerrillas, Federal authorities passed a law in December 1866 that required all able-bodied men over eighteen to register for possible muster into the state militia. Those who refused would be arrested, jailed, and fined twenty-five dollars. They knew that former Confederates would not agree to such an order.

After returning from Texas, Archie Clements sent a letter to the commander in Lexington, Maj. Berryman K. Davis, that any men who reported for militia duty would be treated as enemies. On the morning of December 13, twenty-six guerrillas rode into Lexington in military formation. At their head was Archie Clements; he was followed by David Poole. They hitched their horses in front of the City Hotel and went inside for supper. Afterward they went to see Maj. Bacon Montgomery of the state militia company. Montgomery registered them according to law then told them to leave town at once.

Clements led his men out of town but soon returned with a friend. They went to the City Hotel for drinks. When Montgomery heard Clements was in town, he sent three men to arrest him. As the soldiers approached, Clements pulled his revolvers and started shooting. He then ran out a side door, mounted his horse, and ran out of town. Suddenly, from every window and doorway, soldiers of the state militia aimed their rifles on the lone rider galloping down the street. When the smoke cleared, Clements fell from his horse, face first, his body riddled with bullets.

In southwest Missouri the Federals encouraged armed bands of "regulators" to ride through the night and mete out their own brand of retaliation on former Rebels. In the year after Appomattox, four thousand former Secessionists were murdered in southwest Missouri. The regulators insisted that they would give any returning Rebels "a swift bullet or a short rope."

Peaceful pursuits were denied to former guerrillas. Harrison Trow recalled:

The law which should have protected them was overridden. Indeed, there was no law. The courts were instruments of plunder. The civil officers were cutthroats. Instead of a legal process, there was a vigilance committee. Men were hung because of a very natural desire to keep hold of their property. To the cruel vigor of actual war, there had succeeded the irresponsible despotism of greedy highwaymen buttressed upon assassination. The border counties were overrun with bands of predatory plunderers. Some Confederate soldiers dared not return home and many guerrillas fled the country.[24]

The Federals began closing in on Quantrill's men one by one. Joseph Gibson had gone to Kentucky with Quantrill but returned to Missouri after surrendering to authorities in the Bluegrass State. A few days after returning to his home in Henry County, he was shot just a few feet outside his own door.[25] William Hulse was surrounded at his farm in southeast Independence.

Eighteen heavily armed men hid behind his barn and waited for Hulse to emerge from his house to go to the barn. Then they opened fire without warning. They ran off, leaving Hulse for dead.[26] About the same time two men from Shawneetown, Kansas, killed one of Quantrill's former guerrillas, a soldier named Johnson, in Lee's Summit, Missouri. He had been with Quantrill on the October 17, 1862, Shawneetown raid. Even Quantrill's black bodyguard, Henry Wilson, who had been wounded seven times during the war, was forced into hiding for ten years after the war. It was not until 1874 that Wilson rode into Lawrence and took a job working for the wife of Gov. Charles Robinson. He remained with her until her death. Still, many people in Lawrence threatened to have him hanged.[27]

Another Quantrillian, J. C. Peters, was escaping out of Missouri through western Kansas when he was spotted by a group of vengeful Unionists. They waited in ambush for him to return to where he had his horse tied up. Peters stepped into a barbershop and had his whiskers dyed, then he went into a clothing store for a different set of clothes.

When he entered the store the owner recognized him, shook his hand, and let him pick out a suit of clothes for free. The proprietor asked: "Do you remember one time way down in Missouri a man who was going to be shot by Quantrill's band and had stated he was innocent of the charges laid against him, and you believed him, stood up for him and saved his life? I'm the man." Aided by the storeowner, Peters escaped to Omaha, Nebraska, where he eventually settled before being allowed to return to his home in Liberty years later.[28]

Oliver Shepherd wrote to the Federal commander in Liberty to say he and six of his men wanted to surrender but would only do so if they were allowed to keep their weapons and horses. Shepherd stated, "We must keep our side arms for you know we have personal enemies who would kill us at the first opportunity." They were told they would be given no special terms. Shepherd and his men subsequently surrendered a short time afterward. When they did, the Clay County sheriff arrested two of them, one for murder and the other for horse stealing—crimes committed during the war from which Union soldiers were exempt.[29]

After Theodore Cassell of William Anderson's company surrendered, a band of militia at the home of Elias Thompson shot him down in cold blood in the barn lot. After killing him, a member of the militia amputated Cassell's finger so he could steal his wedding ring.[30]

Cole Younger and his brother Jim tried to return home and live in peace. Jim had accompanied Quantrill into Kentucky and was arrested after

Quantrill's death and taken to the military prison in Alton, Illinois. He was not released until the fall of 1865. Younger's mother, Bursheba Younger, and her smaller children had been driven from Harrisonville in Cass County after Federals had murdered her husband in Jackson County, where jayhawkers forced her to set fire to her house. The family moved to Lafayette County, where fourteen-year-old John was driven into the bush after a failed attempt on his life. The surviving Youngers moved from Lafayette County to Clay County for the duration of the war. Afterward the family returned to Jackson County to renew farming and forget the misery of the last years, but they found no comfort even there.

Cole and his brothers built a comfortable log house for their mother and made rails and fenced in the land. Federals either stole or shot whatever livestock they had. In lieu of horses or mules, the brothers plowed with oxen. They permitted no light to be lit in the house at night and traveled public highways warily. Armed men chased them from their home, and finally a vigilance committee of skulking murderers and red-handed robbers set out at night to kill the brothers.[31]

Cole and Jim knew they had to be armed to stay alive and protect what remained of their family. In January 1866, while the Youngers were living in Lee's Summit, they sent younger brother John into Independence to have a pistol repaired. The gun was loaded even though broken. After John paid for the repairs and picked up the gun, he entered a store with about a dozen customers. One was a former Union soldier named Gilcreas who had recently been released from jail. Someone called out John's name, and Gilcreas went over and kicked the boy. John warned him that he would kill him if he did that again. Gilcreas kicked the boy again, and John pulled his brother's pistol and shot him through the heart. John escaped but was apprehended and brought back to town the following day.

An investigation concluded that Gilcreas was "laboring under a great excitement without proper cause and would undoubtedly have killed the boy" had John not acted. A grand jury refused to review any further facts, considering the coroner's evidence satisfactory.[32]

Afterward a vigilance committee attacked the Younger home, broke in the doors and windows, and rushed upon Bursheba with drawn revolvers. They demanded to know where Cole and James were hiding. When they failed to find the former guerrillas, the soldiers carried John Younger to the barn, placed a rope around his neck, and lifted him off the ground to get him to tell where his brothers had gone. Three times they pulled him off his feet, but he did not say a word and lost consciousness. They laid him on the ground, and with the rope still buried in his flesh, the vigilantes beat him with sticks and the butts of their rifles and hacked at him with knives. A half-hour passed before he came to.

The vigilantes told Bursheba Younger that, if Cole was in the area, they would find him and kill him. Cole and Jim, however, were nowhere near the farm; they had traveled to Sherman, Texas, to scout for a new home for the family. A few days after John's beating, Bursheba Younger died a victim of poor health due to constant deprivation.

Denied an opportunity to live in peace, the Younger and the James brothers turned to outlawry. Their crimes were considered a fair blow at Northern carpetbaggers who were enriching themselves in the economic tur-moil after the war. The two sets of brothers, afterward known as the James-Younger Gang, committed numerous crimes across several states in the years following the war. The same sympathizers they had known during the war supported them despite their crimes. Many of their victims were the railroad barons they viewed as plunderers exploiting the people left destitute by the war. The banks they robbed allegedly were connected to their former North-ern enemies. When the gang's career came to an end in Northfield, Min-nesota, in 1876, the targeted bank was believed to hold a great deal of money belonging to Union Gen. Benjamin F. "The Beast" Butler.

Around Jackson County, former members of jayhawker regiments and the old Missouri State Militia (like Nugent's Regiment) held a majority of offices in the civil government and used their positions to harass their enemies. Har-rison Trow observed: "Some [former Confederates] were killed because of the terrible renown won in the four years war; some were forced to hide them-selves in the unknown of the outlying territories, and some were persecuted and driven into desperate defiance and resistance because they were human and intrepid."[33]

Those former guerrillas who did not flee the country were forced to take to the bush. James Cummins from Clay County grew up in the same neighborhood as the James brothers and attended the same Baptist church. After the war Cummins commented, "When the war was over and I wanted to settle down they [Federals] would not let me, but pursued me with malig-nant hatred."

Another of Quantrill's men who had gone with him into Kentucky, William Gaugh, tried to return home to Kansas City after the war, but his neighbors would not let him. He was forced to flee to a farm in Florence, Kansas. When his identity became known later, he was forced to move back to Jackson County, Missouri.

Morgan T. Mattox returned back home after the war, but a mob gathered when they found out he had ridden with Quantrill and attempted to hang him on the streets of Platte City, Missouri. He escaped and was chased from his home. He was forbidden to see his family for years afterward. He finally settled in Bartlesville, Oklahoma, where he had a reputation as an outstanding citizen.[34]

John Jarrette, a former captain under Quantrill, was living with his family in St. Clair County, Missouri. A mob gathered at his door and shot Jarrette's wife when she opened it. They also shot Jarette then set the house on fire with the couple's children still inside.

On January 20, 1866, Sheriff Holmes of Harrison County, Missouri, tried to serve a warrant for the arrest of Bill Reynolds in Pleasant Hill, Cass County, Missouri, for crimes committed during the war. Holmes and Deputy James Copeland found Reynolds with two other guerrillas, George W. Maddox and N. P. Hayes. When Holmes tried to arrest Reynolds, a fight erupted in the street. The officers killed Hayes and wounded Reynolds, but Reynolds managed to kill both lawmen. Maddox was captured by civilians and turned over to other lawmen. Reynolds fled to his mother's house, where he was followed and captured. He was brought back to town, a distance of seven miles, in the back of a wagon. His head was pillowed on his mother's lap. When the wagon arrived in Pleasant Hill, Allen Copeland, a brother of the slain deputy, rode up and put two bullets in Reynolds's head.[35]

During the summer of 1866 the governor of Kansas submitted to the governor of Missouri a list of three hundred men who had taken part in the 1863 Lawrence raid. Authorities arrested George W. Maddox and Payne Jones and sent them to Lawrence. There they were jailed for several months with no other charges brought against them except that they were Quantrill's men.

Federal vengeance was so prolific many former Confederates felt compelled to become outlaws in order to survive. On February 13, 1866, twelve riders approached the Clay County Savings Bank in Liberty. The robbers made off with more than sixty thousand dollars. On their way out of town they killed a young man who they believed was going to give an alarm. They then made their way south across the Missouri River, just ahead of a posse. A winter snowstorm soon obliterated their tracks.

Blame was assigned to Quantrill's men. Nine men were allegedly recognized: Oliver Shepherd, Bud and Donnie Pence, Frank Gregg, Jim Wilkerson, and Joab Perry, all former guerrillas. An anonymous letter sent to the authorities in Liberty claimed that Jim Anderson, brother to Bill Anderson, was in on the robbery.

On October 30, 1866, two men robbed the Alexander and Mitchell and Company Bank in Lexington, Missouri. The sheriff called in Dave Poole and his brother John, both former guerrillas, to lead the posse and chase the robbers. They got close enough to see five men but could not catch them.[36]

A few months later five men attempted to rob the bank in Savannah, Missouri. An alarm was quickly given, and the robbers left without getting any cash. A posse chased them for miles but eventually lost their trail. The suspects were alleged to be former guerrillas, and two men were supposedly recognized. The two, however, had alibis and were released.[37]

On May 22, 1867, fourteen men rode into Richmond, Missouri. They approached from different directions in small groups. The men met in front of the Hughes and Wasson Bank on the town's square. Only four entered the bank. The rest stayed outside, guarding the streets. A citizen sensed that the bank was being robbed and gave an alarm. He was chased down and shot. Before leaving town the bank robbers went to the city jail to release those held for expressing Southern sentiments. The jailer and his fifteen-year-old son were killed when they resisted. A drunken prisoner at the jail claimed to recognize nine of the men. Based on his statement, warrants were issued for former guerrillas Payne Jones, Dick Burns, Andy McGuire, Tom Little, Ike Flanery, and Allen Parmer.

Parmer was detained but released after his employer collaborated Parmer's claim that he was in St. Louis at the time of the robbery. On May 26 a posse of eighteen men from Kansas City found Payne Jones in a house two miles west of Independence. While they attempted to surround the building at night, Jones rushed from the house and fired into the posse, killing B. H. Wilson. The posse followed him for more than two miles in the dark before losing his trail.

Authorities arrested Tom Little in St. Louis as an accomplice in the Richmond robbery. He was jailed in Warrensburg but presented evidence from prominent citizens who asserted that he was in Dover, Missouri, at the time of the robbery. A mob seized him from the jail and hanged him.[38]

Because of the large number of men involved in the Richmond robbery and murders, every former guerrilla of Quantrill's old company was accused of being one of the robbers. Some ex-guerrillas decided to leave the country, but that did not stop the killing.

Dick Burns was found dead, his skull crushed by an ax, on the farm of John Deering, four miles south of Independence. There was only speculation as to who the murderers were. By the end of the year Andy McGuire was arrested in St. Louis while on his honeymoon with the daughter of John Deering. He was taken to the Richmond city jail and locked up with

James M. Devers, both former guerrillas. On March 20, 1868, a mob of fifteen men stormed the jail and lynched them.

The radicals had made up their minds that they were not going to leave the matter in the hands of the justice system. They would take the law into their own hands if necessary to rid the country of Quantrill's remaining men.

On March 20, 1868, five men robbed the Russellville, Kentucky, bank of twelve thousand dollars. Former guerrilla George Shepherd was arrested in Kentucky and charged with the crime. He was convicted and sentenced to three years in prison.[39] George's cousin, Oliver Shepherd, also a former Quantrill man, was accused of the same crime. On April 4, 1868, a vigilante mob surrounded his house in Jackson County and, in front of his wife and children, shot him twenty times, killing him on his doorstep. An eyewitness reported that Shepherd was unarmed.

On December 7, 1869, the Davies County Savings Bank in Gallatin, Missouri, was robbed of several hundred dollars. A bank employee and one of the townspeople were killed during the robbery. The deaths were reportedly retaliations for wartime grievances. As the robbers left, one thief remarked that the slain banker had caused the death of his brother, Bill Anderson, and he was compelled to avenge him.[40]

The actions of the ex-guerrillas and those who turned outlaw because of the radicals' escalating political pressure after the war made Missouri notorious. For years to come it was known as the "Outlaw State." Eventually, however, the radicals found themselves their own worst enemies. Slowly the political tide turned against them.

The infamous Ironclad Oath enacted in 1865 was repealed in 1870; former Confederates were once again allowed to vote. This was the opportunity the beaten-down Southerners had been waiting for: to return to society with the full stature of normal citizens. No longer would they be forced to accept subjugation or domination from outside forces. They were older and wiser now, and they planned on putting their political future back into their own hands. Former guerrilla Coleman Younger remarked:

> When the war ceased, those of the guerrillas who were not hung or shot, or pursued by posses till they found the hand of man turned against them at every step, settled down to become good citizens in the peaceful walks of life, and the survivors of Quantrill's band may be pardoned, in view of the black paint that has been devoted to them, in calling attention to the fact that of the members of Quantrill's command who have since been entrusted with public place not one had ever betrayed that trust.[41]

Quantrill's adjutant William Gregg added: "Quantrill's command was composed principally of men and boys, from the very best families of Missouri. Many of them are honored citizens of Missouri and other states, many of whom have been honored with high political positions not in Missouri alone, but other states also and none of them have ever defaulted a record of which, I am exceptionally proud."[42]

Many of Quantrill's former men established new pursuits in well-respected careers in their communities. Lee C. Miller practiced medicine in Knobnoster, Johnson County, Missouri. He stated, "We were soldiers fighting in a good cause, and I am not apologizing to anybody for the part I took. Quantrill's men have no apologies to make to anybody."[43]

With the assassination of Jesse James by the hand of one of his own gang, orchestrated by Missouri Gov. Thomas Crittenden, the final pages in the chapter of the end of the Civil War were being turned. Frank James surrendered to authorities soon after his brother's death with the promise that he be allowed to bury his brother. Afterward Frank was brought to trial but never convicted. This finally afforded him an opportunity to settle down to a life of peace.

It had been a long road of Reconstruction for the South. The radicals had seen their rise and fall from power. The politicians who had taken their place were more reconciliatory to ending the drawn-out tensions that had existed since Appomattox.

After twenty-five years of incarceration in a Minnesota prison, Cole Younger was declared a free man. President Teddy Roosevelt pardoned him because he believed he was a man fit for citizenship. Younger returned to live out the remainder of his days where he grew up in Cass County. His name was probably more popular now than when he had fought during the war and during his outlaw days. But now he only wanted to live a respectable life.

He became a Christian and give his life to Christ. He was respected, not for what he had been, but for what he had become.[44] Once as he was passing through Richmond, Missouri, scene of the last battle of his old commander, William Anderson, he discovered that Anderson's grave was not properly marked. Younger held a memorial service for the slain Confederate leader. A slow procession marched four blocks through the town to the cemetery where Anderson's remains were buried. A small hollow square was formed around the gravesite. A minister blessed the remains of the fallen guerrilla.[45]

Many of the former guerrillas who managed to survive the tumultuous years after the war knew that political office would help bring them and their neighbors back into society more quickly than anything else. Several of Quantrill's men gained a great reputation in politics after the war. Henry

Porter, who had been at Centralia and had gone to Kentucky with Quantrill, was elected to the Missouri state legislature to represent Jackson County. He later moved to Texas, where he served as a judge of the county court, and afterward served as a judge of the probate court in the state of Washington.

Pink Gibson, who had fought at the battle of Centralia, served many years as a judge in Johnson County, Missouri. Harry Ogden was only nineteen years old when he joined Quantrill. Afterward he served as the lieutenant governor and a congressman in Louisiana. Fletcher Taylor had lost an arm after fighting in such notable battles as Independence, Lawrence, Baxter Springs, and Centralia. He was elected to the Missouri state legislature. In 1885 James Moore, after serving a term as councilman, was elected mayor of Kansas City. In 1899 he was elected the president of the Kansas City Board of Trade.[46] Jack Liddil had been with Quantrill from the beginning and became a judge for eight years covering the Blue Township in Jackson County.

Because they were known as bold, fearless men, some naturally found their way into law enforcement. John C. Hope served two terms as sheriff of Jackson County after serving many years as a deputy sheriff and a deputy marshal. He later was appointed as the purchasing agent in Kansas City, serving under two mayors who greatly valued the quality of his work. Quantrillian J. M. Tucker was made sheriff of Los Angeles, California, and Jess Hamblett served as the marshal of Lexington, Missouri. William H. Gregg became a deputy sheriff of Jackson County. James A. Hendricks served as deputy sheriff of Lewis and Clark County, Montana, while Lee McMurtry became a sheriff in Wichita County, Texas. Ninian Letton became marshal of Liberty and West Plains, Missouri, and J. M. Short served as marshal and city collector of Lee's Summit, Missouri. Donnie Pence managed to become the sheriff of Nelson County, Kentucky, in 1871, and held the office until his death in 1896. His brother Bud served as his deputy sheriff. Joseph C. Lea, Quantrill's old friend, spent many years after the war as an instructor in the military college of the University of New Mexico.

Conversely, many of Quantrill's old enemies fared poorly after the war. James Lane won an overwhelming reelection to the U.S. Senate in 1865 but found his political career in ruins when he supported the Reconstruction policies of Andrew Johnson. Lane was trying to curry favor from the Executive Office rather than side with the Radical Republicans who supported policies of revenge and retaliation against the conquered South. Lane had always been violently paranoid and highly unbalanced. When he lost his political backing, his instability increased and his past criminal behavior preyed heavily on his conscience. He sought treatment at an insane asylum near Leavenworth while he contemplated his ruined career. His reputation quickly faded, and in the face of depression and scandal, he committed suicide on July 1, 1866. Sen. John James Ingalls, Lane's colleague reported in an April 1893 article that Lane "gained the prize he sought with such fevered ambition; but after many stormy and tempestuous years, Nemesis, inevitable in such careers, demanded retribution. He presumed too far upon the toleration of a constituency, which had honored him so long and forgiven him so much. He transcended the limit, which the greatest cannot pass. He apostatized once too often; and in his second term in the Senate, to avoid impeding exposure, after a tragic interval of despair, died at his own hand."

After the war James G. Blunt, whom Quantrill had defeated at the battle of Baxter Springs, moved to Washington and became a professional claim solicitor. The Justice Department indicted him in 1873 for conspiring to defraud the government. Like Lane, Blunt had a reputation as a womanizer. In 1879 he was committed at St. Elizabeth's Hospital and Insane Asylum in Washington, D.C. Depraved and disease ridden, Blunt died of syphilis on July 25, 1881.[47] Martin Conway, from Lawrence, Kansas, was known as the most radical of the Radical Republicans; he died in the same institution a few months later.[48]

Charles Jennison, the most notorious of all Kansas jayhawkers, was subsequently tried before a general court-martial at Fort Leavenworth, Kansas, on charges of "conduct to the prejudice of good order and military discipline, gross and willful neglect of duty, defrauding the government of the United States, and disobedience of orders." He was also found guilty of arson, robbery, and embezzlement and sentenced to be dishonorably discharged. By threatening to "reveal the records" of other Kansas officers, Jennison escaped justice with only a reprimand.[49] He returned to Leavenworth and ran a gambling house and became head of the local gamblers and saloon toughs.[50]

In the postwar years attention was focused on the survivors of Quantrill's company and their relatives. Rufus Wilson, a newspaperman from Quantrill's hometown of Canal Dover, interviewed Quantrill's mother after the war. He wrote that one of Quantrill's redeeming traits seemed to have been a deep and tender love for his mother. He wrote to her regularly during his western wanderings, and until the war came, he always sent her part of the money he earned. Caroline Clarke Quantrill added that her son "was always a good boy. He was very, very good to me. He never forgot his old mother. Why, he sent me money all the time he was away from home, even when he was a Confederate soldier. He always divided up his pay with me. He was kind and noble." She was shunned by her Northern neighbors because her son had sided with the South, and when she traveled to Missouri after the war, she found many warm feelings from her son's former friends.

While in Ohio, W. W. Scott, Quantrill's childhood friend and erstwhile biographer, accompanied Caroline Quantrill while seeking information for a book he was writing about her son. He told her that her neighbors did not like her and had said some hard things about her. She replied that she knew there was a dreadful low class of people who delighted in slandering and telling lies in Dover. When she visited Jackson County, Mrs. Quantrill commented, "I have met many friends here, more than I ever expected, in fact every one here is a friend of my dear lost son." In commenting on the stories being circulated about her son and Scott's book, she said: "You may as well give up writing history of my dear lost boy, for you never will get anything correct. No one but his men and friends and myself could get up a correct history of him. His men never will enlighten the Yankees on the subject. So what they gather up will be mostly lies."

After the war Kate King Quantrill used the name Kate Clarke and was extremely cautious about keeping her identity secret because of her husband's old enemies. As a result, not much is known about her. Years after the war she allegedly returned to Jackson County, and in 1930 she was living at the Jackson County Home for the Aged, which was situated on land owned by the Younger family before the war. Very few knew her true identity. Suse Younger, the Youngers' former slave, worked at the home, which was run by Emma Younger and her husband, Kit Rose, while Kate King Quantrill was probably living there.

The site of Kate Quantrill's grave is debated. A newspaper article mentioned that she was buried in an unmarked grave in the Maple Hill Cemetery in Kansas, and recently a marker was erected.[51] Another marker that has the inscription, "Kate King Quantrill, 1848–1930, age 82," erected by Fred Ford and Arthur Dealy in the Slaughter Cemetery in Blue Springs, is part of another story.

Ford was a neighbor of Kate's nephew, Arthur Dealy. Kate stayed with Dealy until she was quite elderly, when she was put in the Jackson County Home for the Aged, commonly known as the Old Folks Home or the Poor Farm. When Kate died in 1930, a local mortician with the Ketterlin Funeral Home had the contract to bury paupers from the Old Folks Home in the Maple Hill Cemetery. The body was embalmed at Ketterlin, but the mortician suddenly moved to the Ozarks and left the funeral home full of embalmed bodies. A month passed before Kate's relatives were notified. When Dealy learned that she had not been buried, he and Ford retrieved her body and brought it to the Slaughter Cemetery. There she was quietly laid to rest without notice being given to the newspapers.[52]

Frank James feared that, after his death, someone would steal his body, so he requested that he and his wife be cremated rather than buried. His ashes were then buried in a small plot in Independence, Missouri, on land that saw the first battle between Union and Confederate forces—the battle of Rock Creek—situated halfway between Kansas City and Independence. The gravestones of Frank and his wife show the following inscriptions: Alexander F. James, 1843–1915; Ann Ralston, 1853–1944.[53]

The Civil War should have ended with the deaths and fading memories of the men who fought in it. The imprisonment of former Confederate President Jefferson Davis only served to make him a martyr for the Lost Cause. Lincoln had directed that the defeated Southern leaders would not be sought out, but after his death, the Radical Republicans ignored his wishes. Davis had been arrested and imprisoned on the assumption that he would eventually be brought to trial. But the trial was never held.

The Federal government knew that it could not try Davis for treason without raising the constitutional issue of secession. Edward A. Pollard described this impending confrontation as "the trial of the North." It was to determine whether a man could be punished as a traitor for acting on an opinion that had divided three generations of Americans. Since any trial would have to take place in Virginia, where the "crime" had been committed, the government wisely recognized that it would never be able to convict Davis for treason in a Southern court. The government also did not want its decision for the responsibility for the nonexchange of prisoners to be brought to public light.

Two years had passed since the war had ended and Davis had been imprisoned. By then Congress was more interested in impeaching Andrew Johnson than in trying Davis. If Davis's trial were to be held, Congress would have to admit that the states were sovereign and their union voluntary and that the Founding Fathers of the Constitution agreed that a state could change its form of government, abolishing all that had previously existed. Rather than permit the war itself to be put on trial, the government released Davis on bail on May 13, 1867. The government tried to pardon Davis, but he refused and insisted on a trial. Quietly on February 15, 1869, the case against Davis was dismissed.[54]

All defeated Southern soldiers remembered the war in similar terms and thoughts. During the war Confederate Gen. Patrick Cleburne observed: "Surrender means that the history of this heroic struggle will be written by the enemy; that our youth will be trained by Northern school teachers; will learn from Northern school books their version of the War; will be impressed by all the influences of history and education to regard our gallant dead as traitors, and our maimed veterans as fit subjects for derision."

After the war Robert E. Lee noted: "If I had foreseen the use these people desired to make of their victory, there would have been no surrender at Appomattox, no sir, not by me. Had I seen these results of subjugation, I would have preferred to die at Appomattox with my brave men, my sword in this right hand. I would have never surrendered the army if I had known how the South would have been treated."[55]

With a pride befitting any veteran who felt justified in fighting for a just cause, Warren Welch of Quantrill's old command wrote to many of his former comrades to attend a reunion in 1910. Ben Morrow, who had ridden with Quantrill from the very start, was another organizer and captain of the Quantrill reunions. Beginning in 1898, Jack Liddil, now a county judge, held small informal reunions of guerrillas in his office in Independence and at the deeply wooded plot of Wallace Grove, an old guerrilla rendezvous in Jackson County.[56] Liddil commented: "Ours was a glorious memory of old times and hardships and we will live in after years, not as thieves and robbers, but as devoted and patriotic soldiers that fought, bled and died for what they thought was right."[57] Cole Younger and Frank James tried to live normal lives and make an honest living. They were the main attractions when large-scale reunions were held each August in Jackson County. When the first reunion was held, each guerrilla wore an elegant ribbon and button showing their former leader's name and picture.

President Harry S. Truman even attended some reunions with the observation: "Quantrill and his men were no more bandits than the men on the other side. I've been to reunions of Quantrill's men two or three times. All they were trying to do was protect the property of the Missouri side of the line." When faced with certain death or the obligation to do their duty, these men answered honor's call, closed ranks with their comrades, and ventured forth to fight the enemy.

The remaining members of Quantrill's band had been scattered over the years. Some had gone to Mexico; some stayed in Texas where they had made friends and had taken their families for safety during the war. Others were in other states and living under assumed names for protection. The reunions were a welcomed pastime. They were occasions to conjure up memories with old comrades. One veteran did not necessarily recall what was memorable in another's experience. One recalled what was special only to him: a comrade wounded, a certain charge upon the enemy, a narrow escape, an enemy pursued or captured and paroled or shot, a memory that made the heart beat rapidly and the pulse beat faster. But they all remembered their old leader. They considered themselves Confederate veterans and were quite proud of having served under Quantrill, whose picture they always displayed prominently at their reunions.

Forty years gave the guerrillas time to reflect on Quantrill's character. What were their thoughts? Never did they relinquish their love and devotion for their former leader. The most honored possession of their postwar reunions were the buttons proudly worn on their lapels with a picture of Quantrill attached above an annual reunion ribbon. George Scholl remarked once how he was upset over unqualified authors writing false reports about the former leader whom they all "followed and loved." He added, "We resent to the fullest extent the defamation of his [Quantrill's] reputation and character."[58] Also speaking of his former leader, Harrison Trow reported, "Quantrill differed in some degree from every guerrilla who was either a comrade or his contemporary. He was said to possess extraordinary resource and cunning." It was these traits that brought him renown.

Epilogue
Appendix
Notes
Selected Bibliography
Index

Epilogue

QUANTRILL DISCOVERED early the effective use of modern lightweight rapid-firing weapons. When he first began his organization, it was a small core group. His men established their hiding places among the rough terrain and acquired weapons from their enemies by launching guerrilla attacks against the units that were sent to search for them or from the arsenals of enemy garrisons. After achieving initial success against his enemies, Quantrill increased his attacks in the territory under his control. This gained him wide recognition from outside his area of operations in the political organization of the Confederate government.

With contemporaries like Nathan Bedford Forrest, John Hunt Morgan, and John Singleton Mosby, who also had no formal military training before the war, Quantrill's successes have not achieved the level of recognition that these other military leaders have had simply due to the fact that the western theater of operations took second billing to the larger battles being fought in Virginia and Tennessee. Harrison Trow observed that Quantrill's warfare was described as "one rather of hatred than of opinion. The regular Confederates were fighting for a cause and a nationality, the guerrilla for vengeance. Mementos of murdered kinsmen mingled with their weapons; vows consecrated the act of enlistment and the cry for blood was heard from homestead to homestead. Quantrill became a guerrilla because he had been most savagely dealt with, and he became a chief because he had prudence, firmness, courage, audacity and common sense."[1]

Often Quantrill resorted to conventional warfare when his command became large enough to engage in open challenges to Federal military might. He was able to take the initiative at his choosing. He controlled the rural areas of the countryside, in effect pinning the Union troops up in the large cites and towns, which he was able to attack at his discretion. As a result Federal commanders resorted to ill-advised actions and reacted out of frustration. This made the government troops seem weak and ineffective. It was rare that Quantrill ever reacted to a move by the Federal military, but rather the enemy found themselves always reacting to him.

When Quantrill's organization grew in strength, he could still fight with small groups and still manage to retain overall command, even though his men were often scattered across a large region. He solved this problem by having an elaborate set of signals that enabled him to relay messages quickly across a large area. To do this he had to have the support of the local population.

The guerrillas were fighting for a cause supported by the surrounding population. The local citizens befriended and aided them, and in turn the guerrillas protected the people by protecting their lives and property. When families evacuated their homes for the safer surroundings of eastern Missouri or Texas, Quantrill's men provided escorts for their safe travel. With often the entire population sympathetic to his cause, they provided him with horses, weapons, ammunition, and any supplies that he needed, including hiding places and new recruits.

Quantrill's men cared for these people because they had been recruited from the area. They were mostly young men inured to hardships and whose personal feelings and emotional attachments were to the regions in which they were fighting. This was an added benefit because his recruits intimately knew the area in which they fought and could fight the enemy on the terrain of their choosing. Quantrill's subordinate leaders were slightly older by only a few years than the men they led. Most had prior military experience from fighting in the conventional battles at the start of the war. Aside from Quantrill's military successes, young men joined his command simply due to the popularity of his leadership and the efficient discipline for which he was noted.

His men were tortured when captured; most were killed and mutilated. And Quantrill shared these dangers and hardships. They rarely had enough to eat, and their shelter was often the open sky. The hardships they endured were not for the weak at heart. They were harassed and pursued around the countryside, but what brought them success was their individual bravery coupled with Quantrill's tactics and leadership.

Quantrill was able to strike or avoid the enemy on his own terms. Many commented on his ability to anticipate the enemy's movements, but most of his insights were due to his network of spies in almost every neighborhood and military and civil organization.

He capitalized on his command's abilities. The more difficult the mission, the more glory they achieved, and the more pride and confidence the men had in his leadership. In displaying his leadership, he taught his men to become tactically proficient. Known as an expert rider and pistol shot, Quantrill taught all recruits the art of horseback riding and pistol shooting. When he thought they were ready, he had them train with the rest of his command as a team to confirm that they were fully prepared to go into battle.

A guerrilla's proficiency in these two basic skills was as important to the men he rode with as it was to himself.

Quantrill knew well his men's capabilities, and with the caliber of men who were in his command, he achieved a great degree of success. The guerrillas' shared hardships, dangers, and hard work strengthened unit cohesion and developed an esprit de corps. They fought for each other as much as they fought for anything else. Their honor and allegiance bound them to one another. The guerrilla's only oath when joining was to be true to his fellow guerrillas and to kill Yankees. To this they remained faithful until death. When Quantrill disbanded his men on occasion, he always directed them to stay in small groups of at least two or three. In this way they maintained their unit integrity.

Quantrill's place in history goes beyond his military exploits as a leading guerrilla warrior or his charismatic leadership. His men loved and respected him. Many made names for themselves following Quantrill's example of leadership and daring. James Campbell observed: "Quantrill was the smartest man I ever knew. He had the qualifications of leadership in him. He knew what to do in every emergency. In camp he was gentle and sometimes jolly. He was kind to his men and to prisoners whenever he had any. And he could shoot, ah, how that man could shoot."[2]

Known as a quiet man who talked little and chose his words carefully before speaking, Quantrill was a close friend to only a few, but these were very intimate ones. His men were brave and intensely loyal to him. At one time during the war there was a fifty-thousand-dollar reward on his head, but not one of his men attempted to betray him. J. T. Keller summarized: "Quantrill was a quiet spoken man and he had good judgement. He knew men and how to handle them. He was cautious and laid his plans well. He seemed to know just what to do, and he did it. His men all liked him. He was not at all tyrannical."[3]

Besides being the first military leader to incorporate the principles of modern guerrilla warfare, Quantrill also exhibited outstanding military leadership traits. He studied past military tactics and personalities, which added to his professional knowledge. Descriptions of him portray him as displaying a remarkable degree of military bearing. He always created a favorable impression by the way he carried himself, his appearance and his conduct all through the war. Whenever strangers saw him, they were always impressed with his ability to look, act, and speak like a leader. Stephen B. Elkins, once a prisoner of Quantrill's, recalled that Quantrill had "the eye of a leader. He was not a large man, but you could tell that he was a leader."

Quantrill avoided profanity. His boyhood friend W. W. Scott remembered that "he was temperate and honest. He was remarkably neat in his person." Even before the war, William Stockwell noted that Quantrill paid strict attention to his manner of dress. When Quantrill finally settled in Missouri, Kate King Quantrill recalled being attracted to him because of the way he politely presented himself. Those who survived the war and remembered Quantrill said that what struck them most was that he dressed so neatly even though living in the bush and spending so much time in the saddle.

The most noted quality that Quantrill's men remembered was his decisiveness. He had an uncanny ability to make decisions promptly and to give orders in a clear, forceful manner. Never has it been recorded to the contrary that Quantrill gave anything but clear, concise, and positive orders. Frank James noted, "Every man was brave and had absolute confidence in the gallant leader." Before and during combat Quantrill was able to accumulate the available facts as they transpired and made his decisions accordingly. The ability to be able to make prompt decisions immediately was demonstrated in Quantrill's sound judgment. Several times during his career he found himself surrounded by a numerically superior force. In a very short time he was able to weigh the facts and decide on possible solutions, which resulted in his eventual escape and victory. Harrison Trow commented, "His judgement was clearest and surest when the responsibility was heaviest, and when the difficulties gathered thickest about him."[4]

Qualities less written about but with as much significance as those already mentioned are Quantrill's personal qualities as a military leader. Commanding an army of farm boys and turning them into seasoned combat veterans was an art of leadership that only a person of Quantrill's abilities could master. He displayed a sincere interest in his men and exuberance in the performance of his duties. His optimism carried over to his men, and when the enemy was arranged in large degree against them and when the days looked darkest, Quantrill was able to rally his men to achieve success. In charge of an independent command, Quantrill had to take charge and show initiative in the absence of higher orders. The missions the guerrillas rode on together were arduous and hard. Following their leader's example, Quantrill's men endured pain, fatigue, stress, and hardship with intrepid fortitude. His men followed him despite the mental and physical trials they had to endure. Harrison Trow observed that Quantrill's "constitution was vigorous and his physical endurance equal to an Indian."

As the guerrillas became a formidable fighting force they did indeed develop into a band of brothers. They depended upon one another. When a task or order was assigned, it was taken for granted that it would be carried out without supervision. All his men were professional in the performance of duty and not one failed to carry out a command. James Campbell commented, "When Quantrill gave orders he was obeyed. No man stopped to parley any further."

The men fully trusted their leader's intelligence and judgment. Hiram George claimed that Quantrill never sacrificed a man needlessly. Frank Smith put his trust in Quantrill when he observed how Quantrill meticulously planned every operation. Besides knowing when and where to attack, Quantrill also kept in mind just how and where he was might need to retreat. As a leader he made contingency plans on every possible outcome.

Largely because of this trust and bond, Quantrill's command displayed an integrity uncommon in other units. His men exhibited more moral principles than their Northern counterparts, and after the war they became honest citizens—when given the chance.

Quantrill's sense of justice in dealing with his men displayed itself in his sense of fairness and impartiality. As a band of brothers the guerrillas were intensely loyal to each other. Quantrill's wife remarked that what endeared him greatly to his men was that he would go among them at night and keep watch over them. Quantrill unselfishly gave up his own comfort for the comfort of his men. He looked out for their needs before his own. In deference to his subordinates, George Todd and William Anderson, Quantrill had an ability to deal with others without causing offense. He always treated his peers, his seniors, and his subordinates with respect and courtesy, showing a remarkable degree of maturity in personal affairs.

What superior qualities Quantrill showed in personal traits were second only to his courage. Every man is afraid in combat, but courage is the mental quality that recognizes that fear and enables a man to proceed in the face of it while exhibiting calmness and firmness. James Campbell recalled Quantrill in battle: "Quantrill never got excited, not even in a fight. He was as cool as a cucumber. They called him reckless, but he never unnecessarily endangered the lives of his men." Frank Smith observed Quantrill in battle and noted, "Quantrill never became excited, in fact, the greater the danger, the calmer he was." And Harrison Trow remembered that Quantrill was "one of the coolest and deadliest men in a personal combat known to the border."

While much acclaim is given to other personalities in other theaters of operations during the Civil War, Quantrill has been overlooked as a military leader and the developer of modern guerrilla warfare. Even William Elsey Connelley, Quantrill's most vindictive biographer, had cause to write: "They were the best horsemen in America at that time, and as a mounted military organization perhaps the world has not surpassed that band of horsemen led by Quantrill to Lawrence."[5]

As the wounds heal, as the prejudices eventually fade away, after the lies and half-truths and sensationalism are discovered, sorted out, and discarded, William Clarke Quantrill will be remembered not just for the cause for which he fought but for the traits that made him what he was: a leader of men and a guerrilla warrior.

Appendix

To FURTHER understand William Clarke Quantrill, I asked Lee Knapp, a Kansas City graphoanalyst, to study two samples of his handwriting. He did so without knowing whose handwriting was being analyzed. Graphology, or handwriting analysis, is a science based on analyzing an individual's penmanship to assess personality. Handwriting analysis is sometimes used to screen prospective employees and by attorneys to study potential jurors and witnesses. Handwriting analysis frequently provides insights into a person's character, revealing strengths and weaknesses. The two samples involved in this study are from William Clarke Quantrill and James Henry Lane.

Handwriting Analysis for William Clarke Quantrill

This SPECIMEN shows writing that completely fills the page, has energy, force, is organized, and has a strong forward slant.

The forward slant in the writing is an individual who reacts to emotional situations and tends to be involved in the lives of others. The far forward slant indicates impulsive tendencies. This writer has some traits in his writing that aid him in controlling those impulses. They are pride, caution, dignity, and analytical thinking. These traits can help slow down the emotions and let the mind catch up. The margins show an individual who is a planner, moving away from the past and embracing the future.

People around this writer will find him perplexing. He is an idealist with enduring willpower, initiative, and determination. He can be diplomatic and has strong organizational skills. While not a showman, he desires attention. His pride and dignity will not allow him to overdisplay in dress or social behavior. On the other hand, this writer has a temper, strong prejudices, is defiant to authority, resents imposition, is impatient, and a perfectionist. His force, temper, and analytical skills would make him a bitter opponent. If his will is crossed, he will unleash a fury upon that individual. He allows very few people to get close and often needs space from people.

445

This writer suffers from a bad relationship with his mother. He represses the hate he feels. He feels rejected by her and tries to please her to get the acceptance he felt was denied him as a child. Although a perfectionist, he will never live up to his own expectations, he never feels "good enough." His relationship with his father was poor. The times he needed either the physical or emotional support, it was not there.

Handwriting Analysis for James Henry Lane

THIS IS a writer with a very strong need for praise. His need for approval may take the easy form of seeming to agree with people, even though he doesn't care about them or their feelings or viewpoint. He tries to please people and is inclined to be credulous, yielding, and flirtatious.

In the area of work, he is all business. He works well under pressure and is not apt to get ruffled in a tense or tumultuous situation. Emotional appeals will not work; he will approach business with logic. However, his investigative thinking does not probe deeply but stays within familiar or known areas. Unfortunately, his logic is tainted by his vanity. His high regard for his abilities is excessive.

Self-esteem is so great that the writer is satisfied with superficial thinking or even snap judgments. In his mind he can do no wrong. He may have flashes of brilliance, but that only serves his purpose of exhibiting his knowledge.

This writer rationalizes his narrow-mindedness because he is content with himself as he is. In his point of view he is above question and sees no need to change his opinions about anything. Even if he is aware of his faulty position, he refuses to admit it and holds adamantly to that position.

If his ego is not being gratified, or if he must defend himself in an ego-threatening situation, he can become frustrated and angry. He will use sarcasm as a protective or retaliatory weapon. Any situation that is seen as a threatening superiority of others will be met with punishment or hurtful remarks.

This writer's vanity stems from a lack of emotional bonding with his father. He is the ultimate image of conceit, self-centeredness, and egoism. His vanity is on the verge of insanity.

* * *

TO HELP understand the personality and character of William C. Quantrill, I asked a prominent Kansas City, Missouri, psychologist, Dr. Daniel J. Keyser to compose a psychological report based on historical documentation about Quantrill from eyewitness accounts of those who knew him intimately.

Psychological Report of William Clarke Quantrill

THE PROFILE is based on material gleaned from historical records and furnished . . . from eyewitness accounts and established factual events.

Mr. Quantrill was a short, small man by today's standards, standing less than six feet tall. He was in his midtwenties but seemed younger than his age. He had light blue eyes and sandy hair with a somewhat small, imperial mustache. His face was pale with a touch of tan. His build was slender and muscular with a lean, sinewy general appearance of approximately 150 pounds. He dressed neatly and appeared to be careful with his clothing and personal hygiene. He even polished his fingernails, which had to be rare for a man in his day and of his years. He wore kid gloves, probably more for his appearance than for the protection of his hands. His manner was debonair and polite, though he did not strut or brag. Some people who knew him described him as handsome. One would have to conclude that Mr. Quantrill was very conscious of his appearance, and he had a certain vanity and narcissism about himself. His personality was apparently that of one who was exacting and meticulous. It is also possible to conclude that he was a cut above the general crowd of his era in the care that he would take with himself and the impression he wished to leave with others. He wanted others to see him as poised, calm, and a gentleman. He could well have been that.

Mr. Quantrill was an intelligent man. Though it is not possible to have psychometric data on this, there are conclusions that can be drawn. For instance, Mr. Quantrill was studious and went to Union College, where he graduated when he was sixteen. He even became a teacher in one of the lower departments of the college. He was fond of history, loved to read and took courses in Latin and surveying. He was quick and accurate with figures. In fact, he was regarded as the best mathematician in his county. He also had an analytic ability. He could sort and parse things into component parts and then synthesize them together into a comprehensive whole. His plans were meticulous and complex. Every operation was detailed, with retreat and escapes considered carefully. The costs of each action were counted and the odds of success and failure computed. His judgment bordered on the occult in that he was able to divine likelihoods and outcomes that others could not see. When responsibilities were heavy, his judgments were surest, validating the calmness and pose of his general demeanor. One concludes from the above that Mr. Quantrill was of above average intelligence, probably with an IQ somewhere between 125 and 140. His vocabulary was well above average as can be ascertained from the letters he has written to others. His attention, concentration, judgment, and planning were superior to the general population.

It is common in today's world to assess general intelligence using the Wechsler Adult Intelligence Scale (WAIS). That instrument has subtests of General Information, Arithmetic, Vocabulary, Digit Span, and other tests to measure intellectual performance. Considering his likely performance on these subtests, it is easy to conclude that Mr. Quantrill had above average General Information, superior mathematical ability, superior vocabulary, superior memory and concentration, and superior planning. Tests such as Block Design and Picture Arrangement would have assessed his abilities in analysis and synthesis, and social anticipation and planning. Opposites would have measured his level of abstraction. He would certainly have generated superior scores on all these tests of intelligence. In fact, it is possible the estimated IQ of 125–140 could be conservative.

It has already been hypothesized that Mr. Quantrill was a calm, poised and stable, somewhat rigid personality, of keen intelligence, and touched with narcissism. He was not given to rash actions, clearly was not impulsive, and could even have been described in obsessive/compulsive character terms. His dress was controlled, his actions were controlled, his ideation and intelligence were controlled. and his emotions were tightly controlled. Others described him as "cool as a cucumber." His calmness in emotional situations was known by all. In fact, it was said that the greater the danger, the calmer he became. He was fearless to the point of recklessness. When he led his men into battle, he was in front shouting them forward. However, we must remember that he had thought out and anticipated every eventuality, even to the point of obsessive/compulsive detail. Quite likely, when all the thinking and planning were done, his recklessness was nothing more than his commitment to action and to the total completion of the job. He would be a formidable opponent.

The only break in this poised presentation of self was his laugh. Sometimes a gay, nervous chuckle or giggle could be heard right after he had killed a man. His men found this to be eerie and a little frightening. This point about him is somewhat in dispute according to records and is crucial information. Should this be true, we could be left with a remarkably different personality. Rather than a calm, intelligent, quiet, and meticulous leader of men, we would have an intelligent, cold, psychopath who could outwit his enemies and dispatch them with cruelty and without feeling. Our answer to this issue can be found in the social analysis of Mr. Quantrill.

Socially, Mr. Quantrill is described as of a retiring nature, but with a ready smile for others and a warm heart. He loved his family, and his family loved him. His inner life was apparently more active than his outer life, and few people were accessible to his inner thoughts and emotions. Many people knew him, but he had few close friends. He spoke little to others and some saw him as a loner. Yet, he was clearly a leader and dominant in groups. He was described as kind to his men and to his prisoners. His men did not fear him, and he never quarreled with them. One account has him caring for a wounded man for over an hour. He was polite to women, admired them, and defended them. He was said to have given the order that if any of his men were to curse or abuse a woman, that they should be shot on the spot. He gave the only picture he had of himself to a woman he was attracted to. His relationships with females were always cordial and considerate. These accounts would certainly be in contrast to a person thought to be cruel and psychopathic. A psychopath, or a more disturbed personality, would not be caring toward his men, and would be shallow in his relationships with women. The descriptions are more in keeping with earlier descriptions as a calm, poised, quiet, thoughtful leader who was fearless in battle and who gave no quarter while the battle was on.

In summary, Mr. Quantrill is described as a small, smartly dressed young man of attractive appearance. He carried himself in a poised manner and drew positive responses from others. He was intelligent with an estimated IQ somewhere in the 125–140 vicinity. He would score high on most of the subtests of the WAIS. His vocabulary was superior, as was his mathematical ability, abstraction ability, attention and concentration, and his ability to analyze and synthesize. He had no apparent intellectual weakness. Emotionally, Mr. Quantrill was withdrawn and reserved and rarely given to impulsive action. The few exceptions were expressed in an unusual laugh that could be suggestive of a darker side of his nature or a nervousness that would break through the rigid controls of his personality. Socially, Mr. Quantrill had few friends, and seemed to prefer the role of a more distant, remote leader, than that of confidant and friend. He was respected and well thought of, and even admired.

Notes

INTRODUCTION

1. William Elsey Connelley, *Quantrill and the Border Wars* (1910, reprint, New York: Pageant, 1956), 59–60.
2. Speech of William Gregg at a Quantrill reunion; *Sni-A-Bar (Blue Springs, Mo.) Voice*, August 28, 1908.
3. William Gregg Manuscript, Western Historical Manuscript Collection, University of Missouri.
4. John McCorkle, *Three Years with Quantrill: A True Story Told by His Scout, John McCorkle* (1914, reprint, Norman: University of Oklahoma Press, 1992).
5. Gregg, *Sni-A-Bar (Blue Springs, Mo.) Voice*, August 28, 1908.
6. Edwin H. Simmons, "Why You Should Study History," *Fortitudine—Bulletin of the Marine Corps Historical Program* 25, no. 2 (Fall 1995).

CHAPTER 1: THE EARLY YEARS

1. *Joplin (Mo.) Morning Herald*, April 29, 1881.
2. Duane P. Schultz, *Quantrill's War: The Life and Times of William Clarke Quantrill* (New York: St. Martin's, 1996).
3. *Topeka Mail and Breezem*, April 22, 1898; Quantrill Clippings, vol. 2, pp. 140–41, Kansas State Historical Society, Topeka, Kansas.
4. William Elsey Connelley, *Quantrill and the Border Wars* (1910, reprint, New York: Pageant, 1956), 56.
5. Schultz, *Quantrill's War*, 39.
6. Connelley, *Quantrill and the Border Wars*, 72.
7. "A Southerner's Viewpoint of the Kansas Situation, 1856–1857: The Letters of Lieut. Col. A. J. Hoole, C.S.A.," *Kansas Historical Quarterly* 3, no. 1 (February 1934): 43–56.
8. Albert E. Castel, *A Frontier State at War: Kansas, 1861–1865* (1858, reprint, Westport, Conn.: Greenwood Press, 1979), 20.
9. John Newman Edwards, *Noted Guerrillas, Or the Warfare of the Border* (1877, reprint, Dayton, Ohio: Morningside, 1976), 38.
10. John J. Ingalls quoted in William E. Connelley, "The Lane Family," *Collections of the Kansas State Historical Society* 16 (1923–25): 35–36.
11. Leverett W. Spring, "The Career of a Kansas Politician," *American Historical Review* 4 (October 1898).

12. Ibid.

13. Ingalls, quoted in Connelley, "The Lane Family," 35–36.

14. Connelley, *Quantrill and the Border Wars*, 65.

15. Ibid., 57.

16. Richard Cordley, *A History of Lawrence, Kansas from the First Settlement to the Close of the Rebellion* (1895, reprint, Lawrence: Walsworth, 1976), 170–71; James C. Malin, "Dust Storms: Part One, 1850–1860," *Kansas Historical Quarterly* 14 (May 1946): 133.

17. Cole Younger, *The Story of Cole Younger by Himself* (1903, reprint, St. Paul: Minnesota Historical Society Press, 2000), 9; John P. Burch quoted in Harrison Trow, *Charles W. Quantrell: A True History of His Guerrilla Warfare on the Missouri and Kansas Border During the Civil War of 1861–1865* (Kansas City: n.p., 1923), 144.

18. William G. Cutler, *History of the State of Kansas*, 2 vols. (Chicago: Andreas, 1883), 877; Receipt No. 1288, Kansas State Historical Society Collections; Connelley, *Quantrill and the Border Wars*, 68.

19. Joanne C. Eakin, *Quantrill Letters* (Independence, Mo.: Two Trails, n.d.), August 23, 1857; Connelley, *Quantrill and the Border Wars*, 70.

20. Connelley, *Quantrill and the Border Wars*, 72.

21. Dory DeAngelo, *Voices Across Time: Profiles of Kansas City's Early Residents* (Kansas City: Tapestry, 1987). Majors's thirty-four-hundred-square-foot antebellum home (1856) is still standing at 8145 State Line Road in Kansas City, Missouri. It is the third-oldest structure in the city and one of the earliest wood-frame revival-style homes in the area. It was also one of the first houses in the area to have closets and to use "extravagant" glass windows.

22. Merrit M. Goddard, *The Historical Alexander Majors* (Kansas City: Alexander Majors Chapter, Missouri Society of the Sons of the American Revolution, 1993). Used by permission.

23. "Some Ingalls Letters," *Kansas Historical Collections* 14 (1915–18): 94–122.

24. Connelley, *Quantrill and the Border Wars*, 78.

25. Ibid., 80.

26. Ibid., 82.

27. Other writings indicate that the turning point in Quantrill's life came at a later time at another place, but my research pinpoints this ambush outside Lawrence as the critical moment in his life.

28. Connelley, *Quantrill and the Border Wars*, 82.

29. William Gregg Collection, Western Historical Manuscript Collection, University of Missouri.

30. Ibid.

31. Andrew Jackson Papers, Library of Congress.

32. John Lyde Wilson, *Code Duello* (1838); Sandra K. Gorin, "Battles, Duels, Panics and Skirmishes" (http://www.rootsweb.com/~usgwqury/Ky/Tips).

33. United States, War Department, *The War of the Rebellion: A Compilation of the Official Records of the Union and Confederate Armies*, 128 vols. (Washington, D.C.:

Government Printing Office, 1880–1901) (hereafter referred to as OR), ser. 4, vol. 1, 81–85.

34. Connelley, *Quantrill and the Border Wars*, 90.
35. Ibid., 125.
36. Ibid., 110.
37. Ibid., 125.
38. Quantrill Clippings, vol. 2, Kansas State Historical Society, Topeka, Kansas.
39. Connelley, *Quantrill and the Border Wars*, 104.
40. Castel, *A Frontier State at War*, 43.
41. Susan B. Anthony, Daniel Anthony's sister, was honored for her abolitionist and women's rights efforts by being featured on a U.S. dollar coin.
42. OR, ser. 1, vol. 3, 447, 485, 490; Charles Robinson, *The Kansas Conflict* (1892, reprint, Freeport, N.Y.: Books for Libraries, 1972); Charles Robinson to James Montgomery, May 7, 1861, James Montgomery Papers, Kansas State Historical Society, 111–13; Simeon M. Fox, "The Story of the Seventh Kansas," *Kansas Historical Collections* 8 (1904): 24, 27–30.
43. Connelley, *Quantrill and the Border Wars*, 113–14.
44. Ibid., 136.
45. Younger, *The Story of Cole Younger*, 10.
46. Trow, *Quantrell*, 144.
47. Ibid., 98–102; Frank Smith manuscript, courtesy of Albert Castel.

CHAPTER 2: THE PARIAH STRIKES

1. William Elsey Connelley, *Quantrill and the Border Wars* (1910, reprint, New York: Pageant, 1956), 143.
2. W. L. Potter to W. W. Scott, quoted in ibid., 150.
3. A. J. Walker to W. W. Scott, February 22, 1883, quoted in ibid., 167.
4. *Kansas City Star*, May 23, 1926.
5. John Newman Edwards, *Noted Guerrillas, Or the Warfare of the Border* (1877, reprint, Dayton, Ohio: Morningside, 1976), 44.
6. William Gregg Manuscript, Western Historical Manuscript Collection, University of Missouri.
7. Pearl Wilcox, *Jackson County Pioneers* (Independence, Mo.: n.p., 1975).
8. *Kansas City Journal*, May 12, 1888.
9. Joanne C. Eakin, *Recollections of Quantrill's Guerrillas, As Told by A. J. Walker of Weatherford, Texas to Victor E. Martin in 1910* (Independence, Mo.: Two Trails, 1996), 2.
10. Ibid., 4.
11. Hildegarde R. Herklotz, "Jayhawkers in Missouri, 1858–1863," *Missouri Historical Review* 17, no. 4 (July 1923): 505.
12. William G. Cutler, *History of the State of Kansas*, 2 vols. (Chicago: Andreas, 1883).

13. A. J. Walker's account gives Chalkey T. Lipsey's name as Southwick. At the coroner's inquest, the body was never identified. On October 28, 1861, Southwick joined Company C, Tenth Kansas Jayhawking Regiment.

14. Edwards, *Noted Guerrillas*, 46.

15. Connelley, *Quantrill and the Border Wars*, 82.

16. Frank Smith manuscript, courtesy of Albert Castel.

17. William Gregg Manuscript, Western Historical Manuscript Collection, University of Missouri.

18. Connelley, *Quantrill and the Border Wars*, 186.

19. W. L. Potter, January 20, 1896, in ibid., 187.

20. Richard S. Brownlee, *Gray Ghosts of the Confederacy: Guerrilla Warfare in the West* (1958, reprint, Baton Rouge: Louisiana State University Press, 1984), 43.

21. Solomon Young was President Harry S. Truman's grandfather.

22. See Joanne Chiles Eakin, *Tears and Turmoil: Order No. 11* (Independence, Mo.: Eakin, 1996); Richard L. Miller, *Truman: The Rise to Power* (New York: McGraw-Hill, 1986); Joanne C. Eakin, comp., *Walter Chiles of Jamestown* (Independence, Mo.: Wee Print, 1983).

23. James Montgomery to George Stearns, June 26 and July 5, 1861, George L. Stearns Papers, State Historical Society, Topeka, Kansas.

24. James S. Rollins Papers, February 12, 1862, Kansas Historical Society.

25. Eugene Fitch Ware, *The Lyon Campaign in Missouri* (1861, reprint, Iowa City: Press of the Camp Pope Bookshop, 1991), 190–97. See also Nathaniel Lyon to Thomas Sweeney, July 1, 1861, Thomas J. Sweeny Collection, Huntington, Springfield, Missouri.

26. Nathaniel Lyon to Chester Harding, July 31, 1861, Letters Received, Department of the West, box 10, RG 393; Lyon to John S. Phelps, July 27, 1861, in OR, vol. 1, ser. 3, 408.

27. Nathaniel Lyon to John C. Frémont, August 4, 1861, in OR, vol. 1, ser. 1, 47–48.

28. Jared C. Lobdell, "The Civil War Journal and Letters of John Van DuBois, April 12, 1861 to October 16, 1862," *Missouri Historical Review* 60, no. 1 (October 1966): 27–28; Edwin C. Bearss, *The Battle of Wilson's Creek* (Diamond, Mo.: George Washington Carver Birthplace District Association, 1975), 47; Nathaniel Lyon to Chester Harding, July 31, 1861, Letters Received, Department of the West, box 10, RG 393.

29. William G. Bek, ed., "The Civil War Diary of John T. Buegel, Union Soldier," *Missouri Historical Review* 40, no. 3 (April 1946): 313.

30. www.rootsweb.com-mocivwar/confederates.html submitted by Larry S. Wilcox.

31. Correspondence of Sterling Price, OR.

32. William F. Switzler, *Switzler's Illustrated History of Missouri, from 1541 to 1877* (1879, reprint, New York: Arno Press, 1975), 394.

33. OR, ser. 1, vol. 3, 447; Charles Robinson, *The Kansas Conflict* (New York: Harper & Brothers, 1892), 434–35; Charles Robinson to James Montgomery, May 7, 1861, Montgomery Papers, Kansas State Historical Society, Topeka, Kansas; Kansas, Adju-

tant General's Office, *Report of the Adjutant General of the State of Kansas, 1861–1865* (Topeka: Kansas State Printing Office, 1896), 111–13; *Leavenworth Daily Conservative*, July 31, 1861; C. B. Zulavsky to G. L. Stearns, July 28, 1861, Stearns Papers, Kansas State Historical Society, Topeka, Kansas; Albert Castel, "Kansas Jayhawking Raids into Western Missouri in 1861," *Missouri Historical Review* 54, no. 1 (October 1959): 2.

34. OR, ser. 1, vol. 3, 457–59.
35. Ibid., 487–88.
36. Michael L. Gillespie, *The Civil War Battle of Lexington* (Independence, Mo.: n.p., 1991).
37. Castel, "Kansas Jayhawking Raids into Western Missouri in 1861," 2.
38. Thomas Goodrich, *Black Flag: Guerrilla Warfare on the Western Border, 1861–1865* (Bloomington: Indiana University Press, 1995), 8–10.
39. Gillespie, *Battle of Lexington*, 30.
40. Missouri Historical Company, *History of Lafayette County, Missouri* (St. Louis: Missouri Historical Co., 1881), 50–57.
41. Edwards, *Noted Guerrillas*, 51.
42. Missouri Historical Company, *History of Lafayette County*, 50–57.
43. Gillespie, *Battle of Lexington*, 30.
44. Floyd D. Shoemaker, ed., *Missouri Day by Day*, 2 vols. (Columbia: State Historical Society of Missouri, 1942), 2:156.
45. George T. Maddox, *Hard Trials and Tribulations of an Old Confederate Soldier* (Van Buren, Ark.: Argus, 1897), 9.
46. Edwards, *Noted Guerrillas*, 22.
47. Maddox, *Hard Trials and Tribulations*, 40.
48. D. M. K. Campbell to Leroy Pope Walker, July 26, 1861, OR, ser. 4, vol. 1, 505.
49. Joanne C. Eakin and Donald R. Hale, *Branded As Rebels: A List of Bushwackers, Guerrillas, Partisan Rangers, Confederates and Southern Sympathizers* (Lee's Summit, Mo.: Donald R. Hale, 1993), 306.
50. Roberta Bonnewitz and Louis T. Allen, *Raytown Remembers* (Clinton, Mo.: Raytown Historical Society, n.d.), 42.
51. George L. Hagan, *Tales of Tragedy Trail* (Clinton, Mo.: Printery, 1976), 28–29.
52. Thomas Carney to W. R. Judson, February 23, 1863, in Kansas, Adjutant General's Office, *Report of the Adjutant General of the State of Kansas, 1861–1865*, 84; S. M. Fox, "The Letters of Samuel James Reader, 1861–1863," *Kansas Historical Quarterly* 9 (May 1940): 151; *(Lawrence) Kansas State Journal*, March 13, 1862; *Leavenworth Daily Conservative*, May 27 and August 6, 1863.
53. David M. Hunter to C. G. Halpine, OR, ser. 1, vol. 3, 446; Leverett Wilson Spring, *Kansas: The Prelude to the War for the Union* (1907, reprint, New York: AMS Press, 1973).
54. This correspondence is noted in OR, ser. 1, vol. 3, 446.
55. Ibid., 361.

CHAPTER 3: SOUTHERN HOPES—A SAVIOR APPEARS

1. Richard Cordley, *A History of Lawrence, Kansas from the First Settlement to the Close of the Rebellion* (1895, reprint, Lawrence: Walsworth, 1976).
2. Joanne C. Eakin, *Recollections of Quantrill's Guerrillas, As Told by A. J. Walker of Weatherford, Texas to Victor E. Martin in 1910* (Independence, Mo.: Two Trails, 1996), 13.
3. Walker interview, *Kansas City Journal*, May 12, 1888.
4. Donald R. Hale, *We Rode with Quantrill: Quantrill and the Guerrilla War As Told by the Men and Women Who Were With Him* (Kansas City: Donald R. Hale, 1992), 79.
5. A Kansas soldier fell wounded from his saddle in front of the home of Southerner John B. Saunders. The Saunderses tended his wounds and nursed him back to health. Two years later he commanded a company and was given a list of homes to be burned under General Orders No. 11. The Saunders house was on the list, but because the family had shown this man kindness, the house was spared from the jayhawkers' torch. After the war the family returned to find their home still standing but stripped of its doors and windows and all furnishings except the top of a sewing machine and a broken rocking chair. This house is still standing east of Independence at 17601 R. D. Mize Road. See *Independence (Mo.) Examiner*, February 26, 1962.
6. United Daughters of the Confederacy, Missouri Division, *Reminiscences of the Women of Missouri During the Sixties* (Jefferson City: Stephens, ca. 1913).
7. Cole Younger, *The Story of Cole Younger by Himself* (1903, reprint, St. Paul: Minnesota Historical Society Press, 2000), 1; Carl W. Breihan, *Ride the Razor's Edge: The Younger Brothers Story* (Gretna, La.: Pelican, 1992), 267.
8. Marley Brant, *The Outlaw Youngers: A Confederate Brotherhood* (Lanham, Md.: Madison Books, 1992), 26. Walley was a captain in Company C, Cass County Home Guards, Ninth Kansas Jayhawker Regiment, per military records and pension.
9. OR, ser. 1, vol. 8, 530, 534–38, 551, 576, 831; Caleb Smith to Thomas Ewing, February 27, 1862, Thomas Ewing Papers, Library of Congress; *Leavenworth (Kans.) Daily Conservative*, February 28, 1862.
10. Albert Castel, "Kansas Jayhawking Raids into Western Missouri in 1861," *Missouri Historical Review* 54, no. 1 (October 1959): 2.
11. Richard S. Brownlee, *Gray Ghosts of the Confederacy: Guerrilla Warfare in the West* (1958, reprint, Baton Rouge: Louisiana State University Press, 1984), 47.
12. Breihan, *Razor's Edge*, 32; John Newman Edwards, *Noted Guerrillas* (1877, reprint, Dayton, Ohio: Morningside, 1976), 55; Castel, "Kansas Jayhawking Raids into Western Missouri in 1861," 1–11.
13. W. L. Webb, *Battles and Biographies of Missourians* (Kansas City: Hudson-Kimberly, 1900), 324; *Leavenworth (Kans.) Daily Conservative*, November 13 and 26, 1861; George Miller, *Missouri's Memorable Decade, 1860–1870* (Columbia, Mo.: Stephens, 1898), 76, 89; Union Historical Company, *The History of Jackson County, Missouri* (Kansas City: Union Historical Co., 1881), 271–73.

14. Union Historical Company, *History of Jackson County, Missouri*, 277–78.

15. Albert Castel, *A Frontier State of War: Kansas, 1861–1865* (1958, reprint, Westport, Conn.: Greenwood Press, 1979), 61.

16. Ibid.

17. Castel, "Kansas Jayhawking Raids into Western Missouri in 1861," 1–11; Thomas Carney to W. R. Judson, February 23, 1863; Kansas, Adjutant General's Office, *Report of the Adjutant General of the State of Kansas, 1861–1865* (Topeka: Kansas State Printing Office, 1896), 84; S. M. Fox, "The Letters of Samuel James Reader, 1861–1863," *Kansas Historical Quarterly* 9 (May 1940): 151; Kansas, Adjutant General's Office, *Report of the Adjutant General of the State of Kansas, 1861–1865* (Topeka: Kansas State Printing Office, 1896); *(Lawrence) Kansas State Journal*, March 13, 1862; *Leavenworth (Kans.) Daily Conservative*, May 27 and August 6, 1863.

18. OR, ser. 1, vol. 8, 448–49.

19. Ibid., 507.

20. Ibid., 552.

21. Ibid., 818–19.

22. Rollins Papers, Missouri State Historical Society, Columbia, Missouri.

23. OR, ser. 1, vol. 22, pt. 2, 484–85.

24. Homer Croy, *Last of the Great Outlaws: The Story of Cole Younger* (New York: Duel, Sloan and Pearce, 1956), 14.

25. Dudley Taylor Cornish, *The Sable Arm: Black Troops in the Union Army, 1861–1865* (1956, reprint, Lawrence: University Press of Kansas, 1987), 72.

26. James Montgomery to Gov. Charles Robinson, August 3, 1862, Charles and Sarah T. Robinson Papers, Kansas State Historical Society, Topeka.

27. James C. Worthington to Roy Dunning cited in Croy, *Last of the Great Outlaws*, 215.

28. Daniel R. Anthony to his father, November 24, 1861, cited in Edgar Langsdorf and R. W. Richmond, eds., "Letters of Daniel R. Anthony, 1857–1862: Part One, 1857," *Kansas Historical Quarterly* (Spring 1958): 6–30.

29. Albert Castel, *William Clarke Quantrill: His Life and Times* (1962, reprint, Norman: University of Oklahoma, 1999), 59. Towns such as West Point, Morristown, and many others were destroyed by Kansas jayhawkers and no longer exist today.

30. Webster Moses to Nancy Mowry, December 4, 1861, in Moses Letters, Kansas State Historical Society, Topeka, Kansas.

31. See Kansas, Adjutant General's Office, *Report of the Adjutant General of the State of Kansas, 1861–1865*; Daniel R. Anthony to his father, November 24, 1862, cited in Langsdorf and Richmond, "Letters of Daniel R. Anthony," 6.

32. Simeon Fox to George W. Martin, December 8, 1908, in Fox Papers, Kansas State Historical Society, Topeka, Kansas.

33. Brownlee, *Gray Ghosts*, 169.

34. Ibid.; William S. Rosecrans, letter to the editor, *Cincinnati Gazette*, August 4, 1862.

35. *(St. Louis) Daily Missouri Republican*, December 29, 1861.

36. Ibid.

37. Harrison Trow, *Charles W. Quantrell: A True History of His Guerrilla Warfare on the Missouri and Kansas Border During the Civil War of 1861–1865* (Kansas City: n.p., 1923), 30; Edwards, *Noted Guerrillas*, 52.

38. *Liberty (Mo.) Weekly Tribune*, October 18, 1861.

39. Eakin, *Recollections of Quantrill's Guerrillas*, 17.

40. Hale, *We Rode with Quantrill*, 122.

41. Trow, *Quantrell*, 30–31.

42. Quantrill Clippings, vol. 2, Kansas State Historical Society, Topeka, Kansas.

43. Trow, *Quantrell*, 32.

44. Joanne C. Eakin and Donald R. Hale, *Branded As Rebels: A List of Bushwackers, Guerrillas, Partisan Rangers, Confederates and Southern Sympathizers* (Lee's Summit, Mo.: Donald R. Hale, 1993), 183, 267, 286, 337, 350, 351.

45. Near present-day Lee's Summit and Ess Road, seven miles south of Independence.

46. *OR*, ser. 1, vol. 8, 476–78.

47. Ibid., 496–97.

48. Frank Smith manuscript, courtesy of Albert Castel.

49. Eakin, *Recollections of Quantrill's Guerrillas*, 18; William Gregg Manuscript, Western Historical Manuscript Collection, University of Missouri.

50. Castel, *Frontier State of War*, 137; Union Historical Company, *History of Jackson County*. Redlegs were notorious jayhawkers known for their brutality as well as for the red Moroccan leggings they wore as identification.

51. Ann D. Niepman, "General Orders No. 11 and Border Warfare During the Civil War," *Missouri Historical Review* 66, no. 2 (January 1972): 191.

52. Walter B. Stevens, *Centennial History of Missouri*, 4 vols. (St. Louis: Clarke Publishing Co., 1921), 1:629; Breihan, *Razor's Edge*, 73; Younger, *The Story of Cole Younger*, 32.

53. Kansas City Historical Company, *History of Johnson County, Missouri* (Kansas City: Kansas City Historical Company, 1881).

54. Castel, "Kansas Jayhawking Raids into Western Missouri in 1861," 1–11.

55. Thomas Goodrich, *Black Flag: Guerrilla Warfare on the Western Border, 1861–1865* (Bloomington: Indiana University Press, 1995), 24.

56. *(St. Louis) Daily Missouri Republican*, January 16 and May 8, 1862.

57. John Nicolay and John Hay, eds., *Complete Works of Abe Lincoln*, 12 vols. (New York: F. D. Tandy, 1905), 8:214–20.

58. *OR*, ser. 1, vol. 8, 552.

59. Carl Breihan, *The Killer Legions of Quantrill* (Seattle: Hangman Press, 1971), 25, and idem, *Razor's Edge*, 33; Augustus C. Appler, *The Younger Brothers* (1876, reprint, New York: Fell, 1955), 51–54.

60. Provost Marshal Files, roll 142, National Archives, Washington, D.C.

61. Eakin and Hale, *Branded As Rebels*, 43.

62. USMC Leadership Course 7000 series, Marine Corps Institute, Washington, D.C.

63. Edwards, *Noted Guerrillas*, 15.

64. Napoleon's general, Marshal Joachim Murat, said this about his cavalrymen.

65. S. R. Gleaves, "The Strategic Use of Cavalry," *Journal of the U.S. Cavalry Association* 18 (July 1907): 9, 18–25; George T. Denison, *A History of Cavalry from the Earliest Times* (1913, reprint, Westport, Conn.: Greenwood Press, 1977), 394–95; Theodore H. Rodenbough, ed., *The Cavalry*, vol. 4 of *The Photographic History of the Civil War*, ed. Francis T. Miller, 10 vols. (New York: Review of Reviews, 1911–12), 18–26; J. F. C. Fuller, *Grant and Lee: A Study in Personality and Generalship* (New York: Scribner, 1933), 266–77. For discussion of a European opinion of cavalry for raiding purposes, see Jay Luvaas, *The Military Legacy of the Civil War: The European Inheritance* (1959, reprint, Lawrence: University Press of Kansas, 1988), 2, 66, 85, 104, 114–15, 130, 136, 139, 141–46, 148, 153, 154, 157–58, 222–23, 237–44.

66. Hampton B. Watts, *The Babe of the Company: An Unfolded Leaf from the Forest of Never-To-Be Forgotten Years* (Fayette, Mo.: Democratic Leader Press, 1913), 4.

67. Albert R. Greene, "What I Saw of the Quantrill Raid," *Collections of the Kansas State Historical Society* 13 (1914): 430–51.

68. Niccolo Machiavelli, 1531.

69. Jim Murphy, *The Boys' War: Confederate and Union Soldiers Talk About the Civil War* (New York, Scholastic, 1991), 34.

70. Ned Bradford, *Battles and Leaders of the Civil War* (1956, reprint, New York: Meridian, 1989), 238.

71. Quantrill clippings, vol. 2, Kansas State Historical Society, Topeka, Kansas.

72. Postwar newspaper interview with Kate King, *Kansas City Star*, May 23, 1926.

73. Charles L. Armstrong, "Ambushes: Still Viable As a Combat Tactic," *Marine Corps Gazette* (July 1990).

74. Union Historical Company, *History of Jackson County*, 681–82.

75. Ethylene Ballard Thruston, *Echoes of the Past: A Nostalgic Look at Early Raytown and Jackson County* (Kansas City: Lowell Press, 1973), 125.

76. Paul Brooks, *Legacy of Faith* (Marceline, Mo.: Walsworth, 1992), 20.

77. Today Benjamin Rice's home, along with its slave buildings, is a museum in Raytown, Missouri (Rice-Tremonti Farm Home Museum, 8801 E. 66th Street, Raytown, MO 64133). It is one of very few remaining Southern homes spared by jayhawkers.

78. Warren Welch accounts, Jackson County, Missouri Historical Society, A125 4F1.

79. Jackson County, Missouri Vital Statistics, Marriage Records, KCMo Mid-Continent Public Library.

80. John McCorkle, *Three Years with Quantrill: A True Story Told by His Scout, John McCorkle* (1914, reprint, Norman: University of Oklahoma Press, 1992), 127.

CHAPTER 4: THE MAKING OF A GUERRILLA

1. Union Historical Company, *The History of Jackson County, Missouri* (Kansas City: Union Historical Co., 1881), 466.

2. Joanne C. Eakin and Donald R. Hale, *Branded As Rebels: A List of Bushwackers, Guerrillas, Partisan Rangers, Confederates and Southern Sympathizers* (Lee's Summit, Mo.: Donald R. Hale, 1993), 61.

3. OR, ser. 1, vol. 8, 57.

4. William Elsey Connelley, *Quantrill and the Border Wars* (1910, reprint, New York: Pageant, 1956), 224; William Gregg Manuscript, Western Historical Manuscript Collection, University of Missouri; B. James George Sr., *Confederate and Quantrill Officer* (n.p., 1973).

5. William Gregg Manuscript, Western Historical Manuscript Collection, University of Missouri.

6. OR, ser. 1, vol. 8, 335–36.

7. Donald R. Hale, *They Called Him Bloody Bill: The Life of William Anderson, Missouri Guerrilla* (Clinton, Mo.: Printery, 1992), 4.

8. Daughters of the American Revolution, *Vital Historical Records of Jackson County, Missouri* (Kansas City: DAR, 1934).

9. Union Historical Company, *The History of Jackson County*, 367–70.

10. Brooks, *Legacy of Faith*, 38.

11. William E. Parrish, gen. ed., *A History of Missouri*, 5 vols. (Columbia: University of Missouri Press, 1971–97), 3:84.

12. Ethylene Ballard Thruston, *Echoes of the Past: A Nostalgic Look at Early Raytown and Jackson County* (Kansas City: Lowell Press, 1973), 386–87.

13. Frank Smith manuscript, courtesy of Albert Castel.

14. OR, ser. 1, vol. 8, 611–12.

15. Connelley, *Quantrill and the Border Wars*, 237. Randlett was released on Tuesday, March 18, 1862, at Independence on parole of honor per ibid., 232.

16. John Newman Edwards, *Noted Guerrillas* (1877, reprint, Dayton, Ohio: Morningside, 1976), 77.

17. William Gregg Manuscript, Western Historical Manuscript Collection, University of Missouri; Connelley, *Quantrill and the Border Wars*, 229.

18. *Topeka (Kans.) Capital*, August 21, 1888; Frank Smith manuscript, courtesy of Albert Castel, referencing a story Smith was told by Quantrill's men.

19. William Gregg Manuscript, Western Historical Manuscript Collection, University of Missouri.

20. Eakin and Hale, *Branded As Rebels*, 215.

21. Edwards, *Noted Guerrillas*, 456.

22. William Gregg Manuscript, Western Historical Manuscript Collection, University of Missouri.

23. Thomas Goodrich, *Black Flag: Guerrilla Warfare on the Western Border, 1861–1865* (Bloomington: Indiana University Press, 1995), 25.

24. Connelley, *Quantrill and the Border Wars*, 238; Cole Younger, *The Story of Cole Younger by Himself* (1903, reprint, St. Paul: Minnesota Historical Society Press, 2000), 14.

25. Joanne C. Eakin, *Recollections of Quantrill's Guerrillas, As Told by A. J. Walker of Weatherford, Texas to Victor E. Martin in 1910* (Independence, Mo.: Two Trails, 1996), 19. In August 1862 Nellie Wallace's husband was arrested and held in the Independence jail, awaiting execution for being a Southern sympathizer. When Quantrill attacked the town, he freed Wallace. For this Wallace's daughter Elizabeth was eternally grateful. After the war she offered her home for the Quantrill reunions.

26. Goodrich, *Black Flag*, 31.

27. John McCorkle, *Three Years with Quantrill: A True Story Told by His Scout, John McCorkle* (1914, reprint, Norman: University of Oklahoma Press, 1992), 39–41; Quantrill Clippings, vol. 2, Kansas State Historical Society, Topeka, Kansas.

28. McCorkle, *Three Years with Quantrill*, 39–41.

29. Harrison Trow, *Charles W. Quantrell: A True History of His Guerrilla Warfare on the Missouri and Kansas Border During the Civil War of 1861–1865* (Kansas City: n.p., 1923), 43–50.

30. McCorkle, *Three Years with Quantrill*, 40.

31. Trow, *Quantrell*, 43–50; McCorkle, *Three Years with Quantrill*, 40.

32. Younger, *The Story of Cole Younger*, 14–15.

33. Frank Smith manuscript, courtesy of Albert Castel.

34. McCorkle, *Three Years with Quantrill*, 40.

35. Quantrill Clippings, vol. 2, Kansas State Historical Society, Topeka, Kansas.

36. Frank Smith manuscript, courtesy of Albert Castel; Trow, *Quantrell*, 51–58.

37. Richard S. Brownlee, *Gray Ghosts of the Confederacy: Guerrilla Warfare in the West* (1958, reprint, Baton Rouge: Louisiana State University Press, 1984), 67.

38. Joanne Chiles Eakin, *Warren Welch Remembers: A Civil War Guerrilla from Jackson County, Missouri* (Shawnee Mission, Kans.: Two Trails, 1997), 1.

39. Trow, *Quantrell*, 60.

40. Ibid., 61.

41. Ibid., 64; Edwards, *Noted Guerrillas*, 251.

42. Trow, *Quantrell*, 65; Edwards, *Noted Guerrillas*, 251.

43. Augustus C. Appler, *The Younger Brothers* (1876, reprint, New York: Fell, 1955), 86–87.

44. Trow, *Quantrell*, 70.

45. Ibid., 69–72.

46. Marine Corps Institute Infantry Patrolling, MCI 03.35C. Marine Barracks, Washington, D.C.

47. McCorkle, *Three Years with Quantrill*, 2.

48. OR, ser. 1, vol. 13, 402–3.

49. Ibid., 506; Albert Castel, *William Clarke Quantrill: His Life and Times* (1962, reprint, Norman: University of Oklahoma, 1999), 87.

50. Brownlee, *Gray Ghosts*, 71.

51. OR, ser. 4, vol. 1, 1094, 1098.

52. OR, ser. 1, vol. 13, 835.

53. Homer Croy, *Last of the Great Outlaws: The Story of Cole Younger* (New York: Duel, Sloan and Pearce, 1956), 16–17.

54. Marley Brant, *The Outlaw Youngers: A Confederate Brotherhood* (Lanham, Md.: Madison Books, 1992), 30–31.

55. Younger, *The Story of Cole Younger.*

56. *Kansas City Journal,* August 23, 1903.

CHAPTER 5: BAND OF BROTHERS

1. John Newman Edwards, *Noted Guerrillas, Or the Warfare of the Border* (1877, reprint, Dayton, Ohio: Morningside, 1976), 21.

2. *Independence (Mo.) Examiner,* November 13, 1903; Joanne C. Eakin and Donald R. Hale, *Branded As Rebels: A List of Bushwackers, Guerrillas, Partisan Rangers, Confederates and Southern Sympathizers* (Lee's Summit, Mo.: Donald R. Hale, 1993), 184.

3. Warren Welch Collection, Jackson County Historical Society.

4. Marriage Records of Jackson County, Missouri, 1851–1865, vol. 2.

5. Joanne C. Eakin, *Recollections of Quantrill's Guerrillas, As Told by A. J. Walker of Weatherford, Texas to Victor E. Martin in 1910* (Independence, Mo.: Two Trails, 1996), 18.

6. William Gregg Manuscript, Western Historical Manuscript Collection, University of Missouri.

7. *Western Journal of Commerce,* May 30, 1863.

8. B. James George Sr., *Confederate and Quantrill Officer* (n.p., 1973).

9. This was midway between Kansas City and Independence. The battle of Rock Creek occurred at today's Hill Park on Twenty-third Street and Westport Road in Independence. Frank James and his wife are buried on the north side of Hill Park in a small plot surrounded by a white stone wall. The first conflict is often said to be the battle of Boonville, but the battle of Rock Creek in Jackson County was fought weeks earlier.

10. William Gregg Manuscript, Western Historical Manuscript Collection, University of Missouri.

11. Donald R. Hale, *We Rode with Quantrill: Quantrill and the Guerrilla War As Told by the Men and Women Who Were With Him* (Kansas City: Donald R. Hale, 1992), 130–31.

12. *Kansas City World,* April 28, 1901.

13. Ibid.

14. *Topeka Capital,* July 8, 1898.

15. Eakin and Hale, *Branded As Rebels,* 214.

16. Ethylene Ballard Thruston, *Echoes of the Past: A Nostalgic Look at Early Raytown and Jackson County* (Kansas City: Lowell Press, 1973), 227.

17. Eakin and Hale, *Branded As Rebels,* 466.

18. Burton Rascoe, *Belle Starr, "The Bandit Queen"* (New York: Random House, 1941), 87.

19. Homer Croy, *Jesse James Was My Neighbor* (New York: Duell, Sloan and Pierce, 1949), 28.

20. Eakin and Hale, *Branded As Rebels*, 235.

21. Ibid., 351.

22. Ibid., 368.

23. Ibid., 146–47; Union Historical Company, *The History of Jackson County, Missouri* (Kansas City: Union Historical Co., 1881).

24. Thruston, *Echoes of the Past*, 235.

25. *Kansas City Journal*, August 23, 1902.

26. George T. Maddox, *Hard Trials and Tribulations of an Old Confederate Soldier* (Van Buren, Ark.: Argus, 1897), 75.

27. *Oak Grove (Mo.) Banner*, October 8, 1898.

28. Union Historical Company, *The History of Jackson County, Missouri*, 705.

29. Henry Huston Crittenden, comp., *The Crittenden Memoirs* (New York: Putnam, 1936), 370–71.

30. George L. Hagan, *Tales of Tragedy Trail* (Clinton, Mo.: Printery, 1992), 38–39.

31. Daughters of the American Revolution, *Vital Historical Records of Jackson County, Missouri* (Kansas City: DAR, 1934).

32. Edwards, *Noted Guerrillas*, 177.

33. Crittenden, *Crittenden Memoirs*, 145–46.

34. Hale, *We Rode with Quantrill*, 77.

35. *St. Louis Post Dispatch*, August 24, 1902.

36. OR, ser. 1, vol. 41, pt. 2, 45; Jim Cummins, *Jim Cummins' Book* (1903, reprint, Provo, Utah: Triton Press, 1988).

37. Thomas Goodrich, *Black Flag: Guerrilla Warfare on the Western Border, 1861–1865* (Bloomington: Indiana University Press, 1995), 54; Marley Brant, *The Outlaw Youngers: A Confederate Brotherhood* (Lanham, Md.: Madison Books, 1992), 53.

38. Ike Hall interview with W. W. Scott in Wakefield, Ky., 1887; Connelley, *Quantrill and the Border Wars*, 303.

39. Eakin and Hale, *Branded As Rebels*, 273.

40. Hagan, *Tales of Tragedy Trail*, 28–29.

41. Thomas M. Goodman, *A Thrilling Record: Founded on Facts and Observations Obtained During Ten Days' Experience with Colonel William T. Anderson* (Hawleyville, Iowa: Goodman, 1868).

42. OR, ser. 1, vol. 41, pt. 2, 75.

43. Edwards, *Noted Guerrillas*, 304.

44. Interview with W. W. Scott in Wakefield, Ky., 1887, quoted from Connelley, *Quantrill and the Border Wars*, 302.

45. *Kansas City Post*, August 20, 1909.

46. Edwards, *Noted Guerrillas*, 20.

47. Eakin and Hale, *Branded As Rebels*, 115, 182, 201.

48. Donald R. Hale, *The No Quarterly: Newsletter of the William Clarke Quantrill Society* (April 1998).

49. *Pleasant Hill Times*, September 5, 1924.

50. Maddox, *Hard Trials and Tribulations*, 59, 76.

51. Joanne Chiles Eakin, *Tears and Turmoil: Order No. 11* (Independence, Mo.: Eakin, 1996); United Daughters of the Confederacy, Missouri Division, *Reminiscences of the Women of Missouri During the Sixties* (Jefferson City: Stephens, ca. 1913).

52. *Sni-A-Bar (Blue Springs, Mo.) Voice*, August 28, 1908.

CHAPTER 6: FIELDS OF GLORY

1. *OR*, ser. 1, vol. 43, pt. 2, 374.

2. T. C. Hindman to T. H. Holmes, November 3, 1862, *OR*, ser 1, vol. 13, 48.

3. Richard S. Brownlee, *Gray Ghosts of the Confederacy: Guerrilla Warfare in the West* (1958, reprint, Baton Rouge: Louisiana State University Press, 1984), 92.

4. Mark Grimsley, *The Hard Hand of War: Union Military Policy Toward Southern Civilians, 1861–1865* (New York: Cambridge University Press, 1995).

5. *OR*, ser. 1, vol. 13, 402–3.

6. William Gregg Manuscript, Western Historical Manuscript Collection, University of Missouri.

7. Frank Smith manuscript, courtesy of Albert Castel; William Gregg Manuscript, Western Historical Manuscript Collection, University of Missouri.

8. Harrison Trow, *Charles W. Quantrell: A True History of His Guerrilla Warfare on the Missouri and Kansas Border During the Civil War of 1861–1865* (Kansas City: n.p., 1923), 74.

9. William Elsey Connelley, *Quantrill and the Border Wars* (1910, reprint, New York: Pageant, 1956), 256–58.

10. John Newman Edwards, *Noted Guerrillas, Or the Warfare of the Border* (1877, reprint, Dayton, Ohio: Morningside, 1976), 88–91.

11. Donald R. Hale, *We Rode with Quantrill: Quantrill and the Guerrilla War As Told by the Men and Women Who Were With Him* (Kansas City: Donald R. Hale, 1992), 135.

12. *OR*, ser. 1, vol. 13, 154–60.

13. Capt. Irvin Walley, the man who killed Henry Washington Younger, belonged to Andrew G. Nugent's battalion.

14. Connelley, *Quantrill and the Border Wars*, 262.

15. *OR*, ser. 1, vol. 13, 226.

16. Morgan T. Mattox, interview, by William Elsey Connelley, April 29 or 30, 1909, at Bartlesville, Okla. Quoted in Connelley, *Quantrill and the Border Wars*, 262.

17. The Federals burned down the John Cartmill Wallace home after the battle of Independence. Wallace had come to Jackson County in 1847 and lived between Independence and Kansas City on a hill just north of the old Independence road. Fifteen-year-old Elizabeth C. Wallace was so thankful to Quantrill for saving her

father's life that after the war she offered her home to host the reunions of Quantrill's surviving men.

18. *Oak Grove (Mo.) Banner,* June 10, 1904.

19. W. L. Webb, *Battles and Biographies of Missourians* (Kansas City: Hudson-Kimberly, 1900), 143.

20. Pearl Wilcox, *Jackson County Pioneers* (Independence, Mo.: n.p., 1975), 337–38.

21. John McCorkle, *Three Years with Quantrill: A True Story Told by His Scout, John McCorkle* (1914, reprint, Norman: University of Oklahoma Press, 1992), 32.

22. United Daughters of the Confederacy, Missouri Division, *Reminiscences of the Women of Missouri During the Sixties* (Jefferson City: Stephens, ca. 1913).

23. Joanne Chiles Eakin, *Warren Welch Remembers: A Civil War Guerrilla from Jackson County, Missouri* (Shawnee Mission, Kans.: Two Trails, 1997), 3.

24. McCorkle, *Three Years with Quantrill,* 33; William Gregg Manuscript, Western Historical Manuscript Collection, University of Missouri.

25. Ethylene Ballard Thruston, *Echoes of the Past: A Nostalgic Look at Early Raytown and Jackson County* (Kansas City: Lowell Press, 1973), 259; Leslie Anders, "Fighting the Ghosts at Lone Jack," *Missouri Historical Review* 79, no. 3 (April 1985): 332–56.

26. Carolyn M. Bartels, *The Civil War in Missouri Day by Day, 1861 to 1865* (Shawnee, Kans.: Two Trails, 1992), 65.

27. Albert Castel, *William Clarke Quantrill: His Life and Times* (1962, reprint, Norman: University of Oklahoma, 1999), 87.

28. William M. Paxton, *Annals of Platte County, Missouri* (Kansas City: Hudson-Kimberly Publishing Co., 1897), 330.

29. National Historical Company, *History of Clay and Platte Counties, Missouri* (St. Louis: National Historical Co., 1885), 680–81, 703.

30. Thruston, *Echoes of the Past,* 272.

31. Cole Younger to Harry Hoffman, quoted in Robert Barr Smith, *The Last Hurrah of the James-Younger Gang* (Norman: University of Oklahoma Press, 2001), 30.

32. OR, ser. 1, vol. 13, 251.

33. Ibid., 255.

34. Henry M. Woodsmall was captain of a Southern company from Platte County that came to Jackson County to fight alongside Quantrill until they could join Price's army. National Historical Company, *History of Clay and Platte Counties.*

35. Castel, *Quantrill,* 95.

36. *St. Louis Post Dispatch,* August 24, 1902.

37. *Paola (Kans.) Record,* February 2, 1905.

38. William Gregg Manuscript, Western Historical Manuscript Collection, University of Missouri.

39. *Paola (Kans.) Record,* February 2, 1905.

40. Edward E. Leslie, *The Devil Knows How to Ride: The True Story of William Clarke Quantrill and His Confederate Raiders* (New York: Da Capo Press, 1998), 144–47.

41. Edwards, *Noted Guerrillas,* 120.

42. Newspaper story by C. M. Bowring in Joanne Chiles Eakin, comp., *Diary of a Town: Wellington, Missouri* (Independence, Mo.: Wee Print, 1984).

43. Edwards, *Noted Guerrillas*, 121.

44. Ibid., 122.

45. *OR*, ser. 1, vol. 13, 267–68.

46. *Kansas City Journal Post*, December 20, 1936.

47. National Historical Company, *History of Carrol County, Missouri* (St. Louis: National Historical Co., 1882), 325.

48. William Gregg Manuscript, Western Historical Manuscript Collection, University of Missouri.

49. Report of Capt. Daniel H. David, Fifth Missouri Militia Cavalry to Col. W. R. Penick, Independence, Mo., October 8, 1862, in *OR*, ser. 1, vol. 13, 312,

50. James Williamson, *Mosby's Rangers* (1896, reprint, Alexandria, Va.: Time-Life, 1982).

51. William Gregg Manuscript, Western Historical Manuscript Collection, University of Missouri.

52. Richard Cordley, *Pioneer Days in Kansas* (New York: Pilgrim Press, n.d.).

53. Trow, *Quantrell*, 91–93.

54. McCorkle, *Three Years with Quantrill*, 38.

CHAPTER 7: EARLY SKIRMISHES

1. Harrison Trow, *Charles W. Quantrell: A True History of His Guerrilla Warfare on the Missouri and Kansas Border During the Civil War of 1861–1865* (Kansas City: n.p., 1923), 97–98; Albert Castel, *William Clarke Quantrill: His Life and Times* (1962, reprint, Norman: University of Oklahoma, 1999), 99.

2. William O. Atkeson, *History of Bates County, Missouri* (Cleveland: Historical Publishing Co., 1918).

3. Report of E. B. Brown to John M. Schofield, November 16, 1862, and Ben S. Henry to James G. Blunt, November 11, 1862, in *OR*, ser. 1, vol. 13, 796;

4. *OR*, ser. 1, vol. 13, 33.

5. *OR*, ser. 1, vol. 22, pt. 1, 39–40, 796–97, 821–22.

6. Trow, *Quantrell*, 158; William E. Parrish, *Turbulent Partnership: Missouri and the Union, 1861–1865* (Columbia: University of Missouri Press, 1963), 99.

7. Frank Smith manuscript, courtesy of Albert Castel.

8. Ibid., courtesy of Albert Castel.

9. Following his visit to Richmond, Quantrill returned to Arkansas sometime in January 1863. Records show that on January 21, 1863, he purchased a vest for $9 from Maj. W. H. Hayes, the acting quartermaster at Little Rock, Arkansas, who was in charge of the Chief Clothing Bureau. Records also show that pay voucher #1272 was paid on February 16, 1863, for service from December 1, 1862, to February 3, 1863, in the amount of $280 from Headquarters, District of the Gulf, Mobile, Alabama, to W. C. Quantrill, Captain of Cavalry Scouts, Confederate States of

America. Quantrill was also paid under pay voucher #332, March 4, 1863, for the period from August 7, 1862, to January 1, 1863, in the amount of $672. The voucher reads: "From Pay Master at Mobile, 18 February 1863; 'I have received of Major John Ambler this 4th day of March, 1863, the sum of $672.00 being the amount in full.'" The voucher was signed by W. C. Quantrill, Cavalry Scouts. Three months later, on April 2, 1863, Quantrill also bought a hat for $15 from the quartermaster, Major Haynes.

10. *OR*, ser. 1, vol. 48, pt. 2, 24–25.
11. *OR*, ser. 1, vol. 22, pt. 1, 826–88.
12. *OR*, ser. 1, vol. 22, pt. 2, 17–18.
13. Ibid., 483.
14. *OR*, ser. 1, vol. 13, 455.
15. Trow, *Quantrell*, 106–7.
16. Ibid., 110.
17. Edwards, *Noted Guerrillas*, 141.
18. Trow, *Quantrell*, 110–15.
19. Cole Younger, *The Story of Cole Younger by Himself* (1903, reprint, St. Paul: Minnesota Historical Society Press, 2000), 5–6.
20. Personal account of Reuben Smith, *OR*, ser. 1, vol. 22, pt. 2, 33.
21. *OR*, ser. 1, vol. 8, 478.
22. Trow, *Quantrell*, 115.
23. Cole Younger's winter quarters in 1862–63 was at present-day Lee's Summit Road and Highway 40 in Independence, Missouri.
24. Trow, *Quantrell*, 121–23.
25. *OR*, ser. 1, vol. 22, 320.
26. Joanne C. Eakin and Donald R. Hale, *Branded As Rebels: A List of Bushwackers, Guerrillas, Partisan Rangers, Confederates and Southern Sympathizers* (Lee's Summit, Mo.: Donald R. Hale, 1993), 482–83.
27. John McCorkle, *Three Years with Quantrill: A True Story Told by His Scout, John McCorkle* (1914, reprint, Norman: University of Oklahoma Press, 1992), 67.
28. Benjamin Franklin Parker was from Jackson County and had been given a colonel's commission by James A. Seddon, the Confederate secretary of war, and H. D. Walker, the assistant adjutant general of the Confederate army, and had been given command of the First Missouri Partisan Rangers. Parker's commission, dated May 11, 1863, was found on his body on July 1 at Waverly, Missouri, just a month after the hanging of James Vaughn. See Eakin and Hale, *Branded As Rebels*, 336, 442.
29. Thomas Goodrich, *Black Flag: Guerrilla Warfare on the Western Border, 1861–1865* (Bloomington: Indiana University Press, 1995), 46–47.
30. Trow, *Quantrell*, 163.
31. United Daughters of the Confederacy, Missouri Division, *Reminiscences of the Women of Missouri During the Sixties* (Jefferson City: Stephens, ca. 1913); William Gregg Manuscript, Western Historical Manuscript Collection, University of Missouri;

Walter B. Stevens, *Centennial History of Missouri*, 4 vols. (St. Louis: Clarke Publishing Co., 1921), 1:852.

32. Jacob Hall Family Papers, Jackson County Historical Society, Independence, Mo.
33. Goodrich, *Black Flag*, 23.
34. OR, ser. 1, vol. 34, pt. 2, 13.
35. Operations Against Guerrilla Units, Marine Corps Institute, MCI 03.24G.
36. Augustus C. Appler, *The Younger Brothers* (1876, reprint, New York: Fell, 1955), 65.
37. Ibid., 55.
38. William Gregg Manuscript, Western Historical Manuscript Collection, University of Missouri.
39. Joanne C. Eakin, *Recollections of Quantrill's Guerrillas, As Told by A. J. Walker of Weatherford, Texas to Victor E. Martin in 1910* (Independence, Mo.: Two Trails, 1996), 39. In 1910 this story was published in serial form over a twelve-week span in the *(Weatherford, Tex.) Daily Herald*.
40. Andrea Viotti, *Garibaldi: The Revolutionary and His Men* (Poole [Eng.]: Blandford Press, 1979), 68.

CHAPTER 8: BRUTALITY UNFOLDS

1. Jacob Hall Papers, Jackson County Historical Society, Independence, Mo.
2. John Newman Edwards, *Noted Guerrillas, Or the Warfare of the Border* (1877, reprint, Dayton, Ohio: Morningside, 1976), 161.
3. Harrison Trow, *Charles W. Quantrell: A True History of His Guerrilla Warfare on the Missouri and Kansas Border During the Civil War of 1861–1865* (Kansas City: n.p., 1923), 141.
4. Joanne C. Eakin and Donald R. Hale, *Branded As Rebels: A List of Bushwackers, Guerrillas, Partisan Rangers, Confederates and Southern Sympathizers* (Lee's Summit, Mo.: Donald R. Hale, 1993), 269.
5. Ann D. Niepmann, "General Orders No. 11 and Border Warfare During the Civil War," *Missouri Historical Review* 66, no. 2 (January 1972): 190.
6. W. L. Webb, *Battles and Biographies of Missourians* (Kansas City: Hudson-Kimberly, 1900).
7. Operations Against Guerrilla Units, Marine Corps Institute, MCI 03.24G.
8. Missouri City was called Richfield at the time of the guerrillas' raid. It was three miles east of Independence on the Missouri River.
9. OR, ser. 1, vol. 22, 465.
10. Ibid.
11. William Elsey Connelley, *Quantrill and the Border Wars* (1910, reprint, New York: Pageant, 1956), 302.
12. William Gregg Manuscript, Western Historical Manuscript Collection, University of Missouri; *Sni-A-Bar (Blue Springs, Mo.) Voice*, August 28, 1908; Eakin and Hale, *Branded As Rebels*, 315.

13. Men like Samuel Kimberlin, Jeptha Crawford, John Saunders, and Joseph C. Lea were killed in the presence of their families. See chapter 7.

14. Joseph A. Mudd, *With Porter in North Missouri: A Chapter in the History of the War Between the States* (1909, reprint, Iowa City: Press of the Camp Pope Bookshop, 1992), 316.

15. Albert Castel, "Order No. 11 and the Civil War on the Border," *Missouri Historical Review* 57, no. 4 (July 1963): 359.

16. Sherry Lamb Schirmer and Richard D. McKinzie, *At the Rivers Bend: An Illustrated History of Kansas City, Independence, and Jackson County* (Woodland Hills, Calif.: Windsor, 1982); Charles F. Harris, "Catalyst for Terror: The Collapse of the Women's Prison in Kansas City," *Missouri Historical Review* 89, no. 3 (April 1995): 291.

17. OR, ser. 1, vol. 22, pt. 2, 484–85, 572–74, 579–85.

18. *Kansas City Daily Journal*, June 30, 1863.

19. Niepmann, "General Orders No. 11 and Border Warfare During the Civil War," 185–210.

20. OR, ser. 1, vol. 30, pt. 3, 698.

21. William Gregg was mistaken; Ulysses S. Grant gave this order to Philip H. Sheridan.

22. Niepmann, "General Orders No. 11 and Border Warfare During the Civil War," 191; Albert E. Castel, *A Frontier State at War: Kansas, 1861–1865* (1858, reprint, Westport, Conn.: Greenwood Press, 1979), 122.

23. Edwards, *Noted Guerrillas*, 175.

24. Eakin and Hale, *Branded As Rebels*, 386.

25. OR, ser. 1, vol. 22, pt. 1, 202.

26. John McCorkle, *Three Years with Quantrill: A True Story Told by His Scout, John McCorkle* (1914, reprint, Norman: University of Oklahoma Press, 1992), 68.

27. A partial listing of the Federal troops killed includes the following: From Company E—Cpls. John S. Kirkpatrick and Alexander E. Needham and Pvts. Charles Beauvois, Isaac S. Brubaker, Andrew M. Deal, William Grimes, and Joseph Jackson. From Company K: Cpls. Thomas J. Bell and John N. Cosner and Pvts. Alva J. Cosner, John Lunn, James McCormack, William H. Musson, George W. Phillips, and Casper H. Schroeder. See William G. Cutler, *History of the State of Kansas*, 2 vols. (Chicago: Andreas, 1883), 1:194.

28. William Gregg Manuscript, Western Historical Manuscript Collection, University of Missouri.

29. McCorkle, *Three Years with Quantrill*, 68–69.

30. Cousins of Boone Muir, George and Boone Scholl fought at this skirmish. They were great-grandsons of Daniel Boone. Guerrilla John Ross married the sister of the Scholl brothers. Boone Muir was mistakenly listed as buried in the Smith Cemetery after the June 17 skirmish, but he lived in a Confederate retirement home, died in 1913, and was buried in the Belton, Missouri, cemetery, per Jan Toms, a descendant of Muir.

31. Edwards, *Noted Guerrillas*, 177–78.

32. OR, ser. 1, vol. 22, pt. 2, 460–61.

33. After the ensuing disaster, among the items returned to the families was the satchel of trinkets and dry goods that Nannie Harris McCorkle and Charity McCorkle Kerr had purchased in town. McCorkle's granddaughter believed her grandmother was arrested because she had witnessed the murder of Henry Washington Younger by Federal soldiers, but since Henry Younger was killed more than a year earlier, it seems unlikely that the Union men would have waited so long to murder a witness.

34. Mattie Lykins Bingham, "Recollections of Old Times in Kansas City," *Kansas City Genealogist* 25, nos. 3 and 4 (Summer/Fall 1984): 111–17.

35. Thomas Goodrich, *Black Flag: Guerrilla Warfare on the Western Border, 1861–1865* (Bloomington: Indiana University Press, 1995), 73.

36. Donald R. Hale, *They Called Him Bloody Bill: The Life of William Anderson, Missouri Guerrilla* (Clinton, Mo.: Printery, 1992), 8–9; Edward Thomas Fay and William E. Connelley, interview, March 18, 1918, Kansas State Historical Society, Topeka, Kansas. Fay received the details from Patrick and John Reddington.

37. McCorkle, *Three Years with Quantrill*, 76.

38. Goodrich, *Black Flag*, 73.

39. Trow, *Quantrell*, 128.

40. Ibid., 129.

41. Carl W. Breihan, *Ride the Razor's Edge: The Younger Brothers Story* (Gretna, La.: Pelican, 1992), 66; *Kansas City Post*, May 12, 1912.

42. Thomas Goodrich, *Bloody Dawn: The Story of the Lawrence Massacre* (Kent, Ohio: Kent State University Press, 1992), 8; Darrell Garwood, *Crossroads of America: The Story of Kansas City* (New York: Norton, 1948).

43. *Kansas City Post*, May 29, 1912.

44. *The Trail Guide* (1956): 20–21, Kansas City Posse of the Westerners Records, Special Collections Department, Kansas City Public Library.

45. Goodrich, *Black Flag*, 74.

46. Trow, *Quantrell*, 129.

47. Headquarters, District of the Border, Kansas City, Mo., September 11, 1863, *OR*.

48. C. B. Rollins, "Letters of Caleb Bingham to James S. Rollins, Part 5," *Missouri Historical Review* 33 (January 1938): 62.

49. *Washington Sentinel*, March 9, 1878.

50. McCorkle, *Three Years with Quantrill*, 78–79.

51. William Gregg Manuscript, Western Historical Manuscript Collection, University of Missouri.

CHAPTER 9: FROM LAWRENCE TO LEGEND

1. John Newman Edwards, *Noted Guerrillas, Or the Warfare of the Border* (1877, reprint, Dayton, Ohio: Morningside, 1976), 186.

2. William Gregg Manuscript, Western Historical Manuscript Collection, University of Missouri; *Sni-A-Bar (Blue Springs, Mo.) Voice*, August 28, 1908.

3. Harrison Trow, *Charles W. Quantrell: A True History of His Guerrilla Warfare on the Missouri and Kansas Border During the Civil War of 1861–1865* (Kansas City: n.p., 1923), 23–25.

4. Edwards, *Noted Guerrillas*, 184.

5. William Gregg Manuscript, Western Historical Manuscript Collection, University of Missouri.

6. Thomas Goodrich, *Bloody Dawn: The Story of the Lawrence Massacre* (Kent, Ohio: Kent State University Press, 1992), 38–43.

7. Joanne C. Eakin, *Recollections of Quantrill's Guerrillas, As Told by A. J. Walker of Weatherford, Texas to Victor E. Martin in 1910* (Independence, Mo.: Two Trails, 1996), 56.

8. William Elsey Connelley, *Quantrill and the Border Wars* (1910, reprint, New York: Pageant, 1956), 310.

9. Albert Castel, *William Clarke Quantrill: His Life and Times* (1962, reprint, Norman: University of Oklahoma, 1999), 122.

10. *Lawrence (Kans.) Republican*, May 1, 1861.

11. Goodrich, *Bloody Dawn*, 33.

12. *Lawrence (Kans.) Journal*, January 9, 1862.

13. Ibid., June 13, 1861; December 11, 1862.

14. William Gregg Manuscript, Western Historical Manuscript Collection, University of Missouri.

15. Richard Cordley, *A History of Lawrence, Kansas from the First Settlement to the Close of the Rebellion* (1895, reprint, Lawrence: Walsworth, 1976).

16. *Lawrence (Kans.) Journal*, November 6, 1862; *Lawrence (Kans.) Republican*, November 6, 1862.

17. *Lawrence (Kans.) Journal*, August 6, 1863.

18. Frank Smith manuscript, courtesy of Albert Castel.

19. William Gregg Manuscript, Western Historical Manuscript Collection, University of Missouri.

20. Frank Smith manuscript, courtesy of Albert Castel.

21. Homer Croy, *Last of the Great Outlaws: The Story of Cole Younger* (New York: Duel, Sloan and Pearce, 1956), 19.

22. Quantrill Clippings, vol. 2, Kansas State Historical Society, Topeka, Kansas. Shortly after the raid, Jacob Rote joined Company L, Fifteenth Kansas Jayhawker Regiment. He was murdered in Eudora after the war. See *Kansas City Star*, July 19, 1903.

23. William Gregg Manuscript, Western Historical Manuscript Collection, University of Missouri.

24. *Lawrence (Kans.) Journal*, May 9, 1861.

25. Leverett Wilson Spring, *Kansas: The Prelude to the War for the Union* (1907, reprint, New York: AMS Press, 1973), 287.

26. Eakin, *Recollections of Quantrill's Guerrillas*, 60.

27. John McCorkle, *Three Years with Quantrill: A True Story Told by His Scout, John McCorkle* (1914, reprint, Norman: University of Oklahoma Press, 1992), 80.

28. William Gregg Manuscript, Western Historical Manuscript Collection, University of Missouri.

29. Edwards, *Noted Guerrillas*, 193.

30. Interview with Andy Walker in the *(Weatherford, Tex.) Weekly Herald*, January 15, 1910.

31. Connelley, *Quantrill and the Border Wars*, 194.

32. Quantrill Clippings, vol. 2, Kansas State Historical Society, Topeka, Kansas.

33. William Gregg Manuscript, Western Historical Manuscript Collection, University of Missouri.

34. Trow, *Quantrell*, 147–48.

35. William C. Pollard, *Dark Friday: The Story of Quantrill's Lawrence Raid* (Big Springs, Kans.: Baranski Publishing Co., 1990), 77.

36. Eakin, *Recollections of Quantrill's Guerrillas*, 62.

37. McCorkle, *Three Years with Quantrill*, 80.

38. Spring, *Kansas*, 290.

39. Cordley, *History of Lawrence*, chap. 15, 5–6.

40. Hugh Fisher, *The Gun and the Gospel* (Chicago: Kenwood Press, 1896), 185.

41. Edwards, *Noted Guerrillas*, 199.

42. Cordley, *History of Lawrence*, chap. 15, 5.

43. *Kansas City Post*, March 21, 1915.

44. William G. Cutler, *History of the State of Kansas*, 2 vols. (Chicago: Andreas, 1883), 1:322.

45. Spring, *Kansas*, 270.

46. C. M. Chase to *(Sycamore, Ill.) True Republican and Sentinel*, August 22, 1863, in Chase Letters, cited in Alan W. Farley, "Annals of Quindaro: A Kansas Ghost Town," *Kansas Historical Quarterly* 22, no. 4 (Winter 1956): 305–20.

47. Cordley, *History of Lawrence*, chap. 15, 5–6.

48. Cutler, *History of the State of Kansas*, 1:321.

49. Trow, *Quantrell*, 150.

50. McCorkle, *Three Years with Quantrill*, 80.

51. Spring, *Kansas*, 286.

52. Richard O'Connor, *Buffalo Bill: The Noblest Whiteskin* (New York: Putnam, 1972), 42.

53. *Lawrence (Kans.) Republican*, June 5, 1862.

54. Marley Brant, *The Outlaw Youngers: A Confederate Brotherhood* (Lanham, Md.: Madison Books, 1992), 45.

55. Spring, *Kansas*, 242.

56. *Kansas City Journal*, August 1902.

57. Carl W. Breihan, *Ride the Razor's Edge: The Younger Brothers Story* (Gretna: Pelican, 1992), 114.

58. Brant, *Outlaw Youngers*, 46.

59. William Gregg Manuscript, Western Historical Manuscript Collection, University of Missouri.

60. *Lawrence (Kans.) Journal*, October 17, 1861.

61. Cordley, *History of Lawrence*, chap. 15, 7.

62. Frank Smith manuscript, courtesy of Albert Castel.

63. Cordley, *History of Lawrence*, chap. 15, 8.

64. Connelley, *Quantrill and the Border Wars*, 194; Fisher, *Gun and the Gospel*, 194.

65. Cutler, *History of the State of Kansas*.

66. Spring, *Kansas*, 292.

67. Letters dealing with such charges were written in the 1870s and 1880s, e.g., Boaz Roberts circulated a public notice dated March 13, 1879; Hugh D. Fisher to A. B. Leonard, October 24, 1888; W. H. Makleney to Hugh D. Fisher, April 3, 1885.

68. M542, Rolls 1–10, Cab. 41, Drawer 2, National Archives, Washington, D.C.

69. Frank Smith manuscript, courtesy of Albert Castel.

70. "One of the Sufferers" to S. N. Wood, Lawrence, September 2, 1863. Council Grove Press, September 14, 1863, Kansas State Historical Society, Topeka, Kansas.

71. William Gregg Manuscript, Western Historical Manuscript Collection, University of Missouri.

72. *Quantrill's Raid: The Lawrence Massacre*, brochure produced by the Convention and Visitors Bureau, Lawrence, Kansas.

73. *Western Home Journal*, December 1, 1881.

74. Edwards, *Noted Guerrillas*, 197.

75. Ibid., 196.

76. McCorkle, *Three Years with Quantrill*, 80.

77. Cordley, *History of Lawrence*.

78. Fisher, *Gun and the Gospel*, 188.

79. Albert R. Greene, "What I Saw of the Quantrill Raid," *Collections of the Kansas State Historical Society* 13 (1914): 430–51.

80. Newspapers after the Lawrence raid listed all 148 persons killed. Some have claimed that as many as 300 houses were destroyed, and some even asserted that the entire town was put to the torch. The Lawrence Visitors Bureau brochure map showing the town at the time of the raid identifies 87 buildings as destroyed. During James Lane's 1862 raid on Osceola, Missouri, more than 400 homes were destroyed.

81. William Gregg Manuscript, Western Historical Manuscript Collection, University of Missouri.

Chapter 10: After Lawrence

1. Joanne C. Eakin, *Recollections of Quantrill's Guerrillas, As Told by A. J. Walker of Weatherford, Texas to Victor E. Martin in 1910* (Independence, Mo.: Two Trails, 1996), 65.

2. Albert Castel, *William Clarke Quantrill: His Life and Times* (1962, reprint, Norman: University of Oklahoma, 1999), 136; Frank Smith manuscript, courtesy of Albert Castel.

3. William Gregg Manuscript, Western Historical Manuscript Collection, University of Missouri.

4. William C. Pollard, *Dark Friday: The Story of Quantrill's Lawrence Raid* (Big Springs, Kans.: Baranski Publishing Co., 1990), 86.

5. William Gregg Manuscript, Western Historical Manuscript Collection, University of Missouri.

6. Harrison Trow, *Charles W. Quantrell: A True History of His Guerrilla Warfare on the Missouri and Kansas Border During the Civil War of 1861–1865* (Kansas City: n.p., 1923), 152.

7. John C. Shea, *Reminiscences of Quantrell's Raid upon the City of Lawrence, Kansas: Thrilling Narratives by Living EyeWitnesses* (Kansas City: Isaac P. Moore, 1879).

8. William Gregg Manuscript, Western Historical Manuscript Collection, University of Missouri.

9. Trow, *Quantrell*, 153.

10. Albert R. Greene, "What I Saw of the Quantrill Raid," *Collections of the Kansas State Historical Society* 13 (1914): 440.

11. John McCorkle, *Three Years with Quantrill: A True Story Told by His Scout, John McCorkle* (1914, reprint, Norman: University of Oklahoma Press, 1992), 82.

12. Ibid.

13. Castel, *Quantrill*, 138; Frank Smith manuscript, courtesy of Albert Castel.

14. Greene, "What I Saw of the Quantrill Raid," 444.

15. Donald R. Hale, *We Rode with Quantrill: Quantrill and the Guerrilla War As Told by the Men and Women Who Were With Him* (Kansas City: Donald R. Hale, 1992), 89.

16. William Gregg Manuscript, Western Historical Manuscript Collection, University of Missouri.

17. Eakin, *Recollections of Quantrill's Guerrillas*, 68.

18. Thomas Goodrich, *Black Flag: Guerrilla Warfare on the Western Border, 1861–1865* (Bloomington: Indiana University Press, 1995), 94.

19. Pollard, *Dark Friday*, 90.

20. John Newman Edwards, *Noted Guerrillas, Or the Warfare of the Border* (1877, reprint, Dayton, Ohio: Morningside, 1976), 203.

21. Edwards, *Noted Guerrillas*, 206.

22. Stuart F. Voss, "Town Growth in Central Missouri," *Missouri Historical Review* 66, no. 2 (January 1970): 208.

23. Ibid., 51.

24. Ibid.

25. Goodrich, *Black Flag*, 94–95.

26. *Richmond Examiner*, 1863.

27. Joanne C. Eakin and Donald R. Hale, *Branded As Rebels: A List of Bushwackers, Guerrillas, Partisan Rangers, Confederates and Southern Sympathizers* (Lee's Summit, Mo.: Donald R. Hale, 1993), 416.

28. OR, ser. 1, vol. 22, pt. 2, 482–89.

29. John Speer, *Life of Gen. James H. Lane, "The Liberator of Kansas," with Corroborative Incidents of Pioneer History* (Garden City, Kans.: Speer, 1896); Pollard, *Dark Friday,* 96.
30. Pollard, *Dark Friday,* 98.
31. Albert Castel, "Order No. 11 and the Civil War on the Border," *Missouri Historical Review* 57, no. 4 (July 1963): 359.
32. Lew Larkin, *Bingham: Fighting Artist—The Story of Missouri's Immortal Painter, Patriot, Soldier, and Statesman* (Kansas City: Burton Publishing Co., 1954), 245, 260, 294.
33. William E. Parrish, *Turbulent Partnership: Missouri and the Union, 1861–1865* (Columbia: University of Missouri Press, 1963), 159–60.
34. Goodrich, *Black Flag,* 99.
35. Sherman Bodwell, diary, Kansas State Historical Society, Topeka, Kansas; Goodrich, *Black Flag,* 66.
36. W. L. Davis manuscript, Kansas State Historical Society, Topeka, Kansas.
37. Voss, "Town Growth in Central Missouri," 199–200.
38. Union Historical Company, *The History of Jackson County, Missouri* (Kansas City: Union Historical Co., 1881), 12; Eakin and Hale, *Branded As Rebels,* 223.
39. Missouri Historical Company, *History of Saline County, Missouri* (St. Louis: Missouri Historical Co., 1881); Eakin and Hale, *Branded As Rebels,* 354.
40. Cole Younger, *The Story of Cole Younger by Himself* (1903, reprint, St. Paul: Minnesota Historical Society Press, 2000), 4.
41. Frank Smith manuscript, courtesy of Albert Castel.
42. McCorkle, *Three Years with Quantrill,* 59.
43. Robert Hull was assigned to Company H in Quantrill's company; Eakin and Hale, *Branded As Rebels,* 221; William Gregg Manuscript, Western Historical Manuscript Collection, University of Missouri.
44. Wedington to Clark, October 20, 1863, *OR,* ser. 1, vol. 22, 675.
45. Jacob Hall Family Papers, A111 3F17, Jackson County Historical Society, Independence, Mo.
46. *Leavenworth Daily Times,* June 28, 1862.
47. *OR,* ser. 1, vol. 22, 696.
48. Ibid., 696.
49. Samuel R. Curtis to Ben Loan, September 29, 1862, *OR,* ser. 1, vol. 13, 688–89.
50. *OR,* ser. 1, vol. 22, 696.
51. Lt. James Pond received the Medal of Honor for his actions against Quantrill's guerrillas at the battle of Baxter Springs.
52. Hale, *We Rode with Quantrill,* 59.
53. Ned Bradford, *Battles and Leaders of the Civil War* (1956, reprint, New York: Meridian, 1989), 1:335–36.
54. Eakin, *Recollections of Quantrill's Guerrillas,* 79–80.
55. *OR,* ser. 1, vol. 53, 908–9.
56. Edwards, *Noted Guerrillas,* 221.

CHAPTER 11: HALLOWED GROUND

1. *OR*, ser. 1, vol. 22, pt. 2, 1046.
2. *OR*, ser. 1, vol. 26, pt. 2, 339–40.
3. Ibid., 382–83.
4. Frank Smith manuscript, courtesy of Albert Castel.
5. Joanne C. Eakin, *Recollections of Quantrill's Guerrillas, As Told by A. J. Walker of Weatherford, Texas to Victor E. Martin in 1910* (Independence, Mo.: Two Trails, 1996), 81.
6. For more than a century historians have asserted that Bill Anderson was never married, but recently his marriage license was discovered in Texas. See also John McCorkle, *Three Years with Quantrill: A True Story Told by His Scout, John McCorkle* (1914, reprint, Norman: University of Oklahoma Press, 1992), 97.
7. Jackson County Historical Society, Independence, Mo.
8. Hindman's Confederate Partisan Act for Missouri was dated July 17, 1862, Headquarters of the Trans-Mississippi Department, Little Rock, Arkansas.
9. Frank Smith manuscript, courtesy of Albert Castel.
10. John Newman Edwards, *Noted Guerrillas* (1877, reprint, Dayton, Ohio: Morningside, 1976), 223.
11. Edward E. Leslie, *The Devil Knows How to Ride: The True Story of William Clarke Quantrill and His Confederate Raiders* (New York: Da Capo Press, 1998), 293.
12. Ibid., 296.
13. Eakin, *Recollections of Quantrill's Guerrillas*, 80.
14. Ibid., 83.
15. McCorkle, *Three Years with Quantrill*, 97.
16. *OR*, ser. 1, vol. 34, pt. 1, 678, 941–42.
17. Edwards, *Noted Guerrillas*, 230.
18. Hamp B. Watts, *The Babe of the Company: An Unfolded Leaf from the Forest of Never-To-Be Forgotten Years* (Fayette, Mo.: Democratic Leader Press, 1913), 3.
19. Edwards, *Noted Guerrillas*, 234.
20. Eakin, *Recollections of Quantrill's Guerrillas*, 51–52.
21. Joanne Chiles Eakin, *Warren Welch Remembers: A Civil War Guerrilla from Jackson County, Missouri* (Shawnee Mission, Kans.: Two Trails, 1997), 13.
22. Union Historical Company, *The History of Jackson County, Missouri* (Kansas City: Union Historical Co., 1881), 210–11.
23. Eakin, *Warren Welch Remembers*, 5–6.
24. *OR*, ser. 1, vol. 41, pt. 1, 49–50; pt. 2, 62–63, 189, 246.
25. *OR*, ser. 1, vol. 41, pt. 3, 395.
26. *OR*, ser. 1, vol. 41, pt. 2, 75–77.
27. Joanne C. Eakin and Donald R. Hale, *Branded As Rebels: A List of Bushwackers, Guerrillas, Partisan Rangers, Confederates and Southern Sympathizers* (Lee's Summit, Mo.: Donald R. Hale, 1993), 62–63.

28. W. H. Schrader, memoirs, Brunswick, Mo.; the *(Chariton County, Mo.) Brunswicker,* 1981.

29. Watts, *Babe of the Company,* 13.

30. Buck and ball was a musket load consisting of a large lead ball and several buckshot.

31. Edwards, *Noted Guerrillas,* 236.

32. *Boone's Lick Heritage* 6, no. 1 (March 1998).

33. *Kansas City Star,* May 23, 1926.

34. McCorkle, *Three Years with Quantrill,* 110.

35. The back of a photograph of Bill Anderson in the Jackson County Historical Society, Independence, Mo., lists an address that indicates the Anderson home was in Fayette, Howard County.

36. Frank Smith manuscript, courtesy of Albert Castel.

37. Ibid.; Donald R. Hale, *We Rode with Quantrill: Quantrill and the Guerrilla War As Told by the Men and Women Who Were With Him* (Kansas City: Donald R. Hale, 1992), 109.

38. Watts, *Babe of the Company,* 15–16.

39. OR, ser. 1, vol. 41, pt. 1, 440.

40. Watts, *Babe of the Company,* 16–17.

41. McCorkle, *Three Years with Quantrill,* 111–12.

42. National Historical Company, *History of Howard and Chariton Counties, Missouri* (St. Louis: National Historical Co., 1883), 283.

43. Watts, *Babe of the Company,* 30.

44. Frank Smith manuscript, courtesy of Albert Castel.

45. McCorkle, *Three Years with Quantrill,* 118–19.

46. OR, ser. 1, vol. 41, pt. 1, 441.

47. Gene Owen, "Boonslick Sketches," *Boonville (Mo.) Standard*; Lilburn Kingsbury, "Way Back Yonder," *Cooper County (Mo.) Record*; McCorkle, *Three Years with Quantrill,* 118.

48. Edwards, *Noted Guerrillas,* 293; Jim Cummins, *Jim Cummins' Book* (1903, reprint, Provo, Utah: Triton Press, 1988); George Scholl, letter, collection of Claiborne Scholl Nappier.

49. Albert Castel, *William Clarke Quantrill: His Life and Times* (1962, reprint, Norman: University of Oklahoma, 1999), 189.

50. Harrison Trow, *Charles W. Quantrell: A True History of His Guerrilla Warfare on the Missouri and Kansas Border During the Civil War of 1861–1865* (Kansas City: n.p., 1923), 176–77.

51. Hale, *We Rode with Quantrill,* 104–6.

52. Trow, *Quantrell,* 183–84.

53. Frank Smith manuscript, courtesy of Albert Castel.

54. Donald R. Hale, *They Called Him Bloody Bill: The Life of William Anderson, Missouri Guerrilla* (Clinton, Mo.: Printery, 1992), 57.

55. Frank James interview in Henry Huston Crittenden, comp., *The Crittenden Memoirs* (New York: Putnam, 1936), 338.

56. OR, ser. 1, vol. 41, pt. 1, 440–41; pt. 3, 488, 491, 521, 522, 693; *St. Louis Democrat,* September 28 and 30, 1864.

57. *Topeka Capital,* July 8, 1898.

58. Frank Smith manuscript, courtesy of Albert Castel.

CHAPTER 12: LAST RAID—LAST HOPE

1. OR, ser. 1, vol. 41, pt. 1, 718.

2. *Liberty (Mo.) Tribune,* November 4, 1864; *St. Louis Democrat,* October 28, 1864.

3. OR, ser. 1, vol. 41, pt. 1, pp. 632.

4. Harrison Trow, *Charles W. Quantrell: A True History of His Guerrilla Warfare on the Missouri and Kansas Border During the Civil War of 1861–1865* (Kansas City: n.p., 1923), 218.

5. National Historical Company, *History of Howard and Chariton Counties, Missouri* (St. Louis: National Historical Co., 1883), 289.

6. OR, ser. 1, vol. 41, pt. 1, 431; *St. Louis Democrat,* October 21, and November 14, 1864; National Historical Company, *History of Howard and Chariton Counties, Missouri,* 289.

7. Carolyn Bartels, *Civil War Stories of Missouri* (Shawnee, Kans.: Two Trails, 1995), 84.

8. John McCorkle, *Three Years with Quantrill: A True Story Told by His Scout, John McCorkle* (1914, reprint, Norman: University of Oklahoma Press, 1992), 122.

9. Trow, *Quantrell,* 214.

10. OR, ser. 1, vol. 41, pt. 4, 891–92.

11. H. C. Dryden, interview by William E. Connelley, June 13, 1905, Kansas State Historical Society.

12. *Kansas City Star,* August 16, 1913; Donald R. Hale, *They Called Him Bloody Bill: The Life of William Anderson, Missouri Guerrilla* (Clinton, Mo.: Printery, 1992), 75.

13. Trow, *Quantrell,* 220–21.

14. *Moberly (Mo.) Evening Democrat,* August 15, 1924.

15. Ibid.; OR, ser. 1, vol. 41, pt. 4, 354.

16. Sylvester Akers manuscript, August 21, 1909, quoted in William Elsey Connelley, *Quantrill and the Border Wars* (1910, reprint, New York: Pageant, 1956), 457–58.

17. *Kansas City Star,* May 23, 1926.

18. McCorkle, *Three Years with Quantrill,* 128.

19. John Newman Edwards, *Noted Guerrillas* (1877, reprint, Dayton, Ohio: Morningside, 1976), 383. Among those who answered the call were John McCorkle, his cousins George Wigginton and Thomas Harris, and Harris's brother-in-law, James Lilly. Also present were William, Edward and Henry Noland; Allen Parmer; Jim Little; William Basham; John Barker; Chatham Renick; Foss Key; Richard Glasscock; Jim Younger; William Gaugh; Sylvester Akers; Jack Graham; George Robinson; Tom Evans; Andy McGuire; Payne Jones; John Barnhill; Will Parker; John

Hunter; John Ross; Frank and Jesse James; William Hulse; Clark Hockensmith; Peyton Long; Ben Morrow; John Koger; Donnie and Bud Pence; Oliver Shepherd; David Hilton; Randolph Venable; Richard Burns; Isaac, Tom, George, and Bob Hall; Lee McMurtry; Henry Porter; Joe Gibson; James Williams; Rufus, Robert, and William "Babe" Hudspeth; a guerrilla named Baker; and several others.

20. Edwards, *Noted Guerrillas*, 384–86.
21. Ibid., 389; Donald R. Hale, *We Rode with Quantrill: Quantrill and the Guerrilla War As Told by the Men and Women Who Were With Him* (Kansas City: Donald R. Hale, 1992), 76.
22. Edwards, *Noted Guerrillas*, 390.
23. McCorkle, *Three Years with Quantrill*, 136.
24. Edwards, *Noted Guerrillas*, 391.
25. McCorkle, *Three Years with Quantrill*, 138.
26. Edwards, *Noted Guerrillas*, 392–95.
27. McCorkle, *Three Years with Quantrill*, 140.
28. Edwards, *Noted Guerrillas*, 403.
29. Ibid., 425.
30. Quantrill's men to William Elsey Connelley, Quantrill reunion, August 21, 1909.
31. R. T. Owen to W. W. Scott, October 12, 1888, cited in Connelley, *Quantrill and the Border Wars*, 467.
32. Quantrill Clippings, vol. 2, Kansas State Historical Society, Topeka, Kansas.
33. Edwards, *Noted Guerrillas*, 433.
34. Trow, *Quantrell*, 243.
35. Edwards, *Noted Guerrillas*, 437; Allen Parmer, interview, *Dallas (Tex.) News*, November 27, 1927.
36. Memo of W. W. Scott in Connelley, *Quantrill and the Border Wars*, 35.
37. *Kansas City Star*, May 23, 1926.
38. Ibid.
39. Edwards, *Noted Guerrillas*, 438.
40. *Kansas City Star*, May 23, 1926.

CHAPTER 13: VENGEANCE IS MINE, SAYETH THE LORD

1. W. W. Heartsill, *Fourteen Hundred and 91 Days in the Confederate Army* (1867, reprint, Wilmington, N.C.: Broadfoot, 1987), 244.
2. Abraham Lincoln, Second Inaugural Address, Library of Congress, Washington D.C.
3. LeRoy P. Graf and Ralph W. Haskins, eds., *The Papers of Andrew Johnson*, 16 vols. (Knoxville: University of Tennessee Press, 1967–2000), vol. 7; Eric L. McKitrick, *Andrew Johnson and Reconstruction* (Chicago: University of Chicago Press, 1960), 399.
4. Woodrow Wilson, *A History of the American People*, 10 vols. (New York: Harper & Brothers, 1918).
5. *Missouri Democrat*, October 23, 1863; *Missouri State Times*, October 24, 1863.

6. William E. Parrish, gen. ed., *A History of Missouri*, 5 vols. (Columbia: University of Missouri Press, 1971–97), 1:43.

7. William E. Parrish, *Missouri Under Radical Rule, 1861–1870* (Columbia: University of Missouri Press, 1965).

8. *Missouri Statesman*, September 4 and October 31, 1868.

9. Missouri State Laws, Ralls, 1980.

10. *Liberty (Mo.) Tribune*, November 2, 1866.

11. See Thomas S. Barclay, "The Test Oath for the Clergy in Missouri," *Missouri Historical Review* 18, no. 3 (April 1924): 345–81.

12. Quoted in Thomas S. Barclay, *The Liberal Republican Movement in Missouri, 1865–1871* (Columbia: State Historical Society of Missouri, 1926).

13. Joanne C. Eakin and Donald R. Hale, *Branded As Rebels: A List of Bushwackers, Guerrillas, Partisan Rangers, Confederates and Southern Sympathizers* (Lee's Summit, Mo.: Donald R. Hale, 1993), 39–40.

14. National Historical Company, *History of Clay and Platte Counties, Missouri* (St. Louis: National Historical Co., 1885); Union Historical Company, *The History of Jackson County, Missouri*; *Liberty (Mo.) Tribune*, January 5, 1866; Eakin and Hale, *Branded As Rebels*, 427.

15. Eakin and Hale, *Branded As Rebels*, 211; *Liberty (Mo.) Tribune*, January 5, 1866.

16. Parrish, *Missouri Under Radical Rule*, 91.

17. Harrison Trow, *Charles W. Quantrell: A True History of His Guerrilla Warfare on the Missouri and Kansas Border During the Civil War of 1861–1865* (Kansas City: n.p., 1923), 231–33.

18. Homer Croy, *Jesse James Was My Neighbor* (New York: Duell, Sloan and Pierce, 1949), 39.

19. Trow, *Quantrell*, 248–61.

20. *California (Mo.) Weekly News*, January 14, 1865.

21. OR, ser. 1, vol. 48, pt. 2, 470, 545, 599, 705.

22. Ibid., 705–6, 785, 837–38, 848, 872.

23. *Jefferson City (Mo.) State Times*, May 10, 1867.

24. Trow, *Quantrell*, 261.

25. Eakin and Hale, *Branded As Rebels*, 162. Some disbanded Kansas militia killed John Bishop at a creek crossing south of Westport soon after the war (see ibid., 27).

26. Pearl Wilcox, *Jackson County Pioneers* (Independence, Mo.: n.p., 1975), 394.

27. *Independence (Mo.) Examiner*, September 12, 1931.

28. *Liberty (Mo.) Tribune*, September 5, 1924.

29. *Liberty (Mo.) Tribune*, May 20 and June 29, 1865.

30. Hamp B. Watts, *The Babe of the Company: An Unfolded Leaf from the Forest of Never-To-Be Forgotten Years* (Fayette, Mo.: Democratic Leader Press, 1913), 30.

31. Trow, *Quantrell*, 259.

32. James W. Buel, *The Border Outlaws* (St. Louis: Historical Publishing Co., 1881), 115–17.

33. Trow, *Quantrell*, 253.
34. *Kansas City Post*, September 9, 1921.
35. Buel, *Border Outlaws*, 116.
36. *Lexington (Mo.) Caucasian*, October 31, 1866.
37. *Liberty (Mo.) Tribune*, March 8, 1867; Buel, *Border Outlaws*.
38. *Warrensburg (Mo.) Weekly Journal*, June 5 and 19, 1867.
39. *St. Louis Daily Republican*, March 23 and 26, 1868; Buel, *Border Outlaws*.
40. *Kansas City Times*, December 16, 1869.
41. Cole Younger, *The Story of Cole Younger by Himself* (1903, reprint, St. Paul: Minnesota Historical Society Press, 2000), 60.
42. William Gregg Manuscript, Western Historical Manuscript Collection, University of Missouri.
43. *St. Louis Post Dispatch*, August 24, 1902.
44. Todd Menzies George, *The Conversion of Cole Younger and The Battle of Lone Jack: Early Day Stories* (Kansas City: Lowell Press, 1963), 19.
45. Elmer L. Pigg, "Bloody Bill, Noted Guerrilla of the Civil War," *The Trail Guide* 1, no. 4 (December 1956); Kansas City Posse of the Westerners Records, Special Collections Department, Kansas City Public Library; Donald R. Hale, *They Called Him Bloody Bill: The Life of William Anderson, Missouri Guerrilla* (Clinton, Mo.: Printery, 1992), 112–14.
46. Eakin and Hale, *Branded As Rebels*, 313.
47. James G. Blunt to Henry Z. Curtis, August 10, 1863, Thomas Moonlight Papers, Kansas State Historical Society; James Hanway to Parents, December 9, 1863, James and John Hanway Papers, Kansas State Historical Society.
48. James G. Blunt, "General Blunt's Account of His Civil War Experiences," *Kansas Historical Quarterly* 1, no. 3 (May 1932): 211; William G. Cutler, *History of the State of Kansas*, 2 vols. (Chicago: Andreas, 1883), 302–4.
49. OR, ser. 1, vol. 41, pt. 4, 842–43, 873.
50. *Leavenworth Daily Times*, March 19, 1865; *Leavenworth Daily Conservative*, April 27, 1865.
51. *Kansas City Times*, February 7, 1930.
52. Larry Evans, friend and neighbor of Fred Ford and Arthur Dealy, Kate King's nephew, interviewed by author, 1999, Independence, Mo.
53. The small cemetery surrounded by a white stone wall is in Hill Park, near Twenty-third Street and Westport Road in Independence, Missouri.
54. Edward A. Pollard, *Life of Jefferson Davis* (Philadelphia: National Publishing Co., 1869), 535; John J. Craven and Edward K. Eckert, eds., *"Fiction Distorting Fact": The Prison Life, Annotated by Jefferson Davis* (Macon, Ga.: Mercer University Press, 1987), 131.
55. Robert E. Lee to F. W. Stockdale; see Douglas Southall Freeman, *R. E. Lee: A Biography*, 4 vols. (New York: Scribner, 1934–35), 4:374, n. 7.
56. *Independence (Mo.) Examiner*, August 20, 1909.

57. A125, 4F22, Jackson County Historical Society, Independence, Mo.

58. Scholl Letters, Claiborne Scholl Nappier Collection.

EPILOGUE

1. Harrison Trow, *Charles W. Quantrell: A True History of His Guerrilla Warfare on the Missouri and Kansas Border During the Civil War of 1861–1865* (Kansas City: n.p., 1923), 250.

2. *St. Louis Post Dispatch*, August 24, 1902.

3. Ibid.

4. Trow, *Quantrell*, 251.

5. William Elsey Connelley, *Quantrill and the Border Wars* (1910, reprint, New York: Pageant, 1956), 317.

Selected Bibliography

Anders, Leslie. "Fighting the Ghosts at Lone Jack." *Missouri Historical Review* 79, no. 3 (April 1985): 332–56.

Appler, Augustus C. *The Younger Brothers: Their Life and Character*. 1876. Reprint, New York: Fell, 1955.

Armstrong, Charles L. "Ambushes: Still Viable As a Combat Tactic." *Marine Corps Gazette* (July 1990).

Atkeson, William O. *History of Bates County, Missouri*. Cleveland: Historical Publishing Co., 1918.

Barclay, Thomas S. "The Test Oath for the Clergy in Missouri." *Missouri Historical Review* 18, no. 3 (April 1924): 345–81.

Bartels, Carolyn M. *The Civil War in Missouri Day by Day, 1861 to 1865*. Shawnee, Kans.: Two Trails, 1992.

———. *Civil War Stories of Missouri*. Shawnee, Kans.: Two Trails, 1995.

Bearss, Edwin C. *The Battle of Wilson's Creek*. Diamond, Mo.: George Washington Carver Birthplace District Association, 1975.

Berneking, Carolyn. "A Look at Early Lawrence: Letters from Robert Gaston Elliott." *Kansas Historical Quarterly* 43, no. 3 (Autumn 1977): 282–96.

Bingham, Mattie Lykins. "Recollections of Old Times in Kansas City." *Kansas City Genealogist* 25.

Blunt, James G. "General Blunt's Account of His Civil War Experiences." *Kansas Historical Quarterly* 1, no. 3 (May 1932): 211–65.

Bonnewitz, Roberta L., and Lois T. Allen. *Raytown Remembers*. Clinton, Mo.: Raytown Historical Society, n.d.

Bradford, Ned. *Battles and Leaders of the Civil War*. 1956. Reprint, New York: Meridian, 1989.

Brant, Marley. *The Families of Charles Lee and Henry Washington Younger: A Genealogical Sketch*. Burbank, Calif.: M. Brant, 1986.

———. *The Outlaw Youngers: A Confederate Brotherhood*. Lanham, Md.: Madison Books, 1992.

Breihan, Carl W. *The Complete and Authentic Life of Jesse James*. New York: Frederick Fell, 1953.

———. *The Killer Legions of Quantrill*, Seattle: Hangman Press, 1971.

————. *Quantrill and His Civil War Guerrillas*. 1959. Reprint, New York: Promontory Press, 1974.

————. *Ride the Razor's Edge: The Younger Brothers Story*. Gretna, La.: Pelican, 1992.

————. *Younger Brothers*. San Antonio: Naylor, 1961.

Britton, Wiley. *The Civil War on the Border*. 2 vols. New York: Putnam, 1890–99.

Brooks, Paul. *Legacy of Faith*. Marceline, Mo.: Walsworth, 1992.

Brophy, Patrick, ed. *Bushwhackers of the Border: The Civil War Period in Western Missouri*. 2d rev. ed. Nevada, Mo.: Vernon County Historical Society, 2000.

Brownlee, Richard S. *Gray Ghosts of the Confederacy: Guerrilla Warfare in the West*. 1958. Reprint, Baton Rouge: Louisiana State University Press, 1984.

Brugioni, Dino A. *The Civil War in Missouri: As Seen from the Capital City*. Jefferson City, Mo.: Summers Publishing, 1987.

Buel, James W. *The Border Outlaws*. St. Louis: Historical Publishing Co., 1882.

Burke, John. *Buffalo Bill: The Noblest Whiteskin*. New York: Putnam, 1973.

Carr, Lucien. *Missouri: A Bone of Contention*. 1888. Reprint, New York, AMS Press, 1973.

Castel, Albert E. *A Frontier State at War: Kansas, 1861–1865*. 1858. Reprint, Westport, Conn.: Greenwood Press, 1979.

————. "Kansas Jayhawking Raids into Western Missouri in 1861." *Missouri Historical Review* 54, no. 1 (October 1959): 1–11.

————. *William Clarke Quantrill: His Life and Times*. 1962. Reprint, Norman: University of Oklahoma, 1999.

————, and Thomas Goodrich. *Bloody Bill Anderson: The Short, Savage Life of a Civil War Guerrilla*. Mechanicsburg, Pa.: Stackpole, 1998.

Connelley, William Elsey. *Quantrill and the Border Wars*. 1910. Reprint, New York: Pageant, 1956.

Cordley, Richard. *A History of Lawrence, Kansas from the First Settlement to the Close of the Rebellion*. 1895. Reprint, Lawrence: Walsworth, 1976.

————. *Pioneer Days in Kansas*. New York: Pilgrim Press, n.d.

Cornish, Dudley Taylor. *The Sable Arm: Black Troops in the Union Army, 1861–1865*. 1956. Reprint, Lawrence: University Press of Kansas, 1987.

Craven, John J., and Edward K. Eckert, eds. *"Fiction Distorting Fact": The Prison Life, Annotated by Jefferson Davis*. Macon, Ga.: Mercer University Press, 1987.

Crittenden, Henry Huston, comp. *The Crittenden Memoirs*. New York: Putnam, 1936.

Croy, Homer. *Jesse James Was My Neighbor*. New York: Duell, Sloan and Pearce, 1949.

————. *Last of the Great Outlaws: The Story of Cole Younger*. New York: Duel, Sloan and Pearce, 1956.

Cummins, Jim. *Jim Cummins' Book*. 1903. Reprint, Provo, Utah: Triton Press, 1988.

————. *Jim Cummins the Guerrilla*. Excelsior Springs, Mo.: Daily Journal, 1908.

Cutler, William G. *History of the State of Kansas*, 2 vols. Chicago: Andreas, 1883.

Dalton, Kit. *Under the Black Flag*. 1914. Reprint, Memphis, Tenn.: L. J. Tolbert, 1995.

Daughters of the American Revolution, Kansas City, Missouri. *Vital Historical Records of Jackson County, Missouri, 1826–1876*. Kansas City, Mo.: DAR, 1934.

DeAngelo, Dory. *Voices Across Time: Profiles of Kansas City's Early Residents*. Kansas City: Tapestry, 1987.

Eakin, Joanne Chiles. *The Making of a Missouri Rebel: John P. Webb, 1832–1913*. 3d ed. Shawnee Mission, Kans.: Two Trails, 1995.

————. *Recollections of Quantrill's Guerrillas, As Told by A. J. Walker of Weatherford, Texas to Victor E. Martin in 1910*. Independence, Mo.: Two Trails, 1996.

————. *Tears and Turmoil: Order #11*. Independence, Mo.: Eakin, 1996.

————. *Warren Welch Remembers: A Civil War Guerrilla from Jackson County, Missouri*. Shawnee Mission, Kans.: Two Trails, 1997.

————, comp. *Diary of a Town: Wellington, Missouri*. Independence, Mo.: Wee Print, 1984.

————, and Donald R. Hale. *Branded As Rebels: A List of Bushwackers, Guerrillas, Partisan Rangers, Confederates and Southern Sympathizers*. Lee's Summit, Mo.: Donald R. Hale, 1993.

Edwards, John Newman. *Noted Guerrillas, Or the Warfare of the Border*. 1877. Reprint, Dayton, Ohio: Morningside, 1976.

Fellman, Michael. *Inside War: The Guerrilla Conflict in Missouri During the American Civil War*. New York: Oxford University Press, 1989.

Fischer, Leroy H., ed. *Civil War Battles in the West*. Manhattan, Kans.: Sunflower University Press, 1981.

Fisher, Hugh. *The Gun and the Gospel*. Chicago: Kenwood Press, 1896.

Garwood, Darrell. *Crossroads of America: The Story of Kansas City*. New York: Norton, 1948.

George, B. James, Sr. *Confederate and Quantrill Officer*. N.p., n.d.

————. "The Georges, Pioneers and Rebels." Jackson County Historical Society Archives. Independence, Mo.

————. *The Gregg Biography*. Lawrence Kansas State Historical Society.

George, Todd Menzies. *The Conversion of Cole Younger and The Battle of Lone Jack: Early Day Stories*. Kansas City: Lowell Press, 1963.

Gillespie, Michael L. *The Civil War Battle of Lexington*. Independence, Mo.: n.p., 1991.

Gilmore, Donald L. "Revenge in Kansas, 1863." *History Today* 43 (March 1993).

————. "Total War on the Western Border." *Journal of the West* (July 1996).

Gleaves, S. R. "The Strategic Use of Cavalry," *Journal of the U.S. Cavalry Association* 18 (July 1907).

Goddard, Mrs. Merrit M. "The Historical Alexander Majors." September 1933. Published by the Alexander Majors Chapter, MOSSAR, Kansas City, Mo.

Goodman, Thomas M. A Thrilling Record: Founded on Facts and Observations Obtained During Ten Days' Experience with Colonel William T. Anderson. Hawleyville, Iowa: Goodman, 1868.

Goodrich, Thomas. Black Flag: Guerrilla Warfare on the Western Border, 1861–1865. Bloomington: Indiana University Press, 1995.

———. Bloody Dawn: The Story of the Lawrence Massacre. Kent, Ohio: Kent State University Press, 1992.

Gorin, Sandra K. "Battles, Duels, Panics and Skirmishes." http://cgi.rootsweb.com/~genbbs/genbbs.cgi/USA/Ky/Tips.

Graf, LeRoy P., and Ralph W. Haskins, eds. The Papers of Andrew Johnson. 16 vols. Knoxville: University of Tennessee Press, 1967–2000.

Greene, Albert R. "What I Saw of the Quantrill Raid." Collections of the Kansas State Historical Society 13 (1914): 430–51.

Gregg, William H. "A Little Dab of History Without Embellishment." Western Historical Manuscript Collection, University of Missouri, Columbia.

Grimsley, Mark. The Hard Hand of War: Union Military Policy Toward Southern Civilians, 1861–1865. New York: Cambridge University Press, 1995.

Hagan, George T. Tales of Tragedy Trail Clinton, Mo.: Printery, 1974.

Hale, Donald R. They Called Him Bloody Bill: The Life of William Anderson, Missouri Guerrilla. Clinton, Mo.: Printery, 1992.

———. We Rode with Quantrill: Quantrill and the Guerrilla War As Told by the Men and Women Who Were With Him. Kansas City: Donald R. Hale, 1992.

Harris, Charles F. "Catalyst for Terror: The Collapse of the Women's Prison in Kansas City." Missouri Historical Review 89, no. 3 (April 1995): 290–306.

———. Charley Hart Really Lived. N.p., n.d.

Heartsill, W. W. Fourteen Hundred and 91 Days in the Confederate Army. 1867. Reprint, Wilmington, N.C.: Broadfoot, 1987.

Herklotz, Hildegarde Rose. "Jayhawkers in Missouri, 1858–1863." Missouri Historical Review (October 1923): 64–101.

Hickman, W. Z. History of Jackson County, Missouri. Topeka: Historical Publication Co., 1920.

Hildebrand, Samuel S. Autobiography of Samuel S. Hildebrand, the Renowned Missouri "Bushwhacker." Jefferson City, Mo.: State Times Printing House, 1870.

Hoole, William Stanley, ed. "A Southerner's Viewpoint of the Kansas Situation, 1856–1857: The Letters of Lieut. Col. A. J. Hoole, C.S.A." Kansas Historical Quarterly 3, no. 1 (February 1934): 43–56.

Johnson, Rossiter. Campfires and Battlefields: A Pictorial Narrative of the Civil War. New York: Civil War Press, 1967.

Jones, Virgil Carrington. *Gray Ghosts and Rebel Raiders*. 1956. Reprint, McLean, Va.: EPM Publications, 1988.

Kansas City Historical Company. *The History of Johnson County*. Kansas City: Kansas City Historical Company, 1881.

Keating, Bern. *The Flamboyant Mr. Colt and His Deadly Six-Shooter*. Garden City, N.Y.: Doubleday, 1978.

King, Spencer B., Jr. *Darien: The Death and Rebirth of a Southern Town*. Macon, Ga.: Mercer University Press, 1981.

Larkin, Lew. *Missouri Heritage*. Columbia, Mo.: American Press, 1968.

Lee, Fred L., ed. *The Battle of Westport, October 21–23, 1864*. Kansas City: Westport Historical Society, 1976.

Leftwich, William M. *Martyrdom in Missouri: A History of Religious Proscription, the Seizure of Churches, and the Persecution of Ministers of the Gospel, in the State of Missouri During the Late Civil War, and Under the "Test Oath" of the New Constitution*. 2 vols. St. Louis: S. W. Book and Publishing Co., 1870.

Leslie, Edward E. *The Devil Knows How to Ride: The True Story of William Clarke Quantrill and His Confederate Raiders*. New York: Da Capo Press, 1998.

Lexington (Mo.) Historical Society. *The Battle of Lexington*. Lexington, Mo.: Lexington Historical Society, 1903.

Lincoln, Abraham. *The Complete Works of Abraham Lincoln*. Edited by John G. Nicolay and John Hay. 12 vols. New York: Tandy, 1905.

Maddox, George T. *Hard Trials and Tribulations of an Old Confederate Soldier*. Van Buren, Ark.: Argus, 1897.

Malin, James C. "Dust Storms: Part One, 1850–1860." *Kansas Historical Quarterly* 14, no. 2 (May 1946): 129–44.

McCorkle, John. *Three Years with Quantrill: A True Story Told by His Scout, John McCorkle*. 1914. Reprint, Norman: University of Oklahoma Press, 1992.

McKiernan, F. Mark, and Roger D. Launius, eds. *Missouri Folk Heroes of the 19th Century*. Independence, Mo.: Independence Press, 1989.

McKitrick, Eric L. *Andrew Johnson and Reconstruction*. Chicago: University of Chicago Press, 1960.

Miller, George. *Missouri's Memorable Decade, 1860–1870*. Columbia, Mo.: Stephens, 1898.

Missouri Historical Company. *History of Lafayette County, Missouri*. St. Louis: Missouri Historical Co., 1881.

———. *History of Saline County, Missouri*. St. Louis: Missouri Historical Co., 1881.

Monaghan, Jay. *Civil War on the Western Border, 1854–1865*. 1955. Reprint, Lincoln: University of Nebraska Press, 1985.

Moore, John C. "Major General Sterling Price: A Biography." In vol. 12 of *Confederate Military History*, edited by Clement Evans. 17 vols. 1899. Reprint, Wilmington, N.C.: Broadfoot, 1987–89.

Mudd, Joseph A. *With Porter in North Missouri: A Chapter in the History of the War Between the States*. 1909. Reprint, Iowa City, Iowa: Press of the Camp Pope Bookshop, 1992.

Murphy, Jim. *The Boys' War: Confederate and Union Soldiers Talk About the Civil War*. New York: Clarion Books, 1990.

National Historical Company. *History of Bates County*. St. Louis: National Historical Co., 1883.

————. *History of Carrol County, Missouri*. St. Louis: National Historical Co., 1882.

————. *History of Cass County*. St. Joseph, Mo.: National Historical Publishing Co., 1883.

————. *The History of Cass and Bates Counties, Missouri*. St. Joseph, Mo.: National Historical Co., 1883.

————. *History of Clay and Platte County, Missouri*. St. Louis: National Historical Co., 1885.

————. *History of Howard and Chariton Counties*. St. Louis: National Historical Co., 1883.

————. *History of Howard and Cooper Counties, Missouri*. St. Louis: National Historical Co., 1883.

Oates, Stephen B. *Confederate Cavalry West of the River*. Austin: University of Texas Press, 1992.

O'Connor, Richard. *Buffalo Bill: The Noblest Whiteskin*. New York: Putnam, 1972.

Parrish, William E., gen. ed. *A History of Missouri*. 5 vols. Columbia: University of Missouri Press, 1971–97.

————. *Missouri Under Radical Rule, 1865–1870*. Columbia: University of Missouri Press, 1965.

Paxton, William M. *Annals of Platte County, Missouri*. Kansas City: Hudson-Kimberly Publishing Co., 1897.

Peckham, James. *Gen. Nathaniel Lyon and Missouri in 1861: A Monograph of the Great Rebellion*. New York: American News Co., 1866.

Phillips, Christopher. *Damned Yankee: The Life of General Nathaniel Lyon*. Baton Rouge: Louisiana State University Press, 1996.

Pigg, Elmer L. *Bloody Bill, Noted Guerrilla of the Civil War*. N.p., n.d.

Pollard, Edward A. *Life of Jefferson Davis*. Philadelphia: National Publishing Co., 1869.

Pollard, William C. *Dark Friday: The Story of Quantrill's Lawrence Raid*. Big Springs, Kans.: Baranski Publishing Co., 1990.

Rascoe, Burton. *Belle Starr, "The Bandit Queen."* New York: Random House, 1941.

Robinson, Charles. *The Kansas Conflict.* 1892. Reprint, Freeport, N.Y.: Books for Libraries, 1972.

Rodemyre, Edgar T. *The History of Centralia, Missouri.* Centralia, Mo.: Press of the Centralia Fireside Guard, 1936.

Schultz, Duane P. *Quantrill's War: The Life and Times of William Clarke Quantrill.* New York: St. Martin's, 1996.

Shea, John C. *Reminiscences of Quantrell's Raid upon the City of Lawrence, Kansas: Thrilling Narratives by Living EyeWitnesses.* Kansas City, Mo.: Isaac P. Moore, 1879.

Shoemaker, Floyd D., ed. *Missouri Day by Day.* 2 vols. Columbia: State Historical Society of Missouri, 1942.

Speer, John. *Life of Gen. James H. Lane, "The Liberator of Kansas," with Corroborative Incidents of Pioneer History.* Garden City, Kans.: Speer, 1896.

Spring, Leverett W. "The Career of a Kansas Politician." *American Historical Review* 4 (October 1898).

———. *Kansas: The Prelude to the War for the Union.* 1907. Reprint, New York: AMS Press, 1973.

Starr, Stephen Z. *Jennison's Jayhawkers: A Civil War Cavalry Regiment and Its Commander.* Baton Rouge: Louisiana State University Press, 1973.

Steele, Phillip W. *Jesse and Frank James: The Family History.* Gretna, La.: Pelican, 1987.

———, and Steve Cottrell. *Civil War in the Ozarks.* Gretna, La.: Pelican, 1993.

Swindler, William F. "The Southern Press in Missouri, 1861–1864." *Missouri Historical Review* 35, no. 3 (April 1941): 394–400.

Switzler, William F. *Switzler's Illustrated History of Missouri, from 1541 to 1877.* 1879. Reprint, New York: Arno Press, 1975.

———. *The Trail Guide* 1, no. 4 (December 1956), Kansas City Posse of the Westerners Records, Special Collections Department, Kansas City Public Library.

Thruston, Ethylene Ballard. *Independence (Mo.) Examiner,* May 1, 1941.

———. "Captain Dick Yeager, Quantrill Man." *Western Historical Quarterly,* no. 1 (June 1968).

———. *Echoes of the Past: A Nostalgic Look at Early Raytown and Jackson County.* Kansas City: Lowell Press, 1973.

Trow, Harrison. *Charles W. Quantrell: A True History of His Guerrilla Warfare on the Missouri and Kansas Border During the Civil War of 1861–1865.* Kansas City: n.p., 1923.

Union Historical Company. *The History of Jackson County, Missouri.* Kansas City: Union Historical Co., 1881.

United Daughters of the Confederacy, Missouri Division. *Reminiscences of the Women of Missouri During the Sixties.* Jefferson City: Stephens, ca. 1913.

U.S. Marine Corps Institute. USMC Leadership Course 7000 series.

———. *Infantry Patrolling,* MCI 03.35C. Marine Barracks, Washington, D.C.

————. *Operations Against Guerrilla Units*, MCI 03.24G. Marine Barracks, Washington, D.C.

U.S. War Department. *The War of the Rebellion: A Compilation of Official Records of the Union and Confederate Armies*. 128 vols. Washington, D.C.: Government Printing Office, 1880–1901.

Viotti, Andrea. *Garibaldi: The Revolutionary and His Men*. Poole [Eng.]: Blandford Press, 1979.

Ward, Geoffrey C. *The West: An Illustrated History*. New York: Little, Brown and Co., 1996.

Watson, Thomas Shelby. *The Silent Riders*. Louisville, Ky.: Beechmont Press, 1971.

Watts, Hamp B. *The Babe of the Company: An Unfolded Leaf from the Forest of Never-To-Be Forgotten Years*. Fayette, Mo.: Democratic Leader Press, 1913.

Webb, W. L. *Battles and Biographies of Missourians*. Kansas City: Hudson-Kimberly, 1900.

Wilcox, Pearl. *Jackson County Pioneers*. Independence, Mo.: n.p., 1975.

Williams, Burton J. "Quantrill's Raid on Lawrence: A Question of Complicity." *Kansas Historical Quarterly* 34, no. 2 (Summer 1968): 143–49.

Williamson, James Joseph. *Mosby's Rangers*. 1896. Reprint, Alexandria, Va.: Time-Life, 1982.

Wilson, John Lyde. *Code Duello*. 1838.

Wilson, Woodrow. *A History of the American People*. 10 vols. New York: Harper & Brothers, 1918.

Woodson, W. H. *History of Clay County 1885*. Topeka, Kans.: Historical Publishing Co., 1920.

Younger, Cole. *The Story of Cole Younger by Himself*. 1903. Reprint, St. Paul: Minnesota Historical Society Press, 2000.

Newspapers, Magazines, and Articles

American Historical Review (American Historical Association)

Boone's Lick Heritage (Boonslick Historical Society Quarterly)

Boonville (Mo.) Standard

Border Star (Westport, Mo.)

Brunswicker (Chariton County, Mo.)

California Weekly News (Moniteau County, Mo.)

Cooper County (Mo.) Record

Daily Missouri Republican (St. Louis)

Dallas (Tex.) News

Emporia (Kans.) News

Fortitudine: Bulletin of the Marine Corps Historical Program

Independence (Mo.) Examiner

Jefferson City (Mo.) State Times

Joplin (Mo.) Herald

Kansas City Daily Journal of Commerce

Kansas City Post

Kansas City Star

Kansas City Times

Kansas City World

Kansas Historical Quarterly (Kansas State Historical Society)

Lawrence (Kans.) Daily Journal-World

Lawrence (Kans.) Daily Tribune

Lawrence (Kans.) Herald of Freedom

Lawrence (Kans.) Republican

Lawrence (Kans.) State Journal

Leavenworth (Kans.) Daily Conservative

Leavenworth (Kans.) Daily Times

Lexington (Mo.) Caucasian

Liberty (Mo.) Weekly Tribune

Missouri Historical Review (State Historical Society of Missouri)

Missouri Partisan (Quarterly Journal of the Missouri Division, Sons of Confederate Veterans)

Missouri Statesman (Columbia)

Moberly (Mo.) Evening Democrat

New York Daily Times

New York Herald

Oak Grove (Mo.) Banner

Olathe (Kans.) Mirror

Paola (Kans.) Record

Pleasant Hills (Mo.) Times

Richmond (Va.) Examiner

Sni-A-Bar (Blue Springs, Mo.) Voice

St. Louis Daily Republican

St. Louis Missouri Democrat

St. Louis Post Dispatch

Texas Daily Herald

The No Quarterly (Newsletter of the William Clarke Quantrill Society)

Topeka (Kans.) Capital

Topeka (Kans.) Mail and Breezem

Topeka (Kans.) State Record

U.S. Marine Corps Gazette

Warrensburg (Mo.) Weekly Journal

Washington Sentinel

Archives and Special Collections

Convention and Visitors Bureau, Lawrence Kansas. *Quantrill's Raid: The Lawrence Massacre.*

Evans, Larry. Independence, Missouri. Correspondence and oral history.

Jackson County Historical Society Archives, Independence, Missouri. Various Collections.

Kansas City Public Library, Special Collections Department. Kansas City Posse of the Westerners Records.

Kansas State Historical Society, Topeka, Kansas. Archives collections.

Missouri Historical Society, St. Louis.

Smith, Frank. Fifteen-chapter memoirs of life with Quantrill. Courtesy of Albert Castel.

University of Missouri, Columbia, Mo. James S. Rollins Papers and Western Missouri Historical Manuscript Collection.

Index

Bond, Bradley, 357
Bondi, August, 19
Bonne de Femme Creek, 370
Boone, Daniel Morgan, 99
Bowman, Hiram, 109, 138, 161, 421
Bowring, C. M., 193
Bragg, Braxton, 233
Bragg, Howard, 140, 418
Brannock, Lizzie, 85
Breckinridge, James, 174, 179
Breeden, Martin, 204
Bridgewater, James H., 401–2
Brinker, John, 87, 140, 170
Brooking, Alvin, 98–99, 106–7
Brooking, Henry Clay, 98
Brooks, John W., 53
Broomfield, Ben, 387
Brown, Egbert B., 125, 227
Brown, Frederick, 6
Brown, Harvey, 368
Brown, Jason, 6
Brown, John (abolitionist), 6, 18–20, 24,
    29–30, 63, 74, 279, 329
Brown, John (guerrilla), 145
Brown, John, Jr., 63
Brown, Owen, 6
Brown, Philip, 255–57, 262
Brown, Salmon, 6
Brush Creek, 316
Bryant, David, 187
Bucher, Philip, 265
Buckner, Simon Bolivar, 412
Buel, James T., 166, 173–80, 182
Buffington, J. J., 199
Bull Creek, 26, 312
Bullene, Lathrop, 305
Burbridge, John Q., 388
Burns, Richard "Dick," 390, 398, 428
Burris, John T., 35–36, 130, 189, 192–96, 222,
    225
Burton, Peter, 205
Butts, George N., 349–50

Cameron, Simon, 44
Campbell, Demuel, 202
Campbell, Doc, 305
Campbell, James, 66, 152–53, 172, 184, 232,
    441, 443
Canadian River, 338, 353

Canby, Edward R. S., 412
Carney, Thomas, 319–20
Carter, Al, 367
Carthage, 45–46, 88, 154, 173, 328, 353
Cassell, Theodore, 367, 387, 395, 419, 424
Catherwood, Edwin C., 202, 235, 366
Cave, Jane, 324
Cave, John S., 323
Cavender, Jefferson, 353–54
Centralia, Mo., 80, 109, 137–38, 145, 173,
    376–78, 380–81, 385, 431
Chambers, Barney, 179
Chiles, Dick, 197–98
Chiles, Henry Clay, 12–13, 60, 71, 204
Chiles, Jim Crow, 345–46, 392
Chiles, Joel, 357
Chiles, Kit, 177
Christian, Benjamin, 344, 349
Clark, Charles S., 277, 310, 314, 323, 327
Clark, John B., 205, 387–88
Clark house fight, 119–23, 172, 346
Clarke, Henry S., 23, 296, 299
Clarke, Jerome (Sue Mundy), 402
Clarke, William, 422
Clayton, George M., 150, 215
Clements, Archie 151, 305, 318, 348, 366–67,
    376–77, 380–81, 387, 394, 419–23
Cleveland, Marshall, 24, 42–43, 64, 71–72, 76
Clopper, John Y., 165
Cockrell, Clinton, 76, 207
Cockrell, Francis M., 135, 352
Cockrell, Vard, 150, 183, 185, 352–53
Coffee, John T., 183, 185
Coleman, Charles F., 239, 306, 323–24
Coleman, W. O., 388
Collamore, George Washington, 270, 284, 296
Collins, Buck, 367
Condiff, James, 392
Connelley, William Elsey, 259
Cook, Frank, 191
Cook, John E., 20
Cooper, Douglas H., 336, 338, 341, 343, 352
Copeland, Allen, 427
Copeland, James, 427
Copeland, Levi, 188–90
Cordley, Richard, 273, 284, 300
Cornell, John, 290
Corum, Alfred, 395
Corum, James, 395